THE OXFORD HISTORY OF
THE CHRISTIAN CHURCH

Edited by
Henry and Owen Chadwick

C

The Early Reformation on the Continent

OWEN CHADWICK

OXFORD
UNIVERSITY PRESS

OXFORD

UNIVERSITY PRESS

Great Clarendon Street, Oxford OX2 6DP

Oxford University Press is a department of the University of Oxford.
It furthers the University's objective of excellence in research, scholarship,
and education by publishing worldwide in

Oxford New York

Auckland Bangkok Buenos Aires Cape Town Chennai
Dar es Salaam Delhi Hong Kong Istanbul Karachi Kolkata
Kuala Lumpur Madrid Melbourne Mexico City Mumbai Nairobi
São Paulo Shanghai Singapore Taipei Tokyo Toronto

Oxford is a registered trade mark of Oxford University Press
in the UK and in certain other countries

Published in the United States
By Oxford University Press Inc., New York

First published 2001
First published in paperback 2003

British Library Cataloguing in Publication Data
Data available

Library of Congress Cataloging in Publication Data
Data applied for

ISBN 0–19–826902–1
ISBN 0–19–926578–X (pbk)

1 3 5 7 9 10 8 6 4 2

Typeset in Bembo
by Jayvee, Trivandrum, India
Printed in Great Britain
on acid-free paper by
Biddles Ltd., Guildford & King's Lynn

CONTENTS

ABBREVIATIONS

ADB	*Allgemeine Deutsche Biographie*
ARG	*Archiv für Reformationsgeschichte*
BSLK	*Bekenntnisschriften der evangelisch-lutherischen Kirche*
BW	*Briefwechsel* = Luther's Letters in Weimar edition
CR	Corpus Reformatorum
EKO	*Evangelische Kirchenordnungen des 16. Jahrhunderts*
Ep.	Erasmus's Letters, ed. P. S. Allen
KG	*Kirchengeschichte*
LP	*Letters and Papers, Foreign and Domestic, of the Reign of Henry VIII 1509–47,* ed. J. S. Brewer and others (London, 1862–1920)
MHSJ	*Monumenta Historica Societatis Jesu*
ODC	*The Oxford Dictionary of the Christian Church*
OER	*The Oxford Encyclopaedia of the Reformation*
Op.	*Opera,* especially Calvin's in CR
TR	*Tischreden* = Luther's Table Talk in Weimar edition
TRE	*Theologische Realenzyklopädie*
WA	Luther's Works, Weimar edition
ZKG	*Zeitschrift für Kirchengeschichte*

I

THE BOOK

During the fifteenth century Germans improved the use of metals, with start-ling results. Guns that destroyed less inefficiently, clocks that more or less kept the time, organs that played in tune, and a new way of making books easy for readers.

Johann Gutenberg was an enterprising trader who made money out of pilgrims by selling them looking-glasses and polished stones. For several years he experimented with metal types to make books. He kept borrowing money from friends or kin and seldom repaid his debts. In 1456 he printed the Bible at Mainz; 1,282 pages in two columns to each page, with spaces left for the illuminations that used to be inserted into the old manuscript Bibles, and sometimes known as Mazarin's Bible because the copy belonging to Cardinal Mazarin was important in the study of early printing. Creditors were after him even before he published, and after the Bible was printed he had to sell all his equipment to meet the debts and died in debt despite a pen-sion from the archbishop of Mainz. The invention, so disastrous for its maker, changed the religious and intellectual history of Christendom.

By 1500 we know of some 27,000 printed titles, nearly three-quarters Latin books, but also vernacular books of piety and prayer and works of entertainment. They were carried by traders in wooden trunks or casks and sold at markets, usually unbound. The printers' chief object was the Bible— 94 Latin Bibles by 1500, 16 German Bibles by 1522. Usually it was printed with a commentary.

Convenience was with print. The compositor could experiment with chapter headings, indexes, tables of contents, footnotes. For the first time everyone who wished to read had to master the order of the alphabet—the word alphabet is hardly found in the English language until the second half of the sixteenth century and its earliest use was to mean an index; so late as 1604 an English dictionary needed to tell readers that to use the book they must learn the alphabet. Printers could add lists of misprints or errata, and then lists of books, first of catalogues of books for sale, and then be helped by persons with a new passion or hobby, the bibliophiles; until the Zurich Protestant polymath Conrad Gesner was able to publish (1545) the *Bibliotheca Universalis*, which listed every book and author in Greek, Latin, and Hebrew since printing was invented, about 10,000 books with about 3,000 authors; such lists made it for the first time easier to create an encyclopaedia, so that four years after the *Bibliotheca*, Gesner published an encyclopaedia of theology. Such reference works made a new range of scholarship possible. They were destined not to last, though Gesner's *Bibliotheca* went through three editions. The materials grew too vast to be contained within the volumes.

The copyists of manuscripts were slow to allow themselves beaten by printers. Johannes Trithemius was the Benedictine abbot of Sponheim, and a learned bibliographer. He published (1494) a treatise in praise of copyists who produce books by hand, *De laude scriptorum manualium*. The argument concerned monasteries. By the printing monasteries lost an important resource for their life and devotion. The leisure of the life needed filling. Monks had hands and heads occupied in copying texts, an automatic and worthwhile job, and thus they learnt the texts of the Bible, and it was work which could be started at a fixed time and be left at a fixed time. They used parchment which would last whereas this paper of the printers would not.

Trithemius is often said to be the last defender of the manuscript against its incoming conqueror. This is not right. He thought printing a marvellous invention, a gift of God to humanity.[1] He kept close to the printers at Mainz and printed his own works there. The defence of copying was for monks and for them only. Monks in many abbeys, including his own at Sponheim, murmured that because print is available, this handwriting in which they engage is wasted labour and soul-destroying. Yet from early days the devotional tradition of the monk's life rested in part on copying. The monk must not be idle. He could not say prayers all day. He could not dig the fields all day. The making of manuscripts was useful and kept him from depression and boredom. It was not just mechanical, there was art in it. If copying is abolished what will happen?

The battle for print was easily won. Monasteries were among the earliest institutions to set up printing presses. Trithemius was not slow to print his little treatise in praise of the copyists. His most read book was a manual on the monastic life (*De triplici regione claustralium*) of which he had a thousand copies printed at Mainz and which even into the seventeenth century had to be learnt by German Benedictine novices.

The monks of Sponheim were bitter and rebelled while he was away (1505) and long before the end of the century the Sponheim library was nothing and its books could be found in the Escorial beyond Madrid, or in Rome, or Vienna, or Copenhagen, or Oxford. A French bishop tried to tempt him, and the emperor in Vienna, and the young elector of Brandenburg; but in the year after his fall from Sponheim the prince-bishop

---

[1] Annals of Hirsau ad ann. 1450, ii. 422.

of Würzburg made him abbot of St Jacob in that city and his library there is now almost complete within the library of Würzburg university; but his Würzburg copy of the Gutenberg Bible is that now in the British Library.

Trithemius died in 1516 and never saw what was to happen to the monks within a few years. He was a shining illustration of the northern Renaissance. In that age public opinion despised monks as ignoramuses, and the faster the scholarship of the Renaissance matured the more ignorant they seemed. Though Trithemius bothered little with the Greek language he was truly a man of the Renaissance, learned and a bibliophile. Despite the axioms of his age he still believed that the monastery is the place where learning and piety are married harmoniously.

Educated persons had not trusted texts of copyists because they knew how easily slips crept into the process. The printed book was no more believed without question. At first they were not fully conscious of a dangerous future. Their new invention spread information much faster, and therefore misinformation.

The demands of the private reader affected the trade. Instead of vast volumes for reading on lecterns, they needed small texts for their shelves or pockets. The printers could only do this if they sold many copies and now the demand was there. The pamphlet meant that the printers' trade was the new vehicle for public debate and public quarrel and politics.

At first the printed book was too expensive to get into the hands of teenagers at school or undergraduates except through the university library in the same way as they learnt in the days of manuscripts. But even before the end of the fifteenth century people concerned with education noticed a difference, that learning with the eye was easier and learning with the ear not so indispensable. More people could teach themselves instead of sitting at the feet of a master. And the range of knowledge open to a scholar turned from a sea to an ocean, as was at once shown in several academic careers. Such knowledge could now be acquired without ceaseless travel round the libraries. Scholars still wandered, many thought it necessary to spend a few years in libraries of Italy. No library could yet compare with the libraries of the seventeenth century. The library at Erfurt university which the undergraduate Luther used had about 800 books, though one of the Erfurt colleges had inherited a private library with 1,000 books. At Wittenberg the elector's library was designed to be a university library and grew slowly with wretched grants from the State until it received various libraries from empty monasteries. When it was conquered by a Spanish army in 1547 and moved to Jena it became the basis of the library of Jena university, with 3,000 books.[2] Leipzig university created a good library by taking over the books of nine suppressed monasteries.

---

[2] Eckhard Plumacher, in *TRE* vi. 419, 423.

Libraries that used taxpayers' money could do better; that meant royal libraries, the French king, the king of Hungary until a Turkish army sacked his library, in Italy Medici, Sforza, Visconti, the Pope. Of lesser princes far the most important grew at Heidelberg, capital of the elector Palatine, because it was an older university in Germany and that family liked buying books until the elector Ottheinrich not only joined the princely library to the university library but helped himself almost to bankruptcy during the 1550s through his passion for collecting books. This Palatine library was also fortunate because the only Protestant member of the richest banking family of Germany, the Fugger of Augsburg, happened to be another passionate buyer and bequeathed his collection of books and manuscripts to the Palatine, which thereby became the most magnificent and useful library of Germany; until it was captured by Tilly's Catholic army during the Thirty Years War and was packed up and sent to Rome as a return for the money which the Pope contributed to the military campaign.

The private libraries of a few scholars were weighty but no private citizen could compete with state institutions and monasteries had more urgent needs than buying books. Only one library of a famous humanist survives.

Public libraries in the big towns were started to meet the needs of the municipality. As monasteries collapsed and were dissolved, or as they did not collapse and still were dissolved, they allowed the making of far better public libraries and sometimes the first such library in a town. The books of several monasteries were joined together and became easier of access and a better collection. Nuremberg, though famous for its scholars, had only about 500 books in the city library at the beginning of the century. Thirty-eight years later this library was given the books of all the monasteries in the city and was endowed with the former Dominican friary, a capacious building, to house so many books. The 500 books with which they began were multiplied by ten within fifty years.

The Reformation closed monasteries and put no value on many of their medieval manuscripts, and sometimes used manuscripts to bind modern books and sold the monastic library in the market cheap, and during civil wars like the Peasants' War in Germany monasteries were burnt and their books went up in flames.

The Protestant desire for educated clergy meant a drive for better libraries. Big parish churches put books into the vestry or into the unused house of a canon and made these books accessible to everyone—though mostly it was clergy or schoolteachers who used them. This time of founding libraries lasted from about 1525 for half a century; after which a library of use was too big to house in a room like a vestry and needed a building created for the purpose of being a library. These vestry libraries were quite small. The library of St Nicholas church at Spandau near Berlin had only 38 books at the end of the sixteenth century. When Carlstadt, then a professor at the university of Wittenberg, went to the fighting debate with Johann Eck at the Leipzig Disputation in 1519, he could not rely that the books which he might need would be found in either the city or the university library at Leipzig. He must carry what he might want, and throughout the journey from Wittenberg he needed to sit among a wagon-load of books.[3] The holdings grew by private gifts or bequests. They also might benefit from the books of a former monastery, and in certain Lands (Hesse for example) they were helped by a small but fairly regular grant from the State. In all these libraries a majority of books were about theology because in response to buyers printers published more books in theology than in any other area of knowledge (except books like almanacs). But they also contained classical texts, and slowly a few texts of history and still more slowly a few books on science.

Excitement was in the air. That a town had 2,000 books in its public library does not prove that anyone read them. The number of books which printers published is a better guide to the explosion of knowledge than the state of the libraries because they depended on a market and could not print unless people wished to read. Yet not seldom there are signs of excitement at new learning; at coming to the springs of ancient knowledge which would help them to advance modern knowledge.

Of the biblical languages, it was a long time before many printers possessed Greek type and many never acquired Hebrew type. Cambridge hired a printer of Greek in 1521 but he soon left, Oxford did not get Greek type till 1586. Far the most important centre for Greek printing was in the workshop of Aldus Manutius in Venice, for the Venetian empire in the Aegean made many Greeks seek work in the capital.

Authors were attracted for another reason than clarity and ease of repro-duction. For as long as authors could remember they needed to compete with the censorship, which was a fact of life and continued to be so for a few cen-turies more. To stop the spread of a printed book was possible, by seizing the press and fining or imprisoning printer and author. But from the earliest moment it was seen that this was harder for the censors than the suppression of 300 manuscript copies. Rarely did censors get cooperation from printers who wanted to make a living and wished to sell anything that enough people would buy. This experience soon gave a moral attitude to people engaged in publishing and printing. This new machine was associated with the ability of authors to write what they liked even if the magistrates disliked what they said. Though no one yet talked about freedom, the association between the print-ing press and an antipathy to censorship and repression was not slow to form.

---

[3] *TRE* vi. 419, 421; Martin Brecht, *Martin Luther: Sein Weg zur Reformation* (Stuttgart, 1981), Eng. Trans. J. L. Schaaf, *Martin Luther: His Road to Reformation* (Philadelphia, 1985), 310.

To be a censor of the printed book was one of the most delicate of tasks. Let us take what happened to Robert Estienne, leading printer of Paris.

Henri Estienne, of a distinguished Provençal family, set up a printing press in the student quarter at Paris and so founded a house honourable in the history of knowledge. He worked with famous French scholars and when he died he left behind him the dominant French firm. He was succeeded by his son Robert, who made a big technical improvement by the use of roman and italic lettering and married a humane and able wife and from their home and parenthood the children grew cultured. With his biblical texts and the Latin classics, under his Latinized name of Stephanus, Robert reached out beyond a French public—the best edition of the Latin Bible till then, a good edition of the Greek New Testament, two editions of the Hebrew Old Testament. Though patronized by the Catholic French king his trade went to England and Zurich and Geneva. In 1543 he published easily the best of Latin dictionaries till then. He was that rare combination, a good businessman and a technical expert and a fine scholar; this Thesaurus was his own scholarship, he had tried to persuade well-known scholars to do it and they refused. He was a genius at arrangement and many scholars including John Milton owed some of their quotations to his indexing skill and range and clarity.

The university of Paris criticized his freedom and he promised to submit; then he was prosecuted and submitted. The notes to his excellent Bibles or New Testaments disturbed several of the professors of the university of Paris to whom the State had given the duty of sanctioning new books for publication. Were they to demand that certain passages be deleted for the next edition? or that Bibles should only be issued with lists of errata which they demanded, errors to be marked perhaps with obelisks? If they did the first they accepted that meanwhile the book went on doing what they regarded as damage. If they did the second, as several of them wanted, the task of deciding on errata was long and painful and could lead to disagreement among themselves. The only answer was to ban the whole book, whatever the merits of most of it might be. Since they were then banning a work of the first importance to the development of learning, the reputation of the censors, professors though they might be, sank amid anger and ridicule; and caused the loss of the best printer in Paris.

Such censorship was intolerable to so open a mind and he found himself ever closer to the Protestants and their larger freedom for publishing. He secretly bought a house in Berne and gained the leave of the city to settle there but he had much to lose in Paris and hesitated to go. In 1550, on the pretext of a journey to Lyons, he went instead to Geneva with the aim of being free. Almost at once he made the most radical difference to lay people's study of the Bible yet achieved, by adding the verse numbers (1551, Bibles hitherto had only the chapters—first found in old Hebrew Old Testaments and then taken into early Christian Bibles but not in the modern system till about 1250, probably in the later works of the archbishop of Canterbury, Stephen Langton) and so made reference far easier. He began to publish Protestant books. Among them was the final edition of that classic of divinity, Calvin's *Institutes*.

But when Estienne wrote a tract against the Paris censors (*Ad censuras theologorum parisiensium responsio*, 1552), he did not dream of pleading the still unknown principle that scholarship must be free, or that censorship is wrongful interference with the liberty of minds. His reply was anger and scorn of the way in which the Paris censors had maltreated him personally. Modern readers find the tract unpersuasive. But in it is the sense of freedom at last—he said that he felt like St Peter the apostle being escorted out of his prison by the angel. He did not mention that there was a censorship of books in Geneva.

Censorship was violent. An obscure Paris or Brussels printer, not intending to spread heresy but only to make a living because he knew that people would buy a book, was liable to be arrested and burnt on the marketplace on the ground that the propagator of heresy is as guilty as the proposer of what he propagates. A printer like Estienne was too big and famous a man, too close to the scholars and the academic reputation of France, too near to the king, too symbolic of humanist studies, to be probable fuel for a fire. But it happened with lesser people. The printing press was so new that those who sought to control it did not understand what they did and were liable to become fanatics. The most bizarre decree ever passed by a French government banned *any* new book from being published (13 January 1535). A rule so ruinous for the book-trade and for education had to be altered only six weeks later.

Books were not in themselves 'causes' of the Reformation. Always they were tools for preachers, or for teachers, or rather later for parents. Half-literate or even literate people still preferred to be read to than to try to read for themselves, still wished to have texts explained to them by word of mouth. Many books of course were designed for the smaller public, to teach academics and speakers what they needed. What changed the European churches was new knowledge found by scholars; the movement commonly known by the nineteenth-century term Renaissance. But the invention allowed 'renaissance' to affect many more minds.

Despite the high numbers of sales the trade was complicated because printers wanted to sell more copies by piracy. There was no copyright. The only protection was the refusal of government to license another version (as with the King James Version in England) but this protection reached only so far as the frontier of the State. Normally authors were paid no royalties. Luther earned nothing by his books. When he was offered fees he refused them.

The absence of control beyond a frontier created a further problem for a controversial thinker who wanted to express meaning carefully, for many of the 'unauthorized' printers took less trouble and easily corrupted the text as well as making absurd mistakes that were not corrected in proof.

The printers on the Catholic side had nothing like the same success. They were less common in the printing and sold far fewer copies; and in some states or cities where the publication of reforming literature was forbidden printers complained to the authorities that they would be ruined.

The ease of producing copies benefited everyone who needed many copies of the same book—almanacs, technical handbooks, school textbooks, hymn books or prayer books. The French printed perhaps 100,000 copies of the metrical psalter in a single year, King Philip of Spain printed 22,000 copies of the Catholic breviary so that Spanish clergy could say their offices according to Spanish custom.[4] Henry VIII could order every English parish church to own a Bible and could hope to be obeyed.

In any town of any size the number of persons employed in printing steadily rose until they made a force in the town's economy and among the educated class. Protestant printers were rather less often censored, they could sometimes print works which Catholic censors suppressed, not because of religion—for example Machiavelli, whose political theory was regarded as immoral, or Pietro Aretino, who was obscene, or Rabelais, who satirized the establishments, all three of whom were officially banned by the Catholic Church.

The best of this was more books in schools. Many children must now learn not only reading and writing but Latin and, if they made good progress, Greek. Since not so many adolescents are well adapted to enjoy learning languages until they have advanced beyond the beginnings, punishments in schools grew more common; probably because there were more children in the classes and more schools than because the subjects which they were now expected to learn needed to be driven into their heads.

The oral

Who could read? Estimates of the rate of literacy during the sixteenth century depend upon a small heap of evidence, of which the best is the number of pamphlets printed. The rate of literacy was rising during the sixteenth century. Schools were more numerous and continued to increase in number. But literacy was low at the beginning of the century, and is not a deficiency which can be cured in a moment or by the invention of a machine. It is

[4] Robert M. Kingdon, 'Patronage, Piety and Printing in Sixteenth-Century Europe', in D. Pinkney and T. Ropp (eds.), *Festschrift for Frederick Artz* (Durham, NC, 1964), 29, 34.

probable that two-thirds of the people in any large town of northern Europe and more than three-quarters of the people in the villages depended for information on the spoken rather than the written word. If anyone wanted all the farm labourers to read the New Testament, he would need to wait decades before it was possible, and the printing of a pocket Gospel would not be enough. They might learn a little from the woodcut illustrations which began to lighten copies of the Bible. They might learn a little from the frescos which continued to adorn the walls of churches. They would learn very little indeed, and not without error, unless the woodcut or the fresco was explained to them verbally.

But they nearly all went to church. As reformation progressed, they nearly all went to catechism. The people who taught them the catechism could read and now had better equipment for instructing themselves before they taught others. In church they heard the Bible read, now in the vernacular. Not all the people who listened to a book being read to them, even in their language, would follow it because of the gulf between a literary form and the spoken word and because the ear wanders in its attention. But because they were unable to read (if they were) they would take in the spoken information or poetry or narrative more easily than the literary mind which had come to rely on the eye instead of the ear.

Therefore it is too simple to say that the biblical revival of the Reformation had no influence on ordinary people because most of them could not read. More people could read, many more people read the Bible, and many more people sat under the literate people at classes. The doctrine that oral tradition was not the main source of knowledge has been carried so far in modern work as to question whether pulpits were in any way the main source of religious training and reform. That they were not the only source is self-evident.

But it was a belief of reformers that the Word of God has an innate and convincing power of truth which can take hold of anyone's mind; that all minds are corrupt and therefore are liable to take out of it what they want rather than what it says; that therefore they need the grace of God for right understanding, because only grace can heal the corruption of their mental process; but that this is possible for the simplest and most illiterate person as well as the most learned. They were sure that a mind did not need to be expert to understand what God wanted. Sometimes true faith was more evident in simplicity than among professors at the university. Without humility, they were sure, no one can understand, for the soul must know that it is not self-sufficient, and sometimes humility is easier for the uninstructed than the instructed. Religion does not depend upon being told what to believe. But one who cannot read, or can only read a little, is bound to depend for knowledge of the truth on what is read or spoken; even people who read easily depend on those who can translate Greek or Hebrew. But what is the essence in the Bible is not hard. Scripture comes with a directness and clarity which carries with it light and joy.[5] So it was widely believed and asserted at the time.

From early days the study of the Bible was not simply derived from the pulpit or the catechism or a class set up by the pastor though for most people it was derived only from those, but it was also fostered in groups due to the enterprise of private people who met to talk it over in their homes. Such groups were the places where strange or radical doctrine could be put forward. This was why, quite quickly, pastors who had encouraged laypeople to study the Bible for themselves began to suspect and later to try to prevent such groups for private study. To study was one thing, to start to teach others on poor knowledge was another. In 1525 a layman from Wil in the canton of Zurich wrote to the chief pastor Zwingli to get his permission to read the Bible to anyone who wanted to join him. He confessed that he was no theologian and that his faith was 'simple' but he had learnt of God and it seemed to him wrong that he should need the leave of politicians to expound God's truth from his Bible.[6]

But little groups were inevitable. For we have evidence of argument in the corners of streets, or in the shops. And naturally we have evidence where a layperson misunderstood a text though its meaning was obvious, or of others who cited a text as though they understood it while it was clear that they understood nothing. We also have evidence from demonstrations. If laypeople suspected that a Catholic priest or Protestant pastor taught them wickedly, they might clatter out of church, or shout down the speaker, or throw missiles at the pulpit, or parade in the street. These critics were not only young hotheads from a university, though a mob could well include students. The shouting may be evidence of knowledge misappropriated, but it is indirect evidence of people reading books.

During the twentieth century editors for the first time collected and analysed the pamphlets of that age. Often these were brief, violent in language, on rarer occasions obscene, not only with illustrations but caricatures, many of them anonymous or under a false name of author. They were directed not to the educated but to the common people. As so many were only half-literate we have small means of testing how powerful were these productions; except by the number of copies sold, for they were wanted in large numbers—nearly one pamphlet every year for each German who could read. Most were printed and read in towns. They could contain sermons,

---

[5] One of the best statements of this is in Zwingli's *Von Klarheit und Gewissheit des Wortes Gottes* (*Of the Clarity and Certainty of God's Word*) CR, Zwingli, i. 338 ff.; and cf. Arnold Snyder, 'Word and Power in Reformation Zurich', *ARG* 81 (1990), 263 ff.

[6] Markus Marer to Zwingli, 8 June 1525, Zwingli, *Werke*, viii. 337.

or poems, or tracts, or dialogues. They were vehement, they addressed the passions more than the reason. There were authors brilliant at this form of art, Luther among them. There were authors themselves almost illiterate. Upon the opinions of the common people this new form of literature was epoch-making in the history of the passing of knowledge or alleged knowledge, and probably had more effect than books and must almost have equalled the power of the spoken word as uttered in sermons.

2

THE BIBLE

Since the sixth century the Latin translation of the Bible, the Vulgate, had held the field in western Europe. Most of it was made by St Jerome. When it first appeared it was opposed as a novelty. Jerome translated the Hebrew Old Testament (except for the psalms which he translated from the Greek version) and for his day did it well. He included an older version of most of the Apocryphal books; he translated the four Gospels from the Greek; and adapted an earlier translation for the rest of the New Testament. The oldest copy of the whole which we possess was written in the (later) County of Durham about 700. After that there were various efforts to tidy and correct errors and what is known as the received text was not established finally till the thirteenth century. But it was familiar to all the clergy who used it, and to some laypeople. Theologians used its texts, the liturgies made parts of it familiar by regular recitation, it had taken that quality of sacredness which any well-written words take after long use in a people's prayers. The very name of Jerome had a halo of sacredness in their memory of early Christian saints because he was linked to this foundation of a people's worship.

The scholars' cry of *back to the sources* instantly affected the Vulgate. At first no one except radicals thought that anything but the Latin should be read in church. The quest was to get the right text of the Latin. But now it was possible to test the Latin against the Hebrew for the Old Testament and the Greek for the New Testament.

Because Latin was the international language, and the language of culture as well as the sacred language of the Church, the most weighty part of the new cultural interests lay in the revival of classical studies and the understanding of the ancient world. The school teaching of Latin as a way to understanding law, or science, or divinity, turned towards an understanding of Latin and of Greek as a way towards the apprehension of that which they believed to be the highest literature known to humanity.

Already during the fourteenth century there were two groups of people wanting the Bible in the vernacular: those who resented the Church and wanted biblical truth to be propagated to reform the Church; and those who cared for the Church and wanted laypeople to understand the Bible for the purposes of their private devotion. Even before that poets had put extracts from the Bible, stories or psalmody, into verse for the sake of the laypeople; nor only for the sake of the lay, for at times such poems were recited at meals in monasteries. None of these translations were used in church, only in private devotion. And many church authorities doubted the wisdom of encouraging simple people to read the text of the Bible for themselves. It is wrong to make this a universal axiom and assert that all the medieval Church was afraid of the laity reading the Bible. The authorities were not so much against vernacular Bibles in themselves as against the wild ideas which they expected to come from their use. Where there were educated laity who needed the Bible the authorities were usually happy that they should be helped by a translation. There was an evident correlation between the passages of Scripture selected to be read in lessons in church and those which were chosen for translation; a correlation which proves the existence of the idea that translations were useful to help the laity in their worship. The number of manuscripts from the age just before printing shows how valuable both laity and clergy found such translations.

The moment the printing press started, the spread of translations was of course much wider. At first they were full of mistakes because they copied the manuscripts.

The new work on the text of the Bible did not begin with a desire for translations into language which the people understood. The first and main task looked to be the making right of the Latin translation of the Bible, for they were aware that there were variations in the text.

In 1508 Lefèvre of Etaples, who was a good Latin and Greek scholar, and engaged in recovering better texts of Aristotle and making a harmony of four Latin translations of the psalms, asked the monks of St Germain in Paris how they came out from saying their psalms and what they gained from the devotion. When he examined them he reported that they had not understood the psalms and came away discouraged from the recitation.[1]

Thus not only radicals but humanists, desiring better worship in churches, asked for readings not in Latin but in the languages of the people. Though there were already vernacular versions, demands for better versions, in French or German or Italian or English or Spanish, were to be heard. If these were to content the scholars they could not simply be a German version of the Latin. They also must go direct to the Hebrew and the Greek.

The Dominican friar Santes Pagnino from Lucca was converted to the religious life by the fire of Savonarola in Florence. He was encouraged by Pope Leo X to study the oriental languages, and published at Lyons (1527) a literal translation into Latin of the Hebrew Old Testament and the Greek

---

[1] Lefèvre, Preface to *Quincuplex Psalterium* (a harmony of four Latin texts of the Psalms), ed. Guy Bedouelle (Paris, 1979).

New Testament. Such work, with a pious Catholic intention, not only helped towards a better edition of the Latin but assisted the process whereby the uniqueness of the Vulgate as a sacred book was weakened. He printed his text in verses, but no one took any notice of the verses until Robert Estienne produced his numbering which became the norm. Vernacular translators were helped by Pagnino's literal Latin—Olivétan for a French version, Coverdale for the English.

Not all sensible persons thought that this demand ought to be met. The Bible is a difficult book. Some of it, like chapters from Leviticus, is useless to piety if read in church. It is better that the select parts of the Bible be what is presented to the people, and that is done by the liturgy. The people have a biblical base for their religion because they absorb the prayers of the Church which are based upon the Bible and listen to sermons which expound weightier passages from the Bible. Sermons sometimes misquote and sometimes misrepresent and often bore and on occasion misuse; but they are about the Bible even when they do not move the people. Tell a layperson who is literate to read all through the Bible from beginning to end and the faith will profit little. The texts need to be read in a context of prayer and in the understanding of the Church; and this is achieved by the select readings during the services.

The argument was accepted by leading Protestants as well as Catholics. But among reformers it did nothing to counter the demand that the Bible be available in the vernacular languages. The general vague feeling that much was wrong with the Church and much needed changing for the better; the medieval conviction which they inherited that the Bible is the foundation on which the true Church is based; the perception that print made it possible for laypeople if they were literate to read the Bible as never before—in the face of these convictions the conservative plea, that they must continue as before but with improved Latin texts, was brushed aside as blindness.

The idea with which they started, that they could find a better Vulgate by using the Greek and the Hebrew manuscripts, was soon seen not to be workable. For if they pursued it to the natural end, the Latin translation would no longer look like the Vulgate.

There was another difficulty over the historic text. The world was well accustomed to notes, not only on the New Testament but in it, so well accustomed that a text without notes was unusual. During the early Middle Ages commentators helped the study of the Bible by taking quotations from the early Christian Fathers and writing them into the margins, or between the lines, of manuscripts of the Bible.

These citations of the Fathers were called glosses. They started as a tool for study but because they were entangled physically with the text of the Bible they took an authority of their own. As they gained authority they needed pruning of oddities by copyists; and so there came to be *the* Gloss, called from the fourteenth century the Customary Gloss, *Glossa Ordinaria*. This rather grew than was created. A famous teacher at Laon, Anselm (died 1117), who was a pupil of St Anselm archbishop of Canterbury, had a hand in its growth and collected the glosses on the Psalms and the epistles of St Paul.

Because there was a physical unity between the text of the Bible and the glosses, they affected the way in which the text was understood. When in medieval universities professors lectured about the Bible, they took as their basic texts not only the Vulgate Latin text but the glosses attached to it. The Gloss made the Bible long and heavy to hold and expensive to provide; libraries needed several volumes.

Because of the link printers started to publish the text with the glosses.

Intended as a tool for students, the Gloss was used by the educated and pious to help their reading of the Bible; and in this way the Gloss affected literature as well as theology. Getting rid of the glosses was a principal desire of the reformers in their plea to go back to the pure text of the Bible. Erasmus thought of the Gloss as a prickly hedge through which you have to cut your way to find the truth about God. In the Catholic tradition for a time the glosses were valued the more because reformers rejected them.

Various later medieval writers produced general commentaries on the Bible. Far the most important for this purpose was Nicholas of Lyra of the university of Paris (died 1349) because he knew Hebrew, which then was very rare, and because he produced a commentary (*Postillae perpetuae*) on the whole and because his judgement was often good and because he tried to keep away from mystical speculation or allegory and to go for the literal and moral sense of the text. He used the best of the Jewish commentators and spent time confuting their conclusions when they were against the Christian interpretation. He was so useful that his book was one of the earliest to be printed. Erasmus often found him ridiculous, and especially because his lack of Greek led him into absurdity, but still used him. Luther found him as wrong as one would expect a papist to be but still used him. Lyra had become almost like the glosses, venerated by a link with the Bible, and to some moderns was like a Father of the Church.

But forty years before the Gloss was first printed, one of the best scholars before the age of printing made a start at amendment. Lorenzo Valla was a cantankerous priest who despite doubts about his orthodoxy was a papal secretary in Rome and Naples, and died in 1457. He saw that if the evidence were tested famous documents accepted by the Middle Ages could not be genuine—the Donation of Constantine for example,[2] by which the pope was alleged to have been given secular power over much of western Europe;

---

[2] *De falso credita et ementita Constantini donatione declamatio* (1439).

the writings which passed under the name of St Paul's disciple Dionysius the Areopagite and which as almost apostolic became dominant in the Christian mystical tradition; the letter from Christ to King Abgar of Edessa on the Syrian border, promising to send a disciple to heal him and preach to his people, a letter from very early Syriac story and believed and valued during the Middle Ages.

Living in the age when Greek scholars fled westward from Turkish onslaught, Valla was aware of the Greek manuscript treasures and wrote notes on the Vulgate translation.[3] That testing soon suggested more drastic changes to the Latin text than was at first expected. He inferred that phrases of the Vulgate Latin were errors or misunderstandings from the Greek source. He wrote a different gloss: notes on the New Testament text from the point of view of the language, its meaning and style and grammar. The work was pedantic. Valla was not concerned with theology, only with the right understanding of the text in view of the improved knowledge of ancient Latin and ancient Greek. He floundered as anyone would do who attempted such a comparison for the first time. But he started the effective criticism of the New Testament text. He had no desire to make an edition of the Greek Testament, he only wished to correct the Vulgate.

The Complutensian Polyglot

Cardinal Cisneros was the archbishop of Toledo and the reformer of the Spanish Church on old-fashioned lines. He was a Franciscan of Toledo who became Queen Isabella's confessor. He reformed monasteries in Spain, not without ruthlessness. In 1499, seven years after the Spanish conquered the province of Granada which had been ruled by Muslims for seven centuries and a half, he forced Muslims to become Christian or leave Spain—and many became outward Christians.

The see had a marshy unhealthy estate and palace at Alcalá. There he founded a university which opened after the drainage of the ground. It was designed as a theological university, to supply educated and moral priests to the parishes of Spain. Most of the members were graduates though there were also twenty paying undergraduates in arts and theology. Under the university were seven schools (in intention more) to prepare boys by teaching them Latin and Greek. This study of Greek was new to Spanish education. But Alcalá was not a 'humanist' university because its intention was so dominantly religious rather than literary. In the study of Latin poetry the Christian poets took precedence over Virgil.

---

[3] These Annotations appeared in two editions: the first attacked by Poggio as irreverent to Scripture, the second finished shortly before Valla died and couched more prudently. Erasmus printed these second Annotations in 1505 and learnt much about the New Testament from them.

From an early time in the history of the university, perhaps even before it opened, they projected a new edition of the Bible in the two original languages of Hebrew and Greek and in the Latin translation. Cisneros started with three converted Jews to help with the Hebrew. Later he acquired a Greek professor, originally from Crete, Demetrios Doucas, who had worked in the Aldine press at Venice on the printing of Greek literature. The equipment and the persons were assembled. The New Testament was printed in January 1514, the Old Testament in July 1517. The text of the Vulgate seems mainly due to a Spaniard, Diego López Zúñiga, known by his Latin name of Stunica, and eventually the most famous of the Polyglot authors because he stormed into battle with Erasmus.

They printed the Greek text of the New Testament in beautiful parallel columns with the Latin Vulgate. The manuscripts which they used were not of high quality but the editing was careful and accurate. The editors were conservative. Nevertheless as a first attempt in the modern age this Bible was a scholarly performance.

But the moment the Old Testament was in print, their patron Cardinal Cisneros died. The executors of his will failed to get papal approval for publication until March 1520, and the Bible only began to be sold in 1522. It was in six volumes. They printed only 600 copies. Many of these copies were lost in a shipwreck on the way to Italy. Each copy cost $6\frac{1}{2}$ ducats, far beyond the means of anyone but a well-endowed library. It was soon unobtainable. And meanwhile Erasmus had published his New Testament and captured the market.

Erasmus captured the market not only because he came out first. It mattered who he was, and what he had written before he published the New Testament. No one had heard of Alcalá. Anyone who read books read Erasmus.

He was already a very famous author when he published his New Testament in 1516; the New Testament in Greek, with a Latin translation, printed by Froben at Basel. This quickly became a symbol of what the new learning achieved for the understanding of the Bible. It had the freshness, the excitement, of the best of the Renaissance.

Erasmus knew that he needed protection. He first wrote to Pope Leo X asking him if he might dedicate to him his edition of St Jerome's works. The courteous Medici pope accepted the Jerome dedication and said that he looked forward to the publication of the New Testament. Erasmus had this letter printed. It was a shield.

He entitled his New Testament *Novum Instrumentum*, edited 'after many manuscripts in Greek and Latin both ancient and corrected . . .'. By the Greek edition stood his Latin translation; and then more than half the volume contained explanatory notes, the Annotations; so that the volume was not a pocket affair but contained 986 pages. At that size it could not be intended to be a people's New Testament. Readers disliked the title New Instrument and felt it strange, so later he went back to calling it New Testament.

For several centuries it was assumed that the aim of Erasmus was to find the original Greek text of the New Testament, which indeed was a task characteristic of the best scholarship of that age; that then he needed to provide a Latin translation to replace the canonical Vulgate, so that the many people who did not know Greek but knew Latin could understand what changes he was recommending to the text; and thirdly, that to justify these readings and this translation against critics who were sure to be numerous, he needed scholarly notes and hence the Annotations.

Modern enquiries showed that this logical order is the reverse of what happened. He started with the idea of scholarly notes on the New Testament; like those of Lorenzo Valla whom he admired and whose Annotations he had published. This led him on to the idea of a Latin translation to explain his notes to the world. Then the Latin translation needed the reference to the Greek original in order to justify it, and hence the Greek New Testament was in origin the third and not the first of the tasks which he set before himself.

He knew more Latin and Greek than Valla, he knew and valued Valla's work, he would create an improved series of textual notes; and so we get his Annotations. In these he used Valla extensively, often without saying so.

With his Annotations Erasmus aimed to make the *Latin* text more accurate as a translation and in a better literary style. Plainly it was the second of these aims which would be likely to cause most trouble to the author. It was soon evident to him that he could not justify his changes in the Latin without also publishing a Greek text.

The next question was of quality of Greek text. In the title he claimed to have used many manuscripts, ancient and later. For the Greek he had four manuscripts only; three from the libraries at Basel. He had imagined that the libraries at Basel would contain many early manuscripts, but was disappointed. Three of the four manuscripts were by later standards neither important nor early, but the fourth was of the twelfth century and contained all the New Testament except the Revelation and even now is not despised. He also borrowed a very late manuscript which contains his only Greek text of the Apocalypse, but it included new errors because a secretary copied it badly. It omitted the last six verses so he coolly made his own translation from the Latin into Greek. From his friend John Colet the dean of St Paul's in London he saw three Latin manuscripts from the cathedral library—they no longer exist—and said that they were the most accurate of all. In all parts of the New Testament he sometimes said that he had found another reading, but he did not mention where he found it and some of these readings have not been discovered to this day though there is no evidence that he cheated and that charge is very improbable. Besides manuscripts he also used citations of Scripture in the early Fathers.

In this work he behaved as a true scholar—except that he made notes in pen on the manuscripts which he borrowed—going to see the manuscript and collating it, judging on probabilities from the (then rather vague) age of the manuscript, and aware that his expertise in the Greek and Latin classics was not always a good guide to the grammar used by the authors of the Bible. He knew the rule that the more unlikely reading is likely to be right because the copyist would change what he thought must be wrong but not what seemed to him obvious.

Even when allowance is made for the pioneer nature of the operation, the quality was not up to his own standard of scholarship as shown in other fields. The reason for this was hurry. Froben the printer was the culprit because he was excited at the idea of bringing out a New Testament by the best scholar of the day before the appearance of the forthcoming Spanish Complutensian Polyglot edition which had been announced. Froben was a devout printer who became a close friend of Erasmus and was willing to risk much money for a cause which, in the absence of laws of copyright, had a chance of failing to cover the large expenses. (He put a quaint note in at the beginning of the book, 'If people copy this book illegally, at least let them copy accurately.')

Erasmus knew that he went too fast. As a scholar he did not like what he had done. He wrote to a friend, 'it was more thrown out to the public than edited'. To another he wrote 'I've done six years' work in eight months.' He exaggerated his defects. And he had good assistants at Basel, among them a first class Hebraist, Oecolampadius, to whom the printer Froben also felt a special gratitude for the achievement.

The book made an epoch in the history of the human intelligence. One unique aspect was the number of prefaces. This was a weakness in Erasmus. He could not resist the temptation to write words. Three prefaces were two too many. The first preface was powerful.

This first preface was called 'Encouragement to the Devout Reader'. This is not academic, at times it is emotional. He blamed anyone who wanted to keep the Bible from the common people. For, he said, the Christians neglect the source of Christian truth. They know more about Plato or Aristotle or Averroes. (This was far from accurate.) Yet Christian truth is easy to find by everyone, you do not need to be a professor to discover what it is, you only need a pure and simple and religious heart. Therefore it is more than lawful, it is necessary, that all Christians read the Bible; and so it must be translated for them into the language which they understand. It ought to be in Scottish and Irish, even in Turkish and Arabic. 'I want even the lowliest of women to read the Gospels and the letters of St Paul.' Would that the ploughman at the plough or the weaver at the loom could think of it, or the traveller

lighten a journey with stories from it. Why should we reserve doctrine for
the monks and theologians who are a minority among Christians and some
of them not so good as they ought to be? If princes put it to their people, and
priests preached it, and teachers taught it to their classes, Christendom
would not be divided by wars, nor by the passion for getting rich, nor by so
many lawsuits; and we could bring people to faith more effectively than
by weapons and threats. This knowledge is won by the feelings, by life more
than by argument, by conversion more than reason. Only a few can be
learned, but anyone can be a Christian, 'I dare to say, anyone can be a
theologian.'

This was followed by another preface, called Methodus, 'On Method',
though the result is not methodical. For since he said that this knowledge is
won through feelings and the will and living a life, he left no large place for
rational methods of enquiry. Approach the reading of the New Testament
with a serene mind, not tumultuously, but like a stream flowing calmly. It
needs a thirsty soul, and one thirsting for nothing else in the same way. Then
try to learn the biblical languages—with a good teacher and some courage it
can be done, perfection in them is not needed, but no one can understand a
book without knowing the language of the author who wrote it. 'Do not listen to people who say "Jerome's translation is good enough for me."' There
may be able people who should go to the context of the New Testament—
the Roman world and its history, the geography of Palestine, what light these
throw on the letters of apostles. Incite the young to read the life of Jesus from
birth to resurrection. And then Erasmus drew a portrait of his idea of the true
Christian—Christ created a new people, who look to heaven and by dis-
trusting the certainties of this world have another wealth, another nobility,
another power, another happiness; without envy, with a straight eye, without
lust, a people the greater because humble, with an ideal which looks back to
the purity and simplicity of the child; living day by day like the birds of the
air, not valuing life but looking forward to death, not afraid of tyrants or
Satan, because resting in Christ's protection. If they can they ought to study
the early Christian Fathers; but they need not bother their heads with debates
of medieval schoolmen. They are to beware of common mistranslations—for
example the word Church to mean the clergy, the phrase 'divine worship' to
mean ceremonies.

Critics noticed the self-contradiction and lack of realism. Erasmus tells
everyone to read the Bible but they should all know Latin and Greek and
Hebrew though they need not be perfect in those languages.

Then he added still a third preface, called 'Apology', a defence of the right
and duty of correcting the accepted Latin Vulgate text with the aid of the
Greek original. It is addressed to the professional theologians—I have
sweated blood for your sakes, please do not treat me with ingratitude—this

preface was too self-regarding to introduce a New Testament and the book would have been better without it. He knew that his notes (Annotations) were valuable academically and wished to commend them to the professors.

At the end of the Annotations was printed a letter from his chief helper Oecolampadius in which there is a shining portrait of the atmosphere which surrounded this moment of religion and scholarship. It is a panegyric which Erasmus preferred to omit in later editions; but the reader feels it to be sincere; Oecolampadius, no mean scholar, felt it a privilege to be working with Erasmus, such refined writing with so happy an air, the honour and the delight of literature, powerful scholarship which has left previous interpreters far behind; and yet there is nothing heavy, it is full of grace; we have watched his hours of work, late into the night, consulting manuscripts, comparing commentators, accurate over the tiniest words, and yet everything presented with kindness and generosity and with a happy face, with simplicity and a total absence of arrogance. Erasmus never received a more deserved and more genuine tribute from a friend and colleague.

The learned world was excited and grateful at the appearance of the New Testament. The name of Erasmus, as scholar and as a leader of religious devotion, stood at its summit. He was celebrated; probably no scholar had ever been so widely revered. The public did not buy many copies of his New Testament. The first edition sold 1,200, not rapidly. But because he knew it to be faulty he was already at work on a second edition. This appeared after two years, now called *Novum Testamentum*. Of both editions together Froben the publisher sold 3,300 copies. Therefore it was not the New Testament in everyone's hand, an appeal to the Christian people of Europe. It was an aid to the learned and intended as such. This second edition was that which Luther knew and lies at the base of his German translation of the New Testament and thereby influenced the English translations.

Few readers could manage the Greek, everyone who had a copy could read Latin. The Latin translation was soon printed separately. Erasmus had doubts. He realized that this would draw more abuse upon him for weakening the authority of the Vulgate Latin text.

He had said in the third preface that he had no idea of weakening the Vulgate. He said that he wished the Vulgate to be taught in school, and quoted in sermons, and sung in church. But in the home, in private reading, he claimed, his own translation would help understanding. In his Latin translation he kept nearer the Vulgate than he needed, in order to preserve what familiarity was possible. He did not strive for elegance of style. He said that he intended his translation only for private use. But that meant he wanted a large number of people who had never read the Bible at all, and whose only knowledge of it was by listening to the Latin Epistles and Gospels at mass, to read it for themselves.

A few readers were disturbed by any language that was not the Vulgate. On occasion Erasmus committed the normal sin of translators of prayers by altering the familiar without necessity. His moralism softened the force of St Paul's idea of grace. Because he accepted the axiom that Scripture is easy to understand, he looked for simplicity and so deformed complex texts by thinning them. There are mystical texts and Erasmus was no mystic. But the stone of offence lay in the Annotations. These notes contain a treasure of learning, to illustrate the New Testament from the early Christian Fathers.

But—he was so personal an author. In whatever he wrote he took his readers into his confidence, argued with them, made fun of them, addressed them directly. These so learned Annotations have asides. The tone of the international humorist, mocking and cutting, kept poking in—(St Matthew xi 30 my yoke is easy and my burden is light—contrast what burdens they lay on us now—clothes, fast days, feast days, vows, marriage fees, confession). The notes were less academic than their presence claimed.

As the editions were revised and improved, so the Annotations grew in size, and part of the growth was an answer to critics of his New Testament who were offensive, and he was bad at not refraining from offensive retort.

If the text was decisive for future Protestant Bibles, the Annotations were important. They made a fresh way of explaining. They filled the old function of glosses. They were used by the leading exegetes of the sixteenth and seventeenth centuries and they put the old form of glossing the text, which served several medieval centuries, out of use.

To explain the texts he also wrote Paraphrases. These were published part by part, Romans first, Acts last. They were regarded by the new students of the Bible as very helpful. He could not bear parts of the morality of the Old Testament and explained it away by the traditional use of allegory, though he accepted that the literal meaning was the first to be sought. St Paul in the Paraphrases turned into a renaissance sort of apostle. Some 'explanations' in the Paraphrases are not explanation but preaching. For the Paraphrases aimed at a wider public than the Latin New Testament. They were written in an easy style.

He was asked, are you sure that you are doing right? This Vulgate Bible is familiar to everyone who reads and hears it in church and is used by every preacher; and in a people's devotion familiarity with the words is important. Is it right to unsettle everyone by telling them that the text they use is a wrong translation? Is it right to unsettle them by telling them that a famous text is not in an old Greek manuscript and ought to be ejected from the Bible? May you not be weakening the authority of the Bible among the people?

Erasmus even used the inscription on the cross, that was written in three languages, as an argument for the necessary study of languages—have we to force everyone taking orders to learn Greek and Hebrew and to exclude from the priesthood anyone who has not time nor inclination nor ability for the study of two ancient languages in two strange sorts of lettering?[4]

A Carthusian published a book at Paris against what Erasmus did. He argued thus: We need a single translation of the Bible with which everyone is familiar. If there are several translations there will be arguments over versions and meaning, and the use of texts unfamiliar to worshippers at church services. That will cast a doubt on the authority of the Bible. They tell us that housewives, artisans, labourers, ought to read the Bible for themselves. But no one says, you cannot be saved unless you know the Bible. What people need can be just the Lord's Prayer, and the Creed, and the Ten Commandments, and otherwise the rules of the Church. If we tell everyone they must know all the Bible we tell them to do something impossible for them. And to throw the Bible at them has danger—what will they think of God in the Old Testament when they find Judah and the prostitute, and big-amous patriarchs, and bulls and goats in bloody sacrifices, and the four evan-gelists disagreeing? And what will happen when they find the Bible says nothing about an annual confession, or a Lent fast, or keeping Sunday holy? A Bible is an object, physical, which must be treated with reverence. What sort of reverence will happen to it if it goes into the house of every common man and woman?[5]

To such arguments Erasmus had a short answer. If in our day study proves that a translation is not faithful to the original, no ton of piety ought to stop us from mending it.

To this answer he held in theory. But it did not quite meet all his difficul-ties. The most beloved story of forgiveness in the New Testament was that of the woman taken in adultery. Erasmus did not find it in his older Greek manu-scripts of St John's Gospel. Erasmus kept it in his text. He was right to keep it, at least somewhere in his New Testament. But such cases made the simple answer less easy. Suppose that a text is much used and much beloved in daily worship, and then the students say that old manuscripts suggest this to be wrong—are the worship and long use by the Church, or the new results of researchers, the more weighty? The answer was not clear and there were several places where he found it not clear.

Usually he was consistent in his principle. It was common belief in the Church that St Paul wrote the Epistle to the Hebrews. Erasmus said that he could not have done it. 'If the Church defines that St Paul wrote the Epistle to the Hebrews I shall willingly obey and put my reason in chains, but it is my opinion that he did not.' There was satire in Erasmus.

---

[4] So Jacob Latomus, real name Jacques Masson, a mainstay of the conservative Louvain faculty of theology, in *De trium linguarum et studii theologici ratione* (Antwerp, 1519).

[5] Petrus Sutor, real name Cousturier, *De tralatione* [*sic*] *Bibliae et novarum interpretationum reproba-tione* (Paris, 1524).

The Vulgate had the last clause of the Lord's Prayer—'For thine is the kingdom, the power and the glory . . .'. Most early manuscripts did not have it. The liturgy, and a people's prayers, used and loved it. But Erasmus was not alone in omitting it. The Spaniards of the Polyglot omitted this doxology and explained why.

The Johannine Comma was the name for the insertion of the Holy Trinity into the text of the fifth chapter of the First Epistle of St John: 'there are three that bear record in heaven, the Father, the Word, and the Holy Ghost and these three are one'. The word *comma* meant originally a phrase in a sentence and only later a mark of punctuation. This text was taken to prove the doctrine of the Trinity. By origin it was a Western gloss written into the manuscripts in the fourth century or even earlier, in Africa or Spain, and about a hundred years after Jerome it appeared in some manuscripts of the New Testament. By the age of Charlemagne it was fully established in Latin Bibles. It was an interesting example of the way in which a gloss between the lines of a text could win its way into the main text without fraud by copyists.

The Spaniards of the Polyglot knew that it was not in Greek but though they were not always so conservative they kept the Comma, probably because they did not dare not to print it as part of the text; and this was to have long consequences in history because it affected the Council of Trent and modern Catholicism; until even as late as 1897 the Holy Office in Rome declared the Comma to be authentic, and in 2001 various Anglican clergy read it in church on the first Sunday after Easter.

Unlike the men of the Polyglot, Erasmus did not print it in his first edition. Professional exegetes were more disturbed by this than was well-judged. Erasmus was said to be abandoning the doctrine of the Trinity and opening the door to the wilder forms of heresy of which the Church rid itself with such difficulty in the fourth and fifth centuries.

Erasmus was resentful but wished to appease. Someone in England faked a manuscript which contained the text. Conservatives who had Greek manuscripts started writing the missing text into the margin. An Irish manuscript was found with the addition and this gave Erasmus the weak excuse to avoid trouble by restoring the text in his third edition of the New Testament. Five years later he was able to report that a friend who had examined the Vatican manuscript, far earlier than any manuscript used by Erasmus, had found that the text was not present—but still he kept the text in all his last editions. He defended his integrity as a scholar by pleading that the text was in the Vulgate and therefore St Jerome must have had it in his Greek manuscript; and he could not yet know that St Jerome did not have it in his manuscript and that it was not present in the earliest editions of the Vulgate. Because he kept the text against his better judgement it stayed in the reformed translations and in the English King James Version and in the Book of Common Prayer.

The renaissance of scholarship helped to create the Reformation by its new learning, that is an unshakeable axiom. But despite what the critics of Erasmus alleged, was anyone unsettled in their religious ideas because learned persons showed that all the accepted text of the Bible was not quite so secure as they had supposed? The history of the Comma shows that this is improbable. Decades later, Unitarians in eastern Europe appealed to Erasmus when they tried to justify their rejection of the doctrine of the Trinity. But the doctrine of the Trinity did not rest on the Comma and went on being professed with hardly a hesitation of mind until the coming of the Enlightenment during the eighteenth century or even later. Erasmus himself was important to the coming Reformation, but not because he started an argument among scholars over certain texts. What unsettled minds was the ability to read the Bible in their own language and discover how far from its teachings or practices existing church teaching or practice felt to be. The medieval Church had taught them to revere the Bible as a source of the truth. It tried in its way to encourage them to read the Bible for their devotional life. It proved its system of doctrine with the aid of texts from the Bible and accepted that these had an absolute authority when rightly understood. In this way the medieval Church was the supreme source of the Reformation in Europe because it put forward the Bible as the supreme authority and now when so many more people were able to read the Bible, they found that its contents justified critics of the medieval Church.

Erasmus was helped in his defence because he won an official commendation of his New Testament from Pope Leo X, and printed this praise at the front of every later edition: 'we take much pleasure in your endeavours . . . they show an original and distinguished scholarship . . . we very much rejoice in the explanations which you have added . . . and hope it will help theology and the orthodox faith. God will reward you, and we commend you, and all Christian people will praise you.' It was sent 'To our beloved son Erasmus of Rotterdam, professor of divinity'. That was not quite what Erasmus was, though he was a doctor of divinity at the university of Turin where he had never studied. Erasmus was fortunate in coinciding with the last years of this last of the Renaissance popes.

Hebrew

In 1500 very few Christians knew Hebrew. They had two guides to the Hebrew of the Old Testament; one was the Vulgate translation, for Jerome had done well in Hebrew for his time; and the other was the Septuagint translation, where the Hebrew was turned into Greek for the benefit of Greek-speaking Jews during the third century BC. Yet the new scholarship drove them back to the sources and they must have Hebrew if they were to find the right text of the Old Testament. They could not get on with the Bible until a few Christian scholars acquired a profound knowledge of the Hebrew language.

Since the days when the Septuagint and later Jerome translated, Hebrew developed into a literary and philosophical and poetic language, mainly among the Jews of Muslim Spain. It was a purely literary language. No one spoke it except in prayers, though there are rare traces of certain families or communities using it on the sabbath. In Spain the Jews were many, enough to affect Spanish culture. In that country alone they occupied other professions besides those of physician and banker and scholar. Spain was the centre of gravity of Jewish civilization. The sudden desire of the Spanish to turn them out was bad for Spain, bad for the Jews, and good for the other countries in which they settled.

The conquest of the south caused many Muslims to embrace Christianity. They met Jewish faith and some were attracted to that power in Jewish faith which was the God of Mount Sinai. The Spanish fancied that they saw how Jewish ideas affected the new converts. They ordered the Jews to be Christians or to go.

Numerous Spanish Jews accepted Christian baptism. About 300,000 left Spain, in fearful conditions, and on their journeys they lost people through shipwreck or piracy. They left behind many children who were educated as Christians. Most went to North Africa and Greece and Syria and Egypt. A new centre of gravity was created for the Jewish people in eastern Europe, in Poland and Russia. But these easterners did not for a long time recapture the intellectual leadership of the Jews.

Across Italy, in Rome and Venice and Genoa and a few other towns, there were already Jewish communities. Here ex-Spaniards could settle. Former Spanish Jews were good physicians in Venice and Genoa. And there were scholars: Jews in Italy and Germany who were expert in the language of the Old Testament. There was a chance for Christians to advance in their understanding of the Old Testament.

This path was made difficult by the reluctance of Jews to help. Spanish converts were the best assistants, as one of them, Alfonso de Zamora, was the key Hebraist among the Polyglot translators. But Jews preferred to keep the knowledge of Hebrew away from Christians. They had a sense that the language was sacred and did not want it profaned by 'outsiders'. They also knew that their books contained attacks on Christianity—in the effort to persuade likely converts not to go over—and if they taught Christians to read Hebrew, onslaughts might be found and what might the consequence be? They had a reasonable fear that if a Christian asked to be taught Hebrew the motive was sinister, to search out matter whereby their faith could be slandered. Serious students had difficulty in finding anyone willing to teach them

Hebrew. But little by little they found help; first from converts, later from students still of Jewish faith.

These difficulties are shown in the youth of Conrad Pellican. A Franciscan from the age of fifteen, he was sent by his community to study at the university of Tübingen. On a journey he met a learned Jewish convert to Christianity, who told him how he had attended a debate between Christians and Jews where the Jews won easily because they knew the Old Testament and the Christians did not. Pellican determined to learn Hebrew. He had no grammar and no one to teach him and could find no Jew to help. His superior brought from Mainz a very heavy manuscript of the prophets of the Old Testament, then he learnt the alphabet from a fragment of Jewish poetry, then he went right through the Old Testament trying to understand the Hebrew text with the aid of Jerome's Latin translation. In 1503 he was able to print the first Hebrew grammar in any European language.

Eliahu ben Ascher Hallevi, usually known as Elias the Levite, was born in the Nuremberg ghetto but when he was a young man his family was thrown out of the town and he taught Hebrew in Padua. Later Padua was sacked in the war and he lost his possessions and fled to Rome. When already fifty-five, he found happiness and a good life. The general of the Austin Friars Egidio of Viterbo wanted to learn Hebrew and came across Elias and gave him rooms and stipend and enabled him to dedicate himself to scholarship. His happiness ended with the sack of Rome in 1527, through which he lost rare manuscripts and most of his books, and so he wandered off again. He refused an excellent invitation to teach Hebrew at the Sorbonne because he did not wish to be the only Jew in Paris, and finally passed over to the Protestant world, though not to be a Christian, when he accepted an invitation from Paul Fagius at Isny in south-west Germany to help set up Hebrew fonts for a printing press. On this Isny press he printed most of his own works, which were read by both Jews and Christians. He helped everyone by creating a Hebrew–German lexicon. In Basel the ex-Franciscan Protestant scholar Sebastian Münster translated much of Elias's grammatical work into Latin. The most widely used Hebrew grammar in the Reformation was Münster's re-edition (Basel, 1529) of Elias's grammar.

In Italy the learned Jews and the Christian scholars began to get together. Both had a concern for the scholarship of the ancient world. Because Jews settled in north Italy, they started to print Hebrew books, especially in Venice. They were unofficially allowed to study at the university of Padua. And both Jews and Christians were interested in the cabbala (kabbala, qabbala). At first Jews used the word to mean the tradition of truth. By the early thirteenth century it acquired the meaning of a mysterious truth; that a secret of God was hidden in the symbols of the Old Testament. Some Jewish converts to Christianity believed that the Christian God could be proven by examining this secret. When Moses climbed into the mists of Mount Sinai he received not only the Ten Commandments but instructions which were cast into a hidden form, for at that moment the peoples were not yet ready to see these truths. Hebrew was the original language of the world and therefore in old Hebrew books we may expect to find truths communicated to the earth. These books of the cabbala were kept apart from the common people because their minds must grow before they could understand.

Pico della Mirandola was an Italian humanist and on his travels met and was influenced by a Spanish Jewish convert to Christianity. From this source he 'discovered' the cabbala. He accepted the belief that there was no more convincing proof of the godhead of Christ (outside the Christian revelation) than that which was derived from the cabbala and its mysterious knowledge. He found there the Trinity, and the Incarnation, and the godhead of the Messiah, and the idea of original sin, and reconciliation through the grace of Christ, and demons and angels, and purgatory and hell. He aimed at an apprehension of the divine in which the secret enquiries and Greek philosophy and the study of natural science and a biblical theology should all unite in presenting truth to humanity.

In Germany this idea became fruitful, not just for a mystical link between a few gnostic or muddled Jews and a few gnostic or muddled Christians, but for sane and fruitful enquiry into the Bible; and so made a difference to the coming Reformation.

Reuchlin

Contemporaries regarded him as a prodigy of learning, they put him with Erasmus though he had neither the range nor the fascination. Some also put him with Luther as one of the founders of Protestantism—but he remained a Catholic till death. For most of his life he was a lay lawyer but ran short of money and took up teaching Greek and Hebrew grammar.

Reuchlin was older than Erasmus and reached fame before him with his Greek studies and his Hebrew grammar. He was also more learned than Erasmus in the languages. But Erasmus soon overtook him in reputation and achieved a fame which he could never match; for Erasmus could write charmingly and Reuchlin was heavy and concentrated on philology and could not speak to the multitude. There were no pilgrimages to Reuchlin's house nor statues erected then to his memory. But Hebrew to him was more than a hobby. It was his real life; it was the language of God who by it spoke to the world.

At first he found difficulty in finding a Jew who would help. Reuchlin finally found his instructor when visiting the court of the emperor Frederick III at Linz in Austria, where he met the emperor's personal physician. This was Jechiel Loans, so good a physician that the emperor knighted him, probably a unique fate for a Jew of that age. He had conformed to Christian life, and agreed to teach Reuchlin Hebrew.

Part of Reuchlin's academic drive rested upon the cabbala. He was influenced directly by Pico della Mirandola's wish to marry the mysteries from the Jewish cabbala to the faith of the Old Testament and to Greek philosophical religion. Much of the result was nonsense. He played with numbers and letters in the hope that when the code was broken they would disclose the secrets of God. He believed that God has given to humanity the occult science and that we must recover this and that our knowledge of the Hebrew texts will help us. Through the cabbala we should understand the secrets hidden in the Old Testament (which only those who understood Hebrew could decodify) and then we should see that the mysteries hidden there point forward to the New Testament and confirm the Christian revelation. He believed that the Jews might be converted from their hatred of Christianity (which he supposed them to be full of) by this method.[6]

Helped by the self-taught Conrad Pellican, he published a Hebrew grammar (1506). It sold very few copies. The scholars in universities did not think it worth their attention—with rare exceptions of whom Martin Luther was one. Reuchlin had realized by now that the world was against him; that the Jews disliked what he was doing, and Christians were nervous of a Hebrew Old Testament.

The remote and retiring lawyer became a figure of public controversy, though hardly anyone understood his work and though no one could possibly understand one side of his work because it was not intelligible. And he had a quality which the Renaissance could recognize. 'I revere Jerome, I greatly respect Lyra [the received commentator on the Vulgate]. But above them I love truth because God is truth.'

Reuchlin won fame because a Jew who had been converted to Christianity, Pfefferkorn, publicly advocated that governments should confiscate all Jewish books; the motive being the welfare of the Jewish people, for they would never be happy unless they assimilated into society and that they could not do unless they became Christian and the existence of their own books of worship hindered them from conversion. He did not mind that the effort if attempted would cause extreme persecution, nor that taking books was stealing (he said that it was not stealing if the aim was the benefit of the person from whom the object was taken), nor that the destruction of historic books would be contrary to what the best scholars wanted, nor that people

---

[6] This theory was first put forward in *De verbo mirifico* (1496); fuller in *De arte cabbalistica* (1517), but by then a vaster controversy overshadowed the argument. Reuchlin's works on the cabbala were reprinted Stuttgart, 1964.

like Reuchlin or Pellican would regard such book-burning as a very grave
loss to the understanding of the Old Testament part of the Bible. As the
famous Hebraist in Germany Reuchlin led the resistance to this obscuran-
tism; which made him much more famous, and much more controversial,
and his life unhappier, and his purse emptier; but gathered round his support
the humanist scholars with Erasmus at their head.

The pamphlet war lasted ten years, 1511–21. It ended in Pfefferkorn's formal and Reuchlin's actual victory. During the ten years the question of
Hebrew books was continuously before the educated reader.

The Apocrypha of the Old Testament

One result of the study of Hebrew astonished Christendom; a split between
northern Europe and southern over which were the books of Holy Scripture
to contain the revelation of God to humanity. No one expected this split
when the Renaissance fostered the study of the texts of the Bible.

At or near the end of the Old Testament were books written not in
Hebrew but in Greek. The chief were the books of Wisdom, Ecclesiasticus,
and Maccabees. Jews that were not Greeks excluded them from the list of
books that were inspired. The Greek translation for Jews, the Septuagint,
made no difference between them and other books of the Old Testament.
St Jerome doubted them, and called them 'ecclesiastical books' as opposed to
'canonical books'. In Greek the word *apocryphos* meant hidden; and in later
Greek when applied to books it meant books of which the author is
unknown, and from that it easily came to be used of books where the author
was believed to be a person who wrote a book and then gave it a more famous
name as its author. St Jerome used it in Latin to show his doubt of the non-
Hebrew books[7] and reformers often quoted what Jerome said.

The medieval Catholic Church continued to use these Greek books as a
part of the inspired and canonical Scriptures. The new critics of the north,
first among them Carlstadt, professor at the university of Wittenberg,
quickly resolved the doubt, *de canonicis Scripturis libellus* (1520): the Jews are
right, Hebrew is the language of God, the Old Testament which contains
God's message to his people is written in Hebrew, and the Greek books are
an addition of material about good behaviour but are not truly the Word of
God. In all Protestant editions of the Bible the Greek books were placed
together at the end of the Old Testament, and within a few years were given
the title The Apocrypha, with the definition that these books are not to be
counted as part of Holy Scripture but are useful and good to read.

---

[7] Migne, *Patrologia Latina*, 29. 601 ff.

This was helpful. In the Vulgate for example the books of Daniel and Esther have Greek additions which do not edify.

It did not mean that printers produced the Bible without the Apocrypha. No such edition is known for nearly all the sixteenth century. The books were not part of Holy Scripture but they ought to be printed with it—that remained the view for decades. Though Ecclesiasticus was a moralist in the Apocrypha, and Proverbs was moral in the Old Testament, Ecclesiasticus continued to be widely used in Protestant moral teaching, and with another book of the Apocrypha, Wisdom, appeared, though not extensively, in Protestant calendars and lectionaries for daily reading of the Bible in church or in the home. But everyone agreed that however useful in morality they could not be used to establish or support any doctrinal truth.

In Switzerland laypeople began to ask the obvious question. Why are these books printed in the Bible when they are not inspired nor part of Holy Scripture? Yet even in Switzerland there were no editions of whole Bibles printed without the Apocrypha until the last two decades of the sixteenth century. And then the motive was the wish of the printer to reduce the cost of the book to the client by shortening the Bible in a place where it was evidently possible to omit many pages. Every home ought to possess a Bible—but it is a long book—it is expensive and heavy—if we can rightly shorten it we can help laypeople. This view was taken without regard for the content of the different books. If they wanted to help the religion and morality of the people they would have done far better to omit, say, parts of Leviticus and include parts of Wisdom and Ecclesiasticus. It never occurred to them. The Word of God to the Jews was in Hebrew.

To translate the Bible into the languages which the peoples now spoke was a formidable task. These languages were only during that age finding their maturity as literary languages rather than spoken. To express a paragraph well and clearly they were accustomed to Latin, a language effective and clear by its nature and with a long history in European culture. This Latin varied according to the needs of the user. The philosopher in the schools used a Latin far from the style of the old Roman authors but it was serviceable for its purpose with many technical terms. Italian humanists and then French tried to write Latin like the Romans at their best, Cicero or Caesar. Erasmus wrote beautiful Latin which became a model for schoolchildren for two centuries, it was of the classical style and yet it was living and in no way 'a dead language'.

But these *dialects*—the English could not any longer write like Chaucer, the Germans could not write like the Minnesingers, the French found it easier to make a version because their language was so much nearer Latin. These coming translations of the Bible were to be formative of a literature in each nation, especially in countries where the spoken language was German or a derivative from German, like English, or Dutch, or Swedish, or Danish, or Swiss-German—and in any country where the spoken language was not from the Roman—like Hungary or Finland.

The Germans and the English were fortunate. In each people their first big translator had a touch of genius in the use of words. In both countries this meant that the new German and English Bibles were the most influential of books on the coming vernacular literatures.

In England William Tyndale was educated at Oxford University and then at Cambridge and started by translating one of Erasmus's more radical books, the *Enchiridion*, from Latin into English. Influenced by what was happening in Germany he worked to translate the New Testament but moved to Germany to do it and visited Luther at Wittenberg. But his English translation (first edition 1525) was not imitated from Luther. His text was the Greek of Erasmus and in translating he was helped by Erasmus's Latin and Luther's German. He had clarity and power. The importance of what he did was shown by the generations who afterwards used and were affected by what he had done.

In Saxony Luther was kidnapped for his own safety to the Wartburg castle and had leisure and translated the New Testament. It was done quickly, eleven weeks for the draft, then he went over it with friends. At base he used Erasmus's 1519 edition of the Greek New Testament. The translation appeared without name of author or printer but with woodcuts by Cranach. It had instant success. It cost half a gulden, a week's wage for a craftsman.

The Old Testament did not come out as a unity but in books or parts as they were completed, the first edition of the whole was not till 1534, printed at Wittenberg by Hans Lufft with 117 woodcuts from the workshop of Cranach, and cost 2 gulden 8 groschen or 'about the price of five calves', not within the means of working people. Lay families, even if they had members who could read, at first had not a whole Bible but a part, the Psalms, or a Gospel, or all four Gospels.

Luther was a master of strong direct German and was creative of its literary force. He thought about how a translator should work. In translating he 'interpreted' the text, that is gave some texts of the Old Testament a little Christian slant, and laid himself open to the charge of detractors that he falsified the Scripture. He was criticized by his enemies for adding glosses and prefaces. In his prefaces and in sentences of the translation it could be seen how his mind developed. Even though he translated from the original he was so familiar with the Latin Vulgate, both in study and from its use in services, that the memory of it was still present to him as he worked.

He was free in his attitudes to the inspiration of the text. He would tell his audiences that St James is simply wrong or that the text on giants is nothing to do with physical size (they are arrogant men); he said that Moses is boring because he goes on repeating himself—but troubled hearts are fond of repetitions; or that Moses' wordiness grates on sensitive ears; or that the story of Noah's drunkenness is silly and unprofitable. He did not think much of the last book of the Bible and said so plainly.

He realized that to be an effective translator he must have a mastery of the language, and that for him this meant consultation with colleagues. When he was brought up against a difficulty he took several days or even a fortnight before he could pitch on the right word in German. He often used modern phrases and what was then colloquial language. Luther was never content at what he had done; he and his committee continued to work at revising it for the rest of his life. Even the second edition of the New Testament had already many changes and the corrections continued from edition to edition.

As the various editions came out, there were generally more alterations in the Old Testament than in the New because the knowledge of Hebrew made rapid strides, often with the help of Jewish scholars. Twelve editions of the whole Bible appeared during his life and twenty-one editions of the New Testament; this does not count the pirate editions, nor Emser's Bible for the Catholics which was so largely based on Luther's that the Catholics of Germany went on using Luther's Bible, though they did not know it to be mostly his, until the eighteenth century.

The last edition in which he had a personal part in the emendations appeared during the year before his death. In his last years owners of Bibles liked him to sign his name at the beginning of their copy, with a saying.

The principal translator was not the best scholar in the group. But he knew enough Greek and Hebrew to be able to trust his two experts in the languages, Aurogallus and Melanchthon. The translation triumphed because none of it was written in the jargon of a committee but all by a single mind who possessed a genius to create the first true work of art in the history of German prose.

Swiss-German was so different from Luther's German that they needed to alter many words though they accepted his influence and had his translation at base. Leo Jud was the pastor who was mainly responsible for the Zurich Bible, completed in 1529. As in Wittenberg they continued working at the text in committee, which met regularly in the choir of the minster, but unlike the group at Wittenberg this was a larger body which included laity. One effect of this larger committee was to make them more radical in their choice of words. They left out Luther's prefaces.

Maps

Maps of Palestine had a long history because pilgrims needed them, and later merchants and crusaders. Yet maps in Bibles were part of the Reformation.

In most there were no maps because it was always considered that cost must be reduced. But quite quickly they came into printed Bibles.

At first they were hard to decipher, at least by a modern eye. There were three lands which were specially felt to need maps if readers of the Bible were to understand it. The first, and for a time the most common, was a map of the journey of Moses and the Israelites from Egypt to the Promised Land, when they took forty years to travel the distance from Egypt to Palestine. In a fine Old Testament of 1525 the Zurich printer Froschauer printed an intelligent map of the strange journey. Four years later he printed a map in his whole Bible but put it the wrong way round so that the Mediterranean sea lay east of Palestine. There was an attempt to map the Garden of Eden but that proved difficult because the Book of Genesis said that in it were four rivers and they could find only two.

In the New Testament readers felt a need to follow the journeys of St Paul so a map of the eastern Mediterranean began to be added. A little later they tried for a map of Palestine during the life of Christ.

This map-making had a side benefit, to interest a man like Mercator in the science of map-making and so form a step towards the maps of the modern world.

Illustrated Bibles

The days of early printing produced a marvellous series of illustrated Bibles which were widely used despite their high cost. Of the seventeen German Bibles before Luther fifteen were illustrated. In many German Bibles the illustrations are almost entirely confined to Genesis. In the New Testament it is only the Apocalypse which has an accepted cycle of pictures and the reason for this is not clear. It is extraordinary when the scenes of the life of Christ played such a part in the stained glass and woodwork and therefore in the general world of art and its patrons: Dürer and Schongauer.

Luther's New Testament of 1522 has only initials and the Cranach illustrations of the Apocalypse. The illustrations began to be political and 'applied'. Babylon appeared as papal Rome and the Babylonian whore wore the tiara of the pope. Duke George of Saxony protested about the malice and the tiaras went. Some people thought to see the faces of contemporaries in the pictures but this is not proven. The illustrators liked to be against popes and against monks and to be critical of the upper classes including princes.

There was soon a demand for more illustrations and the illustrators liked to make them more polemical. They sold better if they were nearer to the modern popular press. But they were not only polemical.

In 1524 Wittenberg published the first Danish New Testament and it contained a portrait of the king of Denmark (Christian II) and the Danish arms by Cranach. This was the first case of a prince's portrait appearing at the beginning of a Testament or Bible and it was the first of many; for these vernacular Bibles were partly paid for by grants from royal or princely treasuries. In the last New Testament of Luther's life he approved in proof a title page with himself and his elector John Frederick kneeling before the crucified.

Luther had a hand in choosing the pictures for the complete Bible, and gave orders that they should be simple illustrations of the text and should do nothing that did not serve the text. Still, the anti-papal note remained in the pictures; a new political hint came in when the war of Gog and Magog became the Turks attacking Vienna. There was a new note in the Old Testament in that the pictures sometimes pointed to the New Testament fulfilment of an Old Testament event or prophecy. The New Testament pictures were always fewer and more restrained than those of the Old Testament; except curiously in the Apocalypse, where the tradition of Bible illustrators overcame Luther's scruples that the Apocalypse was not a valuable book.

Luther wanted picture-books of the Bible for children (and for uneducated laity). The first appeared in 1540 with two hundred pictures.

These Wittenberg Bibles had a big influence on printing in other parts of Germany. In Basel Holbein the Younger had a hand in the pictures. The culmination of these illustrated Bibles was the Froschauer Bible of 1545, with fair landscapes and soldiers in modern armour and artistic licence and practical moral lessons. This became the base for the illustrated Bibles of German-speaking Switzerland.

The middle years of the sixteenth century produced the most beautiful Bibles ever printed. The age treated the book—as a physical object—with the deepest reverence. They sought to match its wonder as ethical and religious authority with an attractiveness and dignity of format which would satisfy the devout reader and be a pleasure to handle, even fondle, at the prayer desk.

This desire for a beautiful volume was not compatible with the quest for a book so cheap that it could come into every household. But there was still a demand for the expensive Bible, in well-to-do homes and for reading on lecterns in churches and cathedrals. They used excellent materials in paper and type and illustration. They were in a mood of excitement in the rapid expansion of the trade of bookseller. And they had an advantage denied to their successors in the labour market. The conviction of northern Europe that the monastic life was mistaken threw into the quest for employment educated people who once were monks and now needed work to pay them a stipend and satisfy their minds. A fair number of the proofreaders in the houses printing Bibles were formerly monks. Not only were they available as experts but their labour was cheap. That meant an ability in a publisher to print accurate and fair texts with skilled labour on low wages. This was one of the reasons why the Bibles of Froschauer in Zurich or of De Tournes in Lyons or of Froben and Oporinus in Basel or of Robert Estienne at Geneva were among the most beautiful Bibles ever sold to the people.

These printers were indispensable to the reforming movement, especially where they were themselves devout and in sympathy with its ideals. Consider for example the career of Christoph Froschauer. He was the son of an Augsburg printer who at the age of twenty arrived at Zurich as a wandering apprentice in search of printing work. He found it in the firm of Rüger and when Rüger died he ran it for the widow and after a short time married her and became head of the firm. When Zwingli began the Zurich reform Froschauer was already an eminent citizen of the town and worked closely with Zwingli. He printed books by Luther and Erasmus, then the works of Zwingli as they came out whether books or pamphlets; and then in 1524 a German New Testament and seven years later the first edition of his famous Bible beautifully printed with woodcuts after Hans Holbein; and for the 1545 edition these illustrations were increased by illustrations from the Strasbourg artist Heinrich Vogtherr, whom Froschauer persuaded to come from Strasbourg to live in Zurich as an employee of his firm. When he died in 1564 Froschauer had done as much for the Reformation as the Froben family in Basel.

Verse-numbers

After Robert Estienne produced the Bible where the chapters were divided into numbered verses, they were not quick to be adopted universally despite their manifest convenience.

The new system had two or even three unexpected disadvantages. It divided the paragraphs of the original into separate sentences, so that it was easier to take the single line out of its context. Perhaps it made the sense of a whole passage a little harder for an ordinary reader to penetrate. Because a verse often ended with half a line, the system took up much more space and paper and made a heavier Bible and so put up the cost of printing and raised the price to the customer. But the advantages in quick reference, in biblical study or catechism or preaching or the schoolroom, were so plain that it won its way as indispensable.

Italics

The habit of distinguishing by a different type—smaller or italic—words not in the original but added by the translator as necessary to explain the sense was surprisingly early—the first sign of it is found in 1535.

3

SCHOLARSHIP AND RELIGION

It is not to be controverted that scholarship was a reason for the Reformation and the way in which it went. But that does not mean that all scholars were reformers.

As institutions universities by their nature divide in tension between persons who wish to hand to posterity the best of knowledge as they have so far received it, and those whose interest is to move into new fields. There are new findings and new fashions and new demands from students and these excitements affect what is expected of the curriculum. And there is a great body of existing knowledge acquired by tried methods, and the new lecturers need to persuade their colleagues that what they do is of the same weight and importance as the existing curriculum. The chief study of the older schools was philosophy, especially as applied to problems in divinity. The new schools discovered the excitement of classical literature and history and poetry and deplored the narrowness of the reigning syllabus. Older minds might resent the demand that time and lectures should be given to poetry, which is a matter of taste, and taken away from a hard mental training in logic. This normal division of opinion was made bitter because it was entangled with three debates, of which two were academic and the third had powerful social consequences.

The Renaissance discovered the beauty of Greek language and literature. Medieval universities taught ancient Greek thought, especially the science and philosophy of Aristotle, through the medium of Latin translations, some of which had passed through Arabic. The humanist cry was back to the sources, learn Greek, study the texts. This demand made older lecturers in philosophy uncomfortable. The texts which they knew were now less easy to think correct.

Humanists had also discovered the quality of the best of Latin classical prose. The Latin which university lecturers used for their courses, for teaching and examining and philosophical enquiry, had developed into a language which was effective for its academic purpose, but which was not Cicero's Latin and which he would have despised. Classical scholars found it ridiculous, professors lecturing in 'bad Latin'. This was part of the scorn which humanists felt for their predecessors. The conservatives attacked these newcomers, literature is a lightweight study, standards are lower, lectures are thin, minds are not trained toughly, why should we need Greek which unlike Latin is a dead language? Yet if they did not conform to what students wanted or needed they lost their audience and the university fell into trouble over its budget.

The tension with consequences was the conviction that the old syllabus was a waste of time. We send our young people to listen to lectures where someone discusses an obscure point of divinity to which no one knows or ever could know the answer; when their growing minds must be led to find the glory of literature with its high moral content. The humanists did not think theology bad but as then practised in universities they were sure it was wasted time because dry and remote from the world that mattered. This attitude must lead towards a reconstruction of religious teaching in universities, quickly if humanists won government of the faculties, slowly if conservatives hung on to their methods until they or their successors found that they no longer attracted audiences of students because those students now had no interest in learning the logic and theology of the schools.

When the world came to religious change, the old theologians stood firm. But the scholars were not all for the new. They divided. There is a theory that they divided by age; if older, conservative; if in middle years, wavering; if young, ardent for reformation. The humanist Pirckheimer of Nuremberg was strong for Luther and named when Luther was excommunicated, and afterwards rejected the reform. Melanchthon, the most famous professor of Greek in Germany, was only twenty-one when he became a professor and turned into one of the most celebrated of reformers. The theory has a measure of truth. Yet other reasons affected the way by which humanists went. Pirckheimer was affected by the troubles of his sister, who was an abbess while nunneries were being closed or emptied. Many others held professorial posts in states which refused to go with religious change and if they wanted to keep their pay needed to conform and withdraw into the purely academic area of their lives.

There is a mystery here which historians do not easily solve. Printing, and more books, and more information, helped to cause the Reformation, no one doubts it. The leaders of reform were intellectuals, professors of the university like Luther and Melanchthon in Saxony, leaders in academies of a high standard like Zwingli and Bullinger and Peter Martyr in Zurich, pastors of a rare distinction in learning like Calvin in Geneva or Bucer in Strasbourg. Yet not all learned persons were on the side of change. Padua was the great school of medicine in Europe and remained it after all the changes, Bologna was the great school of law and never lost its Catholic spirit. The universities of Louvain and Cologne and Paris had members so far to the conservative side that they were laughed at as dyed-in-the-wool, but they had rare scholars among their ranks. The university of Ingolstadt in Bavaria had the most unattractive of all conservatives among its professors, yet it held in a chair, despite pressure on him to move to somewhere more forward-looking in its ideas, Reuchlin, who inaugurated the modern study of the Hebrew language.

But we find that in various parts, and not infrequently, the impulse to religious change came not from the teacher, nor from the government, but from the people; not from men or women who were reading their new-printed Bibles with care and diligence and surprise, but from a crowd who suddenly felt nausea towards what was happening in their church. It often started with a cry, not to find better truth than they had, but to rid themselves of a pollution felt to be a stain upon the community. This is what made the unsolved historical question. Was it more that the people felt in their guts that things were wrong and would take action in the only way they knew, by demonstration, to get change? and then when they acted the teachers must step in to guide change and eventually to control it? Or was it more because the teachers said that truth was not being taught from Catholic pulpits and demand for change fitted certain gut-feelings which already existed among the common men and women?

Many academics took time to know where they stood, perhaps most of them. Later we shall meet sudden changes, experiences like conversion. But the humanists were after all academics.

Mosellanus was such a one, not quite sure what the future held. His career was unparalleled as an example of the rustic boy who turned into one of the leading scholars of the age. A choirboy in Trier cathedral, he attended a course at Cologne and learnt Greek; went to teach in a secondary school and then at the age of twenty matriculated in the university of Leipzig, where the professor of Greek was Richard Croke, the famous Englishman who later taught Greek to King Henry VIII. Through Croke Mosellanus mastered the language, and simultaneously published a very humanist book, *Paedologia*, dialogues in Latin for use in school, a best-seller in sixty-five editions during that century alone. For an hour he won a European fame that was more than academic; for when Martin Luther came to Leipzig to defend himself against the attacks of Johann Eck, Duke George ordered Mosellanus to open that historic debate. Mosellanus never showed any sign of being drawn to Luther. His prince, Duke George of the other Saxony, disliked everything Luther stood for and Mosellanus was loyal. And yet he was not comfortable in the university of Leipzig. He thought very little of the historic structure of a university. It pained him that he must call himself by the ridiculous title of Master of Arts. He probably minded that his colleague in the chief Leipzig chair of theology (Hieronymus Dungersheim) thought it his duty to confute Luther with such vehemence. Mosellanus argued for the necessity of Greek and Latin because only so can we understand the Bible. He admired Erasmus. But he did not move. His friends were moving towards opposite sides— one friend was Pflug, who finished as a Catholic bishop, another was Joachim Camerarius, who later created the repute of the university of Leipzig and who became the close friend, and afterwards the biographer, of Melanchthon. Mosellanus died when he was only thirty and it is an interesting guess what he would have done if he had lived to the age of forty-four when Duke George died and the succeeding princes took ducal Saxony, as its people mostly now wanted, under the aegis of the north German Reformation.

When Mosellanus died, a death widely seen as a disaster for his university, two things happened which shed light on the problem. Erasmus wrote a letter (no. 1526) to express his sorrow at the loss and said that to find a worthy successor in the chair of Greek would be no easy task because Duke George would allow no one into the chair unless he was against Luther. But, wrote Erasmus, most of the people who knew enough Greek to be respectable as professors were not against Luther. Then Duke George invited Erasmus himself to recommend the successor. He selected his fellow Dutchman Ceratinus, of whose scholarship he had a high opinion. Ceratinus came, but left for his native land after only three months. It was suspected that he could not be so strong against Luther as his prince desired. Greek studies at Leipzig languished for a few years, until after Duke George's death and the coming back of a truly big Greek philologist, Melanchthon's friend Joachim Camerarius.

Guillaume Budé, Latinized as Budaeus, was the best of French scholars in his age; and though the tradition of the Sorbonne was suspect as too conservative for a humanist generation, Paris was full of scholars. He taught himself Greek and came to be looked upon as the expert in the Greek language. He was patronized by the king and was made royal librarian and helped to create the first piece of what was later to be the great Bibliothèque Nationale. In that office he was able to help the humanists by his influence on the king. He made a profound study of Roman law, later on Roman coinage; and despite the academic nature of these subjects his Roman law contained an onslaught on the scholastic system of jurisprudence and his coinage treated economics and even a communist theory. Did such studies have any effect on what was slowly happening to European religion? All his life he remained a loyal Catholic with sympathies for moderate reformation. Yet, as change began to happen, or those who wished for change became more public, conservative France grew narrower in mind; and after he died in 1540, his wife and children did not feel safe and fled to Calvin's Geneva.

Of these humanist scholars, whose essential interest was classical antiquity, two became symbols of a new reformation. One was Melanchthon, lecturer in Greek at Tübingen university when almost a juvenile and then professor of Greek at the university of Wittenberg from the age of twenty-one. Here it was the place of the chair rather than the work which made him a symbol; for it put him at the right hand of Martin Luther, gave an international academic weight to Luther's university, and placed a steady loyal mind at the side of what Luther wanted to achieve. Melanchthon came to the heart of the Reformation because he went to that special chair. The other was Erasmus. It mattered where he went. It was not a little part of his ability to be a symbol that he changed his place of work from conservative Louvain to a Basel which grew more hostile towards conservatives during the time that he resided there. But it was not his place that mattered most. It was because he was recognized everywhere as a scholar of international fame.

His personal history mattered to the rare psychology which is found in the mature adult. The son of a Dutchman who could not marry his woman because he was related to her within the prohibited degrees, and so illegitimate by birth, he was likely to think from childhood that the rules of the Church were not perfect. The circumstance made him, who later in life was prolific in the freedom with which he expressed his personal emotions, reticent about his early years and for long there was guessing about his youth. He went to a good school at Deventer, good enough to make him like learning Latin and want to know it well. At eighteen, with father dead and the family unable to afford a university, he joined the Augustinian monks at Steyn. For eight years he lived the usual life of a monk, and they won him dispensation from the rule that an illegitimate cannot be ordained priest and he was ordained. But the library of the monastery was important to him. He used it well; there he went on perfecting his Latin, partly by much reading and partly by writing essays. He discovered that he loved writing. The discovery led him to his first sense of mission in life, which was to last all his days. There were devout persons who said that learning was nothing to do with goodness. He determined to show the contrary. His first book, *Antibarbari* (*Against the Barbarians*), had the militancy of youth in this sense. He produced apostolic authority for his case. 'Paul, who was snatched up to the third heaven, sent letters that he might be sent the books in parchment and then argued with Peter about Christian doctrine.' He studied hard; the Fathers of the early Church naturally, but what fascinated him was the ancient Roman world and its literature, now being made available by the new printers. He read Italian humanists, leaders in that Renaissance love of classical literature. In maturity this sense of mission turned into a very intelligent longing that he might help to reconcile the best of literature with the best of religious thought.

In pursuit of books he made the acquaintance on paper of a real scholar, the Italian Lorenzo Valla, the powerful critical mind of the fifteenth century. This meeting was important enough to make Erasmus start an index of Valla's

writings. Valla gave him an ideal of 'eloquence'; that is, how to persuade
people to the truth through the right use of words and accurate information.

His fellow monks could see that he was not happy in his little world and
needed bigger libraries and a wider sphere. Here there is a difficulty, and no
small one because it affects the view of the place of Erasmus in the origins of
the Reformation. Erasmus had an optimistic view of the human race and
what they can achieve morally if they try. That suggests an unbullied childhood and a contented youth and an admiration for at least a few of those
among whom he grew up. In his maturity, when he had long abandoned his
monastic vows, he still accepted that there were monks who were good and
did good. But with that avowal was evident a deep-seated resentment that he
was forced as a child into a way of life for which he was not suited. 'They tied
a halter round my neck.'[1] This resentment turned into a criticism of the vows
which monks take, and the way of life, the quarrelling between religious
orders, the petty disputes inside monastic houses, the hypocrisy of people in
habits who pretend to be revered by the world but behave worse than ordinary men and women. When Erasmus began to write the repute of monks
was not high. By the time he had finished it was far lower still and his satire
was no small contribution to that descent. Something in the house at Steyn
helped to cause this campaign, but we cannot yet know what. When he was
accused of being an apostate monk, he once said that no one blames a man
who flees from captivity by pirates.[2]

They released him on leave of absence to become secretary to the bishop
of Cambrai, presumably in the false belief that one who was so good at writing letters would make a good secretary. Erasmus had no interest in administration and the bishop soon freed him for study at the university of Paris—
and at last, at the age of twenty-nine, he was where, if his family had any
money, he should have been ten years earlier. Henceforth he was in a world
which had everything he wanted except money to live on and comforts to
enjoy—the bed was hard and he was afraid of disease through lack of calories.
Still wearing his monk's habit, still on leave from his monastery, he made ends
meet, though not easily, by coaching in Latin the sons of the rich. Later in life
he was accused of being too intent on money and this struggle for existence
in Paris may have been part of the cause. But he had good libraries, touch
with leading academics like Budé, entry into a leading theological faculty of
Europe.

He studied the scholastic philosophy and qualified himself to be an expert
in theology. But there was something odd about the result. 'Scholastics',
'schoolmen'—these were words which he used with contempt for the rest
of his life. And since that world identified theology with the faculties of

---

[1] *Ep.* 1581 a.   [2] To Lambertus Grunnius (a pseudonym), *Ep.* 447.

universities and their use of logic and syllogism and authoritative texts, there were those afterwards, even into modern times, who defined Erasmus as a scholar but no theologian. Occasionally he thought this of himself. That was misleading. Underneath the apparent doubt of 'theology', there was now a mind expert in the New Testament (but not yet in Greek), and qualified in the early Christian Fathers.

Since he made ends meet by coaching the young, it was the nature of education about which he first wrote. Literature should revive education and through schools transform the culture of Europe. From this time he already had misty ideals of a better society because more cultivated. It was an ideal which assumed the dignity and sacredness of the human being.

Every member of the species should treat every other member with respect, and strive for peace and harmony, and settle disputes by reasonable argument and not by violence. Revolution could never be his ideal. This sweet reasonableness was fostered by religious sensibility, the Christian ideal of gentleness and pity and forgiveness, and of not pushing the self forward. This is the kind of person whom the educator must seek to help grow. The child should discover the wisdom of the centuries and so must know Latin as the key to unlock literature, and must learn the gospel and the truths which it inculcates as the key to moral right and piety. And as children develop they must be led to practise 'eloquence', how to use words that persuade towards the truth, how to see the relationship between the use of words and the perception of truth. It brings precision of mind because words have different meanings in different contexts, and this habit of exactness it is of the first importance to learn at school. He even wrote a book of etiquette for boys— on not blowing the nose on the sleeve, on covering the mouth for a yawn, the ugliness of excessive laughter. No other great scholar, no other serious religious leader, ever wrote a book on the etiquette of polite behaviour. He was not a realist, he said that normally classes must be not more than five in number.[3]

He believed in men and women and what they can do—'as a bird is born to fly, a human being is born to wisdom and an upright life'—'every human can be taught virtue without any hardship'. Such optimism meant that it was hard for him to understand the multitude who knew about original sin, the disciples of St Paul and St Augustine, Martin Luther among them, who believed that humanity can only come to good by a great act of God. His first love for study of the early Fathers was St Jerome the translator of the Bible, and Jerome's theology was not close to St Augustine's.

In 1500 he made his academic name with a publication nothing to do with theology: *Adagiorum Collectanea*, which was a collection of the proverbs he

---

[3] *De pueris instituendis*, in *Opera Omnia*, i, 2, 21 ff.

could find among the Greek and Latin authors, 818 of them, with short explanations. It could not have been done, even at 818, without a vast range of reading. No one thought of the author yet as a possible rebel in the Church. It was just a useful instrument for classical studies. But most proverbs are wise sayings about morality, so that the book contained, in a new and subtle way, the best ethical insights of the ancient world. To each new edition he added proverbs, until there were more than 4,000 of them by the end of his life. And during his last few years when he was controversial, he used his comments for satires on society—kings and their folly, tyrants and wickedness, clergy and their hypocrisy, the need for a purer religion, the futility of war, the stupidity that priests are not allowed to marry. But this was a long way ahead, in the years after his New Testament and into the time when leading Catholic theologians held him up as a rebel. With reverence for the core of religion and for the best of literature, he could be irreverent about everything else from Homer's heroes downwards, and it was impossible for him to be dull.

But the religion of the man came out in something bigger than satire. In 1501, perhaps in Paris perhaps on a visit to the Netherlands, he drafted the first of his devotional books and printed it two years later: *Enchiridion militis christiani*, which was a play on words for it could be translated either as the handbook of a Christian soldier or as the dagger of a Christian soldier. Later in life when he was famous this became a much read book. At first it was read by hardly anyone.

It is a very religious book. Its theology is of the simplest. Let the Christian truly resolve to reform the moral way, to give up the adulteries, decide to be brave instead of timid, look upwards towards the eternal. The fight is hard because of our blindness and our passions and the ease with which we surrender. But we must fight on in the knowledge that this battle cannot be lost because God stands at the side. Parts are platitude. Try hard to do good and you can succeed and God will help. 'No attack by a demon is so overwhelming, no temptation so pressing, that the hard study of the Bible cannot easily defeat them'—'a main part of Christian life is to wish with all one's heart to be a Christian'.

But the conventional morality was turned into something bigger for that generation by the appeal from external rites to the inward spirit—your religion is images and pilgrimages and dressing as a monk and going to mass?—but true religion is of the heart and its way is the gentle following of Christ's precepts, and we must beware of superstitions which many attach to ceremonies.

It was not common to find a moralist whom it was such pleasure to read.

He spent the years from 1506 to 1509 in Italy, mainly at Venice with the great printer Aldus Manutius, and perfecting his Greek. He became, oddly, a doctor of divinity at the university of Turin, which he did not attend. At the house of Manutius it was a rule that all conversation must be carried on in Greek. This Greekizing fraternity in Venice and then in Padua was indispensable to Erasmus's later expertise and to his reforming achievement.

He went on to Rome, where cardinals were kind to him, and then, wondering what to do next, accepted another invitation to England. He stayed in the house of Sir Thomas More and whiled away the time by writing *Encomium Moriae*, which can mean either praise of More or praise of Folly, and it was as the praise of Folly that it infinitely amused the world.[4]

It is folly that keeps the world in being. Unless men were fools they would not marry and chain themselves to women. Unless women were fools they would not marry and face childbirth and little children. Unless powerful men were fools they would not engage in great buildings or causes or trading which carry high risks but which when they come off help humanity. Human beings have a touch of the fraud, and it is better so, we only get along with each other if we pretend in our social relationships, we ought not to strip people of their illusions, those who live with what they hope to be true are happier than those who see things as they are really. How happy the fool who knows nothing and is content to know nothing, contrast the scholar who wastes time and eyesight and health in a profitless assembly of knowledge. What a lot of fools there are—the tribe of theologians writing useless notes on other people's books, men and women who think they will cure toothache by invoking a favourite saint, useless statues, monks who will not touch money but are ready to touch women, censors poring over harmless books to pick a passage as irreverent or scandalous, preachers who paint what happens in hell when they have no knowledge of it whatever, kings who oppress the poor and spend the taxes on their horses, popes who think prayer useless and poverty a sin and to be beaten in war disgraceful and to die on a cross very bad for the Church. And yet the truest and greatest fools are to be honoured—the folly of giving away what one has, and fasting for the sake of God, and forgiving enemies, and the simplicity of the child. The little book was popular because it was daring, because it was written with charm and bite, and because in jest it said things about society which many people now thought needed to be said.

The charm did not conceal, though for some readers it extenuated, the revolutionary innuendoes in the book. It was so amusing that at first not everyone realized its power. Pope Leo X smiled at it. Sir Thomas More

---

[4] *Encomium Moriae* only started to be written in More's house 1509, pirated edition 1511, first proper edition 1512; revised 1514 Strasbourg which contains much material on religion; 1516 from Froben at Basel with more additions. The first part is banter, the second bitterer. New edition in *Opera Omnia* iv. 3. 1999.

defended it. But from 1515 it began to be attacked, and later was formally condemned. Condemnations only added to the sale, there were thirty-six Latin editions before Erasmus died, and translations into French, German, and Czech. It could not be translated into English until after King Henry VIII died, and could only be printed among Erasmus's works in Protestant countries. It did much to help the mood of the educated—the Church affords so much matter for satire that it must be mended.[5]

Then came his New Testament of 1516 and bigger fame and soon far bigger controversy. The few years after that were the summit of his celebrity and his happiness. His name stood for the Bible and the best of its study; for the wish that its texts should be better known, and by working men and women not only by academics; that Greek and Latin and Hebrew should be more studied than they were. Morally his name stood for better education for everyone; for getting away from external religion to a religion of the heart and spirit; for the belief that all is possible and none need despair; for the conviction that humane literature and the best of religion are not opposed but are allies; and for the peace of Europe.

In that year he was regarded not only as a great scholar but as a great religious leader. It mattered to the churches of Europe what his opinions were on how to reform. The elector Frederick of Saxony, a devout Catholic but soon to be the one person whose shield stood between Martin Luther and death, bought every book by Erasmus for his private library.[6]

He was full of hope for society in these years when he was so valued. Telling his friend Wolfgang Capito that he was getting old now (he was about fifty), he would be content to be young again because he thought that they could shortly see the beginning of a new golden age. The great princes have turned to foster peace, there is a rebirth of literature which governments encourage, medical research is making progress, and the study of law led by such as Budé, and mathematics. It will be harder to find progress in theology, so conservative are theologians, but as the knowledge of the three languages (Latin, Greek, and Hebrew) advances so theology will progress in

---

[5] In 1516 someone wrote the antipapal pamphlet *Julius Exclusus*. In this Pope Julius is represented as knocking at the gate of heaven and indignant that he is not let in. The beginning is funny, the later part less interesting than the *Praise of Folly*. Because it seems to have come from Erasmus's circle, many in Europe believed him to be the author, and if so it could not do his Catholic repute anything but much harm. Luther thought he wrote it, so did his Catholic academic foes. He always denied that he was the author. As late as the scholarly Toronto translation of 1986 by Michael J. Heath there was probability that he was not truthful in his denial. Subsequently there has been more inclination to accept Erasmus's denial and it is unsafe to use the *Julius* as 'typical' of Erasmus's less public views on popes. In the year when we know that it was written (though not printed till the next year, 1517) he was engaged on the enormous work connected with the New Testament and it is hard to imagine him finding the time, or changing so radically his mood, to write the *Julius*.

[6] Spalatin to Erasmus, December 1516, in Erasmus, *Ep.* 501.

the universities; an achievement in which he allowed that even he bore a humble part.[7]

Only eight years after he wrote this portrait of a halcyon future, his then beau idéal the French King Francis I crashed in the battle of Pavia and went to a Spanish prison, only ten years later the Renaissance in Rome was ended and the city sacked and almost destroyed by a wild unpaid army of German and Spanish mercenaries.

He lived comfortably at Louvain, with confidence in his powers, no duties to distract him from study and writing, and an international reputation which meant that anything he published would be bought by many. His correspondence was vast, he was made an official adviser to the future emperor Charles V. He won freedom from the pope not to be a monk under a monk's vows (he left off his monk's habit nine years before but went on dressing as a priest) and so was again respectable in his ecclesiastical position—the dispensation did not save him from malicious gossip that he was an apostate monk.[8] Liberal-minded bishops wanted their clergy to read his books and adopt his ideals, kings sought to win a name for culture by persuading him into their court or university.

He did not reflect how many enemies he was making. It was not only the satires like the *Praise of Folly*. He had now published a large volume on a subject where there were experts—his Annotations on the New Testament. Professors in their chairs in France or Italy or Spain or Germany despised this amateur theologian and used the language of scorn; at Alcalá the most formidable, Stunica; in Paris Noel Béda, less extreme than Stunica and less expert, but rough and the mouthpiece of the most famous of universities; Béda's lieutenant at Paris, a Carthusian Sutor (real name, Cousturier); at Louvain Latomus, who published his first shafts against Erasmus by putting them forward as criticisms of Mosellanus of Leipzig; Edward Lee, to be the new archbishop of York, academically not much but far from the most reticent of critics.

The criticisms were of three kinds: technical scholarship, general doubt of Erasmus's proposals, and disloyalty to the authority of the Catholic Church.

Stunica (=Diego Zúñiga) had been working for a few years on the Complutensian text of the New Testament. As soon as he read Erasmus's New Testament he told Cardinal Cisneros that it was full of mistakes. The cardinal preferred to have no public attack on Erasmus but died and so released Stunica. He was a better Hebraist and theologian than Erasmus, and

---

[7] Erasmus to Wolfgang Capito from Antwerp, 26 February 1517, *Ep.* 541.

[8] Julius II in 1506 released him from the authority of his monastic superior. It was a help but not enough. So he applied further to Rome—Leo X, 1517, and again for more freedom from Clement VII, 1525, which ensured that he was so free from monastic vows that he could leave his property by will.

nearly as good in Latin and Greek. But he was arrogant and plausible as well as learned. Erasmus's 1522 edition of his New Testament was better work partly because he profited from Stunica's corrections.

Stunica published *Annotations against Erasmus* and after Erasmus answered he published *Blasphemies of Erasmus* (Rome, 1522). He did not damage Erasmus except with a few of those who mattered at Rome, partly because Erasmus was too big to damage (though that was not Erasmus's opinion of himself), partly because he felt that he must defend the Vulgate on all counts, and partly because he believed Erasmus to have published his New Testament for the sake of personal gain and without any religious motive; than which no charge could be more untrue. He said that he had proved Erasmus to be 'the standard-bearer and head of the Lutheran rebels who were overturning the Church'. '*Erasmus lutherissat.*' And in a letter: 'You'll find him openly sharing the opinions of Arius, Apollinaris, Jovinian, Wycliffites and Hussites, and finally with Luther himself. Erasmus single-handed taught him his heresies and blasphemies, and armed him. Let them call him sun, and moon, and the glory of Germany; Italy calls him impious, Rome mistress of the world judges him a blasphemer, worthy of Luther's fate, i.e. as a Public Enemy of the Church of Rome'.[9]

Rome disliked the tone and delayed publication. But Stunica's campaign began a movement which slowly turned into a heresy-hunt and ended nearly fifty years later when the censors achieved a triumph more overwhelming than Stunica could have predicted.

From the beginning of 1518 Luther's pamphlets appeared in Germany and divided opinion. Erasmus did not read them systematically but what he saw and heard of them he thought to contain much truth. They assailed the ills of the monks which needed assailing. They accused Rome of abusing its authority, which he thought a right charge. They were expressed too sharply for his taste. But he believed it a great error to silence Luther.

In that year he published a new edition of the *Enchiridion* and it was now that the book became famous. For it he wrote a new preface, in which the main part was an attack upon monks for departing from the ideals with which monasteries were founded. In it there was an oblique reference to Luther, though without naming him; and it was clear both that Erasmus approved of him and that he warned him not to be in such a hurry but to go more cautiously.

---

[9] Stunica to Vergara, Rome, 4 May 1522, *Ep.* iv. 630; appendix. Vergara was another from Alcalá in Spain, in Erasmus, *Ep.* 1581. The alleged heresies were not all compatible. Jovinian was against valuing the monastic life above the married, and against an excess of Mary-cult. Arius could not accept the Nicene creed because for him Jesus though divine was lesser than his Father. Apollinaris was the opposite, he believed Jesus so far divine that he did not share all human nature.

The Colloquies

When he was a young tutor at Paris teaching Latin to students, he designed an excellent textbook for learning conversational Latin; debates, but the speakers talked interestingly and were sometimes funny. He did not publish it but pupils were not used to being amused when learning Latin and liked it much. One at least kept a copy. In 1518, at the height of his fame, when the market would buy anything that he wrote, a small group published them through Froben at Basel and did him a disservice, as he thought at first (publishing juvenilia without asking the author's permission), but a service in that it put before the world what became one of his two most popular books. It was given the title *Familiarum colloquiorum formulae*, or rules for intimate conversation in Latin. When he found how the public leapt at them, he took them seriously; to add each time, to make funnier and more satirical, less of a textbook for Latin and more of a literary event, and at last more hostile in its commentary on how churchmen misbehaved, in his last years once or twice scurrilous (the last edition was 1533). The Church had a bad time in the *Praise of Folly*. It had a worse time in the later *Colloquies*—its rules of marriage, cult of saints and superstitions, monks and clergy pretending virtue. Of religious, Franciscans had the worst time. He gave large new handles to critics and did not mind. The *Colloquies* were the second of his books weighty in the background to the Reformation—a hundred editions in his lifetime.

It made a problem for censors. Schoolmasters liked them, boys and girls enjoyed learning Latin, not an invariable experience with textbooks. Adult readers enjoyed them as moderns enjoy a humorous but not scandalous magazine. They were truly useful, for the many people who not only needed to write Latin but to speak it in conversation, how to greet with courtesy or refuse without offence, or even make a common sentence without error. They also presented a vivid lively portrait of social life. More than one Catholic-minded friend asked him to produce a bowdlerized edition of the *Colloquies*. An enterprising Dominican printed a much-altered *Colloquies* without mentioning that anything was changed, and took out every bit that assailed monks and their vows, or clergy, indulgences, or pilgrimages. The faculty of theology at Paris censured sixty-nine texts of the *Colloquies* as either in error or likely to hurt the morals of young people. Catholic moralists alleged that the behaviour of young people brought up on this book grew worse. 'Erasmus scattered weeds everywhere and then said "It was a game, just a joke. I was only teaching Latin."'[10]

It is just a question whether he meant his more outrageous dagger-strokes to be taken seriously. Yet the reader feels about them that underneath the

---

[10] *Ep.* 1581 and 1804 note.

author had a serious purpose to which he was dedicated. He might declare that it was just fun, and he well knew what was humour, but no one could think the humour to be aimless.

In 1533 the school at Wittenberg talked of using the *Colloquies* as a text-book in class. Luther was totally hostile to the plan. 'When I am dying I shall order my children never to read the *Colloquies*. He puts godless opinions into people's mouths.'[11] Nevertheless the Wittenberg school adopted it, they found it too valuable to be without.

Erasmus, always bad at refraining from defending himself, wrote an essay *On the usefulness of the Colloquies*, a catalogue of those which had so far appeared (1526) with the moral which could be drawn from each. Then he added the essay to the next editions of the book. It included a typical sentence: 'Nowadays no one can write a book unless he is surrounded by bodyguards.'[12]

Here was a person whom more than half the world thought to be the leader of everyone who wanted reform in the best sense—that is, reform with loyalty to the Catholic Church and its authority including the pope; and about whom a smaller but potent fraction of the world thought to pursue an impossible task, that the reforms which he wanted would destroy the unity of the Church, and several of his teachings were those of a heretic.

Erasmus was sure that he was a loyal Catholic; was faithful to the authority of the pope even while he assailed the behaviour of popes; disapproved of such clamour for reform so loud that it was bound to divide the Church.

Erasmus quarrelled with opponents—that is, tract-writers who published hostile treatises against him. But one of the most attractive sides of his nature was loyalty to friends even when they disagreed with him. And this was bad for his reputation. What must the Curia of Rome think when they found how he stood by Melanchthon, who was Luther's chief aide? Such friendships became impossible to keep if he was to preserve his reputation as a Catholic. But he was not willing to throw over friends whom he valued even when he thought them wrong.

He regarded the Basel printer Froben as his most intimate friend. Froben was a first-class professional who used Holbein to illuminate his texts. He printed many of the early Christian Fathers as well as Erasmus's New Testament but was not prepared to refuse to publish a scholarly work because its author was thought to be evangelical. He published Luther during the first two years when he was at his controversial fame. Erasmus begged him not to go on publishing Luther, and Froben gave way, but unwillingly. Erasmus felt it a calamity when Froben died in 1527 and mourned him as though he were a member of his family and wrote that everyone who cared about scholarship ought to wear mourning clothes.

---

[11] *TR* i. 397.　　　[12] *De utilitate Coll.* ad init.

Then there was Paul Volz, the Benedictine abbot of Hugshofen near Sélestat in Alsace. He much admired Erasmus, and the admiration was reciprocated for Erasmus dedicated to him the 1518 edition of the *Enchiridion*. In the Peasants' War raiding peasants sacked and burnt his abbey and the fire destroyed his unpublished books. He was left with nothing but his habit. He sought help from the Austrian authorities in Sélestat but they refused on a charge that he was 'one of Luther's followers'. To survive he had no alternative but to move into a reforming town and went to Strasbourg, where he was accepted as one of the preachers. Yet Erasmus continued to regard him as a friend and, worse for his Catholic repute, kept the dedicatory letter to him in the many later editions of the *Enchiridion*.

There was a friendship still graver—with Oecolampadius. By origin a south-west German Heusgen, turned into Hausschein (so that the English called him Huskin) and then into Greek as a humanist, Oecolampadius had the special experience of the Catholic system of confession and penitence by being the canon penitentiary at Basel cathedral. Froben invited him to Basel to help Erasmus with the New Testament because he was excellent in Greek and Hebrew. He made the index for Erasmus's nine-volume edition of St Jerome. This made a close bond between him and Erasmus. Troubled in mind by administering the system of confession and then by the indulgence controversy and what he read of Luther, he became a Brigittine monk near Augsburg with the odd desire that the religious life would settle his mind and prevent him falling from the Catholic faith. When he published a book against the penitentiary system (1521) the Brigittines refused to keep him. After a dramatic wandering he sought refuge in Basel which he already knew so well and where his friend Erasmus now lived.

In June 1523 they made him a professor of the university, where he expounded books of the Old Testament. By the end of the same year he was also a preacher at St Martin's church, where they soon had reforming sermons and services. Only two years later he was convinced that in the holy communion the bread and wine did not become the Body and Blood of Christ; though Christ is given in the holy communion, the bread and wine were not the gift but symbols of the gift. Catholics, and Martin Luther, regarded this as a gross anti-Catholic heresy. Erasmus's attitude was, rationality suggests that Oecolampadius and Zwingli are right; but rationality goes very little way in this mystery and the right thing was to stand by the teaching of the Catholic Church of the centuries.

Oecolampadius argued with him but he stuck to his position. The disagreement could not but make for coolness between them. Yet Erasmus kept the friendship, not so intimately perhaps. He protested if Oecolampadius praised him publicly as though they agreed; he heard that in the pulpit Oecolampadius criticized his opinions about free will. But he never forgot what he owed to him. Conrad Pellican said to Erasmus, so late as 1525, that their close link was a blessing which glorified God. For the Curia in Rome it was something that Erasmus dissented publicly from such a heretic. But it was very bad that they were evidently still friends. Erasmus was long before his time in trying not to allow differences of doctrine to end kind relations; even though he knew that this complicated his life and endangered his happiness.[13]

More remarkably he applied this toleration to books. He did not apply it to books which attacked himself for both in Rome and in Brussels he nego- tiated that government should step in to stop Stunica and Sutor and the others. But he regarded such tracts as offensive propaganda, not as serious scholarship.

The Basel town council sometimes asked him whether they should allow a book to be published. Though against Luther he did not wish them to censor Luther's books which contained good things. The town council asked him what to do when Oecolampadius wrote his book[14] about the holy com- munion, and published it in Strasbourg not to embarrass the Basel council; should they license it for Basel? Erasmus gave them civilized advice. 'This is a scholarly book. The writing is good. I should regard it as truly religious if one could say that of anything so far from the tradition of the Catholic Church, from which I think it dangerous to go.'[15] The Basel council refused the licence. In September 1525 a Catholic friend pleaded with him to write an answer to the book. He simply replied, without blaming either side in the argument, that he had neither time nor knowledge to do what was wanted.[16]

A little later there was another such friendship. Simon Grynaeus was a dedicated adherent of the Reformation when he came to teach Greek at Basel just after Erasmus fled from it (1529). He had been educated at school with Melanchthon and the two were always friends. As a scholar he was spec- tacular because he discovered in the library at the abbey of Lorsch five lost books of the Roman historian Livy.[17] He was rather like Erasmus in moder- ation and good nature but was a devout Protestant. The two scholars corres- ponded with respect and friendliness. Yet by 1525 Grynaeus believed that Oecolampadius was right about the presence in the eucharist, a view which Rome thought the worst of heresies. There was a moment when Erasmus almost quarrelled with Grynaeus but the coolness was nothing to do with his

[13] For the difficulty with Oecolampadius in 1525 see *Ep.* 1538.

[14] *De genuina verborum Domini, Hoc est corpus meum, iuxta vetustissimos authores expositione.*

[15] *Ep.* 1636; cf. 1618, 1620, 1624.   [16] *Ep.* 1616.

[17] These were Livy, books 41–5. Lorsch was one of the oldest monasteries in Germany, ori- ginally Benedictine and once rich, during the ninth century it housed probably the best library in western Europe; then with a chequered history and Premonstratensian. When Grynaeus studied in the library it still had monks; but it came under the Palatinate, which when it became Protestant closed the monastery 1563. It was burnt down by Spanish troops during the Thirty Years War.

opinions, Erasmus thought that on a visit to England Grynaeus did not do what he could to clear up a trouble over Erasmus's money. This friendship could not help Erasmus's reputation with the Roman Curia.

Erasmus was honest in his own defence. He said that he did not condemn the cult of the saints, but people made superstitious prayers to saints and addressed to them requests which they would never make to an ordinarily good person. He was accused of mocking the services of the Church when all he had done was to blame the importing of secular airs of music into churches. He said that we hardly regard as essential to worship a noise which no one can understand. He did not attack ceremonies, he attacked ceremonies as a substitute for true inward religion. He did not attack pilgrimages, he attacked the abuses of pilgrimage, like husbands deserting wives and children to go to Rome or Jerusalem. He did not blame the reciting of psalms, he blamed the compulsory reciting of so many psalms that they became formal and all meaning was lost. He is not a rebel against bishops, he has taught everyone to respect their authority, unless they push their impieties at the faithful. He has not attacked rules, he has attacked too many and too detailed rules, whether of fasting or feasts. He is not banned from putting forward an opinion that private confession was not founded by Christ. He will hold marriage to be a sacrament if the Church holds it to be so, but this is not clear, because great Christian authorities have disagreed. He does not condemn all the schoolmen of the Middle Ages but their learning had become a sophistry and it is right to think afresh from the Bible.

He was accused of denouncing war. He freely confessed the charge. War may be fun for fighters but is no fun for the people. Is it right for a pope to encourage war as he has? to enter into military alliances as he has?

He did not have a particular theology to advocate, it was rather a type of piety. Ancient literature must be part of education and be used to explain Christianity, both in history and in morality. That was to unite the best of literature with the study of the Bible, to make a harmony of the best of religion with the best of culture, for this will prevent the remoteness of religion from the highest of natural aspirations. During the years 1516 to 1520 he expressed what many people thought and gave them a programme of vast influence. Most of the leading reformers came out of an Erasmian background of ideas and hopes.

He allowed that there were reasons why he should be attracted to Luther's camp. 'They want me there, their opponents push me off. If they succeed in suppressing Luther they would not omit to suppress me and all good literature at the same time.' But, he said, he did not want to be a partisan. He wished to stand above the parties in the hope of being a mediator between them. There were parts of Luther which he did not understand and parts with which he disagreed profoundly. And yet—'who in the beginning was not for Luther? It is obvious that the world is full of abuses which will no longer be borne; and destiny draws the world towards purity . . .'.

When Luther was excommunicated, he thought the bull merciless and not the way of a gentle Pope Leo and due to his henchmen.[18] He wanted to postpone such thunder so that the lines of division be not tidy and there would still be room for debate. He thought the bull risked everything for which he stood—literature and culture and the renewal of theology and the true interpretation of the Bible. 'I am grieved to see the gospel doctrine attacked. All they do is silence us, not teach us better. And they teach things totally contrary to the Bible and common sense.'[19] He wrote a letter of protest to Pope Leo: that there was a conspiracy of obscurantists, that he had never approved of Luther's violent language, had asked the printer Froben not to publish Luther's works, advised him not to trouble the peace of the Church, and recognized his own duty to the pope. But it is better to teach people than to burn them.[20]

That 8 October, 1520, a pile of Luther's books was publicly burnt at Louvain. This manifestation edified less than was intended because students threw onto it books of the school-theologians. We do not know whether Erasmus watched the fire nor with what feelings he heard of it. The bull ordered the clergy to preach against the errors of Luther and his disciples. Had they not in their town and university the chief ally of Luther? A Carmelite mounted the pulpit in St Peter's church and preached a sermon which was supposed to be about charity but which declared with force that Erasmus was Luther's man.[21]

To live in a town under a conservative government and be denounced by name from a pulpit was to be in peril. From Germany the firebrand Ulrich von Hutten, who wanted to use Luther to spark a nationalist German revolution, warned Erasmus that his life was in danger from poison or dagger and that he must escape from Louvain. 'If they damn Luther they won't forgive you. Flee, we need you . . . They say that you began all the trouble . . . and that it was you who stirred us up to long for freedom.'[22] Yet Erasmus now uttered the opinion that the bull against Luther was cruel.

The outlawing of Luther at the Diet of Worms, which turned Luther from a monk about whom Germans quarrelled into a religious leader whose name was as famous in Europe as the name of Erasmus, made a crisis in the life of Erasmus. He thought the behaviour of Luther's enemies deplorable, and even touched with madness. He could see now that Luther

---

[18] *Ep.* 1153 to the rector of Louvain university.
[19] *Ep.* 1141.   [20] *Ep.* 1143 from Louvain, 13 September 1520.
[21] *Ep.* 1153, 'dixit me magnopere favisse Luthero'. The speaker was Nicolaas Baachem.
[22] In Erasmus, *Ep.* 1161, 13 November 1520. It is possible that the postman was detained and that this letter never reached Erasmus.

could only succeed if he smashed the unity of the Church and he knew that he could not go that way. He would be loyal to the pope, but he would not attack Luther. He would help each side to be reasonable if he could, he believed in the Catholic Church. This moderate viewpoint, as parties moved towards force, and books were burnt, and preachers in Belgian pulpits were shrill, was impossible for a famous scholar living in Louvain. Erasmus's life was not safe, and his social life was troubled, and his work affected. He said that if he went on living in the Netherlands he would have had to become an executioner.

In 1521 he went to live in Basel. He told Louvain they would see him again in the spring. He was forced out of Louvain, he was not forced to settle in Basel, he had many invitations. A cardinal wanted him at Rome, the French court pressed him to Paris, Zurich offered him citizenship, Saxony suggested a professor's chair at the university of Wittenberg, he even decided to go to Italy. But Basel it was, he was a friend of their printers, and the choice had long consequences for his future, set between Protestants and Catholics.

It was a part-retirement from the campaign to reform Church and society. He could not tell what was about to happen, but he realized that he could not stop it when it was bad nor help it when it was good, and resigned himself with the three words, *fata viam invenient*, 'fate will take us the way it decides'. He was not very comfortable in Basel. He disliked the cost of living.

For the first time he began to regret paragraphs he had written. 'If I had foreseen what would happen to this generation, there are passages in my books which I would not have written or would have written differently.' Evidently he wondered whether to become polemical and partisan and knew that he was not that sort of person. 'Not everyone has strength to become a martyr. I am afraid that if violence came I should follow St Peter's example. When popes and emperors make good edicts, I obey them because it is my religious duty. When they make bad edicts, I put up with it because that is the safe way to behave.'[23]

When he went from Louvain to settle in Basel, the worship of the town was still Catholic. It was a university town, the only university in Switzerland till the modern age. Above all it had Froben his printer to welcome him and for several months to give him hospitality. It had more freedom, to say and write as he wished. The first few years were a serene time despite the clashes of the world outside. No one in Basel would rise in a pulpit to denounce him. (But Guillaume Farel did, not because he was alleged to be a follower of Luther but because he was not Protestant, and as a result Farel was thrown out of the town.) He wrote now his best Catholic devotional books. But he also went on satirizing the abuses of church life, in *Colloquies* which

[23] *Ep.* 1202, 1218.

grew more and more outspoken (useless ceremonies, war, too many saints' days, order to clergy to be unmarried though this had no authority in Scripture or early Church, turning opinions about theology into articles of faith, begging friars, why do not they work instead of begging?—and so on). He lived quietly among his books and costly furniture, not as a hermit but among a pleasant circle of humanist friends. There were local worshippers. Several secretaries travelled for books and papers.

Moderate persons in an immoderate world cannot be at ease. Despite the pleasures of his Basel life, he was under fire from both sides. German reformers could not understand why he did not back them when so many of his opinions agreed with theirs, and accused him of being a coward not prepared to stand up and be counted, or as too intent on his income, a person with a foot in both camps, 'an amphibian'. But by the date when Luther called him the king of amphibians, Luther's objection was no longer that Erasmus vacillated about being a Catholic, but in the opposite direction, that he was a friend of Oecolampadius, of whom Luther and the pope equally disapproved.[24] The savage attack upon him as a compromiser came from his former admirer Ulrich von Hutten, in a pamphlet so virulent that it was hardly to be explained except by Hutten's severe illness—Erasmus has a fine intelligence but no guts. Erasmus made the mistake of answering.[25]

His conservative friends believed that the only way he could rescue his reputation as a Catholic was by writing a book against Luther, a *Contra Lutherum*. They pressed, entreated, almost went on their knees to him—for the Church's sake, for his soul's sake, for the sake of friendship. He said that he had better ways of using his time. Or that his studies had not given him the equipment. Or that Luther wrote in German and he did not read German fluently. Sometimes he was bolder. 'These accusations of Luther,' he wrote to the pope's chaplain, 'these accusations about the greed and corruption of the Roman Curia—would to God they were not true!'[26]

Whatever he did for religion seemed to go wrong in conservative opinion. On Palm Sunday 1522 there was a demonstration in Basel against the rules of fasting. Erasmus wrote a book on the apparently trivial subject, 'On the Ban on Eating Meat on Fast Days'.[27] It was a popular book, for a time one of his most popular. Good aspirations always develop into rules. Then the rules get stuck. They need to keep up with the times and with what general opinion accepts. The law of celibacy is like that. But changes must not be made by demonstrations and mobs, the leaders of the Church must sanction them.

[24] *TR* 3392b, rex amphiboliarum.
[25] Hutten, *Expostulatio* (1523); reply by Erasmus, *Spongia*, same year.
[26] *Ep.* 1358 from Basel, 17 April 1523. This pope was the reformer Adrian VI, which made such a sentence less shocking to Catholics who wanted reform.
[27] *De interdicto esu carnium*, in *Opera Omnia*, ix. 1. 19 ff.

Within only a few years Catholic opinion regarded this as one of his most unCatholic books. He had not intended it to be offensive.

The Roman Curia, after repeatedly inviting him and then pressing him to write against Luther, demanded that he explain his faith. He replied that in his books one might surely find errors but he never doubted any accepted doctrines and claimed to have done better than Luther's public assailants to weaken the cause of Luther. Yet this pressure finally decided him that he must write against Luther. The decision pained him.

There was a story that when the last crusaders were forced to leave Palestine, angels picked up the house of Mary and Joseph at Nazareth, to save it from Muslim hurt, and put it down at Loreto in the Marches of Italy. Much later, and after a cult grew up there, the pope said that this was true and that this house at Loreto was indeed the house of the Holy Family. Pope Julius II confirmed the cult and the best artists of the day adorned the sanctuary. Erasmus believed not at all in the legend. He was against dubious devotion to saints. He mocked pilgrimages to spurious relics. But now, in autumn 1523, he published a mass in honour of Our Lady of Loreto. The mass said nothing about the legend. The rite was simplified. The archbishop of Besançon, who was one of Erasmus's pupils, gave the mass an indulgence of forty days and when Erasmus printed a second edition it included the indulgence—yet he was almost as hostile to indulgences as Luther and thought them bad for morality. Friends were shocked, Luther's men thought it only to be expected of a compromiser.

The moralist in him realized that there was a doctrine of Luther which he thought very wrong. He believed that Luther denied free will. Luther said that God's mercy in saving the soul is overwhelming and he sometimes gave the impression that the individual has no room to choose. To express St Paul's doctrine of grace he used language which could sound extreme—even when the will does the best it can, it is still guilty of mortal sin—if you do good with the aim of getting merit with God, what you do is a sin worthy of hell—and more of the same. Erasmus did not believe that such expressions were helpful or true. He misunderstood Luther to say that people have no free choice in the ordinary conduct of their lives; which was far from Luther's teaching. But Luther's expressions caused distress to others besides Erasmus, because the language sounded fatalistic, as though we can do no good however hard we try, and then God is the author of evil.

He still preferred not to write against Luther. Free will was one of the thorniest areas in philosophy. He did not expect to convert anyone so he had no faith that his writing was useful to anyone but himself. He consoled himself for the ungrateful labour by the thought that henceforth those who accused him of being a Lutheran would have to shut their mouths. But if he must write, here was an area where he could write with a clear conscience.

To the moralist in him a freedom to choose between right and wrong had to be defended at all costs if any belief in right and wrong was to be maintained. He could meet the wishes of his conservative friends, and simultaneously say something which he thought to need saying, and conduct a controversy not on the level of mutual abuse which he had so often preached against, but on a plane of intellectual argument, if he published a book *On the Freedom of the Will* (*De libero arbitrio*). He told Pope Clement VII that he was writing against Luther on this theme. Almost at the same time he published an edition of the *Colloquies* which mocked monks and theologians, magic, popular superstition, absurd relics.

De libero arbitrio was printed by Froben at Basel and was in the shops in September 1524. He sent copies to many people including Henry VIII and Melanchthon but not to Luther. Here, he said, is one of the insoluble problems of philosophy, about which we can know little. What we do know is that we *ought* to live a life that is good because this *ought* is in our conscience. To talk paradoxes about God predestining us is useless—such a subject should only be argued inside lecture-rooms. In the Bible some texts are for free will, some for a chained will, and we are agreed that Scripture cannot contradict itself. What is certain is that we must decide for penitence and ask the mercy of God, and attribute whatever is good in us to God and whatever is bad in us to ourselves. But this means, we can decide.

Luther was then busy with writing a commentary on the book of Deuteronomy and did not read Erasmus's book for more than a year and then only replied because friends told him that he must answer someone who was thought to be a great reformer and yet preferred classical morality to St Paul. When he studied Erasmus's book he found that he agreed with almost none of it and answered, as always when he wound himself up, with vehemence, *De servo arbitrio* (*On the Will that is Not Free*). It was not at all a moderate book and Erasmus rose in wrath and answered it with an equally immoderate book *Hyperaspistes* (*The Champion*).

There was no chance of these two understanding each other on this theme. Erasmus knew that he came to truth, piece by piece, with long years of hard study. Luther had in his background an experience, a Damascus Road. By 'free will' they could not begin to mean the same.

Luther did not answer *Hyperaspistes*. In spring 1526 Erasmus, still reluctant, wrote a second part. This was a wordier but better book, which went back to his ideal of a Christian humanism. Realizing that he persuaded neither side, he wrote what he believed, in a more serene atmosphere, of the soul as free to answer its call. In our sense of God's overwhelming majesty we cannot make him unjust or cruel. We cannot say that revelation alone brings the truths about God because truth is found among pre-Christians like Socrates or Epictetus, it is blind not to recognize that pagan wisdom as a gift of God.

Reason is not always corrupt. Pagan virtue is still virtue. The original sin of nature is not the only source of sin. We are made moral or immoral partly by our childhood, and by the way we are brought up, and by the environment.

The two or rather three books on free will achieved no object. To reformers they did not understand the human predicament. The pope's disciples wanted attacks on Luther and less academic discussion. A few humanist members of the Curia were pleased. But what more of the Curia wanted was aggression against everything Luther stood for, a loud declaration of faith in the pope's authority, and an assertion of the seven sacraments.

Luther and Erasmus were two reformers who wanted many of the same things. Their personalities and methods could hardly have been more different: irony and satire versus passionate appeal; detached scholarship, where the commitment of the heart is almost hidden, versus engagement of the heart, where the underlying scholarship is almost hidden; charming style versus the hammer; fear of politics versus care-nothing for politics; moralist versus theologian; humanist versus ex-schoolman; ex-monk whose study was still a cell, versus ex-monk whose family home was open to all the world. They could hardly be allies even when their goals were the same. Erasmus thought Luther to risk success by extremism, Luther doubted whether so funny a man could be serious. When he met the *Julius Exclusus* and was sure that Erasmus had written it, the most anti-papal satire of the age, he said only that Erasmus is so elegant and so witty that he makes you laugh about the ills of the Church when you ought to weep. Erasmus sighed when the world would not decide to be better, he was sure that it could decide, it only had to take a hold of its will-power, and it is a pity that it fails; Luther saw the world as so corrupt that it could never decide to be better, without an intervention from outside it. He wrongly imagined Erasmus not to be 'engaged'. The chief link between them was the scholar Melanchthon, who revered both and wanted each to understand the other.

As the 1520s moved on, leading scholars at Basel moved also, towards reformation, and with radical suggestions. The best mind in Basel after his own was Oecolampadius. The city now had mass in Latin at several churches and the reformed communion in Swiss-German at others and citizens were free to go to which they liked. In those days no city could remain in so modern an attitude without violence blowing up—attacks on priests from one side, attacks on pastors from the other. Oecolampadius thought it obvious that it was right to abolish the mass and that anyone who thought the contrary rejected gospel truth. The city began to be disturbed and Erasmus hated disturbance. He loved to sit in Froben's garden (this is Jerome Froben, son of his great friend now dead and an heir to the printing firm) and worked there if the weather was fine, but now rough parades were in the street outside to destroy his peace. On 9 February 1529 a crowd of working men seized the market square, and then went round the churches destroying images. In face of this popular movement the city council banned the mass.

The entire personal problem of the origins of the Reformation is encapsulated in the predicament of Erasmus at this moment, the pain of deciding what to do, the decision and its extraordinary consequences.

He was against revolutions, against violence. He was unhappy with a sacrament which departed from the old doctrine of the mass. He could never say that he regarded the Church of Rome as wholly evil though he accepted that much in it needed changing. His place in Basel was hard to keep. It was like living in Louvain before 1521, being the odd man out in a society, though society was now on the other side of him, and here his life was in no danger. What was in danger was his acceptance by Catholics across Europe as a writer whom they could read with profit.

His 'agitation in mind' was what now he called it. He was happy in Basel; liked the community of learned people; enjoyed close friendships; knew he was valued; had access to his favourite printers; and had no need to go. Yet he felt he must go. It took him a month to decide to move and where, and his Basel friends did not know till a week later.

Catholic faculties of theology were still out for his blood. He could not return to Louvain, nor try Paris, nor Cologne. He felt a need to be not far from Basel. He must find a conservative university not too conservative. His preferred place was Speyer on the Rhine, a historic free city with a noble romance cathedral, and then the seat of the Reich supreme court. Curiously it was the place where not many days after Erasmus left Basel, the five German princes lodged the Protest (against the effort to suppress their religious liberties) which created the word Protestant. But Erasmus believed that the place would be noisy with the Rhine trade and decided against. Then King Ferdinand, the Habsburg archduke of Austria, who ruled the Black Forest and was Catholic, proposed a safe shelter at the university of Freiburg im Breisgau, and even offered him a half-finished palace to live in.

The offer did not attract him. He heard that the place was cramped, provincial, and that the inhabitants were superstitious; but this was probably talk by Basel friends trying to stop him from going. Freiburg was nearer, and he had stone, and gout, and travel was painful. He wanted to leave the town without publicity but it was a vain hope and the only result of his desire was to breed the rumour that he was trying to avoid saying goodbye to Oecolampadius. The last thing he wanted was to trample on the long friendship. He invited Oecolampadius to talk in Froben's garden. One side begged the other not to leave, the other side told the one that he was wrong about the presence in the Holy Communion. But it was a friendly and civilized talk. Erasmus confessed to having enjoyed the talk. He said he was sorry to go but he could not seem to approve what was done here in religion.[28] At the quay on the Rhine a few friends came to see him off. It was silent. There was neither abuse nor cheers. Oecolampadius told Simon Grynaeus, 'I think he won't be gone for ever.'[29]

He stayed at Freiburg longer than his friends expected, six years. The new Pope Paul III showed his pleasure at what he thought was a public refusal of Protestantism by conferring upon him the income of a Dutch prebend. Yet he was not happy. He missed the Basel academics and scholarly printers, and found it remote. It was not a bad university, then over seventy years old, small in numbers and with buildings which lasted till the Second World War. Among the Catholic professors were some who approved of him. But there were disadvantages. The grand unfinished house was not comfortable, he preferred to build another for himself. He was burgled, losing his best furniture, and money from cupboards. His health worsened. The faculty of theology was not uncomfortable, yet he felt 'a tumult of theologians'. The local monks 'barked' at him and kept saying that he was a Lutheran.[30]

He went on quietly with his scholarship, editing Augustine and Chrysostom.

At Freiburg he wrote his only direct attack on the Reformation. A Dutch monk Geldenhouwer, who had been a close friend in earlier life, went over to Luther and claimed Erasmus as on his side and used a little-known letter from Erasmus to prove it.[31] *Against the Pseudo-evangelicals* was a true anti-Protestant tract. Much that is called reform is only change. Society can never be perfect. The Church can never be perfect. So let us be moderate. The Church must be mended, the clergy's standards raised; but to say that we must make the Church like that of the apostles is like saying that we must put an adult back into the cradle. 'It is silly to change what is bad into what is bad, it is mad to change what is bad into what is worse'—where he was speaking of bad monks becoming worse ex-monks.

Protestants thought that the purpose was only to persuade Catholics that he was still Catholic. The reader feels more sincerity than that; an old man's sense of tragedy that a movement which he had helped to idealism was failing. If the object was to make Catholics trust him, it did not succeed.

In 1533 from Freiburg he sent a letter to the king of Scotland. It commended to him the mortal enemy of Luther, Cochlaeus, who sought to prevent William Tyndale's English translation of the New Testament from being buyable in Scotland.[32] The heart of his reforming plea was that the

---

[28] Erasmus to Pirckheimer, *Ep.* 2158.
[29] In Erasmus, *Ep.* viii, 2147 note. [30] *Ep.* 2328 and 2868.
[31] Geldenhouwer used Erasmus's *Apologia ad monachos Hispanos*, in *Opera Omnia*, ix. 1. 270; cf. preface at *Ep.* 1879.
[32] *Ep.* 2886.

New Testament should be read by the simplest persons. This letter was not a recantation. But it commended personally a Catholic scholar who was trying to stop the sale of a famous translation.

In the same year he made a serious effort, of the kind we should now call ecumenical, for reconciliation between the sharply dividing Churches: *De sarcienda Ecclesiae Concordia* (*On How to Make Peace in the Church*). It asked for a Catholic Church of tradition which should make the necessary concessions to Protestants. Much of it was devotional meditation, how beautiful is peace and unity in a Church. But it said many things unpalatable to Catholic readers—the hunt for gold, the ambitions of clergymen.

The cult of saints has superstition but we ought to bear with a people's affection. Statues and pictures are silent poetry and you do not blame a bride who kisses her new ring—we ought to bear with people who kiss bones and relics—still, in church it would be better to have no pictures but stories from the Bible. There are doctrines which are mere human opinion but we can put up with them till a council decides. Let the two sides abandon points of doctrine that can lead to no solution. We have too many feast days, and rules of fasting ought not to be rigid, infant baptism is *probably* apostolic. The pope will soon make fair conditions of peace for the Protestants and then the harmony of the Church will be secured.

This book only added to the charges of heresy which conservatives pushed at him. As a result Freiburg was never home as Basel was.

He went on writing; a devotional book on the preparation for death; and then one of his best books, *Ecclesiastes*, a book on how to preach sermons. He had thought about the subject for sixteen years before he published. Since he had never entered pulpits to preach, this was based on reading rather than experience. But it is one of the books which disproves the contention that this was not a theologian.

He was glad to receive honouring letters from the new Pope Paul III, who said, for he had not read much of Erasmus, that he highly praised his excellent doctrine, and addressed him as his beloved son;[33] Erasmus took care to circulate a rumour that the Curia was considering his name as a possible cardinal; still rueful and yet half-proud that he was able to quote to friends the absurdity, which he said was common among friars, that 'Erasmus is the father of Luther; Erasmus laid the eggs and Luther hatched the chickens; Luther, Zwingli, Oecolampadius, and Erasmus are the soldiers of Pilate who crucified Christ.'[34] He was afraid of what the radicals would do if they flooded the earth.

In 1535 he moved back to Basel, to live in the house of Froben the younger. He once said that his home was where his library was—he had sold

---

[33] *Ep.* 3021. Erasmus printed the letter in *De Puritate*.   [34] *Ep.* 2956.

his books to his Polish admirer John a Lasco on condition he could keep them during life. But in old age this was not true. He felt that in coming back to Basel he came home. Basel was quiet now. The city was well-run. Oecolampadius died five years before and Erasmus did not need to face arguments about doctrine. Another close friend Bonifacius Amerbach, who was the chief executor of his will, had become a member of the Reformed Church while Erasmus was at Freiburg and was now the rector of the reviving university and pleaded with Erasmus to come and help its restoration. He told some friends that he went back to see to the printing of *Ecclesiastes*; others that he went back for reasons of health. In Basel they rejoiced at his return and he took a pride in their pleasure. It had long been his home and he was happy to be back.

This did not mean that he identified himself with the Protestants.

In June 1536 he wrote a friendly letter to Philip Melanchthon, blaming Luther for abusing him and saying how everyone threw rocks at him as they did at King David, but addressing this Lutheran leader, whom he had always admired, as 'religious and learned'; and then his last known letter, to the Catholic Goclenius: 'my health forces me to stay in Basel. I have very sincere friends here, which I did not have in Freiburg. Yet, because of the disagreements over doctrine, I would prefer to die somewhere else.'

So he died, at home in a Protestant city on 12 July 1536 and was buried honourably in a Protestant cathedral with a Protestant service and a Protestant sermon by his old pupil Oswald Myconius of whom he did not approve.[35] A Catholic writer could not bear it that he died without a priest to attend him so he later faked evidence for the priest. Protestants also made legends, that monks buzzed throughout the sermon at his funeral, and that night desecrated the new soil of the burial.

He died rich and left his money to help the old and infirm, or promising students, or respectable women who needed work. Amerbach organized the trust, which did excellent work in helping needy students at the university.

It became a question whether Erasmus was a Catholic or a Protestant. Posterity may see that between those names there was less difference than might at first appear, and that a person could have something of both in the heart without a sense of tension. That was not how Europe saw things in the years after Erasmus died. In the battles soon to rage it mattered to propaganda whether either side could claim him. Controversialists of both parties wanted the name of such learning on their side. But both sides hesitated. How could Protestants claim a mocker who attacked Luther so personally and whom

---

[35] When Oecolampadius died they tried to get Simon Grynaeus to succeed him as chief minister but he preferred to remain the professor of Greek so they chose Myconius, who had a good record as a teacher.

Luther denounced and who uttered thoughts on the power of humanity to do good which were not to be reconciled with evangelical conviction of the power of God and the littleness of humanity? Catholics could justly claim that he never separated from the Catholic Church and provided texts indispensable for the study of Catholic tradition. But they could not claim one who attacked popes and doubted doctrines and ruined the prestige of monks and friars. The question was whether an author who did so much to start reformation could be claimed as a critic of that reformation.

At once there were biographies. His humanist friend Beatus Rhenanus, who helped publish the first unsanctioned edition of the *Colloquies*, and aided Froben in accurate printing,[36] wrote an account of the last weeks of which he knew nothing first-hand; but two years later Froben began the *Collected Works* of Erasmus and to this Rhenanus wrote a short life for a preface. Dedicated to the emperor Charles V, it magnified the links between Erasmus and the Catholic emperor. It was open on his good relations with popes, silent on the *Colloquies* and the *Praise of Folly*, drew an affectionate picture of a loyal friend, a kind generous scholar, and Christian of quiet devotion. It observed that he passed severe judgements, especially on superstition and ambition, but did not mention monks nor clergy.

Friedrich Nausea was a lover of Erasmus and mourned his death as though he was his father. He was court chaplain at Vienna and wanted to open the eyes of the world to what they had lost. Within a month of the death he published a *Monodia* of lamentation for a pure life, a master of literature and a mind so free from superstition. Erasmus brought the gospel to ploughmen and weavers, the first to restore the gospel to our age and so did the work of an apostle; the dazzling ornament of the Church; his death was predicted by this year's eclipse. For this stout Catholic, soon to be a bishop, Erasmus was not only equal to the wisest sages of antiquity, he was a saint; with a majestic face, a temperate and moral life, the right ethical standards in what he wrote. Probably the pope will soon give him the title of Blessed. 'Praise for the dead should be without adulation but we can scarcely praise him enough.' All this in 1536. Twenty years later no Catholic bishop could write in such terms.

For this was not the view uppermost in the Curia. Professors said that this was a good man who sometimes did harm, others said that no author who did so much harm could be a good man. In Italy he was still read widely. When the Council of Trent met to make the Church better, more than one speaker argued that it was wrong to condemn all Erasmus or even parts because he did such good to the Catholic Church. This was not the general view of fathers

---

[36] Rhenanus was a true scholar who discovered the text of Velleius Paterculus in the library of a monastery in Alsace and gave it its first edition. At first he welcomed Luther but then reacted. To escape the reform he left Basel four years before Erasmus.

at the Council. Speakers, usually Spanish or Italian, were vocal in condemnation. They said that his faith in human goodness weakened the doctrine of original sin, that he put marriage above virginity and doubted whether marriage is a sacrament, he mocked monks and ridiculed popes, and hesitated about the cult of saints and images. He had the same ideas as Luther but made them sound like pious Catholicism.

In 1555 Paul IV the Inquisitor was elected pope and put all the books of Erasmus on the Index of Prohibited Books whether they were to do with religion or not. This was a shattering victory for the Stunicas, until then several of Erasmus's books were widely used, they were needed in schoolrooms. In Catholic countries they were read by people who did not dare to read Luther but wanted to read a reformer of the Church. They were also read because they were good to read—the New Testament for example, or the Paraphrases, or the *Enchiridion*, and sometimes because they were funny like the *Colloquies*. In places they continued to be read with the author's name removed from the title page.

Selective condemnations, in Spain or Italy or the Netherlands, show what censors really minded. The *Adages* were usually left free for school use and the general reader. The patristic texts were still used. The books on methods of education grew obsolete but were not banned. The *Enchiridion* and the Paraphrases usually escaped. One censor at Antwerp said that Erasmus gave them more trouble and used up more of their time than anyone else.

The blanket condemnation could not survive. Forbidden were *Colloquies*, *Praise of Folly*, the book of marriage, the book about the ban on eating meat, *Lingua*, and the Paraphrase of St Matthew in its Italian translation. *Lingua* needs an explanation because it was far from being an important book. It posed as an ethical study of the tongue and its vices and how to use it well and of the importance of not using it too often, and one is reminded of Thomas Carlyle speaking for hours in praise of silence. There is a passage on how it is better to keep silence when one is attacked, and hardly anyone was less qualified than Erasmus to forbear in that way. There was classical learning with examples. It was written in 1525 when he resented the attacks on him from theologians of Louvain and Paris; and illustrated the crimes which the tongue can commit by examples of slander and calumny drawn openly, though not by name, from his opponents—even using what was heard at their tables—'he is the worst of heretics', 'he is a fellow-conspirator with Luther', 'he knows no theology', 'he is the son of immoral parents'. This was the most devastating attack on friars which he ever wrote—poisonous words from friars posing as good—'has the Holy Spirit ceased to guide? is God's name now a nothing?' There were reasons why they should wish to prohibit this book, though it was never popular like the *Colloquies* or the *Praise of Folly*.

But all other works *on religion* were also banned until they were given expurgated editions approved by the faculties at Louvain or Paris, and they must not carry the name of the author on the title page. So much for that uncontroversial book of devotion the *Enchiridion*. They thought it made physical acts so unimportant that it led devotion away from sacraments and even from certain doctrines.

While Ignatius Loyola was studying at Alcalá, the *Enchiridion* was published in Spain and the university argued about it. The convert student was recommended to read it as a helpful work of devotion. He found it cold and undevotional. After he founded the Jesuits he made a rule that they should not read Erasmus.[37]

In eastern Europe Erasmus gained a strange authority which lowered his reputation further in the West. In his preface to the works of St Hilary he taught how the earliest Christian Fathers had not recognized the Holy Spirit to be divine in the same way that they recognized the Father and the Son. This correct historical observation was seized upon by the groups in Poland and Transylvania who rejected the word Trinity because it did not come in the New Testament. His enemies in the West accused him of reviving the heresy of Arius, who would not allow Jesus to be God in the sense of being equal to his Father. Antonio Possevino was the pope's agent in the eastern lands. He said how many of his works were forbidden, and others only allowed in expurgated versions; how his Arianism had a disastrous effect in Poland; how he ran from his vows and monastery after eight years and became a wanderer for the sake of a career; how he was no solid theologian and his overproduction of books led to many errors; how his salt and bitter wit put into print things indecorous for a clergyman; how Luther drank from his well—and then, sixty years after Erasmus himself quoted it, Possevino cited in a new form the famous *mot* of the egg and the hatching: *Erasmus innuit, Luther irruit. Erasmus parit ova, Luther excludit pullos. Erasmus dubitat, Luther asseverat.* Or, Erasmus did the doubting and then Luther went dogmatic.[38]

To be popular among Protestant thinkers on religion (as distinct from teachers in schools interesting their pupils) was impossible for Erasmus until some of them allowed that he was right about free will. With the school of St Augustine, even of St Paul, Catholic or Protestant, strong against him, with Luther and Zwingli and Calvin and Bucer dominant, this admission

---

[37] The story has been doubted, on the ground that we owe it to Ribadeneira, who wrote his life of Ignatius as late as the end of the 1560s, and in any case says that it happened earlier when he was learning grammar at Barcelona. But Gonzalez in 1555 said it was at Alcalá, and that is the more probable because just then the university was discussing the book. For the ban in the Society see *MHSJ* iv. 359; v. 95 and elsewhere.

[38] Possevino, *Judicium de Erasmo* (Lyons, 1593) repeated in *Apparatus Sacer* (Venice, 1606), i. 388–9.

took time, and hardly happened until near the end of the sixteenth century, and in his native Holland.

He had led scholarship towards reform of the Church, that was undeniable. The Catholic Church had condemned his writings, that was undeniable. Against practices of the Catholic Church he had written much they wanted to say (indulgences, ceremonies, certain sacraments), that was undeniable. He had done great things for the propagation of the reading of the Bible, that was undeniable. But Luther called him an emissary of Satan. His books on free will showed him to be a semi-Pelagian heretic, he thought that the human race could climb to heaven partly by its climbing agility. He seemed to be more a jester than a sober reformer. They doubted whether the tone of the *Colloquies* was the way to make a Church better. Though obviously a reformer he had refused to come out on the Protestant side, he was Mr Facing-Both-Ways. Saner critics did not explain his neutrality by bad motives like miserliness. But they were apt to impugn him for lack of courage. Everyone knew how close a friend he was of Sir Thomas More who died for the pope's authority. On the Catholic side this friendship was awkward for the first biographers of More.

There were three places where criticisms were brushed aside.

Basel was proud that he had felt himself at home there. Citizens knew him personally and enjoyed him. His executors Amerbach and Froben and Episcopius put up a Latin plaque for his grave—'To Erasmus of Rotterdam, a man in every way great, who married to prudence a peerless learning in every sort of discipline; his posterity admires and imitates. We place this to the best of patrons, not to remember his name which is immortal in so many editions and books, a name which will not be forgotten in any company of the educated; but to his mortal body which is laid here.'

Several Swiss leaders of the Reformation kept this high opinion. But not all. In September 1557 Farel, then chief pastor for Vaud, and Beza, then professor of Greek at Lausanne, both colleagues of Calvin, passed through Basel and stopped at an inn. Before a large audience they abused Erasmus, Farel said he was wicked and a heretic, Beza said he was a disciple of the heretic Arius. The news was brought to Amerbach and Froben, who made a solemn protest and declared that it was calumny and even civil law protects the dead from libel.[39]

Twenty-three years later Beza mellowed. In his *Icones*, which were portraits of the leading reformers with short notes on what they did, there was first the list of forerunners beginning with Wyclif, and then the list of those who reformed Germany and the name of Erasmus came second; his 'inexhaustible fertility of genius', and his fame. But he was content to mock

[39] Literati Basileenses Farello et Bezae. Calvin, CR xvi. 2728.

superstition and refused to come out for the right cause. Yet 'good scholar-ship was restored; so let his name stand in this religious place'. Beza did not think he need mention the New Testament.

The second place which had private reasons to revere the memory was Holland, especially Rotterdam. They knew that they had begotten a great Dutchman. Their Church as it became Protestant was Calvinist so this was not without doubt.

While it was still a Catholic country, Prince Philip, soon to be King Philip II of Spain, came to visit Rotterdam in 1549. The municipality erected a wooden statue of Erasmus dressed as a clergyman in homage to the royal visitor. Eight years later, still Catholic, they made a stone statue on the bridge by the market.

In the Dutch war of independence Spanish soldiers used this statue as a target and the pieces fell into the river. The now Protestant city fathers soon made a new statue in wood to replace the stone, with Erasmus preaching (an inappropriate design) and in his hand a Paraphrase. In the 1590s they replaced this with stone, no longer a preacher or clergyman, but now in the gown of a scholar, and the book looks more like the *Colloquies* than a Paraphrase. This again was replaced, in 1622, by the statue that still stands, with a youthful face and a big folio volume.

Pastors objected. One said he was a scoffer at religion, another observed genuflection to the statue as though this was the cult of a saint. The German air raid of May 1940 destroyed the plaque on the house where he was born but missed the statue.[40]

The third place where Protestants felt little doubt was among disciples of Melanchthon. Most Lutherans followed Luther in having small use for Erasmus. Melanchthon, with the same ideals of a harmony of scholarship and religion, had kept his friendship to the end. After Luther died he even wrote an essay in praise of Erasmus. This was a great teacher and great teachers are a gift from God. He admitted there were arguments with Luther but all good men have differences of judgement. The letters of Erasmus in praise of the earlier Luther were often reprinted by evangelical publishers. In the church at Nordhausen Lukas Cranach painted the leading reformers and Erasmus stands among them.

In 1928 the body believed to be that of Erasmus was exhumed. The skel-eton was found to have traces of syphilis. This discovery suggested incongruity. We know the personality of Erasmus and much in his mentality, including distaste, would hate anything liable to lead to venereal disease. Nearly half a century later it was discovered that the wrong body had been exhumed.

[40] Nicolaas van der Blom, 'The Erasmus Statues in Rotterdam', *Erasmus in English*, 6 (Toronto, 1973), 5 ff.

4

DEATH

It has been argued that guilt was invented during the thirteenth or fourteenth century. Any reader of the Old Testament, or the plays of Sophocles and Euripides, knows the contrary. In the twentieth century there was an English teacher of the classics, mild and gentle and serene, who exploded if his pupils argued that conscience was discovered by the disciples of Christ.

Faith is likely to deepen this sense of guilt because it puts forward high ethical ideals, too high for more than a few to come near. Aspiration after a moral ideal and guilt at failure to attain it go hand in hand. When such an ideal became the desire of the peoples it must be accompanied by a more profound sense of frustration, inadequacy, or at its most powerful, despair. When friars, wandering preachers, spoke to their crowds about *saving*, *redeeming*, they spoke to ears which felt comfort in their need.

It has been implied that friar-preachers created the sense of need so that they could then meet it. That is impossible to believe. Pulpits have power, especially where not many can read, but not that much power.

The extreme confessions of personal guilt were usually found in monasteries. Many lukewarm monks lived a pleasant retired life with fresh air and reasonable diet and peace. But the system, being designed by its founders to create idealists, was sometimes sure to succeed. A monk who thought was confronted daily with a beckoning towards a Mount Sion, and if he thought he had attained it he had failed though he did not know it. The perception of sinfulness was sensitive, in a few even to a feeling like the flesh being raw.

This feeling, discomfort at its lowest, physical pain at its worst, was deepened because it was usually accompanied by a vision of judgement to come. Every moment of time precious in the eyes of one's Maker. Born into the world for a purpose, to glorify God and help men and women. All guides to the way of monks or nuns accepted that the bow must not be stretched tense all the time, that rest and relaxation and refreshment, mental as well as physical, was a necessity. But we must stand before our Maker and give account of how we have used our time and be told where we failed and we shall be ashamed and shall be punished.

The mental attitude was not usually pessimism. This same Maker had created a lovely world to inhabit, with music and flowers and streams and clouds and stars and light and sparkling waters, they could rejoice in the pleasures and refinements of so varied a universe.

But it had this end which must be passed. Death was everywhere; no undertakers to hide its grievous manifestations, no chemists to sell drugs except quacks (whose drugs could help, since the buyer believed), no doctors except for the well-to-do, few homes where the dying could go to spend their last weeks or months. Not an end so much as a new beginning—to a life more comfortable or less? For ordinary people approaching death was a hard fact like the need to eat bread and to be accepted stolidly—we are not sure whether this was true, the sources show the articulate classes bothering about their end, did the poor seem to bother less because they could not express their anxiety?

Historians agree that the plague of 1348 and the next three years marked a psychological point in Western consciousness. For a town or village to lose a third of its people and few brave people daring to minister to the infected meant that bodies were everywhere. The towns grew in numbers, people packed more closely together, sanitation and drains had hardly improved since Roman days. The towns knew enough to ban burials in populous areas or dung in the streets, and to isolate lepers, but no one understood the existence of bacteria till the seventeenth century.

The Reformation was always thought to begin because of an argument over death, and the fear of death. Of course religion and death were always connected because religion spoke of another world and another scale of time.

From the early days of Christendom and before, the funeral was more than a getting rid of a useless lump. It was always a duty that the family should inter the body of the dead with reverence. St Augustine had said that the body was that of a person created by God and redeemed by Christ and waiting for the risen life; and therefore must be buried with piety. So they closed the eyes and the mouth, and washed the body, and placed it in a clean shroud or at times, if the person was eminent, in the robes of office; and buried the body with face towards the rising sun, for the Saviour would come from the East. There was no other method of disposal than burial. This was what happened to Jesus and ought to happen to his disciples. Among the Christians the funeral was not only the business of the family. This was a member of a Christian community and the whole community was concerned. It was a religious service, with prayers and hymns, as they followed the bier to the grave.

Could they pray for the dead? The early Christians did so though questions were asked about it and bishops needed to explain why it was done. As time passed it became a 'mass for the dead'—to bless the remains in church in the context of the sacrament, say, a requiem. There was a ritual also for dying people, with an anointing, and forms of prayer. As time passed the hymnody used with the requiem was forbidding. The *Dies Irae*, 'Day of Wrath', written probably by Thomas of Celano in the earlier thirteenth century, was sometimes used as part of the rite:

> Quantus tremor est futurus
> quando judex est venturus,
> cuncta stricte discussurus!

'What terror there will be among us when the judge is coming . . . when the judge takes his seat nothing will remain hidden, nothing will remain unavenged.'

> sed tu bonus fac benigne
> ne perenni cremer igne . . .

'Be kind, don't let me burn for ever. Put me on your right hand among the sheep and not among the goats. While the accursed are thrown into the flames, call me up to be among the blessed.'

This hymn had not won its supremacy as a necessary part of the mass of the dead when reformation began. It became a regular piece of the liturgy of the dead through the Council of Trent half way through the sixteenth century. But already it was widely used.

This sense of judgement was expressed, and helped to make, a doctrine of purgatory. Early Christian writers spoke of a cleansing fire after death whereby the soul is purged. In the third-century Origen this fire is both a cleansing and a punishment. St Augustine was not sure about it. But before the end of the seventh century there were masses for the dead which were connected with the idea of a fire of purgatory. At the start of the eleventh century Odilo the abbot of Cluny introduced a feast of All Souls on 2 November in which masses should be said, and alms should be given, to help the dead. St Thomas Aquinas in the thirteenth century accepted that masses and prayers and almsgiving and indulgences could help the dead in their passing through purgatory. By this time the idea was declared in pulpits as a moral incentive. That their hearers were anxious before the torments of hell and purgatory became a moral impetus in the sermons of popular preachers.

Dante's purgatory was not so well known in the Middle Ages as afterwards but its beautiful picture took for granted the needs of souls in purgatory and the belief that mortals now in the flesh can help them.

These ideas were given point by the practice of indulgences. In the eleventh century appeared the notion that we can do penance for the dead by proxy, and thereby save them from the worst torments which they must endure in the afterlife. This was encouraged by those who cared for the fervour of a people's devotion and was accepted by ordinary folk and was criticized by thinkers who worried that all was not well with the religious doctrines which it implied.

In their preaching to the people the friars used sermons on hellfire—prepare, it can happen any moment, you may have very little time, its consequences are infinite; act now. Then came the plague. There is an association in time between the Black Death of the middle fourteenth century and more gruesome representations of death in art. A link in time does not prove that one was caused by the other. But it has a probability. Types of devotion unknown before made their appearance. The skeleton, to the ancient world a harmless object—let us eat and drink—was frightening.

The devotion was 'democratic'—death is the leveller, it happens to kings as well as beggars. As an instrument of poets and dramatists and mural artists the portrayal of death became a satire. The mayor looks splendid in his robes and chain but he will die tomorrow just like you and me so there is no need to take him seriously. This form of 'democratic' thought could be savage— this mayor who looks splendid secretly takes bribes and will not get away with it because of the Enemy. Since the clergy were ceremonious and well-vestmented in processions through the streets, an artist who hated clergymen had a means of scorn by the use of their skeleton. To the Dominican preacher death was a moral impetus. To the mendicant artist it levelled pope and bishop with the dust.

In 1424–5 we have the first proven example of a 'Dance of Death'. The name is not exact. There were legends that at night once a year the dead in churchyards rise from their graves and dance a ghostly jig. But the 'dance of death' so-called was a series of pictures, on the wall of a cemetery or in glass or carving, where each member of society, especially the respectable, walk hand in hand with a skeleton, who jests at the pomposity and beckons him or her to destruction. It could be anti-clerical but that was because it was against outward pomp and power. The friars used it in their preaching, artists who illustrated books of hours used it in their illustrations, poets and playwrights took up the theme.

The most famous series was engraved by an Erasmian: Hans Holbein the Younger. He composed it at Basel between 1524 and 1526 but it was not published until twelve years later and then at Lyons. A series of pictures of human beings walking with skeletons was likely to be boring as art. One skeleton is like another because it has neither face nor dress. Holbein saved it from tedium not only by his quality as a draftsman but by a variety of scenery, architecture, background and costume. He began with the creation, and the garden of Eden; and the skeleton first appears when Adam and Eve are driven out of the garden and when Adam is forced to dig the soil for his food by the sweat of his brow, death digging at his side. The fifth engraving is of all men's bones, rising up to play as an orchestra, with a drum and trumpets and sackbuts. The pope sits on his throne and the emperor kisses his feet while behind the pope's left ear a skeleton whispers. The emperor wields a supreme authority from his throne while a skeleton clambers about his head. A king (the king of France by his fleur-de-lis) dines at a banquet and a skeleton is one of the waiters; and so with a cardinal, and an empress in a little procession about to fall into an open grave which she hardly sees, and a queen, whose jester in cap and bells has no face but a skull, and a bishop, and a duke, and an abbot whose mitred skeleton tugs at his habit, and an abbess, a nobleman, a canon in full vestments, a judge evidently bribable, a barrister while his skeleton listens courteously to the argument, a senator, a preacher whose skeleton squeezes into the pulpit behind him, a priest going to minister to the dying while ignorant that this is his own last journey and in front of him the skeleton ringing the bell, a monk, a nun who has a lute-playing lover, an old hobbling woman, a physician about to prescribe a cure and he does not know that his own time is come, an astrologer who surveys the heaven above his head and does not see death facing him, a rich man counting his hoard of gold and the skeleton has his hand in the till, a merchant in harbour, a storm at sea and the skeleton breaks the mast to make the crew helpless, an armoured knight run through the back by his enemy for death is not chivalrous, a count, an old man, a countess who tries on a new gown which she will not have time to wear, a lady, a duchess, a pedlar, a ploughman, a little child snatched away from the hearth and waving a wee hand in goodbye to its mother. Then the series ends with the Last Judgement but it is happy, death has vanished.

The engravings are against emperors as much as against popes and cardinals. They are against monks and nuns. But the bishop is quietly resigned to death, the parish priest dies on a noble mission, the preacher about to drop dead grips his audience except for a man asleep at the foot of the pulpit. The series was not against the pastoral clergy.

In the twelfth century an Irish monk of Regensburg wrote down the *Vision of Tnugdal*, a knight who was given the privilege of seeing into the future life. This *Vision* was translated into several languages and affected piety in the later Middle Ages. Guided by his guardian angel he saw sinners roasting in a cauldron and tortured by a flamethrower from the devil and torn by talons; the worst were the rich and the worldly parsons. A vision like this, which was only the most popular of many, had the work of warning the people to repent.

In such a world of thought the idea of purgatory came as relief. It meant that there was an area of the future agony over which a soul or those who loved it could have influence from this earth. And the question for reformers was whether it was a healthy method of warning the soul or creating penitence.

Indulgences

The indulgence grew out of such ideas in the Western earlier Middle Ages and was formulated by the schoolmen as a theory—originally called absolution or relaxation and from the thirteenth century called indulgence—and then during the last two centuries of the Middle Ages became a weighty part of the religious life of the people.

As the system of private confession and penance grew it was necessary that there should be guidance, and then rules, about what penances were to be demanded of the sinner when he or she made confession; and the performance of these penances was a condition for readmission to communion in the Church. For graver sins these penalties could be very demanding. Charity demanded a system of 'equivalents' that were more possible—instead of going on pilgrimage to Compostela give to charity the cost of the journey; if it is impossible to fast on a certain day say psalms instead, and so on. Soon it was agreed that if the penitent could not do it a friend could do it instead. And it was agreed that the penalty could be diminished or remitted at the prayers of the confessor—which affected not only the penalties inflicted by human law but God's punishment for sin.

The theory did not come in without criticism. It was obvious that sin was not forgiven without penitence in the heart; and it was obvious that this system—pay money to help a crusade—had the danger of separating the external act, which won remission of the penalties due to sin, from regret in the soul.

In the thirteenth century St Thomas Aquinas justified the system.[1] Christ has full power to forgive and has passed this fullness to the pope. The Church cannot err and has approved the indulgence. Christ has an inexhaustible grace, a treasure, which he has passed to the Church to dispense. This can be applied to charitable ends. It can release those already suffering from pains which they endure in purgatory.

Such a theory would not be believed unless it met a demand; and the demand was caused by confessors aware that penitents who came to them suffered from the belief in fire and the conviction that their parents or dead children were in an agony which they longed to relieve. Any attack upon indulgences as external acts, which could be dissociated from repentance in the sinner, was bound to carry with it a much deeper attack—a question whether the doctrine of purgatory, as taught in sermons and in pictures on the walls of churches, was true. Various people taught, and more people believed, even by 1300, that the pope has power to free a soul from the pains of purgatory and send that soul to heaven. A few people were still bold

---

[1] *Summa Theologiae*, III Suppl. qq. 25–6 and 71, with some remarkable logic.

enough to criticize what was happening. No one in authority listened to them. The critics were rebels like John Wyclif in England or Jan Hus in Prague or John of Wesel the canon of Worms cathedral, bold enough to be accused of heresy. Yet they grew more vocal in their opinion of what was happening to penitence and their doubt of the system by which mis-penitence was encouraged.

The theory was not so bad as practices which accompanied its use. The Church is always short of money for good causes. Money can always be got from the offer of an indulgence. The money will be used to valuable ends— like paying for a crusade, or building a cathedral, or helping a town by bridg-ing its river.

The sellers of indulgences, collectors of the money, were not concerned about penitence, their business was to pull in money. The churches and clergy in the city of Rome were good at it, for they offered years of remission, sometimes thousands of years, in return for the gifts of the pilgrims. Collectors had a motive to paint what happened in purgatory as agonies, centuries-long pain.

Put at its least offensive thus: the son of a dead father gives alms to the Church. This is self-sacrifice, and in return for it the Church releases the son from the duty to do penance for sin. Then the act of charity is taken up before God and is part of the general self-sacrifice which good men and women do. Thus it is used to help the departed.

Put at its most offensive thus: drop a silver coin into the plate and the soul of your grandmother will fly to heaven. This last was not a caricature. It was preached thus to (and by) people who did not understand and thought only about their beloved who had gone.

The indulgence was now the big source of extra revenue in the Church. To abolish it would be like abolishing modern bazaars, raffles, gift days, spon-sored bicycle rides and fees for entering cathedrals. Wealthy individuals might give large sums for a special object. But the alms of the people came through the bag.

A professor of divinity worthy of the name must ask what was the founda-tion for so strange a doctrine. He need not question the necessity for alms-giving to repair churches or build bridges. He would need to insist that there is no substitute for penitence; to ask whether the Church militant here on earth can control what happens in an unknown world. When he enquired what is the authority under which the indulgence is offered for sale, he would find to his surprise that the authority was modern. So far from it being an ancient custom of the Church, he would find that though the practice was older, its modern understanding could be found neither in Scripture, nor in the longer tradition of the Church, but rested upon modern edicts by the See of Rome.

Rome of the Renaissance needed a cathedral worthy of its grandeur. Pope Julius II decided to rebuild St Peter's, and needed almsgiving, and proclaimed an indulgence. His successor Leo X renewed this indulgence. The estimates were vast, the money came slowly. Partly it came slowly because some states blocked it. Several German governments thought it undesirable that money should flow out of their territories to build a cathedral in Italy and refused to allow preachers of the indulgence across their frontiers.

The archbishoprics and bishoprics of Germany were secular states within the empire as well as diocesan bishoprics. Since their occupants could not marry, the states could not become hereditary; but because they were essential to the structure of power within the empire, they were the possession of families, related to those like Habsburg or Wittelsbach or Hohenzollern who were the potent political clans of Germany. Hence when in 1514 the young Hohenzollern Albert of Brandenburg became at the age of twenty-three archbishop of Mainz, bishop of Magdeburg, and acting bishop of Halberstadt, it was a political act which had the backing of powerful men in both north and south Germany and caused vexation to other powerful men like the elector of Saxony.

To be bishop of three sees and to be bishop under the age of thirty was contrary to church law. He needed dispensation. For this Rome charged him huge fees (52,286 ducats), which he could not afford. Therefore it was agreed that for eight years he should take charge of the German sale of the indulgence to rebuild St Peter's. He and Rome reached a secret agreement. Half the proceeds of the indulgence in his territories should go to the fund for St Peter's. The other half of the proceeds should go to the Fugger bank at Augsburg, which loaned Albert the money to pay Rome the remainder of the fees. Therefore some of the gifts from the people were to end in the good object of rebuilding St Peter's; and some to enable a young ecclesiastic to exercise power; and some to pay bank charges. The people did not know this.

The sale of the indulgence in the Brandenburg Lands was entrusted to the Dominican Johann Tetzel, who was experienced in the work. He could not preach the indulgence at Wittenberg because he could not cross the frontier into Saxony. For more than half a century Saxon rulers had restricted the preaching of indulgences in their lands. Why should Saxon money go to build churches in another country when there was need for churches and bridges at home? Why should money be collected from Saxons on the plea that it would be used for a crusade against the Turks and then the crusade was not launched? Saxon and other rulers were not so much against indulgences as against indulgences which benefited other states.

Tetzel preached the indulgence at Jüterbog just over the Saxon frontier and Wittenbergers went to hear him and to give their alms.

Several people across Europe had doubts about the theology of an indulgence. Two circumstances point to the feeling against indulgences which now was evident. Tetzel's marketing of his wares was specially offensive; and he was not the only such trader whose sayings shocked the more religious among his audience. Secondly, not far from Jüterbog was Wittenberg with its university, and a professor of biblical studies whose objection to indulgences was not in intellectual theory but in morality—they blind ordinary people to the truth about God.

In October 1517 Martin Luther got hold of a copy of the instructions which Archbishop Albert issued to his indulgence-preachers.

The Ninety-five Theses issued by Luther on 31 October 1517 were not a cry to all Germany. They did not denounce all indulgences. They in no way denied papal authority. They were an academic's plea for serious discussion by academics on the rights and wrongs of an indulgence. But this academic, it was evident from the theses, was engaged in his soul as well as his head. He was disturbed that penitence and the conscience should be treated so lightly. He was disturbed by the notion of external guarantees for getting to heaven or for what would happen in the afterlife. He was concerned as a pastor as well as a professor. He denied that indulgence could have any effect on the forgiveness of the soul after death or the shortening of the purgation. The Church can forgive the penalties which it has imposed. But the rest must be left to God. And the way the indulgence is preached gives the people an illusion.

The academic debate for which he asked never happened. The reasons were two: the printing trade, which seized upon these academic theses as an attack upon Rome which all Germany would want to read; and secondly, the growing feeling in Germany that Roman power over the Church in Germany was bad and should be diminished, and that anyone with the courage to attack it should be backed. It took about five months before Luther was well known in Germany. In March 1518 he published his first German pamphlet, *Of Indulgences and the Grace of God* (*Von Ablass und Gnade*). The records of printing show that this was read by far more people than the Ninety-five Theses. Astonishingly quickly it was evident that most articulate German people agreed with Luther.

All reformers agreed that an indulgence was a deception. But what of purgatory? This was an idea much older in Christendom. Natural feeling spoke out for it. They observed people die whose life was partly bad and partly good and could not think that they deserved to fly to heaven without cleansing and could not think that a merciful God would condemn them to torment for ever. The idea that a cleansing process ought to follow death was as natural in the sixteenth century as it was to Augustine in the fifth century.

At first Luther did not challenge the existence of a purgatory though he thought its existence to be more merciful than pictures and sermons painted it. The souls there are not in physical torment, they endure mental agony when they see the consequences of what they did. It is a state where they learn to deepen their love of God and their fellow humans. But he recognized that the existence of purgatory could not be proved from the Bible and people who deny its reality are not heretics. Ten years later he had moved his opinion and published *A Recantation on Purgatory*.[2] Melanchthon laid it down that all purification from sin happens by repentance on this side of the grave and not in the afterlife.[3]

The question arose whether reforming divinity became the thought of the people not because it freed their pockets from the need to subscribe to indulgences or to masses for the dead, but because it freed their minds from fear of pain after death in purgatory or in hell.

It is an unsolved question what these differences in attitudes to the future life made to society. The preaching of the danger of hell, to discourage villainy and bring souls to repent, went on among Protestants as among Catholics. Without a faith in adjustment to a better future by slow cleansing after death the Protestants were confronted by a still starker choice. But it is probable that the fear of what might happen in the future life declined and was slowly replaced by fear of the process of dying. Catholics of the time said that this abolition of purgatory by the reformed led to a decline in moral behaviour by laypeople because it weakened the sanction that if you are a villain you must pay the penalty in the next life if not in this. That is just possible, though only just. What is certain is that the 'assurance' of the reformed, the total confidence in the grace of God, was also a power morally during the next generations.

Postulate a preacher in a pulpit warning his people to prepare for death. Was he more likely to increase their resolution by warning them of torments to come? or by putting before them the reliance on faith and forgiveness now as the cleansing which would enable them to stand before their Maker? Putting this in the form in which it would confront pastors, how would they best help the dying soul during the last hours?

In the old piety of the friars the moment of death, or rather the moments just before death, were the concern of pastors everywhere. In this new world where purgatory had faded but where hell lived on, where you no longer had to plead a list of good actions during your life but could put a simple faith in your Redeemer, the evangelicals continued to advise pastors on what to say when they stood by a deathbed. They even used older Catholic books which gave advice about deathbeds. Like the older pastors though with more force

---

[2] *Widerruf vom Fegfeuer* (1530), *WA* xxx. 2. 367 ff.
[3] *Apology for the Augsburg Confession*, CR xii. 65.

they urged upon the prostrate to reach out with faith and be penitent about the past but look forward with confidence to the future. They drafted rituals, with a prayer for mercy and a reading of texts of forgiveness and a creed. The pastor, or a layperson if needed, was to urge the dying to say words of gratitude, for example a dying husband to his wife, or to commission her or a relative to care for the children. They continued to give the sacrament where the dying person was able to receive it. But they dropped the anointing with the disappearance of Extreme Unction as no true sacrament.

They found a new theme to talk about—whether it is right to encourage the dying, or the wife or children of the dying, to think that they shall see each other again in the world to come. Some people thought this wrong to talk about because it was the reformed principle that we must only say what is in the Bible and there is nothing about this in the Bible. To others it felt a natural part of a Christian hope.

Luther believed in hell. Fearsome pictures of hell he thought deplorable.[4] Many Protestant preachers used hell and judgement to stir their people to repentance and the acceptance of forgiveness; so that the distinction between the older attitudes and the newer was not great.

What now affected reformers was the requiem, masses for the dead. It was clear to them that the piling of masses, perhaps hundreds, in the aim of helping a soul in the afterlife was an absurdity. But can we pray for the dead at all? Luther thought it a family act which people wished to do in private. Melanchthon would do nothing to stop prayers for the dead but rejected masses for the dead which would work by the mere event that they were celebrated and would open the door to mechanical devotion. Calvin was confronted with a request from a French refugee in Montbéliard; here not a few people said when mentioning the departed, a ritual phrase, *to whom may God grant a good and happy resurrection*. Calvin's reply was that this is not wrong to think, that when a friend is buried or when news of a death is brought, 'I will beg that on the last day he and I may share in glory', in this was nothing superstitious. But no formulas, do not let us get such a ritual phrase into common use, let us do nothing there that Scripture does not warrant.[5]

The funeral rites of the Reformation were simplified. The services refrained from prayers for the dead. Since it was an expression of faith in the afterlife, an address by the minister to the people was in place and most Protestant church orders recommended or required at least a short address. This was not wholly an innovation for such homilies were known even in the early days of the Church. But they were not universal and it was only during

[4] *WA* ii. 686ff., from one of his sermons on preparing for death (1519); *WA* xlvii. 441, a sermon on Matthew 23: 1–3 (1537 or 1538); cf. Tarald Rasmussen, in *TRE* xv. 453.
[5] Calvin to Vatellus, 25 September 1562, CR, Calvin xix. 8–9.

the sixteenth century and among Protestants that they began to be so. An address intended to make new life its theme easily turned into a speech about the dead person and became a panegyric or at worst a flattering lie and turned the minds of the hearers away from heaven instead of towards it. They accepted the rule of charity *De mortuis nil nisi bonum*, let the historians express their revulsion later, say nothing bad about the lately dead. They followed Catholics in keeping the passing-bell, which slowly rang out from the church tower for the funeral. In Swiss villages they sounded the bell for a long time and Calvin thought it indecent that bells should sound more for a dead person than for calling the people to church on Sunday, and it was enough to tinkle a little bell to warn mourners it was time to assemble.

In several early hymn books printed by the reformers the only hymns were for use at funerals. For one of them Luther wrote a preface (Klug, 1542) in which he said what he thought should be done about funerals. They were too sad. To carry a coffin is to bear a soul towards salvation. The old customs were wrong because they were so mournful—masses for the dead and vigils and processions and purgatory and other 'hocus-pocus on behalf of the dead'. Purgatory has a torment 'which lets the dead neither rest nor sleep'. We are not to sing dirges at gravesides, but hymns of comfort, rest, forgiveness, life. The funeral is to be decorous and traditional rites well done and a tombstone to adorn the grave because this is a comfort. If there is a wall near the grave it would be good to put a text on it, on peace and falling asleep and the vision of God and '*O death where is thy sting?*'

In many cities the guild was responsible for the funeral of a member. Among Swiss guilds there seemed to be a special desire to avoid any ritual or symbol that could remind the mourners of the Catholic past.

Christ's descent into hell took many more hours of discussion during the sixteenth century than before or after. In the third century, and probably before, Christians accepted that after his death Christ went down into hell and there taught the truth to those who died before his time and even baptized good people among them, and in so doing experienced the full fate of humanity. This came into early ways of prayer as a symbol of the victory over the grave. By the middle of the fourth century it appeared in the Apostles' Creed, and in the Middle Ages it was used as a drama in the mystery plays. The idea was important to reformers as to medieval people. To Luther it meant victory over sin. Calvin understood it differently—Christ underwent the pains of his Father's judgement. But everyone agreed that it was a symbol of truth about the way in which the Redeemer reached out to souls who lived before his earthly time in history.

Medieval devotion centred upon the passion of Jesus, the last hours before his death. It dwelt upon his sharing in agonies, weakness, temptation. The reformers kept it at the centre of devotion. The greatest hymns of the passion

were written by Protestants, though on a medieval tradition of piety—
'*O Sacred Head Sore Wounded*', by the Wittenberg student Paul Gerhardt in
the seventeenth century but deriving from a medieval Latin poem; '*When I
Survey the Wondrous Cross*' by Isaac Watts in the English eighteenth century.

It was in continuity with the Middle Ages. But there were differences.
Because they appealed to the Bible, they could not adorn the story with
graphic detail as the mystery plays did or make it a melodrama by pious
invention. They could not surround it by legends from the early apocryphal
Gospels of the first centuries. They would not have Veronica's handkerchief,
nor even the *pietà*, the beloved statue of the Mother suffering below the cross
with her Son in her lap, because these were not in the Bible and the *pietà* was
not fully developed until the fourteenth century. The Lutherans kept crucifixes in churches, for the most part, but would not have pictures which were
based on legend, so that the pictures in their churches were less varied.
Taught by Erasmus to suspect relics, they could never feel devotion to a phial
said to contain Christ's blood. In their churches Good Friday was an important day in the year, with readings of the passion, but they rejected the long
hours of preaching introduced by religious orders.

5

THE CITY

The Reformation began in towns. That is not surprising. It was connected with higher education, which could only be had in towns. Monasteries were often in deep country and a few of them had excellent libraries and educated monks. But good libraries were more frequent than monks qualified to use them. Several of the educated monks were leading reformers. But the cloisters from which monk-reformers came were in or near towns or sent their young monks to universities in towns.

The link between the town and the coming Reformation is evident in north Italy and France and the Netherlands and the south of England. But it is most evident in Germany and Switzerland. Of the nine most famous reformers, six are associated with a 'free city'—Zwingli and Bullinger with Zurich, Bucer with Strasbourg, Calvin with Geneva; and Erasmus (if we count him) with Oecolampadius at Basel. The other three were one 'team', all at Wittenberg as close colleagues and friends—Luther, Melanchthon and Bugenhagen—and Wittenberg was no free city but the university town in the elector of Saxony's state.

These free cities were not quite 'free' because they lay within the Holy Roman Empire and therefore had a sovereign, the emperor, and were subject to laws which they had not made for themselves, the laws of the Reich, and to a supreme court of the empire, called the Reichskammergericht (literally imperial chamber-court), first created not long before in 1495 as the interpreter of those laws; and to a law-making body, the Reichstag or Diet, which met when the emperor should summon it.

The empire then included all the German coast to modern Holland except for Denmark and Schleswig; to the east it did not include Poland or Hungary, and no one quite knew whether Bohemia was within the borders or not; to the west Alsace and Lorraine and Burgundy; to the south all Switzerland. The medieval claim to be ruler of Italy remained as a ceremonial fiction like the English king's claim to be king of France.

But for two hundred years the emperor's power had faded before the power of the princes and cities until he was the president of a German federation. On his western borders the Spanish ruled the Netherlands and the French had more power in Burgundy and rather more power in Alsace and

Lorraine. The Swiss cantons had taken themselves into their own federation and although they were nominally still a part of the empire, the Swiss cities were out of reach of the emperor's authority. Zurich could decide what the citizens should do without interference from the Reich, though not without the chance of interference from the other cantons. In that sense Zurich was now a truly free city of the empire.

In 1521 there were eighty-five free cities of the empire. Four-fifths of these became or were for a time 'Protestant'. They contained the educated classes who despised the local church machinery, of which there was usually a pile, and who resented interference by the bishop or abbot or (at rare times) the pope. If they were educated in humanist studies their attitude was likely to be critical but it was still critical if they were educated at all, though often not with the radical criticism that could lead towards revolution. Some were people who bought printed books but others hardly ever bought a book though most had the ability to read and write. In the towns the movement quickly had a base in the people so that crowds might move into a church and shout down the Catholic preacher or remove the statues with less decorum than the middle class liked. Usually the urge to reform passed downwards, from middle classes towards artisans rather than from the working class upwards. But there were several exceptions. In Rostock the first reforming congregation was composed of harbour-workers, artisans, and journeymen as well as merchants and members of the university. In Saxony the mining apprentices were among the early adherents of Luther. In Strasbourg and Ulm the artisan was at first more friendly to reformation than the patricians or the merchants.

When it is said that the middle classes in the cities were the protagonists of reformation, it was not so much the leaders of the guilds, who had vested interests in conservatism, nor was it so often the patrician or traditional families who had governed the city, and cared about law and order, and were not sure about change, and might have their daughters in aristocratic nunneries and their sons in canonries; though there are found patricians and leaders of guilds who were strong for reformation. In several chief cities magistrates protected the Reformation.

Towns were nominally under a bishop. The municipal council was more likely to know what to do for the good of the Church than the bishop who was often elsewhere. Berne was under four different bishops for its territory lay in four different dioceses. The city council of Nuremberg was far more powerful than its bishop whose see was in little Bamberg.

Religious motives were mixed with social. In many towns the result of religious reformation was more interest among the citizens about sharing in the government; that is, a nearer approach to a city democracy. In a town like Hamburg this new sharing of the people in the government lasted.

Like many humanists Erasmus preferred monarchy or oligarchy. 'Democracy' meant a mob in the streets of Basel. A state, such people believed, can only be held together without party fighting if it has a single head, or government by a strong committee of the better people. Since power corrupts, such a head or committee must be persons who wish to conform to the laws of God and of that state, and will value the freedom of the people as much as their obedience to law is valued. In Zurich Zwingli was a disciple of Erasmus. But his mind was conditioned by the city-state. He believed that a constitution with a single head must be doubtful because all human beings suffer from original sin and because the sovereign need take no account of the wishes of the people; and because an individual ruler can more easily drive the people into war. All leading reformers agreed in denouncing the absolute power of a dictator. But they still preferred government by an elite. Democracy leads to party strife, demonstrations, and mobs; dictatorships lead to tyranny; the best government is to find 'the best' and let them rule; but they need a legitimate place which they can only receive if they have some form of election from the people.

In most towns where the statistics are known, more of the clergy were conservative than reforming. Since many clergy were paid by endowments which derived from monasteries or chapters, they had personal reasons for voting against change, but of course these selfish reasons were not usually the sole reasons for conservatism. The most conservative of all were usually the canons of the cathedral, or of the collegiate foundations in the town. They were well-endowed and key figures in the conservative establishment. They had a certain protection in the law of the Reich. They were often the last to accept reform. In various towns they needed to die off, one by one, before the town successfully reformed the college or the cathedral.

Ulm: reformed in 1531; clergy for reform, 5; clergy against or neutral, 30— yet the Reformation in Ulm was ardent. Ulm was not untypical.

When change came to a town, it normally came slowly because the municipal council altered its complexion little by little till the reforming members were a majority. Where there was a valued and popular evangelical leader—for example Zurich with Zwingli as its chief pastor—the change happened fast, the council was influenced not only by respect for their chief pastor but by observing the hold which he had among their people. But Zurich was not typical. The slow change at Frankfurt or Basel was nearer to the norm. Members of councils were seldom instructed in theology or the Bible. They had responsibility for decisions but often had a sense of floundering. Change was coming, could not be stopped, where would it lead? how should it be guided? and sometimes they postponed, and postponed again.

Where a council carried the change step by step they had time to reconcile doubters and waverers and try to bring over the antagonists. They could also do more to ensure their legal safety against foes outside who might appeal to Reich law. They could carry out their duty to punish demonstrators in church during services, or prevent attacks on monks and nuns. They could bear in mind clergy whose consciences were troubled, who saw that things were changing but were afraid of what might happen and were not sure that they would approve of it when it did happen and wondered about their stipends and the happiness of their concubines and children. A council's moderation could also help laypeople who loved the devotions of the Catholic liturgy and if there was to be change wanted to maintain that affection in their way of worship.

To the contrary there was a powerful motive for speed, decision. If they delayed they might fail to keep order in the city. They were not far from riot. If they went on allowing Catholics to say mass, in churches or chapels set aside for them, they were faced with a crowd which had got it into its guts that the mass was a pollution of the city. Hesitant government, or slow change, or moderation, could produce worse results for public order than accepting at once what the majority of councillors, their leading pastors, and a majority of the people now thought to be a necessity for the health and prosperity of the city.

Disturbance was of various types. It could arise because a reforming preacher was silenced by the police. (At Minden in a plague the Benedictine abbot imprisoned one of his monks because he preached a reforming sermon, and the crowd broke in and released the prisoner.) Or because the people had learnt a German hymn and interrupted a service by their singing. Or because a historic and ritualistic procession now seemed to bystanders ridiculous if not superstitious and they so mocked it in the streets that the procession turned into a fight (so at Göttingen once). Such processions began to be difficult to hold with dignity. Several chapters or clerical authorities were known to refrain from marching because they feared what might happen. Where a procession was held and thought absurd, there could be a mock rival procession in fancy dress (so in Lüneburg). In a few cities the quarrel was traditional, it was a repeat of old medieval friction between the clergy and the lay leaders of the city (so in Dortmund for example). It could be members of a trade union surrounding a meeting of the council and shouting to interrupt it and here the 'religious content' in the disturbance might be small. It could be people surrounding a meeting of the council to press it to appoint their reforming favourite as the chief preacher in the town—then the 'religious content' was larger. It might be lusty singing of psalms in German during masses in Latin—in Lübeck this was not on the spur of the moment but organized from church to church systematically.

About the growth of lay power over the churches in the towns there was at first nothing 'Protestant'. City councils ordered processions, or in time of plague issued calls to a national day of prayer, or published decrees against luxurious clothing, not because this could issue in class jealousy but because it was offensive to God—yet it was thought offensive to God because it issued in class jealousy. They banned dances at times of service or sometimes on holy days. They tried to ensure that church endowments were used properly, or issued a dispensation that a couple could marry though they were within the prohibited degrees of relationship. The decrees of city councils on dress or behaviour are frequent in years before the Reformation, which shows that they were hard to enforce. The council of Berne, as though it was a sort of pope, declared a very improbable miracle to be authentic.[1]

With monasteries and nunneries they could not interfere so freely, it was harder to trample on church law. But town governments tried to see that a monastery cared for its tenants, and were known to throw a shrew out of a nunnery. Occasionally, with the leave of Rome which they paid for, they suppressed a weak house to use the endowment for a better purpose. Occasionally they levied taxes on houses that were formally exempt from taxation.

The reforming work of the towns did not depend on the presence of a university. Erasmus had ties with universities, and Wittenberg became for a time the most talked-about university in Europe because of its connection with reformation. But famous universities were rocks of conservatism—Louvain, Paris, Cologne, Ingolstadt. Several reforming cities had no university—Geneva, Strasbourg, Zurich, Nuremberg, Hamburg. As they became leaders of reform they founded institutes of higher education which soon carried the reputation of universities and attracted good scholars.

Historic universities educated scholars who became part of the humanist movement and from the humanist world passed among the ranks of reformers: Melanchthon the celebrated example, educated at Heidelberg and Tübingen. In only one case a historic university was important as an institution to the early stages of reform. The university of Basel was opened in 1440. Its founders came out of the Conciliar Movement which tried to reform the Papacy as well as the Church. When their efforts ended in failure the university closed, but the city made sure it was reopened, in 1460, with the bishop of Basel ex officio as its chancellor. From its opening it was the only university in Switzerland for three hundred years, the only Swiss institution to award degrees. Its learning was soon of a European reputation and not only because Erasmus made the city his home and was linked with its professors, Simon Grynaeus in Greek, Castellio in biblical studies, Sebastian

<hr>

[1] Richard Feller, *Geschichte Berns*, ii (Berne, 1953), 95.

Münster and Conrad Pellican in Hebrew; and the great printing houses, with Froben, and Oporinus's publishing of Calvin and of Vesalius the great anatomist and of the first printed Koran, and of the Magdeburg *Centuries* which were to do so much for the study of church history. They educated Zwingli.

But even in Basel, while leading humanists tried to make people read Luther, the majority in the faculties was not for reform. Various professors could hardly bear it when the city appointed Oecolampadius and Pellican as professors. When Erasmus felt that he could stand the changes no longer and left, several professors and students abandoned the university at the same time and for three years the university had to be closed.

As the cry for reform grew louder cities divided in opinion. The council's main duty was to keep order. There were city councils, themselves divided in opinion, where the only option lay in trying to hold the balance between the disputing parties. Basel was one such. The council held the ring so long as it was able—too long as we know. They tried to provide for two different ways of worship at different times in their important church of St Martin's. They forbade the singing of hymns in German because conservatives called this *howling* or *babbling* and were distressed by the noise but reforming congregations took no notice of the council's order, there came points where city magistrates could issue a decree and be fairly sure that it would not be obeyed. They determined that no one should be compelled any longer to attend mass, a decision which only recognized their powerlessness to compel. They said that priests could refuse to celebrate mass in St Martin's and two other churches, but if they failed to do their duty in the remaining churches they must lose their prebends. The clergy must still by law be unmarried but the council made no protest when Oecolampadius married (she was an able woman, later after his death the wife of Capito and lastly of Martin Bucer) and did not attempt to deprive him of his stipend or his post. Then on Good Friday 1528 members of a textile guild removed all the pictures from St Martin's and from the Augustinian monastery. Holding the ring had become impossible, they delayed too long. Just at this moment, the most powerful of the Swiss cities, Berne, by which Basel was often influenced, carried through its reformation.

Basel cathedral celebrated mass at Christmas for the last time in 1528, with the old ceremonies and furnishings and incense and organ and crib; the last moment before violence. The crowd demanded the ejection of Catholic members from the council; and when they did not get their way there came the destruction of pictures, a revolution in which only one person was injured. Oecolampadius was moved to be chief pastor at the cathedral. The majority of the council that remained removed pictures and statues from other churches but in an orderly manner. Amerbach thought it tyranny;

Erasmus and three other humanists left because they could not bear the disorder. But Oecolampadius, a sober humanist who disliked violence, thought the end-result a wonderful grace, a gift which should have come to them before, with the town in harmony at last. And some of his people regarded it as winning a war of liberation against oppressors who used the Church as their instrument to hold down the people.

A town would often be affected by what happened in a nearby town. Ulm was influenced by events in Augsburg, Hamburg by Bremen, Regensburg by Nuremberg, Wismar by Stralsund. Any council which adopted a plan for reformation was uncertain of its place in the law of the Reich. Its first need was to take over pieces of the church endowments to help the welfare of the poor, or create better schools, or to strengthen the parish system. If it tampered thus with historic trusts, might an appeal lie to the supreme court of the Reich on the ground that despite a legal act by the council the act was illegal in a higher authority? Such hesitation could not affect the Swiss towns where the Reich court was too remote and powerless to matter. But it complicated the behaviour of German town councils. Hence, when a powerful city like Nuremberg behaved in a way which might be challenged in the Reich court and it was found that (at first sight) no authority could stop it, that released the reforming parties in other cities, as what happened in Berne affected Basel.

Every big town had citizens who wanted the council to diminish or abolish monasteries, organize poor relief and hospitals, reduce the number of clergy, simplify the services, do more for education, find clergy who knew their Bibles; and if their bishop objected to such evidently right proceedings, to throw off his authority so far as it was not already a piece of ceremony.

This did not depend on the possession of an orator with power of speech. The chief pastor in a town needed to be able to talk because the pulpit was a chief source of information and exhortation. Several towns were fortunate in such speakers, Zurich with Zwingli, Geneva with Calvin, Lausanne with Viret, Nuremberg with Osiander, Strasbourg with Bucer. Such speakers were level-headed as well as cogent.

It did not help a town to have as its chief pastor a wild or over-fervent speaker. In Neuchâtel Guillaume Farel thundered from the pulpit but his ministry was only prevented from disaster by interventions from government, which was the council at Berne. In Waldshut in the German south the reforming leader Hubmaier, an ex-Catholic priest whose alarming utterances had already caused a riot against the Jews and the destruction of the synagogue at Regensburg, so led the town council that the result was occupation by Habsburg soldiers and the end of reform. In the far German north there was a reforming preacher Friedrich, so hot in speech that he won the name 'The Mad Friedrich' and had to be dismissed.

But even a big town did not need an eminent speaker to lead its programme of reform. Frankfurt was probably the richest trading station in
Germany. Here were no prominent leaders for reform. Its council had long
quarrelled with the clergy in the town, especially the monastic houses, and
had an anti-clerical mood.

In 1522 the church at the monastery of St Catharine's in Frankfurt was
opened to preaching which may be called Protestant though the word
Protestant did not yet exist. This first preaching, by Ibach, was typical of the
worse side of the reforming movement. It was easy to stand in a pulpit and say
that the clergy are immoral and they are thieves and robbers and everything
is wrong and you must all go out and do something about it. It was harder to
stand in a pulpit and say what ought to be done about it even if this extreme
utterance were true. Reformation was caused by negation—by a wide
acceptance that what exists will not do—but it could never be what it became
unless it found people to talk of truth in the Church in a way that would
persuade.

Denunciation from the St Catharine's pulpit at Frankfurt only caused violence or demonstrations which were not welcome to those keepers of public
order the city authorities. They ejected Ibach from the city. But there was
beginning to be a demand by the people for 'evangelical preachers'; that
meant, speakers who will tell us the truth out of the Bible and do not appeal
to the customs or decrees of the Catholic Church. Against conservative
clergy there were demonstrations. In such conditions it was easy for monks
or nuns discontented with their way of life to leave their houses. The town
moved slowly but with inevitable steps. They had no pastor who was married
until 1527 and about that time more than one church gave communion in
two kinds. In 1531 the council created a common chest for the poor (which
still exists) and the money for this came partly out of now closed monasteries
and nunneries. Congregations went on demonstrating if mass was said so two
years later the council abolished mass. But it was still a divided council. While
the guilds were solid for reform, even members of the council who were not
conservative were afraid, with reason, of what the emperor and the Reich
supreme court might do.

When the way of worship was under question, the answer was always an
appeal to the Bible.

A reformer stands in a pulpit and says, in the Bible there is no mention that
clergy should be unmarried, on the contrary we find apostles who marry.
Soon various priests in the town marry their concubines or others. By
church law the council should eject them from their parishes and some city
councils for a time obeyed the law. But more councils, confronted with an
appeal to the Bible, saw no cause to be rid of married clergy and good reason
to keep them.

In certain cities neither side could fully prevail. In Frankfurt for example the cathedral was divided between conservatives and reformers because, though the guilds and the crowds were for reform, Reich law gave the chapter of the cathedral rights. In cities where two ways of worship persisted side by side, the one with the Latin mass, the other simplified and in German, one group needed to maintain a very discreet presence (just as the Frankfurt Jews needed to keep their synagogue unmarked in a back street), for demonstrations by the people were easily provoked. Under such conditions a family might divide almost in a modern way. There was a Glauburg family at Frankfurt where two sisters continued to be nuns at nearby Marienthal, and three brothers joined reforming congregations, but two of them where the reformed service was rather traditional and the other where the reformed service swept away everything that reminded worshippers of a traditional liturgy.[2]

Strasbourg is a city with excellent archives where change attracted research by historians. Near enough to France on one side and to Habsburg possessions on the other to be cautious about Catholic power, it could nevertheless move quietly forward with reformation. Its eminent clergy became reformers and the city council in majority liked what they did in their churches. By 1523 the council resolved that no one should preach anything from a pulpit except the gospel, which sounds the least revolutionary of platitudes and was probably intended to be peace-making, but in those days it could be and was taken as a signal for radical change. The council helped to persuade monks and nuns that theirs was not the best way of life and provided pensions where they decided to come out of their cloisters. They did not try to stop their ministers taking ornaments out of churches or making decoration simpler, there was no reason why they should; but they tried for justice by seeing that if someone had given a work of art to the church he or she or the heirs should get it back. As early as 1525 they limited the saying of mass to four chapels, those in the chapter churches. This was drastic but done because if they left mass anywhere in a parish church they risked violence, and because some of them were convinced that it was better to get rid of mass altogether and have a simpler service in German. A year later a large party on the city council wanted to ban mass altogether but could not quite get a majority. They had one riot of 300 people. It was 1529 when they banned mass, nine years after reforming ideals started to penetrate the town. Even then mass went on in private houses and among groups of monks and nuns who maintained an unobtrusive common life. They took the right to choose clergy for parishes, and extended the moral laws of the medieval town, with new parish officers,

---

[2] H. Dechent, *Geschichte der Stadt Frankfurt in der Reformationszeit* (Halle, 1906), 29.

churchwardens, to supervise the morals of both clergy and laypeople. What happened was probably influenced by events up the Rhine at Basel.

In a few places the chief pastor was leader of the city in all senses, with an influence on politics as well as the churches and religion. In Zurich Zwingli was quickly important in politics as well as religious reform. In Geneva, though more slowly, Calvin won a similar dominance. But in other cities the leadership always rested with the council and the chief pastor was but one of its principal advisers. In Berne their chief pastor Haller was not specially influential. In various towns the lay leader of the council was also the leader of reform and this could happen even though the chief pastor was an eminent person whose name was well known across Germany. At Nuremberg they had a big man in the pulpit, Osiander. Yet the leader of reform was a layman, the council secretary Lazarus Spengler. At Strasbourg they had a still bigger man by repute, Martin Bucer. But he was not the leader of Strasbourg reform though he had influence upon it. Jacob Sturm studied law and was affected by reading Erasmus. He joined the Strasbourg council in 1524 and served on it so long that he won weight by wisdom and the way he spoke. He was austere and very religious and they did not find him cheery. Both he and the council relied much on Bucer's advice. But it was not Bucer so much as Sturm who guided the Strasbourg reformation step by step; so that the church property was used for social welfare, a college soon famous was founded which still exists and muddled everyone by being put under another Sturm, Johann, no relation of the city leader. A council moderator like Jacob Sturm was a mixture between a religious man—get a better church by more education and instructed clergy and better moral behaviour—and a political leader who guided the city through the dangers that must ensue—against the threat from the law of the Reich on one side and on the other from politicians in the kingdom of France who had eyes on the borderlands with Germany.

If a council went moderately, the marriage of priests was a difficulty. It was legal to eject a married priest from his cure. That still happened. But now it was not popular with the people. Where a priest married and was ejected and lost his pay, he could be felt to be something of a martyr and this helped the reforming cause.

Niklaus von Wattenwyl was an able and intelligent man who became a priest and with family influence was rewarded. When still a young man he was already canon of three cathedrals and superior of two monasteries and head of a collegiate church and was received with honour by the pope. Everyone expected him to become bishop of Lausanne. Then he realized that much was wrong with the Church and asked for a general council to change it. When he saw that there was no hope of a general council, he became a Protestant and resigned his many rich preferments. The sacrifice was respected and the reforming cause given an impetus.

Where a town was in reforming mood but still needed to take legal decisions, the common expedient was a public disputation between the parties,
reformers and conservatives. These disputations have been scorned as mere
shows, the result was a foregone conclusion. It was a condition of such disputations that each side should draw its arguments only from the Bible. In the
debates conservatives pleaded that the Church was earlier than the Bible and
made the Bible, and therefore customs and doctrines of the Church must be
taken into account. In the mood of that age this argument was abhorrent to
many in the audience. The Church could be seen to be in the wrong, the
only way forward was to change, and the right way to change must be by
going back to the Bible and seeing what was there. The debates always, or
almost always,[3] ended in an evangelical victory. But they should not be
scorned as show. They were necessary to councils made up of people not
expert in religion who needed to have their doubts satisfied by public proof
that they were called upon to decide what was right and had the authority of
the Word of God.

When they had decided for reform they always needed to restrain the
extremist; not only the sudden mob breaking 'idolatrous' windows, but conscientious or misguided or just barbarian individuals. Tramps or unemployed
labourers could fancy that churches were abolished and they could make
them useful. In Berne minster, lately reformed, just emptied of all its statues
and its twenty-six altars but one, Hans Zehender rode a donkey into the nave
to occupy it as a good stable for farm animals. He was fined 20 gulden and
expelled.[4]

The part played by crowds proves how discontent with the Catholic
Church had entered the heads of the common man and woman in many
German and Swiss towns. We need to be 'free'; why should we go on paying
money to an institution which keeps canons in comfort and sends our money
out of the country? Historians have talked of a semi-democratization within
the constitution of the towns. They have asked whether the cause of the
German Reformation was not a social drive on the part of newly conscious
groups of working people. They have asked whether this was not accompanied by a new doctrine in theology. In his 1520 appeal *To the Christian Nobility
of the German Nation* Martin Luther, though himself a monk and a priest,
tried to destroy the belief that under God's law the human race is divided into
two ranks, cleric and lay; the cleric as superior because they care for souls
while the lay care for bodies. He reminded them of New Testament doctrine
that all the Lord's people are priests. The town clerk or the sweeper has as

---

[3] But some Catholic–Protestant debates ended with no victor; e.g. the Disputation of Leipzig in
1519 and the Colloquy of Poissy outside Paris in 1561.
[4] Feller, *Geschichte Berns*, ii. 162.

much of a priesthood as the pastor. All are called to do good to the community, each in a way which is needed under the intention of God for humanity, and are doing a work which can be called priestly.

This opinion that the idea of the priesthood of the laity made a difference to the attitudes of lay urban leaders towards their churches has an attraction, but it also has an air of improbability. Later we shall see how the doctrine made little difference to what happened inside reformed churches. It is more likely that lay leaders used the doctrine to justify a course of action which diminished the privileges or exemptions of the clergy, that is, it became an excuse rather than a motive or cause. Pious laypersons always knew that their work was a 'calling'. Most people had no idea of 'vocation'—an idea which was certainly strengthened by Martin Luther—but got on with earning a living.

Nuremberg was another rich city. For 150 years its industries led the metal trade. Its merchant class was potent and its international relations easy because other powers needed its help. Its news service was important. It had no university and did not found one for another hundred years but that showed how little the culture of those days depended on the endowments of a university. For this was as civilized a city as was to be found in Germany, or anywhere else in Europe, outside Padua and Venice and Florence and Naples and Paris, with poets, and scholars, and musicians like the mastersingers, and chief artists of the age with Dürer at their head. It was supposed to be within the diocese of Bamberg but during the fifteenth century it freed itself from the interference of the bishop.

The government was an oligarchy like that of Venice. Forty-two persons were qualified to serve on the inner council, thirty-four of upper-class families and eight artisans from the town's industries. There was an outer council of 200 but it was used only for information. The townsfolk accepted that this government by the few was 'representative' of them. The council supervised the welfare system run by the religious houses, and every parish had a hospital, and an inn for pilgrims, an orphanage and homes for incurables. They made sure that any money subscribed to the indulgence came to them. They tried to limit the right of sanctuary but failed. The exemption of clergy from the secular courts still gave trouble.

By 1513 they achieved the right to choose the priests for all parishes. The houses of monks and nuns were mostly eager to reform themselves. Many were cultivated, with good libraries, good binding for books, and in St Catharine's nunnery a making of fine tapestries. It was a pious city. In St Lorenz church three masses were sung daily. The numerous private endowed masses were observed. Of the religious orders the people specially revered the Austin Friars and the Franciscans.

In 1516–17 the vicar-general of the Austin Friars Johann von Staupitz came to preach the sermons for Advent and Lent. He was strict with his own order and not without a strand of the mysticism which marked the best in medieval devotion. In the house of the order in Nuremberg he collected round himself a group for study and prayer which came to be called the Sodalitas Staupitziana. The group included nearly all the influential minds in the town including the powerful secretary of the council Lazarus Spengler, and the painter Albrecht Dürer.

For the sermons delivered by Staupitz the Augustinian church was hardly big enough to hold the congregations which he drew. We need to diagnose how he collected such crowds. For everything known about him suggests that this was not a clever orator who knew the tricks of the pulpit, that cannot be the reason for the popularity of his sermons. He was never anything but a serious, sober person who would not scorn the art of presentation but would have no use for devices that make for popularity. He had nothing in him of a demagogue. Could the drawing power only come because he had fresh things to say which people were excited to hear? He told them that the idea of winning heaven by piling up one's good works before God and then pleading one's righteousness was not a Christian idea of God. He told them that indulgences as practised were wrong because they suggested to the purchaser that so sins were forgiven. Such an idea must be untrue because it did not go with the compassion of an all-merciful God. He talked of the love of God and mercy, and of the teaching of God's grace in St Paul's Epistle to the Romans.

Here is the almost insoluble puzzle of the relation between a speaker and his audience. Listening ears are excited by something fresh, but they are not excited by something too fresh because they assume it to be absurd. The town clerk Spengler took down full notes of what the orator said. Something was already in the minds or hearts of those Nuremberg worshippers which made them think that this preacher said what many of them were beginning to recognize but had not made conscious to themselves; for example it was talked about that indulgences as sold in Germany were a racket. Yet the devotion of the town in those days was still pious in a medieval way, with shrines and relics valued as precious and sometimes as wonder-working, with a cult of Mary.

Staupitz did not say in his pulpit that to be a monk or nun was a wrong way of life, he did not believe that it was. Yet among his audience were already persons who, even if they had read no word of Erasmus, doubted the social benefits of such numerous monasteries and nunneries.

In 1517 the affairs of the order took Staupitz away from Nuremberg. He sent to replace himself in the pulpit the best preacher among the Augustinians, the head of their community at Wittenberg, Wenceslaus Linck.

In a pulpit Linck was more sparkling than Staupitz but went the same way in the religious ideas which he taught the people. A bridge was set up between the congregations of Nuremberg and the ideas then being argued about in the university of Wittenberg.

The Nuremberg council now chose as preacher at St Lorenz a young Hebraist who turned into a leading reformer. The council's motive for the choice was not doctrinal. They wanted a pastor who would do good to the system of welfare and believed that he was the man for that pastoral and practical care. Andreas Osiander studied at the very conservative university of Ingolstadt but since his work shows no signs of school divinity, probably he was not taught by the controversial Ingolstadt leader Johann Eck and concentrated on the Greek and Hebrew languages. He admired Reuchlin and Erasmus and Luther. He was no radical nor was the city council. They went slowly in their changes.

But if official policy was to go slowly, individuals could not be stopped from following their consciences. In the New Testament the communion was received in bread and wine. We go back to the Bible. The council had no desire to disturb the people. But in the prevailing mood change was impossible to stop. It was started by the prior of the Austin Friars Volprecht at Easter 1523 and in the next year most people received wine as well as bread and Volprecht had all the service in German. Then the council was confronted with the usual chaos—monks came out of monasteries, which was illegal, and married, which was illegal; services of a traditional ritual were disturbed by shouts or demonstrations; people did not keep the rules of fasting, which was illegal. In June 1524 Osiander designed a conservative form of worship, mostly in German. The council promptly told the two parish churches to restore the rites which they had newly omitted. But they allowed the reading of the Bible in German and allowed the omission of the prayer of sacrifice in the consecration and allowed people to receive in both kinds. But the clergy refused to restore the rites. The bishop of Bamberg excommunicated the clergy and the city took no notice.

In all the towns which went reformed there was a common form in outline:

1. Make the city government the control of church affairs as it was of the State, for the Church was a weighty part of the State.
2. Have forms of worship which the people could understand and which were simpler.
3. Take 'misused' trust funds and apply them to the welfare of the city: the dole for the poor, the hospitals, or education, or the maintenance of pastoral care.

When a trust fund was being misused was a matter of argument. The funds were much needed if the welfare system of the city was to work. The city governments took it for granted that the very numerous endowments to say

thousands of masses were useless and therefore misused. That was not difficult and met few opponents. Much more in dispute were the endowments of
the monasteries. Many citizens now felt that life as a monk was a useless way
and that the endowments which maintained it were misused.

Hamburg

Along the northern coasts were the seafaring towns of the Hanseatic League.
Their merchant class had growing power and pushed against the traditional
rights of clergy or lords. Hamburg was a third of the size of Nuremberg, only
some 15,000 people, and nominally it had not been a free city like
Nuremberg but a town within the duchy of Holstein. But it achieved
actual independence of its duke, its fleet was the best protection against
North Sea pirates and it behaved as a free city, though in imperial law it was
not recognized as free till 1510, nor by the kingdom of Denmark till 1768. Its
bishopric was the historic see of North Europe, founded in the age after
Charlemagne as the base of the missions to Scandinavia, united in 847 as the
bishopric of Bremen-Hamburg which in the late eleventh century had a
diocese reaching so far as the Faeroes and Iceland. Then the Danes started to
found sees and lessened its vast though nominal authority. Disputes within
the union Bremen-Hamburg left Bremen as seat of the archbishop with
a cathedral and Hamburg as place of another cathedral and chapter
whose canons had the right to share in the election of the archbishop of
Bremen.

Hence it was the Hamburg canons who controlled the churches in the
town and their provost who exercised the powers of a bishop; a situation
which invited a local Church–State conflict. These disputes increased in
bitterness because the historic and well-endowed monasteries were exempt
from tax and did not bear the burdens of the little but flourishing state.

During the fifteenth century there were many court cases between
chapter and town and for ten years 1499–1508 an interdict lay on the town.
The townsfolk were pious and full of anti-clerical feeling. The middle classes
protested against the privileges of the canons and the monks, they wanted
more influence over the schools and more say in the choice of parish pastors,
and they despised the canons for not practising what they preached. They
also wanted more part in the town government which was under a select
oligarchy of leading citizens.

The Franciscan friary had a church, of St Mary Magdalene, which was
liked by the people. One of the Franciscans Stephan Kempe preached
reforming sermons and for a time was the heart of the common people's religion. Here was a place where the desire for change in the Church could not
be separated from desire for change in the State.

The chapter was legally entrenched. So the city parishes went ahead—they took the right to choose pastors, and invented their own poor chests, in disregard of the legal rights. The aristocratic council conceded as slowly as possible but step by step and at last, in May 1527, allowed the disputation which was so often the prelude to religious change. The city became Protestant—except that the cathedral still had Catholic masses to which no one outside the chapter was allowed to go, and such canons as had not emigrated were still Catholic and there were continuous lawsuits between city and its canons. The chapter appealed to the Reich supreme court, the emperor issued an order that the chapter be restored to its rights, and the town council took no notice. Nobody won in law, the chapter survived as a quaint relic till the invasion of Napoleon Bonaparte.

Because the council now had church endowments at their command, the development of schools was rapid. They planned a centralized system of welfare and poor law but it proved impracticable and did not happen, the welfare remained locally organized.

Because the archbishop of Bremen was traditionally nothing in Hamburg, and because the provost and chapter of Hamburg were now nothing but plaintiffs in a lawsuit, the clergy needed a hierarchy. In 1532 the council decided to appoint a bishop, to be called superintendent. They found a newcomer among their clergy, a Premonstratensian monk Johannes Aepinus. In north Germany the Premonstratensians were third only to the Franciscans and Austin Friars in the part they played in the Reformation. Aepinus had been imprisoned for heresy in Brandenburg and on release taught in a school on the Baltic at Stralsund until Hamburg went reformed and he came to the city to be one of the parish pastors. Now he was for two decades chief pastor of the town and often its representative abroad, even going to England about the divorce of King Henry VIII and disappointing the king's advisers by thinking the divorce not allowed. His books, like those of Erasmus, were put on the 1559 Index of Prohibited Books, so they must have been widely read.

But because of the strange situation of a non-archbishop outside and a relic-chapter still in the town, the clergy had a polity which was to be unusual though not quite unique in the Reformation. All the parish pastors met at a statutory meeting with Aepinus in the chair and among other agenda exercised criticism of and discipline on the clergy themselves.

Bullinger

Where a city was secure, and became a reformed community, its chief minister started to possess an importance far outside. The chief of these individual pastors to possess a European importance was Calvin. Constitutionally his only place was that of the senior pastor among the pastors at Geneva though that also carried the right to sit on various governing committees. But as the situation developed in France, with a very numerous Reformed Church under persecution or its threat, Geneva became the 'capital' of the French Reformed and Calvin was continually being asked to place ministers or advise on every sort of problem. And since these secure cities were a refuge for those who escaped persecution—John Knox from Scotland, or English who came out from under the reign of Queen Mary, or Netherlanders who fled from the hunt by their Spanish government—the chief pastor at Geneva had effect in Edinburgh, or Cambridge, or Antwerp, or Amsterdam, as well as in Rouen or Lyons. It mattered that the chief pastor should be a famous writer whose books on divinity were read acceptably by many, especially in commentaries on the books of the Bible. It also mattered that he should hold office for long enough to write much and to become well known. It was not trivial that Calvin held his place at Geneva for twenty-four years during which great events happened in Europe.

In the same way the chief minister at Zurich exercised a European import-ance. Zwingli became well known as the reformer of Zurich, rather as Oecolampadius at Basel was known, an eminent reformed theologian. But he had not much time because he was killed after eight years of his reforming programme, though those eight years were formative. His successor Heinrich Bullinger lived much longer, and for forty-four years was the chief pastor of Zurich. Such a length of tenure meant that he had time to gain European weight.

Bullinger's papers began to be properly edited only in recent times. Son of a priest, and a talented boy, he studied at the Catholic university of Cologne, where he found books by Luther and Melanchthon. For six years he taught in a school attached to an abbey near Zurich. There he met Zwingli and married a former nun. He was with Zwingli at the fatal battle of Kappel and escaped to Zurich. At the age of only twenty-seven he was elected chief minister (called antistes) and held that office till his death, so that Zurich-religion became identified in all Europe with the name of Bullinger.

Under the impact of the disastrous battle the council had the feeling that their chief pastor had meddled in politics and it was desirable that the new chief pastor should confine his work to the sphere of religion. In an urban republic like Zurich the borderline between religion and politics was always blurred. But Bullinger was a gentle, moderate person and soon respected for wisdom throughout the city, and after a few years far beyond it. He was the leader of the Swiss Reformation in a way which even Calvin never rivalled, though Calvin's influence extended as far outside Switzerland and some-times, especially in France, further. During his first thirteen years in office Bullinger published commentaries on all the books of the New Testament except the Revelation of St John. These commentaries were not only scholarly, they were easy for the reader to follow. It is a sign of that age that this was a necessary basis for wider influence.

His home was always open and his wife always had refugees to care for. He gained a reputation as a counsellor in troubled marriages. He followed Zwingli's plan of preaching often—almost daily at first, later twice or three times a week—always simply, always explaining a book of the Bible. He maintained Zwingli's 'prophesyings' for the studies of the clergy and devout laity. As England slipped away from a Lutheran discipleship, Zurich became its spiritual adviser. Lady Jane Grey, the most learned young queen that England never quite had, read Bullinger and wrote to him and translated into Greek part of his book about marriage and sent him as a present a piece of her embroidery.[5]

He was in correspondence not only with the English, but with the Hungarians and the Poles, with the king of Denmark and the landgrave of Hesse. His *Decades*, originally written for King Edward VI of England, became in a translation material for sermons from many English pulpits during the reign of Queen Elizabeth.

Here was the city not only dominating its own canton politically but of an importance, mainly intellectual but in part also political, far outside its borders by reason of the eminence of its chief pastor. The same applied to Geneva. It applied to Strasbourg, though not only because of Martin Bucer, there were Capito and the two Sturms. It did not quite apply to Berne, though Berne had excellent scholars, nor to Basel though Basel was the only one of these cities with a university. Where a city grew eminent in this way it attracted scholars who were not all theologians. The classical languages and the study of Hebrew were near to theology but several eminent persons came to these places for the study of language and not for divinity.

This attractiveness gave Zurich one glory which no other city rivalled.

The Zurichers, city dwellers that they were, began a new devotion in Christian thought—the glory of God in mountains.

The seas were long a glory, from the Psalms and the *Odyssey* onwards. They were the easiest means of communication, often the only means; their rivers carried heavy loads through the land, their water carried goods as well as knowledge between the nations. The tops and mists of the mountains were the shrines of gods, like Olympus or Ararat or Sinai or Horeb or Carmel. In the Psalms the mountains skip like rams, Isaiah cried of the beauty not of the mountain but of the feet of him who comes upon it bearing the gospel of peace. Pictures of landscapes were on the walls of houses, made fairer by a distant range. The painters of the Renaissance loved valleys and could not portray them without mountains behind. Their interest in their art began to

---

[5] *Zurich Letters* (1840), iii. 429.

make mountains real instead of conventional; as to paint a real Lake of
Geneva when their work was an altar-piece of the apostles on the Sea
of Galilee. When they wished to portray a saint in a wild solitude, it was their
interest to make the rocks fearful and precipitous.

But for ordinary life mountains were like deserts, a danger to travellers, an
obstruction to makers of roads and the merchants who needed to use them,
a refuge for those who had to flee, a haunt of the criminal, a horror through
which Hannibal's invading army must pass and which when it came into Italy
reached lands, as Livy said, fitter for human beings. Relief from the steam and
noise of cities was pastoral, the poems of Theocritus or the *Eclogues* of Virgil,
the Sabine farmsteads of Horace. The monks began with a quest to get away
from human society but the motive was religious, to avoid sin and cultivate
the sense of the presence of God. Many practised blindness to the material
world. Yet a few of them, St Jerome especially, made appeals to come away
because there is fresh air and the beauty of solitude and the freshness of
nature. And St Francis of Assisi with his hymn to the Sun had a new sense of
'Brother Nature', the union between human beings and their natural environment. Leonardo da Vinci asked rhetorically, 'What moves you, human
being, to leave your home and family and friends and wander through the
hills and valleys—if it is not the natural beauty of the world?'[6]

One may love hills, one does not walk on high alps because one cannot.
Doctors seeking drugs might climb high in search of plants. They did not
enjoy the work. Petrarch climbed Mont Ventoux in Provence, which is
nearly 6,000 feet—that caused comment.

The new knowledge of the Bible among ordinary people made a difference. The first chapter of Genesis is an unforgettable poetic description of
the making of the world when God saw that everything that he made was
good. But there was no sight of mountains in the Garden of Eden.

Persons of a mystic nature meditated on the union between the human
race and the created world. God is in us, God is in his creation of which we
are part, can we say that nature is God? That quiet, unprovocative heretic in
Bucer's Strasbourg, Sebastian Franck, believed that we can: 'Whoever dwells
in nature, dwells in God, for God is nature.' God is beyond all our knowing
and yet he expresses himself in nature.

In Zurich the scholar and scientist Conrad Gesner saw more. Building a
collection of plants to catalogue and analyse, he needed the high ranges. He
found that on the heights he felt a wonder which was akin to a religious
apprehension of the world. The sense of vast physical might and of human
littleness which he felt among the snows was a sacrament of the glory which
the soul feels in its apprehension of God. In 1541 he wrote a letter to a friend

---

[6] Leonardo da Vinci, *Libro di Pittura*, i. 35 and 55; iii. 519 and 530.

on what he found; and later the same year he printed the letter in the preface to his book about milk.[7] Afterwards this letter became a landmark in the link between religious wonder and the mountains:

I have decided to climb a few mountains a year, anyway at least one, about the time the flowers are full out, so long as I can physically. This is partly for science, partly for exercise, and partly for the happiness of my spirit. It is a delight for the feelings—the marvelling at these giant masses, the lifting of my head among the clouds. I don't know how it is that on these astounding heights the soul is affected so deeply and contemplates the work of the greatest of all architects. Human beings have no sense of wonder, they sit at home and do not go out to look at the world's theatre, they hide away in holes like rats in winter, without realizing that the human race was put into the world to know God better through his marvels. They keep their snouts down and never look upward at the stars . . . A lover of wisdom wants to use both kinds of eye—the eye of the body and the eye of the spirit—to observe the paradise which is the earth—of which precipices and peaks and clefts are a part . . . Of all the elements and diversity in nature mountains elicit most sense of wonder.

His physical eyes were short-sighted but his observation sharp.

All this from a person who published vast original works during his life, close friend of Zwingli and the chief humanist in Zurich who suffered the tragedy of losing both his father and Zwingli when they were killed at the battle of Kappel, a person of his desk, doctor of medicine, master of languages and pioneer in linguistics, modest about any achievement and with a child-like faith, the father of bibliography and creator of the science of entomology, discoverer of 200 hitherto unknown plants and a pioneer in the study of fossils—he died from the plague at the age of only fifty-five, with Bullinger at his bedside near the end. In his generation and the next two generations his works were of the first importance in science and scholarship. Later posterity remembered him above all as the person who taught them that the high mountains are another way to see the wonder of the creation and its Maker.

The care of the poor

The old church institutions in the town performed social services that the community could not do without. They provided most of such hospitals as existed, offered dole on a large scale and called it alms for beggars, organized teaching for boys and girls, and through nunneries offered the only available homes for unmarried ladies.

But as a town like Nuremberg tried to organize better provision, it saw how inadequate was what existed. Its leaders hardly considered that an ideal provision was always likely to be impossible. They were filled with an

---

[7] *Libellus de lacte et operibus lactariis*, Preface.

idealism which made them believe, not without reason, that they could greatly improve what was done for the sick and the homeless and the very poor and the boys and girls who needed schooling.

It was now an axiom that the system of dole for beggars encouraged beggars. Constant handouts on the steps of churches were not the way to encourage able-bodied persons to take jobs. Nor were they the best way of helping the sick who ought not to need to drag themselves to the church door or monastery gate to receive their means of livelihood. A piece of this first axiom was an attack upon the idea that poverty is holy. St Francis of Assisi had preached Holy Poverty and the Franciscans had a mission to the poor. But now this devotional ideal seemed more to create than cure poverty.

It had reached the point where beggars were a plague in town life—a wor-shipper in church was disturbed by their pleas, pedestrians in the streets ran a gauntlet of supplications, the ideal of poverty had grown in the countryside and now seemed a menace in an urban community, citizens who loved their city were ashamed of the dirt and disease that was brought by the very poor and their attitude was like the modern who felt that the town was polluted by traffic blocks and petrol fumes, instead of cars cluttering the road then there were too many bodies in rags; anywhere in the town but particularly near the west doors of churches or the gates of monasteries or nunneries; for beggars knew the doctrine that a soul might help a parent to less suffering in the after-life if alms were given to the poor, and were familiar with the soup or bread given out at the doors of religious houses, and knew that monks or nuns were not supposed by their ideals to refuse anyone who asked them for help. The doctrine which moderns called the *heavenly investor* was hardly questioned—to give brings advantage to the giver.

All over northern Europe the attitude to the poor was changing. Many are poor through no fault of theirs. But among the poor were persons who could work and did not, the work-shy. It was at last realized that forms of the teach-ing about poverty had the unwanted effect of increasing the number of work-shy persons because it was more comfortable to live on a dole if the dole was enough for food.

The monastery had the religious duty to give alms to persons who asked. Bad or impoverished religious houses did no such thing, but the idea of a means test before helping a person who came for help was in contrast with the ideals of monks. Towns could be more hard-hearted, and needed to be because when they embarked upon poor relief and poor law they could see the whole need and how the funds at their disposal were not sufficient for that need. They made rules, for example that a person who received dole should not sit all the day idle but should do something useful like weave a basket. The town had more resources and could distinguish different needs more easily than a monastery, for example it could create a home for the blind. Their institutions started to gain from people's wills in the same way as religious houses.

Reformers said that the motive of giving money to the poor was not to push the soul of the giver towards heaven but to save the body and soul of the poor, that is brotherly love and not personal salvation. This motive was an improvement. But it could not be denied that it reduced gifts to the poor, so self-motivated are even the pious.

The beggar was no longer seen as one of God's children who are always with us, but a socially undesirable object. It had to be asserted by Protestant leaders that begging is not dishonourable if it is a necessity. Certain towns made a decent life a condition of receiving alms—a drunken dole-receiver, for example, or a whoremonger, might get a warning or two or three, but if he or she did not reform the name would be struck off the list. In reformed Switzerland these rules were tough, anyone on relief must attend church or be struck off, and so with anyone caught swearing. States often paid mid-wives to see to births from destitute mothers. In Nuremberg the haphazard collections in churches or from house to house were replaced in 1522 by a state-organized collection through the streets, heralded by a bell and a town-crier, and backed by calls from the pulpits. Beggars were registered. A committee of twelve was appointed to administer this welfare and enquire into the circumstances of each person who seemed to be destitute; and these officers had the duty to store food ahead for the poor against the danger of a bad harvest. They maintained the late medieval rule that beggars must wear a badge, so that they could be kept out of pubs. They had the duty also to try to find work for the children of the destitute.

This Nuremberg practice became a model for many German towns even for places of much smaller population. Among the larger it influenced Strasbourg.

A visitor to Strasbourg in 1526 was astonished to find not a beggar on the streets. He noticed that tramps passing through were housed a day and a night at the expense of the town.[8] Strasbourg had the rule of three warnings before someone was taken off the list for ill-behaviour.

The little town of Leisnig in Saxony near Wittenberg gained fame as the start of a new system whereby unused church endowments—for example because a canon had died, or a monastery was empty—should be united into a common chest to be administered by municipal authorities—ten overseers to be appointed, with a strong box secured with four locks—for the good of the poor. It did not work at first in Leisnig because the town council had different ideas from the overseers on how to use spare endowments. But what

---

[8] *Literae virorum eruditorum ad Craneveldium*, ed. H. de Vocht (Louvain, 1928), 515. The witness was on his student travels. For Nuremberg, E. Sehling, *Evangelische Kirchenordnungen,* xi (Leipzig, 1956), 20ff.

happened in Leisnig was fairly typical. All over Germany towns set up common chests for the poor. In the north the chief organizer was Bugenhagen from Wittenberg. He used many words to tell north Germany that the way for a Christian to say thank-you to God is to give more to the needy.

Bugenhagen took seriously the problems of a system of poor relief.

First, it was an axiom that all towns make it illegal to beg. Where were the very poor to be if they were not allowed to lie at the church door? Geneva had officials stationed at the doors of churches to stop a queue.

Second, if they are not begging they must be found work if they are fit enough; the males to the State's work, for example the maintenance of public buildings or highways; the females, if they have no little children and are not nursing elderly or sick relatives, to be used as nurses in the public hospitals or the care of orphan children, it was not expected that they would have any education to enable them to teach in a girls' school.

Third, whence was the state money for welfare to come? The money from the endowments of former monasteries or masses—this was the source from which it came before—but now welfare was less haphazard and therefore more expensive to the State. Leisnig practice lumped all the 'unused' money from the church endowments into a common fund and many church orders followed this example. But it had a difficulty; this central fund for good works also supported the clergy and repaired their manses and bought the needs for church services and kept the church buildings in repair. Since ex officio clergy were important in the distribution of the money for the care of the poor, they had another interest in how the money should be used and what proportion of it should go to the care of the poor. Bugenhagen preferred arrangements where there were two separate funds, one for church and education, another for the poor and sick; this second fund to have trustees who were not clergy though the clergy were likely to know the needs and so would help in allotting grants; and the trustees should be chosen by the community—they were given various names, 'trustees' (*Pfleger*), or 'Almoners' or more religious-sounding names like Levites or deacons.

In the New Testament were deacons who ministered. They gave out the alms and looked after the poor. Stephen and Philip were deacons who preached but they were exceptions. The office was from the first important in that it integrated the work of social care with the worship of the Church. Since the function of the deacon was important as an aid to the bishop, he was soon used by some bishops to help with the conduct of services, and so added a liturgical to his social function, for in a large congregation the bishop needed hands to minister the bread and wine at the sacrament, or to administer unction to the old and sick; and where a calamity occurred like the plague the deacon could be used to help with the great number of funerals. (*His?* Phoebe was a deacon.) The excellence of women as nurses meant that they were respected as church officers and not as church employees; and the need for baptism meant that in emergencies they could minister that sacrament as midwives. But their high place arose from the essential quality of the congregation as a community with duties of social welfare, and for such work the women were necessary. The bishop also had elders/presbyters/priests to help with the sacraments, but for a long time deacons as controllers of alms were the more important of the bishop's aides. The long dispute was settled slowly and ended when the deacon became an office through which a man must pass by ordination before he could be ordained priest. The alms duties of the deacon faded away and were replaced by the growth of begging and the charities of monasteries or colleges.

Abolishing beggars and taking over the funds of old religious houses or charities, the reformers needed officers, trustees, administrators. As they always went to the New Testament if they could, the name of deacon was natural to some of them; Bugenhagen used it in the church orders of north Germany, Calvin was strong that it was the right name for those who ministered in Geneva hospitals. But others preferred to keep the medieval custom, that the deacon was not an alms—or hospital—officer but an assistant cleric on the way to being a priest. England kept that with an ordination for the deacon, Bullinger kept it in Zurich. The difference was considerable, in England the deacon was a clergyman, in Geneva he was a civil servant. Calvin thought of him as one of the church officers, Bucer said that the existence of the deacon as almsgiver was essential to the nature of a church, but the people all knew that he was a state officer. In most churches the new functions of the deacon as a state officer made it impossible to think of him as a clergyman. Calvin said that deacons were of two kinds, those who looked after the poor and those who cared for the sick, and both kinds were to be called deacons. But neither the people nor the officials of the city used the name. State documents went on calling them by their secular offices and not by their church name, for they were seen as persons in the civil service and not as a form of junior cleric. What happened had nothing to do with what pastors of the city said should happen.

But the teaching of Calvin, with the past history of deacons, had a bigger influence in the churches which were under the lead of Calvin—the French Huguenots, the Netherlanders. There the deacon had also liturgical functions, like administering the chalice at the sacrament. Though an almsperson, he was also a junior pastor.

Because women were essential in the proper running of hospitals, it would be natural that the managers of hospitals should be not only deacons but deaconesses. That did happen, but almost exclusively in the Netherlands. Under Netherland influence the synod of Wesel in north-west Germany in 1568 ruled that women of faith and upright life and maturity of years may be ordained for the care of the sick and the prisoners. Even here the idea that they were ordained did not last.

Local governments were acutely aware of the danger that moneys might not go to the right destination; so aware that in places the arrangements look like red tape. Yearly accounts were inadequate, they must be quarterly. The trustees must meet every month, or every fortnight, or Sunday mornings every week. The old monastery rule about borrowing books—that three keys held by three different persons are needed to open the book chest—was applied to the poor chest, no single person could take money out if the sole person present, the city of Magdeburg was fussy enough to order that there be ten keys.

But the old endowments now feeding the poor chest could not reach the need. Where was other money to come from? In each church a collection box stood near the door or the altar, so that worshippers, though no longer pestered, could contribute less individually. Like modern collecting boxes in churches, which go to the fund for maintaining the church and not to the poor because the State has taken that over, they needed a stout lock. Guests at weddings and mourners at funerals lay under a social obligation to remember the poor through these boxes. Collections with a bag or plate happened in church services on Sundays, destination the poor and not 'church expenses' as now, but there were Lands where collections in church happened only on feast days, in Brunswick once a year. In town churches were also chests to receive gifts in kind like bread or eggs, which of course were distributed the day they were received.

And still the need. The towns authorized collections from house to house, almost a tax except in name, but unlike the beggars only on fixed days, once a week in certain towns, four times a year in Mecklenburg, and everywhere after the harvest was gathered in, so that a collection for the poor was associated with harvest festivals. In the entrance halls of the inns were collecting boxes for the alms of travellers passing through.

And still the need. The expenses of the fund must be kept down but it had to employ people—the deacons etc.—trustees had to know who needed, prominent beggars might be frauds, women in real hardship might be too proud to say a word. They had to know who was gravely ill, and how many children were in the house, and whether any occupant was incapable of working through injury. They had to create primary schools for the children from destitute homes, or if mothers were sick, crèches, and training in crafts for boys or in needlework for girls and they were aware that this was one of their more expensive tasks. Where funds were available, they were able to lend at no interest to a poor man trying to set up in a business.

At first sight it is strange that in the states where the Protestants came to control government, they did not provide for the deficits by taxes. They disliked it because in an age when it was impossible to make an income tax fairly collected, taxes meant higher prices for certain commodities and so hurt most of the very people they were trying to help. Although they disliked it very much if gifts made to church were alienated from the intentions of the donors and transferred to help the poor, Oecolampadius in Basel thought it a moral act where it was necessary and not a breach of trust, because the poor were a higher need. He was even prepared, if it were a necessity, to allow the sale of valuable church goods to the same end.[9] The way in which a charity collected was almost a form of income tax. At the seasons or occasions ordered by the State, almoners went round the houses of the better-off asking for money; in theory it was a voluntary gift but in practice it was almost impossible to refuse and almoners noticed whether the gift of a middle-class person was too near the widow's mite to go without comment. But it remained a 'gift'. Calvin was consulted whether a would-be communicant who refused to put anything in the collecting-bag could be rejected from the sacrament, and said not.

Berne invented a system where at the daily sound of the church bell the poor, whose names stood on a list after they passed a test of approval, gathered at an appointed spot to receive vegetables and bread. In the country the list was drawn up by the pastor or the local governor. To achieve this they turned several religious houses into hospices or hospitals. At the gates of these houses the blind and crippled and very poor received the dole—so it was like the old gate of the monastery, except that these recipients had been tested whether they were in need and there were officers who should try to find them paid work. Physicians were appointed by the town to care for the sick—this was not new for formerly there was a town doctor, but now they appointed two or three. They brought pressure to bear upon the rich for contributions, a voluntary-compulsory tax. These charged a fixed fee for attending the childbirths of the rich, a smaller fee for attending the less well-off, and they were ordered to serve the poor 'for God's sake'.[10] Society regarded these physicians as lowly persons in the scale of humanity.

The most interesting of the reforming theorists of social welfare was Hyperius (Gheeraerts, Latinized as Hyperius because he was born at Ypres). He was educated at the university of Paris, where he met the writings of Erasmus and ended as the reformer of Hesse after Bucer's departure from Strasbourg. After his death in 1564 there was published his book on the state care of the poor—*De publica in pauperes beneficentia*—which soon had an English translation as *The Regiment of the Povertie*.

The State is the God-given instrument for the welfare of the people and

[9] Rudolf Wackernagel, *Geschichte der Stadt Basel* (Basel, 1907–24), ii. 394.
[10] See the city ordinance of 1576 in Feller, *Geschichte Berns*, ii. 323.

the suffering among the people must be its particular care; and the task is so large and so complex that only the State has the means to undertake it. Moreover the State for its own good has the political necessity to prevent the burden on society represented by masses of beggars. Of course it has to be a cooperative work, in which the Church and the middle classes and the poor themselves help the State.

How is it to be done? The State must make a record of the poor and how they live and whether they have any means to help themselves. It is the State's duty to ensure that the charities are used for the purposes for which they were intended. With the Church authorities it should appoint in each place three or four guardians of the poor relief and then give them real power—to find out the need, to raise the money to meet it, to distribute it fairly, to keep accurate accounts, and to decide what to do with any surplus. They must regularly visit the houses of those in need, or possibly in need, and have the power to enter them. Hyperius defended this power as no undue interference by the State in private life. They need to know how many people are living under one roof and their age and strength and whether they can work and whether they need medical attention. They should meet twice a week to take decisions and exchange information and deal with complaints and penalize (by reduction of grant) people who gamble away their dole, or drink it away, or are unemployed when they need not be, or are savage to wife or children, or quarrel with their neighbours. They must also try to find work for the able-bodied poor. They have a special duty to look after widows and orphans, and to get old people who need it into homes or hospices.

In modern times reformers have scruples that they cannot accurately find out who is poor and who is not poor without gross interference with liberty, and therefore it is better to be benevolent to a lot of people and not worry too much if some of them pretend to be poor and work by moonlighting. Hyperius had no doubt on this score. Money was too short to allow the State to hand it out to people who were only in a pseudo-need. A 'false' beggar is a thief.

The common chest, an endowment usually from former monasteries or collegiate foundations or funds for private masses and chantry chapels, is to be supplemented by house-to-house collections; collections in church; gifts; bequests; economy through paring down luxuries; sale of church furnishings and church endowments; gifts in kind. There is a voluntary income tax which the better-off pay of their own accord but under moral pressure from the State and the society; so that it is almost a voluntary/compulsory tax on the middle classes.

The categories were: widows, orphans; sick; old and weak; strangers and pilgrims, but especially refugees from persecution—genuine refugees are to be adopted into the community; prisoners of war; people who suffered a calamity like the loss of all their wealth in a storm at sea and so were rich one day and had nothing the next and were ashamed to ask anyone for help— these must be helped privately so that they are not made embarrassed; and students at the university whose families cannot pay their fees. Some of these can help themselves in part. Widows especially young widows are encouraged to marry again; some can earn a partial living as cleaners or teaching in school or in needlework; orphans are to be made to learn a trade and good families must be found to bring them up; the sick must get medical aid with the aim of making them fit to work again but if they are incurable the guardians must provide hospices; cripples are sometimes capable of part-work, for example they can learn a musical instrument or pump an organ. In this way Hyperius conceived of poor relief as not only dole for the unemployed or pensions for the old but medical care and if necessary education both in school and for trades. The reader does nothing but admire Hyperius, but may wonder whether these collections in churches and casual gifts and bequests and a voluntary/compulsory tax rose to anywhere near these needs; not anyway in the town budgets of the sixteenth century.

The movement was wider than that of the reformers. Nuremberg started to create a system of poor relief nearly fifty years before its reformation. The famous book on poor relief, *de subventione pauperum* (1526), was written by a friend of Erasmus, the Spaniard from Bruges in the Netherlands Juan Luis Vives. His family was Jewish in Spain during the bad time and he was a convert, as critical of the Catholic Church as Erasmus but with less hesitation than Erasmus in his loyalty.

Vives' theory was more rigorous than the plans of any Protestant reformer and was hardly repeated before Lenin came; the poor on a census list; begging illegal, beggars punished; to be unemployed illegal except for the sick; the State to ensure jobs for all, which may mean state-run courses for apprentices to learn crafts and hard labour for the unteachable or the unwilling; if a worker cannot earn enough for subsistence, the State to pay a supplement; citizens not to relieve plights which they discover but to report the need to the magistrate. Sources of money: the endowments of charities; the rich; tax-revenue.

The plan, surprising in a Catholic who was accustomed to poor relief through almsgiving by religious orders, was approved by the university of Paris, and is said to have influenced English poor relief under King Edward VI, and probably influenced that citizen of Ypres Hyperius. The impracticable quality was evident because no state could yet organize an NKVD or a Gestapo to cope with those who preferred not to cooperate, and no one could yet realize that if by law everyone must do a job that would mean people pretending to do a job which did not exist. It has been found that Vives' book was less influential than was thought at one time.

Hospitals

Religious orders which specially cared for the sick had been an important part of the Christian contribution to society. The medical services of the Roman empire were mostly in the form of help to out-patients. Much of the development of residential care happened under religious inspiration, the city of Constantinople being pre-eminent in creating such institutions. The wards which they served were seldom good at medicine because few people knew much medicine outside the faculties of medicine in the universities and the fashionable physicians hired by the rich and the powerful. But they cared; physically, that the sick had elementary comforts in bed, and elementary food if they could eat it, and the service of chaplains.

These orders were now being ended by reformation, so that their need must be met in other ways by the city or the State. Everyone, Protestant or Catholic, believed that sickness is a visitation sent from God and that prayer can help and even that miracles can happen to the apparently incurable. Educated people accepted that it was wrong to throw away the help which expert medical persons could give, and experts on the human anatomy and its ills should be used just like experts in law. Everyone agreed that suicide was sin—though moralists held that there could be circumstances when it was not mortal sin and did not lead to damnation; and if a patient refused to have the care of a doctor who knew how to cure the trouble, there was danger of suicide, therefore medicine was needed morally. Such problems of medicine were discussed less in textbooks of medical science than in religious debates—the commentaries on stories of healing in the New Testament, or pastoral discussion on how best to minister to one in danger of death.

In the universities search was in progress—how to cure this French disease which seems to be imported from America and which they were beginning to call syphilis; how the blood moves in the body, how the nervous system works, how muscles behave. This was the scientific exploration which easily crossed the barriers which now divided denominations. It was an international enquiry. The physical predicament of humanity put everything else into the shade. The greatest anatomist of the age, Vesalius, was doctor to the emperor in Brussels and a Catholic and his work was used in all the Protestant faculties of medicine. But not many doctors could as yet employ with discrimination the half-knowledge that existed. They had one benefit from invention. As modern metalwork could now produce letters for printing, and more lethal guns, and truly musical organs, so it could now create surgical instruments less crude to operate.

The ending of religious orders had two bad effects: the nursing might be crude but it had experience of care; and nuns, who had borne the brunt of the care of orphans and senile, were no longer ordered systematically under an abbess. Many of them became nurses in the 'secular' hospitals, which were by no means all new, for often continuity with the old was maintained. Cities founded hospitals and financed them and hired staff to care for them and some of these were former nuns. But nurses were in short supply and some cities made it a condition that if a woman received poor relief she should nurse. Nuns had often been women from middle-class homes with education. Nurses brought in off the streets in return for the dole might be dirtier in their habits and more likely to be drunk. It needed the nineteenth century, with its Florence Nightingale and Theodor Fliedner, to bring the remedy. The Reformed Churches under Swiss influence usually appointed deacons and deaconesses to be in charge of service at the hospitals.

Thanks to the labours of an expert we have an unusual portrait of what happened to the care of the sick in one town, Geneva.[11] Before the changes the town contained seven religious houses, where monks ministered alms and friars begged for alms. There were seven hospitals, each with a priest at its head and an administrator who gave alms to the poor. Each of these seven institutions had a small group of residents, probably fewer than twenty, of the old, the sick, and orphan children. The town council also had a fund for helping poor and sick who were able to go on living at home. Outside the town stood an isolation hospital for contagious diseases and two small homes for lepers.

In reform the council took over the hospitals and created a single general hospital in a big building in the middle of the town, the old nunnery of Sainte-Claire. Begging was illegal. The hospital trust ran relief—bread to the poor in the countryside, in the city it handed out loaves at the door (only to needy whose need had been inspected). It must lodge for a night or a few nights travellers who were too poor to pay. The head was a layman (*hospitalier*) who reported to the trustees (*procureurs*) proposed by the council for election by the voters. They had heavy work. From old church funds they had an endowment for the hospital, so must care for properties and rents. They seldom thought the income enough and often asked the council for a supplement. No tax was allotted to meet their needs. On occasion the council organized a collection for them, usually when a flood of French refugees arrived. When the refugee communities became stable in the town, as the Italians or the French with their own congregations, their people subscribed to a separate fund to help their own members, with their own auditor and nurses and at times a paid physician.

[11] R. M. Kingdon, *Church and Society in Reformation Europe* (London, 1985), 200 f.

The accounts of the French show that Calvin himself was the most generous individual contributor.

Printing allowed many more physicians to know of the historic enquirers into disease. Hippocrates was printed in Latin for the first time in 1525 and the next year in the Greek. Galen had mainly survived in an Arabic translation which was used by doctors in Spain, most of whom were Jews. A Latin translation was printed for the first time in 1490 and the Greek for the first time in 1525. So from that year doctors of medicine had the essence of ancient enquiries at their disposal if they took the trouble, and would know far more of symptoms and the parts of the body even if some of the classical theories were wild. In France Rabelais lectured on both Hippocrates and Galen.

Most practical doctors in the hospitals were not capable of being so near the frontiers of knowledge. They went on in the old ways, mostly derived from Jewish doctors in Arabic Spain, sometimes with cures that might work and sometimes with cures that killed. It was still true that a patient had more chance from faith than from medicine. The plants found in America, and there observed to be used by the Indians against disease, added to the range of possible drugs. But since no one knew much about them they were hardly used. Quinine came into Europe but took some hundred years or more before it persuaded the profession of medicine to take it seriously.

Because priests had been the healers of the common man and woman, and expert doctors were in courts and palaces and the homes of merchants, what was happening to medicine had an effect on the hospitals of reformed towns. The most dramatic was in Basel.

Theophrast von Hohenheim was a Swiss from the shrine village of Einsiedeln who was the son of a doctor and a mother who was a nurse, and is first found practising as a doctor in Salzburg in 1524 but writing controversial tracts on theology which leans, if not towards Protestantism, at least to severe criticism of the Catholic Church, and towards commenting, inadequately, on the Bible. Two years later the now reforming city of Strasbourg hired him to be 'the city doctor'. A year after that Basel, with Erasmus still in residence, hired him, now known as Paracelsus, to be the city doctor with the additional duty to teach medicine at the university; there is evidence, though rather late, that Oecolampadius caused this invitation. Since the lectures attacked with contempt existing physicians and theories of medicine they caused furore and he had to leave Basel very suddenly. Then he wandered round Swiss and south German towns, wherever they would put up with him for a time, Zurich and Nuremberg among the places, and died at Salzburg in 1541. After his death his works were repeatedly published. He was a curious mixture of the charlatan and the real experimentalist and the student of the cabbala which was mystery-mongering. This most notorious of doctors in the age of the Reformation probably had very little effect on the practice of medicine

in the state hospitals, where uneducated nurses and not well-qualified physicians, not a few quacks among them, did their best to make patients
comfortable and relieve suffering. In north Italian hospitals, physicians began
to lecture to students on patients and symptoms. Progress was still delayed by
the deep conviction of reverence for the human body which made dissection
repugnant to many minds, to some minds blasphemous.

6

CONVERSION

Epistrephein. To turn about, originally to turn into one's own heart and come close to reality. In its classical sense it had not meant anything sudden, like lightning on a road to Damascus. It was a time of enlightenment; a growth in better knowledge of oneself; a clearer understanding of the created world. In the Bible it carried the sense of return, a going back to God after being a prodigal. But the Latin *conversus*, someone who is converted, meant a monk who had not yet taken vows to be always a monk, a new member of the community. The first use in a modern sense came when it was applied to Jews who became Christians—they were *conversi* or *conversae*—converts.

The division of Western Christendom by the Reformation widened the term. Catholics became Protestants, Protestants became Catholics. But it was not applied to any such change. It must come from spiritual conviction, an assurance that the soul had found light. It could not rightly be applied to a person who was a Catholic and who when the government went Protestant decided that it was sensible and convenient to be Protestant also; nor could it be applied to a not very devout Catholic who married a devout Protestant and decided for the sake of the unity of the family to be of the same religion as the spouse. It must feel to be a transformation of the soul.

Such a change was marked by an event which everyone could see. A nun left her convent and married. A friar became a Protestant preacher. A Protestant pastor came to believe that he was wrong and was received back into the Roman Catholic Church. The idea of conversion, which formerly described a growth in light which might be slow, was now associated with suddenness, with particular moments. It was now sensible to ask *When? Where* was that person converted? St Augustine's voice in the garden near Milan, like the road to Damascus, was no longer an experience granted by God to select souls. True Christians would be able to trace in their past the time when they took for themselves what those who baptized them under-took for them when they were babies, or more dramatically when they real-ized, as if inspired, that the husks of swine could never satisfy their need.

This word conversion could nevertheless be applied to two special moments. There was a perception, which the soul could feel overwhelming, of new truth. And there was the act of decision which followed this experience.

To the reformers this mattered specially. Many of them were persuaded with St Augustine that the grace of God is irresistible, he comes as he came to Paul and transforms the soul. The Calvinists were more universally convinced, that grace cannot be resisted, than were the disciples of Luther—though some Lutherans were also so persuaded. If I can reject what God offers, then my blessedness depends upon a decision of mine—whereas all experience of grace is sure that everything comes down from above, from outside. So the disciples of Calvin.

The more this idea was pressed, the more likely it seemed that conversion is not a process but a moment. The doctrine led to a new kind of mission-preaching, from near the end of the eighteenth century called *revivalism*, continuous with the old missions of the friars, but with a new edge because of its open acceptance that every soul is near the experience of the Damascus road.

It is very difficult for history to analyse such experiences because they are of the essence of autobiography and no persons judge their past accurately. We know of St Paul because he described what happened to him. Our evidence comes from what people wrote about themselves (which is rare), or what other people took down after hearing them speak, or what other people inferred, and wrote down, after seeing what happened. The historian seeks to describe what people believed to have happened to themselves; which sometimes may not be the same as what they reported to have happened, and yet it is hardly possible to get further into the truth than what they said.

Much the commonest manner of conversion among the leading reformers was the slow process of enlightenment. They studied. The questions to answer were in the air which they breathed. Melanchthon had no 'conversion' in any sense of a great experience. He read books, and went to church, and thought, and taught, and grew in outlook, and was influenced by people whom he met, especially but not only by Luther. Andreas Hyperius, long a Catholic, educated at the two conservative universities of Paris and Louvain, turned into an eminent reformer. No one has found anywhere in his life that could be called a moment of enlightenment. We know little about his youth because he came from Ypres in the Netherlands and the Ypres city archive was destroyed during the First World War. The most important part of it seems to have been the reading of his fellow countryman Erasmus, but other people and other experiences entered in.

One external event which could affect sudden decisions was a tragedy or near-tragedy likely to affect the emotion. In Zurich Zwingli was like Melanchthon thus far, in that his course to reform was by study and thought and being a pupil, direct or indirect, of Erasmus. At one time he was reading a work of Erasmus in bed every night. It was said of him that he knew nothing of the spiritual experiences which drove Luther into a monastery and then into what was described as a feverish searching of the Scriptures. Philip Schaff, who had a profound knowledge of the Swiss Reformation, said of him that he had no 'severe struggle', nor 'violent crisis', 'his conversion was a gradual intellectual process'.[1] Because Zwingli was a Swiss reformer there has been search for an emotional experience which could have altered his religious perception. As parish priest of Glarus he received money from Rome for his help with supplying Swiss mercenaries to papal armies, and for all his critical humanist education did not begin with any antipathy to popes. He went as an army chaplain to the Swiss force in Italy and that convinced him of the wrongness of the mercenary system. For the three years from 1516 he was the parish priest of Einsiedeln with its great abbey and place of pilgrimage.

Later in his life he always placed his reception of evangelical truth within those three years. It is not clear how this happened. The Erasmian in him disliked superstitious behaviour which he witnessed in pilgrims who came to the famous shrine and its healing image of the Virgin. He disliked what happened in the parish when the pope's envoy came to sell the indulgence. Popes hiring mercenaries for war—simple folk behaving superstitiously—hard study by an able mind of the Bible and the Church Fathers—was this enough to explain a deep religious change? Though a priest of the Catholic Church he had a woman, in Catholic Switzerland that was hardly regarded as sin, certainly not sin like a marriage; but probably more than one woman—the moral change was neither sudden nor dramatic. Till 1520 he still drew his pension from the pope.

It has been put forward that the emotional experience must have come when he served his parish in the plague. He became priest of the Great Minster (the leading parish church) at Zurich in December 1518. Seven months later the plague broke out in the town. It killed a third of the people. He served the sick and dying for some five weeks until he caught the germs and was gravely ill and almost died. No human being could work within such a calamity without being affected emotionally. The classic Reformation historian Merle d'Aubigné, who assumed that everyone's conversion is sudden, recorded as the moment of grace, in morals and in religion, this experience of other people's deaths and of near-death. That Zwingli was much touched is proved because though not naturally a very poetic person he wrote short almost staccato but devout and prayerful lyrics on the soul that faces mortal illness and feels to be near death and then comes to recovery.

We can track the converting effect of an experience of suffering in a few others. Menno Simons was a Catholic priest in the Netherlands. The news

[1] Philip Schaff, *History of the Reformation*, 3rd edn. (Grand Rapids, 1986), ii. 27.

from Germany caused him to doubt whether the doctrine of transubstantiation in the eucharist could be true. As he celebrated the sacrament he kept
wondering whether what he was doing was what he was taught to do. After
a vacillation of two years he decided that after his prayer of consecration the
bread was still bread and the wine still wine. But he continued as a Catholic
priest and pastor and did not broadcast his new opinion which carried physical danger. He read Luther and tried to be careful to preach out of the Bible.

Then he heard from a neighbouring Dutch parish how a man who denied
that babies should be baptized was burnt as a heretic. From that moment he
doubted whether infant baptism could be right. This was an intellectual
doubt like the doubt about the eucharist, but in the autobiographical passage
in which he described it, there is a suggestion that the emotional experience
of the burning had something to do with it. He did not leave his priesthood.

By that year 1531, still a Catholic priest and ministering in a Catholic
parish, he was sure that it is wrong to baptize babies; that the anabaptists who
taught that it was wrong might be mistaken in several of their beliefs but not
in their main doctrine. He needed to minister as a pastor to anabaptists in the
parish and seems to have argued against their views. To the west in Münster
an anabaptist army was defending the city against siege and it made another
religious agony inside him—the anabaptists were right not to want the baptism of babies but they were absolutely wrong to engage in violence for their
cause.[2] This feeling was sharpened by a nearer calamity. Not far from the
parish was Oldeklooster, a monastic house. It was forcibly occupied in spring
1535 by a band of anabaptists led by men of Münster, among whom was Peter
Simons who may have been Menno's brother. A government force took the
monastery after a siege of eight days and killed in battle or executed afterwards most of the occupiers. This massacre was the experience which caused
earlier doubts to take over his mind:

These people were mistaken. Yet their blood felt hot on my heart. I could not bear
it. My soul could not rest for thinking about it. These misguided people were so
sincere that they were willing to sacrifice their lives for their faith; and meanwhile I
sat well-fed in a parish where I doubted.[3]

His outspokenness made his presence in the parish dangerous. In January
1536 he left his parish and priesthood at last and began an underground life,
without quite knowing where he was going. He was baptized, and married.

---

[2] More than one modern scholar has taught that this condemnation of Münster and anabaptist
violence was only in retrospect and that in the early days he was influenced by Münster positively.
Undoubtedly his mind at the time was still moving. But there is no evidence that he ever approved
of violence; what he admired was the sincerity of faith which made violent people willing to risk
death for their cause.

[3] *Over een Schrift tegen Gellium Faber*, in Menno Simons, *Opera Omnia Theologica* (Amsterdam,
1681), 256 ff.

After a time a group of anabaptists begged him to help and teach them. The entreaty still caused him agony, whether he could identify himself with a group which could not yet be called a denomination and which had so lately committed acts of violence.

Cases are found where the reading of the Bible, or a fresh translation of the Bible, had a transforming effect upon the personality. In Cambridge Thomas Bilney was a newly ordained priest when he obtained a copy of the New Testament edited by Erasmus and freshly translated into Latin. It was not the Greek original but Erasmus's Latin which had the power. The language of St Paul came upon him with freshness. 'Immediately I felt a marvellous comfort and quietness, insomuch as my bruised bones leapt for joy.' *Immediately*—he felt suddenness in the transforming. But the effect came upon his already *bruised bones* so that he found his soul to be in need before the illumination came.

He did not resign his Catholic priesthood or become Protestant—the word did not then exist. He was a strong critic of 'external religion', including choir music in church. Like Erasmus he was against pilgrimages to Walsingham or Canterbury and attacked the superstitions connected with relics and the invocation of saints. But he went on accepting the authority of the pope and the sacrifice of the mass and the doctrine of transubstantiation, and still thought that Martin Luther was a wicked heretic. Others in the university gathered round him to discuss Luther's books, and St Paul's thought—especially Hugh Latimer, who had just delivered for a degree a vehement dissertation against Melanchthon and afterwards believed that he owed his 'conversion' to knowing Bilney, to whom he went to make his confession.

A comparable form of conversion is found in Frederick of Pfalz-Simmern. There was marriage to a devout wife; but more important later was the study of the Bible for himself. The prince did not begin life pious, among German princely weddings which were alcoholic his wedding was uniquely drunken. Marriage to his devout wife did not produce what the Calvinists were later to call conversion, but it made him a Protestant because wife and family were Protestant. He did not openly declare himself Protestant until nine years after his marriage, and still fought on the emperor's side against the Protestant princes in the Schmalkaldic war.

Then the accidents of heredity brought him unexpectedly to be the Elector Palatine, and so one of the seven chief princes of Germany. The Palatinate was already a Lutheran state with a church led by a tough, determined Lutheran pastor. But a Rhineland state had influences from Switzerland. Church and university were divided about the doctrines of Luther and the doctrines of Zwingli. The new elector met a city and Land disturbed by the disagreement. His first reaction was to tell them all to say nothing about the disputation. He appealed to Melanchthon and won a letter from that peaceable soul supporting his desire for silence. No stern order to the divines, nor his dismissal of the chief pastor as too controversial, nor his letter from Melanchthon, stilled the strife in the Land. Willy-nilly the elector was thrown into the predicament that he must decide between one of these schools of divinity and that he was not qualified to make the decision.

He took the task very seriously. He began the work of understanding the arguments of both sides. He did not read the divines. He did not open books written by Zwingli or Calvin. All the autumn of 1559 he studied the Bible, sometimes far into the night, even at the risk of health. The letters of his Lutheran wife showed a growing worry that his loyalty to the evangelical cause was weakening. His personal physician was a dedicated disciple of Zwingli, Thomas Erastus, curiously famous to the English later as the founder of 'Erastianism'. But court influences pulled both ways. The final acceptance of Swiss church order and Swiss divinity was due to Frederick's private study of the Bible and the religious consequences in the heart which followed. Every worldly motive—from family life to political protection of the Palatinate in the conflicts within Germany—was against what he decided. He took the decision because he was sure that he had found the truth for himself.

Another prince of whose internal debate we know was George of Anhalt. This was a small principality not far from Wittenberg and Magdeburg, with its capital at Dessau. The ruling father died when his three sons were young and left their mother as regent. She was granddaughter to Podiebrad the Hussite king of Bohemia and so might be expected to be anti-clerical, and in Luther's first two years after the indulgence she was not unfriendly to him. Her third son George could remember with distaste the preacher of the indulgence Bartholomew declaring that the pardon was of such power that even if a man raped the Blessed Virgin he could be forgiven. But when Luther's language grew hefty, and a Wittenberg mob damaged pictures in church, and monasteries were dissolved, and peasants rose in rebellion, she turned away from this programme of reformation and as a pious Catholic trained her sons to be not only pious Catholics but hostile to these reformers. Young George accepted the common Catholic opinion of the innovators—the Protestants teach that you can be as bad as you like and still go to heaven, doing good is useless.

As the third son he was provided with church posts. At the age of eleven he was canon of Merseburg, soon after he was also canon of Magdeburg, and he was ordained priest at the age of seventeen. But he was given a good tutor, the humanist Helt. Together they studied the Bible, and church history, and Greek and Hebrew. This education caused stress. He was a pious Catholic who resented this alleged Reformation. But Bible and church history together caused doubts about Catholic faith and practice. Loyalty to his

mother, and loyalty to his Church, and love of the richness of Catholic ceremonial, and resentment at the supposed doctrine 'doing good is useless',
conflicted with an intellectual criticism in his mind. He worked long hours,
night after night with his problem. Sleeplessness and anxiety made it worse.

'What can I do? I have found the stones on which I built to be tumbling.
Shall I turn to Luther?—yet I hear he condemns doing good. In the Peasants'
Revolt I saw with my own eyes what people say was caused by such teaching. . . . I have pain in the guts because I was taught that this teaching brought
neither happiness nor prosperity, and its adherents were punished by God and
fell into poverty. One side, a tumbling building. The other side, teaching held
to be unchristian. How can I act conscientiously? God knows how many
sleepless nights I have passed, or what horrors I have felt.'

He consulted his bishop, the archbishop of Magdeburg, who begged him
to remain a Catholic because a prince who was a priest was destined to the
most glittering and powerful career in Church and State. This was not a
cogent argument to a mind in his predicament.

Then it was 1530 and the Diet of Augsburg and the publication of
Melanchthon's Augsburg Confession. The text opened George's eyes. The
goal of reform, it declared, was no revolution but the Catholic religion
trimmed of its modern errors and unwarranted practices. George read the
Confutatio, the Catholic counter-document. The first draft of this was fierce,
with lists of Lutheran heresies, but was rejected by the emperor as too violent
in language; and the new draft was not too immoderate. Yet George disliked
it even to disgust.

He had no single person responsible for his 'conversion'. He found his
own way. Melanchthon's persuasiveness made it possible for him to surmount
a barrier which Luther's thunder raised. It was easier for George that at this
moment his Catholic mother died. The pull of family loyalty faded.

He began by thinking a few changes would be enough. Let clergy marry.
Give the cup to the communicants. Diminish unmeaning ceremony. Events
proved that it was false to call such changes 'minor'.

In the next year a sick person in Dessau asked to receive the chalice at his
communion. Should he give it? His archbishop refused to allow such a
breach of the law. Their court chaplain refused to give it. George could not
think it right to refuse such a request. From that moment he knew that he was
on the side of reform. The court chaplain disappeared. In 1532 the three
brothers, who ruled Anhalt as a triumvirate, accepted a court chaplain recommended by Luther, Nicholas Hausmann. It still helped that Hausmann
was celibate. The choice of Hausmann opened a friendship with Luther.

The break with other members of the family was painful. They were
reminded of their mother. For three years George did not make his conversion public. He held two Catholic posts, canon of Magdeburg and dean of

Merseburg, and showed no sign that he wondered whether he ought to resign either, in both spheres good could be done. Even in Dessau change was very slow, not for two years did they buy a large chalice from a monastery to give the sacrament to a large number of communicants.

The emotional changes usually happened in countries where the decision carried instant danger. If a leading person, clergy or lay, became an open Protestant in most of Italy, most of France, all of Spain and all of the Netherlands, even for five years in the England of Mary, that decision brought danger of death very near. It meant flight, a self-imposed exile; and so was a big personal decision, to emigrate for one's faith. Such persons would not go unless their faith mattered deeply to them.

The moment which historians can observe is not the internal decision but the arrival in a foreign country. Robert Estienne, greatest printer in France, suddenly arrived in Geneva—we cannot be free enough in Paris, he found, Catholicism carries with it an excess of censorship for true scholarship.

Calvin left France for Strasbourg and first came to Geneva by accident. There was violence in Paris against Protestants and Cop, a close friend of Calvin, was notorious to government. Later in life Calvin said that he experienced *subita conversio*.[4] What was this suddenness? He never explained it further. He must mean more than a sudden realization that he must flee from the country for his life. He must mean that there came a sudden religious conviction.

This idea is suspect for two reasons. First, his divinity of the grace of God demanded suddenness; grace came, the soul cannot resist. Was it possible that he shaped the memory of his own long past in the light of this faith? Secondly, the mind is a hard, rational mind. He was a scholar who was associated when young with the best of Parisian humanism. He learnt from academics of a high standard in classical studies who were uncomfortable with the Catholic conservatism in the university of Paris. There was an intellectual grounding which could have led toward his change. If there was suddenness in religious apprehension, certainly it had a prehistory in the development of the mind.

Nevertheless those who came out from under persecution after risking their lives often used emotional language of a strength that disclosed deep feeling. Calvin, apparently so stable and so convinced of truth and so rational, could at times use words which betray fire underneath, to modern reading they ring with evidence of internal insecurity. 'I would rather die a hundred deaths than . . .' do such and such. 'I would much rather be burnt by the papists than torn in pieces by my own neighbours' (this because preachers in the Berne territory said he was a heretic); 'my only consolation is that death will come soon' (it was ten years away); 'If you only knew the tenth part of

---

[4] *Comm. in Psalmos*, preface, CR xxxi. 21.

the atrocious wrongs they inflict on me your kindness would groan at such suffering'.[5] Such language even came into his penning of diplomatic documents, a task at which his coherence and clarity normally made him an excellent drafter: 'we would rather face death and ruin of property, city, wives and children, than turn aside from our reformation by a single point or word'—this for a meeting with the Bernese who were the protectors of Geneva but did not like everything that happened there; and the language was overblown, most Genevans would change more than a few details for the sake of their wives and children.

Guillaume Farel became the most emotional preacher among French-speaking Protestants. He was of an ecclesiastical family and went to study at the university of Paris, where he started to doubt things that happened in the Church but remained a devout Catholic. He was taught by Lefèvre of Etaples, a moderate reforming humanist; but here the 'conversion' was gradual. He helped Lefèvre to make a French translation of the New Testament. In 1523 he took the decision to emigrate and went to Basel, where Oecolampadius gave him a home in his house. So he learnt to be part of the world of Zwingli and Oecolampadius but not, emphatically not, of the world of Erasmus though Erasmus was also in Basel and was another friend of Oecolampadius.

Quarter of a century later he tried to describe his conversion in a letter to a French friend at Lausanne.[6] He described his deep faith in Catholicism and loyalty to the pope; and then he read the Bible 'because the pope gave it authority' and noticed contradictions but thought that he had not understood rightly. He spent hours on his knees before statues of the saints and there said the services of the Church. Then he met Lefèvre of Etaples, who showed him how merit is nothing and all is of God's grace. Many years later he remembered the change as 'sudden'. The evidence suggests that it took about three years.

That it felt sudden is shown by the instant extremism of language about the pit out of which he had been brought. So extreme that after the first three of his sermons Erasmus persuaded the council to expel him from Basel.

Here was a person who became convinced of the need for religious change by his biblical study but continually extended his ideas by needing to preach them and then was taken into a wider world of 'Protestant' leaders.

Red-bearded, short, with knobbly cheek-bones and a big mouth and radiating eyes, Farel was well educated and yet no thinker but an evangelist, bold and rash, brimming with energy and simplicity of faith. His sermons were

---

[5] CR xv. 40, 357; Calvin to Wolphius, December 1557; xv. 271 to Toussaint, 1554.

[6] *Epistre à tous seigneurs* (1548); originally a private letter to a friend in Lausanne, printed in *Guillaume Farel 1489–1565*, by various authors (Neuchâtel, 1930), 104 ff.

like a storm at sea. He knew the Bible and found his certainties in it and his conversation and devotions were full of biblical language. To persuade the thoughtful he was little use. As a writer he was heavy and confused. As an orator to the people he was agreed to be the most powerful that that age knew. The few ideas were put across with force, but with numerous interjections, humorous and graphic even vulgar—with cries that denounced enemies and summoned his side to victory—God cannot fail you, you are his champions and he makes you conquerors, these ruffians and exploiters are worthless and will vanish like smoke. The motto on his seal ran *Quid volo nisi ardeat*, 'I want nothing else but that the soul shall be on fire.'

He passed through the French-speaking districts of western Switzerland that lay under the protectorate of Berne, causing conversions, enthusiasm, and horror. His work was unique to the Reformation. Except in this one area Protestant churches were not normally made by travelling missionaries moving from pulpit to pulpit and village to village like medieval friars or later Methodists. They were made by priests in city parishes, persuaded that the way of reform was right and setting out to teach their people. They might use, for example, a wandering Franciscan to help them, though this was not the usual way towards change. But Farel was an itinerant, protected only from stones or lynching by letters from the Berne government which he carried on his person. If they threw him out of a town he was soon back. On occasion a priest rose in church after he spoke to tell people that what Farel said was not true. Priests hid their relics and monks hid their valuables when they heard that he was on the way. He arrived at a church during mass and preached with such vehemence that the people started taking down the images and the priests fled in vestments to the manse. Once he knocked over a wooden wayside pulpit. In other villages the priests were wholly in favour of Farel but needed as much instruction as the people. Once a foe sent horses galloping through his assembly, once he was badly hurt when two men banged his head against the wall of a chapel, once he was stoned by a gang of women, once a crowd tried to throw him into the river and he was rescued by being locked in the local prison.

Farel was the nearest among the reformers to a Savonarola of the past or to an American evangelist from the eighteenth century onward.

Others were moved more by a preacher than by a book or books. The dramatic case is Galeazzo Caracciolo, son and heir of the Marquis of Vico and one of the great aristocrats of Italy.

His conversion by sermons had a ground prepared. Living in a luxurious palace near Naples he attended the religious study group led by the Spaniard Juan de Valdés. It was primarily a study of the Bible but Valdés was influenced by ideas from Luther. A few years later Caracciolo attended the sermons of a famous preacher, Peter Martyr Vermigli.

Martyr was the son of one of Savonarola's disciples at Florence. He entered the Augustinian order and they found he was a great preacher and an able theologian. From 1533 he was the prior of a convent at Naples. There he started reading works by the German reformers and was persuaded. Still a Catholic priest and a prior, he preached in 1540–1 a series of sermons which Caracciolo attended. The eventual result was one of the most dramatic of changes—a rich young man leaving family, and wealth, and home for the sake of true religion.[7] Perhaps Martyr's personal example influenced him. Not long after the sermons, in the next year, Martyr realized that he had to leave and went like most Italian converts to Switzerland, until Bucer found the right place for him as professor of theology at Strasbourg.

Of all these converts if they can be called converts in a narrow sense as distinct from minds which grew slowly, Luther was the most dramatic and the most illuminating. He was unique and the uniqueness made part of his force.

Most reformers were affected in their origins by humanism; from middle-class homes, well educated in modern scholarship. Not so Luther. He liked to remember that he was a peasant by origin though it was only just true because his miner father had risen in the ranks of the workforce. Still, there were nine children so nothing but strict simplicity could be in the house. His university of Erfurt just then, when he was there in 1501–5, began to be affected by the humanists. They did not touch Luther's course, which was the traditional systematic training in the logic of the schoolmen. His father wanted him to be a lawyer so he turned post-graduate to law. The sources are strangely thin for what then happened. There are signs of discontent with the new subject, and of anxiety about the plague. But what afterwards was overwhelming in his retrospect was the lightning flash that struck so near to him on the road, 2 June 1505, that he cried a vow, 'St Anne save me and I will be a monk.'

Not everyone who cried in a moment's fear would afterwards fulfil the vow. There must have been preparation in the mind for this first 'conversion'. To his father's disapproval, it brought him to the then best monastery in Erfurt, the house of the Austin Friars, the order of which he was to be a member for eighteen years and which he was almost to destroy. There is no sign later of a special devotion to St Anne, the mother of the Virgin Mary.

Here was not a person who became a monk, like so many, to get a good education or to know that they could have a secure life. This was a person committed to fulfil the moral ideal to which he was vowed; so committed that he was soon in turmoil at the failures. To most people temptation is hardly an alarming word. In Luther the word *Anfechtung* meant assault upon

---

[7] N. Balbani, *Historia della vita di Galeazzo Caracciolo* (Geneva, 1587), Eng. trans. M. Betts (London, 1907), 13–16; Benedetto Croce, *Vite di avventure di fede e di passione* (Bari, 1936), 192–3.

the personality. To a newly ordained priest the first mass was and is a formidable religious experience. To prepare for it he read Gabriel Biel's commentary on the consecration prayer at mass (*Explicatio Canonis Missae*).[8] Biel did not understate what happened to the priest. It was a meeting with God face to face. The experience deepened Luther's sense of sin and tumult of mind. His superior Staupitz tried to help him with teaching about the grace and mercy of God; and did help him because it became his deepest conviction in religion.

From 1512 for the next thirty-four years till death Luther was professor of biblical studies at the young university of Wittenberg in electoral Saxony.

In this time came 'the experience in the tower' which is usually regarded as his true conversion. It is not so mysterious as Calvin's but it still has mystery. No one knows when it came; though we know more or less where, not in a church or a storm but in one of the rooms (not sure which) of the tower inside the monastery of the Austin Friars in Wittenberg. Naturally we know of it from autobiography. But the main piece of self-description came from many years later, Luther's preface to the first volume of his collected works, which was published in 1545 the year before he died. There he dates the big change of heart and ideas from about the time just after the theses over indulgences, the winter of 1517–18. He was hard at work on the study of the Epistle to the Romans and when he worked at the texts of the Bible he worked with his feelings as well as his intellect. He says that he lashed at the texts trying to drive the meaning out of them. It was Romans 1: 17, 'The just shall live by faith.'

According to his memory he felt an overwhelming enlightenment of the mind that the justice of God is not a demand upon the soul but a pure gift of grace to be received through faith. The difficulty of this memory consists in our knowledge of his earlier lectures as a professor on St Paul's Epistles and how far he had already come, first with the aid of Staupitz and then through his own thought and study and moral experience of fighting temptation. Various scholars have dated the moment in the tower to a time several years before the protest against indulgences. The difficulty is only apparent. A person may know something well for a few years and yet have a sudden sensation that *this* is what is meant, especially meant for his own soul. He had supposed that God is righteous and demands of humans that they try for righteousness and is just and so punishes them when they fail. As a monk he lived a good

---

[8] Biel died in 1495 while Luther was at school. He was partly a product of the university of Erfurt but became a leading member of the educational order the Brothers of the Common Life and his last work was as professor of theology at the university of Tübingen. In philosophy a leading nominalist. The *Explicatio* (originally *Sacri canonis missae expositio*, 1488) was a vast book and needed epitomes, which prove how it was in demand. Modern edition ed. H. O. Oberman and W. J. Courtenay, 4 vols. (Wiesbaden, 1963–7).

life and yet knew that he was nothing before this terrible judgement. He wanted to love God but was more inclined to hate a divine taskmaster. Now the freedom of grace seemed to him to come pouring in suddenly.

Minds usually develop in two ways. They try to explain, and cannot explain unless they are clear to themselves. If they meet opponents who argue against them, their defence clamours for a fuller explanation of what they meant. Luther's mind was affected by his critics. He had assailed indulgences, he had not meant to assail the pope. His enemies said that in assailing indulgences he assailed the authority of the pope and the Church. Being the person that he was he asked himself whether they were right.

To be told by Rome that he was suspect for heresy, then that he was a notorious heretic; to defend himself in the home of the Fugger bankers at Augsburg in an interview with the able Dominican Cardinal Cajetan (was there a treasure of the Church from which popes could dispense pardons?— Luther realized that he believed in no such treasure, the meeting was more a shouting match on Cajetan's side than a debate); to be at imminent physical risk (Cajetan was empowered to seize him, a senior Austin Friar in Germany—the Curia avoided asking Staupitz—was ordered to seize him, his elector Frederick was asked by Rome to seize him and was sent the honour of the Golden Rose in the hope that he would seize him, friends including Staupitz were thinking up schemes to save him from certain death, there was even a plan that he should be apparently kidnapped to take him to a safe place); to discover that an academic was willy-nilly a political object; to appeal from a pope who was not properly informed to a pope better informed; then, seeing that the pope was informed, appealing from the pope to a general council—there was still a long way to go for his mind; for in January 1519 he drafted a submissive letter to the pope—that he cannot bear the pope's anger; he cannot retract on indulgences because it would hurt the Church if he did; he said he regarded the power of the Roman Church as above everything except the authority of Jesus Christ. He recommended people to obey it. He accepted the invocation of saints. He was sure that souls suffered in purgatory. He did not send this letter. There was far to go before he was the leader of a Reformation.

There were two moments of crux in the growth of the mind; the Leipzig disputation in July 1519 and the Diet of Worms in spring 1521.

If Luther's mind was to grow he must be protected and given time. The elector of Saxony Frederick the Wise was a devout Catholic who loved relics but was influenced in religion by Staupitz and the Augustinians and liked humanists and patronized art and good music and was proud of his new university where Luther was now the famous professor. He was also the most skilful and experienced operator in the tortuous politics of Germany. Luther embarrassed him as someone bad for his reputation. He chose excellent advisers and listened to them. He thought Luther might be wrong but was not prepared to hand over a person becoming so important in his Land without serious enquiry before impartial judges. Frederick the Wise was not indispensable to the coming Reformation. If Luther had been killed in 1520 the death would not have stopped reformation, we have seen too many causes driving towards change which had nothing to do with Luther's person. But Frederick's protection made what was to happen much more dramatic and so conditioned the development of Protestantism, even though when he died in 1525 there were still no persons called Protestants.

Leipzig was the main town of the other Saxony, not Luther's Saxony. The professor Johann Eck at the Bavarian university of Ingolstadt had attacked Luther on indulgences. Luther's colleague at Wittenberg Carlstadt attacked Eck wordily, in 406 theses. They agreed to meet at Leipzig to debate the issues. All this so far was in a fairly civilized academic atmosphere. A debate between Eck and Carlstadt was arranged—with great difficulty, the theologians at Leipzig and the local bishop predicted that it would make more trouble and tried to prevent it but were overruled by Duke George. Luther went as a spectator. Eck was a powerful debater and drew Luther into the argument by controverting positions which were Luther's and which Carlstadt had not touched. Luther was not willing to be attacked without replying—this was a weakness which afflicted him all his life—and after doubt till the last minute whether the duke would give him leave to talk, came into the debate.

The coming debate was given much publicity beforehand, for this was no longer about indulgences but about the pope's power. In the Middle Ages radicals had attacked the pope's power by their pens or in heresy trials. But this event at Leipzig was new and historic. For the first time in Christian history two opposing theologians were to debate the primacy of the pope not in a heresy trial or a lawcourt but in academic public debate as a question of truth or error. Educated Germans expected what would happen with excitement and trepidation.

The state of minds about the meeting is shown by the escort—200 students of Wittenberg university came to Leipzig to see that their famous professor was fairly treated and they arrived carrying weapons. On the other side Leipzig monks were afraid what the presence of a firebrand in the city might do to their monastery. The debate lasted from 27 June till 16 July 1519 and bored the undergraduates. Even the Leipzig theologians were said to have dropped off into naps.

The pleasant Leipzig humanist Peter Mosellanus observed Luther and described him. Gaunt with worry and hard work but full of life; the face always happy-looking; knowing the Bible well and able to cite texts at will; owning enough Greek and Hebrew for his purposes; in private life friendly, with nothing sour about him, often witty in conversation; but in public debate too fierce in denunciation, fiercer than is right for a mind seeking for new ways of truth.

Mosellanus observed Eck. Solid physique, you would think him a butcher; a harsh voice often too loud; astonishing memory; not quick nor subtle, a heaper of information, he likes to display his knowledge and so batter the audience who are not capable of judging the argument.

Luther said the pope erred. He now believed, with a middling knowledge of history, that papal supremacy, in the West only, rose during the last 400 years. He did not deny that it was an earthly arrangement of church administration which should be respected. In the traditional mode of critics of popes since the Great Schism he had appealed from the pope to a general council. But the Council of Constance, admitted by everyone to be such a general council, had condemned John Hus and caused him to be killed as a heretic. Luther is teaching some of what Hus taught. Therefore Luther is teaching not only that popes can err but that general councils can err, and no authority is left to the Church. The argument was powerful and Luther could do nothing but accept its truth; except for the last inference that there is now no authority in the Christian Church. The Bible is the only unerring authority under which the Church stands.

Until this drama in a kind of courtroom in Leipzig he had not realized that this was what he thought. Eck seemed to have won a debate with a victory which must shatter Luther's still vague programme of reform. Soon after the debate Eck was the first to use the word 'Lutherans' abusively, to mean persons who are heretics and disciples of Luther. What he had achieved was to push Luther from being a critic of papal authority into a more radical course—but hardly yet radical. He did not believe that he was a Hussite. He did not deny that general councils had authority, he only disbelieved that they could not err. He was against popes, and against indulgences, and like many in the modern universities he was against the school theologians, with the difference that most were humanists and therefore against them, and Luther was against them though he was no humanist but because he was religious. He was still very troubled internally. He still looked upon Staupitz as his father-figure and longed for comfort from him and did not get it. He had a dream in which Staupitz left him and he shed tears but then Staupitz promised to come back and the dream ended happily.[9]

An individual cannot cause a whole movement of ideas and peoples. But one person may come to symbolize such a change in human affairs, and be made a figurehead, and be looked upon afterwards as the maker of the movement, and during the crisis that comes upon conventional society his or her words or fate make the difference to the way changes go. The drama comes

---

[9] *BW* i. 202, Luther to Staupitz, 3 October 1519.

to be seen as the centre of the long process of change, a wide movement of many minds is understood in the light of the drama.

So it was with Luther. And in his career the supreme moment of symbol, which turned him from a monk troublesome to the authorities into a figure of European weight, was his appearance at the Diet of Worms.

Germany must condemn this heretic and execute him. He attacked indulgences which meant that he denied the pope's authority. Eck showed how he denied that a general council is infallible and asserted that an appeal lies from a general council to the Bible. In 1520, basing himself on the idea of the priesthood of all believers, Luther wrote the tract *An den christlichen Adel* (*To the Christian Nobility of the German Nation*), summoning the German princes to reform the Church. It clinched the belief of conservatives that this was a dangerous heretic. It was exceptional among Luther's works.

It was dedicated to the new young emperor Charles V and to his own friend Amsdorf, who came of a noble family. It was a programme of what needed reform, and appealed to the German complaints, the gravamina, against the see of Rome.

Princes have no right to interfere in churches? On the contrary. They have a vocation for the welfare of their people. According to the New Testament (1 Peter 2: 9) all Christian people are priests and all have the right to help the Church where it is necessary. If a ruler has power to call a town clerk who misbehaves into account, a ruler must have the right to call a pastor who misbehaves to account. Even if Rome misleads, the ruler has a duty to prevent the error.

What then should rulers do now? If the list of things which need altering is long, it becomes a programme of reform not so vague. Too many cardinals—too lavish robes—kissing toes—bishops being secular lords—limit the orders of begging friars and unite their houses and ban begging, let the city councils care for the poor—too many pilgrimages—abolish the permanent vows for monks which tie unsuitable people to the monastery—abolish compulsory celibacy for the clergy—reduce the number of masses for the dead—do not make more saints—stop indulgences and abolish brotherhoods—educate both boys and girls far better. In a second edition he added more things they should be against—drunkenness, flaunting costumes, excessive rates of interest charged by banks especially the Fugger, and brothels. Not all these demands were specially to do with a programme which later would be called Protestant. Conservative reformers wanted many of them though they did not see how to get them and so were less vehement about them. And they needed to defend celibacy for the clergy and indulgences and permanent vows for monks, which in the climate of opinion were now hard to defend. They could reasonably defend the idea that there is a real

distinction between the priesthood shared by all Christians and the special
priesthood given to persons selected to minister sacraments.

The months from 1519 to early 1521 were full of controversial pamphlets,
Luther versus A or B or C, the enemy pouring vitriol on Luther and Luther
unable to refrain from pouring vitriol in return. From the tiresomeness
sometimes wildness of the pamphlet war, it is easy to imagine that Luther's
mind was no longer developing. In certain broad ways it was already set—let
us go back to the Bible and judge the Church by it; let us get rid of all idea of
human merit and see that all goodness is the gift of God; teach lay Christians
that they have a duty to see that the Church and its members are better;
improve education, indeed make it universal if that were possible; free souls
bound by law to what is not their vocation—a young girl put into a nunnery
as a child who by law must remain in a nunnery all her life; a young man
ordained as a priest who by law for the rest of his years may not marry—free
them—which means the overthrow of canon law as it exists.

But underneath the war there was a movement of the mind, especially
about sacraments. It was doctrine that there were seven sacraments—baptism, the holy communion, confession, confirmation, marriage, ordination,
extreme unction. In the Bible Luther only found three of these seven, the
first three. He did not deny that there should be prayers at a wedding, or an
ordination, or by the dying. He now denied that these prayers had a promise
from God like the first three, they were not in the same way outward signs of
a gift of divine grace.

But the big change was in the understanding of the mass. This was taught
to be a sacrifice we offer to God, the sacrifice of Calvary. If so, it is something
good we do—and is regarded by the people as the good that they do; yet it is
an overwhelming gift from on high. But it was during these months he was
first sure of the biggest change which the future Protestants were to make to
the Catholic doctrine of the mass—it is not a sacrifice and they ought to
remove from the form of service language suggesting that it is. There is a sacrifice of praise and thanksgiving by the people, but not a sacrifice of Christ.

The practical consequences of this change were great. The frequent private masses—masses for the souls of the dead—ought to stop. This sacrament
is an act of a congregation, in the true sense a *communion*. So the people
should hear the words of consecration of the bread and wine, to share in it—
for it was the custom that these words should be said silently by the priest.

In October 1520 he shocked some of Germany by putting these changes
into a book with an excess of strength, *A Preface to the Babylonian Captivity of
the Church*. As the title said, this was fierce against Rome, thief of the freedom
of Christians. But in ideas the most important piece was the doctrine of
sacraments: three only; in the communion the laypeople to receive the cup;
the Lord is present in the gifts at communion but we are ordered to believe in

transubstantiation which is doubtful doctrine; no sacrifice but that of praise. On the other sacraments the radical part was that on ordination. Since the Bible has nothing about it, it is a way which the Church has ordered to get clergy. So clergy should not only be free to marry if they wish, they should be elected and it should be possible to stop them being priests if necessary. The chief work of the priest is not saying mass but preaching the Word. Every priest should be a preacher/teacher.

This was the most radical book that Luther ever wrote and he wrote many more books during the next quarter of a century. It caused more hostility to him in Germany than any other of his books. It made many Germans feel at last, this is less a reformer than a heretic.

The bull threatening excommunication, *Exsurge Domine* ('Rise up O Lord'), was dated Rome 15 June and placarded at St Peter's on 24 July 1520. On 10 October 1520 it arrived at Wittenberg. The authors did not yet know the big books just published. They listed forty-one heresies from Luther's books (these forty-one supplied by Johann Eck)—indulgences and confession; the eucharist and it is a heresy to ask that laypeople be given the chalice; attacks on pope and councils; denying the necessity of good works; doubting whether it is right to burn heretics. It banned him from preaching, ordered his books to be burnt, and gave him sixty days to recant or he would be excommunicated. If he failed to recant anyone might seize him, and ought to.

Eck was to publish the bull in Germany. The other nuncio for Germany Aleander, who was the Vatican librarian and a humanist, was ordered to ensure that the emperor Charles V did what ought to happen. The emperor was urgently needed to bring pressure upon the elector Frederick of Saxony not to protect his subject.

Eck did not find it easy to publish the bull in Germany. In a few places there were disturbances when it was tried. In some towns Luther's books were burnt successfully, yet not without trouble. No longer was Luther just a professor. He was a symbol of liberty for the people. It was symbolic that a month later he published what became his most celebrated essay under the title *Of the Freedom of a Christian*. This freedom of which he wrote was not the freedom which concerned the young men who mobbed Eck, or the undergraduates at Erfurt university who threw the bull into the river. It was freedom of the soul through faith.

The bull completed the change of mind from pious monk, loyal to popes, into rebel. Melanchthon invited anyone who cared for gospel truth to be spectators at the burning of the bull outside the Elster gate at Wittenberg. Luther's lieutenant Agricola went round trying to persuade scholars to give up folio volumes of schoolmen like Aquinas and Scotus, so that they could be burnt on the pyre. The professors liked to keep the folios on their shelves. Several editions of canon law were sacrificed, and they cheerfully threw away pamphlets by Eck. When the fire went merrily Luther threw onto it the copy of the bull. Then the undergraduates marched in procession and sang as they went.

Luther never regretted this pyre. He thought it afterwards one of his very best acts. He never questioned that books which propagate grave error ought to be burnt.

Hardly anyone doubted that the probable outcome of what was a looming battle could only be Luther's death. The weight against him was such—an emperor and a pope in harness, several of the leading princes and archbishops of Germany, force of every variety that mattered. Luther himself was aware of the probable outcome. It is likely that this would have affected his mind. As the outlook of refugees from persecution in France or the Netherlands was affected by danger to their lives, from Calvin downwards, so in the winter of 1520-1 with Luther.

They could not kill this professor of theology out of hand. He must appear, be allowed to defend himself, argue with the great, even to be an item in the agenda of a parliament. He was not someone whose world was the quarrels of the monks or the disputes of universities. He was debated as earnestly as taxes or war.

So the first person to turn Luther from a professor into a symbol was the head of his state, Frederick the elector of Saxony. Luther was a respected academic in his new university. He was now a very popular person. The papal nuncios wanted Frederick to cause Luther to be burnt—once a person was excommunicated for such heresy there was nothing left for the State to do but kill. Frederick, not yet called the Wise but winning the title even during his life, was resolute not to be high-handed and was well aware of Luther's popularity. His own religion was conservative and medieval though influenced by Staupitz and the Franciscans. Luther might be wrong, Frederick was not sure. But he ought to be heard. He had a political motive, his people would hate him if he turned over Luther to be killed without a trial. But it is clear that in his mind more than politics was at stake. Justice must be seen to be done.

The Diet of Worms

The agenda of this Reich parliament was urgent: how to keep internal peace in the Reich, how to encourage trade, how to protect Germany from the Turkish armies in Hungary. The delegates started by caring little about a tiresome Saxon monk. The people who forced Luther into the agenda, and so changed the fate of the Reformation, were the two papal legates Aleander and Caracciolo. These two had just cause for anxiety. Pictures of Luther with a halo or a dove descending were being sold in the streets of Worms.

The two legates did not mean to push Luther into the diet. The bull had excommunicated this heretic, the emperor's duty was to outlaw him and execute him. There was no place for debate. If Luther appeared at the diet the laymen would argue and so interfere in a sphere which belonged to the Church. No sane person could plead that the books were not heretical. Luther must not go to Worms. Aleander provided the emperor with text after text—Luther does not believe in purgatory, nor the right of the pope to make laws, nor the presence of Christ in the eucharist, nor free will, nor saints, nor monks' vows.

The elector Frederick insisted to the emperor that Luther should be given a fair hearing and a safe-conduct. It was the estates at the diet who forced the emperor to give way. Leading members of the diet told the emperor that the common people of Germany stood behind Luther and they could not answer for public order if this monk were condemned without a hearing. The gravamina, the list of complaints which German diets liked to pass against the pope even though they were as Catholic as possible, made some think that Luther might be useful to get their way over gravamina.

When Luther heard that he was invited or ordered to the diet he was very pleased. He expected that in Worms he could put his case in the face of Germany and the world. Many of his friends were afraid. Even if he were given a safe-conduct he would still be at grave risk if he went. It was well known that a hundred years before, John Hus went to the Council of Constance under a safe-conduct and was burnt for heresy on the plea that safe-conducts are not valid for persons convicted of heresy. Luther was cheerful in saying, not without an amusing little touch of pride, that he was himself a worse heretic than Hus.

Most managers of the diet—not all, several thought that disaster would follow—agreed with the emperor that in the circumstances Luther must come. But they all agreed that there must be no argument with him, he must not be allowed to present his case before this parliament. He must answer one question only—these books you have written, so contrary to the faith of our fathers, do you stand by what is in them? If he said yes, then the emperor could at once issue the decree of capital condemnation. If he said no, then he recanted, and they could allow him to discuss moderate criticism of the ecclesiastical system. That was the plan.

A copy of the charges, that is of the texts deemed heretical, was sent to Wittenberg. He saw that if he went to Worms he would meet a demand to recant with a threat attached. He saw also not only that he must go to Worms but that he had no intention of recanting. Inside himself he knew that he had to risk whatever lay ahead.

Not all the advisers of Frederick the Wise were sure that this was the right decision. He would be declared a heretic, then the safe-conduct would be invalid, then he could be killed. Several Saxon civil servants recommended that he should not go. The more influential took the contrary view. They thought that nothing could please the emperor and the legate Aleander more than if Luther refused to come. He was more at risk and not less if he failed to appear.

On 2 April 1521, travel expenses paid by the university, Luther set off in a covered wagon and with the belief that almost certainly he went to his death. Monks' rules said that monks must travel in pairs so he had with him an Austin Friar named Petzensteiner, and two other friends, one of them Amsdorf. That the diet was right in resolving that they could not act ruthlessly to so popular a person was proved by the journey. The towns received him ceremoniously, mayors came out to greet him, topers in bars drank his health. When he entered Worms trumpeters sounded out from the cathedral.

On 17 April, the day after he arrived, he was summoned to appear before the diet. He dressed in his habit as an Austin Friar and observers noticed the strong, rough look under the tonsure. His books were piled on a bench. He was asked whether he wrote these books and whether he wished to recant anything that was in them.

He answered so softly that not all could hear what he said. The books contained many statements about the truths of religion and it would be wrong to say yes or no without consideration. He had expected questions on selected texts or particular propositions, not an umbrella demand about thousands of pages which it was absurd to lump together. The answer of a plea for time to think was compelling. They lectured him on the need for peace and unity in the Church and then gave him one day to consider. It has been proven historically that parliaments are impossible substitutes for lawcourts.

Next day the diet had more pressing business and he must wait till 6 p.m. to appear, when the evening made lights necessary in the overcrowded hall full of sweaty people. He was asked the same question as yesterday. Because yesterday he asked for time to consider and sounded uncertain, they expected him to recant.

This time everyone could hear his answer. He begged their pardon if he were not familiar with the ways of such high company as theirs, he had lived his life in a monastery out of the world. In writing books his only desire was to be of service to God. He could not abandon these books but allowed that in so many there might be mistakes which came into print because he was stupid or careless or biased. As to recanting the books were of three kinds:

books of devotion with no controversy in them, no one could want him to drop these;

books against the popes, and since all Germany is full of complaints against the pope, and the same complaints are common in other countries, he could

not abandon these books because recanting would only help tyranny—
'Good God what a tool of wickedness I should be if I recanted these!'

books against individuals who defended the popes. He confessed that in
these he had sometimes written too sharply, more sharply than befitted a
monk and a professor. But the cause was right, so he could not abandon
these.

Now he said that he was willing to be judged by the Bible. If they persuaded him that he was wrong out of the Bible, he would recant willingly and
burn his books with his own hands.

The prosecutor, the chancellor of Trier, refused the plea that all the books
be not lumped together. They are all harmful and heretical and against the
traditions of the Church. Will you recant or not? This demand brought the
answer which made Worms more a symbol than a diet. 'So long as my conscience is held prisoner to the Word of God, I can recant nothing and will
recant nothing, because to do something contrary to my conscience would
endanger my salvation. So help me God. Amen.'

The emperor told the diet that from his family he was a protector of
the Catholic Church. Twenty-one years old, he spoke with passion. For the
Church he would give his kingdoms and friends and body and soul; he was
sorry now that he had not got rid of Luther before the diet met. But he must
respect the safe-conduct. Then he would proceed against the heretic with his
full authority.

The diet asked him for time, perhaps Luther could still be persuaded by
discussion. Three more days were allowed for private talks with Luther. A
committee was chosen. Luther's sudden giant stature in the Reich can be
judged by the persons chosen for this committee—to argue with an allegedly
heretical Saxon monk they appointed two electors—Brandenburg and Trier,
two of the seven chief officers of empire after the emperor, both known to be
against Luther; Duke George of the other Saxony who was vehement against
Luther; two other bishops, one of them Luther's diocesan the bishop of
Brandenburg; the great scholar Peutinger from Augsburg, and four others
one of whom, Count George of Wertheim, was known to be on Luther's
side. The committee met Luther at 6 a.m. in the lodging of the archbishop of
Trier. It was a civilized meeting. They discussed. It was like a seminar. They
moved away from crude demands to recant every jot.

But at the second session, with many of the committee gone, four others
came in, one of them Luther's lieutenant Amsdorf, another a specialist in controversy against Luther, Cochlaeus, who held a Catholic deanery at Frankfurt
and thought Luther a maniac. The minutes show Luther the stronger, violent
language against him answered by silence. Next day the two real scholars on
the committee, Peutinger and Vehus, argued with Luther for three hours. It

was a new argument, from policy—obstinacy will destroy everything you want, submission will save the best of the reforming programme.

That evening the committee gave up the struggle. Cochlaeus, returning to his Frankfurt deanery, found that hardly anyone would speak to him. The emperor sent a message to Luther that the safe-conduct was still valid but that he must be home within three weeks and then the emperor would proceed against him.

Frederick the Wise had decided that Luther must be saved from death. He must be put in a place of safety. But he, the elector, must not know the plan. He must not be in trouble with the emperor. He could not protect 'the heretic' publicly. Luther must disappear. This was quietly told to Luther's escort before he even left Worms on 26 April.

On 4 May he greeted his relatives at Möhra near Eisenach and with Amsdorf and the friar Petzensteiner was driven over the hills. In a wooded glade the cart was ambushed by a group of armed horsemen. The friar leapt out and ran away and disappeared from history. Amsdorf shouted protests. They pulled Luther roughly from the cart—but he had time to pick up his Hebrew Bible and his New Testament—and forced him to run along the road by one of the horses until they were out of sight. Then they stopped, changed their manner, and gave him a horse; and travelled by back lanes and in the black evening to avert pursuit and arrived at the Wartburg Castle before midnight.

Was he murdered? In the Netherlands Albrecht Dürer heard the news and thought his death a disaster for the cause of God and the gospel. Was this the breach of the safe-conduct which so many feared? Three weeks later the edict against Luther was approved by the remnant of the diet. Legally Luther was now an outlaw in the German empire. Legally his books could not be read nor sold. Anyone who fed him or sheltered him was guilty. It was the legal duty of every German to arrest him and send him prisoner to the emperor.

The elector Frederick the Wise took only this much notice of the edict, that he was supposed not to know that Luther was alive and well and in hiding within Saxony, and that in the four following years during which he protected Luther he was careful never to meet him face to face.

Life in the Wartburg was disguised. He had to dress as a knight; to grow his beard and the hair on the head to hide the tonsure (in beard and abundant curling moustache like a sergeant-major's he looked rather handsome, Cranach later did a woodcut); was addressed as Junker George; lived in the room usually occupied by distinguished prisoners. No one outside the elector's staff knew where he was. Sometimes he argued about religion with the commander of the castle who was his gaoler. He did not like the solitude, he was not fit to be an anchorite. He needed to talk with Staupitz, or Melanchthon, and could not. He disliked the food because it was too rich for him and because he got little exercise. Solitariness was suffering, it brought fights with demons which howled into his psyche.

The kidnapping at Möhra grew to be a piece of the symbol that was the Diet of Worms. Like the refusal to recant before a mighty assembly, the ambush and the hiding in the fortress had that element of the melodramatic which could turn a person into a legend. The papal legates and Charles V and the elector Frederick had transformed a monk, with whom one could argue, into the figurehead of a mighty movement. Reformation depended on many minds and many different ideas. The Diet of Worms and its aftermath possessed the quality to associate it for ever in the memory of Europe with a single mind.

He had unquenchable energy and a powerful mind which thought for itself—not often subtle, sometimes crude, but stirring and provocative and never resting content with someone else's conventional channel; and despite the heavy-handedness on certain subjects, it could attain profound insights. The intellectual bludgeon and the real penetration and moments of rare sensitivity combined to make him a potent influence on students.

The reading of the New Testament in the edition of Erasmus helped him to form his mind.

He was a person of many words, more in pen than through the mouth, and some of the books are too long for the matter, but he was never obscure, everything was plain, the fault is repetition and not contortion of the mind. He could easily be caustic, and could explode, but inside he was emotional, and deeply distrustful of himself, and not at all arrogant. He was liable to intense depressions which he tried to cure in faith, but in earlier life he needed his superior Staupitz to help as well as his psalms, and later in life he needed his wife to help as well as his psalms. He had sparkling eyes, and loved flowers, and dug vegetables. He put his heart into everything, and exposed the personality. He was uninhibited in saying what he thought, and that was to make his interior the best-known of the sixteenth century. Calvin people admired and never knew, Erasmus they admired and were friends but few of them knew, Luther they admired or hated and knew all about him because he said exactly what he thought, even about himself.

7

MARRIAGE OF THE CLERGY

In the earliest Christian age the clergy could marry. The wish to keep them unmarried arose from the same movement of ideas which begot the monk and nun, the belief that a person can be more dedicated in prayer, or in pastoral service, if not 'burdened' with the ties of a family. There was something also of an experience that sexuality is inseparable from lust and so contains or easily can contain something of sin. By AD 400 many leaders of the Western Church were persuaded that to be unmarried is best for ministers, and that the married state usually made for lower standards—of prayerfulness, and especially of unselfishness, because the need to provide for children is the source of prudence in money or even avarice.

The greatest council of church history, the Council of Nicaea in 325, refused a motion that the clergy must stop living with their wives. The East accepted a rule that while bishops must be unmarried, the parish clergy could be and should be married—only, they must be married *before* ordination. The West was rigorous, in theory. Pope Siricius in 386 ordered all clergy, bishops, priests, and deacons, to be unmarried. Until the eleventh century most Western parishes took little notice. Then Pope Gregory VII embarked upon a plan to drive wives out of vicarages, the motive being to prevent church endowments passing to the heirs of the priests. He ordered that married priests should not lead worship. The effect would have stopped worship in many country parishes if it had been obeyed rigorously and it was not. But the notion that only unmarried priests are proper priests was stamped into the articulate part of the Western Church. A more serious consequence was to replace wives with mistresses or concubines. Parishes knew enough to disapprove wives but accepted that a woman in the priest's house was a necessity or forgivable. Bishops fined priests with women but most bishops did not mind if they kept them and many bishops had their own women.

Luther's attack, following those of Erasmus, upon the law which had such consequences, caused priests to disregard the law, not by living with women which was not new, but by making them wives through a sacrament in church. Three priests married, one of them Bernhardi a former student of Luther. Archbishop Albert demanded that the elector of Saxony surrender Bernhardi for punishment. The elector referred the request to a commission, before which Melanchthon argued that as priests in the early Church married Bernhardi was blameless and if he could not keep a vow of celibacy it was moral that he should marry. This last argument did not please Luther then immured in the Wartburg.

Luther the unmarried monk now sang the praise of marriage more loudly. The state of marriage is the noblest condition in creation. So they were made in the Garden of Eden. They keep together, have children, bring them up to God's glory. And after the fall they still need each other—mutual help, the desire for a human partner, the power of the sexual drive are all anchored in creation and therefore the will of the Creator. However the sexual act is affected by lust, it is in marriage acceptable to God. Here he supported the second traditional ground for marriage—the protection from unchastity, the 'hospital of the sick'. Exceptional people have the gift of continence—but for most of the human race marriage is the norm. The stream of love flows on— in the creation and nurturing of children. Marriage is part of the secular world but leads the pair into the spiritual world.

He was not romantic about marriage. He knew that married people can be unhappy as well as happy, that their personalities are tried as they live together, that children can be a dividing as well as a uniting force, that boredom can set in, that a marriage resting only on the first passions was likely not to last—he did not imagine the married state to be like the Garden of Eden.

Monks were leaving their cloisters, and then nuns, and nuns were more at risk in that world unless they had a family to go back to. If a nun was persuaded that her way of life was wrong what was she to do? Nine nuns from a community at Nimschen, over the border in the other and still conservative Saxony, were unsettled by Luther's writings and consulted him. If they left their cloister they would commit an illegal act in that Land. Luther arranged to smuggle the nuns out. A friend at Torgau had a cart which went to trade in fish at the convent, and put the nuns in his cart, still in their habits, and brought them over the border. It was the night of Easter Eve 1523. The nine came to Wittenberg and as months passed by most of them found husbands. At first several people refused to receive renegades into their house and Luther laboured hard to place them.

The last unmarried was Catherine von Bora. She worked as a housemaid and refused with decision to marry a husband whom Luther's friends found for her, no less than the rector of the university. A young patrician wanted to marry her but his family refused to allow the union. She even suggested that she ought to marry Luther or his lieutenant Amsdorf. She was sixteen years younger than Luther and he found her manner proud.

Friends told Luther he ought to marry; to set an example, but they may have noticed the bachelor-mess at the Austin Friars. He consulted his father who wanted a grandchild and was vehement in favour. He was anxious—

they might say he became a reformer because he could not control his lust—
and worried whether it was right for an outlaw to ask a woman to share his
danger.

Early in June 1525 he accepted the arguments of his friends and agreed that
he ought to marry. Reasons?—he believed in the marriage of priests, and
would set an example. 'I hope it will make the angels laugh and the devils
weep.'[1] These are reasons of someone who will soon marry but is not in love.
A few days later he married Catherine von Bora in the presence of
Bugenhagen, parish priest of Wittenberg, on 13 June 1525 and a fortnight
after that the wedding was publicly feasted in the streets with a procession to
the music of fifes and a banquet.

Though friends had pressed him to the act, others were grieved when it
happened. No one asked what was the opinion of Catherine about marrying
a renegade monk so much older, it was obvious to everyone that an ex-nun
must find a husband. What they asked was whether it would diminish
Luther's influence, and might make the charge easy that all this reform was
only about lust. Melanchthon thought the marriage lamentable. He wrote a
letter which his first editor altered before he printed it. The original text
showed that Melanchthon could only suppose that the nuns of Nimschen
had 'captivated' him. But he came to the wedding. They put up with gossip—
someone printed a pamphlet that Catherine threw off her habit and went to
Wittenberg like a chorus-girl and lived in sin with Luther. Erasmus was satirical when he heard of the marriage. Whether or not Melanchthon minded
such scandal for propaganda, as he thought about the interest of reform, there
is no sign that Luther minded.

His attitude to sexuality changed. To the end of his life he associated the
reproductive system with the transmission of original sin. But this became
intellectual and not emotional. Not in love with her on the day he married
her, he was deeply in love with her six months later. That December 1525 he
wrote to his friend Spalatin a letter on the occasion of his (Spalatin's) marriage. He refused the invitation to the wedding because the roads were not
safe in the aftermath of the peasant troubles. Then he added words which earlier editors of his letters refused to print. In Spalatin's parish of Altenburg
there was a row because their parish priest was marrying. Luther told him to
take no notice of these critics. Marriage is a gift of God. 'When you sleep
with your Catherine and embrace her, think this—"This is a human being,

---

[1] Luther to Spalatin, 16 June 1525, *BW* iii. 533. Spalatin was an early humanist graduate of
Wittenberg university before Luther arrived there and was ordained as a Catholic priest and became
tutor to John Frederick the son of the elector's brother John. He did much to protect Luther when
the indulgence controversy broke out. Frederick the Wise stayed unmarried and died in 1525 and
was succeeded by John and therefore John Frederick became the elector of Saxony when John
died in 1532.

the best little creature of God, and Christ has given her to me. Praise and glory to him." On the evening of the day when I calculate you will receive this letter, I will love my wife in the same way and have you in my memory and so we shall be together.'[2]

Catherine Luther moved into the Black Cloister and their six children were born there. But this was not all the population of the large old ex-monastery, for Catherine's aunt moved in and several orphan children who were nieces or nephews of Luther; and then they put up students who needed accommodation. This was often in return for services like secretarial help. Then there were bedrooms for travelling pastors and bedrooms for the staff which Catherine needed.

The main meal of the house was at 10 a.m. (for they began work at dawn) and Luther and Catherine dined together with the household. Occasionally till the end of his life Luther maintained the monastic custom of silence during meals. But mostly it was talk, and with the students there, and the visiting pastors, and an intelligent wife, it was often good talk. Luther was so lively a conversationalist, and so revered by everyone present except Catherine, that first one student and then another started to take notes of what he said; and afterwards, in their own room, wrote up their notes. Luther did not mind and even when he said something outrageous (which was not rare in his conversation) he never told anyone not to put it down. His wife once said amusedly that they were getting so much free instruction that they ought to pay a fee.

It cannot always have been easy to get down what he said, for his talk rollicked away in a curious macaronic mixture in German and Latin, not saying one sentence in German and another in Latin but tumbling up both languages in the same sentence.

A very few of the people present—especially if they were humanist scholars and understood the nature of historical sources—thought that if such and such saying were noted it might survive and then diminish Luther's reputation. It was the way of a lively conversationalist to throw off remarks on the spur of the moment—provocative, or extreme, or coarse. Catherine once rebuked him publicly at table for being too rough, but only once so far as we know. Philip Melanchthon, the best scholar who ever dined at that table, saw the danger for the future and asked one of the note-takers to be careful what he recorded. But one by one they slammed it all down; and eventually one of them, Aurifaber, who became Luther's secretary during the last few months of Luther's life and therefore had not long to sit at that table, made a collection.

Two kinds of remark by Luther were to prove the wisdom of Melanchthon. One was the earthy. Luther was a miner's son and not a

[2] *BW* iii. 635.

Victorian gentleman in his manner of speech. It used to be thought that he said some things in Latin, as Edward Gibbon used to put the obscene into Latin footnotes, in 'the decent obscurity of a learned language', so that his wife should not understand, but it is now proved that she understood Latin. The second was the freedom with Scripture. If he did not like what was in the Bible he said so. Some defenders of Luther said that he could not possibly have said what the note-takers made him say and therefore the Table Talk was a forgery. It did not appear among Luther's *Collected Works* for more than two hundred years.

In the midst of attacks upon the papists or the disciples of Zwingli, or explanations of difficult passages of Scripture, or judgements on urgent ethical cases, or fun, or leg-pulling, we get a live picture of the relation between the husband and the wife. Once they record him as saying 'There is no sweeter union than that in a good marriage.' He was amusing about it and when he proposed a bridegroom's health he told him that he should be content with the usual custom and be lord of the house while his wife was not at home. He was grateful that he had helped to end the belief that the single life was morally higher than the married, and even more grateful that he had attacked the pretend-single life so common among Catholic clergy and helped to end social discrimination against women who were concubines of priests. He retained a masculine view of the female sex, that they were in part created for the purpose of helping males to live without pollution.

He admired Catherine—she spoke German well. One scribe records him as saying *eloquentia mulierum periculosa*, 'articulate women are dangerous',[3] but the context shows that he was pulling her leg. In public she treated him with deference, calling him Doctor and never using the affectionate *Du* (thou). But he signed himself to her 'my true love'. He admired her faith, especially when she thought she was dying and like the nun that she used to be repeated one verse of the psalms more than a thousand times and he prayed hard that she would survive.

Their marriage had tragedies. Of the six children a girl died after eight months, another girl died at thirteen in the arms of her father, with Catherine weeping in the room but not feeling able to come closer. Four children reached adulthood and did well, which was not easy for the offspring of the most famous person in Europe and says something about his wife. Luther wanted one son to be a soldier and two to be scholars and one to farm. It did not happen. Hans married the daughter of the theologian Cruciger and became a well-regarded lawyer. Martin lived quietly in ill-health at Wittenberg and died at the age of thirty-three. Paul became an eminent doctor of medicine but with the misfortune to become court physician

---

[3] *TR* iv. 4081.

in Berlin at a time when that Brandenburg court was corrupt. Margaretha married an able East Prussian and bore nine children.

This was not the first clerical marriage. The wave of opinion, that wives are better than concubines, was unstoppable. But historically Catherine was a person of the first importance. Her parents placed her in the nunnery when she was ten years old. She lived in the nunnery for fourteen years with no experience of the world, all her adult experience was that of a nun. As an adolescent she had taken vows of chastity and obedience which now she broke. She married a man who was breaking a vow of celibacy which he had taken too young and who did not then love her but took her for reasons of public policy.

There was a belief that if a monk or nun produced a baby, that child was sure to be deficient in body or mind. If Catherine's first baby had come deformed it would have struck no little blow at the Reformation. It would have struck a blow if the marriage had ended in divorce or separation, and a lesser hurt but still a hurt if she had proved to be a shrew. It mattered to many more than Luther that she proved herself not only lovable but a woman of capacity.

Luther married Melanchthon to Catherine Krapp, daughter of a former councillor of Wittenberg, in 1520. There was no legal difficulty because Melanchthon was not a priest. He started with a large lack of enthusiasm, his university colleagues pushed him into it to settle him and stop him overworking. The children made the difference. He rocked the cradle while he read his book, cared personally for their education. Three of the four children reached adult years and one of them, Anna, fitted his ideal of a learned and cultivated woman. She made a disastrous marriage, to the philologist George Sabinus, who turned out faithless and a bully. It cost Melanchthon scruples to get him made founding head of the new Protestant university of Königsberg. In 1544 he deliberated how to get her a divorce, but she died three years later exhausted with six children in ten years of marriage. The son Philip married secretly at the age of eighteen and Luther demanded that the marriage be held invalid but it continued. The second daughter Magdalen married the medical professor Caspar Peucer, a man after Melanchthon's heart in intellectual interests and friendliness.

At the Diet of Nuremberg in 1522–3 the estates were required to penalize priests who married and they refused. At the Diet of Speyer in 1526 the reforming estates demanded leave for priests to marry and were in effect allowed to sanction it until a general council should decide. That meant that more clergy married and did not wait for the problematical general council. The Diet of Speyer in 1529 tried to withdraw the temporary concession. At the Diet of Augsburg in 1530 Melanchthon pleaded that since the clergy of the early Church were allowed to marry, the marriage of the clergy should freely be conceded as one of those 'minor matters' about which there need be no lasting disagreement. Erasmus from a distance tried to persuade the diet to accept that clerical celibacy should be voluntary but it would not.

The arguments *for* were (1) the Bible has married clergy and we are trying to follow the Bible; (2) the result of the rule is too much whoredom; (3) the Eastern Churches have clergy who are married so that it is not even a Catholic rule. The arguments *against* were expressed by a provincial synod at Salzburg in 1537. In Austria and Bohemia King Ferdinand was losing priests steadily to the Protestants because they wished to marry. He tried to persuade the Salzburg council to accept that celibacy ought to be voluntary. They refused. Their theologians said that marriage of clergy in the early Church was a temporary concession because then priests were too few; that though St Peter had a wife and a daughter Petronilla he left them for the sake of his apostolate. Such marriages are not the best thing for the Church. The priest is committed to prayer and sacraments and is hindered by marriage. The minister of God must have no business other than God's business. What happens among the Greeks and the Protestants only goes to show that celibacy is better. The marriage of priests is public prostitution and such priests should be excommunicated.[4] (Petronilla appears in the Roman martyrology as the daughter of St Peter and was perhaps a real early martyr and it was an early gnostic legend which made her Peter's daughter by the association of the names. She was invoked against fever and the danger of travel, and has an altar in St Peter's at Rome.)

These were not moderates. But the moderate Cardinal Contarini defended celibacy against Melanchthon.[5]

To the contrary, the arguments of one parish priest were direct. He held a Catholic parish and ministered as a priest and the parishioners approved of him. The visitors in the diocese found that he had a wife and ordered him to get rid of her. He said this: (1) I might not have the gift of continence; (2) married, I can more easily approach loose women to bring them to a better state; (3) the vicarage is a better-run place as we are. No one but the Protestants gained when he was expelled.

Georg Witzel

The career of Georg Witzel showed the anxieties which occurred in these years when it was not yet certain what would happen over clerical marriage. At the university of Erfurt he learnt humanism and became an ardent admirer

---

[4] *Acta Reformationis Catholicae*, ed. G. Pfeilschifter (Regensburg, 1959), ii. 319f.
[5] *Confutatio articulorum seu quaestionum Lutheranorum*, ed. Friedrich Hünemann (Münster, 1923), *de caelibatu* at 14–16.

of Erasmus, and acquired the desire to reform the Church by going back to the sources. He went off to study at Wittenberg but his father ordered him home and pushed him into ordination as a Catholic priest. His sermons started as evangelical, he soon married, and before long he was no longer in a Catholic parish but an evangelical pastor. He was an evangelical with traditional attitudes and criticized what evangelicals did and spent a time in gaol. In 1531 he returned formally to the Catholic Church—but was a married priest, and was given a little back-street congregation in Eisleben with the right to preach but not to celebrate sacraments. He was driven from place to place and at last found shelter with his wife at Fulda.

At Fulda was the great abbey with the bones of St Boniface the English founder of German Christianity. It was an independent state under a prince-abbot who, because of the origins, had the repute and rank of being the most important monk in Germany, and ruled a house which in its flowering had the best teachers and the best copyists of manuscripts and the best school of miniatures in the empire. But now his state was weak, its security hung upon the emperor. The monks were noblemen and worldly, the pastors ill-educated though the library was famous. Protestant convictions spread among the people. Witzel sought shelter there because the then prince-abbot allowed priests to marry and to administer communion in two kinds.

Witzel was now working for reunion. He regarded the marriage of clergy as a custom on which Christians could agree to differ. He could not believe that it was more moral to keep a concubine than a wife. Popes who ordered this, he believed, could not foresee the evils which would happen. He could not believe that any true authority would order a father to put away his children because he was a priest. Inside himself he suffered. He would not desert his family, yet he longed to exercise his priestly office. But he was obedient, and refrained.

The curious thing is the swing in public opinion in different directions. Early in the century the common people respected their priest if he was celibate but expected him to have a mistress and did not mind; and this meant a public acceptance of a private marriage, quiet cohabitation, but not of ceremonious marriage. Half a century later there is evidence of opposite waves of opinion in different parts of Germany. In the north unmarried priests might be suspect, in the south married priests were disapproved or hunted out of their parishes. But public opinion had swung less far than it looks. In both south and north the people were less rigid than their articulate leaders. The visitation records of Catholic dioceses still show a lot of Catholic priests with women and show them keeping their women and their children with the full backing of their parishioners. The Cologne visitation of 1569 reported that twenty out of thirty-six priests had concubines and yet had the full support of their people. It became a mark of a difference of denomination, whether the woman was called a wife or a housekeeper. In Protestant parishes as in Catholic, people still preferred the woman not to be too prominent. If a Catholic priest called the woman 'my wife', it began to be a sure sign that he moved towards Protestantism. Even strong anti-Protestant priests could be happy over the children. The Praemonstratensian monk Engelbert Korte ministered to one of the parishes served by the monastery, Clarholz in the Rhineland. He had ten children in the vicarage. When his wife/woman died he went back to live in the monastery and this record of multiplication did not stop him being elected prior. That did not turn out quite well because later one of the sons claimed that the monastery misappropriated family property and arrived with an armed band to claim his rights.[6]

The reaction against celibacy brought the assumption that a pastor was truly effective in his vocation if he was married, for marriage protected him from scandal and allowed him to go wherever he wished among his people. Though it was recognized that some men have no vocation to marry and it was right for them to be single, this was not the common expectation. If a pastor's wife died the bereaved was allowed little time for mourning, friends looked for another partner. Calvin looked for Viret's sake and found a lady whom he thought suitable and wanted to propose as Viret's proxy but the plan failed. Viret was less active but accepted the idea, and at last the second marriage came and was even happier than the first.

If someone preferred to remain unmarried he was suspect not for homosexuality but for clinging to the relics of popery. Conrad Pellican came from his Franciscan friary to Zwingli's Zurich and had no desire to marry. But he found that the people suspected a former Franciscan of believing that the unmarried way is higher morally. Colleagues kept offering him brides. So he married, and afterwards was glad that he had, and was an affectionate father.

This was not the rule everywhere. Hausmann, chief pastor of Zwickau, remained unmarried. Zwingli did not press Pellican to marry. In Neuchâtel Farel ministered for decades without marrying. He often preached about the beauty of marriage but did not marry. Suddenly it happened when he was sixty-nine. Far from being pleased his friends were astonished and grieved because of the age of the bride, a devout seventeen-year-old who was the daughter of his housekeeper. He went to Geneva to beg Calvin's support and did not get it and could not persuade Calvin to accept an invitation to the wedding. The scandal quickly passed and the marriage was accepted and there was a son who died at the age of four, three years after his father.

---

[6] August Franzen, *Zölibat und Priesterehe in der Auseinandersetzung der Reformationzeit und der katholischen Reform des 16. Jahrhundert* (Münster, 1969), 96. Korte was elected prior though the Counter-Reformation was then ardent—1603.

While Calvin served as a pastor in the French refugee congregation at Strasbourg, he was advised that he set a bad example by remaining a bachelor. He rejected a suggestion that he should marry a woman who would bring a good dowry. He said he did not mind about beauty, he would like a wife who was modest and thrifty and would care for her husband's health.[7] He found an anabaptist's widow, who like himself was a refugee from persecution, Idelette de Bure. She made a difference to him. Severe and workaholic, he made disciples but not friends. Idelette became one of the three or four people in the world who could be said to be an intimate. She gave him a son who died at once. After ten years of marriage she died and he mourned her truly.

He never married again. And here is a puzzle. Most pastors of whom we know in that age and who lost a wife too young, came under pressure to marry again. A pastor ought to have a wife, that was now a social expectation. Yet after Idelette died there is no sign of any persuasion directed to Calvin to find a new wife. Perhaps his friends thought he had no time for a home.

There were Catholic priests with concubines who became evangelical pastors but did not marry their woman because they thought it wrong for a priest to marry. (Did any of them wonder whether their parishioners would like it if they turned her into a wife? We have no evidence.) In 1542 Corvinus,[8] himself a former Cistercian converted by reading the books of Erasmus and Luther, conducted a visitation of the evangelical churches in the Land of Lippe. He found several pastors, former priests, who had concubines but had not married. As the years passed this became ever more difficult in reformed parishes. *Either marry the woman or put her away*—first the disciplinary authorities and then in time the people began to insist.

Some clergy were attracted to the Reformation because it made their women respectable and their children legitimate. But this was not at first an obvious attraction. Many parishioners, used to the rule of celibacy, were not sure about a wife and for them the wife might be less respectable than the mistress. And were the children legitimate? Reich law said that the children of priests were bastards. Could they for example inherit? Until 1555 there were legal problems over clergy's children in evangelical lands, because lawyers ruled that the law still held them to be bastards. In places there were hot arguments with jurists. So late as 1610 the Anglican bishop of Sodor and Man had to ensure that the children of clergy on the Isle of Man were not treated by lawyers as bastards.

---

[7] Calvin to Farel, 19 May 1539, Calvin, CR x. 1. 348.
[8] Corvinus expounded the Epistles and Gospels well (English version 1550; last edition 1902 in USA); advised Philip of Hesse; superintendent of Brunswick-Calenberg; in prison for three years for resisting the Augsburg Interim, 1548.

In eastern Europe—Hungary, Slovenia, Eastern Poland—there were many members of the Orthodox Church, in which parish priests, not bishops nor monks, must be married. Therefore it ought to have been easier for Roman Catholic priests to marry their women and be acceptable to their congregations. But it was not. The Catholic people were conscious of the difference between denominations and did not like it blurred.

No one raised the modern argument over celibacy that unmarried priests or pastors can more easily stand up to persecution because they have no responsibilities for a wife and children. In the Reformation the fault was rather the other way—the ruthlessness with which leaders sent pastors to risk death without much consideration for their wife and children.

Protestant ministers in Paris risked death. Gaspard Carmel had to flee from Paris in the affair of the Placards in 1534, studied at the university of Basel, was ordained as a pastor and sent to Paris. He came on leave to Geneva where his wife and children were in safety and stayed quite a time. While he was away the persecution in Paris worsened. Could he stay safe in Geneva while his flock was in such danger? Calvin, to whom all French ministers looked for guidance, ruled that he could not. 'Nothing gets over the one sentence in the gospel, *whoever looks back is not worthy of me.* I allow that he has obligations to his wife and children, but everything which takes us away from Christ is strong. I know this is difficult, but that makes victory (over the temptation) more glorious.' But then Calvin said that he could come and explain the situation of the Church and then his own difficulties and ask for grace that someone else may be appointed to go. 'This delay must be as short as possible.'[9] Under this pressure on the conscience Carmel went back into France and used various assumed names and was given a special mission to evangelize in Brittany where he worked as a pastor for three or four years.

When his successor Des Gallars was in Paris there was a manhunt for Protestants in the city. Calvin was considerate to the family in Geneva to see that they did not know what was happening, but did not encourage Des Gallars to leave Paris. That had a generosity because Des Gallars had for years been a minister in Geneva and one of Calvin's closest colleagues. He volunteered for Paris in the crisis there of 1557 but was only able to stay one year before he was relieved.[10]

The next pastor in Paris, Macard, was married to Calvin's niece. Under orders to go to Paris he found that he was sad to leave his wife and children

---

[9] Beza to Farel, 11 November 1557, Calvin, *Op.* xvi. 691.

[10] Des Gallars was sent to London in 1560 when the French congregation there appealed to Calvin for a minister, and a year later a deacon went from London to Geneva to bring over his wife and children. The English climate was bad for his health and his last years were spent with the queen of Navarre at whose deathbed he ministered. He translated into Latin various books which Calvin wrote in French.

and his flourishing Geneva congregation. When the time came for him to be withdrawn from Paris because of the risk, he said that he preferred consideration of the family not to weigh in the decision; but there is a hint in the letter that they did weigh with Calvin. With another pastor these considerations weighed heavily. In 1560, replying to an urgent request from the parish of Montélimar, Calvin sent them a pastor to be temporary. But he would not allow them to keep him for more than a short time. He has a wife and children. His wife is ill. He cannot leave her for long. If he left her too long he would be thought inhuman.[11]

All reforming lands faced the new problem of the clergyman's widow. His concubine was cast adrift at his death because she was not supposed to exist. The pastor's widow concerned the parish and the bishop and the town council. The church in Norway for example, strongly Lutheran under Danish influence, had rules for clergy widows. For a year after the pastor's death (that was longer than in some church orders) she was allowed to live in the parsonage. Then the parish must find her and her children somewhere to live. But the new pastor if unmarried was encouraged to solve the difficulty by marrying her, pressure was strong, it was almost a social obligation. This meant that sometimes the parson's wife was much older than he was and when his wife died he then married a younger girl who in turn might become a young widow.[12]

There were cases where the existence of a wife and children protected the husband. If he had a family, an authority did not like to be so rigorous against the husband for fear of what would happen to the wife and children. This happened with one of the famous reformers of evangelical Germany— Matthias Flacius Illyricus. Though not formally a pastor he had more religious influence than most pastors. He married the daughter of a pastor whose work he admired. When she died in her twelfth childbirth, he was left with eight boys and three daughters and did not know how to cook. Friends told him he must marry again and looked about for brides. Flacius asked whether any sane woman would marry a widower of advanced years with so many children and no job and no stipend and now so unpopular that no one would give him a job? He said that a bride ought to be middle class and good-looking, she need not have money. They found him the daughter of a Regensburg pastor. She had courage and accepted. She shared his travail and exiles from state to state, once hiding from a passing band of 300 imperial horse, once in Antwerp under immediate threat from Spanish troops. He survived better with her than without her, her presence touched hearts. The family found shelter in the White Ladies nunnery at Frankfurt, now run by a

[11] *Op.* xviii. 65–6, undated letter.
[12] A. A. and C. F. Wisløff, *Norsk kirkehistorie* (Oslo, 1966), i. 549–60.

Protestant prioress tough enough to take no notice of the city government when they ordered her to expel this refugee family. Flacius died before they were expelled; the city was mean enough to refuse him a church service at burial but allowed his widow to become a Frankfurt citizen and two years later she married the headmaster of a Frankfurt school.

8

MONKS AND NUNS

Many leaders of reform were monks or friars. For centuries the religious orders threw up men or women or movements which transformed the Church. Now they did so again. This was not a sign of decadence but its opposite. They were unpopular with the common people. Among so large a number it was easy to find bad monks. But in the long tradition of prayer and charity could be found some very good. Luther began reform because he was a good monk, not because he was a worse variety of that calling.

More reformers were friars than monks. Erasmus was an Augustinian canon bored with the life; another such canon was Peter Martyr Vermigli, most influential of Italian Protestants who changed though not at all bored with the life. Only two important reformers were Benedictines, Ambrose Blarer of Constance and Wolfgang Musculus in Augsburg, but this did not mean that Benedictines were rare among reformers. Corvinus was a Cistercian. Oecolampadius was a Brigittine monk (the order of St Bridget of Sweden) but he was unique in that he entered a lately founded monastery in an effort to stave off his growing doubts and settle his mind in a Catholic way. Lefèvre of Etaples wanted to be a monk but was prevented by ill-health.

But friars were nearer the people and less shut behind walls. Luther was an Augustinian Eremite (Austin Friar) but he rightly thought of himself as a monk. Martin Bucer was a Dominican; but it was rare to find Dominicans among reformers, one vocation of the order was resistance to doubtful innovation in ideas, usually their houses were steady against incoming Protestants. The Franciscans, with their memory of a founder who rebelled against stuffy authorities and was a man of the people among the people, were most likely to generate reformers. The two eminent Hebraists after Reuchlin, Sebastian Münster and Conrad Pellican, were both Franciscans before they turned to the Reformation. The Italian Bernardino Ochino was a Franciscan Observant before he felt the need for a stricter discipline and turned to the new Franciscan order of the Capuchins. Francis Lambert, child of a secretary at the pope's palace and the first Frenchman openly to espouse reform, was an itinerant Franciscan preacher who came from Avignon and went to Wittenberg and was housed by Luther in the Austin Friars. He was unpredictable, neither Zwingli nor Bucer could quite do with him and he found his work when he was invited to help the Reformation in Hesse. Several of Luther's best helpers were monks or friars. In Hamburg and Rostock the Franciscan communities were among the first preachers of reform. Luther did not react against a wretched corrupt house of friars. He was a member of a community religious and inspiring, with its authority in Johann von Staupitz, one of the best friars in Germany.

As Luther grew more radical after the argument over indulgences, he did not at first question whether to be a monk was a right way of life and was still himself a monk. The first thing he questioned was whether it could be right for young people to take life vows to follow a way of life which they had not long experienced. But the nature of his private spiritual growth—the torment over striving to do good and earn merit—led him first to question the biblical and ethical teaching given in monasteries, and then to ask the radical question, is this teaching given and this moral practised because of the structure of the way of life?

After he had been kidnapped for his own safety and was hidden in the Wartburg castle, he heard that monks at Wittenberg, among them several from his own house, had left their monasteries. He was forced to ask himself whether they were wrong and realized that he could not say that they were wrong. The result was a booklet 'On Monastic Vows' (*De votis monasticis*). The first page was dramatic. It was a dedication of the book to his father who had tried to dissuade him from entering a monastery; moved by religious crisis he had taken no notice of the plea. In this dedication he apologized to his father as one who had sinned against the command to honour one's father and mother and now recognized that the decision was a mistake and he hoped that by his experience and advice he would free other souls from the same error of thinking that a call to the monastic life was a call which took precedence over the ordinary duties to one's parents.[1]

The book argued thus: the monk's way has no authority in Scripture. The founder of the way, St Antony, chose to be a hermit but took no vow about it. If anyone has taken a vow then he or she has no need to keep it but ought to be set free from it. He confessed he thought at first that it was priests and not monks who should be free from the vow of celibacy but now he realized that no human being ought to be under a lifelong vow to refrain from marriage; and cited 1 Timothy 4: 1–3 'some shall depart from the faith . . . forbidding people to marry'. A community should be like a school, which anyone can join and anyone can leave when he or she likes—whereas, because of vows, monasteries are composed of people in prison for life.

But a life dedicated to prayer, could it only be achieved behind walls which keep out the world? The highest of all commands is to do good to one's

---

[1] *WA* viii. 573–4.

family and one's neighbours. The worship of God lies not in the monastic office but in this charity to fellow humans. He soon reached the conclusion, connected with his memory, that the monastic services can be undevotional repetition—'voices like tubes and trumpets rather than true worshippers'.[2]

Luther was moving onward. He accepted that a man might rightly choose to become a monk to discipline himself and learn how to serve his neighbour better; that a woman might choose to become a nun because she feels a vocation but she must not imagine it is the ideal way of life or the most sacrificial. He now had a fundamental doubt. This way of life shouts to the world that this is the good life and every other form of Christian way is on a lower level, and for the sake of true Christian communities we have to be rid of that notion.

Though Luther's attitude was influential, the movement against monks was far wider in its origins. Among the working people was a belief that monks were among the oppressors of the poor—witness the attacks of peasants in the Peasants' War. Town governments were sure that they could not get adequate welfare or schools or hospitals unless they took endowments which kept going a handful of monks.

When the Westphalian county of Lippe took a reforming church order, neither town council nor town churchmen behaved badly to their monks and nuns. Yet the text of the church order stated their objections thus: They set themselves up as better than other people, so are Pharisees. They wear peculiar clothes which separate them from humanity and are intended to make them look as though they are holy. They make their vows equal to the sacrament of baptism, which is false. They lower the reputation of other Christian vocations more than is right. And their way contradicts Holy Scripture which does not send people out of this world.[3]

To be a monk in north or central Germany was to be unpopular and they were at times unsafe to come out in the streets in their habits, even if they went to church in their habits. For months the nuns of St Bridget in Stralsund were liable to be pelted with mud or even stones if they appeared in their habits.

Under such conditions a religious must believe in vocation to persist. Many went there as minors and might by now want a chance to get out of that way which bored them. Others realized as adults that they were attracted towards the other sex. The law said that they must stay in their houses until death, and to avoid this fate without becoming a runaway it needed special leave, usually in scholarship, as Erasmus or Sebastian Münster or Conrad Pellican left their communities. But in reforming areas no government would now enforce the law against monks or nuns who walked out.

---

[2] 'Fistulae, tubae, sambucae', *WA* viii. 622.
[3] Alois Schröer, *Die Reformation in Westfalen* (Münster, 1979), i. 161 ff.

Monks were more likely to leave than nuns. Monks could face, or imagined that they could face, an unfamiliar world and had a reasonable chance
of jobs unless they were too old. Nuns might or might not find husbands and
if they did not their future would be hard to secure. Many nuns came from
the middle class or higher where the idea of a paid job was demeaning. The
longest, toughest resistance to attempts to dissolve religious houses came
from nuns.

But not all nuns persisted. Like monks they did not wish to be unpopular
with the people. They asked themselves the hitherto unaskable question
whether what they were doing was the best of ways and whether one could
do more good to one's neighbour and the world by coming out.

The nunnery of Poor Clares at Königsfelden in Switzerland was a house
for the daughters of south German and Swiss aristocrats. They were educated
nuns so they read Luther and Zwingli. They decided that their way of life was
not right. They asked their official protector to release them from the legal
obligation to remain in the nunnery till death. Their protector was the still
conservative council at Berne. The council asked chaplains and relatives of
the nuns to persuade them to think again. It tried out the idea that if the nuns
were allowed an easier rule of life they would not be so discontented with
their lot. A majority among the nuns would have none of this. With reluctance the Berne council felt that it could do nothing but give the nuns the
right to choose freely whether they left or stayed, and allowed departing nuns
to take with them what they or their families had contributed in money or
clothes or possessions. Several of them married at once and it caused a sensation when one was publicly betrothed in Berne cathedral. All this was five
years before Berne could be said finally to be a reforming city. It was still
ejecting priests who married from their parishes and stipends. The council
did not act by majority out of a conviction that nunneries were wrong, or
even out of the persuasion that a nun's individual conscience ought to be free
to choose another way of life. It acted as governments do, to make the best
out of a situation that they do not quite like. It was only later, in 1528, that the
Berne government formally dissolved Königsfelden.

If monks or nuns could leave their cloister if they wished and then be no
longer runaways nor guilty of an offence against the law but persons who
found like Erasmus that they were in the wrong vocation and now chose
another occupation, it weakened struts of the system because it reflected
on the vow of obedience and on the vow of stability in the house until
death. If a monk was free to leave when he decided, what happened to the
community, or the vows of obedience which they took? The question was
whether a free right to leave was compatible with the existence of monasteries and nunneries as they had been known for so many centuries in the
Church.

So the doubt whether so many women and men should be tied to the unmarried life behind high walls threw up a radical notion; whether the monastic ideal could any longer be seen to be a practicable way of life; and, what would happen, if many communities collapsed or were closed, to the endowments and the land and the buildings which sustained them.

A famous monastery which dissolved itself under the changing opinion of those years was the Wittenberg house of the Austin Friars. It was called the Black Cloister though they wore white inside the house, because in public the habit was black. At the end of 1521 there were thirty friars, in February 1522 there were not more than six, then one or two more joined, then the number fell to three who included Luther. Many of them took secular jobs and many of them married. The house was not suitable for three friars, for it was constructed in forty individual cells, with a large refectory and a large dormitory and a ramshackle whitewashed wooden chapel propped up by beams on both sides. The friars had started to build a permanent chapel but had not finished and in the yard there was the builder's mess. Luther was attached to this plainest of chapels for there he preached some of his first sermons from a little pulpit made of planks. The friars called it Bethlehem.

Nevertheless Luther continued to live in the rambling pile and went on wearing his habit until October 1524. Even then he felt it painful and diffi-cult to put off his habit and appear in ordinary clothes outside the house like a layman. He looked about for someone who could order him to leave off his cowl but there seemed to be no one with that authority.

The first effect of the friars leaving was the poverty of the house because every person who left had the right to a share of the contribution which he made to the endowment when he was admitted and the whole endowment was small. Appeals to the elector of Saxony gained a right for Luther to con-tinue permanently in occupation of the Black Cloister and the other two friars were given plots of land belonging to the Black Cloister on which they built little houses.[4]

Luther's book on monastic vows had an impetus in the flight from monas-teries, and in none more frequently than Luther's own order. He had told the world that monastic vows were mistaken. The Erfurt house and the Wittenberg house lost many of their people. One of the Augustinian brothers of Luther's Wittenberg community, Gabriel Zwilling, told the world that no man can be saved wearing a cowl. First a few friars left, then a crowd. Many of them took secular jobs and married; and we cannot judge how happy were these sudden marriages by people trained to believe that it was wrong to fall in love. Early in 1522 the Augustinian general meeting for

---

[4] Eighteen years after Luther's death the town of Wittenberg bought the Black Cloister from Luther's children.

Thuringia and Meissen voted that anyone who wished could go and anyone who wished could stay. But this was too moderate for the situation. In certain towns if a monk wanted to keep his vow and turned up at mass in the cowl, he might be thrown out of church by students. And if a commodious rambling convent was left with two or three inhabitants uncomfortable among its echoing halls, a town had eyes for better use of the property.

During the next few years one house after another lost its people and was closed. The Augustinians lost 69 houses out of 160 within ten years. Soon princes or town councils dissolved little houses as useless and turned their endowments to ends which they regarded as more useful. Monks left inside a Protestant town found that they needed to live a very inconspicuous life, and sometimes if they went out they were mocked. In places war destroyed what was left by their Christian critics. The Austin Friars had twenty-five houses in the province of Hungary. They lost every one. A few vanished because Protestant ideas made headway, more because they were loot in a civil war and Turks did the rest.

A monastery was easier to leave than a nunnery but it was not easy. The vow was not forgotten. Luther dressed and behaved as a monk for three years after he told the world that he was sure this way of life was mistaken. Staupitz, who helped him towards his understanding of St Paul and the grace of God, could not go the way of his pupil. Staupitz had a true sense of the spirituality in the cloistered life. While his houses tumbled, he kept to the rule, but when they fell, and because he was now suspect to Catholic authorities as partly responsible for a rebel monk, he transferred himself (June 1522) to be a Benedictine monk at Salzburg. The cardinal of Salzburg soon made him abbot of the house though the monks did not want him. We know more of his teaching because there the nuns took down his sermons. But he was now a troubled soul. He criticized Luther for attacking so many outward things of the Church, especially monks; yet he believed Luther right in his essentials of faith and refused to abandon his friendship and loyalty. He was much deeper than Erasmus into the best of medieval thought; yet like Erasmus, who also wished to stay a Catholic, his books were all put on the Index of Prohibited Books; and sixty years after his death an abbot of his monastery at Salzburg solemnly burnt all his papers; while two of his books, *On True Faith* and *On the Right Love of God*, were often reprinted by Protestants who valued the affectionate side of medieval mystic thought.

If the monastery lay in a Land where law still insisted that runaway monks or nuns were to be chased and brought back, were they to face the risk of going? By what means get away? Was it a Christian act to flee in the night and in disguise? Not all monks in a house, and in a nunnery fewer of the nuns, were likely to be convinced that this way of life is wrong and the house must dissolve itself. Loyalty to friends and other members of the community disturbed consciences. Worse monks had worse feelings—they went into a monastery not to need to earn a living, why should the community throw them into unemployment in a world with no dole?

If a house dissolved itself whether by a drift away or by a vote, it left one or two or three or four fathers living in a house too vast for them and in poverty because those who went took pensions from the endowment. Then the State stepped in—to turn out the remnant, and join them to an existing house with a bigger remnant, and persuade them to accept pensions.

If the State did not step in, tragedy could ensue. At Hasselt in East Frisia was a community of Hospitallers. The brothers voted to dissolve the house and go. A single brother insisted on staying. While walls crumbled and windows fell out, he miserably occupied a room or two, still wearing his habit; not alone, for he married the monastery cook and said that he did it to quiet his conscience. The Hospitallers discovered the lady and threatened him with discipline and ordered him to leave but he refused to come out. Tormented by his conscience inside the half-ruined monastery and threatened by Catholics outside, he was found hanging from one of the broken windows. We do not know what happened to his wife. But after the house lay empty for several years the East Frisian government stepped in at last, took over the property, repaired it, turned it into a nursing home for the mentally deficient brother of the count, demolished the monastery chapel, and used its stones to build a prison in the town of Stickhausen.[5] Meanwhile the Hospitallers pursued their case in the imperial courts to get the property back and after thirty years of endeavour succeeded; Hasselt was not finally secularized until the age of Napoleon.

Erasmus, who had told the world more humorously than anyone else that there were too many monks and that their numbers ought to be diminished, did not like the result that he saw. The beggar who was once respectable because he was a friar was still a beggar and despised because he was a tramp. Monks who had gone after whores from their monasteries chased whores more openly when they left their monasteries. A kleptomaniac was better coped with by an abbot than when the town had to face the results of his thieving. 'I know some', wrote Erasmus in a letter warning a friend against leaving his monastery, 'who were deluded by the dream of freedom and left their monasteries and dressed like laymen and found wives. And ever since they have been poor, not at home in their world, despised by family and friends. You do not realize how lucky you are to be out of so wretched a society.'[6]

Others easily found their right vocation when they left and without trouble of mind. Some delayed their departure, where they could, that is,

---

[5] Heinrich Reimers, *Die Säkularisation der Klöster in Ostfriesland* (Aurich, 1906), 12, 40–1.

[6] *Ep.* 1887 from Basel, 15 October 1527.

where the house was not collapsing about them, until suitable work was possible. Many monks became parish pastors. Sebastian Münster, leader in the
study of Hebrew and then the creator of modern geography, was a Franciscan
who entered the order for the sake of higher education. His superiors saw
that his mind was exceptional and gave him excellent schooling and prepared
him for ordination as a priest and allowed him the chance of using Reuchlin's
Hebrew library at Stuttgart and (probably through Reuchlin) to meet
Melanchthon. By 1519, still a Franciscan, he was teaching in Basel and
worked on Hebrew texts and translated ten of Luther's sermons. Then the
order sent him to Heidelberg to teach Hebrew. He appears quietly to have
slipped off a few years after he was convinced that the way of the
Reformation was right and only after he had found another good chance of
scholarship. The mind showed no sign of agony.

In Hamburg the Franciscan house led reformation. Friars were ardent for
reform, most accepted it and left their house and married and took jobs. A
few stayed. Nearly all the Dominicans in the town were steady against
change, most left the town, their prior went off to Speyer to prosecute the
council before the Reich supreme court, a few old members remained in
buildings too spacious and so were moved into the Franciscan house and the
Dominican priory became a poor house for women. The Cistercian nuns of
Reinbeck, to which the upper classes sent unmarried daughters, were led by
their prioress to opt for reformation. The Hamburg difficulty came over the
rich Cistercian convent of Harvestehude, where the nuns were resolute
against change and had an abbess tough enough to stand against any town
council. After three troubled years the nuns consented to move on condition
that they remained the owners of the property. Then the town turned the
place into an evangelical community for the daughters and widows of
citizens.

All over north Germany this solution was not uncommon. Monkish life
was bad—that began to be agreed—so there ought not to be nuns. But society still needed homes for unmarried ladies, and these homes appeared often
in old nunneries and looked like them; though with simpler services in
German and with a reformed pastor as chaplain and they might or might not
be allowed to wear a habit very like the nun's habit and they were sometimes
under pressure to do a useful task like running a girls' school.

At Pinneberg just outside Hamburg was a nunnery of special importance,
the Uetersen community. It housed the unmarried daughters of aristocrats of
Schleswig-Holstein and of rich citizens of Hamburg; that is, it met social
need and had power; the more power because technically it lay under the rule
of a count, from a junior branch of the Holstein family. In 1533 nuns were
allowed to leave if they liked but those who stayed went on keeping the rule
and wearing the habit. After nine years King Christian III of Denmark, who

was also duke of Holstein, arrived to take strong action; he drove out the priests who said mass and put in an evangelical chaplain. The majority of the nuns stayed Catholic and for a time got back a priest to say mass; so the king/duke sent another evangelical chaplain and turned the nunnery into an evangelical college for ladies; that is, the community went on keeping the rule, but with reformed services in Low German. This long, fairly serene, resistance meant that Pinneberg was the last territory in Schleswig-Holstein to be reformed; not finally until 1561.

The worst disturbances came in communities when they were divided, and especially in monasteries of the countryside which were secluded. They served as homes for the younger sons and the unmarried daughters of squires. When a government went reformed, as a mere matter of human rights it always abolished the canon law that a monk or nun who left the house without leave of the superior or higher church authority committed illegality. If the State did not enforce a Protestant chaplain upon them, it always allowed them to invite a Protestant chaplain if they wished. But 'they' who wished meant the majority; so there were nunneries where the superior and the larger number of nuns forced Protestant services on a handful of nuns who loved the ancient ways and thought what was done was both illegal and immoral; and there were nunneries where a minority of nuns longed for services in German and less archaic rules and knew that they had the support of many in the world outside, and could not change the old ways in which the majority of nuns in the house stood fast. Such divided houses could be very unhappy. They need not be, in various communities monks or nuns retained their loyalty to each other and the community while they agreed to disagree—but this civilized tolerance lasted nowhere longer than a few years at most, by its nature the predicament was too tense for the happiness of the house.

At the Cistercian nunnery of Itzehoe on the edge of the marshes in Schleswig twenty-eight nuns wanted their services in German. The abbess, backed by the remaining thirteen nuns, refused to allow it.[7] At the Franciscan house in Basel Conrad Pellican was a friar who wanted change. The house contained the most scandalous friar in the city. When reformed and conservative walked in the same cloister and ate in the common refectory and worshipped together in the chapel, no one could be comfortable. Pellican dared not eat the food in the refectory until a friend tasted it. He accepted Zwingli's offer of the chair of Hebrew at Zurich partly because the Basel friary was rent, and arrived in reformed Zurich still wearing a Franciscan habit.[8] In the

---

[7] Erich Hoffmann, in W. Göbell (ed.), *Schleswig-Holsteinische Kirchengeschichte* (Neumünster, 1982), iii. 153. Eventually the State forced the reformed service on the nunnery.

[8] C. Zürcher, *Konrad Pellikans Werke in Zürich 1526–56* (Zurich, 1975), 20.

Cistercian nunnery at Rechentshofen in Württemberg it came to a bloody fight between old-minded nuns and nuns who wanted change.[9] At Gengenbach in Swabia the majority of monks were reformers in opinion and elected as the new abbot an open disciple of Calvin, an election which did not lead to harmony.[10] Salem was a historic Swabian house of the Cistercians with a famous scriptorium. It treated its tenants hard and was in trouble during the Peasants' War. Unlike others of the area, peasants could enter the house as monks and a monk of peasant family could be elected abbot. The house bought Luther's works plentifully for its library. At Norden in East Frisia was a Dominican house. One of the friars Heinrich Reese believed that reformation was right and went round the towns challenging opponents to a disputation, and came into the friary church and put a Bible and Concordance below the pulpit and from the pulpit defended reform. His fellow Dominicans offered little resistance. Conservatives found a champion in the abbot of nearby Marienthal abbey. The debate ended with Reese coming down from his pulpit and renouncing both his habit and his membership of the order. He became parish pastor at Norden. Then several of his fellow Dominicans accepted work as pastors of other reformed parishes. Then the prior disappeared carrying off the valuables, the house was not viable, the count bought out the survivors with pensions.

This running away of the Dominican prior, though illegal, was not theft in a moral sense. As a community was about to dissolve, or felt its surviving members to be under threat either from its own brothers or from government, despairing conservatives wanted to remove the valuables—whether because they were sacred like pyxes or chalices or candlesticks or relics or (less often) folio volumes, or furniture or 'private' possessions because they might enable a smaller community to continue somewhere else. The Cistercian house at Maulbronn was assigned as the house to which monks of half-dissolved houses, who wished to continue to live as monks, could collect. Therefore it was peopled with the stoutest of conservatives or the old who needed care. But then the abbot Johann von Lienzingen ran away to Speyer with the precious bits and the account books and tried to govern the house from a distance—until a group of his monks followed him.[11]

Where a monastery was in turmoil, it was essential for government to send in commissioners to list the property. In many houses monks cooperated in making these inventories. But elsewhere the appearance of the commissioners was felt, especially by nuns, to be a sordid and illegal intrusion into their peace and a threat to their future. Cataloguing often speeded the process of

[9] H. Hermelink, *Geschichte der evangelischen Kirche in Württemberg* (Stuttgart, 1949), 69.

[10] *Die Territorien des Reichs im Zeitalter der Reformation und Konfessionalisierung*, ed. Anton Schindling and Walter Ziegler (Münster, 1989–93), s.v. Swabia.

[11] Hermelink, *Geschichte der evangelischen Kirche*, 66–7.

dissolution though it had no such open intention. It was intensely unpopular. The Cistercian abbey of Herrenalb in the Black Forest had an abbot and
sixteen monks. It had importance by reason of its endowments and in the past
did well artistically. But the house was sacked in the Peasants' War and never
recovered. When government tried to reform, the abbot and nine monks
decided to stay, seven monks decided to leave and accept pensions. It took a
posse of eighty men to collect the valuables of the house by force. Even so the
abbot was accused three years later of hiding wealth and was put into prison.
The house was half-restored in the reaction of 1548, but in the next years
became a Lutheran community, not to be finally secularized till the age of
Napoleon.

At Greifswald in Pomerania was a historic Cistercian house, the Eldena
(who is St Hilda). Its management was conservative for a special reason, that
it was tied to the university of Greifswald which was conservative. It sent
monks to that university for their higher education and from the university
students it gained novices. But when parents refused to send their offspring
to so conservative a place of education, the university failed, lectures ceased,
the Eldena novices were no more. The abbot sent out letters and agents to
attract novices, in vain. He laid on lectures to replace the university lectures.
Young monks drifted away.

Inside the community his sub-prior led the reforming party. Several young
monks were sent to the bishop to be ordained and on the way stopped at an
inn where they found a book with a preface by Bugenhagen. They took
down quotations. Then they stayed in a monastery, where the chaplain of
the house sold them Melanchthon's commentary on the Epistle to the
Romans.[12] At their ordination to be priests they heard the bishop say the
words 'Go ye into all the world . . .' and felt contradiction between this charge
and their enclosed way of life. The Eldena monastery fell apart. Abbot and
prior and several monks stayed there till they died.[13]

Many ordinary people believed that mass must be stopped from being celebrated in churches if the life of the town was to be clean. Did that apply to
mass celebrated quietly by a priest in someone's home? Was the chapel of a
monastery the private room of a family or another public church providing
services for anyone? Most monastery chapels accepted lay worshippers at
their services.

[12] Melanchthon lectured on Romans in 1520–1 but did not print the lectures. However, a student took his notes of the lectures and showed them to Luther who was pleased and printed them
without asking Melanchthon; and then, still without authority, Johann Agricola published a
German translation. Therefore Melanchthon in 1532 printed a new commentary on Romans
(much extended in 1540) partly with the aim of sinking the unauthorized version *quam ego plane non
agnosco.* Since the Eldena monks bought the copy after 1532 it cannot be determined which edition
they bought, but there is a phrase in the sources which suggests that it was the earlier.

[13] Hellmuth Heyden, *Die Kirchen Greifswald und ihre Geschichte* (Berlin, 1965), 98.

Therefore—may a government close all monasteries and nunneries for the sake of the Church and the good of society? This was a different question from government making sense of endowments where a dissolving community left a chaos.

Against: a government has no such right. This is a historic way of life in Christendom. To take the money of monasteries is like confiscating money from citizens.

For: if monks are bad for the Church they are the institution which needs change most and that means their abolition, unless we allow older monks and nuns who wish to remain to continue their way of life till death.

The For and Against were argued at the meeting of the Schmalkaldic League in February 1537. The delegates of Charles V said that reforming states stole property by closing monasteries. The Protestant delegates said that this was a wrong way of life which had bad consequences for society and its moral welfare. Even if in justice they allowed former monks to keep pensions they must be right to close monasteries. Melanchthon and Bugenhagen were present and agreed. If a parish is served by an unworthy priest, he must be turned out and the stipend given to someone better. The State does nothing else when it closes a monastery. This money was a gift or gifts directed to help people to Christian ways of life and worship, which is what monasteries fail to do. The property is rightly transferred to other purposes which can be seen to be in God's service.

Unlike dissolutions in England and the Protestant cantons of Switzerland, the process in Germany was without a coherent pattern. Reforming government must bear in mind the law of the Reich. The Reich supreme court was not very effective when plaintiffs objected to a property being taken but it was not wholly ineffective. From policy as well as a sense of justice, reformers preferred not to drive out monks. They hoped that monks would decide to go.

Therefore pressure began on surviving monks where there were enough of them to make a workable community. Show them the attraction of a pension. Prove that work was available outside. Explain how their ideal was wrong or impracticable. Stop them buying Catholic books. Install a reformed preacher as their chaplain. Order that they be present at his sermons. Prevent them wearing their habits in the streets (an order necessary for their protection) or more harshly stop them wearing habits in the house— again necessary in certain towns or villages to avert assault upon the premises. Make the community accept the German language instead of Latin for prayers and hymns.

These forced chaplains were unpopular among monks and nuns and it is not likely that sympathetic ears would be open or that sermons persuaded. This was not always true. At the Cistercian house of Bebenhausen in Württemberg the preacher was an old Wittenberg student Hans Schmölz, who did his work so well that nineteen out of thirty-five monks accepted the reformed way and five became evangelical pastors. Bebenhausen was made Protestant in 1535 and twenty years later became an evangelical community which ran a school. It was finally secularized in the age of Napoleon when it was turned into a royal hunting lodge.

Monks were less conservative than nuns about forms of prayer. They were less likely to object to services in German and a reformed way of worship because it was a reverent liturgy and could be used by Catholics. The nuns were more resolute and in certain houses preferred no sacraments at all to a Protestant sacrament, even for years on end; and their saddest loss in this principle was the absence of a sacrament at death. In monasteries where there were priests, Latin mass continued privately after it was illegal, and in more humane Protestant states survivors were allowed their Latin mass without the need for it to be secret. But this last was hard for government to concede because the saying of mass would become known in the town and could provoke physical attacks from fanatics; and it was hard to reconcile with the tender consciences of magistrates who believed they had a duty to get rid of whatever was wrong in worship. In towns like Frankfurt am Main the mass was preserved at a particular church under a Reich treaty with Catholics and then the mass was secure and surviving monks could attend—but this was much less easy for any Catholic laypeople in the town.

It was a general rule that no house could receive novices and therefore must die out in time. This was liable to exceptions. At various nunneries in East Frisia nuns were encouraged to leave but if they decided to stay were allowed to do so and then when they grew too old to look after themselves the State allowed them younger nuns as a way of caring for the old. Such exceptions were rare.

Nuremberg was one of the early towns to reform and also a town where nuns held out longest. Monks left their houses quickly and many nuns also. Then the council tried to bring over the survivors; banned monks from entering nunneries to hear confessions or preach; stopped them from accepting novices; ordered all houses to use the reformed service. Several houses took no notice of this last order. The council sent in preachers whom the nuns refused to hear. There was a problem when a mother claimed back her daughter from a nunnery and the nun refused to come out and the council gave the mother the legal right to fetch her away—but who was to use force? There was another problem when nuns from convents out in the countryside, burnt or threatened by peasant bands, sought refuge in the city and then the duty to help refugees took precedence over the duty to persuade nuns not to be nuns.

In Nuremberg nuns had an unusual defender—a great abbess, Charitas Pirckheimer, sister to a famous humanist, one of the powerful men of the town. Like a few others her community of St Clare continued, without novices, legally with a reformed way of worship but actually with the Latin. They listened without enthusiasm to Protestant sermons. To Charitas and her Poor Clares Osiander preached thirty-four sermons on Sundays and holy days during the summer of 1525. For a few years the communications between Osiander and the abbess were tense. Eight years later the little group of surviving nuns were not known in the city, they lived quiet lives as though in a ghetto, which they may have thought a contemplative way. The last nun at St Catherine's did not die till 1596.

The social class of monk and nun was often different. Many monks came from working-class homes, many nuns from middle-class homes. This meant that, by culture or education or habits, not all ex-monks were seen as suitable husbands for ex-nuns and vice versa. Ducal Saxony, separate from electoral Saxony, was Catholic till the change of ruler in 1539. Duke George's successor Heinrich decided to reform and as part of it to dissolve the religious houses. But when nuns began to be turned out of their convents, their families protested to the duke. They asked what good could come of driving out the girls to disgrace their kin by marrying tailors and cobblers and runaway monks? For a time the nuns were allowed to continue in those convents.

We have a study of what happened to nuns in the great city of Augsburg when it accepted reform. There were seven nunneries and one community of canonesses. St Clara was a troubled house before any reform and the nuns did not resist dissolution. Many left, the rest gave it to the city council in return for pensions, and the building became a home for waifs and strays. Two other convents were likewise dissolved easily. But there was a Dominican nunnery of upper-class daughters, forty-four nuns with thirteen lay sisters, a rich house, St Catherine's. It drifted downhill, at Christmas 1547 ten nuns went to mass and seven to the evangelical sacrament. In such a drift there were the two sores, no new younger nuns to look after the older, and division in the house. But the council made it unhappier still. There was a Benedictine house of St Nicholas where nuns had left but ten stayed as stout conservatives. The council believed that these nuns were in secret communication with the nearest powerful Catholic ruler, the duke of Bavaria. They ordered them to join the nuns of St Catherine's. To transport them in carts, while ten nuns shrieked through the streets, took forty policemen.[14]

Dissolution was less harsh because there were still Catholic lands with monastic houses ready to receive monks and nuns who emigrated from a country which wanted to be rid of them. Those who felt that they could not

---

[14] Angelika Nowicki-Pastuschka, *Frauen in der Reformation: Untersuchungen zum Verhalten von Frauen in den Reichstädten Augsburg und Nürnberg zur reformatorischen Bewegung zwischen 1517 und 1537* (Pfaffenweiler, 1990), 74–5.

abandon their way of life went southward, to the Tyrol or Bavaria or the Austrian lands, a journey not easy for the old and the old were more likely than the young to want to travel.

In German Lands where convents were allowed to die out slowly, civic need could build up pressure against them. The Observant Franciscans still had a house near the middle of the prosperous North Sea port of Emden. By 1543 it was so evangelical a town that it appointed a famous reformer as its superintendent, the Pole John a Lasco (Laski), the scholar who had inherited the library of Erasmus. Yet in the centre of this Protestant city, with commodious buildings and a pleasant garden, a small and still diminishing community of Franciscans continued with their old way of life, except that they did not beg, nor walk the streets in their habits; two of them obeyed orders by attending sermons at the parish church, and sermons were preached in their chapel by reformed preachers. A council might have regarded this as enough. It seemed to a Lasco extraordinary, in the high age of reforming conquest, to allow a Catholic mass at the heart of the capital of the Land. He did not think of it as wise toleration but as disobedience to the Word of God. And the pressure built up all the time. Emden was a sanctuary for thousands fleeing from persecution in the Catholic Netherlands, made uncompromising by their experience of suffering. This flight brought valuable craftsmen into Emden. But it brought many destitute and every month the need for hospitals and poor houses grew more urgent—and there on a prime site in the middle of the town sat seven Observant friars.

The town's first idea was to take the garden and build a poor house. But the cry for space still grew and in 1556 the friars said they were ready to leave. They were treated generously. Their chapel became a parish church, their buildings a guest house.[15]

But in that northern district nuns continued; legally not allowed mass, they went on with it quietly. The Praemonstratensian nunnery at Blauhus, which in 1562 still had thirteen nuns with two Catholic chaplains, lost its great organ to Emden parish church. A few ancient nuns in other houses drifted on, uncomfortably, often in debt and with few to care for them as they aged, into the 1580s.

When a town's debate about nunneries happened, it could be frightening for nuns; many had been there since childhood, the outside world an unknown menace. In Catholic Geneva in 1532 the bells of the city sounded and the Poor Clares in their ignorance assumed that it was an alarum which heralded the attack of Protestants and soon they would all be driven out of their house and forced to marry. During the next riot in the city the mother abbess put ashes on the heads of all the nuns and they processed round the

---

[15] Reimers, *Säkularisation*, 32.

cloister singing *Misericordia*. They still sang their daily offices. But inside the nunneries were souls persuaded that this way which they had undertaken with a solemn vow, and in which they were held prisoner till death, was not the right way for them.

The defenders of nuns were vehement. These girls had taken an honourable vow. They lived in a respectable community. If they come out they break a vow, and they enter a world for which most of them are not fitted by experience and not a few will end in the gutter. It is said to be a way contrary to the highest Christian ideal of loving one's neighbour and yet it has existed within the Christian community for more than a thousand years and has history on its side. If it is so unnatural a way of life why have so many people chosen to live it?

No one in northern or western Switzerland was persuaded by such an argument. In German Lands it was often convincing. Many states accepted that a community life for unmarried women was an acceptable and even good institution and should be allowed to remain and if it was in an old nunnery that was right. Naturally the community should worship with reformed services. Some states tried to insist that it should educate girls or help with nursing.

The astonishing survival was the house of the Brothers of the Common Life at Herford in Westphalia. The state was a prince-abbey founded early during the ninth century by a son or grandson of Charlemagne to be a headquarters for education and evangelism in Saxony. The abbess was not only the head of the convent but ruler of the State, though she left secular matters to a freely elected council. She was Anna von Limburg (1523–65). Her presence slowed change. For a time there was even a little house of Luther's order the Austin Friars, five men but despite their life as monks leading the town in reform. In 1532 the people would not stand mass in churches and invaded them to remove candles and pyxes.

The Brothers of the Common Life went on as a religious community. They accepted the way of worship in German but still wore their habits and kept the three *rules* of celibacy and poverty and obedience though no longer as *vows*. The bishop of Paderborn resented them as heretics and imprisoned two of them. On the other side the Protestant council and townsfolk and parish pastors resented that they were still there as a sort of Catholic survival. The council demanded that they come out, dissolve themselves, marry, breed children, help the world to get on, and let the town found a school in their buildings. The Augustinians and Franciscans in Herford had dissolved their houses and handed the property to the town, why not the Brothers?

The community now knew where it was. They had evangelical sacraments, read the Bible, had services in German, did not have vows, what was wrong with living a common life and wearing a habit? They did not suppose that being unmarried was a surer way to heaven than marriage. They appealed to Luther, who was once a pupil of the Brothers' school in Magdeburg. He found nothing unchristian in what they were doing, and told the town to leave them, and their fellow-community of sisters, untroubled. He defended their wearing of the habit. He said he was of the opinion that the country would be better off if all religious communities behaved as they did; that they were living according to the gospel and he wished all monasteries of the past had lived like them. 'Your habit and your customs which you have so laudably preserved are in no way contrary to the gospel but help its progress against the fanatics who want to pull everything down.' He sent all the brothers and sisters a greeting from his wife and children.[16]

The town council and the reformed clergy of the town gave way about the habits and allowed the two communities to survive. Then they thought of depriving them of the right to accept novices on the plea that an institution with celibacy, even though without vows and voluntary, ought not to be allowed to continue. 'What' asked Melanchthon 'is this new doctrine which forbids people to stay unmarried? St Paul says it is better not to marry if someone has the gift of continence, so that he or she can better serve the work of the Church.'[17]

Luther preferred that monasteries be schools. The town demanded that the house become a public elementary school—it already had a good Latin school. The Brothers agreed. They chose a master, he was ragged by the children. The town told Luther how bad was the school and demanded the right to turn the house wholly into a school. Luther talked of the council as the new Pharisees and wrote a fierce letter—he has heard that fanatics in Herford threaten the Brothers that they cannot be blessed in their way of life. Yet they put away all papist superstition, and in Christian freedom even if in their habit lead a disciplined life and after the teaching of the apostles keep themselves by the work of their hands. These Brothers help the gospel and do not hurt it. If the council forces them into a school for which they are not suited they will give the town a bad name. In his Table Talk Luther spoke of the very pious virgins who were Sisters of the community at Herford. He said that he felt compassion for them and believed that they ought to be left to do what they thought right.[18]

---

[16] *BW* vi. 249, 254–5 (1532).

[17] Melanchthon to the Brothers of Herford, 4 July 1533, *BW* vi. 472. '*Quid est hoc novum dogma omnibus interdicere continentiam? Paulus aperte ait melius esse non nubere, si quis continere possit, et addit causam, ut expeditius servire possint ecclesiis.*'

[18] Luther to the town council, 24 October 1534, *BW* vii. 113–14; *TR* iv. 89, no. 4031, 30 September 1538. The text has the nuns at Erfurt, but the editors are confident that the name is a textual error through a mishearing by the recorder and that Luther said and meant the Herford sisters.

In all this correspondence it is plain that the heart of Luther was engaged on the side of the conservatives. He had not forgotten the better side of the monastery in his own upbringing and religious development.

The Sisters at Herford lasted till 1565 when they were starved out. The long battle had an odd effect on the Brothers. The more they had to fight against the council, the more good they saw in the old world. They started to join the old Roman Catholic minority that survived in the town under the aegis of the Catholic abbess, and do what they could for their freedom; until, five years after the Sisters closed, they decided to leave Herford. Then happened the strangest event of all: the town council, which had fought for so many years to get rid of a Protestant community, decided to continue one in the same house now empty and fill it with a community of evangelical brothers who would bind themselves to remain unmarried and to live the religious life.

The abbey of Herford as a state remained officially Catholic until the princess–abbess Anna died in 1565. Her successor was installed with the old rites and ceremonies but under her it all became evangelical, with a community of ladies who were evangelical instead of Catholic nuns. So in a reformed world continued the foundation of a son of Charlemagne. In 1804 Prussia turned the community into a place for any denomination but it remained mostly Lutheran till modern times.

Herford was not the only community defended by Luther from Protestant attacks. At Oldenstadt in the Land of Lüneburg a Benedictine nunnery had been founded in 970 under the emperor Otto II. A century and a half later it failed and Benedictine monks from Corvey recolonized it. Abbot Gottschalk was convinced by Luther's writings against vows and sought to alter the Benedictine rule. But Lüneburg was one of the earliest Protestant states, and its rulers owed painful debts. Duke Ernst pressed upon all the religious houses. Two Franciscan communities, the second at Celle, were forced to leave. Cistercians left voluntarily, mainly because they knew they were no longer wanted. Abbot Gottschalk felt a doubt about himself. He asked Luther for pastoral advice—he had thought he should be a monk till death, could he continue as a monk in these new circumstances? Luther answered laconically. Yes, he could stay.[19] Gottschalk happily handed over to Duke Ernst the administration of the goods of the house, it made a religious life easier if he were relieved of these chores.

Six years later the duke took away the library to make it available to the public—he left the monks their theology and prayer books, and left Gottschalk his personal library. Abbot Gottschalk died in 1541 still a

---

[19] *BW* iv. 391, 28 February 1528. Cf. Heinz-Meinold Stamm, *Luthers Stellung zur Ordensleben* (Wiesbaden, 1980), 127–43.

Benedictine abbot presiding over a community of Benedictines, even if the rule had been altered.

Westphalia in the north-west was a pattern of little states and towns. It needed not to be too radical in change because its western regions were in striking distance of Brussels where lay the headquarters of a Spanish army. It was also less typical because it started with fewer communities than other parts of Germany of the size: 63 foundations of which 28 were male and 32 female; plus 17 colleges or chapters with secular canons (5) and canonesses (12).

Of the 28 male houses, 15 dissolved themselves or were dissolved, 11 remained Roman Catholic, one became a Protestant Community.

The Cistercian abbey of Loccum was an independent state and remained Catholic, in name, for all the earlier decades of the Reformation, but turned to be evangelical after 1591 and yet remained celibate till 1878 and survives as a Protestant abbey to this day.

Of the Westphalian female houses, 14 were dissolved, 10 were turned into communities of Protestant ladies, 8 were kept as Roman Catholic nunneries.[20]

In comparison with most of northern Germany the figures show a balance more favourable to Catholics. The result depended on a fairly tolerant policy by the rulers with respect for the Reich law which protected old rights. They also show that more than a quarter of the nunneries were turned into Protestant communities and a few were willing to accept Catholic members.

On the Baltic coast Mecklenburg made a contrast. Here the monasteries were founded as outposts in the great Cistercian movement of the twelfth and thirteenth centuries to evangelize and civilize this remote north-east German coast. Indispensable to the eastward colonization they flowered during the thirteenth century but their remoteness made control impossible and by the fourteenth century they were in a bad way; bottom was when Pope Benedict XII said that the house at Doberan was in the last stages of desolation and despised by the people and a den of sorcerers and a haunt of brigands.[21] By the time reform was in the air there was little resistance.

Many houses dissolved themselves. Not till 1552 did the duke start to dissolve those that still survived.

Cistercian abbey Dargun: March 1552; no resistance. The abbot became the pastor of the local parish and married. The building came to Duke Ulrich who turned it into his country seat.

Doberan, of which the repute was higher than Pope Benedict XII suggested, was the oldest religious house in Mecklenburg, with graves of

---

[20] Statistics in Alois Schröer, *Die Reformation in Westfalen: der Glaubenskampf einer Landschaft* (Münster, 1983), i. 529 ff.

[21] Benedict XII, *Lettres Communes analysées d'après les registres dit d'Avignon et du Vatican*, ed. J. M. Vidal (Paris, 1910), ii. 284, no. 8155.

Mecklenburg princes. To survive they already had to sell their precious furnishings. Many buildings were already demolished before 1500. Monks disappeared and left the abbot and five monks all old and weak and incapable of
running the property. They made it over voluntarily to the duke. The abbot
retired with pension to the daughter-house of Pelplin in West Prussia, which
being under Polish suzerainty had a chance of survival, though barely. The
house of Doberan was demolished, the materials for government buildings;
the church was sacked during the Thirty Years War but remained a noble
monument. Secularized in 1823, it became the cathedral of the diocese of
Kulm and a seminary of ordinands, most of whom were murdered by the
SS in October 1939.

At Marienehe near Rostock, Carthusian, the prior resisted toughly and
ended by carrying off the deeds and goods to another Carthusian house.

Tempzin bei Brüel, Antonian—these were the order of the Hospital
Brothers of St Antony of Egypt, founded at the time of the crusades with the
special mission to care for St Antony's fire, a form of epilepsy. Only the superior was there and he moved out and the house came to the duke. The church
was newly completed and after four decades became the parish church and
though Lutheran still housed a colossal statue of St Antony.

Rehna nunnery, Premonstratensian. By 1541 eight nuns were left of
whom five were evangelical. The nuns were pensioned eleven years later and
their beautiful church remained in use.

Malchow—the nuns accepted that it was to be a home for the elderly and
that they must receive no new young novices.

The nunnery of Poor Clares at Ribnitz resisted with the protection of a
ducal abbess. Duke John Albert personally argued with the nuns for a whole
day but in vain. They still sang their hours in Latin 'the language of the angels'
and were fully Catholic till about 1572 and then became an evangelical community for the unmarried daughters of the nobility, still in their habits, with
the right to receive novices on the understanding that anyone could leave
if she wished. They accepted German for their services but tried to teach a
little Latin in a girls' school.

Thus several Mecklenburg nunneries adjusted to a new life, quietly and
not unhappily, sometimes making a new community life not unlike the old.
But there were a few Mecklenburg nunneries capable of a resistance which
tested the will of reforming governments. If nuns were numerous and determined, no government liked to use force against pious old ladies.

Dobbertin had thirty nuns, only two were for reform. They finally
accepted a preacher (if unmarried) and the sacrament in two kinds and the
removal of a few pictures and an amended version of their hymn book. But
when the pictures were removed, especially one of St Mary, there was a
tumult of shrieking nuns. When the visitors came for the third time the nuns

flung stones and pails of water and stools at them singing *Salve regina miseri-cordiae*. The nuns won the battle and for the next five years were not disturbed. In the end they became a home for elderly ladies, a few Catholics among them.

Endowments

The endowments of dissolved houses were meant to provide an income for the pensions of the members and then for the needs of the State, but as these were church endowments their primary destinations were expected to be the parish, the pastor, the hospital, the dole, the school, the university, the students of the university—anything that was good for pastoral welfare or health or education. It was a widespread opinion that government in a crisis justifiably used monastic money, even to paying its debts or saving from bankruptcy, for these objects helped society and so were indirectly part of social welfare. In such emergencies Catholic sovereigns stripped monasteries and churches of their 'surplus' silver and there was no reason why the habit should not continue among people who held the silver to be useless or misused.

At Luther's table in 1544 one of those present said that princes turned evangelical to steal church property. Luther replied 'The opposite is true. Ferdinand (of Austria) and the emperor and the bishop of Mainz do it . . . The Bavarians are the worst, they have rich monasteries. My elector and the landgrave have poor monasteries . . .'[22] But he hated what he saw as misappropriation. He shared the general opinion among reformers that all money for charity, as endowments of monasteries could be said to be, ought to remain for charitable objects.

Towns took less of the money for secular purposes than did princes. The treasury of a prince was more likely to be empty, in his wider country areas the control of officials and squires was looser. The worst cases of misappropriation of monastic lands happened when there were years of uncertainty whether that Land would or would not join the Reformation. During vacillation local lords could do much as they liked and they liked most to pocket monasteries. These were also the years when an abbot or prior was most likely to flee with the valuables.

If a state was bankrupt it was acceptable in Catholic times for church money to help save it. But bankruptcy could have more than one cause. Joachim II, elector of Brandenburg 1535–71, the first Protestant elector, was extravagant. His court was expensive, his way of life beyond his means, he loved building, he put the State into intolerable debt. When he reconstructed a church with church money it was the most expensive of buildings, with

---

[22] *TR* v. 306, no. 5663.

golden statues of Christ and Mary and silver statues of the apostles. He used two monasteries to pay the stipend of the court-marshal, and built a fortress with the proceeds of monastery property and abbey silver. His civil servants followed his example. In Brandenburg of 1550 thirty religious houses were in the possession of noblemen with chateaux. Brandenburg, especially in his earlier years, was the classic example of how the monastic moneys ought not to have been used.

A series of visitations established better order in the charities. In the end fifty-two houses out of sixty-six came into state ownership, three were given to the university of Frankfurt an der Oder and to Latin schools. The State used some of the money for various church purposes and especially for many more schools. How far the improvement was due to the Brandenburg general superintendent through much of the period, Johann Agricola, is not clear. His successor, working with an economical elector, may have had more to do with it.[23]

The worst consequence of the debts was not the disappearance of monastery money. In his troubles Joachim II used Jewish advisers and borrowed through their agency. Michel Jude lived in high style at the court and his wife and he enjoyed much favour. He died in an accident and his family were expelled and his heirs dunned the elector for debts. A successor Lippold was made the protector of Jews in the Land and was entrusted with very confidential business like secret payments to the elector's mistresses and very public business like the mint. These 'court-Jews' brought a hatred among the people; so that after Joachim's death Lippold was tortured and confessed incredible crime and mobs sacked the houses of the Jews and the government expelled Jews from the Land. There were nastier consequences of misgovernment than the alienation of church money.

In certain Lands the process was slow because the legal situation was in doubt under Reich law. Lippe was an evangelical state which wanted to dissolve its monasteries. Yet the Catholic bishop of Paderborn had rights and his blocking meant years of delay, so that some were not dissolved till 1571 though much earlier they were not allowed novices. But in the end most of the endowments went to charity. Three of the nunneries continued as communities for Protestant ladies. The house of the Windesheim nuns at Lemgo became a Latin school.[24] The property of the Augustinian canons at

---

[23] Colleague of Luther at the university of Wittenberg, his secretary at the Leipzig disputation, then preacher and headmaster at his birthplace Eisleben, he quarrelled with Luther acrimoniously in 1540 because Agricola seemed to deny the place of law in justification ('antinomian controversy') and to get away from Wittenberg accepted the work at Berlin. Died 1566.

[24] The monastery at Windesheim in Holland was founded by the Brothers of the Common Life in 1387. Other houses joined them—marvellous expansion, about 300 houses in a century. All male houses were dissolved in the age of Napoleon; to be re-created as a male order in 1961.

Blomberg and of the Observant Franciscans at Lemgo went to the State, which created a trust for education and charity.

No one thought the buildings sacred. If a monastery was empty and stood useless in the country it could be sold (proceeds to go to a church fund, ideally), and the stones used for any good object. Stone from monasteries made prisons, dungeons, forts. They were adapted for schools or poorhouses or hospitals, or to repair parish churches.

What happened in Hesse under the landgrave Philip has been studied in detail and made a good model. In 1526 the Synod of Homburg allowed monks and nuns to leave their convents if they wished and appointed visitors to look into the state of the religious houses. At this point many monks and nuns left, and the visitors were immediately confronted with the decision, what to do with the property. The *Landtag* (Hesse parliament) decided that if the religious wanted to continue in prayer and study they could; that if they went out they were to be paid compensation; that money was to found a university at Marburg; and other money was to be used to support the poor and 'other needs of the State'. In the next two years visitors went round the monasteries, many accepted the pensions and many did not.

Marburg was founded, the earliest Protestant university. Four hospitals were created, three survived into the twentieth century; two nunneries were left as communities for the daughters of the upper classes; student grants were created to send poor young people to the university; a school to prepare for the university was founded; pastors' stipends were raised and regulated; poor chests were created or supplemented in the towns; other schools and parishes were created; several abbey churches became parish churches. The State kept some of the endowment.

Like most reforms, it worked more cumbersomely than this sounds.

Outside the gates of Magdeburg was the rich Benedictine house of Berge, founded by the emperor Otto the Great. When the town went evangelical, the situation of the monks was impossible and a mob looted the abbey. Benedictine life continued under miserable difficulty which grew until 1549 when a Catholic army besieged the town. Under this threat the town council could not afford a Catholic outpost not far from its walls and destroyed the abbey and the church and took away organ and choirstalls and bells and silver and archives. Still the house continued with a few monks and rich property but neither abbey nor church. In 1561 they elected a new abbot, Peter Ulner, a Benedictine from Holland, who was an able administrator. He rebuilt the abbey with a new and smaller church and mended the finances. His position was tenable only if he was friendly with the evangelical town council. In 1565 he preached a Lutheran sermon in his church, brought German hymns into use, and reformed the liturgy of the mass. Then he started to train evangelical ordinands and founded a school in the abbey and built a library. So a historic Ottonian house, felt to be no longer useful in its old function, was turned into a valuable place of reformed education. It continued till the time of Napoleon.

As a general rule:

1. The object of reforming powers was to close monasteries and nunneries because they were undesirable and because they could not carry out their Reformation without the closure.

2. A minority of monks were forced to leave their houses; for many left of their own will. As Erasmus said, there were far too many monks for the health of the institution and many monks then in monasteries had no 'vocation' thereto. Probably a majority of nuns were forced to leave their houses though many left freely. The worst happened when local officials, told to get nuns out of a convent somehow, bullied helpless and determined ladies. But many nuns were allowed to stay on in their houses provided they partly conformed to the new evangelical environment; but with a problem of ageing and care of the old as novices were refused to them.

3. A pension from the endowments of the house was paid to those who left, whether they left of their free will or because they were thrust out. If a superior helped the dissolution the pension might be good; and better monks easily found new work as pastors. But poorer states paid poor pensions.

4. Those who wished to continue as contemplatives or as Benedictine-type monks of a regular life had to move to another part of Germany or to another country. For the old the journey could be formidable.

5. It was easier for the monk who went out than for the nun because he was not dependent upon finding someone to marry and there were more jobs available to him. Many of the Protestant parishes in the next two decades were staffed by pastors who were former monks. In ex-monks the publishers had a unique source of educated men as ill-paid proofreaders and compositors of learned texts. The schools needed teachers, the universities needed scholars.

6. In this vast transfer of property from a series of private corporations to the State there was room for hanky-panky, especially over the movable articles of any value, or when the State was desperate for money to balance its budget, or when the government of that state was not in control of its greedy lords or officials. But many funds were transferred to schools, universities, parishes, stipends of clergy, and the welfare institutions from hospices to hospitals.

7. There was no sign of regret, all across the reforming world, that something valuable in a historic way of prayer or charity was being lost to Christendom. In his long memory Martin Luther showed signs of understanding the stature of the dedicated life and proved this practically by his

stalwart defence of the Brothers and nuns at Herford; and with Lutheranism communities of unmarried men and women continued into modern times. But the attitude rested on conviction that the way of the Bible could not justify withdrawal from normal social life; and that it was so essential to prove that the world is God-given, and that no soul needed to retreat from it to be holy, that Catholic orders were better gone.

Philip Melanchthon was liable to depressions. At one time he fell into a deep depression because his son-in-law George Sabinus was so unkind to his daughter. Then he wanted not to see anyone or speak to anyone. Luther worried about him and consulted Cruciger and others on how to help him. 'I get depressions and temptations—then I find company, which is a good form of consolation. A person is not strong if sad and solitary even if fortified by Scripture. . . . Monks and hermits—invention of Satan; outside God's plan and order. By creation every human being is a political or an economic or an ecclesiastical person. No one escapes this condition of life except by a miracle. So far as we can, we must not live alone.'[25]

At another time: 'Papists and anabaptists say that if you wish to know Christ, try to be alone, don't mix with people. This is diabolical advice. . . . You cannot help your neighbours unless you keep company with them. Solitude is against marriage, against earning a living, against taking a part in politics—and against a Christ-like life, for he did not like to be alone, he stirred trouble for a government, always had people about him, was never alone except to pray. Down with people who say *Like to be alone for so you will be pure in heart.*'[26]

The consequence for women

Literature shows how the life of women, at least of those in the educated classes, differed in the sixteenth century from the life of their predecessors; but why is not clear; whether from the rise of a more numerous middle class, or from the growing number of educated women, or from the decline of nunneries, or from one of those mysterious social axioms which take hold of a society and leave history to guess at the reasons. Reformation had the ideal of a universal education though it could not achieve it and this meant many more girls at school though the provision for their education never rivalled that for boys except among the upper classes. The new insistence on teaching, by sermon or catechism or printed tract, meant that numerous women were familiar with the Bible and a few were expert in theology and held their own with male disputants.

---

[25] *TR* iii. 592–3, no. 3754 (1538).   [26] *TR* ii. 50–1, no. 1329 (1532).

The Reformation changed the ideal of the virgin dedicated to God as the highest ideal of womanhood, to the ideal of wife and mother. But historians crudely guess that with dangers of male birth and of war and the longer life of women the number of adult women was larger than the number of men, perhaps by as much as 10 per cent. It has been reckoned that 40 per cent of women at the end of the Middle Ages were single but it is hard to find evidence to make this more than conjecture. No one doubts an excess of women. For centuries society met this excess by nunneries. Working-class women were needed in the fields, or the textile industries, or as midwives, or shopkeepers, or cleaners, or in taverns; and there was an ill-paid but risky employment for prostitutes. Working-class parents who had enough money for a dowry, or could find a foundation which gave grants for dowries to the daughters of poor parents, sent their child into a nunnery, it was a secure way of life, the chance of rise in social respect for the girl and her family, and an opening to a little education. And among the middle and upper classes the nunnery was the only respectable future for a girl who did not marry and there must be some because enough husbands did not exist. And girls chose to be nuns, as in all ages, because they wished to dedicate themselves to God, or at times for lesser motives like fear of childbirth or of maternal responsibility.

Reformers tried to sweep prostitutes off the streets. They refused to allow novices to enter nunneries. They tried to persuade nuns in their houses to leave. It was a question what the unmarried women were to do.

Nothing need stop them continuing to live in a family home and say their prayers. There were priests and ex-monks who looked for wives. With many more schools for girls there was a need for more women as teachers. With a more developed welfare system there was a need for almoners and carers. With a growing middle class there was a need for more domestic servants. The nursing care of the pregnant and the old and the orphan, which nuns often looked after, was still a need and more of a need because there was a more enquiring system for finding out who must have help. A rising population wanted more midwives and on several occasions there were female doctors in gynaecology. Many church orders expected the midwife to baptize, especially when the baby was in danger.

It has been argued that the closing of so many nunneries was a loss to the female sex because it abolished so many posts of responsibility—prioresses, abbesses, etc.; a sphere in which males still had authority as directors of souls and confessors but being an outside authority were weaker because at a remove. To the contrary it has been argued that the number of truly responsible posts was few and in those days of plentiful nunneries the average convent was not filled with dedicated and wise women, so that life in such a nunnery was disciplined in the sense of being unfree and at times was a petty

tyranny with humiliations and solitary confinement and corporal punishment. It was argued on this side that reformation opened doors to women in
three ways; by encouraging more individual liberty; by offering education to
girls; and by releasing many women upon the world instead of shutting them
up in cells.

A feminist scholar examined change in Augsburg and argued this plea to
be mistaken. The town created a more patriarchal society and continued the
refusal to allow women to share in the workshop system. The ideal was home
and family and the ideal of womanhood was centred even more upon her
hearth. This argument went further in speculation about the nature and
effect of private devotion. Previously the Blessed Virgin had been for many
simpler people a mother-god. Reformers regarded that as an excess, a bit of
the clutter if not superstition which pushed between the soul and its
Redeemer. On this theory they took away from the female sex a supreme
cult figure with whom women could identify; and in their weakening of
devotion to saints they deprived the sex of feminine models for imitation and
reverence.[27] The argument is awkward because Mary was the saint of the
home; of childbirth and parenthood; modesty; readiness to accept providence, and to endure suffering in the beloved. To diminish her cult in
society would hardly be likely to add to an opinion that women were too
confined to the home. Perhaps the contrary.

There were three ways, two usual and one unusual, in which women of
the evangelical countries exercised influence or even power. More than one
reforming prince owed conversion to his wife and what happened afterwards
in his state was affected by her attitude. In one area women were exceptionally effective, the street demonstration. They were less liable to severity of
punishment and their voices carried further.

Amid the society of upper-class ladies examples may be taken from wives
of the Hohenzollern family.

The elector of Brandenburg, Joachim I, was the brother of Archishop
Albert of Mainz and himself a convinced astrologer and dedicated opponent
of the Reformation. He married Elizabeth of the royal house of Denmark
because there seemed to be a chance (which turned out to be vain) that she
might bring him part of Schleswig-Holstein. She remained a pious Catholic
for thirty-five years of her life and seven years of marriage. During the
middle 1520s her personal physician introduced her to Martin Luther's
writings and at much the same time her brother the king of Denmark lost
his throne and became a Protestant. Unlike her brother's, hers was a true
religious conversion.

---

[27] Lyndal Roper, *The Holy Household* (Oxford, 1989).

In the autumn of 1525 she complained to Duke Albert of Prussia that her husband was hostile to the Word of God. Joachim showed zeal that his wife should not desert the Catholic faith. He seemed to hate her; and she attributed this hatred not only to the growing cleavage in religion, but to the presence of another woman in his life.

Returning from Breslau in May 1527 he found that she had received communion in both kinds on Easter Day. He was scandalized and determined on violence unless she promised to recant. But he dealt with a convert: 'Christ who saved me twice can save me for the third time if it is his will; if not, his will be done.'[28] Joachim summoned his three bishops and various abbots and doctors of divinity and asked whether he could put her to death. They advised that he could not. Then could he put her away publicly? They said it was possible but they would not advise it. They thought it better that he should shut her up in a castle.

Joachim gave her till Easter 1528 to recant. She sent a secret message to Elector John of Saxony asking if she might come. The answer was Yes; and so she fled to Torgau on a farm wagon in the dress of a peasant girl. Joachim publicly accused her of stealing money and furniture and papers and how she complained of him to his estates as mean. She replied that she gave a few bits of her furniture to her brother; the money she took was only six gulden; and the paper was a pawn-ticket.

Both Luther and Melanchthon had a doubt. Was it right to encourage a wife to desert a husband?

Everyone tried to find conditions acceptable for her return. But for her a sine qua non was the right to pray as she thought right and receive a reformed sacrament, and Joachim rejected any such plan. So she lived in a Saxon castle, often with too little money, and wrote letters to influence her two sons, and befriended her local Lutheran pastor, and studied the Bible and the writings of the reformers, until it was said 'She can put male doctors of Scripture to shame.' During the middle 1530s she stayed at Wittenberg and grew closer to Luther personally. He found her in sickness of body and turmoil of mind and pitied her and judged that she was a holy person.

When Joachim I died in 1535 Brandenburg was divided between his two sons, Joachim II as the elector of Brandenburg, Johann (Hans) of Küstrin as the margrave of Neumark. Both sons pleaded with their mother to come home. They were different, Joachim II was conservative, loved ritual and vestments and choirs, and sometimes conducted the choir himself. But he went along with moderate Protestant change, like the chalice and the marriage of clergy, and consulted Melanchthon. Hans, though almost as convinced an astrologer as his father, was more vigorous in reform. His laws on behaviour were unusual, the penalty for swearing was twice as high for noblemen as for commoners.

Elizabeth was not sure that all was well; the Catholic rites which Brandenburg maintained she could not approve, she was not happy when Joachim married a second wife Hedwig who was a Pole and kept Catholic services in her private chapel and could hardly speak German, and she lamented Joachim's choice of a court chaplain and general superintendent, Agricola, for she knew that he and Luther had quarrelled. She hesitated; and did not return home for five years. When at last she came she lived quietly at Spandau not without a little influence on her sons; and when she died Agricola, of whom she disapproved so warmly, preached her funeral sermon in which he described her as 'expert in theology, a true saint, a child of God'.[29]

The Pole Electress Hedwig broke a thigh and damaged her back in the collapse of a floor at a hunting lodge and spent the last twenty-two years of her life in invalid retirement. A mistress took her place, Anna Sydow, daughter of a civil servant, probably the first 'ducal' mistress to be recognized publicly in a Protestant country. Joachim II treated her as his wife. The people minded that she sometimes wore male costume when she went out with him, but excused the relationship because of the invalid Pole. She grew quite rich. He gave her a daughter whom the emperor made into a countess. When Joachim died his son immediately locked her up. She does not seem to have affected religion except that her brother-in-law became court chaplain and then the dean.

Joachim's brother Hans of Küstrin had a very different wife. Seven years before he was a Protestant he was betrothed at the age of sixteen to Katharina, daughter of the strenuous opponent of Protestants, Heinrich of Brunswick, and married her when he was twenty-three. When he became a decided Protestant she went with him and then he was tough in dissolving all the monasteries and nunneries and collegiate foundations, not without the use of force, and of appropriating church silver. Many schools were founded, even in larger villages, though there the verger was usually the schoolmaster. She gave him two daughters and no male child, so that the two parts of Brandenburg were later reunited. But she had ideas about industry for the prosperity of the people. Granted an estate she imported into it Dutch textile workers and then built a paper mill and a printing press, and remained the manager of the 'new town' and its various concerns. The people loved her and called her 'Mother Katy'.

[29] Johannes Schultze, *Die Mark Brandenburg* (Berlin, 1964), iv. 95; E. D. M. Kirchner, *Die Churfürstinnen und Königinnen auf der Throne der Hohenzollern* (Berlin, 1866–70), i. 232–90.

Certainly the old mode of influencing politics—the vision of a pious person, whereby Bridget of Sweden or Catherine of Siena bombarded popes and monarchs with warnings and exhortations and commands from God and thereby made a difference, or seemed to make a difference, to what politicians did, was no longer open to women in a Protestant world. In Wittenberg or Geneva such spirituals were more likely to be shut up as mentally disturbed.

An eminent scholar surveyed the family law of the Reformation and reached this conclusion:

The first generation of Protestant reformers died believing they had released women into the world by establishing them firmly at the centre of the home and family life, no longer to suffer the withdrawn, culturally circumscribed, sexually repressed, male-regulated life of a cloister. And they believed children would never again be consigned at an early age to involuntary celibacy but would henceforth remain in the home, objects of constant parental love and wrath, until they were all properly married.[30]

[30] S. Ozment, *When Fathers Ruled: Family Life in Reformation Europe* (Cambridge, Mass., 1983), 49.

9

THE NEW SERVICES

Everyone agreed that services in church should be simpler, with less elaborate ritual; that they should be in the language which the people understood; and that they should contain nothing which was contrary to Scripture or could not be justified from Scripture. No one doubted that Christians pray on Sunday the Lord's Day; that the sacrament of holy communion was the chief Christian service, and because the apostles received both bread and wine that was right for all Christians; that services should be apostolic in that they communicated the Christian gospel and therefore there should be teaching-preaching, more of it than most congregations had experienced, and that this preaching should be based upon the Bible; that ministers of services should not simply be able to repeat forms of words but must be able to teach and so must receive training; that part of their teaching must be to instruct the growing young so that they understood the essence of the gospel and what they did when they shared in the sacrament. That was much that they agreed.

It was also agreed that the congregation should be a people that took part with the clergy and did not sit or stand silent while the clergy read the service or the choir sang. How this could be done was harder. Half of many congregations could not read, so that they could not be expected to join in words of praise or penitence unless they were taught to say them from memory; and if they needed books, enough books even for a hundred people in a village was as yet a prohibitive expense. A choir could practise its music and be trained to sing beautifully. If the congregation were encouraged to join what would happen to beauty? If, as every reformer believed, no worship was complete without a declaration of the Word of God, it was possible that the time during which the congregation did not participate would be longer because they must sit silent to listen.

Those who thought about prayer and praise recognized another difficulty in what they now had to do. They knew that familiarity with the words of prayer is an aid to worship. This was not as sore a problem as a modern age has found it because the majority of the congregation was not familiar with the old prayers, and hardly used them meaningfully, since they were in Latin. To put them into German, French, English, Danish, etc. would speed up the familiarity with which ordinary people could take prayers into their cherished possession. Nevertheless some recognized that it would help if the new language which the people understood kept close to the old Latin which a minority half-understood.

This was made more complex because the people began to have an influence on the way in which they worshipped. A reformer respectful of the past and beloved ways of prayer—like Martin Luther when he started thinking of all this—might say, keep the mass in Latin, the choir will be helped by the old cadences, the people will know where they are in the service—but cut out from the Latin prayers what is not scriptural doctrine, like the sacrifice of Christ at the altar; shorten the prolonged choral twiddles which keep the people passive; give the people the cup as well as the bread at communion; let the readings be in the language they know; and teach them truth from the pulpit. Then they would feel the service the same service as the old but they will like the readings in their language and be glad they receive the cup at communion; and so there will be no feeling of radical change or of a congregation disorientated because it has lost its bearings in the way of worship.

But in many places the people were less conservative than those who led their prayers. If it had penetrated their heads, or their bellies, that mass was pollution, they resented a service too like mass. They wanted more radical simplicity. That affected what the drafters of services could do. And there were drafters of services who wanted a radical simplicity whatever their people liked. At Michaelmas 1521 a congregation at Wittenberg received communion in both kinds without waiting for any authority to tell them to do so; and their young professor Melanchthon thought they did right. And when the people were engaged, it was easy for a spell-binding uninstructed preacher to climb into the pulpit and abhor the iniquity of mass and proclaim how everything must be changed. In Wittenberg it was an Austin Friar Gabriel Zwilling—stay away from mass, it is idolatry, it is superstition, it is a memorial, it is not a sacrifice (6 October 1521). From his brother-friars he had so much sympathy that his prior stopped all saying of mass in the monastery.

In such moods there was not time for wise liturgists to sit on a committee and draft forms of service. The students of the university could not wait. In the parish church that 3 December they stopped priests who were trying to celebrate early private masses and when the time came for high mass they seized the service books and drove the priests from the altar. The next day forty students crashed into the Franciscan house and broke an altar.

Forty students breaking one wooden altar would change nothing. But the town stood at a turning-point. The people knew little about the mass, or arguments on its nature, but had the belly-sense that what happened was corruption to which men and women with consciences ought not to conform, that priests were doing wrong by them; and that pay was the reason why this happened. There had to be revised forms of service if the people were going to accept them. These revisions must be achieved without disturbance in church and therefore soon. They must also be achieved legally—which meant with the leave of the elector Frederick the Wise of Saxony; who decided, since he had a divided town and university and chapter, that no innovation be made. But the people would make the innovations whether he said so or not; and because he said not, they would be unruly.

On Christmas Eve in Wittenberg a crowd banged into the parish church and knocked the lamps about and disturbed the service with popular songs. The police arrived and they retired to sing songs in the churchyard. In the Christmas morning at All Saints the archdeacon and dean of the theological faculty, Carlstadt, invited all the two thousand people to participate in a reformed service that day and every Sunday afterwards. He wore lay clothes to preach; talked of how you could not prepare yourself to receive by outward rules but only by penitence and faith in the heart. Here is forgiveness of sins and it needs no private absolution from a priest. Then he went to the altar and celebrated the mass in Latin; but left out the words which contained the language of sacrifice; and left out the elevation; and then he gave them all communion from the chalice as well as from the paten. The communicants took the bread and the chalice with their hands. It was the first of the reformed services: the old liturgy, still in Latin, with much simplified ritual, with a sermon, with the omission of the idea of sacrifice, and a distribution in two kinds. Except for the use of Latin, and except for the reformed refusal to accept that lay clothes were appropriate for the celebrant, it remained the pattern of a reformed sacrament. On New Year's Day almost all the city of Wittenberg received the communion in both kinds. Some of the Saxon country clergy began to distribute the communion in both kinds. Some of them wore vestments, a few wore simpler vestments or none.

In those months where everything seemed possible, it was hard to gather the right mood for the new and it was easy to offend taste by an attempt at innovation which could be mocked. At Ellenburg Friar Gabriel Zwilling's first attempt at reformed vestments was ludicrous. This did not mean that the first uncertain efforts would last. Zwilling later became a sober and respected Lutheran pastor, eventually at the elector's seat at Torgau, and so loyal to the Reformation that when it was assailed by force thirty-seven years later he was ejected from his parish for refusal to compromise.

Apart from the question of using Latin or vestments, there was the doubt about art and music. If it is right to simplify so as to be rid of the clutter which seemed to put furniture between the worshipper and God, does that doctrine apply to painting or statues or music? Are the arts a help to the soul—as architects should try to build a house of God worthy of the high end which is its purpose, should its decoration inside be the best which human artists can devise? Statues and certain paintings were suspect because they had been the focus of superstition among the people. But the doubt was wider than that. Perhaps artistic decoration diverted the soul away from the one thought that matters and blocked the single-minded apprehension of the divine.

The argument for a form of service in German was now powerful and by some was already felt urgent. In Allstedt Thomas Müntzer started to use a form in German. The first such printed form was already used in that year 1522 by the Carmelite prior at Nördlingen. Wherever these German forms were used it was found that the people liked them and that they met a need. Other places began to follow the example. The Nördlingen form said that a priest is not needed to celebrate the sacrament. Its order was: confession, absolution, invocation of the Holy Spirit, preface and Sanctus, consecration prayer, Our Father, O Lamb of God, elevation, kiss of peace, communion, Te Deum, and final prayer. This form was often printed and was used in several other German cities, including for a short time Nuremberg and Strasbourg. The people of Germany liked to have their prayers in a language they could understand; and they liked to have their way of worship in the manner to which they were accustomed since they were children. The new German liturgy fulfilled both these desires. They understood better; but what happened in church was much like what happened to them before; and the two chief differences were that they must not mind if they knew that their pastor was married and they were offered the chalice as well as the paten when they went to receive.

Wittenberg, which everyone looked upon as the leader, was slower to use German. This was due partly to the elector Frederick the Wise and partly to Luther. The elector was shocked by the disturbances which accompanied the changes in Wittenberg—the fanaticism of three 'prophets' out of Zwickau who claimed to be God-inspired, the way in which the orderly removal of pictures and altars from churches by the town council was made disorderly by excited crowds who joined the officials and lent too-willing hands. The elector was not one who liked to interfere. But he also had the Reich to consider. He could not afford to weaken the place of Saxony within the empire, not merely by rescuing an outlaw in Luther (a rescue not supposed to be known), but by becoming scandalous through the empire by what happened in church. His relative George, duke of the other Saxony, laid a formal complaint with the Reich government. The bishop of Meissen tried to intervene with the elector to stop this new liturgy. Nor could the elector wish that such notoriety could hurt a young and now famous university which was an ornament and an economic benefit to his state. Parents began to recall their sons home from their studies.

Luther, so radical in public affairs, was a conservative in devotion. In spite
of the risk to an outlaw he returned from the Wartburg to Wittenberg on
6 March 1522 and at once faced the problem of forms of service. He was sure
that changes were needed but was also sure that the feelings of persons who
loved forms of prayer to which they were accustomed ought to be respected;
care of a people's faith must mean gradualness.

His two basic documents were the *Form of the Mass* (*Formula Missae*) of
1523 where everything was taken still to be in Latin—because this was the
international language, and the historic language, and good for the young
people who were learning Latin—and published two years later, the *German
Mass* (*Deutsche Messe*).

He took two or three more years than reformers elsewhere in Germany to
arrive at the result but when at last he moved it was the influential change. No
early forms of reformed worship had a more general influence than these two
little books. They followed the order of the Roman mass almost exactly,
except that the consecration prayer was confined to the words of institution
and there was no formal offertory and there was always a sermon. The 'tone'
of the service was a little more educating than the old, it should explain to the
people what they are doing. Liturgical experts afterwards accused him of
being an amateur in ordering ways of worship but he had more effect on
them than any expert in the history of liturgy.

In the 1523 rite he did not mind candles nor incense, if a congregation
wanted them they were free to use them. He was against mixing water with
the wine but if the people thought that right he did not mind. He allowed the
minister to say the words of institution silently if they found that reverent. He
liked an elevation of the sacrament but recognized that this was for the 'weak
in faith' because they were used to it. He accepted the old vestments but said
there was to be no pomp. Private confession beforehand was not to be
demanded but it was good. The Agnus Dei, O Lamb of God, should be sung.
It is absolutely necessary that communion be given to the people in wine as
well as bread. At mass there should be German hymns. Weekday masses
should be discontinued but the daily offices of prayer, mattins, evensong,
compline, are biblical and good. The German mass provided that everyone
should sing the Creed in German, that men and women should continue to sit
on opposite sides of the church, and that the women should come up to receive
communion after the men. He turned against customs like the Lenten veil,
and palms on Palm Sunday, and long hours of preaching on Good Friday.

About these new experiments in public worship the evangelicals had a
sense of excitement. They felt gratitude that they had come back to a way of
prayer nearer the prayers among apostles and the earliest Christians.

During the first thirty or forty years of Reformation services, there was a
freedom to alter, modify, further experiment, as the local pastor or his people

judged edifying. But throughout history such freedom has proved more risky than the desire for reverence and good taste tolerates. From 1550 onwards the state authorities, advised by committees of pastors or by consistories of mixed lay and clerical membership, controlled the forms and such liturgies were made part of the law of the Land. The forms then approved lasted, with insignificant changes, until the earlier half of the nineteenth century.

Everyone must receive the wine as well as the bread. Chalices must be larger, and the jugs on the credence table, and as various rites went on mixing water with the wine, jugs also for water, usually of glass. The old monstrance for displaying the sacrament to adoration (if the church inherited a monstrance, it was far from universal in Catholic churches then) was removed and usually sold. The pyx for reserving the sacrament was not needed because the bread and wine were believed by the evangelical theologians to be sacred during their use at communion but not when in an aumbry or cupboard. But a number of evangelical churches used the pyx as a ciborium or vessel for carrying the bread at the offertory.

Questions remained to solve:

1. A conservative might receive the bread and leave the altar. Must he or she be excommunicated for refusing to receive the wine? No: respect a weak faith but still faith.
2. Private masses are wrong. Suppose the pastor arrives to celebrate an announced communion, and no one else comes, may he celebrate? Most thought that he could not though he should read prayers. But this opinion was not universal.
3. Is it permissible to have a daily mass with communion? Yes (Catholic rule).
4. Transubstantiation is very wrong but the bread and wine become the body and blood of Christ, or (Calvin, Bucer) communicants receive the body and blood. In the former, Lutheran doctrine, is there a moment in the service when these elements become specially sacred? Does it happen, as Catholics said, at the words of the consecration said by the priest? Or does it happen as the communicant receives the gift?

Johann Saliger came young from persecuted Antwerp to be evangelical pastor in Lübeck. He held with vehemence that the first of these must be the truth. (1) It agrees with the evidence of Scripture, This is my Body. (2) The other idea, presence in receiving and not before, opens the way to the Swiss idea which has the danger of making Presence not an objective presence but dependent on the faith of the communicant. (3) There is a practical consequence: suppose at the communion the bread is finished and more is needed, must more be consecrated or does that not matter?

In Lübeck Saliger and a colleague were accused of Catholicizing and had to leave. He was given a parish in Rostock on condition he kept silence on the question. But he could not keep silence. When he was called a papist he charged the critics with being Calvinists, and Rostock was disturbed. Both sides had their defenders, Saliger had to leave Rostock for Wismar where everyone was on his side. The argument was not settled and could not be. For everyone was agreed that the gift was not dependent on the faith of the communicant though only persons with faith received it to their blessing.

The altar was originally the table which in the early Church the Christians needed for the bread and wine, and at first it could be used for other purposes of that household. But by AD 120 the table could already be called 'a place of sacrifice'; for already the eucharist was a remembrance of the crucifixion and shared in that sacrifice, and the language of sacrifice was not slow to grow round its understanding. But still the table was commonly called a table. As Latin-speakers were converted to the Church, they found it natural not only to use *mensa* (a table), but *ara* (an altar), and then *altare*. There were those who disliked this, it seemed to hint that nasty customs of heathen temples might have parallels among Christians. When by the third century they ceased to be content with private rooms but had halls set apart for worship, the table became a piece of furniture only used for the purpose of worship, like the speaker's dais and the bishop's chair. In each place of worship was no more than one altar and it was still movable. By 600, the age of Pope Gregory the Great, there could be several altars in one church—but only in the West. For reasons of convenience it stood on steps, to be visible to the congregation. Often it now had the shape less of a table than of a box, the object being that the body of a saint might lie beneath the table. It was not long nor wide because nothing might be put upon it, except the book of the Gospels, chalice, and paten, which hardly needed space; until the twelfth century the cross would stand behind it, so also candles for light. It attracted ornament, even gold and silver. It had become a holy place rather than a table. Only clergy were supposed to approach it. When the idea of asylum grew up, fugitives from the police were regarded as unpursuable if they took refuge at the altar because it was holy ground. From soon after 1200 the ornamented and often beautiful reredoses appeared as a backcloth to the altar.

The way the Reformation started meant that something must be done about altars. They were associated with sacrifice which was now thought to be a wrong view of holy communion. They appeared in numerous corners of the church and then were associated with a cult of saints, or with relics, and had pictures on the reredos which critics now found distasteful. If it was not a place of sacrifice should it be called an altar?

Luther believed it should still be raised, that was convenience. Nothing wrong with candles, people must see. Nothing wrong with a crucifix on the altar, it reminds worshippers of that which they should specially remember at the sacrament. Almost all evangelicals followed his example, they left the altars in their churches. Many churches left the side-altars but did not use them for worship. They liked to change the pictures into portrayals of the sacraments and the preaching of the Word.

Zwingli was radical. The altar is a table. It should be of wood, and movable. For the sacrament it should be brought down to the middle of the church among the people. The name of altar was slowly driven out of use as misleading. To the visitor the marked difference from the Lutherans was the posture at receiving the sacrament. In the north the communicants still came up to the altar to receive bread and wine kneeling from the hands of the pastor(s), in all the Swiss Reformed Churches worshippers sat round and passed the bread and the cup from hand to hand. This last was the marked difference for the visitor. The liturgy was simpler and more unlike the mass though it kept the essence: readings of the New Testament, penitence, Creed (Apostles Creed instead of the Nicene for ease of understanding), Our Father, consecration prayer. The aim and spirit of the whole was quietness and contemplation.

Confession

The sacrament of confession was suspect to Protestants. It had been compulsory. In small Catholic communities there were social penalties for not going to an annual private confession to a priest. In the Middle Ages bishops had wanted to make it compulsory at least three times a year (Christmas and Whitsuntide as well as Easter) but the fourth Lateran Council of 1215 recognized that this was impracticable and made the rule of once a year. Naturally such a rule must carry with it 'the secret of the confessional', the absolute duty of the priest not to pass on what he learnt in confession.

Catholic churches began about 1400 to have chairs which were the place of confession and which were usually placed near the altar. The confessional boxes familiar to later Catholics were post-Reformation. Priests wore stoles as signs of their spiritual authority and in the absolution it was the custom to lay their hands upon the head of the penitent.

In its ideas of penance the sacrament had not been far from the world of the indulgence which had gone so manifestly wrong. Murderers and thieves went to the confessional because they must but omitted to mention their crime which perhaps did not trouble their conscience. At the other end pious nuns went to confession because it was thought pious and perhaps in examining their conscience for sin could only locate a passing disinclination to say the prayers of None. The reason for the demand had only been fully explained in the high Middle Ages, that the priest had full power, by applying the Redeemer's work, to wipe away all the sins which had been committed since baptism, if the sinner was truly contrite. The form of words in which the priest declares 'I absolve you . . .' was late, only made the rule by Pope Eugenius IV in 1439.

Luther when a monk had seen the better side of pastoral care in the use of confession. But he also suffered from its worse side, to make a soul through introspection horrified at its own sinfulness, to make fear rather than faith the centre of devotional life. Hence he resisted, successfully, Protestant demands that confession was bad and must be abolished; while at the same time he tried to rid the sacrament of what he regarded as its wrongful features in practice.

Sacrament is not the wrong word; for though the Reformed in Switzerland declared that in the Bible only two sacraments could be found, communion and baptism, the evangelicals of Germany accepted three sacraments which included confession, and appealed to the scriptural text in James 5: 16, 'confess your sins one to another'. In Lutheran church orders and catechisms confession was continued, always as a preparation before going to the communion. It usually happened on the Saturday evening before a day of communion.

Evangelicals believed in the confessional in this form as a means of devotion and moral discipline. They disliked three parts of the tradition: first, the burden, so that people's consciences were tormented into thinking that they must search out every little thing to say to the priest; secondly, where the confessor tried to frighten penitents so that they would go often to confession; and thirdly where the confessing person used it as a ritual to be fulfilled without true penitence. Since the best Catholics agreed on these later points, Protestant writing on how confession should be reformed had much in common with that among reforming Catholics.

In Catholic confessionals there was a custom of much questioning. Most comers were not articulate, might not even know what was sin and what was not, they needed helping to see, the confessor was expected to be dominant—did you do? have you been? In Basel Oecolampadius regarded such confessors as psycho-tyrants and laid down the rule that if going to confession was not liberation it was not a right way of confession.

If this was true of a confession expected before communion at Easter, it was even truer of a deathbed confession, where evangelicals hated pain caused to a dying person by insistence that he or she be reminded in detail of what they did wrong; rather they should be reminded of their baptism, and their membership of Christ's servants, and the free grace which God offered to them. Many Catholics agreed.

Does the declaration of forgiveness after confession need a priest to say the words? That was Catholic rule, the authority to bind and loose given to the priest at ordination. But Catholics could conceive exceptions—for example a prisoner awaiting execution could receive absolution from any fellow

Christian. Evangelical ideas sounded rather different but in practice were much the same. They agreed that an ordained pastor should be the minister of forgiveness. But they seemed to expect that more emergencies might occur when a lay confessor was needed, and Luther believed that in such emergencies a woman or even a minor could be the minister of absolution.[1]

The custom that absolution should be symbolized by the confessor laying hands upon the head of the penitent continued among the Lutherans. In north Germany and Scandinavia the sacrament of confession was an important part of church life until the Thirty Years War. It did not vanish after that but during the later seventeenth century evangelical critics began to share the view of the Swiss Reformed.

The Swiss Reformed abolished private confession, as sacrament. They insisted instead that there be a general confession, penitence by all the congregation at the beginning of the service and that the minister should declare to the people that the penitent share in the Redeemer's forgiveness. They accepted that persons with troubled consciences could go to the pastor privately and seek his advice and receive a declaration of absolution. But this was nothing to do with the liturgy, had no necessary connection with a sacrament, was not likely to take place in church, and was a form of private consultation within the pastor's care.

In a few evangelical towns the council wanted to provide for persons who did not wish to come to private confession. The liturgy, it was argued (as among the Swiss), ought to contain a general confession of penitence. This proposal ran into tough opposition. If we provide a general confession, shall we persuade the people that private confession is not needed whereas it is a helpful moral discipline? In Nuremberg Osiander, without aid from his pastor-colleagues, hotly resisted the introduction of a general absolution, even to the extent of disobeying the magistrates when he framed the church order, and had to be overruled. Even then he went on preaching fiercely against it—devil's work, anyone who designs this form of service is led by Satan, and so on. The council kept it in the service but allowed Osiander not to use it and things were easier though he still denounced it.

Hymns

Christians inherited their first hymns from the Jewish psalms. In the third century began to be written specially Christian hymns not drawn from the psalms and it was at once seen that if a hymn is to be sung by many people four short lines is the easiest meter; the four-line stanza became much the commonest. But as a collection of songs to be sung by the congregation the hymn

---

[1] *WA* ii. 716, *Ein Sermon von dem Sacrament der Busse* (1519).

book dates from the Reformation. The people had been allowed a few hymns at great festivals, and were familiar with the carol, and in later medieval Germany where friars made a popular sermon into the whole of the service they sometimes sang a German hymn before and after. But there were no hymns in most services, people could not read. If they were sung they were sung by choirs.

But now printers could produce hymn books, and more worshippers were able to read.

Luther asked for poets who should take the hymns of the Middle Ages and make them available and should write more hymns which should be suitable for use in worship. In the preface to the Wittenberg hymnal of 1524 he wrote: 'I am not of the opinion that the gospel should bring down the arts . . . All the arts, and especially music, ought to be used in the service of God who made them.'[2] In his conversation he would from time to time assert that Satan is against music; or say 'Music is a glorious gift of God and near theology.'[3] He loved it himself, was moved as he played his lute, found joy and a lifting from his melancholies, and liked to hear the birds especially nightingales at their song and believed that if people were singing they could not be villainous. He wrote to several of his friends asking them to compose hymns.[4]

It had never been easy to define how a hymn differs from a popular song for unison singing. Appropriateness depended on the subject of the song, but not only that, the mode of expression, the poetic quality, its power as a ve-hicle of reverence or sincerity of feeling. Doggerel did not make a hymn. It must also be suitable for constant repetition in the way that a good prayer was constantly repeated and never boring as the staple of a people's devotion. It was also discovered that a religious song suitable for singing in the home may not be right for a congregation. Certain hymns started as household poetry and were only slowly accepted by public assemblies as fitting.

Luther told his friends not to use slang, nor pretentious words, the words must be easy to understand but also be fitting and pure. He helped to invent the metrical psalm for congregations; that is, the translation of psalms into German metrical stanzas in such a form that a body of people could sing them in unison. This was soon the important part of Protestant hymn books. For a long time in the Swiss tradition from Zurich to Scotland, which sus-pected words used in church if they were not in the Bible, the metrical psalter became the hymn book.

The first Lutheran hymns were printed in little sheets, a single hymn or two or three. Printers collected them. Churches in Wittenberg sang them before the end of 1523.

---

[2] *WA* xxxv. 475.   [3] *TR* ii. 2387.
[4] *Rhymed Preface for all Good Hymnbooks*, in *WA* xxxv. 483–4; a preface to Johann Walther's 1538 poem in praise of music, *Lob und Preis der löblichen Kunst Musica.*

Early in 1524 was the first hymn book. It had a charming title: 'Christian hymns canticles and psalms composed out of Holy Scripture according to the pure Word of God by a few very learned men; for use in church as they already do in Wittenberg'. These few learned authors were Luther (four hymns) Paul Speratus (three hymns) and an unknown who wrote the other. Luther was no romantic poet, sometimes he used crude language, but always he could be understood by the people, always the words were short, tough, vivid, and always power in faith came through the words. He used rhyme and alliteration but not to excess. He also wrote or selected tunes for his hymns. All hymn books of that century printed music as well as words, but only the tune. It was a later economy when printers published the words without the music.

Luther's own first proper hymn seems to have been his German translation of Psalm 130, 'Out of the deep have I called unto thee.' This hymn became obligatory at funerals in Saxony. It was sung at Luther's own funeral. But far his most famous hymn, '*Ein feste Burg*' ('A Safe Stronghold our God is Still'), a rendering of Psalm 46, did not appear until a hymn book of 1531. It was a song of faith in crisis and perfectly represented his personality. It tended to be used on special occasions, at national needs. His most used hymn, probably, was the hymn 'Lord Keep us Steadfast in thy Word' ('*Erhalt uns Herr bei deinem Wort*') probably written about 1541, widely sung because the makers of German church services liked to order it at or near the end of services. Its use could not last in Luther's own wording because it was written for children to sing at a time of fear from Turkish invasion and the first verse talks of Turks and papists trying to tumble Christ from his throne, and even the sixteenth century felt this not to be appropriate in a congregational hymn.

The eight hymns of 1524—the little book was put together from hymns on separate single sheets—soon became, later that year, Johann Walther's book of forty-three hymns with a preface by Luther: the *Geistliche Gesangbüchlein*. Walther was a friend of Luther and a true musician and choir-trained and he meant this book more for the choir than the people. Everywhere among the reforming churches these collections grew year by year in reprints. Part of the success, and the instant affection of people who used them, came because their music was based upon the German folk song. The German people had a tradition of folk lieder, and guilds to back it, such as the Mastersingers of Nuremberg.

Five years later the printer Klug at Wittenberg produced a hymn book authorized by Luther and this became the standard from which most later Lutheran hymn books were developed. Each hymn had its author's name and each feast day was given a woodcut and the book reflected the liturgical year. The last before Luther's death was a Leipzig hymn book with 127 hymns. This took hymns from sources wider than Luther would have liked if he had known, for example from anabaptists. It was ornamented with artistic skill.

When after Luther's death the legends of his virtue grew, he was imagined to have written many of the hymns, even a hundred or more. The actual number is not certain but nothing like that and it may be four. But his conviction of the glory of music and of how the people must be led to sing in their worship was far more influential than the number of hymns of which he was the author, it set the Lutheran churches on the way to the oratorio and towards Johann Sebastian Bach.

He wanted the psalms translated into rhyming poetry but never tried to produce a rhyming psalter of all 150 psalms. The first such metrical psalter was produced at Augsburg but was not good because to be a success it must be not only intelligible but poetic and musical.

Calvin made the use of metrical psalms one of the conditions for his accepting work in Geneva. He likewise was able to use language about music that was not puritan—a gift of God for the pleasure of humanity, blessed with the hidden power of moving hearts, it helps mortals to join their praises with the angels. He had views about music which made musicians uncomfortable. Music in church ought never to be light but sober and majestic and the musicians doubted whether the distinction between heavy and light music was always plain. He disliked harmony in church, music ought always to sing in unison, and the four different parts of a choir were always a distraction; whereas musicians if worthy of the name were bound to love harmony.

They were fortunate in Geneva that they had at their disposal the third of the psalter translated into French verse by Clément Marot, whose career was extraordinary and who influenced French and Swiss French-speaking Protestants more than anyone but Calvin. This hymn-writer was not a pious person struggling to be a poet, but a true poet hoping that perhaps he might be a pious person.

He was a lively court poet of love and flattery, charming with the ladies, a poet within the circle of French humanists. He was not at first a Protestant though he was satirical about monks and thought celibacy an impossible demand except for rare souls who have a gift from God, and he had a good knowledge of the Bible. Not being a priest his conscience was not confronted with any of the public acts which might get him into trouble. King Francis I liked him and his work, the king's sister Queen Marguerite of Navarre, who was the patroness of humanists and some who were almost Protestants, gave him protection.

Then in 1534 came the affair of the Placards and like Calvin he thought it prudent to disappear. He took refuge in Ferrara with Duchess Renée, who was a Protestant to her husband's horror but as the daughter of King Louis XII of France was hard to quell. After a time in Venice Marot returned home and recanted in Lyons in a rite which included a ceremonial whipping and was restored to the favour of King Francis. He wrote epigrams and verses not all of which were in harmony with the future hymn-writer of the Reformed Churches.

In 1539 appeared at Strasbourg a collection of metrical psalms from various hands, including twelve by Marot. Yet he was still a chamberlain at the Catholic court of Paris. Two years later, while he was still in Paris, an Antwerp printer added eighteen more psalms by Marot. It could not last and at the end of 1542 he fled to Geneva and the Sorbonne put his psalms among books banned. In Geneva a book of fifty psalms by Marot appeared. He was only in Geneva for just over a year and was encouraged to go on with the psalter and became a friend of the good musician Louis Bourgeois. But he was short of money and with his amiable lax character was not in harmony with small-town Geneva and was found playing dice with a woman in a tavern one evening and was not prosecuted but was not comfortable and left for the mountains of Savoy. Most refugees in Geneva loved the town for its quiet order but Marot now wrote a poem in which he described it as hell. He died in Italy in September 1544. Later the Inquisition removed all traces of his tomb.

His psalms were only a third of the Reformed psalter because he never wrote more. Theodore Beza took up the work and finished all 150 psalms in 1562—but he was an accurate translator not a poet. Marot's psalms had astonishing success, they went to more than 500 editions between 1539 and the end of that century, beloved for a simple, moving use of the vernacular. Because they were of the psalms their popularity surpassed every other collection of French lyric poetry.

The quality is proved by what happened in Germany. Various writers tried their hand at a poetic psalter in German. It was difficult, the German language did not easily marry the old rhythms. But much the most successful appeared with a German translation of the Geneva psalter. Ambrosius Lobwasser was unusual for such a translator. The son of a miner, he rose to be professor of law at the university of Leipzig. Working round the legal faculties of various universities, he spent time at Paris and in France discovered Marot's psalms, probably when the complete psalter appeared in 1562. Duke Albert of Prussia captured him to be professor of law at Königsberg, where he spent the rest of his career. Though a devout Lutheran and without sympathy for Calvinists, in his spare time he turned the Geneva psalter into German metrical psalms (published 1573). It was clear and poetic and simple; and as more Germans became disciples of the Swiss, Lobwasser was the hymn book of the German Reformed Churches. He could not be so popular among the Lutherans because their hymn books contained other poetry besides psalms whereas the only hymns which the Reformed would allow were psalms.

The sale of early hymn books was not so extensive as might be supposed; for congregations sang hymns from memory and sometimes the only persons in church to have a copy of the text in front of their eyes were the pastor and his cantor; though in big churches the trained choir had copies. Hymn books were sold more than this suggests for many people bought them not for use in church but for private use in the home. This was truer in the Swiss Reformed tradition where the Geneva metrical psalter came into homes nearly as universally as the Bible.

The sermon

Sermons had their structure and method. If the people were to be taught they must be taught well. The new training of clergy took trouble to make sure that they understood the rights and wrongs of public utterance.

Even at a famous level there was variety. Luther could be a compelling preacher, with free outpourings and understanding of emotion and sense of moral endeavour, and he had the huge advantage of being regarded by his audience as a hero and by some of them as an odd sort of saint. He never preached old sermons a second time though he was willing to write sermons for a diffident pastor to deliver; and his published sermons were preached in many evangelical churches where the local pastor felt that he could not write his own. He disapproved of too fast a delivery, and thought that persons from whom words flow down in a cascade attract listeners but do not touch them. 'Volubility does not affect an audience, even if some of them like it.'[5] Equally he disapproved of speakers who tried to sound clever in the pulpit, he met utterances intended more to raise the reputation of the speaker than the faith or morals of the listeners. He did not like waffle. 'Open your mouth, say something to the point, shut your mouth.'[6]

Calvin lay back on his bed thinking out what to say, but he could preach or lecture without notes and usually took with him only the Greek or Hebrew text of the Bible to expound. The words went flowing out of him. Every other week he preached every weekday and every Sunday he preached twice, that is 260 sermons in a year, with very numerous lectures in addition. Anyone who tries to speak knows that in a far lower frequency of utterance no one can talk sense all the time because no one, not even a person who takes so short a time for sleep as Calvin, has time to suck in enough to make good what goes out; not at least without an excess of repetition. But audiences were not bored. They were supposed to go to church but did not need to go to Calvin's church and most preferred it. His sermons were not amusing nor anecdotal. They were not decked with the devices of eloquence; they did not come over with passion, though sometimes interesting through vehemence of denunciation; they had none of Luther's fun and fewer flashes

---

[5] *TR* v. 5199.　　[6] *TR* iv. 5171.

of original insight; but they thumped away, like a battery of hits that landed on target, with clarity of thought, style, and arrangement, reinforced by the manifest conviction of truth in the speaker. No witness said that he had a musical voice. It was weight which listeners felt.

The order was so clear that it was easy to take notes. The foreign refugees found it harder to follow the spoken word and in 1549 they found a French shorthand expert to take down the sermon; and after that every sermon was committed to paper and then bound and made available to readers. Only in this way did a body of what he said pass to posterity. When he saw his own commentaries on Scripture in this form he was astonished at the accuracy with which they were recorded. Since the matter was good and he would not himself have prepared so much for publication, the reformed world owed a debt to this busy scribe.

Probably Pierre Viret, the only eminent Swiss to take charge of parishes in France, mainly because his weak health demanded a warmer climate, was the most attractive preacher of all the reformers. His face was cadaverous and could alarm the hearers. But the voice and manner and words were persuasive, with warmth and vitality and conviction, not fierce but caressing the ear and the mind, easy to listen to, in touch with the sitters under the pulpit, seeming to come among their personal circumstances, drawing the less pious. The sermons were long, an hour to an hour and a half, but the people did not wish them shorter.[7]

Sine verbo non potest cognosci Deus.[8] Whether they had gifts as speakers or not, all the reformers had the highest sense of the vocation of the preacher. The gospel of God is a Word, ministers are sent to declare that, they are not aiming to interest ears, they are vehicles of God's forgiveness, they affect and console the conscience. Luther imagined the minister in a dialogue with a text from the Bible.

At an age when he was but lately a graduate, Melanchthon was rash enough to write two books telling clergy how to preach.[9] He did the same with more experience fourteen years later. This humanist looked back to the classical theory of speaking. Luther had no special theory of preaching but to take a Bible and draw out its meaning. Melanchthon believed that preachers must be trained in the art of speaking in public and that rules could be set for this purpose. He perceived the difficulty that rhetoric is easily corrupt and hardly marries the simplicity at which the reformers aimed. Nevertheless the speaker cannot dispense with a schooling in what he does. Since Melanchthon was the most influential reformer of them all on the way in which pastors were trained, this doctrine had a lasting influence on the habits

---

[7] J. Barnaud, *Pierre Viret* (Nieuwkoop, 1973), 540–2.   [8] Luther in *WA* xxxi. 1. 333.
[9] *De rhetorica* (1519); *Institutiones rhetoricae* (1521); *de officio concionatoris* (1535).

of evangelical preachers and the structure of their sermons. He was later accused of allowing artifice into a ministry which above all other ministries ought to be free from artifice. To such a charge he had an answer. If you have to speak in public—which is no easy vocation except for the rarest of creatures—you ought to do all you can to discover how to avoid its frequent mistakes.

In Hesse another reforming humanist, Hyperius of Marburg, tried the same instruction to preachers nearly two decades later, and this must have been found useful because it needed a second and enlarged edition.[10] He took the ancient axiom that the object of a speech is *docere, delectare, flectere*, that is to teach, to make enjoyable, and to persuade. He made a parallel with this trilogy in the virtues of faith and charity and hope; and used the old scheme of the rhetoricians:

inventio—find material to speak about—that is, find a subject which is good for the people and is easy for them to understand and is worth talking about;

dispositio—arrange it, so that it is clear to yourself and therefore to the people;

elocutio—speak it—audibly so that they can hear it, in simplicity so that they can understand it, in such a way that they can remember at least some of it, and in such a way that they will want to listen to it;

pronuntiatio—speak it with force and conviction.

The old rhetoricians held that the art came in making the words attractive to hear. This reformer believed the most important part was *inventio*—choosing a subject worth talking about.

Luther called a sermon which expounded Scripture a *Postil*. The word came from the medieval Latin *postilla*. No one is sure of the origin. It may be from *post illa*, 'after those words of the text'. In England there was a verb, to postil, meaning to make comments on Gospel or Epistle. Hidden in the Wartburg Luther wrote sermons and called them postils, the word came into common use in German. A book of postils was often read from pulpits where the pastor did not feel able to preach or his superiors believed with or without reason that he could not preach.

Often the sermon flowed along with the biblical text, phrase after phrase, verse after verse, explaining, commenting, paraphrasing. If there was no reason why they should stop when the next words beckoned, and they improvised as they went, they were in danger of length. On the pulpit ledge was an hour-glass. This useful instrument had not long been plentiful but began to be indispensable in the navigation of oceans and so was manufactured and

---

[10] Hyperius, *De formandis concionibus* (1552; enlarged 1562).

became an item of church furnishing. Listeners watched the dripping sand but preachers who grew older and were full of matter took little notice of the sand. The congregation at Neuchâtel complained to Lausanne and Geneva about the length of Farel's sermons as he got older, and both Calvin and Viret warned him. At Wittenberg Bugenhagen's sermons were regarded as an intellectual treat but their length was killing for the congregation.

The sermons of the earlier sixteenth century could not be the works of art of the seventeenth century. It took time to make a Lancelot Andrewes or a John Donne or a Bossuet, and it took a more educated audience. Early reforming preachers talked too often for that, little time to prepare and less time to memorize, an ignorant people. Often a sermon was nearer to the catechism than to the formal beauties of a later age when poets and scholars gave of their best to that means of communication, and a sermon was art and literature as well as gospel.

Prophesyings in the Swiss tradition

In Zurich Zwingli created an aid to preaching which was taken up in all the churches of the Swiss tradition, including English Puritan congregations. He called it by a misleading name, *prophesyings*. This made it sound as though the meeting was full of charismatic utterance. But it was a sober seminar to discuss and expound texts of the Bible and given its name because the next Sunday or later the preachers were able to explain the texts from their pulpit. Zwingli did not wish to follow the Swiss habit of sending ordinands away to universities. So he must create a system of biblical teaching with professors of as high a standard as could be found in universities. He opened his 'Prophesying' on 19 June 1523, at 8 a.m. All the clergy of the city must attend; senior ordinands also; a few clergy came in from the country parishes. They had a prayer; then a student read a text of the Old Testament in Latin from the old Catholic Vulgate. Then a Hebraist read the same text from the Hebrew and translated it word by word into Latin and drew attention to the differences between the original Hebrew and the Vulgate. Then Zwingli himself read the same text from the Greek Septuagint; and then in Latin drew together the conclusions reached from studying the text in the three languages; after which Zwingli's lieutenant Leo Jud gave a German translation of what Zwingli had just explained in Latin; and this German explanation became the basis of what the clergy said in their pulpits on Sunday. It was a scholarly affair when it began; after Zwingli attracted Conrad Pellican, one of the two or three top Hebraists in Europe, and then Pellican's pupil Theodor Bibliander who was soon as expert as his master, it became the best seminar for biblical study anywhere in Europe, Catholic or Protestant. When Zwingli was killed, his successor Bullinger thought he had enough to do as chief pastor and handed over to Bibliander Zwingli's former duties of expounding the Greek text in the prophesying and of summing up of the result of the seminar. From 1541 they supplemented it with instruction in the natural sciences and secured Conrad Gesner, one of the eminent scientists of Europe.

To sit under a long sermon by a middling preacher was an affliction, and the weight of sin, temptation, and forgiveness expressed in words might sound heavy with gloom. But the leading mood of this devotion was warm; partly because the psalms were brought home to the people who came to know many by heart, and the psalms made one of the great books of poetry in the world's literature and abounded with praise and trust and aspiration.

The reformers set out to make lay folk share in the prayers of the Church. With the hymn/metrical psalm this was achieved. But they also reacted against what they took to be a huge ignorance of gospel truth. There must be teaching. If parts of the service were regarded as a vehicle for information, even if the lesson was about the Bible, then it was not like a corporate act but like a schoolmaster talking to pupils. In the eyes of reformers the crime of the medieval liturgy was its clericalism. Without seeing the peril, they brought back a new form of clericalism and made the role of the pastor as bulky as that of the former priest.

In days while the priest celebrated the mass, males gathered round the door and chatted and might only come in for the consecration. Now they might sleep or be passive except when they were allowed to sing. In time they also began to hang about outside the porch until the time neared for the hymn before sermon.

The records of visitations do not show vast affection by ordinary people for their way of worship (except their singing). Visitations pick on what is wrong and what is wrong is usually the exception. But they point to sufficient evidence of boredom, inattention, sleep, whispered conversation and in rare cases resentment. If the change in the way of worship is summarized too simply as a change from learning with the eye to learning with the ear, then they learnt little with the eye in the old days, and in the new days it was mostly the middle class who learnt with the ear. The old church was darker, its walls had more colour, it had altars in every niche and statues at the pillars and might have a pyx hanging. And now the people felt this to be crowding as though it had something to do with idolatry or even oppression, and expected white walls and light glass and nothing to distract their minds from holy table and Bible and pulpit. This clarity had its simpler variety of 'sensuousness'.

Protestant worship demanded a new interior for the church. It did not at first need new churches because everywhere there were churches in plenty. So old churches were adapted in their furnishing and ornaments. It took money and time if new churches were to be built, less money to adapt the old. And sheer conservatism kept a pattern designed for another purpose. If a church was to be a preaching house, transepts were not the best spaces for making words audible. The people associated the best churches with transepts, they expected town churches to have transepts.

But the way of worship made a difference to what was needed. Pastor and people needed to be accessible to each other rather than set apart by a high screen. The people needed to be able to hear the sermon. They must be able not just to look at the sacrament from a distance but to gather round to receive it. The first signs of a new conception of a church interior were found in the chapels of princes—that of the elector of Saxony at Torgau which Luther consecrated in 1544 with no place of the choir separate (a form copied when Elector Maurice built his castle chapel at Dresden a few years later) and of the duke of Pomerania at Stettin in 1577, where the shape was nearer to that of a preaching hall. If the choir was kept in the architecture, it was made plain that the space was no longer reserved for the clergy but was the place of the laity also, especially at the time of sacraments. The axiom was still accepted that a church ought not to look like a secular building, its purpose distinguished it from town halls or covered markets.

In Switzerland and France and Holland the principles were pushed further. Zwingli and Calvin thought excess of decoration unfitting, though they wanted order and cleanliness. Since the important moment was the proclamation of the Word, and its reception in faith by the people, the altar was moved away from the apse at the east end and became the holy table, brought down so that people could sit round it under the pulpit, also at the centre of the church.

In the sermons of friars, older people or pregnant women brought stools into church. That still happened. But seats were necessary to the preaching; and new-built or new-altered churches might need galleries. In princely chapels there was a seating plan—princes and the court in the gallery, servants of the court and others in the nave below. Ordinary churches also had customary plans, gentry at the front or to one side, guilds paid for benches for their members, benches near the door for the poor, and before 1600 even village churches had stools provided by the church and not brought by their owners. Men and women sat separately.

Vestments

All religions and cultures have special garments for those who lead prayer to God. At times they were simply the best clothes of the day, like those worn by ordinary citizens at feasts. More commonly as in the Old Testament they had a special cut or shape to which symbolism was attributed. They were usually more colourful than ordinary clothes for the practical reason that the person wearing them needed to be observed by a crowd; but also for the same reason that they tried to beautify churches, God must be honoured with the best that we have and an elaboration which would be pretentious in ordinary life is right in the context of worship.

The Christians took from the Jews none of their rules about costume. The apostolic leaders of prayer wore ordinary clothes; no doubt their better clothes, such as were suitable for feasts. But a white garment was soon found appropriate for people taking part in a service; visible to the people and symbolic of purity. And then bishops and priests were distinguished by a shoulder cloak with a little more colour. Gradually these vestments became so customary that as ordinary clothes changed their fashion the clothes of officiants in church remained the same and so were no longer like ordinary clothes but were 'vestments' only worn for the purpose of conducting prayers. Ranks which were marked out in civil society—the prefect or high civil servant—had an effect and it seemed right to mark higher clergy also with badges of rank.

As the earlier Middle Ages developed these costumes they grew complex; on top of the original white garment or alb, the cloak of the priest or bishop called *paenula* and later a *casula* or chasuble, and the belt or girdle which was needed to hold them together. There was a little scarf for the neck called the amice, and special gloves, and special shoes, and a little cloth hanging from the left arm which was originally a sign of rank and was called the maniple, and a coloured band called a stole which probably started out of the handkerchief used for wiping the nose but became universal in the costume of the clergy as a band hung round the shoulders and another sign of rank.

The Reformation divided on what it was right to do. Everyone was agreed on simplicity. Not a single reformed bishop nor superintendent anywhere, not even in conservative England, wore a medieval bishop's garments.

This putting away of clothes which sometimes were ornamented gave a good opportunity for scandal among persons who disliked what was happening. If a valuable article of clothing vanished, it was easy to spread a hard rumour that the new pastor or prelate put it to his own uses. The most dramatic story of this sort concerned the Prussian bishop of Samland. It was said that when he became a Protestant he destroyed his mitre and out of the precious stones made ornaments for his wife.

Such stories should not be believed too readily. We may take the Samland mitre as an example. When Prussia became Protestant, the Teutonic Knights who administered its castles needed to follow Duke Albert in being secularized. One knight, Philipp von Creutz, was in charge of several castles and was asked by Albert whether he accepted the new regime. He said with reluctance that he did. Nevertheless a year later Albert relieved him of his post, and he did not forgive. In the Teutonic Knights archives at Dresden is a report which he wrote, not long afterwards, describing the events in Prussia. The report is against those events as will be expected from the circumstances of its writing. The bishop was accused of becoming evangelical only because he lusted after a wife. He removed his *infel* which was ornamented with precious stones and turned them into decoration for his wife. *Infel* or *inful* was used to mean vestments generally, but often included those for the head, more generally for secular magnates than for mitres. The anti-Protestant historian of the nineteenth century Johannes Janssen, engaged in the thunderous battle between Bismarck and German Catholics, took this story as characteristic of what was happening; but did not mention the extreme bias of the source or the improbability that the angry knight could know anything of what the bishop did except by hearsay.[11]

In Switzerland Zwingli inclined to the opinion that because of the priesthood of the laity there ought to be no difference in costume between the people and their ministers. But this was not what the people were found to want, and soon the Reformed of the Swiss tradition, from France to Scotland, accepted the black academic gown as the proper garment in which to lead worship and preach from a pulpit. Luther was more conservative and most Lutherans followed him. Clothes are not matters of conscience or principle, the people are used to chasubles, let us not disturb their ways unnecessarily. Bugenhagen, responsible for much of the organization, agreed. Thus evangelical churches, though with wide variety of detail, often kept mass vestments though simplified; the maniple, special shoes, etc. vanished as clutter. Some churches had the custom that the minister wore the chasuble to celebrate but the black gown to preach as this was a teaching function. Other Lutheran churches preferred to change the chasuble for a white garment and there, though not rapidly, the alb or surplice became the custom. If a church ceased to use its vestments it was normal for them to be rewoven into altar hangings or to be sold and the money put into the poor chest. In Hungary the Lutheran bishop Bornemisza always preached in lay clothes, but that was very unusual, the more distant the church the more likely to be conservative.[12]

In 1548 the surplice became controversial among Protestants. By the Interim forced through the Diet of Augsburg that year, all Protestant churches were ordered to recover a good measure of Catholic ceremonial. No one minded a surplice in theory, it was simple and symbolic of purity and had history. What they minded was being ordered to wear a surplice by a

[11] Report of Philipp von Creutz in *Scriptores Rerum Prussicarum*, ed. T. Hirsch, v (1874), 377–8; Johannes Janssen, *Geschichte des deutschen Volkes* (Freiburg im Breisgau, 1881–94), iii. 73.
[12] A. S. Unghváry, *The Hungarian Protestant Reformation in the Sixteenth Century under the Ottoman Impact* (Lewiston, 1989), 247–8.

Catholic emperor who had no right to give any such order. Hence the wearing or not caused passionate debate among Protestants. Its restoration, or a refusal to restore it, would show whether that church was prepared on grounds of conscience to resist a ruler who had force. When the storm of the Interim blew over, the result was twofold: churches which restored it were found to like it and kept it for decades afterwards; churches which resisted hastened the general decline of the surplice in favour of the black gown.

The academic gown developed into the long black cassock or talar which was worn by pastors outside church services. During the later sixteenth century laymen started wearing ruffs, and slowly ruffs became of obligation as neckbands to the black talar and are still used in Scandinavia. By a circuitous route through the Counter-Reformation they were the origin of the modern clerical collar.

Outside church there was less difference in garb between cleric and lay. The pastor wore the shape of clothes which laymen wore. But there was a difference, for the tradition that priests should appear in black, unless they had the habit of a monastic order which was brown or grey or white, persisted among the Protestant churches and colourful clothes which laypeople wore were regarded as reprehensible in pastors. Because a church service was a public occasion those who came had usually put on their better clothes unless they were beggars who had no other clothes or wished to show their desperation. Now beggars were banned. But better clothes were less shiny and threadbare at the front of the congregation than near the door. Better clothes did not mean the height of masculine or feminine fashion, that was ostentation and sin.

The organ

Organs had been known since the ancient world as a way to make secular music. They were suspect to Puritans as near drunkenness or debauchery. Theodoric the Visigoth won praise because the moral customs of his court were so high that no one was allowed to play the organ. St Cecilia, afterwards by a paradox the patron saint of music, was represented as going to her death closing her ears to the temptations of the organ.

But this way to make sound was too useful for filling the wide spaces of churches. From the Carolingian age onwards the instrument came into some monastery churches or cathedrals, but as a solo instrument, not at first in a marriage with a choir. By the eleventh century the visitor would find an organ inside nearly all the big churches, whether cathedrals or abbeys. But they were crude instruments, the player hit the keys with his fists, it was physical work. There was a survival of this, for in the German language people talked about 'banging on the organ' centuries after they ceased to bang. As yet the instruments were not capable of the subtleties needed to marry with a choir. In twelfth-century England it reminded Aelred of Rievaulx not of sweetness like a voice but a crash of thunder, that 'terrible blast of the bellows'.[13] It was more like the earlier custom of putting worshippers into the right mood by sounding a peal of the church bells. The organ was not then part of worship but a filling of empty space at the side of worship—except, and it was an important except, they could sound a note which guided the voice of the priest to the right key in the mass as he began to sing the gloria or the creed.

By the end of the thirteenth century organs began to be used in harmony with choirs. When Dante arrived at purgatory, the moment he pushed through the gate he heard a distant choir singing Te Deum with sweet voices and it reminded him of what he heard from choirs in Italy and how they were sometimes accompanied by the organ and if they were they might be inaudible because of the organ (Purgatorio 9, at the end); which suggests that in Italy choirs and organs often went together. A little later Hamburg used its organ to help the choir sing psalms. When Magdeburg received the emperor Charles IV and his empress in 1377, they sang a Te Deum which was accompanied on the organ. In the big spaces—cathedrals, collegiate churches, abbey churches—it had established its utility though not quite its beauty. Enemies were not silent. St Thomas Aquinas said that musical instruments do more to make worshippers comfortable than put them in the right frame of mind for prayer.[14] The feeling lasted. To this day they have kept an organ out of the Sistine Chapel.

The result of this hesitant union between the organ and the church choir was a demand for better organs. The new metal industry of 1500 supplied the need with organs which began to be magnificent in cathedrals, as at Antwerp. That which was built at Innsbruck in the emperor's chapel, with a beautiful painting of the Annunciation on the case, still exists. By then the priest at the altar was given a note from the organ at the beginning of each bit of the liturgy. They had reed stops and flutes and tremulants and two manuals and pedals. The range of sound was widening and its colour more delicate. Those responsible for worship had realized that music from the organ at the beginning, not yet called a 'voluntary', could help to put the worshippers in the right mood for the service. But the more they played in church, the more critics accused them of introducing obscene noises into the services. And not only this. Musicians wanted more time, and a bigger part; and, out of weakness or agreement, priests shortened the mass to meet their wishes. At Catholic Cologne in 1536 the priests were blamed because for the sake of

---

[13] *Speculum caritatis*, 2. 23, Migne, *Patrologia Latina*, 195. 571.
[14] *Summa Theologiae*, 2. 2. q. 91 art. 2.

making time for the music they omitted the reading of the Epistle and the Creed and the Preface and even the Lord's Prayer.[15] Elsewhere there were congregations which did not like services growing to such length when organists added so many minutes of music.

Country churches did not afford organs.

The arrival of the organ in worship caused a different criticism. If we intone or chant the psalms the people can know what we are saying. If we chant them with the organ the words are blurred, the people do not hear.

The reformers started with the instinct that these complex sounds of choir and organ were an intrusion into Christian worship. We want the Bible and we want the Word preached and we want prayers and we want the people to sing the praises. But trills and twiddles and choir-performances are a piece of theatre not an aid to devotion, an invasion by musicians into a prayerful world in which they should have only a restricted place.

Reformed Switzerland went vehemently against organs in worship. Zwingli liked music but for the sake of simplicity preferred to do without it in church. Because they were not yet used to organs which accompanied congregational singing, and knew only organs which served trained choirs and their gyrations, organs appeared to the Zurichers to be a danger to worship. Zurich threw out all singing in church and did not let hymns back until almost the end of the century. From Switzerland came the saddest stories of organists weeping as they watched the removal of an instrument which they loved, at Zurich and Berne for example. The Berne organ was sold to the town of Sitten (Sion) for a bargain price. Hans Kotter was organist at Catholic Fribourg in Switzerland but became a Protestant and was thrown out of the canton. He sought refuge at Berne but Berne had no organ for him to play so he spent the rest of his life teaching in school despite journeys to be employed again on an organ.

This feeling existed elsewhere than in Switzerland. Carlstadt said that organ music was empty noise, acceptable in a theatre but wholly out of place in a church. In Nuremberg Osiander wanted the organs silenced. He based this desire on 1 Corinthians 14, where St Paul did not want the people to speak in an unknown tongue and organ-accompanied words have the effect of an unknown tongue. For several years the organs of Nuremberg ceased. Luther did not love organs. He thought them apt to 'titillate the soul'[16] and never sang the praise of the organ as an aid to worship. But he accepted the rightness of choirs in worship and by his day the organ was an accepted

---

[15] Provincial Synod of Cologne, presided over by Archbishop Hermann von Wied, who later became a Protestant, canon 2. 12; in J. D. Mansi, *Sacr. Conciliorum Amplissima Collectio*, xxxii. col. 1227.

[16] 'nihil ad spiritum . . . istis titillationibus', *Ad librum Ambrosii Catharini Responsio* (1521), *WA* vii. 765.

partner with choirs in great churches. Several early Lutheran church orders provided that organists be chosen and be given adequate pay. Hamburg had four organists for their chief church, who made up their stipends by teaching music.

In 1536 Wolfgang Musculus, at that time a well-known preacher in Augsburg, visited Wittenberg and attended mass and recorded what he saw.[17] The organ was used antiphonally with the choir at the Kyrie Eleison, and the singing of the Gloria, and again to introduce the singing of the Creed, then it sounded out after the elevation to introduce the singing of the Agnus Dei.

The Protestants inherited larger churches which contained an organ. The Lutherans did not remove them but continued to use them. As the century advanced more organs were built for evangelical churches. They did not accompany the people singing hymns. They were a help to the choir parts of the service. There were members of congregations who thought that hymns were the real worship and the organ was part of the musicians' game.

But in big spaces the power of the organ was found to help to unify a numerous assembly trying to sing together. They found it useful to play over the tune of the hymn which the people were about to sing and did not know. The link between organ and hymn was slow to form. The organ did not normally accompany the hymn until well into the seventeenth century. It still had its critics—make the people sing with the organ and they will stop meaning the words of hymns; give the organ and choir their heads and they will take over worship and the people will again be passive—why should we turn churches into concert halls? But once accepted as an aid to hymn-singing the instrument was too useful to be without and even in the countryside little churches started trying to get hold of cheap and simple organs. By the middle of the seventeenth century Nuremberg took it for granted that organs accompanied the singing of the congregation and that this was a long evangelical tradition. The change may be seen in the appearance of the word 'voluntary'. The use of 'voluntary' to mean a piece of music played by the organist at the beginning or end of the service first appeared in the English language at the end of the sixteenth century; and since it meant that the organist played whatever he wished, it was not part of the service, which implied that the organ was part of the service during its celebration.

---

[17] He came on the business of negotiating the Wittenberg Concord of that year, the partial agreement between Luther and Bucer on the doctrine of the eucharist. Earlier he had been Bucer's secretary. He was one of the signatories of the Concord. Musculus's *Itinerarium*, in *Analecta Lutherana*, ed. Theodor Kolde (1883), 217 ff.

Fasts

Moses fasted forty days on Mount Sinai, Jesus in the desert. It was thought to be a tool against temptation by establishing control over the weak will. It could be used to express penitence, or mourning at a death, especially Good Friday which cast its shadow over all Fridays. Early in the Christian use the midweek Wednesday was added as a pious exercise. Such uses had deep roots in Jewish and Christian tradition. Even in the Old Testament critics saw peril—if you think all is well when you fast, while you should be charitable and obey the laws of God. Jesus' freedom from rules of the Pharisees was linked to such critics.

The Catholic Church established rules, not the same in different lands; until the Lent of forty days established at Rome about 700. At much the same time the fast before Christmas was forming, which led to the creation of the season of Advent. In time the days before ordinations were added as right for ordinands to prepare themselves and for others to pray for them ('Ember days', so called in English since Anglo-Saxon times, probably a corruption of the Latin *quattuor tempora* = four times a year). Monks believed in fasting as armour against the attacks of demons. The rules came into canon law. To eat fish was allowed, fasting means to abstain from meat. Excess of fasting is bad because God gave the good things of the world for humanity to enjoy and to be fit to serve others. The canons became too complex for the subject with which they dealt.

When canon law came under fire after 1520, the rules of fasting were inevitably in trouble. The Reformation had nothing to say against fasting, only against fasting made compulsory by the State, fasting as a *legal* obligation. Zwingli's reform at Zurich began its course with a protest about a fine for eating sausages in Lent 1522. The trivial dispute was used by Zwingli to make an assault upon the right of the Church to make laws about civil life. Everyone was afraid of a plan to win heaven by obeying rules. Luther had an extra reason for criticism, he fasted in his monastery on a rule justified by the belief that fasting weakened sexual desire, and thought this an illusion. People must be fit to do their work in the world and therefore ought not to weaken their bodies. But he accepted that a fast is a useful form of self-denial—for some people, the needs of bodies vary. He commended the discipline in his Smaller Catechism.

Calvin was more coherent. Fasting helps devotion, encourages self-restraint, makes prayer easier, and is a physical aid to a mood of penitence in the soul. He perceived the social objection to law—poor people are stopped from eating meat, the better-off can eat deliciously on dishes that contain no meat.[18]

---

[18] All this in *Institutes* iv. 12. 15 ff.

Yet he accepted that in times of crisis governments could arrange national days of prayer and fasting, and all the states with Reformed Churches practised this. Martin Bucer agreed. He thought the English State very wrong to ban meat in Lent when the motive was nothing to do with religion but to help trawlermen in the North Sea fishing fleet.

Saints

Medieval devotion and preaching dedicated itself to saints. The reformers had more Bible to preach about, their range of subjects was wider. But they almost deprived themselves of saints as subjects for sermons. It was indispensable that the sermon must be about a text from the Bible, otherwise it was not a sermon. The exception to this rule was the funeral sermon when, though the speaker must talk about the biblical faith concerning the dead, he might also talk about the dead person especially if the dead were a benefactor of the community. This exception showed how saints were part of Christian memory and could not quite be jettisoned.

At first the need seemed to be to diminish them almost out of sight. Saints' days, they felt, were holidays when people had nothing to do but drink and lust, to be rid of so many holidays is moral improvement, ask the State that Sundays alone be public holidays except for Christmas and Ascension, and Sundays shall be kept as a day of quiet and rest and prayer. Governments were willing but realized that they must not hastily deprive working people of holidays to which they were accustomed and therefore old saints' days remained at first days when people could work or not. Town councils, wanting their workers to have at least one holiday a month besides Sundays, preferred that more days should be kept, usually the days of the twelve apostles and three feasts of the Virgin. Martin Bucer wished to be rid of all weekday holidays including Christmas and Epiphany and Ascension, but people were not willing to be so austere. Swiss churches mostly went on celebrating Christmas for a time. But Neuchâtel finally suppressed it in 1582 because their pastors told them it encouraged 'horrible superstitions' and it was not revived there till early in the eighteenth century. Zwingli wanted to be rid of everything that was not New Testament but the council of Zurich insisted on keeping the patron saints of the town, Felix and Regula.[19]

Saints outside the New Testament did not get into evangelical calendars, with two exceptions. In some of his church orders in north Germany Bugenhagen allowed St Laurence. He really existed, a Roman cleric of the

---

[19] These two were said to have died at Zurich in the persecution of Maximin, their day 11 September. The relics were moved for safety to Andermatt in the Catholic mountain canton of Uri.

third century, who had a cult by the early fourth century and then developed a legend part of which was derived from the stories of other saints of the same name. Roasted, he became the patron saint of cooks and bakers and of the poor generally, and was weighty in peasant life. In Germany he had a special importance that he won the victory over the Hungarians at Lechfeld in 955. To encourage people to receive communion each quarter they needed an autumn date (Christmas for winter, Easter for spring, Whitsun for summer) and some evangelical orders retained a form of All Saints Day (1 November) for this reason. England was an exception in not letting Good Friday become a working day.

The northern ports Hamburg and Lübeck, with their Baltic trade, wanted St Anskar who was the apostle of Scandinavia. In his church orders Bugenhagen had an annual day of thanksgiving for the introduction of the Reformation. A few of these northern church orders put a harvest festival into their calendars.

Luther was no enthusiast for the doctrine that saints must be ejected, we have to be patient about what the people want and not mind if they still treasure the communion of the saints but we should teach that invocation of the saints is wrong because although we may hope that saints in heaven pray for us, our prayer should be directed towards one higher than the saints. In his own pulpit he went on preaching about saints and was quite sorry to have lost so many of them. Once he even said that we ought to keep St Barbara. She was more surprising than Laurence, for she was patron saint of gunners and bell-makers, but more important, she helped in fires and pestilences, and branches were cut on her day to flower at Christmas time so that in Germany she was a customary bit of the Christmas celebration linked to presents to children.

In 1544 Luther's friend Major published a book about the saints, *Vitae Patrum*, for which Luther willingly wrote a preface. The book is strange. It is a form of the *Vitae Patrum* of the fifth century, that is lives of the early hermits and monks of the Egyptian desert; but this version is somewhat bowdlerized. It includes the Life of St Antony the first hermit, a life which is attributed to St Athanasius, and ends with a salutation to the reader; *after* which, evidently as an afterthought, because it has no page numbers, the Life of St Simeon Stylites, whose life on the top of a pillar in Syria was not a way of life which Protestants approved.

In 1559 Caspar Goltwurm made what was till modern times the only serious Protestant effort outside England, to create a calendar of saints for the liturgy. He chose thirteen names before the Reformation and forty-nine Protestant martyrs, and gave each a little biography and tried to avoid legend and sometimes gave his sources.[20] No church used this calendar. Eber made a

---

[20] Frieder Schulz, in *TRE* xiv. 668.

calendar and Melanchthon wrote a postil on how it is useful to study the lives of good people and so be helped to learn the history of the Church.[21] Evidently this was designed for schools not church.

This memory of saints by Luther and his contemporaries hardly lasted among the Lutheran churches, and had to be revived in the twentieth century because of the martyrs of the Nazi era.

Jean Crespin

When moderns read the names on war memorials of the First World War, they suffer a sadness at the loss to humanity by the vanishing of so many thousands of young men. The French civil wars of the sixteenth century, called the wars of religion though religion was not the only reason for the fights, gave observers something of the same sensation. This feeling took a literary form.

Jean Crespin came from Arras, which was then under Spanish rule, trained as a lawyer and practised in Paris. Watching the death of a Protestant martyr converted him to the reform. He was proved to have attended a Huguenot meeting and fled to Strasbourg and then Geneva, apparently because he admired Calvin and with the aim of setting up a printing house. The printing was excellent, in Geneva he was regarded as chief rival to Estienne.

In 1554 appeared the *Book of the Martyrs*; his martyrs were mostly French or Flemish. He took trouble about what happened, wrote well, constantly sought for new information, and won the public. It started small but the cases multiplied and by 1560 it was a folio volume. It had editions into the seventeenth century and was translated into several languages but not into English till later because in England John Foxe did the same work a few years after with an equal attractiveness.[22]

---

[21] CR xxiv. 351.

[22] The Geneva edition of 1570 (the title then *History of the True Witnesses to the Truth of the Gospel*) was given a facsimile at Liège, 1964.

10

CHURCH ORDER

Ordination

The classical doctrine of the ministry spoke of 'indelible character'—once a person is ordained priest he cannot lose the authority which is there implanted—to celebrate sacraments, preach and administer absolution to penitents. The ordained person is a priest for life whether or not he exercises the office, and even if he is dismissed from pastoral care or unfrocked, he cannot be reordained if penitence is allowed, but under proper discipline is simply restored.

In his outspoken treatises of 1520, before his thought matured, especially in the tract *On the Babylonian Captivity of the Church,* Luther wrote with passion of how in the New Testament all God's people are priests. Every baptized person who has faith shares in the priesthood of Christ and has the power of priesthood in the Church. Therefore it is not true that the clergy are given power which is not given to the laypeople. There are not two classes in the Church, there are only Christians with different work to do. Hence there is no such thing as an indelible character except in baptism. A person is made pastor of a parish as another person is made the town clerk. He can be dismissed or resign from the office as he can be dismissed or resign from being town clerk. He holds the minister's rank only while he performs the duty of a minister. If he does not preach he is not a minister. The office of a minister is a sacred vocation, but so is the vocation of the town clerk or any other lawful vocation.

Then may any Christian celebrate the sacrament? may a woman? may a child if he or she understands what is being done? In the early years there are texts which come near assent to this logic—but not women because St Paul orders their silence in church. And it was soon clear, still clearer when Melanchthon defined it, that every minister needs to be called to his work by the Church—whether through election by the parishioners, or authority from other ministers. The doctrine of the priesthood of the laity was more confined than appeared at first. It justified responsible lay authorities—like a government—interfering in the arrangements of a Church to make it better. And in emergencies rules had to be waived—a midwife could baptize a baby in danger of death, a lay prisoner could absolve another prisoner who was dying when no prison chaplain was available, because they also shared in Christ's priesthood. On the island where a Christian community is wrecked with no priest, can they elect a priest for themselves and receive the sacrament?—an instance which hardly anyone believed in as possible until they met it at Macao in the Second World War.

There had been a *hierarchy*, pope—cardinal—archbishop—bishop—priest—deacon—subdeacon—minor orders. In theory all this was waved away. Scholarship generally accepted then and since that in the New Testament the office of a bishop is the same rank as the office of a priest/presbyter. Because the evangelicals did not believe in a sacrifice in the eucharist they dropped words like *sacerdos* which suggested a sacrificing priest. There is only one rank, whether called minister or pastor or preacher (*Prediger*), this last was favoured by evangelicals because they wanted to remind everyone that the declaration of the Word of God is the first work of ministry. In the New Testament are deacons, but they were chiefly for welfare, and are therefore a lay ministry and do not contradict the assertion that there is only one rank among the clergy. No hierarchy.

But some ministers are more important than others? the pastor of a big town of many educated people compared with the pastor of a little village where few could read? Then there were Protestant bishops. And where there were no bishops they found that the welfare and discipline of the clergy needed higher clergy, called superintendents, and in places they might need still higher clergy called general superintendents, and the people sometimes went on calling such higher pastors by the New Testament word bishops. Later among the Lutheran churches we find odd titles—in the electorate of Brunswick-Lüneburg the office Anglicans and Swedes would have called archbishop was 'director of all the churches of the electorate'.[1]

If all the Lord's people are priests is there any need for a rite of ordination? From the absence of evidence in the New Testament Luther and his successors were sure that ordination is not a sacrament. Should they appoint a man to the post of parish pastor as they appointed a man to be the town clerk, sit him in a chair and tell him to get on with the work? To the displeasure of its chief pastor Osiander (no hierarchy but a chief pastor), Nuremberg took this view of the matter, for most of the sixteenth century its only form of ordination was examination followed by appointment.

For several years Wittenberg needed no rite of ordination. They had plenty of ex-monks who had been validly ordained as priests and then became reformed pastors. But these must die off and then the question of ordination rose. The first Wittenberg ordination was in 1535. The laying on

---

[1] Molanus, 1705, *ZKG* 1889, 10. 409.

of hands was reverent and historic and not superstitious, and unlike the Nuremberg council Luther accepted that a rite of ordination was needed. The form of service developed more conservatively than he expected, and this was chiefly due to his organizer Bugenhagen.[2]

It was agreed not to be a matter of principle that the laying on of hands should be the sacramental act which ordained and called to service as a preacher or pastor. But because good people held that it was a matter of principle, trouble came if it was omitted. Without it the authority of preachers was doubted. It was better that it should be the rite so that the conscience of everyone should be at rest.

Although in theory the office of the town clerk was as sacred as the work of the pastor, that was not what the people felt. They more easily found consolation in the words of their preacher than in tax demands delivered from the town council. It felt more natural to use the old word 'consecration' when a person was chosen to be a pastor; and to the ordinand it felt more natural to understand that he consecrated himself to God as he undertook this responsibility for other people's souls.

Johannes Freder lived as a student in Luther's house, the old Austin Friars at Wittenberg. He was first the preacher at Hamburg but was not ordained by a rite because the authority was the cathedral chapter which was still Catholic and refused to lay hands on a Protestant. Freder knew that he had a call from the congregation and the surrounding pastors and the city council and was only not ceremonially ordained through a local Catholic survival which would soon disappear; and in these circumstances he thought his ordination by rite a matter of indifference.

But seven years later he was made the superintendent at the Baltic port of Stralsund. At this point the general superintendent of Pomerania, Knipstro, ordered that he must be properly ordained with the laying on of hands. As Freder had already ministered for seven years he thought that to consent would cast his earlier ministry into doubt, and he refused the demand. He was deprived of the post to which he was chosen. Three years after that, in 1550, he was made superintendent of the island of Rügen in the Baltic. Knipstro again challenged his right to minister. Freder published a booklet *On the Laying On of Hands* (*Van Uplegginge der Hande*) in which he argued that a rite of ordination was not a necessity, and that he ministered though he had never been ordained in that way. An appeal went to Wittenberg, where Luther was dead and Melanchthon and Bugenhagen were supreme. They replied that though the laying on of hands is not a necessity for a valid ministry, it is a laudable and apostolic custom, and they held against Freder's plea.

---

[2] As early as 1525 Luther himself ordained Georg Rörer to be a Wittenberg deacon, with the laying on of hands in the parish church of Wittenberg.

Freder then allowed himself to receive the laying on of hands from the Danish bishop of Roskild, in which diocese the island of Rügen lay. This ordination in its turn was challenged locally, so Freder resigned, and at last, with his ordination from a bishop, was made superintendent at the Baltic port of Wismar where they accepted him without a doubt.[3] There were many circumstances in evangelical Germany where it was better to be ordained with the laying on of hands because then no one challenged the authority.

Though the notion of indelible character through ordination was rejected emphatically (because it was feared to make cleric and lay different kinds of being), it was normal in evangelical churches to avoid a reordination—for example when a pastor changed parishes, or returned to parish work after an interval.

In the south-west the new problem of authority was put by Guillaume Farel. He preached, and few doubted that like any layperson whose duty was to spread the gospel, he could preach in church halls or barns or market squares, which indeed he often did; and then because people invited him or even when they did not, he went into pulpits; defending himself against critics and abuse with the text which all wandering preachers used, from Franciscans to Methodists, that in the New Testament was a command that every Christian should go out into the world and preach the gospel.

But he had a qualm whether if he were invited to celebrate the sacrament he could do so. At first he did not need to face this doubt but then he was made preacher at Montbéliard, on the French–German border under the Lutheran Duchy of Württemberg, where other refugees from the French persecution gathered. They wished for the sacrament in the simpler reformed form and in French. He asked himself whether as they had officially chosen him as preacher of the Word, that included a commission to celebrate the sacrament. He hesitated for a time, especially because the priests and Lutheran pastors of the town were much against him, and then decided that his calling by the congregation must give him the right to celebrate the sacrament which they needed. Still feeling the desire that someone eminent should tell him that he was right, he asked his friend Oecolampadius at Basel whether he approved the decision. Oecolampadius approved.[4] This was not every reformer's opinion, for the call of the Church must be established clearly.

---

[3] Karl Schmaltz, *Kirchengeschichte Mecklenburgs*, 3 vols. (Berlin, 1935–52), i. 46. At Wismar Freder made the Low German text of the Church Order. He died in 1562 and was succeeded as superintendent by Wigand the historian. Melanchthon and Bugenhagen's judgement in CR vii. 740 ff.

[4] Oecolampadius to Zwingli, 21 November 1524, in Zwingli, *Op.* viii, in CR xcv. 252.

Visitations

The office of the bishop in the Lutheran churches lasted and lasts in all the Scandinavian churches. It did not last in Germany except in the form of the superintendents. For in most German Lands church government was easier by a committee with state authority—the consistory, part clergy part lawyers—they needed lawyers because reform interfered with existing legal rights. There was no choice. Government of the Church solely by the upper clergy, with laypeople having no part, had proved to be a bad form of church government. If the laity were to take any part in the Church, the only way came through organs of the State.

The duty of the bishop in caring for the Church had been called since the age of Charlemagne the *visitation*. In the Middle Ages it was an illusion, the idea of the bishop riding round personally to see that the parish priests did their duty and that his parishioners behaved morally; the vast western dioceses were too big, the manifold duties of the bishop in the State more pressing. His junior officials carried out what visitation was done. There existed handbooks for visitors and in their aims they were not unlike the much more systematic visitations of the Reformation and Counter-Reformation. But they hardly happened. Idealists sometimes called for the revival of visitations that the Church might be made more like its ideal, and good bishops practised them and kept a record of the proceedings now valuable to historians. But one difficulty was that even if zeal wanted reforms, implementing the reforms suggested by the visitors cut across the laws of the land and needed the State's power. The big difference came when Luther taught that this was the vocation of the State and not of bishops. Under an order elicited from the elector John of Saxony, Melanchthon wrote an *Instruction for Visitors*, to which Luther added a preface. It became a much-used guide for the reform of parishes.[5] It stated itself as a conscious revival of an ancient practice long neglected. It started a regular series of Saxon visitations: 1528 onward, 1533 onward, then not till 1555.

Visitations took time from many people and were some expense to the State. They were not popular with parsons who were reformed, nor with squires who were found not to be contributing as they ought to the maintenance of their parish. But they had some control over ex-monastic endowments and so were welcomed in parishes because they could help with the repair of church or manse and above all could help the starting of a new school. Parishioners also liked it when they outed an impossible or grossly immoral pastor.

---

[5] *Unterricht der Visitatoren an die Pfarrherrn* (1528); CR xxvi. 42–96.

The first visitors were a mixed committee of clergy and laity, nominated by the State: theologians, high civil servants, and in time also representatives of the people. This was not a standing commission, but a committee appointed solely for the one visitation. This changed when the superintendents were in office because they were permanent and were always members of the visiting committee. But unlike the medieval bishop they had no prison nor power to punish culprits, they could only inform the State authority. Yet they needed part of such power, for example to get rid of immoral clergy. So from the later 1530s the Wittenberg theologians recommended to the State that there be a mixed commission, under the name *consistory*, of clergy and lawyers who should have power to reform. The first consistory started work in 1539 and in the end this method became, not quickly, the universal system of church government in all the German evangelical churches. There were odd variations. In Brunswick-Lüneburg all the consistory was composed of civil servants. In Württemberg there was a *synod* (called by that name), a regular meeting of the general superintendents with authority over the various visitations. Such a body appointed pastors and sometimes schoolteachers, administered the 'patronage of the crown', the management of church endowments. In some Lands the consistory was also the marriage court (as it was in Geneva), in others marriage and divorce were under a separate court.

Luther and Melanchthon had little qualms, whether an excess of State power over the Church was thus conceded. But since there was no alternative the qualms were put aside. They did not object to the system, only to its abuses. They accepted that they faced an emergency. Luther called his elector a *Notbischof*, a bishop for a time of crisis. To maintain church independence of the State was a little easier in Lands where a powerful university drew students from other Lands. Then the freedom of the university corporation, with the theologians as its weighty faculty, spilt over into a measure of freedom for the church organs.

Visitations in Anhalt in 1544–5 are an example. Seventy parishes, 125 churches and chapels, but several parishes had no pastor. The visitors deprived a few clergy as inadequate or immoral, ordered some clergy to go on a course of study and pass an examination. They found one parson whose qualification was a previous training as a clown. The squires all approved of reform as a general idea but this approval did not stop them using their right as patron to appoint illiterates, often the verger or a farm labourer—but sometimes they could find no one else. Several manses had roofs with holes and broken windows. The visitors told the patrons they must only present educated men of good behaviour. The new cups for communion were not all satisfactory, one parson used a tankard. Priests still had concubines, and were ordered either to marry them or to put them away.

Here the visitors could see the need for mercy. An old priest could not wish to marry an illiterate but if he put her away, who would care for his needs? and how would she manage? They consulted Luther, who did not wish them to be rigid. It was agreed that older clergy might keep their women.

They found few laypeople who could manage the catechism. They were pleased with the schools in the town parishes, there were no schools in the villages. The visitors sought to turn vergers into teachers and accepted that a village school in winter might need to keep children warm with straw, which the children were to be asked to bring.[6]

The new system of consistories and visitations worked well all the century, in the promotion of better pastoral care in the parishes and better education. Naturally there were moments of local crisis in Church and State. One example: In the autumn of 1560 the university of Jena was in turmoil—demonstrations against professors, violence by students, congregations stamping out of church, a tumult during the main service. The duke held the professors' rigidity partly responsible and banned them from preaching. Has a secular government power to stop a pastor from preaching in his proper pulpit? They said that the duke attacked the freedom of the Church. Then, the duke created a new consistory, stronger, on which the professors did not sit and which was created without any reference to the church authorities (though among the members were the four superintendents). The professors said that this was a gross interference with church liberties; the new consistory would license publications and they said that the right to publish freely was inherent in the freedom to preach.

The question being raised was whether in crises of public order the usual liberties could rightly be suspended by the secular authority as responsible for order.

Bugenhagen

All over north Germany Johannes Bugenhagen, called Pomeranus because of his birth and youth in Pomerania, designed the new church orders.

He was a northern schoolmaster and priest who made his school well known. Erasmus was the first influence to reform when he read *The Praise of Folly*. Then someone gave him Luther's *Babylonish Captivity* and the reading shocked him, he was puzzled and disturbed. He wrote to Luther and said that he was confused, he did not understand the relation between faith and doing good. He asked for a rule of life. Luther sent him *The Freedom of a Christian*

---

[6] F. Westphal, *Georg der Gottselige zu Anhalt, sein Werden und Wirken* (Leipzig, 1907), 46–8.

Man, there is no need for a rule of life, the Holy Spirit will guide. He went to study at Wittenberg and soon was a friend of Melanchthon and then of Luther. He read Luther *On Monastic Vows*, and this was another shock, so powerful that Melanchthon mentioned it at his funeral. Clergy were starting to marry, he became engaged but his fiancée broke off the engagement for fear of disgrace at marrying a priest; so he married Walpurga and they lived in a miserable house on almost no pay. We know almost nothing about Walpurga, but she bore six children.

In 1524 the pastor of Wittenberg died. The chapter had the right to appoint. They chose Linck, excellent preacher. He refused. They chose Amsdorf, a man so close to Luther. He refused. After awkward delay the town council stepped in and offered it to Bugenhagen, who accepted, the chapter did not try to stop this breach of their rights. Bugenhagen remained town pastor of Wittenberg for thirty-four years till his death. He had gifts as pastor, greater gifts as organizer, and published commentaries on books of the Bible which later were expected to be in the private libraries of parish pastors.

A council or prince would need advice in reforming the Land or the town. They looked to Wittenberg for an expert who could show them how. The town of Brunswick was the first outside Wittenberg to summon Bugenhagen to organize its reformation, in 1528, and from that year he was repeatedly on leave from his Wittenberg parish on similar missions, sometimes for months at a time. He refused a series of tempting invitations including two bishops' sees. One reason why the north wanted him urgently was his Pomeranian native language, Low German, for so he could make himself understood from Hamburg to Copenhagen and from the Dutch border to the Polish. He was a practical man who realized that every situation which he met was unique and was willing to spend many hours in finding out what would be best for the place which then he advised. All his church orders had a common pattern. But his was not a rigid mind, he recognized that circumstances change and the needs of a church with them so that a church order was not unchangeable but might be adapted to a new situation—provided it remained faithful to the Word of God.

He could not get all he wanted. He wished the community, that is the people, to have a say in the choice of their pastors but often the historical rights of patrons were protected by law and sometimes the check on a patron's choice was only the clergy. He wanted bishops of small dioceses but preferred the word superintendent or superattendant to the word bishop. He wanted deacons for the welfare system and regarded these deacons as laypersons. All through the north he presided over reform; Hamburg, Danzig, Lübeck, his native Pomerania, Schleswig-Holstein. In Denmark he crowned the king and consecrated the reformed bishops.

Excommunication

Everyone was agreed that the use of excommunication—'the ban'—was deplorable. Like most things medieval the theory was better than the practice. It was accepted that a church could not go on allowing a glaring sinner or notorious criminal to continue to participate in sacred rites, to the scandal of ordinary folk. It was recognized that there ought to be a place for repentance, and it was the hardened who should suffer this penalty; that there were two aims neither of which should be forgotten, the aims of any penal system: the vindication of justice and the bringing of a bad person to a more moral and less anti-social way of life. But during the last two centuries of the Middle Ages it was used by the officers of bishops to penalize trivial offences; collected debts, like the payment of tithes, became a dubious means of securing that in stock dealings buyers stood to their word. It was used far too often, and hence was frequently disregarded. Penalties were supposed to be enforced by the secular courts but often they refused to inflict the penalties which church courts agreed or recommended. It was the least spiritual of penalties and cast its shadow over the greatest of sacraments.

The Council of Constance after 1414 demanded reform of the institution and something was done but the old ways continued, a practice offensive and trivial.

Yet a church needed discipline. Reformers had no idea of destroying what discipline there was, they wished to make it more effective that people might be moral. The border between sin and crime was not easy to draw. Any church must use the ultimate penalty of withdrawing the right of membership. In that society excommunication carried civil loss—customers refused to buy at that shop, former friends rejected invitations to that house.

Luther's own theory was that this was a purely spiritual penalty and had nothing to do with disadvantages in social life; its aim, reform, punishment that is a medicine. But since there is scandal, reconciliation needs not only penitence in the sinner but a public act of the Church—the congregation or its representatives.

In the social expectations of that age such a theory was too spiritual or too weak. Once the consistories were constituted, they had power to exclude from communion; and since they had a constitution from the State they could recommend penalties to the State authorities, and such a penalty as fines remained in the system of discipline. For a time representatives from the congregation were members of the court, but this acceptance of a congregational right to speak did not stay long.

Later certain evangelical Lands accepted it as law that an excommunicated person must be avoided in social life—Prussia in 1570 for example; and where it was not the law of the Land, the people were used to it and largely followed the old penalty.

Hence unavoidable conflicts between Church and State. The pastor believed himself to possess the absolute right, I am the only one who can decide whether or not this adulterer may come to communion. The magistrate thought that any penalty inflicted upon a citizen without due process of law and witnesses and the courts was not compatible with state authority; and could not be imposed at the whim of a pastor or an emotion of scandal moving a congregation. In several territories there were long battles between clergy who were sure that they had this right and magistrates who resisted their demands. In Mecklenburg the clergy fought over years, at last not unsuccessfully, to ensure that a committee of clergy could excommunicate. But in the end no state could allow a free right of excommunication to any pastor or any committee of clergy on which the State was not represented.

A crisis of Church and State in the very Protestant town of Jena in 1560 was in part caused because a pastor excommunicated one of his lay parishioners who was professor of law at the university: the offence, he declared in public that we can learn Christian truths out of the Roman philosopher Seneca. The offended pastor probably did not know that several early Christians supposed that Seneca must be a Christian, so noble were his moral opinions. The professor's undergraduates were incensed and when the pastor died two months later they sang a Te Deum outside his manse. With a likelihood of disorder as well as injustice, no sane government could risk allowing such a penalty to be uttered without appeal to a state court—at least, to a court which, if composed of clergy, should be legally advised and have the confidence of the state authority.

In Basel Oecolampadius had the useful experience of having once been canon penitentiary in a Catholic diocese. From that past he inherited the conviction that it was the church authorities and not the State which must exercise the discipline of the Church. When Basel was reformed he proposed that there should be a church court, presided over by a lay elder and composed of pastors and lay elders. When the plan came before the town council, it met vocal opponents. They consulted Berne, and Zwingli in Zurich. Both replied that the exercise of moral discipline is the duty of the State. Unlike other Swiss cities Basel decided that each congregation should constitute a committee for moral oversight composed of two members of the council and one of the congregation—but not the pastor, who should however be consulted. Therefore Oecolampadius won none of the principle for which he contended.

In Zurich Zwingli's friend Leo Jud was shocked by what led to Zwingli's death in 1531 and lost all confidence in the council. His conscience was troubled that he was a 'servant of a state church'. He demanded the separation of Church and State, the community should elect elders to a committee which with the pastors should have authority over morals. But Zwingli's successor Bullinger agreed with Zwingli, moral discipline is the duty of the State and should be handed over to representatives of the community and these could be magistrates or a committee of elders. In Zurich it had been given to the magistrates. Any attempt to alter it would fail. It was the business of a magistrate, not of a pastor, to punish. Leo Jud was not persuaded for he said that the handing over of this power to the magistrate was a fiction. Yet he respected Bullinger and worked with him loyally.

Whenever others in western Switzerland, like Calvin or Farel, struggled for the right of a church court to excommunicate, Bullinger always gave advice which cautioned against that constitution. Erastus, after whom Erastianism was named by the English, was born at Baden near Zurich and all his life was a disciple of Bullinger.

For Geneva Calvin created the most systematic of such moral provisions. He did not easily succeed in this. It took him fourteen years of friction between Church and State and at least two battles. He won his way by 1555, a success ensured because French refugees from persecution poured into the city. The worst battle was in 1552–3. A leading citizen, Philibert Berthelier, was excommunicated by the consistory. He appealed to the council, which lifted the excommunication. Calvin said that he would leave the city, and the pastors refused to give Berthelier communion. Other cases at the same time caused the council to deny the right of the consistory to excommunicate. The council knew that Berne took the dimmest view of Calvin's action. But the elections of the next two years gave Calvin's men a majority on the council, in May 1555 his leading opponents fled to Berne, and the consistory achieved almost total independence of the council. Calvin seemed to have won all for which he contended, that it is the church authorities who control excommunication. The council struggled to keep a right to interfere, with a little success, but did not meddle with excommunication.

In theory discipline was exercised by the whole congregation with their pastors and elders. The members of the congregation are to report immoralities which might otherwise be unknown to the pastors and elders. The sinner is to be brought before this consistory and if he or she is penitent a time of exclusion from communion is enough but in a public place in church so that everyone sees that penance is being done. If they are not penitent then the consistory is to hand them to the secular magistrates for punishment, which in extreme cases could mean exile or death. The consistory, and not the main committee of the town council, is the supreme authority over morals. That looks as though the Church and not the State is supreme. But the three main committees of the city government chose the elders, and from their own members. The pastors could suggest names of persons to be elected elder but had no control over the result. Before such elections Calvin normally preached, to urge the choice of truly moral persons. Thus the lay administrators of the discipline were elected by organs of the State who were themselves elected by the people. In one aspect the consistory with its control over behaviour was a church committee, in another aspect it was an instrument of state power.

The Geneva discipline was not universally successful. Two witnesses reported to the consistory that at times of sermon the taverns were full. Prostitutes were banned but they kept reappearing. Skittles were illegal but still the people played. Dancing was banned but a pastor walked by a house, and heard dancing within and went in to stop it and the dancers banged his head.

Yet the city was cleaned up. Adulterers, swearers, witches, shoppers who spent luxuriously, blasphemers, crypto-Catholics, misbehaviour at services, possession of Catholic books, using the miraculous powers of holy water for healing, all had a bad time. For visitors who liked a town to be clean, with a churchgoing people well-mannered, with good schools and a good college and good music, free of beggars or pickpockets or visible prostitutes, Geneva was a model, and the envy of many in Protestant Europe. If they envied the result they did not often wish to copy the methods by which it was achieved.

Berne gave a home to the chief opponent of Calvin on this theory of Church and State.

Wolfgang Musculus (Müslin) was a Benedictine monk and prior who was brought into the reform by reading Luther's books. He married and wrote as Bucer's secretary and then was invited to serve among the reforming pastors in the great city of Augsburg. Here he was soon the leader of reform and was weighty in making the structure of a reformed and populous city. When in 1547–8 Augsburg was forced by the emperor's army to accept Catholic restoration, he took refuge at Berne. He refused many invitations, including one by Archbishop Cranmer to England, and could have gone back to Augsburg. But he stayed in Berne and they used him as professor of Greek and Hebrew. There he became eminent through reforming Europe, by sane commentaries on the Bible and by translations into Latin of many of the Greek Fathers.

He became the theorist of Berne in the argument with Calvin over church government (*Loci Communes* (1560), many times reprinted, often translated). Are Calvin and his allies right in thinking that the New Testament offers us a model for the structure of Church and State? That cannot be right because primitive Christian congregations were working where the only link with the State was persecution. If we go back to the Bible for our lesson, it can only be to the models in the Old Testament, where are societies in which there is no distinction of church law versus state law and where the magistrates/kings also have their place in the spiritual care of the people. He imagined government to be like parents in a household, with responsibility not only for feeding and clothing the young and keeping them safe, but for helping them to grow to be educated persons and moral beings.

In this theory:

The government can
secure public safety, get rid of murderers and robbers;
maintain public honesty;
get rid of whoredoms and adultery and songs or dancing or garments which encourage wantonness;
see that no one lives unemployed;
see that no one lives only on the interest from investments (those governments which stop Jews from earning their livings in the ordinary ways are very wrong);
sanction laws on religion;
appoint ministers where they are needed, and appoint degrees of ministers at pastoral need, see that they teach rightly, and care for the sacraments;
care for the schools;
see that church endowment goes to its proper ends (ministers, widows, orphans).

For all these church duties it (or he) must have advice from qualified clergy because it cannot know enough without help.

The government cannot
save us from disease;
run our family lives or stop all quarrels between neighbours;
teach;
minister sacraments;
judge cases which come to the consistory court;
govern except according to the laws of God.

Suppose a tyrant. The Christian must suffer though it is not wrong to flee (Musculus had fled at the Interim). Eschew criminal means of revenge.

A Christian may not do criminal acts if ordered by a criminal government. The plea that they are forced does not stand.

May a tyrant be killed? If a governor fails to defend his people from their enemies may they defend themselves? No answer is possible; it depends on rare and special circumstances.

Musculus was the theorist of the doctrine which the English called after the name of Erastus; despite his key provision, that the State cannot judge cases in the consistory.

In Geneva Calvin disliked the way this was put. In Zurich it was welcome.

Bishops

The bishoprics were incorporated into the reformed churches in four ways:

1. The reformed church took no more notice of the bishop's rights. This might mean a fight. There was a battle at Geneva which the town won. It might mean that the bishop accepted that he could do nothing and went into retirement hoping that one day his old rights would be restored.

2. The bishop accepted the evangelical faith and reformed his territories accordingly with advice from Wittenberg. This happened in Prussia, and in rare dioceses in Scandinavia.

3. A bishop of the old faith died and the canons who had the right of election elected someone of the evangelical faith. This was the commonest way in which dioceses of Germany were reformed.

Legally the election afterwards needed approval from Rome. The electors might send a name to Rome and Rome would approve because it hoped that all was well. Or they might not bother to send anything to Rome, knowing that the mission would be useless.

4. A bishop of the old faith, in a see now surrounded by reforming states, died. The canons, though under pressure, refused to elect a Protestant successor or elected a Catholic. This happened rarely. When it did happen, neighbouring Protestant states stepped in either to secure an election better for them or to get rid of the bishop's authority altogether. But quite often they needed many canons to die off before they could win a majority for a reforming bishop, then the process could take decades while a powerless Catholic bishop sat hermit-like amid a diocese of Protestant clergy.

The New Testament sometimes talks as though in the earliest Church the bishop and the presbyter held the same office. As the work of the congregations developed, the representative quality of the bishop became ever clearer, and it was held that the jurisdiction of the priests derived from their bishop. But from the time of St Jerome about 400, it was accepted that there was 'a basic equality' between bishop and priests.

As the western Roman empire broke in pieces, the bishops were seen by the people as their best hope of justice and order. They were usually from old senatorial families of Roman descent and necessarily performed high offices in the State. Here was the making of that medieval pattern which created the prince-bishoprics of the German empire, and the pope's state in central Italy, and such giant-bishops as him of Durham who was a key in the defence of the Northumbrian border against the Scots. Even into the sixteenth century and after, the German bishops were almost all of noble families. These seemed remote from what the reformers were looking for.

They did not assume that bishops should be abolished. The early Church honoured them for wise reasons. But they found it hard to accept that a bishop should govern as a secular prince. They believed the mixing up of spiritual and secular authority to be what caused some of the ills of the Church. A few Catholic bishops agreed with them. Georg von Polentz, who was the bishop of Samland, happily surrendered his secular rights to the duke of Prussia and remained bishop of the diocese like an Anglican or Swedish bishop. His neighbour the bishop of Pomesania followed his example. The pair were not quite the only. But for one of the great sees to imitate them—Mainz, Salzburg, Trier, Cologne, Vienna—would cause bouleversement in that area, even a chance of European war. The archbishop of Cologne tried it on and there was soon a Catholic army in Cologne.

So it was necessary for the reformers to create a new kind of bishop. They accepted the doctrine of St Jerome that the two orders of the ministry are in essence one. Nevertheless because they needed them they had to select certain preachers and make them bishops. Mostly they preferred not to call them bishops, though why the name superintendent sounded better it is not now easy to see. The people often preferred to go on using the old name. The superintendent had no secular power, and a smaller area to care for, so that the vast dioceses of the Middle Ages which had made bishops invisible disappeared. Good bishops liked to sound a little modest now. When Prince George of Anhalt became a Protestant bishop, and his official title was Bishop, he still preferred to sign himself Georgius Presbyter.

Because bishop and presbyter were believed to be equal in rank, there seemed no reason why a presbyter should not consecrate someone to the office of bishop. In England and in Sweden, two conservative reformations, they took trouble that new bishops should be made bishop by other bishops in the historic way. The German reformers did not feel this important.

In 1542 they needed a bishop for Naumburg, a see which went back to before 1000. Luther's friend Amsdorf was chosen. Amsdorf was consecrated to the see by Luther himself. Luther even wrote a little book for the purpose, *The Way to Consecrate a Truly Christian Bishop.*[7]

Three years later George of Anhalt, who had been validly ordained as a Catholic priest, and was now the godliest of evangelicals, was made chief superintendent (a disguised way of saying archbishop) of Albertine Saxony. In this situation it was he who decided that he must be consecrated. He looked about for a bishop in the historic succession who was now evangelical—the nearest was a bishop in Brandenburg but he died; there were the two Prussian bishops but he was discouraged by the distance; he seems to

---

[7] *Exempel, einen rechten christlichen Bischof zu weihen, WA* liii. 231. But only two canons attended Amsdorf's consecration and he was never comfortable and after two years was ejected by the war.

have thought of Hermann von Wied, the archbishop of Cologne, who just then was turning to the Reformation—and again the distance was too great, with a risk of being cut off by marching troops. So he invited nearby Martin Luther, whom he held to be a true bishop ('God's blessing does not depend upon an external tradition'). In Merseburg cathedral on 2 August 1545 he was consecrated by the laying on of hands of Luther and the Saxon superintendents.

In 1537 King Christian III of Denmark was reforming his kingdom, a work for which he must have church money. The bishops, all but two of whom were less satisfactory as pastors than this sounds, refused to give way. So he must have new bishops. There were leading reforming pastors to consecrate. The government could have asked for the help of the Swedes to send bishops in the apostolic succession, but the politics of the moment made that unthinkable. In Danish eyes the Wittenberg leaders were more apostolic than any other bishops they could see. So they invited Bugenhagen, who had the extra advantage that he could speak Low German which many Danes understood. He consecrated the seven new bishops at Copenhagen, not without too long a sermon. Officially they were to be called superintendents. The people called them bishops.

In 1539 Albert of Prussia had the duty of nominating a new man to be archbishop of Riga and chose his brother. He asked Wittenberg, first, whether the bishop-elect must be consecrated in a Catholic way with leave from Rome, and, secondly, whether legally he must become a member of the Teutonic Order (from which this old right to nominate descended). Luther was resolute that the new archbishop must not be consecrated in the Catholic form.

Five years later the two dukes of Pomerania, uncle and nephew, had the duty of nominating a bishop of the see of Kammin. One of the dukes was Protestant the other less so; and they could not agree on a candidate. The uncle proposed a boy of seventeen years from his family and was faced with thunder from Wittenberg at the outrage. For a time there was despair, they talked of sending Bugenhagen, himself a Pomeranian, to act as bishop for the time being. But at last they agreed and a Pomeranian pastor was elected.

In all the areas under Swiss influence bishops vanished. Their theory of church government arose out of the practice of municipal government, in which a bishop had no place. Calvin claimed that his presbyterian theory of church government was that ordered by the New Testament and was a necessity for a Church organized according to the will of God.

In France there were many Catholic bishops and naturally some of them favoured the reform.

Caraccioli, an Italian prince who became bishop of Troyes, was present on the Catholic side at the Colloquy of Poissy between Catholics and

Protestants and was persuaded by what he heard from the Protestants. He was a preacher, bishops rarely entered pulpits. He said that he wished to be a Protestant but would remain the bishop of his see and keep the benefices which went with it. He took the title 'Bishop and minister of the holy gospel to the Church of God which is at Troyes'. He implied that other French bishops were ready to follow his example. Calvin was totally against the idea that someone could be a true reformed and bishop of a Catholic see with benefices.[8] Eventually Caraccioli resigned the see in return for a pension.

The bishop of Nevers, Spifame, became a Huguenot but there was no suggestion that he could stay a bishop, he left for Geneva where he came to a bad end. Not all the Catholic bishops who converted were as Calvin would wish. The bishop of Montauban fell in love, resigned his see, got rid of his benefices by selling them, married his lady, and retreated to Geneva where he lived comfortably on the proceeds of a barony which he had acquired with doubtful morality.[9] The French reformed hardly boasted of the conversion of a Catholic bishop of Montauban.

The bishop of Beauvais was the cardinal of Châtillon and famous as a leader of the Huguenot churches. He was deprived of all his benefices and appeared as a Huguenot military commander under the title the count of Beauvais. After peace was made he wore again his cardinal's robes and was excommunicated. Then he married and escaped dramatically to England where Queen Elizabeth received him and 'Madame la cardinale' with magnificence and he became a useful envoy for the French Protestants in England and was buried at Canterbury, admired by those who knew him.

The Roman Inquisition in 1563 summoned eight French bishops to answer a charge of heresy and fixed their names on the walls of Rome. This was unique. The Roman Inquisition was not quarter of a century old. Summoning so many French bishops at once was a sign not only of panic but of inexperience. The charges are of interest.

The bishop of Valence, a Dominican Jean de Montluc, denies transubstantiation and wants to give communion in two kinds and allows and even uses prayers in French and preaches in a hat and wants a union of two churches with a common creed. He had publicly demanded that Protestants be tolerated, and had attacked the cult of images. A prelate might see good in the Protestant ideals and yet wish to remain as Catholic as possible. Rome was specially worried about Montluc of Valence. Pope Pius V deprived him of his see but neither Montluc nor the French government took the least notice and he remained bishop of Valence.

The archbishop of Aix, Jean de Chaumont, was an archbishop from the

---

[8] Calvin, CR xix. 120 ff.
[9] Janine Garrisson-Estèbe, *Protestants du Midi: 1559–1598* (Toulouse, 1980), 21.

age of twenty-seven. He was converted to the reformed faith, and did what he could to persuade his clergy and his diocese. When Pope Pius V declared him removed from his see he did not question the verdict but went up into his cathedral pulpit on Christmas Day, said why the pope was wrong, and then threw off the cross and the mitre which he was wearing, walked out of the cathedral and joined the Huguenot congregation in the town. He married and rose to be a commander in the civil war. For 25 years there was no resident archbishop of Aix.

François de Noailles, of a famous family of aristocrats, was bishop of Dax. His son was to be a close friend of the cardinal of Châtillon, and it was difficult to prosecute someone because he was a friend of an alleged heretic. Rome made an effort to try him but failed and he remained as bishop not of the see of Dax but by the cardinal of Châtillon's wish bishop of Châtillon's see of Beauvais.

Claude Regin succeeded a Protestant, Roussel, as bishop of Oloron. Rome said that he did not wear a bishop's garments nor a tonsure and was 'notorious'. Pius V deprived him but he continued as bishop.

Charles Guillard was bishop of Chartres. He caused an ex-monk now a Protestant to preach in his cathedral and himself was known to attend Huguenot services in the city. Pius V declared him deprived—but no one took any notice, except the inhabitants; for when he caused another Huguenot to preach in the cathedral, the congregation made an uproar and there was riot outside in the town and the bishop vanished into retirement.

The bishop of Lescar, Louis d'Albret, was said to have compelled his clergy to attend Protestant sermons in the cathedral and later would watch the statues and pictures of the cathedral being destroyed without making any attempt to stop it. He put Protestant refugees to be pastors in parishes. He also remained a Catholic bishop although or because his see was within the kingdom of Navarre where his queen and relative Jeanne d'Albret befriended Protestants and tried to ban the saying of mass in Lescar. There was still a Catholic chapter with legal rights in Lescar.

The last of the eight bishops summoned by the Roman Inquisition was Jean de Saint-Gelais, who was bishop of Uzès. The charge was that he celebrated mass and gave communion in two kinds and gave communion to Cardinal de Châtillon.

Of the eight bishops summoned or deprived, two (Caraccioli of Troyes and the archbishop of Aix) became open Protestants. Two were evidently bishops loyal to the pope and Rome fussed about detail. The other four continued in their sees, as bishops with reforming sympathies, whatever the Inquisition said. That was partly through Roman error of judgement. The French government might be Catholic but was absolutely unwilling to allow eight bishops to be tried outside France.

Unlike what could happen in north Germany and Scandinavia, and to a less extent in England and Scotland, if they crossed from Catholic to Protestant, they could hardly remain bishops.[10]

Not only Catholics objected if a French bishop became a Protestant. Roussel was a priest who became reformed and passed time in Strasbourg. He was one of those who collected in Navarre. There, though now a convinced reformed pastor, he was offered the see of Oloron and accepted. Calvin was upset that a reforming pastor should become a bishop and protested. Roussel was fatally injured when a pulpit collapsed while he was preaching. Naturally there was rumour that enemies had sawn through the pedestal.

---

[10] A. Degert, 'Procès de huit évêques français', *Revue des Questions historiques*, lxxvii (1904), 61–108.

II

CREED

All the reforming churches ended up with creeds: called Articles of Faith, *Bekenntnisschriften* (statements of creed), in Latin confessio, credo, articuli fidei, regula fidei.

From the viewpoint of the pew, these did not feel important. Anglican worshippers only bothered with their Thirty-Nine Articles if they were bored during a sermon and whiled away the time by browsing in the back pages of the Prayer Book. Lutherans and Reformed were no different. It was in hymns and the words of prayers that theology made an impact upon the people. But for the Church at large such statements mattered because they were an attempt by a Christian community to express in brief the way in which it should speak about the gospel which it received and was sent to communicate. They had begun with the simplest and shortest—*Kyrios Jesus*, Jesus is Lord.

The idea behind the first such Protestant documents was not negative. The intention was not to say, the Church of Rome is wrong in some statements it makes officially. The object was wider—this is the belief of the Christian Church. But the one could not help but merge into the other even if the intention remained positive.

Meanwhile many former Catholic priests were ministers in reforming churches. All their communities were formed on the plea that the Bible is the safeguard of truth. Then lines needed laying down on how pastors should teach from their pulpits. No previous 'creeds' had quite tried to serve this purpose. The Apostles' Creed was used at baptisms. The so-called Nicene Creed was the ecumenical creed but had slightly different forms in East and West.

The idea was not rapid in coming to expression. In 1533 Melanchthon talked in the university about the need for a body of doctrine, *corpus doctrinae*, and meant by that a general statement of Catholic faith—'a teaching pure and in accordance with the gospel'—which would be valid for all the churches and exclude the errors of fanatics or extremists. A few years later, as church orders were drafted for reforming territories, Melanchthon's colleagues composed within the church order a list of documents which made the *corpus doctrinae* for that Land. The most influential during the earlier period was drafted by Melanchthon himself not long before his death, in winter 1559–60—sometimes known because of its chief author as the *Corpus doctrinae Philippicum*.

These bodies of doctrine always consisted of lists of previous statements. Normally they contained

1. The three creeds of the early Fathers (Apostles, Nicene, Athanasian).
2. The Augsburg Confession, presented to the emperor and the imperial diet in 1530 as a statement of what evangelical Christians believe—mostly this was drafted by Melanchthon. It became the work of a committee which used language which probably he would not have chosen but essentially it was his Confession. It had the merit that its language enabled as many Protestants as possible to accept it, and it showed Catholics how Protestants agreed with them in main points of faith. This destined it to permanent value in German history.

Its principal author did not imagine that he wrote a creed. He thought it a document for discussion with Catholics, his personal effort.

Of all the bodies of doctrine this was the only part which received recognition in the Reich as a profession of faith which it was legal for any state to profess; made Reich law in the two diets of 1555 and 1648. It took a few years before it achieved the status proving the inner orthodoxy of a person or state. After Luther's death the university of Wittenberg compelled doctors to accept it before they took the doctor's degree.

3. Melanchthon's Apology. At the Diet of Augsburg 1530 a committee of Catholics drafted a reply (*Confutation*) to the Augsburg Confession—principal author Johann Eck, a fierce drafter; a summary of what conservatives objected to in evangelical reform: seven sacraments and celibacy of clergy and mass in Latin and communion in one kind are essential, the doctrine of sacrifice in the mass, the life of monks, the jurisdiction of bishops. They did not print this for reasons of diplomacy. But into the resolutions of the diet it was proposed that the Augsburg Confession was with good scriptural and other grounds rejected. So the Confession needed more instant defence.

Melanchthon was at once given the task of answering this *Confutation*. The result was the Apology. A quick draft was ready to give the emperor but he was prevented from receiving it. So Melanchthon started to work over it to make something better and worked during the journey home and went on for a few months at Wittenberg and it was ready in May 1531. In many of the *corpora doctrinae* the Augsburg Confession was treated as inseparable from the Apology. It now contained a systematic doctrine of justification by faith.

4. The Schmalkald Articles. In 1536, hearing the pope's plan for a general council which turned eventually into the Council of Trent, the elector John Frederick of Saxony asked Luther for a statement of faith which could

be used to send to the coming council. Luther was very ill and wrote the draft in the mood of a person who writes a witness to his faith before he dies. He consulted a few of the Wittenberg divines (Agricola and Amsdorf and Spalatin) but it remained his personal testimony—he could not at the time write so he dictated it. After it was argued about in a wider context other theologians took part, especially Melanchthon who added a little treatise on the authority of the pope.[1] But the atmosphere of the document, that at bottom it was the last will and testament of Martin Luther as a religious thinker, gave it a permanent authority; and the Saxon elector John Frederick revered it as Martin Luther's message from the sickbed where he expected to die and made sure that his church treated it with the reverence which such a document deserved.

The papers were brought to the meeting of the Schmalkald League in 1537, which did not formally approve them. Next year, 1538, they were published; and then they were taken up into various of the *corpora doctrinae* under the name the Schmalkald Articles.

They were more detailed, and so more restrictive or binding on preachers than the Augsburg Confession. To believe in justification by faith alone became an essential; to reject purgatory, relics, indulgences, pilgrimages, invocation of saints, monasteries, the doctrine of the pope's authority, became necessary; and by a statement which was not in Luther's original text, and which Melanchthon tried to soften, the doctrine of real presence at the eucharist became necessary.

As early as 1553, the credal status of these articles was shown when the edition of that year altered Luther's *I* in two phrases such as *I believe* into *We*.[2] Certain Lands imposed them more narrowly than others. At its most severe, the new university of Jena in 1558 demanded their acceptance not only by all professors but by all students.

Thus the main credal statement of evangelicals had become the Augsburg Confession with the Apology, and the Schmalkald Articles.

5. Luther's Shorter Catechism was often added.

6. Melanchthon's *Instructions to the Saxon Visitors* of 1528 were sometimes added.

Hence these 'creeds' were framed in a way different from the creeds of antiquity. They were statements, originally personal statements (by two known authors, Melanchthon and Luther) and then accepted and slightly modified by others; designed first with the object of explaining to the emperor, or the pope, or the diet or the pope's Council of Trent, not only how they believed in the gospel but why they must criticize parts of the teaching of the Church among Catholics; and secondly, in effect much more

---

[1] *Tractatus de potestate et primatu papae*, BSLK, 469 ff.   [2] *TRE* xxx. 217 (Klaus Breuer).

importantly, giving pastors in parishes the structure of doctrine which should lie beneath their teaching of Scripture to their people.

For fifty years of the sixteenth century much of the theologians' time was taken with weighing and agreeing such *corpora doctrinae*. Yet to the churches the ways of worship were far more important than articles of faith. The German Encyclopaedia recognized it for England when it said that the Anglican articles of faith were the Book of Common Prayer. In Germany the argument was far more relevant to the people when it concerned whether the emperor could force them to use surplices in church, or compel them to accept that there are seven sacraments. But the Reformation had begun in a protest about truth. The way in which Christian truth was expressed mattered deeply to everyone who thought about how the Church could be made better. That meant, trying formally to exclude the teaching of error from the pulpits of a church; and that meant, framing articles which ordinands or persons appointed to a parish should accept *ex animo*.

The Reformed Churches of the Swiss tradition made no comparable effort to accept creeds which would be of general validity. A city-church might draft a statement of the faith for a particular purpose and have it accepted by another city or cities. But they also used the pleas of individuals—for example Zwingli's *The Reason of Faith* (*Ratio Fidei*, 1523) which he sent as an explanation to the emperor in 1530. These documents by famous Swiss minds sometimes took the place of articles of faith. Calvin's *Institutes*, in its final version a very large book, became so famous and so revered that in the churches of that tradition it was treated as though it was an unusually long creed. Out of it three countries composed articles—France, Confessio Gallicana, 1559; Scotland, Confessio Scotica, 1560; Netherlands, Confessio Belgica, 1562.

In Geneva Theodore Beza wrote a book called *The Confession of the Christian Faith* (1560) which the Hungarians used to turn into a creed.

The early Swiss creeds which aimed at an acceptance beyond that of one city or canton were (1) Confessio Helvetica, 1536, later called prior; (2) Confessio Helvetica posterior, 1562. But as in Germany the various *corpora doctrinae* were less important than Luther's catechism or the way of worship, these Swiss Confessions were less weighty in the life of the Church than the big books by the theologians or the catechisms which arose out of them.

As Calvin's *Institutes*, though not a creed, had the force of a creed in many churches of the Swiss tradition, one Lutheran book had for a time this quality in north Germany. While Luther was hidden in the Wartburg, Melanchthon in Wittenberg worked on a textbook of Christian doctrine and gave lectures. Students published their notes of the lectures without asking him. He was cross (he was only twenty-three) and decided to print a considered treatment. He called it *Loci Communes* (*Commonplaces*), literally texts or themes that are familiar. It was intended as an outline of the topics which students of the Bible should consider especially—how school interpretations have been wrong and how the Bible is useful for the moral life. The book was neither systematic nor profound. Its author lamented it as inadequate. Luther liked it and it became the standard textbook for instruction in Christian doctrine. Early in the 1540s Melanchthon rewrote it, and his last edition of 1559 is four times the length of the original book. Even during his life it went through some fifty printings. Its highest praise came in Luther's Table Talk; 'Next to Holy Scripture there is no better book.'[3] This verdict was the generosity of private friendship.

The eucharist

German evangelicals could not trust the Swiss divines despite the force and coherence of such as Calvin or Bullinger. They did not agree about Church and State nor always about the idea of God's election. But these alone would not have caused breach in communion between them. The separating difference was that over the nature of the presence at the sacrament.

In the Church of the Fathers language about the holy communion was varied. At first they could use words like 'the figure of the Body', or at the communion Christ presents again his Body, *repraesentat*. But they did not intend what later was argued, a distinction between the *figure* and its *truth*. They might talk of bread and wine being symbols, but less in our way of using the word than in the belief that the symbol was the object which it represented. They already took care that the bread for the communion was guarded from irreverence even when it was not in actual use at the liturgy. With the Greek philosophical background of the penetration of material things by an ideal or spiritual world, the sense of presence was easily accepted and they felt no need to define a theology of presence in the sacrament. The Last Supper continues down the generations, Christ giving himself to his disciples for eternal life. Then at the end of the fourth century St Ambrose of Milan taught his people that the bread and wine are 'changed' into the Body and Blood by Christ's word. St Augustine soon afterwards, with his sense of the social mission of Christianity and the vocation of the Church, quite disturbed posterity by the sentence 'It is you' (i.e. the Christians, the Body of Christ) 'who are the sacrament (*mysterium*) on the Lord's table.' The language was more symbolic than that of Ambrose and these two Western authors were appealed to in the arguments of the Middle Ages. So early as the ninth

[3] *TR* v. 5511. Abridged English translation of the *Loci Communes* by L. J. Satre and W. Pauck, *Library of Christian Classics*, 19 (1969), from R. Stupperich's 1952 selection.

century there are signs of priests, out of reverence, reading the consecrating words of the Last Supper in a low voice. Now began new definition—the flesh of the eucharist is the same substance as the flesh that was born from Mary—and such a definition met critics, the big arguments of the Middle Ages began.

In the eleventh century Berengar of Tours said that the bread and wine could be nothing but symbols and the Lord cannot be actually present in the body because his body ascended into heaven and is with God the Father. This radical attitude provoked more definition—the substance of the bread and wine, that is the inner essence of the two elements, is changed into the substance of the Body of Christ. The word *transubstantiation*[4] to describe this change appeared first during the twelfth century but it arose directly out of the reaction to Berengar. Because they could not bear the purely symbolic, there were those who went offensively to the other extreme—at communion the Body of Christ is chewed by the teeth of the communicants. These extreme phrases were not found among the best minds. But by the time of St Thomas Aquinas in the thirteenth century he regarded it as heretical to say that after consecration the bread and wine are still present with the Body of Christ.

The teaching made possible the practice of giving communion only in the bread; which was needed in northern lands where no wine was growable, and was desired by priests nervous of spilling wine or of irreverence when communicating a large congregation; though this was rare, once or twice or at most three times in the year. The teaching also encouraged the feast of Corpus Christi as a special yearly procession of the sacrament, first celebrated at Liège in 1246, after which it met resistance but then was accepted for the whole (Western) Church only eighteen years later.[5]

Then, late in the Middle Ages, came the Nominalist philosophers with the axiom that the particular thing is what is real and generalities describing the thing are but words and not reality. At one time when historians wrote about the causes of the Reformation they were accustomed to list Nominalism. More recently the world doubted whether a people can be so moved to action by subtle philosophical thought. But in this single place it mattered. Transubstantiation contradicted Nominalist theory of truth. It said that the idea or essence of the bread changes and does not leave behind bread but only the outward appearance of bread.

For the Nominalist the outward appearance is part of the essence of the bread. They were too orthodox to deny the teaching of the Church, that the

[4] A word first found in Bandinelli's *Sentences*, c.1150; first used in church law by the Lateran Council of 1215.

[5] Cf. Colin Morris, *The Papal Monarchy*, Oxford History of the Christian Church (Oxford, 1989), 375, 469.

bread changes into what is not bread. But they said the change was not revealed in Scripture and was irrational, therefore its truth was a sign of God's almighty power and of the great authority of the Church.

And once the authority of the Church was challenged, for example over indulgences, transubstantiation, which now rested only on that authority, dropped.

But Luther was not dropping the faith of the centuries since Berengar. He jettisoned what he took to be a piece of philosophical error. The bread is bread after consecration. But it is made his Body. Can we say that he is *in* the bread? We can. All are agreed that it is a spiritual gift, but can we also say that there is a bodily consuming? We can.

What mattered to Luther was the objective nature of the gift, 'outside us'. He was wholly agreed that only persons with faith can benefit from the gift. But if we say, this is a gift which comes to us through faith (of which the bread and wine are symbols) Luther believed that there is a risk that the Presence is believed to be manufactured by our faith.

To the contrary: Zwingli and the Swiss were afraid of the old superstitions which transubstantiation had allowed, with simple people treating the consecrated bread as an amulet. Zwingli accepted that God used material signs and symbols to convey his blessings. But we cannot think the bread is the actual fleshly body, it is a symbol of the body. He understood 'This is my Body' to have the sense 'This is a symbol of my Body', 'This signifies my Body.' The chief purpose of the sacrament is the *remembering* of the Last Supper and the cross that followed. But this is not a *mere* remembering. As it presents cross and risen life to the communicant it is the vehicle of the gift of Christ through the Spirit. And as a common meal it is a corporate act, the centre and the making of the Church which is his Body. Hence he made a difference between the divine and human natures. The human body of Christ is in heaven and not here. It is the divine nature which is given through the sacrament.

In this way the reforming churches were divided by an article of the Creed. There were three attempts to bridge the gulf:

1. Luther met Zwingli at Marburg, 1529.

A political pressure, especially from the landgrave Philip of Hesse who thought this argument was about words, underlay the meeting. Under threat from a Catholic emperor Protestants must try to be united. The theologians took no notice of the politicians and hammered away at truth from the Bible. But they were the most powerful team of reforming theologians ever seen in one place during the history of the Reformation: Luther and Melanchthon from Wittenberg, Oecolampadius from Basel, Zwingli from Zurich, Jacob Sturm and Martin Bucer from Strasbourg, Brenz from Württemberg, Osiander from Nuremberg. Calvin and Bullinger were not yet well enough known. They all talked German and the landgrave was present throughout. In the middle of the room was a table at which Luther and Melanchthon sat on one side, Zwingli and Oecolampadius sat on the other, for these four were admitted to be the leading arguers for each school. This was the famous table on which Luther wrote with chalk the Latin words of consecration, *Hoc est corpus meum*, This is my Body.

Oecolampadius said it must be metaphor. Luther said that Christ's command had made a bodily eating a spiritual event. They went on for three days but attained nothing further except civilized aspiration that there might be less division. Those ecumenical minds Bucer and Melanchthon tried to find formulas of compromise and failed to persuade either side to accept them. The Swiss proposed that they agree to disagree—they could be Christians in full communion with each other and yet hold different doctrines on the sacrament. The Lutherans said that this was not possible. But otherwise they agreed on common articles of faith. Hence the Marburg Colloquy did not do the harm which used to be attributed to it. There was a confession of an evangelical faith.

2. Suffering all the time from the illusion that it was only needful to find the right formulas and union could be achieved, and tireless in the pursuit of the union of the churches, Martin Bucer achieved a change which made a big difference to the future of Germany.

In 1534 he put forward the preposition 'with'. The gift of the Body of Christ is given WITH the bread; avoid 'IN the bread' or 'symbolized by the bread'. God gave two things simultaneously—bread and wine to the body, spiritual gift to the soul. That Christmas he happened to meet Melanchthon at Kassel and persuaded him, another ecumenical mind, that this was a possible way to find more unity and not untrue to the New Testament.

3. Melanchthon tried again to see if he could not alter the phrases of the Augsburg Confession and so make language which both sides would accept. Because the document started as his personal draft and was only beginning to take the status of a creed, he did not see why he should not amend the text in the light of mature consideration. He had long been thinking about the history of the eucharist. He was persuaded by Oecolampadius that the early Church had more than one definition of the nature of the eucharist. Then in various consultations he met Martin Bucer, with his ecumenical aspiration and his use of the word *with*. Though he believed Luther to be right, that in the words 'This is my Body', *is* meant *it is* and not *it symbolizes*, he respected Bucer's way of putting it as sufficient for truth and could not see why it should be rejected as heresy. This was not easy for him because he was very close to Luther who believed it was indeed heresy.

In September 1540 Melanchthon made a revised text of the Augsburg Confession. This won the name *Confessio Augustana Variata*.

'In the Lord's Supper they [the evangelicals] teach that with the bread and wine the body and blood of Christ are truly given to those who receive.'

Many Swiss could accept it and at first the Germans did not realize how important was the change in the drafting. But ten years later, when controversy made Melanchthon suspect to the strict disciples of Luther, they sometimes focused upon this Variata text to prove that Melanchthon was not faithful to his master.

The Variata had long consequences in the history of Germany. The Lutheran states in general insisted on the unvaried (*Invariata*) 1530 text of the Augsburg Confession. But little by little certain German states preferred the Variata; either because like the Palatinate they were influenced by Swiss ideas coming through Strasbourg and the Rhineland, or because they were attracted by Melanchthon's moderation and ecumenical spirit. The crux was when the Variata text was accepted by the diet as a legally valid edition of the Augsburg Confession; and therefore, once any Land which accepted the Augsburg Confession could claim toleration in the Reich, the heirs of Oecolampadius and Calvin assumed toleration because they could sign this version of the Confession. The claim was not quite assured. The Diet of Augsburg in 1566 accepted it as correct but many Lutherans refused to allow that ruling. Nevertheless the existence of Melanchthon's Variata during the years from 1555 to 1618 helped to keep Germany from civil war.

Calvin accepted Bucer's doctrine, *with the bread*. In 1549 he reached an agreement with Bullinger, the so-called *Consensus Tigurinus*, so that all the Swiss churches could be said to be united on this issue. The publication of this agreement caused a wave of criticism from the more severe Lutherans, led by Joachim Westphal who was then a pastor at Hamburg. Calvin's reply, *Secunda Defensio*,[6] was a cry of faith in the basic unity of Lutheran and Reformed. It made no difference. The strict Lutherans were sure that Calvinists departed from the Catholic faith of the centuries which was right because of the plainest words of Scripture. Thus Lutheran and Reformed were divided till modern times by these views of the nature of the Presence in the eucharist.

Since each German Land was self-governing in its church, the *corpus doctrinae* varied from Land to Land; not at base, which was always the Augsburg Confession and the Apology and almost always the Schmalkald Articles. This variety caused disputes especially when a pastor from one Land was to be given a ministry in another, or when the theologians of a Land university assailed the ideas of the theologians of another Land university. Argument begot a desire for more precision of language; and more precise formulas were narrower language and so made argument more common.

[6] 1556, Calvin, CR ix. 50–120.

There were three chief reasons why precision should be sought.

The pope was busy with the Council of Trent, which was engaged in repudiating what Protestants taught. That made Melanchthon's moderation about Catholicism not adequate to Protestant needs.

Since there was dispute with the Calvinists over the Presence in the sacrament, there needed to be definition about Presence in the sacrament.

Because the doctrine of justification by faith alone was at the heart of the faith professed by Protestants, it needed argument how to define it rightly; especially on the part which human decision has in accepting faith.

Because a university was now a power in its Land, and theology was the most influential faculty and its professors were often the best paid, some of the best German minds of the sixteenth and earlier seventeenth centuries were to be found in the chairs of divinity. Piece by piece they built up a structure of faith, a coherent system which might be called a Summa. This could not be done by resting on Luther, whose mind was not of system but of insights. German historians called what happened the Confessionalizing, where the word confession was used to mean creed, and where more modern commentators defined the time as the age of Lutheran Orthodoxy. Though it had a philosophical basis in the theories of Aristotle, it took little notice of the Summas of the Middle Ages, its centre was the study of texts and teachings in the Bible while it took some account of the early Christian Fathers and the ways in which they interpreted the Bible. Its fruition came in the seventeenth century. But already in the early decades after Luther's death, it began with systems such as that of Hyperius in the university of Marburg, or of Daniel Chyträus, who had sat under Luther's lectures and lived in Melanchthon's house and went to the then dismal university of Rostock and became not only its famous professor of theology but the reviver of the university.[7]

Since the church of every Land was independent, each decided its own *corpus doctrinae*, but this was usually the same as others for the most part because it must include the early creeds and the Augsburg Confession and Apology and normally the Schmalkald Articles. But from the 1550s it was asked whether there could not be a *corpus doctrinae* agreed between all the evangelical Lands. Because of so wide a common agreement which no one denied, this was expected to be simple. It was not. Like other university faculties theologians could be fierce with each other, and any Land could be strong in insisting on what it wished. After Luther's death Melanchthon had not the same uniting power for reasons which we shall see later. It took quarter of a century, till the fifty-year celebration of the Augsburg Confession in 1580, till a *corpus doctrinae* was agreed—called the Formula of

---

[7] Hyperius, *De Theologo* (1556); Chyträus, *De Studio Theologiae* (1560).

Concord, received by most Lutheran states. In Lands like Saxony and Württemberg this received legal status, as that to which pastors and teachers and professors of theology must assent. Though rejected by a few Lands, it was accepted later in Germany as a concluding landmark in the early stages of evangelical thought.

In the Reformed Churches a similar process was observable—good minds, this time not mostly in universities but in academies, developing thought in relation to the controversies of the day and the new information from better texts. There was a big difference, for they had in their foundation a theologian of system, it was truer to call Reformed divinity by the name Calvinism than it was to call German evangelical divinity by the name Lutheranism.

12

EDUCATION

Catechism

The near-universal form of teaching in reforming Europe, in many villages the only form at first was the catechism. The word came from *echo*, personalized by the Greeks as Echo the nymph of the mountains, a cry that returned across the valley. So the earliest form of teaching was an echo—the teacher says a sentence, the pupils repeat it. St Paul used *catechumen* to mean a person under instruction in the faith. The early Christians knew of instruction by question and answer before the convert was baptized and confirmed. A simple creed like the Apostles' Creed was an outcome of the method. All through the Middle Ages the West believed that this creed was given to the Church by the apostles even though the form in which we now use it is first found as late as 710; it was thought that in the years of persecution the Creed was kept private to the Christian community, a 'secret of the faith'. When the Greek archbishop of Ephesus came to Ferrara in 1438 and said that if there had been such a creed originally it would have been mentioned in the Acts of the Apostles, he shocked his audience. Renaissance scholars like Valla did not doubt that the Apostles' Creed was very early, but they queried whether it could be given by the apostles.

Since new Christians from the fifth century were nearly all babies, the class before baptism disappeared. Yet priests concerned with the ignorance of their people used the method, even in the eleventh century there are traces of religious instruction by question and answer. In the later Middle Ages it came to a syllabus: four passages which the growing child ought to know—the Lord's Prayer, the Apostles' Creed, the Ten Commandments, and the Hail Mary; together with a first confession of sin.

In English the first known use of the word catechism is in 1506 by Wynkyn de Worde. Three years later John Colet ordered boys at his newfounded school at St Paul's to learn the catechism; the verb goes back half a century before that; yet even in 1540 Archbishop Cranmer of Canterbury needed to explain what a catechism is, an instruction in religion for young people.

The most popular catechism of the Reformation was Martin Luther's Shorter Catechism.[1]

Early in his career Luther asked himself what a reformed catechism ought to be. He dropped the Hail Mary but thought that the other three parts were the right base for instruction and to them should be added a simple explanation of the two sacraments of baptism and holy communion. The first book called a Catechism, for the purpose of teaching the young, was put out by a Lutheran in 1528. The following year Luther published two forms of catechism, the Shorter and the Longer. Since these two became famous the Christian Church hereafter adopted the word catechism to describe such a book.

He was moved to write it because he went on a visitation of the parishes and discovered an abyss of ignorance about the elements of faith and extraordinary inability in pastors to communicate the Christian religion. He thought about it as 'a little Bible for laypeople'.[2]

The atmosphere was new in that it used the Ten Commandments to the end of devotion. In the second section on the Creed he made it personal—God has made *me*, my body and soul, eyes and ears and limbs, my reason and my senses; my clothes and shoes, my food and drink, my home and wife and child and garden and animals, and has given the protection and care that I need—and all this though I do not deserve it; so I am to be grateful and praise him and serve him. And through his Son he has redeemed me and won me from sin and death and the devil. If this personal quality in the catechism is true of commandments and creed it is truer still of the questions and answers on the Our Father.

After the three historic pieces of religious education came (1) question and answer on the sacraments with forgiveness as the key—baptism as the water of regeneration, confession (this bit was added on second thoughts), the receiving of the Body and Blood with its basic texts of the Bible; (2) a form of family prayer on getting up and before going to bed; and (3) added later, a short exhortation on how each member of a household ought to behave, including their obedience to the magistrate and their attention to the teachers and pastors.

Part of its strength rested on his feeling that it helped him. He said that when he fell into one of his moods of temptation, he would recite its words to himself; 'I am a doctor and a preacher . . . but I must remain, and I happily remain, a child learning the catechism.'

Wittenberg printed it with devotional material added, psalms and hymns and illustrations. It was in no sense a complete textbook of Christian

---

[1] By its original title *Der kleiner Katechismus fur* [*sic*] *die gemeine Pfarrherr und Prediger* (first appeared 1529), edition of 1531 in *WA* xxx. 1. 239 ff.

[2] *WA* xxx. 1. 27; *TR* v. 581; for Luther's catechisms see Hans-Jürgen Fraas, in *TRE* xvii. 723.

doctrine. Yet it had the heart of Luther's thought—justification by faith, a soul simultaneously a sinner and made righteous through Christ, forgiveness as the essence of the gift in the sacraments. It was one of his best achievements, to take the old material for the instruction of the young or illiterate and make it fresher and more devotional. The Wittenberg church order required its public recitation.

Henceforth all Lutheran catechisms depended on these two catechisms. It became a holy book. Later editions expanded it with Bible texts and parables. After Luther's death several editions put his portrait as a frontispiece.

Successors found it too important to leave alone. They extended it, packed it, expounded it, decorated it, until it looked more like a treatise on dogma than a pastoral affection for the young. They tried to push into it their safeguards against error in theology; Opitz[3] even added a catalogue of heresies. Teachers in schools or parish Sunday schools adapted it. Then children learnt the explanations by heart and the matter to learn was bulkier and the last state was worse than the first. Gradually they went back to the Shorter Catechism as Luther left it. Wherever Bugenhagen reformed the churches of north Germany he took with him the Shorter Catechism.

The catechism was not confined to what were later called Sunday schools. Catechism services happened where all the people answered the questions of minister or schoolmaster or verger, so that the many who could not read learnt the answers as well as the literate; with one piece of the catechism on one Sunday and the next the following Sunday. They were tools to educate adults. When a verger led them they were confined to learning the text, when a good preacher led them he expanded the exercise into something better than repetition, such as explanation of prayers or psalms. In 1552 Bugenhagen said that he had preached fifty times on the catechism, and later a collection of his catechism-sermons was printed. Usually these catechism-services happened at 2 p.m. on Sunday. These texts became the syllabus for religious education in schools.

This had an effect on the language. It gave a biblical colouring to ordinary speech. It affected families because parents helped their children with the homework of learning. There are known cases of children being able to answer questions from the catechism at the age of four.

The Swiss tradition of instruction for the young began with a little book by Zwingli on the education of children in the faith (*Kurzer christlicher Unterweisung*). All the leaders of the Reformed tradition tried to draft such help. Calvin took his own *Institutes*, a long work of adult theology, and made

---

[3] Opitz succeeded in 1571 at the age of twenty-nine to the chief pastorate at Regensburg; which found him too controversial and reluctantly dismissed him. He went to Vienna where he sometimes had congregations of 8,000 evangelicals; but counter-reformation was coming to Austria and he was again dismissed and died young.

a summary for children. Luther made a short question and answer and others heaped it into a dogmatic treatise. Calvin took a dogmatic treatise and slimmed it down for children. Luther had seventy-eight questions, Calvin had 373. (The Anglican catechism in its final form had twenty-five questions, and was blamed by Calvinists for brevity.)

The climax in the Reformed tradition was the Heidelberg Catechism of 1563.[4] It drew a little from the south German text of Luther's Shorter Catechism. Its success was international, because of the affection which it inspired among young and old. It was longer than Luther's (129 questions) and demanded more of the children. It was very clear, and biblical. It had much of the same personal and devotional quality as Luther's. It took it for granted, and was afterwards blamed for taking it for granted, that young people learning these answers are among God's people and will be brought to blessedness. It also owed its power to the moderation with which it stated doctrine. One big difference between Lutheran and Calvinist thought concerned predestination. For Luther providence was a mystery hidden in the lap of God and we cannot probe further than the texts of the Bible. For Calvin it was an essential truth for Christian life—the sense of our nothingness as we are called to the eternal purpose—and must be proclaimed to the people. Yet the Heidelberg Catechism had nothing on the subject of reprobation to eternal damnation and little on the idea of God's election. It has more sense of assurance—that is, a conviction that I am called to eternal life—as its doctrine of faith was longer and more expounded.

The Swiss could not use Luther's Catechism. It talked of three sacraments, they were sure there were two. Lutherans were happy with pictures in church, Reformed were not. The Presence in the sacrament was believed to be so wide a difference that they dare not use each other's catechisms.

Confirmation

This course of religious education lacked at first a focus, a conclusion that was a symbol of a stage of life completed. Parents and godparents had brought the baby to the font. After eleven to fifteen years the child could understand much of what they had then professed, and could learn the catechism, and should receive the faith consciously and be granted by the Church full membership and the right to receive holy communion. This climax of catechism was soon called confirmation.

---

[4] Authors, Olevianus and Ursinus. Olevianus studied at Geneva, under Calvin, at Zurich under Peter Martyr, and at Lausanne under Beza, so he could hardly have had a better religious education. Expelled from his birthplace Trier he won fame as a preacher at Heidelberg. He had charm and business ability. Ursinus was a Wittenberg graduate and pupil of Melanchthon. He was recommended by Peter Martyr for the chair of theology at Heidelberg in 1561. He was a retiring scholar.

In the earliest rites of baptism, after the immersion into water or pouring of water, came a laying on of hands, in the East an anointing with oil by the priest ('the seal'), in the West a laying on of hands by the bishop. These rites were associated with 'the gift of the Holy Spirit', the grace that enabled the new Christian to live as a Christian soul. As the number of Christians grew it was impossible for the bishop to be present at all baptisms. Hence the priest baptized the baby, and later at another service the bishop laid on his hands. So the rite of Christian admission was divided into two, and both parts were later to be called sacraments.

But then the Church converted barbarian tribes, and the bishop now had to care for areas as wide as a county or wider, and travel was neither comfortable nor safe. The theory still preferred confirmation to be near in time to the christening. But the rite must have a bishop; the bishop was hardly ever there; the children waited, sometimes till their teens. In the early Church confirmation was the climax of the rite of admission. Now perforce it became an optional extra and the weight rested on the cleansing water of baptism. Gradually the hand-laying dropped out of use and anointing was the way the gift was symbolized. The meaning of confirmation was a sending out, strengthened by the Holy Spirit, to do the Church's work in the world. From this idea of strengthening came the word *confirmatio* as a Western name.

The reformers saw no scriptural grounds for calling confirmation a sacrament, which in any case was so largely disused. Baptism admitted to the Church, what need of any addition?

All over reformed Christendom the catechism had a climax for the young. They met in church and there professed their baptismal faith. There was no laying on of hands, no bishop was present (but in electoral Brandenburg it was confined to the bishop and in Wolfenbüttel to his equivalent the superintendent). A few churches used the laying on of hands but made it clear that this was a blessing and not a sacrament.

In Strasbourg Martin Bucer made the key connection between catechism and confirmation. He won the idea partly from Erasmus but also from reading the early Fathers, where he found confirmation to be a sacrament. Zwingli had begun to make the link from his own reading of the Fathers. Erasmus, then in Basel, had proposed[5] that the instructed young should formally take upon themselves the vows of baptism when they reached the years of puberty. Erasmus did not link this with confirmation. Bucer thought hard about a link between the early sacrament and the instruction of the young or of the convert. This taking of the vows at the end of catechism was rightly the confirmation of the early Church; for it should be solemnized with the laying on of hands and would surely be accompanied by God's gift for the needs of the soul.

---

[5] Erasmus, *Opera Omnia* (1706), vii. 31. It was 1522.

He had much influence in Hesse and found that the Marburg reformer Hyperius agreed with the plan. It became part of the Hessian church order in 1538–9.

The innovation took a historic rite which had become meaningless by time and not only gave it a use but made it a prayerful moment of religious education. Its use persuaded two contemporaries who ensured it a future. Melanchthon was persuaded that Bucer was right and henceforth confirmation was accepted among the Lutheran churches. In England Thomas Cranmer believed that Bucer was right and took it into the first English Prayer Book of 1549.

A catechism class taught Scripture, not the three Rs the base of education. But it did encourage learning to read. And no one could teach the Bible without communicating hints to a basic education: a sense of the past, of the passage of time in history, and of the progress of the human race; even a part-misleading but part-true sense of geography; for no one could understand the Old Testament without knowing vaguely about Egypt and Mesopotamia and Palestine, nor understand the New Testament without knowing vaguely about the Mediterranean and Roman rule. Pontius Pilate needed background.

Society was disturbed and this meant that at first fewer students went to the university and for a short time fewer children went to school, because monks' schools were shut and chantry priests had at times taught children and universities were impoverished by the ending of grants from monasteries. The diminution was not usually drastic except in places where war or civil strife took their toll.

The early example of a common town chest, Leisnig in Saxony, ordered that former mendicant houses are to be turned into (or kept as) schools for boys and girls.[6] In 1524 Luther wrote to German towns asking them to establish and maintain schools, and stated why. Most parents cannot read or write. They cannot pass on to children the need for education. They cannot hire a schoolteacher because they have no money. The State must provide the school and pay the teacher.[7]

In the first flush of enthusiasm, certain towns promised free education for everyone and passed a law that every child between six and fourteen must attend (so Berne, 1536).[8] They never had the resources in buildings or teachers or money to make this practicable though it was attempted, much more in towns than in villages. Primary schools in the countryside often owed more to the zeal of a pastor than the efforts of a government board. Luther threatened with hellfire parents who refused to send intelligent children to

---

[6] *WA* xii. 15.   [7] *WA* xv. 27–53.

[8] Richard Feller, *Geschichte Berns*, ii (Berne, 1953), 283.

school—to educate, he said, 'is to render an extraordinary service to God'.[9] The average number of persons who could read and write rose steadily but not fast. In 1570 a Swiss town councillor died who had held many of the chief municipal offices though he could neither read nor write—by that date the chronicler records this as exceptional.[10] Perhaps it was rare in Switzerland. But the Saxon visitation forty-seven years after that mentions councillors who could neither read nor write.[11]

The evangelical ideal was near the portrait of the good schoolboy which Erasmus drew in the *Colloquies*. As he gets up he invokes the name of God, and thanks for the rest of the past night, and says a prayer that the coming day be blest. If he passes a church on the way to school he salutes the Lord and the saints. At school he works well, says grace at lunch, plays games in the afternoon, then back to school; at home he has supper and then reads pleasant stories. Going to bed he kneels and reviews the day and is penitent if need be, and commends himself to God and goes to sleep. If he is bored by the sermon on Sunday he reads the Bible. If he comes across obscenities in books, he skips.[12] Luther had very minor disagreements with this ideal. Erasmus's boy used the sign of the cross and remembered the saints, Luther's did not.

Though a boy or girl no longer needed to know Latin to understand much of the services in church, it was an axiom of good education that it must include the learning of Latin because pastors, lawyers, civil servants, and doctors of medicine could not do without it, nor indeed anyone who wished to understand the general culture of western Europe. Parents who wanted their children to go into business thought that they needed only knowledge of their own language and the ability to add and subtract and multiply and were not keen on the expense of a school to learn Latin. Luther denounced them. A craftsman and a woman managing a household, he said, are not at a disadvantage if they are capable of reading books and carrying on an intelligent conversation. They need to know what is happening in the world, and to understand something of history, and see how this generation has its due work in the passing of current affairs. Luther was willing to advocate education on the ground of the pleasures to which it opened the way. In all that world of humanism knowledge of the ancient classical world was indispensable to understanding the best thought of the present day.[13]

---

[9] *WA* xxx. 2. 532; written in 1530, to Lazarus Spengler at Nuremberg.

[10] Haller's Chronicle ap. Feller, *Geschichte Berns*, ii. 284.

[11] D. A. Tholuck, *Das kirchliche Leben des siebzehnten Jahrhundert*, i (Berlin, 1861), 232.

[12] Erasmus Colloquies, *Confabulatio Pia*, first printed 1522. Erasmus's picture may have been influenced by his friend John Colet; cf. Thompson (ed.), *Colloquies*, 88 ff.

[13] *WA* xv. 27–53, *An die Ratsherren aller Städte deutschen Lands, dass die christliche Schulen aufrichten und halten sollen* (1524): a moving open letter.

He saw no difference between the sexes. Girls should be educated in Latin too, if possible, they also ought to be able to read books and engage in conversation and have the door opened to them towards the pleasures which books brought. He was the more likely to think this because he had an intelligent wife who knew some Latin—but he was an advocate of girls' education before he married or had any children, and Catherine learnt her Latin at a nunnery school now suppressed. In August 1527 Luther invited Else von Kanitz to set up a girls' school in Wittenberg and offered her board and lodging in his home.[14]

During the later Middle Ages towns founded schools. But education was still thought to be the vocation of the clergy and even in the fifteenth century there was a fight at Heidelberg university whether a professor of medicine could be a layman and the dispute had to be settled by a ruling from the pope. But many schools were hardly good places of education and all reformers appealed to princes and town councils to create effective institutions. 'To see that churches and schools are in a good way is the highest duty of rulers,' wrote Melanchthon in 1543,[15] an example of the professor of Greek pleading for more money for his university from the State. Government must ensure that teachers have knowledge, virtue, wisdom—and adequate pay; but it also meant that everyone in a town had a moral duty to care whether their school did well and if necessary collect money for its further needs. Melanchthon said that a (civilized) state cannot exist without a people that can do sums, and understand the calendar, and know some geography and history, and study a language; if the people cannot do these things the community is a society of animals where power rests with the strong because there can be no law. Schools are essential to the Church, you cannot carve clergymen out of the best wood in the world, they must be educated, with a knowledge of language and history and antiquity. But the State has the same interest in training its servants and its citizens.

The medieval school was conceived of as a church school, for usually it was founded and financed by a church endowment even if the towns began to use taxpayers' money to create schools. This axiom did not change quickly. As the reforming states founded their church orders, they normally assumed that the provision of schools was part of that. But it was bound to change since the greater provision of schools could only be achieved with the substantial support of state funds; because the old monastic endowments which helped education were now controlled by state officers; and because since lawyers chosen by the State helped the leading clergy to see that all was well or at least

---

[14] *BW* iv. 236.

[15] CR xi. 612, 618, *De conjunctione scholarum*; cf. CR xi. 108, *in laudem novae scholae* (= the new school at Nuremberg).

better in the parishes, they joined with the clergy in looking after schools. In the Middle Ages the system was provision by the Church with state aid; this did not change instantly; but by 1600 north Germany assumed that the system was provision by the State with the aid of the Church.

It was no easy task. Collect teachers and if they are zealous they may think that the only education that matters is knowledge of the Bible. Parents could not see the point of education and must often be exhorted or pressed. Princes shelled out taxpayers' money with reluctance for any object whatever and if they were economizing, and they were usually economizing, it was easiest to economize on schools and universities.

Melanchthon won in his lifetime the title Educator of Germany and it was justified. Though he wrote theological textbooks as well as textbooks on many other subjects, he always felt that his work was that of a teacher and not of a theologian. He was never ordained and said that it was not his vocation to be a pastor. He dedicated his life to creating schools, making schools better, creating universities, making universities better; all of which meant making teachers more able to communicate knowledge, and pastors better equipped for their pulpits, and professors more likely to look for truth. The field open for his work was huge; schools being founded all over Germany, at first with no proper plan for how they should be run or what they should teach as syllabus, with no ministers of education to appeal to; and universities existing in Catholic forms regarded by many Protestants as obsolete and harmful; with a need for new universities to supply the better training for doctors of medicine and civil servants and lawyers and pastors which the modern states needed badly.

He first started to engage in the work in 1525, with school plans for Eisleben and Nuremberg. Three classes: (1) how to read; (2) read and learn Latin— Terence, Virgil; learn to speak; try to write poetry, and how to write letters or stories; (3) upper form preparing for university—study the rules of dialectic and rhetoric—if good at Latin, start Greek, a few might start Hebrew; mathematics and music (an hour of music daily). General axiom, all this study is only a success if it is linked to religion—*studia et pietas*. There should be short services morning and evening. He wished the children not to be overburdened, therefore not too many subjects for study. He rejected controversy in the classroom, for example do not attack popes. But there was little special religious education; though those learning Greek would be led to St Paul's Romans; by 1528 he planned for two hours a week of RE. But he thought St John and Romans and Isaiah too difficult for the second class, start them in the top form. The mood of the time made Melanchthon afraid that educators would think theology to be the only subject that mattered; and he was determined that general education was what counted, in which religion and morals, which were the vital parts in educating citizens, must be integrated into a wider culture.

Melanchthon loved education—the making of society and the way to truth—but was no blind optimist. He gave a lecture to an audience of elementary schoolteachers. He was depressed, for he took as his theme 'The Miseries of Schoolteachers', '*De miseriis paedagogorum*'.[16] They must cope with gross behaviour which children learnt at home and with children without interest in learning and who must be told something six hundred times before they take it in, and who enjoy annoying the teacher in class—so that to help them is harder than showing a camel how to dance or a donkey how to play the harp. To be a labourer in a mill is more comfortable work.

And when the child gets on, and learns Latin, and writes exercises that are sense, then the teacher must correct them, and Melanchthon thought the worst teachers to be those who took no trouble over correction, because it needs time and care—to show a pupil where a sentence is ambiguous, or the style is rough, or where something is untrue. The teacher has not only to show enthusiasm, but to generate enthusiasm in young people who have none. And the behaviour, especially of boys, whom it is hard to keep away from bars and gaming—if success, then that teacher must have a special gift from God. By bad behaviour teachers are driven to the cane, and themselves suffer that they have to use so wretched an expedient. Do we give them any thanks for this suffering they endure? We give them derisory pay; their pupils have no idea that they deserve gratitude; parents think that if the child does well it is due to the child, if badly it is due to the teaching.

This depressing picture was written by someone who loved young people, and cared passionately for knowledge; and in spite of it all saw the great tasks which teachers did for humanity, and recognized that at times they had joy in seeing how young minds develop, and was grateful for them, and knew that the future of Church and State rested upon their very partial success. Many in his audience would have been taught by him personally and used textbooks which he wrote. For he wrote textbooks on several subjects of the curriculum and they continued to be used into the next century.

Money: make towns the source, more than princes, townsmen feel a direct responsibility for their schools; persuade the rich to pay fees so that the poor can go. Buildings: turn monasteries into schools. Erect schools for the girls separate from the boys and make nunneries schools for girls. Do not make schools remote, if possible put them in towns because of the greater oversight. Make sure teaching in church and school agree.

The point most questioned by contemporaries was the reluctance to teach Greek in schools except to a few better pupils, on the ground that the children must know Latin and must not be overburdened; the language which

[16] CR xi. 121.

made the Renaissance, the sacred language of the New Testament. There were teachers who could not bear not to teach it.

Johann Sturm

All over Germany persons who cared about education did what they could for the newer form of education, part humanist part reformed. Melanchthon was exceptional, but several others, among them his biographer Camerarius at Leipzig, were influential. The most famous was the creator of the school at Strasbourg, Johann Sturm. Not only did he create a good school. He wrote on the nature of education and this made him known outside Germany. In England Roger Ascham the tutor to the future Queen Elizabeth I christened a son Johannes Sturm Ascham. Even the Jesuits, when they reformed Catholic schools, owed something to Sturm.

He was well educated at the conservative university of Louvain and got work in a firm that published classical books. He married a learned French girl and together they set up a hostel for students at the university of Paris and he gave lectures on classical texts in the university. Then the affair of the Placards with its persecution of Protestants, which drove Calvin out of France towards Strasbourg, allowed that town council to bring Sturm to come and reorganize their schools. Martin Bucer had tried to persuade the council to found a university but they refused on grounds of cost. The coming of Sturm was an alternative.

He remained in Strasbourg from 1537 until his death fifty-two years later—though as is the fate of those who stay too long they outed him from his place before the end, not without bitterness, and left him in his last years pottering among his flowers and his bees.

His official post was as the rector of the gymnasium, that is the chief secondary school of the town. He must have tried those under him because he was the sort of leader who is always issuing instructions. He was very fortunate in refugees whom he could find to teach—especially Calvin for a time, and still more a fine scholar in the ex-Augustinian who had fled from Italy, Peter Martyr Vermigli; and for a short time Wolfgang Capito, who had been a close adviser of Archbishop Albert of Mainz but was hardly a refugee for with the pope's permission he had long enjoyed a prebend in Strasbourg; but he now joined the reformers in Strasbourg and became Martin Bucer's chief colleague, a good Hebraist and wise.

School for ten years of life. Like Erasmus and Melanchthon Sturm believed that the best education combined religion and morals with advanced study in classical literatures. Like Melanchthon he did not wish to exclude history or the sciences, which they both regarded as essential. But these were rather supplements to the courses than the main endeavour. More than Melanchthon he was an elitist. What the State needs is good and informed and wise citizens. Our job is to produce the best, brilliant minds if we can, they are what Church and State need. If young people have not got the gifts that make this possible, they deserve less consideration by the educator. Why should we waste time and money in trying to teach the unteachable? (If beggars go on begging after they are ordered not to, throw them out of the State.) But recognize that certain minds are slow to develop so do not reject them from elementary education. Where children have got the capacity the State must provide the means for their education if their parents cannot do it. Like Bucer and after Bucer was dead he tried to make the city found a university but they were economical and created an academy of higher studies and made Sturm its rector.

Because he wished to educate the elite he did not shrink from demand. His nine-year-old was reading the *Aeneid* in Latin, his eleven-year-old *Aesop's Fables* in Greek, his twelve-year-old Aristotle's *Logic*. At fourteen they began Hebrew. His doctrine was: Read the original texts, not modern books about the texts. There should be small classes, eight or ten persons. As they grew there were lectures on natural sciences and law and medicine and theology; not compulsory but Sturm encouraged the older young to attend lectures off their special subject. He did not want narrow specialism but with his demands on time he could hardly avoid it. He accepted that prizes and competition encouraged the young. He believed that the *only* purpose of government is to promote education, it is education that creates a healthy and peaceful society and State. He wanted sport in moderation as a help to make school enjoyable but was so intent on the mind of the pupil that he hardly left time for exercise or for doing nothing. He accepted that his ideal was too high for human achievement. There is a modest sentence: 'We scarcely reach at the age of fifty what undergraduates are expected to achieve.' He wanted women to have the same advantages and believed that the studies of Princess Elizabeth (the future queen of England) set a good example to girls. The State should honour teachers, not only by liberal stipends but in other ways, on the plea that whatever is not honoured is despised by common folk. Naturally he did not get his way about liberal stipends.

The disciples of Melanchthon wanted the State to offer education to everyone; an aspiration very hard to achieve in a shortage of money and teachers, impossible if all education is elitist and pupils must be ten in a class and teachers well paid.

The expansion of school education made rapid progress after its first shaky start while the monastic endowments were being partly turned into education and after the pensions of monks and nuns were less needed. By 1520 there were 89 schools in all the Land of Württemberg. Eighty years later there were more than 400 schools. Catholic Lands were founding schools also but still by clergy and religious orders more than by the State, and so were not usually so systematic as yet. In countries under the influence of Calvin or Bullinger there was a determination to see that everyone could read so that they read the Bible—and the quality which Scottish education in the end obtained over English was connected with this tradition.

Ordinary workers were not easily persuaded that their children needed school, the first need was a labouring pair of hands as quickly as possible. Many were still less persuaded that it was worth having schools for girls, the luggage which they needed was nothing to do with the ability to read and write. These moods or axioms were slow to be overcome. By 1630, a little more than a hundred years after Luther demanded schools for girls as well as boys in every parish, Amsterdam, in a Calvinist country with high ideals of education, allowed statistics of how many could write their name when they signed the marriage register at their marriages. One in every three men signed with a cross, but two in every three women.[17] That might seem poor by modern standards but compared with what had been before it was remarkable.

The theatre in education

The reformers found a tradition of a people's theatre, usually written by priests, and often derived from incidents in the Bible. There was no objection to performing the plays in church, which was the only meeting hall of most communities. But they were also performed in the street or the market square or the village green. The most religious were the mystery plays about Christ's life and death, but there were plays on extraordinary events from the lives of saints, or sometimes plain old-fashioned morality with symbolic characters like Envy. They were an important teaching instrument in an illiterate world.

This custom of drama the reformers had no desire to be without. Most of them liked it much. It stood for that communication of biblical truths which they specially wanted to bring home to their people. It was a part of social life and of education which Protestants continued to share with Catholics. The Lutherans had one advantage over the Calvinists in that they accepted the Apocrypha as good material for biblical teaching and in the apocryphal books came two or three of the best, and in the case of Tobit the funniest, stories at which the people could take pleasure; and even if the tales of Tobit and Susannah and Judith were not in all respects edifying, they made people enjoy drama which was straight out of the Bible and so ensured that they thought the Bible to be a book which was not remote. But they could also use the

[17] *OER* ii. 431 (R. A. Houston, valuable article).

stage for the purposes of propaganda which in their minds was not partisan but a form of education. As Catholic theatre could use characters to play Protestant villains, reforming theatre might represent the pope in the most unfortunate of circumstances and costumes and usually as an agent or vehicle for the activity of flying demons. Even if the pope was not thus portrayed, scenes might still be lightened or weighted by the popping up of devils, who served a theatrical purpose, though in intention but not always in effect more frightening, like that of idiots or jesters in making a contrast with the actions of the leading players. Before the Reformation had won over a town, and it was still officially Catholic, the critics of priests and of superstitions used the stage as a privileged platform to utter their mocking and their satire, a popular form of what Erasmus did for an educated class in his *Colloquies*. These jests from actors, which by an anachronism can be called anti-clerical, led to unsystematic bans and censorship by city councils. But censors have always found the maximum difficulty in deciding when a sentence is funny and when it is blasphemous or only in bad taste. It began to be as acceptable, for example, to pillory indulgence-sellers as openly and as comically as Geoffrey Chaucer had pilloried his Pardoner.

It was not without criticism in the reforming communities. A schoolmaster in Dresden was blamed by his people for acting in a play by Terence—they said that it must be wrong for Christians to act in non-Christian plays. His pastor asked Luther for advice and Luther said that comedies should be put on in schools because so the pupils learn Latin and also learn easily about human nature and adult society. But he warned against a schoolmaster reading the Bible in the same way that he taught a comedy in the formroom. Yet he liked the idea if the life of Christ was portrayed in schools. Once at least he had a student play put on in his own house. Melanchthon took the same view. At Dessau in Anhalt the schoolmaster put on a play in church on Palm Sunday 1543 and was criticized by the ex-Catholic priest who was his pastor. He appealed to Wittenberg with the question, 'Is it right to put on plays of sacred history in poetry or comedy in a sacred or secular place?' The Wittenbergers supported him. Melanchthon said that it was good for the young to see a representation of the resurrection and other histories of the life of Jesus.[18]

The exception was the passion. Plays on the passion were rare. One was performed in Zurich, and Hans Sachs put on one in Nuremberg. Luther thought it could make a sentimental attitude to suffering. The crucifixion was too sacred to be portrayed. It could also be dangerous. At a passion play put on in Pomerania the actor who played Christ received a mortal wound from the spear of the actor who played the soldier and as he fell from the cross

[18] Luther to Prince George of Anhalt, 5 April 1543, *BW* x. 284–6.

killed one of the escort, whose brother then killed the soldier in revenge and himself was later executed for murder—so that the passion play caused four deaths.[19] They soon banned or tried to ban such portrayals, though old customs of some towns, inherited from the mystery plays, were not altered easily.

Later reforming Catholics eventually followed their example, until there was only one surviving passion play, that of Oberammergau in the Bavarian Alps. Among the Protestants passion plays stopped much earlier. Stricter Protestants hated legends, so that they would not countenance plays of incidents from the lives of saints outside the Bible; and when they found texts from the medieval mystery plays which had freely embellished their stories, they sometimes destroyed the copies.

In the Old Testament the kidnapping of Joseph was used for its obvious morals; the golden calf of Moses, as a lesson against superstition; David and Goliath for courage in faith, David and Absalom on sons' duties to fathers; Naboth's vineyard as an attack against oppression and robbery; Daniel and the lions were naturally very popular, and the burning fiery furnace, but so were Elisha and Elijah and Jonah. The story of Esther easily lent itself to drama.

In the New Testament the subjects were less numerous because the books contained less dramatic narrative and the themes were confined to the Gospels and the Acts of the Apostles. John the Baptist was a favourite subject; Christmas as in the Middle Ages was commonest of all. The twelve-year-old Jesus teaching in the Temple was liked, and the marriage at Cana, and the feeding of the five thousand, and Dives and Lazarus which was a play against the wealthy and their corruption and was specially valued by social radicals; Zacchaeus and his tree, and the prodigal son, and what happened to the apostles.

Usually the scenery was very simple, but the authors at least did not shrink from adding conversations to bring the story to life. They stayed close to the story of the Bible but were free with the words which explained it.

A new type was the historical play. Show from the past the struggle between good kings and bad popes. If it is dangerous for a debating society to discuss publicly whether the present authorities behave badly, put on a play about a misbehaving ruler of 300 years or a millennium ago and then authority will not stop it but the audience will take the point. This historical method began to be much used by reforming playwrights. But many plays on both sides contained no propaganda. They were simply intended to show the people how things happened in the Bible story.

[19] Hugo Holstein, *Die Reformation im Spiegelbilde der dramatischen Literatur der 16. Jahrhunderts* (Halle, 1886), 31.

At Nuremberg Hans Sachs the Mastersinger began to write plays while the city was still Catholic. When the city was Protestant he dedicated himself to producing biblical and secular plays, humorous or tragic but always with a moral intention. He started with Abraham sacrificing Isaac, then Esther, later Cain and Abel; and he did not shrink from making it clear that Cain and Abel had to know the catechism.

Such plays were not intended only for classrooms. Pastors and even mayors of towns used such biblical plays as ways of educating their adult people in true history. Some of the scenes were the same as those selected by the medieval mystery plays, like the coming of the Three Wise Men, or John the Baptist. From the Old Testament nothing was so common as Cain and Abel because the moral was so plain and dramatic. The sacrifice of Isaac was popular because it pictured strong faith even against natural instincts. The marriage of Isaac and Rebecca became a lesson in godly marriage. One of the most popular came from an unexpected author: Theodore Beza, to be the heir and intimate and biographer of Calvin. Shortly after he became a Protestant, he wrote a play at Lausanne in French (1550) on the sacrifice of Isaac by his father Abraham; entitled *Abraham sacrifiant*. The grim primitive story is turned into a charming moral, with Sarah in her grief and a band of shepherds. This was not only easy to read and to act, and brought tears to the eyes of audiences, but was a landmark in early French literature. It was widely used, ten editions in the sixteenth century and translated into several languages. The English poet Arthur Golding printed an English version for the court of Queen Elizabeth.[20]

Plays were a good way to learn Latin as well as the stories in the Bible. Melanchthon's first publication was an edition of the works of Terence, a book widely bought and liked by Erasmus. To use the plays of Terence and Plautus, bowdlerized, was a historic way of teaching Latin because they made pupils talk Latin. So the same might be tried with the Bible. The old mystery plays of the Middle Ages had tried it but were now disapproved by reformers because they were full of legend. They stuck more closely to the text of the Bible.

If a Christianized Terence in Latin was useful in school, it was obvious that the same in German could be used in teaching adults who knew no Latin, and early among the Lutherans such plays were produced in the German language. There were good plays and many more bad plays, because the driving desire to educate bred moral platitudes, too frequent sermons in the mouths of heroes or heroines, too many words altogether.

[20] *The Tragedie of Abraham's Sacrifice* (1575). Golding started as a translator of famous Latin texts like Caesar and Seneca and Ovid (the last the *Metamorphoses* in verse and very popular, known to Shakespeare) but in the mid-Elizabethan age he turned to translate from the Swiss theologians revered by the Puritans—Calvin, Beza, Bullinger.

Swiss reformers began with the same ideas. But before long the Puritan tradition came to suspect that plays on the Bible were not fitting and should not be allowed. They met the same objection as that against mystery plays—they interfered with the plain words of Scripture. To make them alive as drama the authors put words into the mouths of their characters which came from their imagination, and even extra characters, not mentioned in the Bible, like Beza's band of shepherds at Abraham's sacrifice. After a time that was felt to be unacceptable. Beza never wrote another play.

The university

A consequence of the Reformation was the reshaping of the university. At first this was very difficult, conservative teachers leaving or being pushed out, radical teachers denying that conventional teaching was of any use, peasants' war making travel dangerous, incidence of the plague during which members of universities might evacuate their town—there was a moment when there were those who doubted whether the university of Wittenberg could survive and it was worse at Erfurt and Frankfurt on the Oder and Rostock and Greifswald. There was a doubt whether if such places succeeded in surviving they could find professors qualified enough to make a good university. Wittenberg survived much more easily than the others named, and chiefly because of its two or even three, later four or five, names with an international reputation.

The historic Catholic universities of Tübingen and Heidelberg and Leipzig and Greifswald were made reformed universities. This was not easy. Professors used to old ways of doing things did not accept what was put to them as a better way. Like Erasmus when Basel university was reformed, several professors in German universities refused to continue at what they regarded as a different institution. The Catholic university of Rostock closed altogether and the closure was long enough to make the refounded body feel a new institution. The Catholic university at Frankfurt on the Oder was not so difficult because it was founded recently, in 1506, and was a weak affair; the river was good for communications, but the distant site had a political motive, instead of starting their university at Berlin (which would have been sensible[21]) the Land of Brandenburg wanted to encourage their underpopulated eastern border. It was soon in trouble as students headed for Wittenberg and by 1536 there were only forty students. Even before the Land itself was officially Protestant, the university of Frankfurt was guided by Melanchthon, whose son-in-law George Sabinus went there as a leading professor.

---

[21] The university of Berlin was not founded until 1810.

New universities were needed in the Protestant Lands. Marburg in Hesse was the first—Silesia had founded Liegnitz university earlier but it closed quickly.

If a university hesitated for years between the old and the new it was likely to have a bad time, as Rostock and Basel had to close and be reopened. Probably the university with the worst time because of inner dispute between old and new was Luther's own Alma Mater at Erfurt. It had been founded by a pope or anti-pope in the great Schism of the Papacy, but at the end of the sixteenth century it became a leader in the humanist campaign in German universities with demands for less schoolmen and better Latin styles and knowledge of Greek and different textbooks and less ancient ways of lecturing. Spalatin, who became Luther's friend, was a leader on the humanist side. This had the result that in the chequered history of Erfurt university its flowering came during the first twenty years of the sixteenth century.

Then the conditions made for sudden collapse. It was too near Wittenberg and none of its professors had the drawing power of the Wittenberg names. Worse, it was divided in two ways. Politically, the town quickly went Protestant but the university was under the jurisdiction of its ex officio chancellor the archbishop of Mainz. Intellectually, though humanists like Spalatin were for Luther, more of them were for Erasmus and against Luther. So they were uncomfortable in their town and rent internally. They never prospered again as in the flowering of humanism. Prussia abolished the university during the age of Napoleon.

Marburg was typical. There was no privilege from the Pope. Its first buildings were former houses of the friars and the Brethren of the Common Life. Its duty was conceived as that of training pastors to serve in the parishes. It had the same four faculties as other universities, and endowed residences as colleges for many students. Latin and Greek must be taught, canon law must not be taught. The professors must all be evangelicals.

Protestant universities increased the weight of universities in society. Bishops were less important or nothing, university faculties were indispensable to the reforming practice of church government. They were certifying the preachers whom everyone now wished to be educated, and all the better schoolteachers whom society now needed even if they were not valued as they merited; and the young who would become the civil servants of the reformed state. Their professors of theology had influence in allowing future pastors to go forward to ordination. They preferred students not to be ordained immediately after their university course but to teach in school for a year or two.

The loss of endowment made for urgent needs. Medieval universities were partly endowed from monastic funds. Protestant rulers continued to finance universities out of the income of canonries or the endowment of now dissolved monasteries. But they had other needs for these monies, far more was dedicated to schools and part to public needs like highways. The attempt to create a state system of education took money which earlier went to universities. The dependence on the State also meant that governments more easily interfered with universities in ways which academics were liable to resent: for example the choice of professors. Governments acted like this before the Reformation, Melanchthon would hardly have been elected at the age of twenty-one to the chair of Greek in the university of Wittenberg unless government had interfered with what the professors wanted. But with universities created or revived by state aid it was commoner. Albert of Prussia, not the most academic of dukes, steadily took decisions in *his* new university of Königsberg. Governments were known to fix the stipends of the professors and as many of them now were married that made a problem. At Wittenberg for example the pay of the professors was adequate, on a scale according to the importance of the subject—theologians and then lawyers most pay, language teachers (Greek and Hebrew less low), and scientists not top professors of medicine least pay. Though the stipends were adequate they did not compare with those in the civil service. The elector of Saxony's wine steward had three times the stipend of his professors.

In the 1550s professors were still unable to lecture on many texts which they needed until the load of new books arrived from the Frankfurt book fair or unless they first dictated to their class the matter which they would afterwards expound. This dictating was a medieval method but it bored the young who fell away from lectures where this happened.

All universities had grants to help poor students. These aids were not plentiful. The best went to help poor ordinands at a residential college.

Student habits were traditional. Senior members struggled with drunkenness, and noise at the carnival, and the wearing of weapons and the use of catapults, and student debt, and the running up of bills unpaid to landlords.

Protestant universities had difficulty at first about degrees. A degree was associated with the old university and its schoolmen, and the history that the right to award degrees depended on leave from Rome. There were persons who carefully made it public that though they attended a university they had not so far demeaned themselves as to take its degree. The title Bachelor of Arts sounded quaint. As for higher degrees, the question was asked, 'If an institution is rational, what is the point of the title of doctor?' Even so eminent a scholar as Simon Grynaeus at the university of Basel, though willing to become a doctor, refused to become a doctor with the traditional ceremonies and there was a quarrel in the city, he was accused of endangering his work by obstinacy; but he won and was elected rector of the university.[22] At

[22] *Amerbachkorrespondenz*, v. 172, no. 2269; the quarrel was partly healed by Wolfgang Capito; cf. Capito to Amerbach, 19 April 1540 from Strasbourg, ibid., no. 2389.

Wittenberg in the 1520s the BA degree was despised and the ceremonies for taking it were mocked as a game for lads. Probably three-quarters of the undergraduates of Wittenberg never took a degree. But anyone who wished to go on to the higher faculties—law, medicine, theology—must be qualified by a BA degree, so that it was taken by anyone who wished to be a civil servant, or a physician, or a theologian. Melanchthon was not afraid of saying that courses at the university should be chosen with an eye to future usefulness.

Melanchthon, who had more effect on German universities than any other single person, strenuously defended the traditional ways for students, in two respects. The first was examinations, doubted by various critics as useless or harmful to education. He said: They demand accuracy, and so stimulate care in enquiry. They ensure that the degree will mean something. And they help the students to self-knowledge, cut them down to size if they are vain, raise them to endeavour if they are diffident. The second was the degree. He held the taking of the degree to be a moment of the first importance in a life and therefore to be marked with due solemnity. He reminded them (wrongly) of the origins of the phrase Bachelor of Arts, as coming from *baccalaureus*, the laurel berry which was so high an award in the ancient world. The degree ensures that students follow an ordered curriculum for the mind, without it teachers would be shooting up 'like mushrooms' overnight.[23]

As in the Middle Ages the top degree was that of Doctor of Divinity. It was rare. It took a course of six years at a Protestant university. It was doubted at first whether married scholars were eligible and it was soon agreed that they were.

The course of study in theology demanded a full knowledge of the Bible, New Testament before Old, with commentaries for the hard places; a structure of doctrine with St Paul's Epistle to the Romans at its centre; selected books of the Latin Fathers Augustine and Jerome. The student must be practised in refuting 'the errors of our age', for example the assertion that babies should not be baptized, or that oaths are wrong, or university degrees useless. The Greek of the New Testament was necessary, the Hebrew of the Old Testament desired but not always compulsory. The classical text of the past, Peter Lombard's *Sentences*, had vanished.

Not only the professors of theology but the other chairs were bound to persons who professed the approved Christian doctrines. Osiander of Nuremberg protested at this in its application to chairs other than divinity, he thought it narrowing. But it had a continuity with the habits, if not the rules, of the past.

---

[23] These mushrooms are a saying of Cruciger, *De Ordine Discendi* (1531), in CR xi. 212—'*subito sicut fungi nascuntur nobis theologi iurisconsulti et medici*'.

Melanchthon loved his university and could sound Utopian about it. He imagined a group of professors, free of envy or dislike of each other, devoid of ambition, who know that they need God's help to fulfil the onerous task of higher education, and that their vocation is holy, given by God to help humanity. He asked that lecturers as they went into a hall to give their lecture should remember that they are going to talk in the presence of God. His later experience of universities did not bear out this pride.

Everyone lectured in Latin but threw out vernacular phrases or words to enlighten students. Melanchthon was amusing about students who pick up a book here and a book there, tired after a dipping—*tumultuaria lectio*—apparently seeking to know a lot. He reminded them of Martial's epigram, 'The man who lives everywhere lives nowhere', and the rule of the younger Pliny, 'Read much but not many books', '*multum non multa*'. Many graduated without being able to compose a Latin speech, when they had to make one they often tried to persuade Melanchthon to write it for them. He complained to Spalatin: 'Most of the young make the mistake of thinking that they do all they need if they listen to a lot of lectures.'[24]

The key to the rising standards of university study and research lay in the languages. Erasmus and his successors told the world that they must understand the Bible; and that meant advanced study of Greek and Hebrew. In these two fields they began to produce first-class scholarship. And if a university possessed one department of the first rank that always had an effect upon quality in other departments. To be expert in Greek was to be expert in more than the New Testament. In the university of Basel Simon Grynaeus transformed the study of classical literature.

Travel

The Renaissance had left a desire for knowledge among the young. As soon as he was old enough to travel alone the Croat Flacius sought out Venice and then headed for Basel to sit at the feet of Grynaeus and then knew that he must go north to the most famous of places of learning, Wittenberg, and be taught by Luther and Melanchthon. Such academic migrations were not always northward. Danes and Norwegians also headed for Wittenberg, though it might be also for Rostock or a north German university if it was not Copenhagen. Catholic universities of excellence still drew Protestant young people: Padua traditionally the best of universities for medicine, Bologna traditionally the best of universities for law, even Paris with its reputation in theology still pulled at Germans or Swiss or English who wished to know more about the subject they had made their own. Well-to-do Swiss

[24] CR i. 584.

families usually sent their children abroad for further education, especially to the Sorbonne in Paris, even if they came from German-speaking Switzerland. For this purpose there were grants. The Swiss exodus continued despite the Reformation. Sons of Protestants who aimed to be lawyers continued to seek training at Padua or Bologna. The Swiss at Paris were discouraged in 1549 when they were ordered to attend mass. For a time Swiss Protestants were inclined to prefer France or northern Italy to the German universities, partly because of historic reputation, and partly because they doubted Lutheran influence on their children. Theologians no longer needed universities for advanced study when Zurich and Geneva founded the two best higher academies for theology in all Europe though they had no universities.

Travel for study was a charity which attracted good bequests, and even some state grants. But scholars needed to find most of their own cost. If government paid for travel it usually insisted that the student return to employment in that state. The libraries had no periodicals but there was a lively exchange of letters about newly published books and their quality.

Bullinger of Zurich sent his son on a study-tour of universities. The advice which he gave to the young man when he set out survived:

1. Fear God. Be humble before God. Have a firm faith. Pray that your faith may be active in charity.

Pray for your country—parents—friends. Always end prayers with the Lord's Prayer.

Use the Te Deum as an act of praise.

Read three chapters of the Bible every day.

2. Be reticent—more willing to listen than to speak.

3. Try to learn Hebrew and Greek as well as Latin; and some history, and some philosophy, and some science.

4. Keep the body clean and the clothes tidy but do not wear clothes that will cause comment.

5. Don't eat too much. Don't drink too much.

6. Keep your conversation cheerful, and moderate, and free from malice.[25]

---

[25] Carl Pestalozzi, *Heinrich Bullinger, Leben und ausgewählte Schriften* (Elberfeld, 1858), 588 ff.

13

DIVORCE

Marriage rites were the ceremonies about which laypeople cared most. In the bride's ring, or the undertakings of the pair, or the white robe of the bride, even the veil of the bride, the people's emotions were engaged, it was an inner part of a family experience. They did not feel conservative about the words which were used except for the words in which bride and bridegroom solemnly accepted each other and those in which the priest/pastor declared they were man and wife. About the 'sacramental' acts they wanted their habits observed.

Across Christendom there had been local variety of custom. Even German Lands close to each other might have slightly different customs in their way of celebration.

Luther allowed much variety in detail. The marriage must be in church and before witnesses. The pastor declared the meaning of marriage and the duties of the pair marrying. Scripture was read. The bride and bridegroom were then asked, either at the church door or before coming to the altar or holy table, whether they accepted each other and would be faithful. In the Lutheran tradition two rings were exchanged, in the Swiss Reformed no ring. Then the pastor joined their hands and declared that they were man and wife and used the text of St Matthew 19: 6 'Those whom God hath joined together let no one put asunder.' In the north German rites it was then usual for the couple to go in procession to the altar, where the pastor would say prayers for them and their children. A ring or rings came into the Reformed tradition when the Palatinate, which began its reformation as a Lutheran state, became part of the Reformed tradition after 1562. The strength of the Reformed tradition went back to Calvin. No one wrote a better biblical exhortation to the marrying couple. But none of the Continental rites measured up to the genius of Archbishop Cranmer in England.

All law ruled that secret marriages were not valid. The rule succeeded thus far, in ensuring (1) two witnesses to every marriage; (2) the entry of the marriage in the marriage register—registers were an innovation of the Reformation (Nuremberg 1524, Zurich 1525, by 1600 universal); and (3) banns to be read in church beforehand. This last was not an innovation except it was more insisted on—there was a medieval word *bannus*, meaning an announcement of a future wedding, already a custom in the twelfth century and ordered by various councils which prohibited marriages unless the banns were first read. The English Prayer Book and the Council of Trent both ruled that the banns be read on three Sundays.

Premarital intercourse

This was illegal and there were penalties in law (Zurich 10 pfennig) but they did not in fact penalize parents who produced babies unexpectedly early, other than by social disapproval. The penalties were hardly enforceable. In country areas people went on taking the betrothal to be the marriage and might not bother with marriage in church until the first baby was born and sometimes held the baptism on the same day as the wedding. This was one reason why authorities said that the engagement does *not* make the marriage. In country districts custom was more potent than anything authorities said. In Geneva one of the charges against Gruet was that he could see no wrong whatever in premarital intercourse provided both parties consented. At Strasbourg a girl had a white wedding and afterwards danced at a party and three hours later bore a baby. The magistrates discussed whether to penalize her. They decided that it would be wrong to single her out.

Illegitimate children

A girl with a baby born out of wedlock was disreputable and a middle-class girl in this predicament could not go to parties. Except for ostracism the children did not suffer or were not supposed to suffer. But they did if the mother was penalized.

The system is proved to be successful by the low rates of illegitimacy. It is accepted that growth in the size of towns puts up the number of illegitimate babies as many more of the human race are cast into each other's company. But in Strasbourg during the 1560s only some 8 per cent of babies were born within eight months of the marriage and during the thirty years after 1560 the rate of illegitimate births was low for a modern city, less than 1 per cent.

Penalties for an unmarried mother could be severe. They varied much. Geneva was famous for severity, Strasbourg more compassionate, Venice famous among Protestants for debauchery.[1]

---

[1] L. J. Abray, *The People's Reformation: Magistrates, Clergy and Commons in Strasbourg 1500–1598* (Oxford, 1985), 190–1.

Prostitutes

All states and societies were against brothels. It was not easy to know what to do. A reforming programme which was in part a drive for the sacredness of humanity and of the sexual relationship could not imagine that it should not include the abolition of prostitutes. But was it so certain that society would gain if prostitutes were treated with violence? And with human instincts being what they are was it certain that what pastors wanted could be achieved? Pastors were apt to think magistrates lax, magistrates were apt to think pastors rigid. But in some cities (Augsburg for a time) the magistrates were tougher than the pastors.

In Zurich a brothel continued despite everything the pastors could do and was not merely winked at but was supervised by government, which stopped married men entering its doors. In Strasbourg a senator twice tried to get the magistrates to allow more brothels with the aim of protecting girls or married women from harassment. His motions failed.[2] Lausanne on its reform expelled all prostitutes from the town but the pimp quietly came back and reopened in his mother's house. In the Lutheran cities of Wismar and Rostock the pastors demanded that all brothels be closed and met blank refusal from the magistrates.

Prohibited degrees

All societies had rules about close family relationships in marriage. Leviticus 18 was the guide to Christian rules. Someone must not marry another person to whom she or he was related by blood. This universal rule was then defined by a long succession of persons, starting with sisters and brothers and parents, whom no one could marry because the relationship of blood was too close. The doubt was whether to interpret Leviticus by its letter—in which case for example first cousins could marry because that marriage is not explicitly banned in Leviticus; or whether the specified bans only illustrated a wider ban and marriage between any quite close relations like first cousins could not rightly be allowed by law or the Church.

At first Christian bishops, when they began to be concerned about marriages, decided according to no rules but according to the pastoral merits of the case. During the sixth century they banned the third degree of relationship (father–son two degrees, grandfather–grandchild three degrees). But by the ninth century it was vastly extended in the Western Church, to the

---

[2] Zurich: Steven Ozment, *When Fathers Ruled: Family Life in Reformation Europe* (Cambridge, Mass., 1983), 33; Strasbourg: L. J. Abray, *The People's Reformation: Magistrates, Clergy and Commons in Strasbourg 1520–1598* (Ithaca, 1985), 191–2; Lausanne: J. Barnaud, *Pierre Viret* (reprinted Nieuwkoop, 1973), 151, 255.

seventh degree—which meant that no one should marry someone to whom he or she was remotely related; and in little village communities, which were immovable because they were all tied to the soil, and where everyone was related to everyone else, it was impossible as law and was a way of producing large numbers of families who lived together without marriage.

Lawyers were kind in casuistical arguments for calculating degrees of relationship and thus diminishing the sternness of the law. But the rule was defended by medical arguments that such family marriages produced mad or deformed children. The great canonist Gratian included in his collection a letter from Pope Gregory that marriage between first cousins cannot produce children. Finally, realizing the damage, the Lateran Council of 1215 reduced the number of degrees to four. That still meant that first cousins could not marry.

The reformers thought this was legalism. They did not doubt that incest is wicked but their instinct was to suppose that canon law is fussy and freedom a desirable goal. Luther accepted the provisions in Leviticus but said that nothing need stop first cousins marrying.[3] Johannes Brenz in Württemberg wrote a book to plead that in marriage affairs the literal word of the Old Testament is not for us. We need laws that suit our problems and the laws of nature.

But lawyers suspected an excess of liberty about marriages within a family. Marriage with a deceased wife's sister—or like King Henry VIII, with a deceased brother's wife—the plea that it could affect a marriage where the younger sister of a wife lived in or near the household, an argument that was used into the twentieth century. Zurich banned marriage with a deceased wife's sister in 1530, Nuremberg soon afterwards, Strasbourg later. Luther began by thinking that marriage with a deceased wife's sister was permissible and that the ban on it was one of the fussy prescriptions of the medieval past. But he changed his mind.[4]

Divorce

In this reforming world marriage is expected to be normal. Because celibates are diminished and mistresses somewhat diminished there will be more marriages and therefore more broken marriages, mistresses deserted by their men are now going to be wives deserted by their husbands. So a consequence of reform must be the provision of a divorce law.

Like their predecessors Protestants disliked divorce. They made provision in their laws for divorce because they saw that it was necessary. But the

---

[3] *On Marriage, WA* x. 2. 280.

[4] Luther: permissible, *WA* x. 2. 281 (1522); not permissible, a letter of 1535, *BW* vii. 152, no. 2171.

provision which they made was hedged about and then their courts interpreted the law more restrictively than its letter demanded.

St Matthew's Gospel allowed divorce for adultery. The other Gospels did not mention this exception. The medieval Church slowly framed the idea that marriage was a sacrament and could not be dissolved. But though the essence of the sacrament was the promise of the bridal pair to each other, the union was not final until consummated by the sexual act. This enabled impotence to be a ground of annulment—not a divorce because it was a declaration that the marriage never happened. Even in the later Middle Ages lawyers commonly used the plea of impotence to achieve what in effect was a divorce and so to circumvent the rule that marriage is indissoluble.

From early in his reforming years Luther denied that marriage is a sacrament. It is the concern of the State as the bond of society rather than the Church as part of worship. It is *res politica*, except so far as it brings cases of conscience. But the more radical of such utterances were to do with practical cases. A fiancé murdered and ran away. Luther was asked whether the fiancée was still committed to him. Hence the negative about *res politica*.[5]

The lawyers needed to develop a system. To achieve this each side, churchmen and lawyers, had to trespass into the sphere of the other. In a legal difficulty evangelical theologians gave opinions without hesitation that they pushed into what legal experts ought to decide. Luther might say that marriage was an affair of the State but he and his pastors constantly intervened in what the State ought to do. Over most of Protestant Europe the courts set up to cope with marriage problems consisted of some clergy and some lawyers.

But the idea that Luther made divorce into a secular affair and in that way made it possible for Christians is an idea of the Enlightenment of the eighteenth century and bears small relation to the sources of the sixteenth century. Luther blamed the contortions of canonists over nullity and thought hard about the welfare of families and unhappy couples, and realized that to provide divorce was necessary to the well-being of humanity. Long after he denied that marriage is a sacrament and the theology of his Church accepted that negative, he was capable of talking loosely of marriage as sacramental; meaning by that how it is a symbol of the union between Christ and his Church.[6] But since divorce led to endless legal problems, and made special difficulties over children, there must be a body of law and system of courts to regulate it. There was no reason why divorce should not be provided where humanity would be befitted by its provision. But in Luther's writings about marriage, the denial that marriage is a sacrament played a smaller part than has been assumed. What led him to his view of the need for divorce was not the interpretation of the Bible but his observation as a pastor. The Edict of

---

[5] *TR* iv. 111, no. 4068.   [6] *WA* xxiv. 422.

the Diet of Worms which made him an outlaw listed among its grounds that 'he has shamefully and incredibly soiled the indestructible law of holy marriage'.

The Bible ruled that divorce is possible only because of adultery.[7] Oecolampadius wanted to restrict divorce to that ground alone. This single reason was not enough for any government that wanted to take sensible care of a people.

Most reformers agreed also on impotence and desertion. Unlike the Catholic law not everyone was agreed on impotence. In parts of Switzerland it was framed thus, sickness is no ground for divorce, illness is a time when the spouse is most needed, impotence is a form of illness, therefore it is no ground for divorce. A Swiss synod decreed the law that *impotence when caused by sorcerers* is no ground for divorce.[8]

Desertion was not so easy to frame in law. A young man went to serve in the army in a foreign country, or travelled to one or more foreign universities for his higher education. The reformers assumed in all divorce cases that there was a guilty party. They hardly ever came near the recognition that there could be faults on both sides. If the pair came to such unhappiness that they could not live together and yet nothing happened which the lawyers could accept as a ground for divorce, then the only resource was to separate and live apart. What destroyed the marriage—disappearing, or sleeping with some-one else—was an act which could often be proved to have happened. But neither desertion nor adultery were easy to prove in courts. This was a reason why Protestant marriage courts were reluctant to grant divorces.

When adultery was so prominent, the fear of a collusive adultery must appear. We are unhappy together, we both want to marry again, let one of us commit adultery, though neither of us has the least desire to do so, to achieve freedom. This very modern question was raised by the pastor of Dinkelsbühl, who asked the advice of Osiander at Nuremberg and received conventional but unhelpful advice.[9]

Courts varied in the length of time which they demanded to qualify for 'desertion'; the most liberal, as short as one year, sometimes three, or four or seven, at the most severe even ten. Desertion had to be 'wicked', and the deserted spouse must show that she (probably a she) made serious enquiries after the other spouse's whereabouts.

---

[7] St Paul in 1 Corinthians 7 also allowed a Christian to remarry if the non-Christian spouse deserted because of the difference of religion. This was known as the Pauline exception. In the sixteenth century hardly anyone came under this provision and it hardly entered the reformers' discussions.

[8] Synod of Neuchâtel, 1551; text in Calvin, *Op.* xiv. 61, *Ep.* 1456.

[9] Osiander, *Gesamtausgabe*, viii, ed. G. Müller and G. Seebass, *Briefe*, nos. 3, 202–4; undated, probably 1543. See the spouse faking adultery in Calvin, *Op.* xiv, *Epp.* 1622–5, 1627, 1635.

An obvious case of 'desertion' was that of a refugee in fear of his or her life who fled the land and the spouse refused to go. Strasbourg and Geneva were most likely to meet such cases from the French persecution.

This situation produced a famous divorce case. Galeazzo Caracciolo was the Naples aristocrat converted to a reformed faith by the sermons of Peter Martyr. Happily married to a devout Catholic and with six children and heir to a marquisate, it took him ten years before he decided he must follow his soul-guide Peter Martyr to Switzerland. He chose Geneva where there was already an Italian congregation. Geneva was proud of him. Here was a person who from sole conviction of truth left wealth and family and eminent public station.

Was there anywhere in Europe that he and his wife could live together? His father suggested Venice. The Grisons in eastern Switzerland was the best hope, they had Protestant and Catholic congregations. He tried to persuade his family to come but they would not.

Here was a husband in the same situation as a refugee from France whose spouse refused to come. Could he marry again in Geneva? Calvin preferred no divorce but his motive was policy, it would give a handle to Catholic critics. Zurich was consulted and a strong board which included Bernardino Ochino and Bullinger and Peter Martyr (this last entered thus for the second time into a key moment of Caracciolo's life) recommended that divorce be granted. So Geneva allowed the divorce and two months later he married a French refugee widow and the second marriage was long and happy.

The reluctance to concede divorce for desertion was a sign of the dislike of divorce. Their experience of the law of celibacy convinced them that if they kept people without the possibility of marriage for long periods they promoted fornication or brothels. Bugenhagen wrote a furious passage against the iniquity of papal and other laws which held that an abandoned wife was married for life and could not remarry. He regarded desertion as worse than adultery, in adultery there was still a chance that all would come right, when a husband vanished he left a desperate wife and children whom neighbours were more likely to despise than pity.[10]

Adultery destroys marriage, to destroy a marriage is a crime worthy of death—the opinion existed but came up against the charitable view of most men and women that such personal relations of a man and a woman might be too complex for rigid rules to be just. Geneva was unique in the amount of backing in the town for very severe penalties for adultery. Even in Geneva this belief was slow to collect support.

---

[10] Ozment, *When Fathers Ruled*, 92; from Bugenhagen, *Vom Ehebruch und Weglauffen*, (Wittenberg, 1540), P to R.

The draconian opinion rested in part on an appeal to the laws of Moses: Leviticus 20: 10, 'If a man commits adultery with his neighbour's wife, both adulterer and adulteress shall be put to death.'

But the Bible could not justify death for the first offence because Jesus prevented the death of an adulteress and gave her a second chance. When Calvin arrived in Geneva the law prescribed a whipping and exile. Throughout his time there this remained the law. Calvin thought that the city should be purified of stain and the old Jewish law should be enacted. During the years when he dominated the city they did not introduce the death penalty. Seven years before he died there was discussion whether to pass such a law but no law passed.

Soon after he died the council accepted the opinion and passed the law of 1566—death for adultery not for fornication. Modern examination of the Genevan court records shows that before the law was passed the death penalty was inflicted on very few people (1560 case: woman drowned, man executed). All the known cases were aggravated—one was a second offence, two were persistent prostitutes.

Calvin's successor Beza wrote a considered treatment *On Separation and Divorce* (*Tractatio de repudiis et divortiis*). He held divorce allowable for (1) circumstances where the rite was null—e.g. of minors; (2) all forms of desertion—a deserter destroys the marriage; (3) adultery but death should only be inflicted in cases of extreme provocation and could not be a normal penalty. All good authorities, he said, allow the innocent party to remarry and he hesitantly allowed the guilty party to remarry.

In Basel the law allowed death for adultery but it was never inflicted.[11]

Alone of the reforming leaders Martin Bucer allowed incompatibility as a ground why divorce might be allowed. It was after he had been forced to flee from Strasbourg and took refuge in England where he wrote his last work, *De Regno Christi*, which he presented to King Edward VI on 21 October 1550 while he also commented on the proposed Book of Common Prayer and so affected the future worship in the Church of Engand. Often accused of being verbose and voluble, he wrote in *De Regno Christi* a clear-headed crisp book. The reader remembers that as a young Dominican he was trained in the syllogisms of St Thomas Aquinas.

On divorce he was very near a modern understanding. He recognized that a purpose of marriage is to bring children into the world and care for them so that they grow aright. But there is a prior condition—that there shall be a

---

[11] Robert M. Kingdon, *Adultery and Divorce in Calvin's Geneva* (Harvard, 1995), 179; cf. T. M. Safley, *Let No Man Put Asunder: The Control of Marriage in the German South-West* (Kirksville, 1984), 35, 191.

true union of hearts in the two spouses. Hence there is a whole range of acts which could justify divorce (desertion, impotence, permanently contagious disease, madness of one spouse) and it comes to a declaration that there can be separation by mutual consent; and since to make a man and woman live singly because they are separate is asking for trouble, the separation by consent must be recognized by the State as a ground for divorce; though in such cases the husband must provide by money or property for the wife, and if she is pregnant she must not remarry for a year.[12] 'Sex is not the ultimate aim of marriage—look at Joseph and Mary . . . The ultimate aim is the sharing in everything, divine and human, in friendship.' But sex of course is a normal part of marriage. Some men and women are called to a life of celibacy but it is wrong to say that their way is morally higher than the married, and it is blasphemy to say that sex is sin.

In modern times some have argued that the reforming ban on secret marriages was one way of putting down the female sex. Before it the girl of fourteen could freely commit herself to another without anyone being able to interfere. It was thus a way of liberty from parental control. But it was also a way of producing unhappiness and girls who were impregnated by a boy able afterwards to deny that he had anything to do with the child. It is nevertheless true that the reformers' attitudes did strengthen parental control over teenage children and sometimes over children of their student years or its equivalent. But they did not strengthen it as much as might be imagined because the reformers still held that marriage was made by the consent of the partners; that no young person ought to be or could be compelled to marry another by the influence of parents; that if the parents refused their leave unreasonably the young couple could have access to the courts.

At times other grounds for divorce were accepted by leading reformers: refusal of matrimonial rights (Luther and Brenz only, not others); cruelty (Melanchthon, Bugenhagen). But the courts decided such matters as they thought right pastorally. For example, in Geneva Bonville maltreated his wife. Was it everyone's duty to try to reconcile the couple and so save a marriage? They asked Calvin, who might be expected to think principle more important than individual happiness. He replied with an emphatic negative to any plan for a reconciliation. The man was a brute and the wife ought to be allowed to be as far away from him as possible.

In none of the main Reformation bodies—that is, except among some groups of anabaptists—was difference of faith between spouses a ground for divorce. But it was hardly expected to occur.

---

[12] Bucer, *De Regno Christi*, ii. chs. 37–8.

Henry VIII

England asked the advice of the European universities and the leading theologians.

Henry had married his brother's widow, Catherine of Aragon. She seemed unable to bear him a male heir, which, after so long a civil war, was a crying need of the English State. Was it possible the marriage was not blessed because it was invalid, being illegal by Leviticus 18: 16 and within the prohibited degrees? The pope had dispensed Henry from the law. But half Europe now thought that popes had no power whatever to dispense from what was laid down in the Bible. That was how the question came. Catherine's own point—Leviticus is irrelevant because her marriage with Arthur was never consummated and was no marriage, so she had not married her deceased husband's brother—was not that which concerned the European universities. The consummation of the first marriage, though probably it did not happen, had been formally and publicly accepted. There was also the text of Deuteronomy 25: 5 which ordered a brother to marry the widow of his dead brother—but only if they previously lived together which could not be said of Arthur and Henry VIII.

The English government sent to consult the European universities on whether the Bible banned a man from marrying his brother's widow, and if so whether the pope has the power to dispense a man from the ban. It was their interest to believe that the answer to these questions would be yes and no. They did not consult German universities but French and north Italian and Spanish as well as Oxford and Cambridge. They did not at first consult the Protestant leaders because this was a Catholic government trying to bring evidence in a papal court to persuade the pope to do something. They were very successful. The two Spanish universities at Salamanca and Alcalá held that the marriage with Catherine was valid because the Bible did not ban it and the pope had the power to dispense from the canonical ban. The theologians at Angers university near Brittany agreed. But almost everyone else held as the English wanted, not only Oxford and Cambridge but the historic universities of Europe, from Bologna and Padua to Paris—though the Paris theologians, as distinct from the university, divided. The king was a Catholic. It mattered to his side what St Augustine or St Ambrose had said, and what popes had ruled. He and his staff had to make a case for the divorce in a papal court. The king's men discovered in European libraries a mass of materials in his favour, much of it controvertible, much of it ready to be used in such a Catholic context, and of no relevance to those whose opinions were asked in Wittenberg or Basel or Strasbourg. But there was one Catholic with the freedom of the Protestants—unlike the king's Catholic advisers like John Fisher or the Spanish scholar Vives, the pope himself need take no notice of his own

Catholic authorities if he thought it in the interests of the Church and the moral law. Pope Clement VII, finding himself in everyone else's impasse, suggested to three English agents that perhaps the king's bigamy would be the answer and that he could give the dispensation for it—but he talked vaguely and hesitantly, not sure that it would do.[13]

At first the Protestant leaders were not consulted formally. Their opinions would not influence a papal court, which was what the English needed. Nevertheless this affair which was the talk of Europe must be matter for argument in Wittenberg or Strasbourg or Basel or Zurich.

The Protestant divines were in a simpler position than the Catholics who were consulted because they did not have to think about whether what they said would influence the pope, or what the Fathers had said, or whether the text could be allegorized, or whether popes had laid anything down. They needed only to rest on two planks—what Scripture said about marriage, and what were the pastoral needs of the personal situation. Nevertheless since the meaning of the texts of the books of Moses had been a source of argument for centuries, they naturally disagreed about the first of these planks, that is whether the Bible did or did not ban Henry VIII from marrying his brother's widow. Nor were they unanimous when they turned to the pastoral predicament. Catherine of Aragon must be treated rightly. If Henry were forced to keep her the evidence showed that he was now repelled by her and passionate about another woman; so that it was very probable that if he were forced to keep her as his queen, her life would be very unhappy. Why did he not take the second woman as a mistress and dump the queen in a splendid castle? That would solve everyone's problem except Catherine's happiness—but not, those who knew about politics observed sincerely, and not only to please Henry, that civil war was too close in the English past to risk the absence of a male heir and it was now believed that Catherine was incapable of such an achievement. Protestant divines found this question much more difficult than did many of the Catholics who could say, St Thomas laid it down . . . The pope has decided . . . They perforce dealt less in authorities and more in pastoral care. Catherine's happiness—the king's morality—the king's happiness—the needs of the English State—the biblical discouragement, to put no stronger word, of marriage to a deceased husband's brother.

Simon Grynaeus the professor of Greek at Basel was on study leave in England and was sent to consult Protestant leaders. He came to Martin Bucer

---

[13] The three were Casale, *LP* iv. 6627; Benet (then the English ambassador in Rome, and a canon of Salisbury and a man who secretly wanted Catherine to win the case), *LP* iv. 6705; Ghinucci (the Sienese who was then non-resident bishop of Worcester), *LP* iv. appendix 261. Benet said that he suspected the pope was only playing for time. Ghinucci reported that though he seemed to consider it seriously, he mentioned objections to such a plan, especially that the emperor Charles V, who was Catherine's nephew, would disapprove.

at Strasbourg and put three arguments on paper: (1) Continental universities agreed that the pope had no power to dispense in such a case; (2) King Henry believed the prohibition in the Bible applied to his case; (3) if no male heir, civil war over the succession probably.

Bucer was a sore disappointment to the English. He could see nothing wrong with marriage to the widow of a dead brother. The laws of Moses did not now apply. Henry took a wife who married him in good faith and Church and State accepted the marriage, it could not now be undone. The king ought not to inflict a terrible fate on an innocent woman. Yet there was an impasse— Henry could not put away his wife morally yet he must have a male heir for the State—and this could only be solved by making the second woman a wife so that her child was legal. Was monogamy in all cases so absolute a law? The patriarchs and heroes of the Old Testament? King David? If this were allowed, it would be much better for Catherine of Aragon. But Bucer nevertheless denied that the possibility of bigamy could apply to the case of King Henry.

An incompatibility will be observed between Bucer's position in 1531 and his liberality when he was a professor in England twenty years later. In his old age he asserted that it was not the slightest use trying to keep an impossible marriage going and that divorce should be available to such couples. In 1531 he held the doctrine, if the marriage does not work, say that it is best if the man tries to keep it going—but without quite saying so, wink at the presence of a mistress—even in this case, where there are political arguments, perhaps involving war or peace, for making the mistress into a queen and therefore a wife. He blamed Henry when he married Anne Boleyn.

This opinion of Bucer, that in certain circumstances bigamy might be a moral possibility as the lesser of two evils, got known round the Rhineland and offended Oecolampadius at Basel who knew that it would scandalize the churches and Bucer must be persuaded that it was wrong—more in the spirit of Muhammad than of Christ. Monogamy is the rule of society, it is the thrust of the New Testament, if bigamy is allowed to anyone there will be vast damage to family life.[14]

Zwingli and Oecolampadius held without hesitation. Leviticus is valid, the marriage with Henry was invalid, the king may marry a wife not Catherine. Luther and Melanchthon said the opposite. Leviticus does not now bind. The marriage with Catherine was valid. Catherine's fate must not be made a tragedy. There are no grounds for divorce. If it is absolutely necessary for the English State to have a valid male heir, the king would do better to marry again and have two wives and then Catherine's lot will not be so miserable. Even Erasmus was drawn in, though his opinion was not asked. He

---

[14] Oecolampadius in Zwingli, *Op.* (Leipzig, 1935), xi. 581–2; Luther in *BW* vi. 178–9; Melanchthon, CR ii. 521–6.

started by thinking the king immoral, then he saw both sides, and in the end hardly knew which side he preferred.[15]

Unlike the English, who were not yet members of a Protestant church, the continental divines could wash their hands of the argument over the royal divorce. Melanchthon wrote to Bucer a weary letter that he wished to have nothing more to do with it.[16] But eight years later they met a similar case in Germany which struck at the heart of their reforming movement: the love life of Philip the landgrave of Hesse.

Philip the landgrave of Hesse was important to the German Reformation. He ruled from 1518 (when he was only fourteen) till 1555. He became a disciple of the reformers soon after the Diet of Worms and reformed his territory with the advice of Melanchthon. Of the Protestant princes he was the most aggressive. His effective little army was indispensable to the cause in its defence against the threat from the emperor Charles V. He did most to beat down the peasants in the Peasants' War. In 1534 he achieved a political act which was decisive: the restoration of Duke Ulrich to his dukedom in Württemberg, which made sure that south-west Germany, like the north, would be Protestant. For twelve or thirteen years Philip was the anchor of the reforming cause in the politics of the German Reich.

It is an argument whether he ever had a profound religious faith. After 1526 he never went to the sacrament, but for honourable reasons which will appear. He thought of pure religion as a depending on the Bible and getting rid of drunkenness and prostitution.

At the age of twenty Philip married Christine the daughter of Duke George of Saxony. There was no affection at the start, the motive was political. She was ugly but pious. According to her husband she had bouts of drunkenness. When Philip went Protestant, Duke George was fierce to his son-in-law. The marriage cannot have been all unhappiness because she gave him ten children, and when late in life he finally got out of prison his first visit was to her grave. During the 1530s his state of Hesse was steadily and well reorganized in the reforming sense.

By sexual adventure he contracted syphilis and in 1538 was seriously ill of it. With his religious advisers he tormented himself about the incongruity of his life; a reforming leader married to a woman and unhappy with her. His illness made him long to be free of promiscuities. He had refused to receive the sacrament because he was afraid of eating and drinking judgement on himself. He asked whether under this predicament of the soul he might be allowed to marry another woman, a lady of the court, Margarete von der Sale, who refused to sleep with him unless they were married. He did not

[15] Erasmus, *Epp.* 2040, 2826, 2846.   [16] CR ii. 552.

suggest that a divorce with Christine or a legal nullity be rigged up. Unlike King Henry VIII he had no desire to be rid of his first wife altogether.

He appealed to the patriarchs of the Old Testament who were not punished by God though they had more than one wife. He also found a pope who during the crusades, it was said, had licensed a Count von Gleichen to marry two wives.[17]

It was a tribute to the pastoral warmth of Martin Bucer that he had become Philip's chief spiritual adviser though he was not one of the pastors in the Land of Hesse. This closeness now placed Bucer in the worst pastoral predicament of his life. Philip asked Bucer to sanction the second marriage and persuade Luther to agree. His arguments were frank. If bigamy were not allowed, his body would force him to be an adulterer. The Bible nowhere condemns bigamy but strenuously condemns adultery. If they had suggested it to Henry VIII so that England could gain a male heir to the throne, they ought to allow it to preserve a man from being an adulterer.

Bucer thought the act immoral and knew that if it happened it would hurt the reforming cause. He was totally against what was proposed. He also felt sensitively and painfully for Philip's predicament; and knew that if this mainstay of the Reformation fell into ruin of character it would hurt many more people than himself. It was first put to Bucer by Philip's physician as a question of health.

Privately Bucer came to moral compromise—as he was dealing with a soul in a sickness of the spirit, an emergency solution might be argued to be acceptable; Philip should keep his first wife Christine, and marry Margarete, and so satisfy his conscience; but the marriage must be as secret as any secret of the confessional; Margarete must be kept in such a way that the world would think her only a mistress, then it could not cause scandal nor hurt society; for the people, if they knew anything about it, would suppose that this was the so common case of a ruler having a mistress as well as a wife.

The laws against bigamy rested primarily on canon law and canon law was dead among the theologians though not quite among the lawyers who still had to appeal to it in certain cases. Bucer thought that it would be a really bad thing to happen, for the long Christian tradition, the Christian care of the

---

[17] Count von Gleichen's dispensation was mentioned by Bucer, *BW* viii. 633 and was narrated by Melanchthon when he lectured in his university on history, *CR* xx. 591. According to this, von Gleichen on crusade was captured. The Muslim commander's daughter was attracted to him and he was promised life and liberty if he would marry her. He agreed, the queen gave him a ship. On arrival at Venice he found a courier asking him to go to Rome. He told the pope everything, was absolved, and the second marriage was declared valid like the first; and when he reached home at Erfurt, the first wife received the second. The only offspring came from the first wife. For the whole question see *BW* viii. 635; *CR* iii. 851–65.

family, the Christian sense of the rights of a woman, all spoke loudly against what was proposed. But he was not willing to say that in all cases it was impossible because there were so many instances in the Old Testament some of which were evidently blessed by God, and apart from that a terrible pastoral predicament needed solving whatever rules or customs said. Starting by rigid resistance to Philip's desire, he came to feel it was probably the only solution, on the absolute condition that it was not known.

After an interview with Philip in which he tried vainly to stop him, he went on to Wittenberg to try to persuade Luther and Melanchthon that his solution of the moral crisis was the least bad. This was put as a moral question of possibility. Luther was not told of the existence of Margarete von der Sale, about whom even Bucer did not yet know.

Luther's memorandum on the subject agreed in all respects with the conclusion that Bucer had reached. Marriage to one spouse must be the rule. No marriage to two spouses could be allowed—as a rule. But if a marriage came into deep trouble, and could only be saved by allowing the possibility of another woman, there was a case for thinking that a second wife would be better than a mistress—better for the second woman, better for the first wife than divorce, and better for the husband whose personality would not be at continual war with itself over the illegalities of adultery. But since monogamy must be the rule, the second marriage must be secret, and be a comfort only to the conscience of the man. It did not matter if all the courtiers regarded her as the prince's mistress, ladies often so familiar in royal establishments.

Philip persuaded his first wife to sign a deed that she did not object to his marriage to Margarete provided her own children kept their rights, and then married Margarete. Bucer and Melanchthon were brought to the wedding on 4 March 1540 by an invitation which did not tell them what they were being invited to. Philip's conscience was content. He went to communion, for the first time for fourteen years.

That Bucer was nourished as a Dominican, and Luther as an Austin Friar, may have caused such an otherworldliness as to think such a historical moment was possible to keep secret. Less than two months after the wedding day rumours were everywhere, in July the story reached England. Christine's family were outraged and wanted publicity. Philip himself wanted publicity, it helped his inner being to know that this was a real wife. Confronted by danger to the reforming cause in grave adverse publicity, both Bucer and Luther advised Philip to deny that he had a second wife if challenged, for monogamy must be the rule. There may be circumstances when to tell a lie is holy because it averts worse evil—they cited Rahab the harlot in the book of Joshua, who was praised because she protected the Israelite spies, when they were hunted, saying that they went out through the city gate as dark fell, though they were hidden under the flax on the roof of her house.[18] Entering a moral maze Bucer and Luther found it more entangling than they expected, and Melanchthon had a breakdown over it. The elector of Saxony told Luther how disturbed he was. Luther said at his dining-table, 'If I am asked, are you happy at what happened, I'd say NO! If I could change things I would. Since I can't change it, I'll put up with it.'[19]

Christine bore Philip ten children, Margarete bore him eight. That had an effect on the German future. He had undertaken to Christine before the second marriage that only her children should have the rights as heirs. Nevertheless the consequence of so many children meant the political division of the Land of Hesse after his death and it was never again to be so powerful in Germany as during Philip's prosperity.

More immediately the bigamy destroyed his reputation, weakened him in the face of the emperor and the Reich, and brought nearer the military threat which faced German Protestants.

Ochino and the question of right

The moral argument was felt to be real. If it is certain that a male cannot be faithful to his wife, and he is driven to resort to another woman, is it better all round, for the children as well as the two women, if the second is allowed to be a wife and is not treated as though she were a harlot? Or is this opening of the door to a bigamous marriage, however narrowly controlled by the State, likely to be appalling in its consequences for family life and society?

This argument made a calamity in the evening of life of an excellent leader of reform, the Italian Capuchin Bernardino Ochino.

After his various exiles—from Italy because of the Inquisition, from the Italian community at Augsburg because of the emperor, from the Italian congregation in London because of Queen Mary—he was made pastor to the Italian congregation which came out of Locarno for faith and was settled in Zurich. His origin in Franciscan practice was not a training in being a man of the world and what was to happen proved the absence of discretion. Zurich more than once blamed him for his outspokenness. But he had an original mind, was well read, and was revered by the refugee Italians to whom he ministered. Bullinger the most influential man in Zurich was godfather to one of his children, Peter Martyr the other famous refugee Italian teaching theology in Zurich remained a friend till he died, John Foxe from London, in composing his history of the martyrs, asked him for information about Italians who had been martyred for their Protestant faith.

---

[18] Rahab in Bucer to Philip, 18 July 1540, in *Briefwechsel Landgraf Philipp's des Grossmütigen von Hessen mit Bucer*, ed. Max Lenz (Leipzig, 1880), i. 193.

[19] Luther to Elector John Frederick, 10 June 1540, *BW* ix. 133–4.

He published booklets which bothered the pastors in Zurich—a tract which might imply that debate on predestination was not useful, then a catechism. They asked him not to publish anything more without consulting them. He took no notice of this request; for soon afterwards in 1563 he published at Basel *Thirty Dialogues*, two volumes in Latin, a remarkable book.

The Reformation was doing much to clean up the sex industry. But still prostitutes were found though their lot was harder, and still men deserted their wives or kept a mistress round the corner, and still women could bear their husbands no longer, and the marriage courts had to provide for divorces which they tried to make as rare as possible. This ex-celibate and ex-Franciscan, a widower and the father of children, had read and meditated upon the case of Philip of Hesse nearly quarter of a century before; and now raised the question as a moral debate, whether it is right that in all situations the only answer is faithfulness to the single spouse. Philip of Hesse had a selfish motive. Ochino had no motive but pastoral concern for people whose marriage ran into intolerable difficulties.

A Carthusian monk Johannes Lening became an evangelical pastor in Hesse and wrote for the sake of his prince a tract defending bigamy, not quite outright because there must be special moral circumstances, but in such a way as to defend Philip, under the title *The Dialogue of Neobulus*. The evangelical world regarded Lening with a certain contempt as unprincipled and ambitious. Without mentioning the source (which was a mistake, he would more easily have defended himself later if he had mentioned his source), Ochino put the arguments of Neobulus into the mouth of his debater Telipolygamus, who pleaded that marriage to more than one spouse may in certain circumstances be permissible. Telipolygamus argued that the Old Testament allows polygamy; that St Paul says a bishop must be the husband of one wife, which implies that those not bishops might have more than one. Ochino retorts simply that to marry more than one wife is immoral. That is, the effect of the *Dialogue* is to make the Bible utter no ban on polygamy, what is against it is the natural law of nations. If someone has more than one wife it offends the conscience of society, which legislates against it; and it is God's will that we obey the law. Ochino keeps saying that monogamy is the only moral relation between the man and the woman. But then, says the troubled soul with a troubled body, what am I to do? Ochino replied, be faithful to your wife and pray for continence. But suppose, says the troubled one, I pray for continence and it is not given to me? Then, said Ochino, you must do whatever you are led to do by God. But it is not possible for God to lead anyone to commit bigamy.

At the fair in Basel that year the Zurichers were blamed for encouraging immorality because they allowed Ochino to publish scandalous things. One attacker said that Ochino tried to justify polygamy. The Zurichers reported the attack to the Zurich authorities. Bullinger and Gualter and Wolf examined the book on 22 November 1563. They reported to the council that it did not defend monogamy adequately. The same day, with a haste that amounted to injustice, the Zurich council voted to expel Ochino from the city. There were three charges: (1) he printed a book in Basel which got round the system of licensing books in Zurich; (2) he wrote about polygamy and other matters in such a way as to hurt the Christian religion; and (3) he lowered the reputation of Zurich with other towns. He was not charged with teaching that bigamy is morally possible, but only that he wrote about such things in a way to raise doubt. There was other material in the essays to give the council pause, though they did not make it a charge: in Dialogue 19 was a debate on the arguments against the doctrine of the Trinity though Ochino came to an orthodox conclusion; in Dialogue 20 a strong doubt whether people ought ever to be executed for their faith.

He said that they misunderstood what he tried to do in his essays, and had no idea that he could not publish in Basel.[20] They insisted that he go. There was a social problem. On the one hand the Italian congregation tried to keep him and wept at his going. On the other hand the story got about among the people that he taught polygamy, and he was at risk if he walked out at night.

His wife had died and he left with his four children for Basel where the ministers were not unfriendly but the council were worried over their reputation if they kept him. Mulhouse refused him and he passed the winter in Nuremberg and then moved on to Frankfurt, where he wrote an unpleasant tract against Bullinger and the behaviour of Zurich. Poland, where there were Italian refugees among the young Protestant congregations, invited him, but then the king ordered all foreigners to leave Poland and he left, not before three of the children died of the plague. He came back into Moravia and found refuge in an Italian anabaptist's house and died. We do not know what happened to the surviving child.

This was the saddest fate of any of the evangelical leaders. Here was a person whose Franciscan spirituality had led him towards a Protestant faith and who had a thinking mind and suffered for his faith from his own people and from the English and from the Germans and finally, through an indiscretion of old age, from the city where he at last found his vocation.[21]

[20] The legality of the printing at Basel was not quite clear, though Ochino had every reason for thinking that it was. The manuscript came to the printer Perna, who took it to Amerbach, who did not read Italian easily and passed it for advice to Curione. Castellio translated it into Latin but did not ask leave to print because that was the printer's duty. Perna printed it on the supposition that as neither Amerbach nor Curione had objected that was equivalent to a leave to print. Cf. Roland H. Bainton, *Bernardino Ochino* (Florence, 1940), 140. Ochino had been warned by ministers not to publish outside Zurich. He believed, no doubt correctly, that a warning from ministers was not equal to an order from the council.

[21] Because of the late visit to Poland, where unitarians were then beginning to prosper, and his death in an anabaptist refuge, unitarians afterwards claimed him as one of themselves. Of that there is no reliable evidence.

14

IN THE COUNTRY

The emperor Louis the Pious made a law in the year 818 that every parish church must have a house for the priest with a garden. In those days priests were not supposed to be married but often had women who were accepted as wives. When Hildebrand and his disciples hunted against priests' women to stop parishes becoming hereditary and because they regarded the single life as morally higher than the married, priests' women turned into house-keepers (though they might still have children) and the parish manse with its garden was still needed. The garden was necessary because the country priest was so poor that he must feed himself, if he could, by cultivating his own soil to get vegetables for himself and his family, and, if it were large enough, to earn a little by selling its produce. If the priest had no concubine, there were usually others in the house—like a lay parish worker and his or her family. Children of the priest, legitimate or not, were necessary to the economics of the house because they were indispensable to labour in the glebe. The Reformation did not begin the social situation where a family lived in the vicarage.

But it was also true that many country churches had never obeyed the emperor Louis the Pious. They needed no manse because if they had services even infrequently a monk might come over from a monastery with links to the parish. If he stayed the night he slept in the vestry. And country churches of this sort might have their own priest who lived all his time in one room. The Reformation inherited parishes where the manse was little but the vestry with a shed built on and the ground to cultivate was tiny. Their pastors were at first poorer than the priests because the fees for masses did not come and for many priests in the country this was a main source of income. In cer-tain parishes the pastor was given the old monastery and might live uncom-fortably in small unheated rooms too many for his needs.

They now wanted married clergy and educated clergy which must in time mean educated wives. The average rural manse was hardly a place for such a woman. But for the moment they could not hope to remedy that and all they sought was marriage instead of concubinage. Visitations ordered that a pastor should either marry his concubine or put her away. The parish had the duty to maintain the manse but this could be quite beyond its resources.

That over the years the authorities and the parishes did well about the provision of housing is proved by evidence that when the Thirty Years War came
wandering bands of mercenaries selected vicarages as promising places to
loot.

Country pastors like priests before them were poor and their life was very
like that of their parishioners and so they did not gain the respect due to one
looked up to because he had more education and more means to help in
times of need, but they retained, what was not always an advantage, the village sense that the pastor was 'one of us'. Their wives went out to earn if they
could be spared from the young children, and the children went out to work
if they were not needed on the glebe.

The pastor had one expense from which the parish ought to have saved
him and often did not—the cost of books. The parish would pay for the Bible
and prayer books and hymn book that were used in church (at first more
likely one or two hymn books, not many, for few of the people read easily).
But the pastor was encouraged by the bishop/superintendent or the visitors
to own a few books regarded as indispensable for his work. In north Germany
the pastor was urged to own selected works of Luther—perhaps 20 gulden—
and books by Melanchthon and Bugenhagen; expensive objects still, so that
a middling-size library for a pastor would cost 200 or 300 gulden, more than
he could earn in three years. Therefore in many manses of the countryside
there were no such books. The Schleswig church order of 1542 listed the
books which clergy need: a Bible, Melanchthon's *Apology* and *Commonplaces*
(two expositions of the Creed), Luther's *Shorter Catechism*, Bugenhagen on
Psalm 29 (which explains baptism), the instructions given by the Saxon visitors to their parishes, and a copy of this church order (so that they can know
the right way to run a parish).

Visitors tried to ensure that manses had one room set aside for the pastor,
as a place where he could give private interviews, and as a room away from
his family where he could study and prepare sermons. It was years before this
was achieved in remote parishes and many pastors still felt incapable of
preparing sermons and when/if they preached read from a collection of sermons like Luther's Postils.

Visitations show that despite the melting of silver in crises of the State or
Church and the putting of silver from monastery chapels to other uses, silver
survived in the parish churches for a long time, and this was not the new chalices needed to give communion in wine to the laypeople, but the old silver
that no one now needed, piled up in the vestry, pyxes, monstrances, censers,
bowls for holy oil; in 1540 the large village of Gartz on the Oder still had
twenty-five chalices.[1] Safes were insecure, visitations not infrequently report

---

[1] Hellmuth Heyden, *Neue Aufsätze zur Kirchengeschichte Pommerns* (Cologne, 1965), 56.

the theft of a chalice. Parishes were known to sell old chalices to afford the purchase of books. The disused liturgical books, Latin missals and breviaries, were still to be found in many vestries, not valued but just clutter and not thrown away. It is possible that one or two of them were used by the pastor, for example the *Golden Legend*, the stories of the saints, which was often in the Catholic sacristy and now to be found still in church libraries and might with care be useful to the evangelical preacher.

The church bells might be taken in a crisis over war and the need for metal for artillery but they still rang from church towers to remind people of the frequent services, and even on saints' days which were no longer a public holiday, and mourners did not think a funeral reverent without the sound of a bell. The people still liked the bell to be rung in storms for they remembered the lore that the bell was a lightning conductor, and a defence against the demons of the storms, a belief however which was fading. Candlesticks were inherited from the past and these were valued and benefactors under the reform gave more candelabra to the Church, for they were needed for light and people still liked them for reverence. The collection plate was in most churches a new item of furniture for in the old world the begging was in the streets, and this in-church begging was organized and supervised so that everyone knew its destination, which was usually to the poor but sometimes to other church objects like repairs.

In most Lands burials were allowed in church till about 1800 but the fee was costly. The peasants had the right of free burial in the churchyard and they could do and were expected to do their own digging. The churchyard was used as pasture for cattle and sheep, and sometimes pigs rootled at the graves, and boys and girls used the space for games.

The customs and orders varied in different regions. It will be best to take six more distant countrysides where evidence is in part available: (1) the peasant republic in the marshlands of south-west Jutland; (2) the broad lands to the east of Germany with few towns, mostly in the duchy of Prussia; (3) the mountain region of the reformed districts of western Switzerland; (4) the French countryside; (5) the churches of Iceland, distantly governed from Denmark; and (6) the attempt to reform the very remote Moldavia, nominally under the sovereignty of the Ottoman Turks.

Dithmarschen was remote not because of distance but through the fens which protected it on one side and the rough infertile land on the other. The people were fisherfolk and smallholders along the North Sea coast between the Elbe and the Eider. Charlemagne conquered them and made them a Gau (Dietmars Gau) but after his empire failed they built their local independence as a republic. The archbishop of Bremen claimed them and the bishop of Schleswig, but they took little notice of either. They eventually allowed the archbishop to station a representative in their council but disregarded his vote. The government consisted of forty-eight elected persons but they could not be turned out for the office was held for life. In 1474 the king of Denmark claimed the sovereignty but when in 1500 his successor King Hans tried to enforce it and invaded them, he was beaten with great loss among the marshes. They vowed that if they won the battle they would found a nunnery in gratitude. The victory felt to be a miracle so they founded a house of Benedictine nuns at the site of the battle. This did not prosper, for nuns were never quite safe in remote country, so they moved it to Lunden and turned it into a Franciscan house. All this showed the Catholic sentiments of the peasant republic. They had no university, hardly a school, not a single library. As they had no town of any size, they did not have the usual place for reforming ideas to take hold.

From the remote past the Hamburg chapter, their nearest big town in Germany, had vestigial rights over their church affairs. Unsettlement had reached them, because in 1523 the council took the resolution to throw off all allegiance to Hamburg. A couple of their young men heard there was a university at Wittenberg and went there to try it out. A group heard that at Bremen there was a remarkable preacher who taught reform and invited him. This was the Dutch Augustinian Henry of Zutphen, who had studied at Wittenberg and then returned to Antwerp where he just escaped being burnt. In Bremen the reforming party was feeling its strength, and protected him from the archbishop and made him their chief preacher.

In Dithmarschen they begged him to come. Dominicans from Lunden organized his kidnapping and he died as a martyr in 1524. But here it is hard to find any evidence that the blood of the martyr was a seed of the Church. On all sides they were surrounded by states going evangelical, they could not escape the wave of opinion. Soon they banned the mass. In many areas of this so recently devout Catholic land of peasants, there was almost no opposition to the incoming of Protestantism, priests came over to be reformed pastors. A few parishes resisted, the Franciscans at Lunden stayed till the regents abolished them.

Possessing no literate class, they could not supply their own pastors and if they were to have schools and evangelical worship they must import. Incoming clergy were astonished and grieved at old customs of the fen-landers, like the right of vendetta, and the right to loot ships wrecked on the coast, and started to change this historic little community which they regarded as an obsolete form of society. The regents accepted an evangelical church order in 1533 but it is characteristic that we do not know its provisions because no copy has been found. In 1559 the republic was finally forced to accept incorporation into the duchy of Schleswig-Holstein. Simultaneously its own church order vanished and it was placed under the church order of

Schleswig-Holstein, destined to a long history into modern times. They were still a long way from the provision of many schools. It was still more than a century before there was a Schleswig university at Kiel in the buildings of a former Franciscan house; the only German university to experience a decade of Russian rule but not the only German university to have its buildings destroyed during the Second World War.[2]

Prussia

Except for the town of Königsberg, prosperous from the sea and the Hanseatic League, with its medieval cathedral and the castle which was the headquarters of the grand master of the Knights of the Teutonic Order, Prussia was almost all rural. Under its name a new and Protestant great power was created but it was far from great when the Reformation began. The country was made and settled by the Teutonic Order which arose, like nearly all knightly orders, out of the crusades in Palestine. They began at the German hospital in Acre about 1190 and were brought into the northern Balkans by the king of Hungary to help defend him from eastern invaders. A Polish duke brought them further north to defend his dukedom against attacks by barbarian Prussians. They led a crusade against the Prussian tribes and by 1231 governed a very large area—ruled by Germans, but not part of the Reich.

As Christian knights of a religious order they were bound to monastic vows of chastity, obedience, and poverty. The obedience was owed to their head, the elected grand master, and they must be unmarried. When they were already governing wide lands on the Vistula and round Königsberg, and depended partly for prosperity on the grain trade, the pope released them from the vow of poverty. By the fourteenth century, after many disasters, they ruled the future East Prussia, part of eastern Pomerania including Danzig (Gdansk), and northward part of the Baltic coast including Estonia. There they attracted settlers from northern and central Germany and embarked upon a civilizing process among peoples who till then were tribal and anarchic. The land was underpopulated and poor, and wars with Poles or each other ruined many villages and drove out many priests. Since they possessed many endowments in Germany and the Tyrol, they also had a 'German master' for these territories who was supposed to be subject to the grand master but was not; and up the Baltic coast there was 'the Livland master', who helped to protect various bishops' territories in what are now Lithuania, Latvia, and Estonia, who was supposed to be under the grand master but was too inaccessible and was not.

---

[2] The university of Königsberg in East Prussia ended at the Russian occupation of 1945.

As Poland grew to be a power it resented this religious order cutting it from the Baltic and forced the knights to surrender part of their territory and for the rest of it to be vassals of Poland. But in what was to be East Prussia, round Königsberg where the grand master had his headquarters, they were still a state that counted. By the time that Luther became famous they were in political trouble. The knights occupied their castles like country residences but made their fortunes and went away. The State was run by lay civil servants or squires, many of them lawyers, who were not noble enough by birth to be admitted knights of the order and could not share in the top decisions. The knights had to be unmarried but they did not do without women, which out of the three vows left only the vow of obedience to the grand master. Being in theory monks they were supposed to lead a simple life but the grand master had a retinue of 400 in his castle. The outward ceremonies were very religious as befitted a religious order; the face of the blessed Virgin on coins, solemn pilgrimages by the grand master on state occasions, the indulgence of 1517 was widely bought.

They needed a military commander as their head and not many such commanders were unmarried. Albert of Brandenburg-Ansbach was elected grand master at the age of twenty-one, partly because his family was one of the great princely families of the German Reich, and partly because his father was famous as a general under the emperor Maximilian. He was a relative of the family which ruled Brandenburg and therefore of Archbishop Albert of Mainz. The Brandenburg family was related to the king of Poland and the order hoped that so their conflict with Poland could be eased. Albert went through the ceremonies which a grand master was expected to attend, with apparent piety; he encouraged the houses of the Franciscans and made new foundations 'to bring blessedness to the poor ignorant and unbelieving people';[3] and yet, even in the early years, there were signs that he regarded the ceremonies with detachment and even on occasion with amusement. The order was fortunate to pitch on a man of such effectiveness. He understood how it was necessary to turn the land of the order into a real state which kept up with the times. Others saw the need and had plans for coping. The bishop of Pomesania, one of the dioceses in Prussia, had a plan for making the king of Poland the hereditary grand master. The Order of St John of Jerusalem, which was driven out of Rhodes by the Turks after a heroic defence in 1522, and as yet had not Malta as a home, wondered whether they should join with the Teutonic Knights and take up the mission in eastern Europe. Albert must do something to reform the order before others had other plans. He began to act independently. In 1523 the see of Pomesania fell vacant and the Poles thought they should persuade Rome to appoint a Pole. Albert could not

---

[3] Walther Hubatsch, *Geschichte der evangelischen Kirche Ostpreussens* (Göttingen, 1968), i. 5.

afford to have a Pole in a Prussian see so he arranged the admission of Dr Queiss to the order and then persuaded the chapter to elect him; all this without reference to Rome.

The State looked to be on the verge of breakdown. The artisans in Königsberg resented their government. If a Teutonic knight went out alone in the streets wearing the white cloak of the order he was not safe from assault and was likely to be insulted.

The citizens looked westward to Wittenberg and its teaching for political rescue. In 1523 the three parish communities in Königsberg joined in asking the municipal councillors to bring in the reform. Martin Luther heard what was happening and sent Johannes Briesmann, a Franciscan who had joined the reform. Still in his Franciscan habit, Briesmann preached the first reformed sermon in the cathedral at Königsberg. The effect was unusual. The sermon persuaded the bishop, Georg von Polentz, bishop of Samland.

Polentz had been trained as a lawyer and was a secretary in the Curia at Rome and then served in the administration of the emperor Maximilian. There he met Albert of Hohenzollern. When Albert became a Teutonic knight, Polentz also enlisted in the order. In 1519, though he knew no theology, the chapter of Samland elected him their bishop. He was hastily ordained deacon and priest to qualify him for the see and he was enthroned with regular Catholic rites. Albert made him the deputy of the grand master. In that office it was as plain to him as to Albert that the Teutonic State could not go on as it was.

In a packed cathedral on Christmas Day 1523 Polentz celebrated the first reformed rite ever presided over by a bishop of the Catholic Church. The news of this sermon by a bishop raced across evangelical Germany. In the next year the bishop introduced Luther's German form of baptism and German hymns started to be sung in East Prussian congregations.

That June 1523 Albert sent a message to Wittenberg that he would like to consult Luther about the way to reform his order, and sent him the statutes. He was nervous because the messenger was ordered to burn the letter. Five months later Albert went to Wittenberg to meet Luther in person, on 29 November 1523. He had questions to ask which showed he had qualms. They were more fundamental than about the statutes, over the problem whether the pope and bishops had authority in the Christian Church. He probably asked for a written opinion. In any case Luther sent him one; and then wrote a more direct pamphlet, characteristic of its author: *Exhortation to the Knights of the Teutonic Order that they Lay Aside False Chastity and Assume the True Chastity of Wedlock.*[4] Albert had political reasons for wanting this.

---

[4] Albert to Luther, 14 June 1523, in *BW* iii. 86. Answer on authority in the Church, *BW* iii. 207–19; *An die Herren deutschs Ordens*, *WA* xii. 228 ff.

Because the knights had to be unmarried they kept leaving Prussia and weakened the State. Married they might stay and build government.

Luther recommended to Albert that he should receive Speratus as the guide to reform. Speratus became the real reformer of Prussia. He never liked Prussia. He was a Catholic priest from Augsburg in south Germany and never quite settled in the north. He married secretly and so was thrown out of a canonry at Würzburg cathedral, and was a pastor in Bohemia till the bishop put him into gaol. So he went to Wittenberg and devoted himself to translating Luther's Latin works into German and helping Luther with hymns, for he was a poet and a hymnwriter.

Albert met him at Luther's house when he visited Wittenberg and invited him to Prussia. He created a service book, a hymn book, and the first Prussian church order. Churches with evangelical services were crammed, Catholic conservatives had little hold on the people or the church organization. Hardly a Land in Germany was more easily reformed—so far as its German population was concerned. They made a common chest for the poor and sick, and banned novices in monasteries, and urged monks to go out and get jobs and wives. In the country the people destroyed pictures or trees that were the goal of a cult.

The second bishop was the diocesan of Pomesania, Erhard von Queiss. He was another lawyer trained at Bologna and was commended to Albert as useful for the diplomatic service. He became bishop of Pomesania to give him a title for his diplomatic missions, he was not consecrated as a bishop and unlike Polentz had no confirmation from the pope. He was hardly respected by the people. But he was more active in evangelical reform than they expected. He ordered clergy to teach two sacraments of the gospel and not seven, to stop pilgrimages, processions, and daily mass, and allowed them to marry if they liked. He said nothing about doctrine, or preaching. Then he married, handed over the secular jurisdiction of the see to Duke Albert, and died in 1529.

For during 1524–5 the grand master of the Teutonic Order was turned into a duke. The leading administrators in the State asked that it should become a secular state. To do that needed authority from Pope and Emperor and nobody could imagine that either Clement VII or Charles V would agree.

On Palm Sunday 1525 Albert the grand master of the Teutonic Order went to Cracow the capital of Poland and knelt to do homage for all the possessions of the order to the king of Poland, and in return came back to Königsberg as the secular duke of Prussia with the arms of the black eagle. Hardly anyone in the eastern domains of the order resisted him. The estates and members of the order in central and southern Germany broke away and under the Deutschmeister, 'the master of the German part of the order', survived as celibate or allegedly so and Catholic until Napoleon Bonaparte swept them all away. Bishop Polentz of Samland, who was legally a prince-bishop, gave away his secular rights to the new duke of Prussia and kept only his religious and ecclesiastical rights. The resident knights in their old castles in the countryside easily turned themselves into hereditary squires and liked the change. The master of the knights in Livland for a time went on the old way but the Protestant movement along the Baltic was so strong that in the end he too dissolved the order of the knights.

Albert's chancellor from 1526 was Friedrich Fischer, once like Speratus a canon of Würzburg cathedral, who had married a nun. In 1526 Albert married Dorothea of Denmark in a marriage service which was wholly evangelical, conducted by the two bishops Queiss and Polentz. She was the first woman to live openly in the old grand master's castle, and was a prayerful evangelical and an excellent wife. The marriage was necessary to the stability of the State. But in the circle of Charles V it gave more ground for pillorying the duke of Prussia as an apostate monk. The book of private prayers which Albert chose for her had many editions and became one of the most widely used evangelical collections of prayers in the sixteenth century. Under the altered title of *A Tinderbox of Christian Prayer* it was the first collection of prayers in a Finnish translation. She went about among the poor like a medieval queen and was beloved by the people.[5] She died young leaving no male heir; a disaster for Prussia because the next wife of Albert was mentally deficient.

In their far-flung rural dioceses the two bishops directed a reform of worship on the lines suggested by Wittenberg. They kept the Latin language for chanted parts but otherwise put the service into German and used Luther's earliest hymn book. They kept some of the service in Latin because in parts of Prussia more people understood Latin than German. They tried to get interpreters to be present at sacraments on high festivals to explain service and sermon to those who knew no or little German. But this seems to have been directed more at visiting traders than at the rustic poor who spoke different languages within Prussia.

In these expanses of sparsely peopled land, the lot of a conscientious bishop was not happy. If he determined unlike his predecessors to get around to such distances and be a true pastor, there were many obstacles. When Queiss of Pomesania died, Speratus became bishop of the see, a person with a scrupulous conscience. He understood no word of Polish and most of his people did not speak German. He must make long journeys over country where roads hardly existed. He had the duty of helping pastors to make evangelical Christians out of a people still with old heathen customs and an odd faith in magic and touches of a more superstitious Catholicism. He worked

---

[5] Walther Hubatsch, *Geschichte der evangelischen Kirche Ostpreussens*, i. 18.

under an illusion that he only had to teach with decision an elementary series of Christian doctrines and all would be well or at least better—and perhaps at times they were better. He could hardly support himself, still less give alms to the needy, because the endowments of the see were devastated by Polish war, and like many of his country pastors he had to support himself with the produce of his glebe. The country Catholic priests in great majority came over easily to the Reformation, he had far less trouble in finding pastors than might be expected, they could hardly do other in the countryside if they were to keep themselves and their women in bread and they preferred their women as wives. But it had the complexity that many priests read the service they were told to read but hardly knew what evangelical reformation was about. Speratus was miserable. To be bishop of Pomesania during those years, if one was to be happy, it was useful not to be so good a man nor so scrupulous about his duty.

Nowhere in Prussia, except in the new-founded university at Königsberg, was there any theological argument between Catholic and Protestant. It was perhaps the one Land of the Reich where this was true. No one outside the university, where the professors were nearly all imported, knew enough theology to argue. The people did not mind, they had the same pastors as before, and much the same sort of service but (if they spoke German) liked the German part and received the chalice at the sacrament with pleasure; and though visitors came round and rebuked them for magic or superstitions, visitors were like the bishop, they could not often appear and when they went away little changed.

There began to be village schools. The people liked these institutions so long as they did not remove children during weeks when labour was needed in the fields. Labour was not only needed at harvest time.

For the bishops and pastors it was a difficulty that those who did not speak German spoke three different languages: Prussian itself, Lithuanian, and Masurian.

Prussian was already a Germanized language with so much mixture of German settlers. A monk had lately produced the first inadequate Prussian dictionary and translated the Our Father into Prussian. Albert took trouble and in 1545 saw that a catechism in Prussian was published and in 1561 a better one, with forms of baptism and marriage, was created through the care of the court chaplain Funk. They found it very hard to find enough pastors who could communicate with Prussians except by the German which most of them were beginning to know. Churches in the Prussian area had two pulpits, the second for the interpreter to translate the preacher. But the Prussian language was dying fast. The last traces are found early in the seventeenth century.

On the northern border were Lithuanian countrymen. The university of Königsberg had grants for students who would learn Lithuanian, and grants for students from the Lithuanian-speaking area. These were intended to produce the pastors for that part of the duchy. It was hard work, for in 1545 there was only one pastor in all the duchy who could take a service in Lithuanian.[6] Bishop Speratus did all he could to find people, and the first professor of theology at the university Rapagalen was a Lithuanian, but he died too soon. In 1547 there was a Lithuanian catechism and hymn book and two years later a form for baptism.

The Masurians spoke a sort of Polish and there were obvious reasons why the university of Königsberg should do all it could to encourage Polish translations. This was much easier to achieve because many Poles knew German and some Germans knew Polish.

The inhabitants of the eastern Baltic coast had been converted by missionaries during the thirteenth century and left under five ecclesiastical rulers— four bishops of whom Riga was the archbishop, and the master of that branch of the Teutonic Knights. Their rulers the bishops and the Teutonic master were recognized as princes of the Holy Roman Empire. There were constitutional struggles—bishops versus master of the knights, squires and municipal counsellors versus master and bishops. But no one had questioned the Catholicism or the ecclesiastical rule. In this remote region the clergy usually had concubines and no bishop felt it possible to enforce the rule of celibacy. The towns had more clergy than they needed, it was hard to find priests willing to serve the country people.

All the eastern Baltic coast had close links with the Hanseatic trading towns to the west, especially Lübeck. Most of the clergy were of German descent and more of them were educated in Germany.

One effect was municipal power over the churches instead of bishop's power because in a rough region only the municipality had the force to protect church buildings and keep order. They started to administer the property and make an inventory of what furniture survived and open poor chests and expel monks because the presence of monks provoked mobs and because they wanted the monastic money for municipal purposes. Only in Reval the cathedral stood firm in its Catholicism, protected by the Teutonic Knights, until as late as 1565 when it was conquered by the Swedes; and two other monasteries survived, one for twenty years and one for nearly fifty, until it was ended by Russian invasion.

In near-chaos they needed reformed services urgently. Briesmann was sent from Königsberg to Riga to get evangelical order, and stayed for four years. His work included a hymn book in Low German and in 1533 his order of service became legal in Riga and Reval and Dorpat. The form of service was

---

[6] Hubatsch, *Geschichte der evangelischen Kirche Ostpreussens*, i. 89.

more conservative than that of Königsberg to respect the Catholic feelings of the people. This church order was more sketchy than the careful orders drafted by Bugenhagen for most of north Germany and Denmark. There was no formal creed but since they needed someone to tell them what was right if a pastor was accused of teaching error in the pulpit, they became dependent on advice from Wittenberg.

In Riga the Letts did the manual work and had their own altar in St Peter's. Before the Reformation the Franciscans had a special preacher to the Letts. The reform converted one of the parish churches to be a church for the Letts with services in the Lett language; but it was very hard to find anyone who could conduct the service without sounding foreign for the pastors were mostly German. We can only be certain of eight Lett-speaking pastors in all the sixteenth century and several were probably Germans who learned the language.[7] However, something was achieved because through these preachers Lettish was created for the first time as a written language. In Reval there was a post of lecturer/preacher in Estonian and at Dorpat there was another such post. In Reval was published a catechism in two languages, German and Estonian, which was printed by Lufft in Wittenberg and is the oldest book in the Estonian language; but the Reval authorities banned it because they disliked the effects on their Estonians of knowing the catechism. The conversion of the Lett and Estonian peasants, who still practised non-Christian customs (especially goodly meals for the dead being placed in their graves, or prayers to the gods of the forests), was a task beyond any instant success and took generations. The creation of the Estonian and Lettish written languages was a service of the reforming movement.

Country parishes in western Switzerland

Neuchâtel, the important town of western Switzerland after Geneva, was under the rule of Jeanne de Hochberg who through her husband was of one of the leading families in France. In Neuchâtel she had a governor from 1529 to 1552, Georges de Rive. The canons dominated the church and the town, and were all well-born and well-endowed and always in dispute with the clergy in the town over tithe and much else, and owned not a mind among them capable of standing up to Farel. In 1529 he appeared in the town with a recommendation from Berne and tried to preach but was only allowed to preach in houses or streets and then only after Berne protested that he must not be silenced. In July 1530 he came there again. Not being allowed a church, he preached in the street and the squares and the pubs. Then,

---

[7] Reinhard Wittram (ed.), *Baltische Kirchengeschichte* (Göttingen, 1956), 43, 86ff.

with the help of Berne, he was given a gatehouse chapel from which he removed the images. Berne again told Farel to restrain his zeal. He answered by placarding the city with notices that anyone who said mass was a murderer and thief. The resulting prosecution gave him useful publicity and a chance to talk truly of how faith is different from buying paradise.

A Bernese army was returning from protecting Geneva in a threat from Savoy and a Neuchâtel detachment had views in favour of Farel and did not mind violence. After a sermon on 23 October 1530 zealots cut off the noses of images and pushed sticks through their eyes. The next day which was Monday the destruction or purification was systematic. The governor could only rescue a few ornaments into his castle. Canons were beaten when they tried to protect the statues. Participants felt that they shared in a divine work of cleansing. They were powerful because so many were young Swiss soldiers returning from the Geneva campaign in which a Catholic threat was the enemy.

The Neuchâtel town council by majority decided for the reform. They promised not to trouble the monasteries nor to hurt priests who were loyal to the old ways. This promise was impossible to fulfil because Berne was now resolute that the mass should be illegal everywhere in its territory and protectorates.

The change at Neuchâtel affected all the villages round, the area in the hills of Bienne, the places in the southern Jura mountains. The middle class people liked it because nearly all church property was redirected to social welfare. A few months later at Orbe, not far away, there were blows between Catholics and reformed about what happened in church. Catholic Fribourg had rights there as well as Protestant Berne. Berne sent Farel into Orbe. Farel was shouted down when he entered the pulpit and had to be rescued by the bailiff. He tried to preach in the market square early next morning but with the same result. He tried again in the afternoon when women pulled at his clothes and pushed him to the ground. The Berne government fined the people of Orbe and ordered them to listen to Farel. Armed with this verdict Farel preached for a week, twice a day, in one of the Orbe churches. He had about ten people to hear what he said. He tried again later and preached in the church of the Poor Clares at Orbe but this confirmed the nuns in their resolution to stand by their old faith. An agreement between Fribourg and Berne finally achieved that the evangelicals could share a church at Orbe with the Catholics, so long as they held their sermons in the early morning. Farel had no sense in him of discouragement. He had a certainty that his cause would conquer in the end and he need only persevere. And it did. In 1554 Fribourg accepted that Orbe could decide by a referendum. The reformed party won the vote by three to two, and the altars and statues were removed.

Even the government of Berne protested to Farel that people had complained about him as violent and as a breaker of images and that he was not to pass the limits of his office of a preacher of the gospel and was to show the people in what limits the gospel makes us free. But the memories of this campaign left legends among the people of the Jura cantons and stories were told and embellished and exaggerated and became a part of folk memory.

Naturally the effects were not made only by a single speaker. Wherever Farel went he found sympathizers among the people; the schoolmaster, or the local priest, or a musician, or a group of merchants, or a friar from a religious house in that region, or some of the younger monks in a monastery, or a young man like Pierre Viret, the future reformer of Lausanne, who was the tailor's son at Orbe and had already acquired reforming opinions as an undergraduate at the university of Paris. As everywhere else the politics and the religion were not far apart. These western lordships were old feudal units, chaotic and weak, and depended on the protectorate of Berne which was now a Protestant state. The middle class wanted the archaic feudalism demolished; and because the apparent power and real powerlessness of the prince-bishop of Basel was one of those feudalisms, that did not incline the educated people any more towards the old Church. No more than elsewhere were they fond of rich chapters and monasteries. Farel was a superlative popular preacher. But some among the listeners were predisposed to welcome everything that he said.

The great issue, between the old and the new, was partly political and partly constitutional and partly social and partly religious. But religion was what everyone understood and felt. The religious issue appeared stark, as though it was nothing to do with politics—simplicity versus ceremony, French prayer versus Latin, Bible versus the decrees of the church hierarchy, light and lack of clutter versus images and statues and little altars, marriage versus celibacy—these were clear to everyone as an either–or. Many people were hardly aware that within this tension so passionate lay also the future of the cantons and the security of the Swiss Confederation.

Bienne itself was part of the prince-bishopric of Basel but had long achieved local secular independence; and curiously in church matters lay within the diocese of Lausanne. From 1507 they had as their pastor the humanist Thomas Wyttenbach, formerly a professor at Basel where he taught Zwingli and Leo Jud. From 1523 he was publicly a disciple of his old pupil Zwingli and began so to teach, and the next year married. When Berne went reformed in 1528 the effect upon Bienne was instant. They removed the ornaments from the churches without violence and reformed the neighbouring districts where most of the Catholic priests came over to the Reformation. Of the twelve canons of the house at St Imier eight remained

Catholic and were given a pension; four turned reformed but one of the four subsequently repented of the change.

Since unusually the village pastors before and after the change are often known, a comparison becomes possible.

village	incumbent/curate	
	before	*after*
St Blaise	non–resident canon; curate had not said mass for six months	young French preacher of culture and piety
Serrières	man of little religion	he accepted reform
Corcelles	Benedictine not liked	refugee from Paris, did well
Colombier	canon who fled	Lausanne priest, deep piety, accepted reform
Bevaix	Benedictine not liked	French humanist from Strasbourg (Andronicus) for two years then cousin of last curé
Pontareuse	good man, ardent, conservative	Frenchman, Basel graduate
Béroche	old man, tired and dis– regarded; accepted reform and resigned	native of region, ignorant but warm
Môtiers	curé who lived with his servant, married her later though he refused reform	Frenchman; hosier at Geneva
Saint Sulpice	local man as priest	the same man
Verrières	served by chaplain	stepson of Lausanne book– seller; mind too independent for Farel, had to move; succeeded by cousin of Farel who was not safe with women and was dismissed
Cornaux	served from St Blaise	good man who could not win parish over
Landeron	irreducibly Catholic (Catholic squire)	preacher never more than temporary

Here are twelve villages. One never accepted the Reformation. Of the other eleven: four of the priests in charge before the change were rather disreputable and two more were unpopular. When the incumbent was a monk or appointed by monks he was likely to be resented by the people.[8]

To replace them: two of the existing incumbents stayed and continued in their parish as reformed pastors. Neither was much good. Four were served by former Catholic priests now reformed and these were good. Six were given to French refugees as pastors. The standard of education among the clergy rose dramatically. Three were cultivated men, one a well-known humanist. In one parish the second of the reformed pastors was a disgrace, appointed only because he was related to Farel. All the newcomers had a difficult time; partly from conservatives in their parishes but more from peasants who thought reform freed them from their church burdens and did not want to pay dues to keep the clergy. In some parishes there was a fairly quick turnover of pastors because they were impoverished. But with the exception of Landeron, the evidence showed that within a few years even parishioners who had resisted innovation defended it after they had grown accustomed to it. This change of mind did not need a new generation of children who had known nothing else. Probably the muse of the French language was important in the reconciliation. Certainly the use of the metrical psalm and congregational hymn helped them. More slowly, taking the endowments of a local monastery and starting a village school, or making better provision for the poor and sick, helped the people to like the new system. It is also likely that the somewhat higher standard among their clergy contributed. That more than half the new clergy were not Swiss but French did not delay the reconciliation; any more than at Geneva where a party hated Calvin but hardly at all because he was French. Farel was French but revered, far from universally but in many parishes, as *their* reformer. They were able to call on educated Frenchmen who had fled from France for the sake of religion and therefore were people with consciences, and like most refugees they fell in the world, needed work and a stipend, and were happy to find their mission in a little village.

In such villages it is possible to see how the organization of the Church took shape. In theory the old mess of jurisdictions between bishop and feudal lord and monastery gave way to a system where the government of the State said what ought to be done; a simplified way of service in the French language (largely translated from Berne's German simplified service) written by Farel and then approved by the ministers in Berne; a system of moral and marriage regulation ordered by the State, and appointments to parishes made by the State.

But in the country districts the reformed pastors were a long way from Berne and had their initiative. They met, to settle their problems, give advice to each other, join for prayers, and accept mutual rebuke, a devotion which

---

[8] Jules Pétremand, in *Guillaume Farel* (Neuchâtel, 1930), 362 ff.

was called the *censure*. In the censure the meeting questioned the pastor about his faith and the performance of his duty and the state of the parish and even about his way of life and his family. Once this voluntary institution formed it gained authority. Berne needed it for advice on who should be the next pastor of a parish. It was not long before it became the effective chooser of the new incumbents of parishes. Thereby the disputes between Church and State could not be avoided on such a matter as discipline—the pastors' desire for the right to excommunicate, the State's conviction that there must be a right of appeal to their court.

The number of clergy was fewer but then in old days it had been unwarrantably high. The village of Neuville had 800 souls but in Catholic times the incumbent had four curates, or one clergyman for every 160 souls. As these numerous clergy had not enough to do, the numbers were not always a help. The reformed parish was at first hard put to it to find one pastor, especially one capable of preaching a sermon that was not hocus–pocus, so the number of clergy dropped sharply. Despite the old endowments they did not inherit a church that was in good repair. Reformed freedom with endowments made this a little easier, yet often the church remained in disrepair, whether the people were Catholic or Protestant mattered less than that they were poor.

France

A country where humanists were able and respected would be sure to see Protestants among its citizens. A canon of Rouen cathedral who died in 1524 was found to have books by Martin Luther in his possession.[9] In the 1530s the Paris Parlement, composed of conservative lawyers and against 'heresy', announced the names of seventy-three 'Lutherans'. Of these fifty-one are known. A few noblemen, a few women, one doctor of divinity (Cairoli), one poet (Marot), a future pastor of Montbéliard Gaspard Carmel, two priests, six Augustinians, the principal of a college, various teachers, precentors at the chapel royal; but also tradesmen—printers, booksellers, pedlars of books, engravers, jewellers, painters, cobblers, coopers, innkeepers, shopkeepers. So the 'Lutherans' came from across society. More were educated than not, many were connected with publishing or printing or education, but plenty were not.

In the slow hidden spread of reforming ideas Paris lay more under the eye of government than did big cities of the provinces, Rouen or Lyons or Orléans. In these towns there was no class difference between Catholic and Protestant—both sides drew from all classes though perhaps the poorest of

---

[9] Philip Benedict, *Rouen during the Wars of Religion* (Cambridge, 1981), 50. John Viénot, *Histoire de la Réforme française des origines à l'Edit de Nantes* (Paris, 1926), i. 127.

the poor and the richest of the rich were likely to be Catholic and the average rate of literacy was higher among Protestants.

Yet there is no certain evidence of an organized Protestant congregation in France until 1541; organized in the sense of being more than a few friends meeting in a private room for the study of the Bible. It was in Meaux, where Bishop Briçonnet had earlier fostered biblical study and reform but then had been forced to cease such encouragement. The first congregation in Paris is not found till 1555. These are late dates compared with Germany, yet the country was not short of educated people and the condition of the Catholic hierarchy and some of its clergy clamoured for reform.

The prime reason was effective persecution. That not only killed Protestants, it created strong reforming churches over the border, in Strasbourg, or Frankfurt, or Montbéliard, or Geneva. Three thousand three hundred French people asked for refuge at Geneva during the 1550s alone. The flight of Estienne or Calvin or Farel was part of a wave of emigration. The western French-speaking side of Switzerland depended for its reforming prosperity on these incomers.

In 1559 King Henry II, who was physically strong and liked sports, went in for a joust and was killed by his opponent's lance into his eye. Since the constitution of France was almost absolute government by the king and the heir was only fifteen years old and married to the child queen Mary later Queen of Scots, there was a vacuum of government with the usual consequence of a jockeying for power—apparent end of persecution, a feeling by the reformed that they might soon be granted toleration. In Rouen 3,000 people met every Sunday in the square outside the cathedral for a reformed service. For three years the reformed congregations hardly hesitated to meet, though many accepted that they could not meet in Catholic churches but must meet in barns or in the open air.

But where a whole town or rather its large majority went reformed this meeting in the open air, when the churches were almost empty, became absurd. Nîmes in the south had a Protestant congregation for thirteen years and by 1560 it was a reformed town.

In the year after Henry II's death there first appeared the word Huguenot to describe the French reformed. The origins are still in doubt. Most historians thought it obvious that the word was a French corruption of the Swiss-German Eidgenossen, or allies, confederates in western Switzerland against the duke of Savoy (Berne, Geneva, Fribourg). As early as 1530 there was a French form in Geneva, *eiguenots*. But in its historic meaning of French Protestants it is first found in a letter of 16 June 1561 from Theodore Beza to Bullinger about the reformed in Lyons.[10] The letter shows that it was a word

---

[10] *Correspondance de Théodore de Bèze*, ed. H. Aubert, iii (Geneva, 1963), 111.

of abuse by opponents. Early Huguenot authors had another explanation for the word; from a story of a gate at Tours called after King Hugh (Hugues— probably Hugh Capet) near which a secret congregation of Protestants met by night. There is no written evidence for its use till 1560 but one Huguenot testified that he heard it in speech nine years before. In English the word was first found in 1565, also as a term of abuse from an enemy. Various modern scholars have thought it a combination, the Eidgenossen who met near King Hugues' gate at Tours. Unlike other nicknames it was accepted by the reformed, and eventually won its way into state documents.

French country congregations

In 1559 the French reformed held a national synod in Paris to which all Huguenot congregations were to send representatives. Only twelve congregations sent delegates. They discovered, so they claimed, that there were 2,500 congregations of Protestants in France. If this were true many French villages had a congregation. But this figure was the highest in the history of France. This was propaganda, to persuade Queen Catherine de Médicis the regent that the reformed were numerous and that toleration was the only sane policy. They were numerous enough to make toleration the only sane policy but not so numerous as they said and the world was not ripe for toleration yet. Contemporary estimates were impressions, from a half to a tenth of the country. Modern attempts to find these congregations have ended in failure. The nearest probable estimate is 1,400 congregations of which two-thirds were in the south of the country. At the end of the civil wars King Henry IV found 694 public churches and 257 private chapels and 800 ministers and 274,000 families or about a million and a quarter people. But this did not include that country which now contains most French Protestants and which was still for many years to be part of the German Reich, Alsace. The 1872 and 1883 censuses, when Alsace was not part of France, recorded about 600,000 Protestants. But long before that King Louis XIV had driven out many Huguenots, to England or America or Germany or Switzerland.[11]

The years 1559, 1560, 1561 witnessed a vast expansion of Protestant meetings through France, especially across the south. Often the congregations were several thousand. In Toulouse a congregation which began with three persons needed two pastors three years later. At Gien they started with four people meeting in a garden and soon had to move to a field and four months later were crying out for a pastor. At Orléans the pastors gave communion in a meadow to five or six thousand.

[11] Janine Garrisson-Estèbe, *Protestants du Midi 1559–1598* (Toulouse, 1980), 64 ff.; E. Doumergue, *Calvin*, 7 vols. (Lausanne, 1899–1917), vii. 345 ff.

The reforming faith was not spreading mainly by preachers sent out from Geneva. It spread among the people who then asked Geneva for pastors. Not all the people. If a town went reformed by majority, others conformed because they needed marriage and baptism and funerals and the services of the church. If the squire of a district went reformed, there were tenants who did what he wanted them to do. People did not always accept conversion as individuals, they followed the surge of the day. When a town was deciding to be reformed, a body of the people could sweep and be swept into the movement. The change was far from being guided by squires. Villages without a single landlord abolished mass and had prayers in French and asked for a pastor.

Under this reformed system the congregation was governed by a consistory; and not seldom in France the elders of the consistory, and even deacons, were in office before they had a pastor. Normally these elders were leading citizens in the community. The consistory was supposed to alternate its membership and elect new members but under French conditions this was seldom possible. The 'election' of new members was in fact by co-opting. Once a pastor was in office he influenced the choice. There was no democratic choice by all the community; or, if this happened exceptionally, it was not to be approved. In theory the community could disapprove the choice of the officers chosen for them but this never seems to have happened and there was almost no chance that it could happen.

The consistory had to approve the choice of pastor and could depose an unworthy pastor but in reality the pastor was often given to them from outside, put to them by neighbouring ministers. It met once a week (no pay but a small fine for absence without excuse). It kept minutes, in country places ungrammatical. It raised the stipend of the pastor—partly by administering former Catholic endowments but partly by a levy—and where the levy was not paid would go out and get it or a substitute in kind. In war this was their hardest task and took most time. It had also to administer the money for the care of the poor. This money more often came from gifts or legacies or Sunday collections, but it could also mean a levy. The consistory must make sure that the congregation was run well, in its bellringers and verger and music and repairs. It administered the moral discipline—in the villages the visiting of houses was not needed—if necessary by penalties, admonition, exclusion from communion. Drunkenness made a small proportion only; dancing (which was hard to stop, the French of all social classes loved dancing, and it had defenders who said that Scripture nowhere banned it), cabarets, banquets, blasphemy, luxury in dress, 'coquetry', including hair and paint—urban behaviour this, less in the villages; hence there were occasional cases where villages were given a pastor from the town and were shocked at the fashion worn by his wife. They were against pubs—because they may encourage drunkenness, take men away from home and family, promote gambling at cards, and if girls go there they risk sordid treatment. They usually expelled prostitutes and this had the effect that women drifted round hedges in nearby fields. The consistory could try to make sure that adults took proper care of their old parents.

They also spent time trying to reconcile quarrelling neighbours and were used as arbitrators in disputes. They had very little difficulty getting the people to attend church despite the length of sermons. They had little difficulty finding the right people to come forward for the various lay duties. This was probably the most important innovation of the Calvinist tradition in western Europe—the laypeople were not a democracy but they felt to be the Church and came forward to do the work of their church and did not assume that the clergy must do all because often there were no clergy to do anything. They felt responsible for the welfare of the people—in providing not only a home for the sick and a dole for the poor, but full employment in the community and a universal education including money for those who could not afford to pay. Full employment was not an impossibility when so many males were needed in war, the difficulty was shortage of labour. Good education was hard to provide, because the schoolmaster was often an ordinand who soon moved away, and because money for stipends was very short.

Communion was held four times a year and in the weeks immediately before it there was moral enquiry and devotional preparation. One of the times was Christmas, for Calvin abolished Christmas and other presbyterian churches followed; but the Huguenots kept the Christmas festival. Catechism was a weighty part of the pastor's duty and this raised a difficulty because Calvin's 'simple' catechism was not simple enough for the people. The psalms, usually of Marot though in the south they had to be in the Occitan version of the southern dialect,[12] were well known and much beloved and said from memory; and the knowledge of the Bible's histories is proved to have been remarkable even among people who could hardly read. They had baptisms inside church services unless there was a risk of death to the child; and they were hostile to traditional mourning at funerals, like black clothes and women's veils and sermons about the dead. The doctrine of purgatory vanished easily but not the desire to pray for the beloved dead. Because they had begun as a church without enough pastors and with no public churches, family prayers and Bible reading in the house spread in France more quickly than in any other part of the reforming world; for at first it was all they could safely do to practise their religion. Here the head of the household and not a pastor normally presided; as in the house of Gaspard

---

[12] Pierre de Garros translated the Psalms into Gascon and dedicated the version to Jeanne d'Albret (1565). Cf. Garrisson-Estèbe, *Protestants du Midi*, 279. There was a translation into Béarnais in 1583.

Coligny; but as pastors became available they could be sent as chaplains to the homes of landowners. The marriage laws were strict but did not differ from the Swiss reformed rules.

Village congregations met before there was any village pastor. But pastors they must get before long. For a time there were extreme forms of pluralism, two pastors trying to look after some fifty country churches. They could only appeal to Geneva which sent all it could, but before long Calvin said 'We are at the end of our resources.'[13]

At first there were only three colleges to train Huguenot pastors, Lausanne and Geneva and Nîmes. Later colleges were founded at Orthez in Béarn and at Orléans. But Geneva had the repute, and was safe as a place to study. In prestige it far outweighed the others and had the merit that it already trained a good number of French refugees who could be expected to want to go back into parishes in France and even if they did not want could be sent. Then new Huguenot congregations in France could find among themselves a young man or two with vocations and send them to be trained at Geneva. Often the need was so desperate that this training at Geneva was of the sketchiest. Sometimes ordinands at Geneva lived under assumed names so that they could less easily be traced and that complicated the task not only of the Inquisition but of the historian. Sometimes the young or not so young man was in Geneva for a few weeks only. A number of them needed to travel through France under an assumed name and it was prudent not to carry upon their person documents which suggested their mission. Sometimes they changed their names when they moved parishes.

The congregation of the village of Valdrome near Die listened to a Dominican preaching. In the middle of the sermon he declared that he was of the reformed faith and came down and took off his habit. The village applied to the Huguenot pastor at Die who came over to organize them. The villagers then elected the Dominican as their pastor, gave him a certificate of excellent morals, had him tested by the nearest three reformed pastors, and decided that they would find the money to send him to study at Geneva— 'two or three months'. It was not much. Calvin must have been suspicious. The next village near Die, Chastillon, knew a schoolmaster in Die 'of very modest attainments' and when it became reformed they elected this school-master as their pastor. They too subscribed to send him to Geneva—for two or three months. It was a condition of these subscriptions of money that Geneva should send him back to the paying parish and not direct him to another ministry; whereas normally Geneva made it a condition of admitting ordinands to the pastorate that they should go where they were sent, and exacted an oath that this rule should be obeyed.

---

[13] Calvin, CR xviii. 466–7.

Nicolas Folion was a Carmelite who became a Protestant and went to study at Geneva. But he was educated and was needed so urgently in France that after four months Geneva sent him first to Marseilles and then to Toulouse. Here he was a pastor for two years and was overwhelmed with the care of people and with administration, so that pastoral duties took all the time and he had not a moment to continue his studies. Then he went as pastor at Saint-Germain-en-Laye near Paris, which had a very educated congregation, and discovered how embarrassed he was at his own ignorance. He pleaded that he be given time away from the ministry to deepen his studies in the biblical languages. 'I find myself so uneducated when I am in the company of gentlemen and ladies.' He did not ask to go to Geneva because by then Orléans, the Huguenot headquarters in the civil war that divided France, had opened a college. His family was at Orléans. But he still asked Geneva for permission.[14]

In this crisis of an expanding church with few pastors, Jacques Berthet was sent to two villages near Orléans. The parishes found him not up to it and would not install him. So he was trained in a parish not far away, in preaching and pastoral care and catechism, for more than ten months, and then a parish asked for him and he was admitted as pastor.[15]

Dialect was a problem, as in Germany. The pastor who spoke the French of the north could not easily be understood in villages of the south and vice versa. Dialects limited the freedom in placing ministers. In the old priests it mattered less because their function was to say the sacramental words in Latin. Reformed parishes demanded that their pastor explain the Bible in sentences they could follow.

In this 'crisis of vocations'—far more people wanting ministers than there were ministers—Switzerland denuded itself. Geneva closed one of its churches because it was short of pastors. Parishes in the Vaud amalgamated. Berne allowed more than sixty of its pastors into France, Neuchâtel sent nineteen. There was a moment when Lausanne had not a single pastor for its own pulpits.[16]

In Geneva they had access to a good library. In the parishes of France the books that they needed were not so common. We have the list of books owned by one French pastor; ten in all apart from the Bible: two commentaries by Luther, two by Calvin (Isaiah and Romans), a Paraphrase by Erasmus (St John), Ramus on philosophy and two books on dialectic by Sturm and Caesarius,[17] Erasmus's book on how to write letters, and the decree of

---

[14] Folion to Calvin, CR xix. 31.

[15] R. M. Kingdon, *Geneva and the Coming of the French Wars of Religion* (Geneva, 1956), 11.

[16] Kingdon, *Geneva and the Coming of the French Wars*, 80; for Lausanne, H. Vuilleumier, *Histoire de l'Eglise réformée du pays de Vaud sous la regime bernois* (Lausanne, 1927–33), i. 681.

[17] Caesarius: Greek scholar at Cologne, pupil of Lefèvre, remained Catholic.

King Henry II of France against the Lutherans. But when he was sent to be pastor at Le Havre in Normandy, a post of danger, he did not think it right to risk the loss of these books by carrying them in his luggage. Probably the only book he took with him to Normandy was his Bible.[18]

About one in ten pastors were ex-Roman Catholic priests. A minority of these continued to minister in their old parishes and that was happy for the people if this was a good man. Nearly a fifth of the pastors came from noble families (in the fairly wide French meaning of the word nobility) because they had the education needed. A respectable number were graduates, there were even three professors of theology. About one in six was son of a Catholic priest, or soon son of a reformed pastor.

Pay was very difficult. They did not always have Catholic benefices as endowment. Tithe continued but pay was normally in arrears, with free but poor housing.

Standards were high and about one in ten pastors failed to reach them. Causes of dismissal: immorality, bad as teacher, wife's behaviour, neglecting pastoral care to practise medicine, truculence with colleague, dividing the congregation, iconoclasm over church ornaments, harshness to the people. There was the pastor who said he was a marvellous preacher, the parish which said they could not do without a marvellous preacher, the pastor who discovered on arrival he was too timid to preach at all, the pastor who was once a monk and whose manner was too reminiscent of his past, the pastor who disturbed people by thinking it wrong ever to kill anyone because of his or her religion, the pastor who shocked Calvin by leading his people in a riot to destroy the local Catholic statues, a village in the Venaissin which supposed that it satisfactorily reformed itself by smashing the ornaments in church. Not all could be as it ought to be. But the conditions made for courage and character. Calvin preferred future French pastors to serve a time in a Swiss parish, usually as deacons or catechists or schoolmasters, before they departed for such responsibility.

This was why Calvin—hated by a party in Geneva, disapproved by the Bernese without whose help Geneva could not resist a siege, respected but not fully accepted by Zurich and Strasbourg, resented by all the Lutherans except Melanchthon—became during the last five years of his life a person with European weight. In those very years the Huguenot churches grew amazingly. Calvin, as the leading voice of the Company of Pastors in Geneva, could supply the ministers, not enough but some, whom they needed. He could supply guidance in the organization of a young church and ethical verdicts on disputed issues and the accuracy and clarity of theology which would be necessary for the new preachers. He was their chief anchor outside

---

[18] Books of Jean Chambeli, listed in Kingdon, *Geneva and the Coming of the French Wars*, 16.

France. They besieged him with letters of request for people and advice. He was exhausted by it and was already ill and there are those who thought that the burden of the French churches contributed to his early death.

This work made a large difference to what happened in Geneva in the argument between Church and State. Normally a city council would need to approve such activity. The Geneva council in its fear of France preferred to know nothing officially about it. The consistory and the Company of Pastors acted on their own authority and did not need nor wish to consult the secular authorities of their State.[19] In 1561 the French government formally told the government of Geneva that the troubles of France were due to the pastors which they sent and these must be recalled. The Geneva council examined Calvin and other ministers and then felt able to draft a reply to the king denying that it had sent a single pastor into France.[20] It allowed that the ministers had done so but said that the pastors had tried everything to avoid and to repress sedition. The council took the precaution of telling Berne what had happened.

Navarre

The little kingdom along the Pyrenees had once been a big kingdom but Spain gradually annexed the southern parts. In 1516 King Ferdinand of Aragon annexed the last lands on the Spanish side of the mountains. They retained a local autonomy which in later centuries changed Spanish history. That left a small and weak French kingdom dependent upon the French kings. However small it still had a measure of independence. But it could not behave too independently and if it were ever to recover any of its Spanish lands it needed the French king. If the French king insisted on being very Catholic Navarre could not be too unCatholic. It had no towns of any size.

Marguerite of Angoulême was the elder sister of the French king Francis I. At the age of thirty-three she was already a widow and two years later married for political reasons Henri d'Albret the king of Navarre, who was much younger than she and was a king almost without a state. In Nérac and Pau she held courts where humanists gathered under her patronage. To encourage the scholars at that date was also to encourage reformation. Famous names went to Navarre for shelter: Rabelais the most famous, Lefèvre, Marot with most effect upon the Protestant religion. Probably not without the help of her scholars but certainly with her mind engaged she wrote short stories and letters and poetry and a devotional book, *The Mirror of a Sinful Soul*, which

[19] In 1557 Calvin asked the council's leave for a right to send ministers to Paris as they thought fit, CR xxi. 681–2; Kingdon, *Geneva and the Coming of the French Wars*, 33–4; and this was conceded with a note in the minutes that it would be bad if the government were known to have said this.

[20] Calvin, CR xviii. 343–5.

Queen Elizabeth of England translated into English. She was not in a mean-ingful sense a 'Protestant', but knew Latin, French, Italian, and Spanish and later learnt some Hebrew and Greek. Erasmus admired her. She was Erasmian in her dislike of superstition, and of too many monks as its pro-moters; a character of kindness and gentleness and laughter, with a mystical religious nature which was not compatible with the rigidity of doctrine led by conservatives in the university of Paris. She founded the first hospice in Paris for poor sick children. She read tracts by Luther and did not reject their contents but she remained a Catholic with a broad mind though she had friendly letters with Melanchthon and gave hospitality in Navarre to several Frenchmen who were Protestants.

She conformed to the mass and certain other rites with which she was not quite comfortable because her reforming chaplain Gérard Roussel persuaded her that these were not matters of principle. Her husband, who maltreated her, came into her boudoir and found Gérard Roussel and Farel at prayers and slapped her in the face.[21] She left a single child, Jeanne d'Albret, who was the mother of the only Protestant king that France ever had and the first maker of a true form of large-scale toleration.

In Jeanne d'Albret's Béarn and Navarre she was a Protestant queen with a conscience who reigned over a countryside of villages many of which were still Catholic, and under the political protection of the government of France which tried to be fiercely Catholic. That meant danger. Many of her people were Basques who spoke only Basque and felt nearer to their kin across the mountains in Spanish Pamplona than to their French-speaking government in Pau. There was almost a racial or language divide between her Catholics and her Protestants. But her French-speaking subjects did not all welcome the changes suggested. Some of the earlier reforming sermons in villages were heckled by the people, at Oloron they caused riot, other such sermons were given to tiny congregations of six or seven hearers. Ban usury and sor-cery and papal provisions and burials inside churches and gambling and dan-cing—and the banning of these last two met hard resistance, she was accused of wanting the people to be angels. She had a conscience, whatever the danger she felt a duty to make her people better, she wanted to cleanse her land of superstition, and get rid of images, and bring in good teachers and Bibles. Fortunately for her and her work her advisers persuaded her that she could not achieve reformation except little by little, in places where the people wished for it.

---

[21] Jeanne d'Albret to de Gourdon, 22 August 1555; Nancy Lyman Roelker, *Queen of Navarre Jeanne d'Albret* (Cambridge, Mass., 1968), 127. Gérard Roussel was a pupil of Lefèvre and a human-ist scholar. He was a canon of Meaux in the reforming time of Bishop Briçonnet, after which he fled with Lefèvre to Strasbourg. He returned to Paris and was in trouble but in 1536 became bishop of Oloron in Navarre. See p. 229.

In 1560 she felt able to make it public to her people that she was of the reformed faith. She was helped when Pope Pius IV summoned her to appear at Rome on a charge of heresy, and this was a boon to her because it swung the French government, which suspected her, into her defence. For a time, until invasion by Catholic armies in the third civil war, Béarn was a conscientious attempt at a reformed French-speaking state.

In the year of her death, 1572, Jeanne asked the Huguenot pastor of Nay, Nicolas de Bordenave, to write the history of her time, and the government made him a grant for the expenses. Like Thucydides he imagined speeches for his characters. But despite the extreme situation of civil war and martyrdoms he was not bitter. Later the text fell into the hands of a Catholic writer who altered or suppressed or mutilated passages. Eventually its true text could be almost recovered and it made a rare source for the Reformation in Béarn and Navarre.

Iceland

Iceland lay under Norwegian rule which meant Danish rule. Its church, within the province of Trondheim in Norway, was powerful both as a Catholic body and in the government of the island. Most of its bishops were Norwegians or Danes and in the later Middle Ages some were mere adventurers but the two last Catholic bishops were Icelanders by birth and both had the high secular dignity of being members of the Norwegian cabinet. Most bishops and pastors had wives. Jon Arason the last Catholic bishop of Holar had his wife and four sons and two daughters in his palace. Because of the fishing trade German trawlers came and there was a church for Germans who sailed out of Hamburg and Bremen, towns which after 1530 were evangelical. Here the reform became known. There were also a few young Icelanders who had studied at north German universities. Soon there were groups to study the Bible and read books of reformers.

Oddur Gottskalksson was sent to study in Denmark and Germany. Here he was persuaded that the evangelical way was right, though he was one of those for whom it was not easy to decide for reform, he saw both sides of the argument, it was an agony which needed prayer night after night that he might be shown the truth, and his eventual decision for reform felt to him like a conversion. Yet he never sought ordination, was never a parish pastor, but dedicated his life to translating books which would help reformation. To translate the New Testament and not to be discovered he made a secret study in a stable. Since the Icelandic printing press was controlled by the bishops he could not print it in Iceland but must travel and published it at Roskilde in 1540. Like so many of the good early translations into the vernacular the book was powerful in the development of the Icelandic language.

In 1537 King Christian III of Denmark formally organized the reformation of the Danish church with the aid of Bugenhagen and re-established
Danish rule over Norway and evidently the reform was to be applied to
Iceland. As was proved in the similar case of England with Ireland, Denmark
could hardly maintain its secular authority in Iceland unless Iceland's church
conformed. Both bishops refused to accept the new church order. The
bishop of Skalholt issued a pastoral letter that the teaching of Luther was a
new and false heresy.

At Whitsun 1538 the Danish governor occupied a rich monastery and
seized treasures and mishandled monks who resisted. It was felt to be gross
provocation. The bishop's men were roused and killed both the Danish governor and his bodyguard.

Bishop Ogmund of Skalholt, who was going blind, resigned the see and
the Alting (Icelandic Parliament) elected Gissur Einarsson, aged twenty-five,
in strict church law too young to be a bishop. But this was not like the
election of minors as bishops from political motives in both Catholic and
Protestant Germany, for Gissur was a devout soul and one of the few
Icelanders who, with the shortage of grants, had the chance of study in
Germany. When he came back he quietly led a group for the study of the
Bible in the evangelical sense but stayed loyal to his bishop. Elected bishop by
the Alting, he sailed to Copenhagen to be confirmed, won the respect of the
Danes, and on his return tried to reform his diocese. But the people did not
want reformation and Bishop Ogmund was still there and a source of resistance. The Danes arrested Ogmund on the (probably false) charge that he was
responsible for the murder of the governor and he died at sea on the way to
face criminal proceedings in Denmark.

Gissur might be young but in such painful circumstances he was a very
good bishop. He worked hard to get rid of Catholic customs but in such a
way that he did not try to force persons who were stout in resistance and left
his fiercely Catholic colleague Arason of Holar to continue the determination not to reform. He tried to make the priests marry their women and as
in north Germany they were not reluctant, especially as he won the change
in law which allowed their widows and children, being now legal, to inherit.
He translated parts of the Old Testament into Icelandic. He managed to keep
the church property for the Church. He used monastic endowments and
buildings for schools and seminaries for the clergy. Iceland owed him much
and it was a calamity when he died at the age of thirty-three.

The result was a little war of religion. The Alting elected another evangelical
whom Copenhagen confirmed—these successive elections of evangelicals by the Alting show change in the attitudes of the educated on the island.
But Bishop Arason of Holar declared the election invalid, seized the cathedral of Skalholt by force and purified it from heresy, treated Gissur less

humanely than he had been treated by Gissur, for he dug up his corpse and threw it out of the churchyard, put the bishop-elect in prison, and announced that he was not only the bishop of Holar but the acting bishop of Skalholt. He held the two sees in Catholic orthodoxy for two years.

It could not last. Two years later Protestants in 'his' diocese of Skalholt made a coup and put him and two of his sons in gaol. The divided state of feeling was shown when the Danish governor dare not put him on trial but beheaded all three out of hand.

The result was bad. The state power had to establish its authority by force. That meant seizure of church property, endowments which Gissur had saved for church uses taken ruthlessly into the state treasury.

In these conditions it was not clear that evangelical teaching or church practices had established themselves among the Icelandic people. Few seemed to mind the loss of monasteries, or the replacement of bishops who professed allegiance to the pope (but were disapproved in Rome for their non-episcopal ways of life) by bishops who rejected the authority of Rome and appealed to the Bible. Both Norway and Iceland became very evangelical countries but it took them till towards the end of the sixteenth century with the grandchildren of those who experienced the change. In Iceland it became clear during the long decades of 1571–1627, when Gudbrand Torláksson was bishop of Hólar. The Icelandic Bible was ready in 1584, the psalm book five years later, both important for the maturity of the Icelandic language and the culture of the island. Confirmations became regular, Luther's Shorter Catechism was the norm. The best of Icelandic psalmody was written by the poet Jon Thorsteinsson who was murdered when Barbary corsairs raided the island in 1627. The last Catholic bishop was deported from the Faroe Islands as early as 1538.

Moldavia

At the far eastern end of the Carpathian range a mixture of Romanians and Vlachs founded during the fourteenth century a principality of Moldavia under a ruler known as a voivode, a word used in Slavonic languages to mean governor. It included the Bukovina, where was the capital Suceava, and along the Black Sea in what is now Bessarabia. The inhabitants were Eastern Orthodox with a Slavonic liturgy and mostly illiterate. The Hungarians and the crusading knights had come this way and had claimed sovereignty but by the fifteenth century Moldavia was an autonomous state and flourishing. Its economy was mostly peasant farming and fishing but not only, for it lay on one route from the manufacturing industries of Germany and the West to the Black Sea and to trade with the East, and exacted fees for the passage of goods.

In 1484 the Turks brought the country into trouble because they cut this trade route. The voivode paid an annual tribute of corn (called a gift) to the Turks at Constantinople but was guaranteed in return his autonomy and freedom for the religion of his people. From 1492 to the Congress of Berlin in 1878 Moldavia was under nominal Turkish suzerainty.

From an early time of the Byzantine empire the Romanians professed the faith of the Eastern Orthodox Church, and this became part of their nationality because it was soul-independence first from Hungarian lords who were Roman Catholics and later from the Turkish overlords. Though their language was not Slav they adopted many Slav words in church matters. There was an Orthodox archbishop in Suceava. Moldavian monks went to and fro to monasteries in Bulgaria and Serbia. A Protestant movement would not meet here a dilapidated Roman Catholic Church, but a church which, though equally dilapidated, must have less in common with Protestants and therefore find them harder to understand, and a church like the Roman Catholic Church in Ireland, a piece of national consciousness against a dominant outside power.

Just across the mountains were Germans, the German colonists of Siebenbürgen, the 'seven cities'. From 1200 to about 1350 Germans trekked eastward into open spaces. They settled along the Baltic coast, in what are now the Baltic states. And they pushed into the Balkans, with their biggest colony along the mountains at Siebenbürgen. Though far from their original land for so long, they retained the German language and sent their children westward for university education. When Luther came it took twenty years or more and an able reformer Johannes Honter, but then almost all were loyal and practising Lutherans, with an evangelical German liturgy and church order.

Thus there came Germans into Moldavia, partly as trading agents, partly from Siebenbürgen as settlers. But they were never more than a few. They had no chance of setting up a German-speaking church. When the Hungarians had been stronger there were Catholic missions but they were of the type of the Teutonic Order, more strong-armed than persuasive. Dominicans and Franciscans tried without any more success than the knights. They built churches and a cathedral but few survived into the sixteenth century except as ruins. At Sereth there were healings at a shrine in St John's Monastery. A pilgrim to Jerusalem bought a chalice-veil and with it touched sacred objects of the Holy Land, and the sick came to Sereth to seek healing. All this was destroyed in a fight; but up to the age of the Reformation pilgrims came to relics. There were still Catholic bishops of Moldavian sees but none now came to Moldavia.

Even when Siebenbürgen went Lutheran during the 1540s there is no evidence of Protestant faith among the few Germans in Moldavia. When

Protestantism at last came into Moldavia, in a strong-armed form like that of the Teutonic Knights, it came upon a people who were all members of the Eastern Orthodox Church. It was the one place in Europe where advancing Lutheranism met not Western Catholics, nor tribes like Prussians, but historic Byzantine Orthodoxy.

Jacob Heraclides was an astonishing character. He grew up in the island of Samos in the Aegean, and then studied in Crete which was a Greek piece of the Venetian empire. He went westward and came to Wittenberg early in the 1550s where Melanchthon was kind to him and where he learnt the evangelical faith. But he needed a living and earned it by serving as a mercenary in the army of Charles V. With Melanchthon's commendation he wandered into the service of Duke Albert of Prussia, who passed him on to Prince Radziwill of Lithuania and then into the service of the king of Poland. The king and Prince Radziwill recommended him to the voivode of Moldavia, Alexander IV Lapuchneanu. He was brave and charming and educated, with a knowledge of Greek and Latin.

Voivode Alexander depended on Turkish backing and Turkish guards and ruled as a tyrant and was hated. The arrival of a soldier of fortune from Poland seemed to the people to make the chance of an overthrow of tyranny. The conspiracy was discovered and Heraclides fled to Siebenbürgen and then Vienna to persuade the emperor to help him. He collected mercenaries and invaded Moldavia and the invasion collapsed. In the next year 1561 he invaded again with only 1,600 horse but many of Alexander's soldiers came over to his mercenaries and he was master of Moldavia: an educated Protestant soldier who was a Greek by origin but who had rejected his Greek Orthodox origin and now ruled an illiterate people for whom the Greek Orthodox religion was a way of life. He took the Greek title 'despot' of Moldavia but sometimes called himself king.

He had led his campaign as a crusade for the truth of the Bible against the superstitions and corruptions of decadent Christianity or Islam. His letters showed a consciousness of being God's agent to build a bulwark of Christian faith against the Ottoman world. He wanted educated immigrants and thought of his land as a sanctuary for Protestants fleeing from the west. He was prudent enough to continue paying the tribute to the sultan. He kept himself secure with a Hungarian bodyguard.

He summoned learned doctors of the Reformation to come eastward to help him reform and educate. He invited one of the best mathematicians in Europe, Copernicus's chief assistant Johannes Rhaeticus: but in vain. He tried to get Melanchthon's learned son-in-law Caspar Peucer, and Justus Jonas the son of Luther's lieutenant. He persuaded Curione, the son of the Italian refugee who was a professor at the university of Basel, to come to be his chancellor—but not for long, Heraclides distrusted him. Most importantly he persuaded a Pole who was a friend of Calvin and whose divinity was Swiss rather than Lutheran, Johannes Lusinius or Lusinski, with a Polish wife from a noble family. He was given as his see the town of Kotnar. Since Kotnar was inhabited by Germans and Hungarians, it is probable that the first duty of Lusinski was to these. This is more likely because Lusinski was made the judge in divorce cases of Germans and Hungarians, while Heraclides reserved divorce cases among the Romanians to himself.

In Kotnar they founded a college for higher education together with a library. They chose for its head a German Protestant, Johannes Sommer, without whose evidence we should know much less about the drama of Heraclides.

In south-west Germany Ungnad ran a printing press for publishing reforming books translated into Slavonic languages, Slovene or Serbo-Croat. He heard of what was happening in Moldavia and sent a messenger offering to translate the Bible into Romanian and asked Heraclides to send scholars who would help him with the task.

Heraclides saw that he needed to treat the Orthodox of his land with consideration and not hurry them to change their ways. He was crowned king by three Orthodox bishops. He appeared at their liturgies and walked in their processions. Some of his coins showed the face of the Virgin. At Epiphany he walked in the procession according to custom, carrying his crown and sceptre. At first he was a friend to the Orthodox metropolitans.

This did not please the reformers whom he had invited to join him and who supposed that he was polluting his and their faith. *Cur victor princeps numina victa colit?*[22] they asked, 'Why should a conquering king worship the gods of the conquered?'

They drove him onward to reform the interior of the churches—especially in the cult of saints and devout customs of the people. He began to absent himself from church or go out before the consecration, and was even believed to be laughing in church when he witnessed something that he thought superstition. He did not now conceal his belief that there were alterations necessary and had no longer any wish to do so. Observers thought him to show a special aversion to monks, almost as if the sight of them hurt his eyes. At home he held private reformed services and invited his friends and was cross when they did not come. He encouraged the printing of Slavonic texts of the Gospels.

He tried to persuade the chief Moldavians by meetings and sermons that change was necessary; that these ceremonies which were so outward were not the essence of religion which was of the heart; and he told the chiefs that

---

[22] Johannes Sommer, *De clade Moldavica*, elegiac poem; E. Benz, *Wittenberg und Byzanz* (Marburg, 1949), 54.

they were credulous, and blamed them for sticking to old usages out of consideration for the affections of their simpler people. He said that the land had fallen away from faith and it was necessary to come back to the truth and he was bringing that truth into the land. He invited leading clergy to meetings and held debates with them. He tried to prove to them that their doctrine of God was untrue and that they could only found truth on the teaching of the Bible. The crunch came when he told them that he would not rest until he had cleansed the land of its superstitions.

He tried to alter what he saw as the shadier moral customs of the land. The prevailing law allowed unusually easy divorce. Any man or woman who held that the marriage did not work—the man hardly needed to give a reason, the woman only needed to claim that she was abused or maltreated—could on payment of a not large sum be given a divorce without the other party being able to object. Among the results of this system of unilateral divorce was a certain amount of bigamy and a certain amount of polyandry; which Moldavian society of that date did not mind.

Heraclides was as bold as his word. He created a church order, with a reformed rite. No one attended these services except his personal friends. When he tried to persuade the chiefs to appear at them, his method of persuasion was such that they believed themselves in danger if they failed to attend. The clergy were totally against him and the people followed them; and as he met the resistance of the clergy he began to abuse them as not only ignorant and yellow but immoral; judgements which had a measure of truth but it was not wisdom at that moment to say so. Bishop Lusinius could not tolerate the laxity of a system of unilateral divorce. He said that marriage was a sacred pledge and that no partner ought to be able to end it at will. He tried to get the law and custom changed and to institute stricter rules before a divorce could be granted. Bishop Lusinius died suddenly in 1562 and was buried by his widow in the church at Jassy but people who knew how he was hated suspected poison.

As everywhere else, to reform needed a large transfer of money—to create schools, hire teachers, make better pastorates, fund welfare for the poor; money only to be got by diminishing the endowments of monasteries or shrines. Heraclides had a still higher priority—to pay the mercenaries who kept him in power. He began to take precious possessions belonging to monasteries and churches; not brazenly, but under the conduct of visitations. Yet certain seizures were crude because they included icons and reliquaries and crucifixes. It shocked the faithful when they found not merely that a reliquary which they revered was melted down to make coins but that the coins bore the head of the king, which felt blasphemous.

Clergy and people agreed that king and bishop were heretics and soon it was put about that the king was an atheist. At street corners they whispered that their king was a heretic or a Jew. Then Heraclides married a Protestant Pole, daughter of the castellan of Cracow who was believed to be stalwart among Polish heretics. It was bad enough that their king should not marry a Moldavian.

The monks and clergy demanded protection. The chiefs saw that their previous tyrant Alexander was less bad than this Protestant. The death of Heraclides felt like a placating of God for the crimes which Moldavia had committed. The leader of revolt talked to his soldiers of churches plundered, of sacred furnishings treated as booty, of foreign accursed ways of worship brought into the land, of priests shamefully treated because they defended the tradition of their fathers, 'and now his foreign wife comes!'[23] The rebellion was a crusade against the Reformation in this form.

Heraclides was deserted and many of his Hungarian bodyguard killed. He rode into the rebels' camp dressed as a king and asked to be allowed to leave the country or to retire to a monastery but he was beheaded on the spot.

They strangled the bishop's widow. The schools that had been founded were destroyed. If a German was found he was killed whether or not he was anything to do with Heraclides. Thus ended the Reformation in Moldavia. Mercifully for history the head of the college Johannes Sommer escaped disguised as a Romanian peasant.

Perhaps it was not quite the end. The hated despot was given a funeral service lasting three hours at the German church in Suceava, so for a time there were places where German Protestants could still pray. And his mangled body was placed in a tomb, which was observed by a traveller as still there nearly a hundred years later. And twenty-four years after his death the Moldavian government ordered all evangelical preachers to leave the land. So for a time they had been allowed to remain, or to creep back over the mountains from Siebenbürgen.

The attempted reformation in Moravia began with the peaceable Melanchthon but he died before it was practicable. Then it was entangled with a leader who was both a Protestant and a soldier of fortune and whose own past in Orthodox religion made him incapable of treating its prelates or congregations wisely. Cruder histories used to assume that after 1555 *cujus regio ejus religio* was always the rule, and that whatever faith the prince professed the people had to conform. But it was not so with Mary Queen of Scots at one end of Europe, nor with Heraclides at the other.

---

[23] Vita Gratiani, 206, in Benz, *Wittenberg und Byzanz*, 57. Cf. Hugo Weczerka, *Das mittelalterliche und frühzeitliche Deutschtum im Fürstentum Moldau* (Munich, 1960); literature in Krista Zach s.v. Rümanien, *TRE* xxix. 473.

15

RESISTANCE JUSTIFIED

The gun now affected war. Basel had a harquebus by 1371. But its range was short, it was slow to load. Its successor the musket is first mentioned in 1523, a word not used in England in this sense for another sixty years. Neither harquebus nor musket took the place of pike and spear and lance during all the earlier Reformation. These new weapons were supplements to steel, they frightened the enemy by noise. The 'advance' was not so much the discovery of an explosive, known for two centuries, but the ability of the new metal-workers to make gun barrels strong enough to withstand explosion inside, and the alchemists to purify the powder in the saltpetre.

Guns began to be useful to batter the walls of a town, where fire could be leisurely. In a battle they were almost useless. On the rare occasions when they were effective the wounds which they inflicted were unpleasant so that moralists believed them immoral—(devils' work according to Luther)—and various commanders ordered that no quarter be given to enemy 'soldiers' who used firearms—gunners were not yet regarded as real soldiers but as mechanics to aid the army. Captured artillerymen were known to be fired out of their own guns. It was widely believed that the inventor of a bomb with gunpowder was a German alchemist, a Franciscan at Freiburg, a canon at Constance who taught at the university of Paris, named by posterity Berthold Schwartz, but the Schwartz part of his name was a mistake by a humanist, he was just Berthold. Guns are first mentioned in the 1334 siege of Merseburg which was the castle of the bishop of Constance. This afforded material for those who disliked monks. Sebastian Münster the ex-Franciscan believed that the devil in person led Berthold to his discovery. Others took the opposite view. War is bad, win it as soon as possible, victory ends killing, if gunpowder helps victory it is moral to use it. Jacob Wimpheling, good humanist, thought the invention one of the claims of Germans to pre-eminence.

The dominance of the knight in war ended more because the Swiss infantry square discovered how cavalry charges could be resisted. The army of the earlier sixteenth century was more 'democratic', more like a trade union, more apt to mutiny for higher pay. The mercenary army was different in spirit. They did not wish to be at risk, for they fought for no cause. Money was the condition of war and pay was usually in arrears. They regularly substituted booty for pay, commanders could hardly stop the sack of towns. The number of deserters rose and that meant brigands and roads unsafe. In the 1530s Guicciardini observed how civilian experience changed in his generation, they saw plundering and murder more often.[1]

Guns made the marches of armies slower. But they were a lesser reason for a snail's pace. Because guns were not yet effective against soldiers they still wore or carried heavy armour, metal was not discarded as useless for the whole sixteenth century. And armies carried along women who helped with the baggage and in camp and were essential to prevent rape of civilians. When the French war of religion broke out, the Protestant army had no prostitutes in its train and an observer commented how marvellous was this behaviour. The commander Admiral Coligny replied that it could not last long.

One of the best mercenaries was Georg von Frundsberg, a Swabian from a noble Tyrolese family, a professional soldier from the age of nineteen. He adapted the changes in the art of war for his troops with such success that soon he was the most trusted mercenary commander of the emperor and fought in the Italian campaigns against the pope and reduced the castles of robber barons and drove Duke Ulrich of Württemberg out of his duchy. There was a story how he watched Martin Luther at the Diet of Worms and was heard to say, 'Little monk, you go a hard road,' but the story has no contemporary source. He became a folk hero sung in popular poems. During the Peasants' War he commanded the only regular army in south Germany and was the only commander to come out of the war without a stain on his reputation.

The wars in Italy gave him a hatred of popes. Both he and his wife inclined towards the reformers and their teaching. In 1526 the pope raised the League of Cognac to smash the emperor's power in Italy. Charles V appealed to Frundsberg who raised his own army and joined the imperialists in north Italy and meant to join the march on Rome which ended in so terrible a sack of the city, but he was spared that by a stroke which left him gravely ill. He made his peace with the pope and returned home to die, and left a message to the world that it should have peace and not war.

Appeals for peace were more evocative in the new conditions. Since war was an innate condition of society no one who had to take practical decisions took the least notice. But the appeals were louder, heard more widely.

One of Erasmus's famous essays, today his best-known commentary on one of his proverbs, is the Adage *Dulce bellum inexpertis*, war is only enjoyable by people who have not tried it.[2] Nothing is more loathsome than war,

---

[1] Guicciardini, *Storia d'Italia* (Bari, 1929), ii. 245.
[2] *Adagia* (1515) 4. 1. 1; Eng. trans. in M. M. Phillips, *The 'Adages' of Erasmus* (Cambridge, 1964), 308 ff.

nothing more unworthy of a human being, let alone a Christian. Yet everyone accepts it as a normal part of life; preachers tell men from pulpits that if
they fight under this or that banner their sins will be forgiven, armies go to
war carrying a cross on their flags.

The human body, created without fangs or horns or talons, was never
designed to fight. Nature produced the frame as weak and soft and unarmed
and in need of friendship and with an inner spark that is divine and lifts the
soul towards the good. Dress this gentle being in armour, make him blow
bugles and thrash drums, pour blood all over a field; then mothers lose their
sons and wives their husbands and children their fathers, and crops are burnt
and churches desecrated and girls raped and the people destitute—a universal demoralization, a hundred thousand noble creatures turned into brutes.
We start these horrors for trivial reasons. And Christ told us to turn the other
cheek and resist not evil and pray every day that God's will be done.

We are told that war is lawful when it is just. What is just? War declared by
any prince for any reason against anybody. But may not it be right to fight for
justice? Everyone thinks his cause just. A teacher of Christian ethics never
approves of war. Perhaps at times he allows it to be permissible, but with
reluctance and sorrow.

They plead that it is right to sentence a murderer to death, therefore it is
right to fight in a just cause. What a difference between the two cases, in the
one a convicted person, in the other only an accusation; in the one case the
suffering falls on the criminal, in the other it falls on countless innocent
persons. Of course we need an agency to settle disputes about which we
might go to war—a parliament of the wise, with experience.

He wrote *Querela Pacis*, the 'Complaint of the Lady Peace' whom every
nation rejects and almost kills—published in Basel with Froben 1517, then
twenty-six editions in his lifetime.[3] The essay had a political motive in that
imperial policy then wanted friendship with France. But it was a text which
was accepted as far above the moment, it framed what was felt to be a great
ideal. The Lady appeals to the better nature of mankind, their rationality, the
gentleness in their make-up, the affections of the family, and the influence of
Christ—and then, princes go to war for trivial causes, and bishops back
them, and preachers cry up the war, and the pope leads an army into battle,
and everyone hires mercenaries who destroy the country which hires them;
go to a prince's court and everyone looks suave and behind the scenes they
are planning to kill; go to a cathedral and you see everywhere the cross the
symbol of peace and all the clergy look pious, and they justify war by pleading the bloody battles of the Old Testament which do not commend what
they allege but are allegories of the tearing of sin from the heart. 'Whoever

---

[3] *Opera Omnia*, iv. (Amsterdam, 1977), 2.

preaches up war is preaching up Antichrist.' Crusades? Crusades alleged to be a war for God are a sacrilege against God. Recognize that Christ is the foundation on which true peace rests. Remember the characteristic language of Christians, 'Peace be with you,' 'Love one another,' 'Our Father,' 'Resist not evil.' Every word of Christianity talks of the harmony of humanity, and every Christian person is engaged in or affected by war. Christians use machinery made by demons to drop bombs on other Christians—no one can believe that guns were invented by mankind—and yet we call these devilish machines by the names of apostles. The most criminal of all excuses for war is to strengthen the home government—a war will distract the people from working against its rulers and unite them against a foreign foe; so a government does well out of the miseries of its subjects. We should banish such tyrants to an island at the furthest corner of the world. Even priests preach the rightness of war and as they speak from their pulpits their mouths are dirty. There is almost no kind of peace, even unjust, which is not better than a state of war, even if it were thought a just war.

'But I have another opinion if barbarian tribes are invading and Christian soldiers have a duty to defend the peace of their people.'

Racial division? The English dislike the French for no reason except that they are French. They dislike the Scots for no reason except that they are Scots. Germans versus French, Spaniards versus French—and for no reason.

The Lady ended by an emotional appeal to princes, and priests, and Pope Leo X, and the king of France, and King Henry VIII, and the Holy Roman Emperor Maximilian, and 'young Charles', soon to succeed as the emperor Charles V—let Christ inspire.

Querela Pacis was another simple moral essay which had no influence on what politicians did. But in 1517 Europeans were less cynical about appeals for peace than they were to be in the eighteenth century or the age of the League of Nations. It was resonant among many readers and identified the name of Erasmus with ideals that raised hope.

The *Landsknecht* was a new political force. He made the Swiss an independent state. He sacked Rome for the first time since the Dark Ages. He was the defender of realms and the protector of Europe from the Turks. He broke the power of the feudal knights and increased the power and the debts of princes. He helped rulers to govern less inefficiently and made them desperate for money. In Italy, if popes were to be free, he forced them to be commanders and if possible rich. He was partly the cause of the low spiritual reputation of Rome which helped to provoke the coming reformation.

The troubled times left problems of conscience for soldiers. In the Peasants' War a colonel with a distinguished record, von Kram, who had fought in France and Italy, found himself in a war where well-armed troops killed badly armed peasants. He asked himself what he was doing. Two months after the massacre at the battle of Frankenhausen, he appealed to Martin Luther to explain, for at that moment Luther was notorious for telling governments that it was right to slay murdering, robbing peasants. The colonel doubted whether he served in a profession which was compatible with being a real Christian.

Luther was not one to decline such a challenge. In discussions he heard soldiers say that if they thought too much about what they were doing they could not do it, so it was better not to ask questions. His feeling that the answer was not obvious came out in the title of the little book of late 1526: *Whether Soldiers, Too, Can Be Saved.*[4]

Society cannot do without soldiers. To be a soldier is an occupation no different from other vocations as service to the community. They may have to hurt people, as a judge or executioner must for the sake of justice, a surgeon amputating for the sake of health. The soldier can be paid, John the Baptist only condemned soldiers if they abused their power to rob. If war is wrong, the punishment of criminals must be wrong. But that means, the only reason for going to war is to stop wrong.

A profession may be godly though misusable—for example that of a judge. That corrupt judges exist does not mean that good people should not become judges. On the contrary. So with soldiers. Since soldiers exist and cannot be abolished, they had better be upright people. Sometimes a soldier cuts off legs or kills but the aim is to protect the woman, the child, the honour and peace of society.

War is a great plague but at times it prevents a greater plague, like the country being overrun by barbarians. War needs to be just—that is, out of a conviction that only so can we see that justice is done.

Suppose that a soldier's lord or employer engages in an immoral war? If the soldier is certain that the war is immoral he must refuse to serve. If he is not sure he should give his employer the benefit of the doubt because to do one's duty is also a moral right.

Whoever starts a war is wrong. Fight only when you have no wish to fight. No war is just unless you can say *I am forced to fight*. But if they have to fight they do not play games. As was his way Luther put this recognition into a form to shock. 'Once there is a just war, the hand that wields the sword is not man's but God's. It is not man but God who hangs and breaks on the wheel and beheads and strangles.'

Humanism was international. Erasmus was as international a figure as the pope; though it was a sign of a growth in national feeling that not only the

---

[4] *Ob Kriegsleute auch in seligen Stande sein können*, WA xix. 623–62.

Dutch but the Germans and the French tried to claim him as a member of their own race. Erasmus was a European, Latin was his means of communication.

It is far from certain that historians can detect anything in the sixteenth century of the sort that the nineteenth century was going to call 'nationalism'. Even in the nineteenth and twentieth centuries, the heyday of 'nationalism', a mass of ordinary people felt none of the sentiments which society in its propaganda attributed to them. Many German peasants thought themselves to be peasants, as if the workers of the world had more in common with each other than with knights or barons or parsons of whatever race; and it was true, for usually the world of which they were workers was bounded by a radius of about fifty miles.

The sense of nationality is something to do with the historical sense. A nation cannot find itself unless it knows that it has common experiences in the past. Therefore the Renaissance, with its coming historical sensibility, must be something to do with a rising sense of nationality among educated people. The English who fought at Shakespeare's Agincourt were more English in their patriotism than the soldiers who fought at the real battle.

Among the German humanists one was young and ardent for reformation by force, Ulrich von Hutten. His career raised this question of nationality. The Catholic Church was an international organization, its law was almost the same in every state, its capital was the legal centre of Europe. Two hundred or more years before, the different kings or governments of Europe started to take less notice of the dictates of Rome. The claim to be above the nations was accepted when it was convenient and rejected when it was not. But were these separate governments, which knew more about local affairs than distant courts in Rome or Avignon, representing anything that could be called a 'nation'? When Henry VIII threw off Roman power and Roman canon law in England, did he represent anything like an English 'patriotism' which wanted England to be powerful and resented interference from abroad? Was the pope unpopular in Germany not because he was thought to teach erroneous religion but because he was not German and no one not a German ought to wield power in Germany?

Hutten, though a humanist and owning links with the community of scholars across all the frontiers, was a German 'nationalist'. Luther criticized the pope because he misled the religion of the people. Hutten resented the pope because he took money out of Germany.

Disobedience to the State

St Paul to the Romans, chapter 13: a subject owes obedience to the State even when its head is a scoundrel. The State is necessary to human welfare and part of divine order.

If the State orders an immoral act it is a duty to disobey. It can be no one's moral duty to commit immorality. But we must not try to overthrow the State. We need it, without it everything would be civil war and murder. Disobey an immoral state and take the consequences. But do not start revolution, which always leads to murder. In essence such was Christian doctrine, taught by medieval political thinkers and by early reformers. The Peasants' Revolt did nothing but confirm the doctrine: obey the State, not to obey makes worse immoralities.

During the 1520s Germany slowly divided in religion, which meant a split in politics. The Catholic emperor was powerful with the riches of Spain and its discoveries in the Americas, prosperous with the wealth of the Netherlands, brother of Ferdinand the archduke of Austria who was also king of Bohemia. Like all sovereigns he was bound by a constitution, he needed a diet. And as the diets of the 1520s met, there were ever more representatives who liked what Luther stood for.

Charles V was a Catholic Netherlander or Burgundian by sympathy and education, a romantic determined to be a true knight and lover of the idea of fame, but a hard-headed politician resolute to maintain the possessions of the Habsburg family, without popular appeal to crowds for he was reserved and at times cold, but respected as a person of conscience, with a sensation that the weight of a world rested upon his back; aware of his vast empire with pride, but glum at the vast debts which he inherited, especially to the Fugger bank; a man with strength of character, who could wait his time, and took thought, and had no dash; who chose sane advisers and used them well but was his own master in the end; who liked the detail of administration and could not always see wood for trees but nothing like his son the later Philip II who wasted hours in poring over work which a secretary could do. Charles had a medieval sense of the vocation of the emperor, called of God to the highest office in Christendom, with a divine mission to defend it against the Turks and to secure law and order and Catholic faith.

He could not speak German and did not well understand Germany. Through the 1520s and 1530s the evangelical cause prospered because the emperor thought it a problem less important compared with what really mattered, the protection of the Habsburg possessions against the French, and that meant frustrating French allies in Italy (among them usually the pope). He achieved much. He established the power of the Spanish crown in Spain, prepared for its union with Portugal, ensured Spanish predominance in Italy, created stronger government in the Spanish Netherlands, and effectively separated them from the Holy Roman Empire that was Germany. To achieve all this, with lasting consequences for southern Europe, he failed to stop the Turks coming into Hungary, and allowed Protestants to achieve equality with Catholics in Germany.

Since the Diet of Worms and his only meeting with Luther, he was sure that Lutheranism was a heresy which the State must suppress. About personal piety he was reticent. He thought the pope often behaved dreadfully and saw no reason to take undue notice of what popes did. He told his son to honour the pope, performed correctly the duties of the Church, left by will 30,000 masses to be said for his soul. But even in the piles of letters to his family he hardly said anything personal about religion. He was not ascetic for he ate huge meals and drank iced beer in capacious tankards at unsuitable hours. Accustomed to power since his teens he grew more bad-tempered or scornful about those with whom he disagreed. Yet he was affectionate, in love with his wife Isabella of Portugal and his children especially his son the future Philip II. He chose moderate chancellors yet had no sympathy for moderate reformers like the Erasmians nor papalist reformers like the Jesuits. He never doubted that the Church of Rome was right about doctrine though he accepted the view of his advisers that it was guilty of abuses which it was an emperor's duty to help cure. He had the right to appoint to hundreds of church offices, and did his best to choose good people, but then made use of the appointments in his political interest and never doubted that he did well, and cheerfully took bishops away from their pastoral cares to serve in state offices. He was happy to mortgage the income of the Spanish military orders to the Fugger bank to which he owed unimaginable debts. But his testament of 1548 to his son Philip placed faith at the centre—'in the things of this world there is a lot of doubt, the only general law I can give you is to trust in God and you will show this faith best by defending the Church'. 'Pope Paul often breaks his word, he has no real care for Christendom, he has behaved badly over the business of summoning a council—but you must honour his office, and he is an old man.' His last will encouraged his son to back the Spanish Inquisition and on his deathbed he advised him to be stern with the Lutherans.

Sooner or later Charles V was bound to attack the Protestants. To gain time he conceded at the Diet of Nuremberg of 1532 a toleration to the evangelicals—those already evangelicals, not to any new adherents—until a council should meet soon and decide the dispute. He allowed the various suits in the Reich supreme court for the taking of Catholic property to be stopped for the time. In 1539 at the Frankfurt *Anstand* ('courteous truce') he postponed again by renewing the concession and asking for debates on the possibility of reunion. But already for several years the Protestants debated among themselves the moral issue—if the emperor attacks evangelical Lands for the sake of religion, are they justified in resisting his armies?

Everyone agrees that a householder may resist a violent intruder; therefore any state may resist another state making an aggressive war. If Bavaria a

Catholic Land attacked Saxony a Protestant Land, no one doubted that Saxony could resist. But to the emperor all the Reich owed allegiance. What if the emperor declared that the Protestant Lands were in breach of Reich law and ordered Bavaria to attack—could Saxony fight against 'agents' of the emperor? Or worse, if the emperor came in person, at the head of an army of mercenaries whom he had hired in Italy and Spain, could Saxony resist morally? Or worse yet, for the political moralists, if intelligence showed that Catholics collected an army to assail the Protestants, could Protestants attack first, to make sure that the other side did not win? i.e. in certain circumstances was it morally justified to launch a preventive war, not to resist aggression but to forestall the aggressors before they moved their guns?

In 1528 intelligence came to Philip of Hesse that Saxony and Hesse were about to be invaded. The news was false, it was a lie propagated scandalously.[5] Philip believed it, and talked of defensive war. Since Saxony was his ally, this misinformation started the long moral debate about the rightfulness of resistance.

Luther was one of the first to be consulted. He was clear:

If Catholic princes attack, of course they are right to resist as they would resist any illegal aggressor.

If these princes claim the authority of the emperor, they should not be believed, the emperor should be given the benefit of the doubt.

To attack first, a preventive war, is immoral. If Hesse starts such a war Saxony would be wrong to join.

When Philip of Hesse heard this advice he was ironical. Why should we sit still while good pastors are hanged and preachers of truth driven out? Is it better to let the house burn down or to take precautions beforehand to stop the outbreak of fire? If it is my duty to protect my subjects, is it only my duty to protect them when they are dead?

Melanchthon and Luther rejected the argument. They said that if their side attacked first, it would be more immoral than acts of revolutionaries in the Peasants' War.[6] But from a year later everyone was afraid of civil war in

---

[5] That it was a lie is curiously uncertain still. Otto von Pack, a Saxon squire, was taken as a political adviser by Philip of Hesse. He told Philip that he had evidence how a secret league of Catholic princes had been formed at Breslau with the aim of deposing Elector John of Saxony and Philip because they allowed Lutherans—the league, Austria, Bavaria, Duke George of Saxony and the three bishops Bamberg and Würzburg and Salzburg. In the end of May 1528 (preventive war) Hessian troops were ready on the frontier of the two sees and Germany was very close to civil war though Elector John refused to take part on Philip's side. The Catholics denied any such league or plan; and in return for the archbishop Albert of Mainz surrendering spiritual authority over Hesse and electoral Saxony, the army stood down. Did Pack pretend, or had he real information—or did Philip pretend, using him, because he wanted an excuse for a preventive war? Later before his execution Pack confessed that he invented the story—but the confession was elicited under torture.

[6] *BW* iv. 423.

Germany. Lazarus Spengler the reforming town clerk of Nuremberg was flat that to resist the emperor is impossible. He thought it lawful to defend Christendom against Turkish invasion but all wars between Christians are immoral.

From one of the Lutheran leaders came a surprising opinion in the opposite sense. Bugenhagen advised that they might freely resist the emperor if he acted unjustly. A prince is put there to protect his people and this duty is overriding and is not cancelled if the overlord is the aggressor. Elector John of Saxony, anxious because more scrupulous about moral right than Philip of Hesse, put the question in a new form. Spengler versus Bugenhagen—which is right? He pointed out that at his election Charles V had promised not to use force against German princes. What may the princes do if the emperor breaks so solemn an undertaking?

On 6 March 1530 Luther sent a considered reply to the elector. By natural law a human being has the right to resist injustice. By faith a Christian has no right to resist injustice but only to suffer. Therefore if the motive is to *defend the gospel*, the elector has no right to resist the emperor. But if the emperor tries to force his princes to kill or exile their subjects, then the princes have a still higher duty—to protect their subjects from injustice. Otherwise they would become mini-tyrants themselves under a larger tyrant.

Luther's mind had moved. But it was still too complex or confused for the crisis which confronted them.

During the winter of 1530–31 all the leading evangelicals except Luther surrendered to Bugenhagen. They did not like what they did. They realized the danger that it might be lawful for any private individual to use violence against a lawful authority behaving unlawfully—which none of them would accept. And Luther, who deeply disliked the position into which events were dragging him, continued to make them uneasy. He had an axiom from which he would never shift. It cannot be right to defend the things of God by force, by war. He detested all the arguments used on the other side. It grieved him that three friends whose opinions he trusted, Melanchthon and Bugenhagen and Amsdorf, pushed him to accept that resistance is inevitable and therefore right.

Those on Luther's side, like Lazarus Spengler, argued that civil war can destroy Germany and end in anarchy; and that if persecution has to happen, history shows that it helps the Church to be its purer self.

From other quarters came different arguments. Spengler's pastor Osiander was cool about St Paul and his order to obey the magistrate. He cannot have meant us to obey a magistrate who behaves unjustly. All magistrates are ordained of God. If the chief magistrate behaves wickedly lesser magistrates also have their divine vocation, which includes stopping his wickedness. Martin Bucer published the remarkable argument. He was writing a commentary on the awkward text of the Sermon on the Mount—'Resist not evil.' Dictators are not within the intention of God. Power is always dispersed. There is no state in which power is not shared among many people. The supreme magistrate is a president, and if he falls for example to extortion, lesser authorities must resist with weapons, for justice is supreme over all. 'Resist not evil' is said to private individuals. Anyone who tries to make one person absolute in a state acts contrary to God's command.[7] St Paul said, Obey the powers that be, in the plural. He did not say, obey the single power that exists.

As danger loomed and Luther in the pain of his old age grew more passionate in his expressions, and as the conflict between necessity and his Christian doctrine looked unrealistic, he came to accept a fight; not precisely against the emperor to whom as head of the Reich they all owed loyalty; but because the pope was bad and had no claim to their allegiance, and if Charles V went to war he acted not as emperor but as the colonel of the pope's army; against such anyone might and should fight—unconditionally.[8] For all the unreality of this document, it enabled Melanchthon to use it in justifying resistance when the war exploded.

Luther had realized now that he could not stop his side from arming. He thought they were wrong; but he was resigned, whatever he said for peace they would take no notice, and if he went on saying publicly that they should not resist, he helped the propaganda of the other side. The denial of war for the sake of God was potent in him still. But he could do nothing and it was better to be silent and see how Providence would lead the nations.

Fortunately for his peace of mind he died four months before the armies marched.

This theory of resistance, destined to so long a future, did not mean that if a ruler becomes a tyrant, any country girl can stick a knife into him in his bath, or any army officer can plant a bomb in a handbag under his table. It gave the private citizen no right of resistance, only the duty to disobey and suffer. It was the responsible magistrates who had the right: a Parliament versus King Charles I of England, an Estates-General versus Louis XVI of France.

In the year of evangelical conversion to a limited right of resistance, Zwingli was killed serving in the ranks when a Zurich army was defeated at the battle of Kappel.

---

[7] Bucer, *In Sacra Quatuor Evangelia Enarrationes Perpetuae*, 54 verso (Robert Estienne, Geneva, 1553): '*Qui in unum transferre hominem conatur potestatem quam quidem Deus, ut rebus humanis maxime conducebat, dispartitus est in plurimos, is ordinationi Dei resistit.*' Bucer dedicated the commentary to Fox the bishop of Hereford.

[8] *Zirkulardisputation, WA* xxix. 2. 35–51.

In August 1531 he wrote a secret and martial memorandum to the Zurich council. The Catholic forest cantons must be overthrown. They persecute the truth and have fallen from God. Switzerland must be given a central government by Zurich and Berne. Such a war would be in accordance with the will of God as the Old Testament proves. The memorandum had no effect because a preventive war was started by the forest cantons who could not afford to let a blockade by Zurich continue.

Zurich did not take the attack seriously and their commander treated the enemy considerately because he imagined that Swiss would hardly fight Swiss unless hired to do so by warring Italians and the campaign would end in threats and a bloodless agreement. The battle of Kappel on 11 October 1531 lasted scarcely quarter of an hour when an outnumbered force of Zurichers was overrun and lost 400 men (the forest cantons lost 100), among them loyal sons of the Reformation. Zwingli went with the army as a chaplain and prayed with them outside a church. He had long had a premonition that he would die violently. In the battle he bore his halberd in the third line and encouraged others and leapt forward into the second line and was badly wounded. He was still alive when the mountaineers found him after the battle. By shaking his head he refused to do penance or invoke the saints, so he was murdered, or put out of his suffering, by an ex-mercenary officer from Unterwalden. Then his body was quartered and burnt as that of a heretic.

In the battle died seven other pastors from the city and eighteen from the countryside including the former prior of Einsiedeln abbey and the abbot of Kappel. This abbot, Wolfgang Rüppli, was elected in 1519, reformed his abbey, created a school there which taught trades as well as Latin, put the abbey under the protection of Zurich, and married a Zurich girl. He hated the war but felt bound to serve. Four of his monks were killed in the battle.[9]

The situations in Germany and Switzerland were opposite. In Germany a powerful Catholic party threatened to overthrow the Reformation in all the Lands of the Reich. In Switzerland the powerful reformed majority threatened to impose their faith and practice upon conservative mountaineers. In Switzerland the minority had no qualms that it was right to engage in preventive war.

The question arose whether Zwingli was a martyr, as clearly as evangelicals burnt at the stake. Some said that he died in the cause of truth which he sought to defend from Catholic aggression. He was murdered, not killed, as he lay wounded under a hedge. His successor Bullinger, in his *History of the Reformation*, was sure that he was a martyr for God. He described how Zwingli had predicted his own death from the pulpit, how his killer was a mercenary, one of those against whom he spent his life preaching; and

---

[9] Bullinger, *Reformationsgeschichte*, ed. J. J. Hottinger and H. H. Vögeli, iii (Zurich, 1840), 151.

printed an elegiac Latin ode—how he died for his country and for Christ and for religion, and proved his teaching by shedding his blood for it; the enemy thought they could make his memory disappear by burning his corpse, but it only made his name more illustrious.[10]

Oswald Myconius was Zwingli's first biographer, five years after the death. He moved to Basel (where he preached the funeral sermon of Erasmus) to succeed Oecolampadius there because he did not like the effect of Kappel and Zwingli's death on the church in Zurich; but he worked closely with Zwingli for the entire period of the Zurich Reformation, so that he was a qualified biographer. He watched the Zurich army go out to fight, a chaotic straggling confusion, and at nightfall met the messenger coming from the battlefield with the news. Though the body was burnt, the Zurichers went out under the truce and hunted through the ashes, and by a miracle found Zwingli's heart whole, intact.[11]

This was not everyone's opinion. Erasmus was pleased at the death. Luther, with his axiom that no one can defend the truth of God with guns, thought it ridiculous to think of him as a martyr.[12]

The Schmalkald League. This was the military defensive alliance between Hesse and Saxony, which two minor princes and several cities joined; the cities including the Hanseatic towns of Bremen and Lübeck which were too far away to matter; Magdeburg in the centre, which was strong; and to the south, more at risk if war came than anything further north, Strasbourg, Ulm, and Constance with three others. The aim was stated to be the defence of true religion. Five years later it was larger, and formidable; with the duke of Württemberg who had strength, four more princes who had not, and strong cities like Brunswick and Frankfurt and Hamburg, the last too far away to count. The league was weaker than it looked because it had no clear unified system of command if it had to fight. It also suffered because just when it began to be needed its most aggressive commander Philip of Hesse lost influence by his bigamy. It was strong enough to block the suits against Protestants in the Reich imperial court. But it had no hope of breaking Catholic power in the three Catholic archbishoprics of the Rhineland which were under the protection of the Spanish army in Brussels, and could not even try to help the archbishop of Cologne, Hermann von Wied, when he became a Protestant. Big Protestant states refused to join—the city of Nuremberg; Brandenburg where the elector Joachim II was evangelical from 1541; ducal

---

[10] Bullinger, *Reformationsgeschichte*, iii. 168.

[11] Life of Zwingli (1536), in *Vitae quatuor Reformatorum* (Berlin, 1841) (these four lives are Luther by Melanchthon, Melanchthon by Camerarius, Zwingli by Myconius and Calvin by Beza).

[12] Luther to Duke Albert of Prussia, April 1532, *WA* xxx. 3. 550; and cf. Luther's *Kurzes Bekenntnis vom heiligen Sakrament* (1544), *WA* liv. 154.

Saxony, where the new duke Maurice had no religion in him but must be Protestant because his duchy was Protestant.

In 1542 the Schmalkald League took over by force the last stiffly anti-evangelical Land in north Germany, Brunswick—the Land, not the city which was already Protestant. No one could fail to observe (1) that this was aggression; (2) that the evangelical leaders still suffered scruples over the morality of such an act; and (3) that the breach in Reich law would win support for Charles V.

The war began in June 1546 and was over in April 1547. Charles had an able and experienced general, the Spanish duke of Alba. He also had on his side some of the Protestants who believed this not to be a war of religion but about the true constitution of the Reich; especially Maurice of ducal Saxony. The Battle of Mühlberg on 24 April 1547 made the elector of Saxony John Frederick a prisoner, Philip of Hesse was imprisoned by a trick, the Schmalkald League was ended, the emperor controlled southern and central Germany. It was certain that all Germany was not about to become Protestant.

Charles V held an embattled diet at Augsburg, lately a Protestant city and now not; from September 1547 to June 1548, the longest diet of the century; embattled because the presence of Italian and Spanish troops meant that he could force through almost what he liked. He knew that he could not drive Germany back to the pope's allegiance. His aim must be compromise; to unite the country on a moderate Catholic programme which most Protestants might at least tolerate. The pope would disapprove. But he regarded the pope as negligible. So far from the pope cooperating with the emperor over a religious policy for Germany he was at that moment negotiating with the French and even the Turks for a military league against the emperor. There should be an interim settlement until a free general council should decide.

Thus the name Interim became the slogan which caused the second wave of Protestant argument over the rightness or wrongness of resistance to the emperor; this time, much bitterer, and more anguished. In the 1530s to argue for resistance was to argue for self-defence; in the four years from 1548 to argue for resistance was to invite invasion by mercenaries. In the earlier debate moralists who wanted non-resistance were respected by their opponents. In this debate moralists who wanted non-resistance were accused of treachery to the cause of God.

Perhaps Charles V had a chance of reuniting Germany if his Interim applied to everyone, all Catholics as well as all Protestants. Then it could be represented not as the politics of power but as a wise Christian attempt at reunion of the Church. He would demand that church services be Catholic in ritual, that the pope's authority be *nominally* recognized, that certain doctrines like the seven sacraments be accepted though with no need to profess the range of doctrines which the Roman Curia demanded, for he intended to allow an evangelical interpretation of the crucial texts as on justification by faith; priests could marry; any church which wished to receive the holy communion in wine as well as bread could do so. He fancied that he could persuade the evangelicals that his demands touched little things like ritual or clothes in church which no one who wished for Christian unity and had not a fanatical conscience could mind. He knew that he must declare they must accept the pope but was willing if they did honour to the pope and accepted his authority and took no notice of what he said.

But when the text of the Interim was published on 15 May 1548 it alarmed Protestants by not being a settlement for everyone but only for them. During the private meetings beforehand the Catholic estates made it clear to Charles that they would refuse to cooperate if they were touched, they were not prepared to allow married clergymen or communion in both kinds. It was hard enough for them to allow it in Protestant states and they did not dream of allowing it in their own. Catholics who argued for the Interim lost credit with Catholics. That Catholic would-be ecumenicist Georg Witzel, from his refuge at Fulda, wrote two tracts in favour of the Interim and dared not publish them if he were to retain the respect of Catholics; and worse, his record made him suspect for being the author of the Interim, a rumour which worried him.[13]

Hence the Interim was no longer a settlement for Germany and in the long run could not work.

Charles V tried to compensate by issuing a reform programme for the Catholic estates (*Formula reformationis*), traditional in demands.[14] Very few Catholic estates took any notice of it.

The army of Charles V occupied Frankfurt but the Lutheran preachers were allowed to stay in their pulpits. The city accepted the Interim, and clergy could marry and communion be in two kinds but many of the rites and ceremonies, including fast days and days of the Blessed Virgin, returned to the Catholic form and the preachers were not allowed to preach against the Interim or the points about which there was argument. The Protestants suffered a big loss in that their share in the cathedral was removed from them and it became exclusively Catholic and remained so. They lost two other parish churches which remained Catholic till modern times, and kept five parish churches and two chapels.

---

[13] Witzel to Pflug, 8 October 1548, in *Correspondance J. Pflug*, ed. J. V. Pollet, iii (Leiden, 1977), 144.

[14] Only priests to be consecrated bishops; pluralities reduced; pastors to be properly trained; bishops to visit parishes and hold synods and have power to visit the exempt like chapters; try to create schools and libraries; clergy to preach, and so to study the Bible.

The result of the Interim proved how acceptable was the Reformation to most of the people of central and northern Germany. Nowhere among the reformed states can be found any popular movement for the restoration of the old. Even under the pressure of Spanish troops the reformed communities showed no sign of wishing for a restoration.

Charles V told one prince who made objections that if that was what he thought he could expect Spanish soldiers in his Land. Pastors who resisted Catholic revival were hunted out or imprisoned, fled to Switzerland or England or north Germany where only Brunswick (Land not city) and Oldenburg formally accepted the Interim. Some went to Prussia where Duke Albert badly needed pastors. Citizens who resisted had soldiers quartered in their houses. Augsburg, Reutlingen, Ulm were forced to conform.

More than one town closed all its services and confined worship to prayers in private houses. Pastors who had been driven out were sometimes used as 'schoolmasters' or 'catechists' or 'sick-visitors' and under such titles carried on a back-street ministry, so far as possible concealed from the eyes of imperial agents. From behind the scenes rose a flood of pamphlets against the emperor and the Catholic Church. The pamphlet war revived as never since the hot days of the 1520s.

As towns perforce accepted the Interim, pastors were forced to leave— Johannes Brenz fleeing by night from Schwäbisch Hall when a Spanish officer came to arrest him, Martin Bucer from Strasbourg, Frecht from Ulm and many another, several hundred. Martin Frecht the reformer at Ulm suffered calamity. Son of the head of the shoemakers guild at Ulm, he went to the university of Heidelberg where he met Oecolampadius and Bucer and Brenz, and helped to reform the university. From 1537 he was chief pastor at Ulm. When they lost the war and could do nothing but accept imperial orders about church services, he was vehement that they should not conform. He was very severely treated, being chained in a fortress with five colleagues. Sick, and ruined financially, he was finally released under an amnesty in March 1549 but exiled for life from Ulm. He spent most of the remainder of his days in destitute exile trying to get rehabilitated and his exile to be lifted. By June 1552, when everything was better for the evangelicals, Duke Christoph of Württemberg, Duke Ulrich's son, made him a professor at Tübingen where he was beloved. In the last year of his life he was allowed to visit his former flock at Ulm.

The towns nearest to the threat from the emperor's armies were Augsburg, Regensburg, Nuremberg, and all the free cities of south Germany including Strasbourg but not the Swiss except for their northern edge at Constance. The fate of Constance was a lesson to everyone and affected what happened over resistance. The historic free city fought the imperial army and after a bloody fight on the Rhine bridge was annexed to the Habsburg dominions and recatholicized ruthlessly. Its pastor Blarer, who till then had a far more than local weight in the reformation of southern Germany, escaped but during the rest of a long life was not again in an important post, he found a pastorate in a modest Swiss parish. Constance taught southern Germany that it was better to conform outwardly, and then some part of the reform could be preserved, whereas total resistance risked all. Observing the fate of Constance, Strasbourg decided that it must be rid of Martin Bucer and he found refuge at Cambridge.

Nuremberg was a powerful city and a mainstay of the Protestant cause. When the university of Wittenberg was forced by the war to close, many of its students arrived as refugees in Nuremberg and the two pastors Osiander and Veit Dietrich organized teaching for them. The council knew that its safety, even its freedom, depended on accepting much of what the emperor demanded. It was also aware that without the aid of its pastors it could not persuade the people to conform to the revived parts of Catholicism—another sign of the speed with which public opinion or even more, public depth of feeling, had changed since the first coming of the reform. Therefore much hung upon the attitude of their pastor of many years service, Osiander.

As they suspected that Osiander would not cooperate they appealed first to Melanchthon because they hoped that his ecumenical mind would be more willing to compromise. They asked preachers to be moderate in pulpits lest their sermons jeopardize the delicate negotiations with the emperor. With less hope of success they ordered that Luther's hymn *Erhalt uns, Herr, bei deinem Wort*,[15] which during the conflict had become a war cry of the Reformation, should only be sung in the early mornings. His colleague Veit Dietrich was ill with gout and could not walk. But when he preached, the sermons were as uncompromising as Osiander's; on one Sunday more so, for he attacked the justice of the town's method of collecting taxes—and this had two political sides—to make citizens discontented with the city's government, and to blame that government for raising large sums of money at the emperor's demands for help.[16] Dietrich discovered that two Nuremberg makers of furniture were doing very well in making a gold-ornamented bed for King Ferdinand, and preached on the parable about Dives and Lazarus.

The council begged the preachers to conform at least in part without compromising their allegiance to the gospel. They ordered Osiander and

---

[15] Probably written 1541—in Klug's hymn book of 1543 it was entitled 'a hymn for children to sing against the two chief enemies of Christ, the pope and the Turks'. In English (*Lord Keep us Steadfast in thy Word*) it never won comparable fame.

[16] The difference between help from Nuremberg to the Schmalkaldic League and help to the emperor was remarkable. To the Protestant side 200,000 gulden promised, only 45,000 gulden went. To the Catholic side, with Catholic soldiers in the town, 13,500 gulden went but also the right to enlist troops in areas round about. Bernhard Klaus, *Veit Dietrich* (Nuremberg, 1958), 264.

Dietrich not to mix religion and politics in a pulpit. There was trouble any-way because when imperial officers ransacked the house in Schwäbisch Hall from which Brenz had just fled, they discovered letters to Brenz from Osiander and Dietrich, who were very rude about the emperor and worse, for they disclosed the help which officially neutral Nuremberg gave to the Protestant armies in the war. But the council was strong. Even as the duke of Alba approached the town with his Spanish force, they abolished the use of the Ave Maria, 'Hail Mary full of grace', which was still said in certain churches. When Alba arrived, the council refused to give a much-needed police protection to monks or friars walking the streets in their habits, they were told that they walked out at their own risk.

In June 1547 the council ended the pastorate of Dietrich. Wisely, they made the reason the letter to Brenz and not the sermons, for then they could say that the State did not silence the Word of God.

In July 1547 the emperor came in person to Nuremberg, carrying as pris-oners the elector of Saxony whom he was depriving of his electorship, and Philip of Hesse whom he had seized by a trick. The city had a bad time and the council did not dare to notice the presence of the two evangelical leaders. But as soon as Charles V went away the evangelical services were celebrated again. In one way it was easier for the council, since vestments at mass and candles on the altar had never been abolished in the Nuremberg reformation, so no one could claim weakness that they were used.

On the Interim Osiander accepted fasts and feast-days and welcomed pri-vate confession—the last he wanted for the good of morals. He would con-sent to no other change in the way of worship. Then he attacked the emperor in a sermon and was in worse trouble.

Finally the council of Nuremberg ordered that all churches should on 11 November 1548 make the changes prescribed by the Interim. One parish church, St Sebald, obeyed. Osiander resigned and vanished. His disappear-ance broke resistance. No one knew where he had gone. Three months later he appeared in Königsberg—a big gain for Duke Albert of Prussia who became devoted to him. Here he became professor of theology at the young university and later an acting bishop. Nuremberg was left with the blot of having refused a pension to the pastor who led their reform and helped them in the Peasants' War and published Copernicus and resisted the bigamy of the landgrave and served the city faithfully for nearly twenty-eight years. Duke Albert tried to persuade Veit Dietrich to come too. As gout and lumbago, swollen feet, and paralysed hands hardly let him get out of bed, he could not travel and remained in Nuremberg, a silenced dissenter, till his death next year. Duke Albert sent gifts to his widow.

In Regensburg they postponed answering the demand to accept the Interim and hoped that passing time would change their predicament but it did not. The council pleaded with the emperor that they were much troubled and asked to be allowed to remain as they were until the future church council decided. The answer was a threat which shattered the Regensburg council.

On 30 June 1548 after more threats the Regensburg council accepted the Interim unconditionally because they could do no other. Their ministers Noppus and Gallus left the city in the middle of that night. The next day was Sunday and congregations arrived at churches to find no pastors and the doors locked.

Regensburgers blamed the clergy for deserting them in their trial. Melanchthon thought that they were wrong to go, they should have stayed to help. Noppus and Gallus said that if they preached they must denounce the Interim and that was now illegal, there was nothing else to do but go.

On 3 February 1549 the council found a curate who consented to celebrate the Interim liturgy, and a congregation of thirty appeared, to pray with Latin hymns, the Agnus Dei, the elevation, a German litany sung by the choir, and the sacrament with wine as well as bread to the communicants. For a time they kept this 'interim-liturgy' going—until people showed how they disliked it, and the irritation of the Catholic bishop was a worry.

The question came again, what were laypeople to do? They needed their babies baptizing, that could be done by a midwife. They needed to bury their kin, that they could do without a pastor. Were they to leave their daughters unmarried though living with a man? Marriage had a civil as well as a religious effect. Were they to deprive themselves of communion and confession or might they go to the Roman Catholic priest?—for they could find an occasional Roman Catholic willing to give communion in two kinds. They could teach their children, and study the Bible, and read printed evangelical sermons. In December 1551 apprentices met on Sundays at the cemetery outside the walls and read the Gospel of the day and a Postil. The council banned the meetings, the bishop threatened to tell the emperor. The young took no notice of the ban or the threat.

During the war Melanchthon and his family and Luther's widow Catherine fled to Zerbst. There they did not feel safe, and Catherine Luther wanted to go as far as Denmark. They moved to Magdeburg first, where they were sheltered in the house of the earlier canon George of Anhalt, and then moved southward again to Nordhausen. It was a time of misery for Melanchthon did not know what to do. It looked as though his and Luther's life's work might be ruined, and his daughter Anna died in Königsberg. He wrote a little book of consolation in suffering; and as with the most famous of authors on consolation, Boethius, the best such books are written by those who need to console themselves.

In June 1547 he learnt that Maurice, now Elector Maurice of Saxony by reward, for the emperor had deprived John Frederick of his electoral rank and much of his Saxon territory and given it to Duke Maurice, intended to reopen the university of Wittenberg, inside the territory which Albertine (Maurice's) Saxony had acquired by the war. Melanchthon's friend Cruciger had stayed at the closed university as a symbolic rector, and two days after the emperor's army marched out he invited the professors to come back. To Melanchthon Wittenberg was the star, the anchor of the Reformation. He believed that its prosperity was identified with the welfare of the evangelical cause. He was sure that if the university could reopen he ought to go back there to help.

He did not trust Maurice. Hardly any evangelicals trusted Maurice. But he was contented with an assurance from Maurice that pure doctrine should be taught at Wittenberg and so he went. Not being versed in worldly politics he would not see that Maurice needed his name for political reasons and not religious; or if he had a glimmer of that he hoped it not to be true and he must trust a solemn assurance. Maurice was a usurper in the former electoral Saxony and if Melanchthon revived the most famous university in Germany the new ruler was being raised towards legality because the most respected name in Germany was prepared to work for him.

He told Maurice that the Interim was impossible to accept. If it were imposed by force he was against resistance because resistance would tear the churches further apart. But he predicted great trouble if it were enforced.

Politically Maurice could not do without the Interim. He needed peace with the emperor. Somehow he must try to bring over Melanchthon. He asked his counsellor Carlowitz to see what he could do. Carlowitz was a disciple of Erasmus and moderate enough to be a good mediator with Melanchthon, and had sufficient repute of being on the Protestant side because he was the civil servant used in the management of former monastic property and in the reform of the university of Leipzig. Because he stood near Maurice in the war, he earned the hatred of Protestants as another Judas, 'godless lawyer'.

Carlowitz wrote Melanchthon a letter—that it was his duty to accept compromise because it was the only way of avoiding more war in Germany. Melanchthon replied with a letter for which many Lutherans never forgave him:

At times earlier in life I followed Luther too slavishly. There were occasions when he decided something more because he was pugnacious than because he saw what was needed for the good of the people. By nature I am not a controversialist, I love peace . . . I will gladly work to reconcile the churches. But I am not willing to accept any change in doctrine, for that would create trouble, nor will I consent that good people should be driven out of the Church.[17]

[17] CR vi. 880 ff.

Carlowitz made the letter public in many copies. In Augsburg it was passed from hand to hand.

Evangelicals were horrified at this admission that Luther sometimes acted because he was quarrelsome, and that Melanchthon followed him 'slavishly'. They thought it an avowal that Melanchthon was not a true interpreter of Luther. In the nineteenth century even Leopold von Ranke was glum that he wrote the letter to Carlowitz. They excused him—the man was a pure scholar, and could not understand how what he said mattered to the politics of the State. But Ranke was still sad—that this truly good man, so soon after his prince suffered calamity and his close friend and leader had died, should write a letter attacking that leader. Even professors, said Ranke sententiously, are no longer private persons when they are entangled in great events.[18]

But Duke Maurice needed an agreement, for political reasons. What could the Wittenberg professors accept? How far would they compromise?—obviously not on 'essentials' but what was essential? The theologians met again and again, at the duke's order, and got nowhere. After repeated failures, and realizing that if the Protestants were rigid they risked losing their heartland in electoral Saxony, Melanchthon agreed at the end of December 1548 to a moderate form of the Interim, known to history, though not at first to contemporaries, as the Leipzig Interim. It was not published, except in a summary.

This Interim declared: The Church shall not teach anything contrary to the Scriptures and therefore its teaching is to be accepted; pastors are to obey bishops; confirmation and extreme unction are to be allowed as they were among the early Christians; confession and absolution are to be taught but no one is to be forced to confess a list of sins; the words of the mass are not to carry the words of a meritorious sacrifice; many traditional ceremonies are to be kept (bell-ringing, vestments, etc.); pastors may marry; the Friday fast from meat is to be observed during Lent; clergymen are to wear dress which shows they are clergymen. Melanchthon did not want this but believed that he had conceded nothing essential to faith and the rest could be tolerated for the sake of peace. Constance showed how refusal to compromise led to devastation of Protestant churches. It was better to agree what one could agree.

Clothes? Must a pastor wear a surplice in church? Some Lutheran churches had kept the custom. No one could say that to wear white would hurt his conscience. It was an *adiaphoron*, a 'thing indifferent', which churches could order or not. If authority ruled that a surplice should be worn, because that was reverent or because it would help the churches back to peace, many priests/pastors would obey the rule and think anyone who

---

[18] Ranke, *Deutsche Geschichte im Zeitalter der Reformation* (Vienna edn., 1971), 1047.

refused to wear it was a trouble-maker. The peace of the churches was a true Christian goal.

But why is authority making this rule? Not because it wishes to make churches more reverent, but because the emperor commanded. By commanding, the State has turned a garment, trivial in itself, into a piece of forcing unwanted religious practices upon tender consciences. Pastors felt a duty to resist, not because a garment was important, but because a hostile state made it important.

Melanchthon suffered from two illusions which were not his fault but which hurt him. He still did not know that the Interim was only for Protestants. In earlier weeks he imagined that the Interim applied to all Germany and so had the merit, among its demerits, of being an attempt at Christian reunion. Secondly, when the 'Leipzig Interim' had become the question, he had no idea that most of Germany knew nothing of a difference between the Augsburg Interim and any modification of it. He was prepared to work with an Interim specially modified for Saxony. For the outside world the two Interims were not distinguishable.

The moral doubt about resistance to lawful authority reached its climax at Magdeburg. The famous city on the Elbe, founded by Otto the Great as a centre of civilization and Christianity towards the Slavs to the eastward and with its newer cathedral consecrated in 1363, had long fought for its rights against its archbishop and easily accepted reform. For nearly quarter of a century it had been a Protestant city with its chief pastor Luther's uncomplicated and uncompromising friend and disciple Nikolaus von Amsdorf, nephew of Staupitz who had so helped the young Luther in religious devotion. Luther preached there to huge crowds too numerous for any church to contain. George Major made the secondary school one of the best new schools in all Germany.

Amsdorf's attachment was exceptional, his past experience of Luther included not only the Leipzig Disputation and the Diet of Worms but the office of godfather to Luther's daughter Magdalen. When Luther thought that he was dying, it was Amsdorf to whom he commended the care of his wife Catherine. When the see of Naumburg fell vacant (its Catholic bishop had hardly visited it), Luther persuaded a reluctant Amsdorf to leave Magdeburg and (after Saxon politics against the chapter which had elected the Catholic Pflug, when some of the town council wanted a Protestant bishop) he was consecrated by Luther himself as bishop with elaborate rites, to reform this Catholic diocese. Amsdorf was unmarried and learned and pastoral and in a different world would have made an excellent bishop. He spent four years of depression at his frustrations as bishop among a half-hostile people until war came and the army of Charles V turned him out and installed Pflug, and Amsdorf returned with relief to Magdeburg. He had no doubt that he was a valid bishop in the Church for he often described himself as an exile.

Strongly Protestant Magdeburg had a chapter protected by Reich law and still Catholic. When Archbishop Albert of Mainz and Magdeburg, he of the indulgence, died in 1545, the canons of the cathedral lost their protector and could not remain in the town as Catholic but from outside the city they struggled to maintain Catholic rights. The new archbishop of Magdeburg, Johann Albrecht, demanded that the city accept the Interim.

The city had no intention of conforming to the Interim but asked for time to consider and during this breathing-space planned resistance. It made guns out of the bells of former monasteries. At the side of Amsdorf strong-minded refugees collected, especially two of rare ability, Gallus who had fled from Regensburg to Wittenberg but now felt uncomfortable with Melanchthon's moderation, and Flacius Illyricus from Wittenberg for the same discomfort.

In 1550 Charles V declared Magdeburg under the ban of empire and sent Elector Maurice of Saxony as the imperial agent to enforce the ban and besiege the town. The siege was long, the defence resisted stoutly. While it held it became a heroic symbol to evangelical Germany, like Malta to Britain during the Second World War. Poems were written in its honour, churches were crammed at special prayers for the safety of Magdeburg. Observers believed that it was saving not only itself, but the well-being and continuance of the Reformation. Inside the town there were prayers at noon, workers knelt in the streets.

The pastors of the city, Amsdorf at their head and Gallus among them, published a *Confession and Apology of the Magdeburg Pastors and Ministers*[19] which was at once famous as the justification of resistance—on the basis beginning to be agreed, that where the chief magistrate acts immorally or as a tyrant, the lesser magistrates have not only a right but a duty to resist, if necessary by force. The document was probably written by Gallus and took a European importance. If a superior government tries to suppress religious truth, lesser magistrates must resist. No government of any state has the right to tell churches how they are to worship God. If it is said that this is all about trivial things, clothes and ceremonies, that is false; worship and faith are so inseparable that what we do inside a church affects what we believe.

After twelve months Maurice was tired of the siege, which harmed him with his own Saxons. The Magdeburgers were also tired, their trade destroyed, guerrilla war in the countryside round. The two sides reached a unique form of treaty. The outward provisions looked as if they contented the emperor—the town surrenders, apologizes to the emperor, pays

---

[19] *Confessio et apologia pastorum et reliquorum ministrorum ecclesiae Magdeburgensis* (13 April 1550), simultaneous Latin and German editions.

reparations and demolishes its fortifications. If these were the real conditions Magdeburg would not have surrendered. But in private meetings Maurice agreed that the only things that must happen were the handing over of the town to the protection of a Saxon garrison—the word 'surrender' was carefully avoided—and the release of prisoners of war without a ransom. Magdeburg need not conform to the Interim, need not expel its refugees, no citizen nor *Landsknecht* would be prosecuted, its historic liberties should remain. This extraordinary combination of a public pseudo-treaty with a real private treaty could only happen if the leaders of the town trusted Maurice. The pastors trusted him not for a moment—a traitor to the evangelical cause—and tried to persuade the council to refuse the offer. But the council needed peace and Maurice was allowed on 7 November 1551 to bring his troops into the city. Before the statue of Otto the Great the city fathers handed him the keys and then he carried out his promise that they should keep their historic freedoms.

This long fight had other consequences than the start to destroying the policy of Charles V.

Magdeburg was revered in Protestant Germany. But not all Protestants thought that it was right. There might be a danger in seeming to have a war over whether or not surplices should be worn in church. The policy of Joachim II of Brandenburg or Frederick of the Palatinate was to accept the Interim and then allow clergy to use what their leaders deemed tolerable. Melanchthon thought the Interim lamentable, and forced the change to the Leipzig Interim for the new Saxony under Maurice, but found the result possible and certainly better than war. Since he was revered as Luther's colleague and Luther's heir, he had followers, Bugenhagen among them.

Because Magdeburg was so famous as the resister, Amsdorf was for a short time hailed as the leader of no compromise. But soon a layman in Magdeburg took his place in national reputation: Matthias Flacius Illyricus, not yet thirty years old. Melanchthon and his followers called their uncompromising critics by the name Flacians.

Flacius had a Croat father and an Italian mother and went to school in Venice, where there were Protestants but at grave risk, so his first acquired faith was martyr-minded. He went over the mountains to seek a good education, first at Augsburg where they sent him on to Simon Grynaeus as the famous Greek scholar in Basel. But Wittenberg was like a magnet beckoning him onward, nothing else would do, he headed northward again. During the journey he had a second big experience. He was miserable, partly perhaps from homesickness, but in soul, despairing, contemplating suicide, with a loss of interest in books and the study of languages, tormenting himself at sin. He delayed the journey to Wittenberg, as if he did not yet dare to face Luther and Melanchthon.

When at last he arrived, Melanchthon received him kindly and helped his studies and paid out of his own pocket for part of the expenses and arranged students for him to teach and so earn fees. In both the lecture rooms of Luther and Melanchthon he sat still in waves of despair and doubt in and out of the soul. He went to consult the university chaplain, who passed him on to Bugenhagen; who compared his case with that of Luther more than a quarter of a century before—by faith from despair to trust and assurance. Bugenhagen passed him on to personal meetings with Luther. Flacius felt these meetings with Luther to be like another conversion. He had been shown how to find faith and his despair vanished.

At the age of twenty-four he was appointed the professor of Hebrew. He married and it was a happy time—the only happy time of a long troubled life.

His gratitudes to Luther and Melanchthon were different. To Melanchthon he owed kindness and intellectual well-being, to Luther he owed his soul. If there came to be posthumous disagreement between Luther and Melanchthon, it was Luther who commanded.

Flacius fled to Magdeburg in the war and when peace came returned to Wittenberg, still to teach Hebrew. Then he realized he could not stay in Saxony or be one who conformed to the Interim. He went back to Magdeburg and worked as a proofreader. Magdeburg was then a militant city and he became its most militant pamphleteer. Since he dared to say what others were too kind to say, within a few months he was, next to Bugenhagen and Melanchthon, the most famous Lutheran writer in Germany. No one else liked to attack Melanchthon so personally. Flacius said that with God's help he would smash the windows which Melanchthon and Elector Maurice were constructing for the Church; and soon was telling the Wittenbergers that they aimed to crucify Christ afresh and to make room for the Roman Barabbas.

Such an extreme onslaught upon a revered person made Flacius a person never to be forgiven among some evangelicals. But he said certain things which even congregations wanted to hear. Does it really matter whether we wear a white garment in church? It does not matter—but it matters because it is happening not from a motive of reverence but at the orders of a papistical sovereign for whom it is the first step towards ending an evangelical reformation. And he could plead a powerful argument. Cry the freedom of the Church, the iniquity of state interference in its way of worship. These Saxon surplices owe their origin not to reverence but to fear.

Congregations were affected because they now loved German hymns. The Interim wanted Latin hymns. Flacius movingly praised the way in which the piety of German people had been deepened by the German hymn, how the words came into their homes and memories.

Daniel could have prayed with the window open or shut. Whether it was shut was 'indifferent'? Confession of faith demanded that it be open.[20]

In 1552 the change of sides by Maurice of Saxony produced the treaty of Passau and the safety of all the evangelical Lands and the vanishing of the Interim. But it did not end the arguments which the disagreements over resistance to the Interim caused.

Flacius moved to be a professor at Jena whence he continued to pour out attacks on Melanchthon.

Melanchthon died on 19 April 1560, while several hundred students waited silently outside his house. He was the quiet mind who owed his European stature to being Luther's lieutenant, but was much more than a lieutenant. After Luther died in 1546 he lost the leadership which reformers expected of him, and through unpretentiousness and simplicity and openness of mind never thrust himself forward and never led a campaign, and yet was no one's reflection, and in no way a second fiddle, but an authentic creator of the German Reformation.

Apparently he lived a happy life, revered all over Europe, even by some Roman Catholics, and liked by a large band of grateful pupils. But call no one happy until death, and the last thirteen years were misery. He carried the burden of sensitivity, and a thin skin, and bore a suffering sense of diffidence about his own scholarship and achievements, at times moods of self-torment. Even in the best of his years he was an academic who grieved that he must do so many chores for the sake of the ecumenical Church.

As he thought about his coming death, he jotted notes on a scrap of paper, and the dying seldom see matters quite straight. What he wrote moved posterity to the heart, and elicited their protective instinct for a wounded man, and damaged his own repute further, and hurt the later reputation of good minds among his contemporaries.

On the left side:

> At death you will be free from sin
> You will be set free from care and from the fury of the theologians.

On the right side:

> you will come to Light
> you will see God and his Son.
> You will penetrate the mysteries which here you could not
>   understand—why we are made as we are, and the nature
>   of the union of God and Man in Christ.

---

[20] *De veris et falsis adiaphoris* (Magdeburg, 1549).

For more than three centuries the world thought of Luther as the creative mind and Melanchthon as his hard-working shadow. This opinion was altered in modern times.

He felt a deep debt to Luther. After Luther's death this made him stick to the university of Wittenberg despite the loss of reputation that this would entail in the circumstances of the Interim. But Luther also owed Melanchthon a debt. To have as his lieutenant an eminent humanist, regarded by Erasmus as the most promising of the younger scholars, famous through Europe for his editions of the classics and his Greek and Latin grammars, gave an academic weight to the university of Wittenberg which Luther alone could not have won. He was not like Luther a hymnwriter. His commentaries on the Bible did not strike home like Luther's. But he could not write the disastrous pamphlets which on occasion flowed from Luther's pen when he was roused. To be a moderate in an immoderate Europe was the chief source of his misery. Sometimes he was able to amend Luther's excesses or soften a harshness. He tried hard, and risked much, to make Luther's doctrine of the eucharist more ecumenical, and failed, yet the attempt helped Germany. The great Bible translation was Luther's and Luther's style; but from the moment he began to revise it for the correct meaning Melanchthon was one of the little group at his side.

A big part of the debt was personal friendship. That was not easy. Luther was full of courage, humour, insight, pastoral affection. But his temperament was explosive and he was not always comfortable as a colleague. His wife could cope serenely. But Melanchthon lived for twenty-seven years in proximity to this person who suffered much from the stone and was often in pain and whose judgement in later years the severity of pain affected. Their single quarrel came when Luther thought Melanchthon far too feeble as in 1544 he sought to help the archbishop of Cologne, Hermann von Wied, to become a Protestant. For two months they were hardly on speaking terms and those weeks were the only time when Melanchthon felt that perhaps he should accept a chair at another university. The long friendship was a feat, from both sides. That Luther could stand so stoutly to a moderate mind helped to make 'Lutheranism' potent.

He gave Luther's funeral address to the university. His voice was moved. He said that this was a hero, and compared him to Paul and Augustine, a mind creative, who recalled the Church to its true origins, like one of the Fathers of the early Church.[21]

There was already a plan to publish Luther's collected works. The second volume now came out and Melanchthon took the chance to write a preface which was the first Life of Luther. Modern scholarship has suspected that he

---

[21] CR xi. 726 ff.

made his hero even more heroic than the truth. He described how at the Ninety-Five Theses against indulgences Luther nailed the theses to the church door at Wittenberg and those hammer blows became a celebrated symbol of the Luther saga. But this is the first information about a hammer and contemporary evidence suggests that the theses were issued as a paper rather than nailed anywhere. It was retorted that a close friend of Luther could hardly have been wrong about so big a moment. But at that time Melanchthon was a lecturer at Tübingen, not knowing that he was to spend his life in Wittenberg.

He was fortunate, more fortunate than Luther, in his biographer. Joachim Camerarius was a Greek scholar who at the age of twenty-one came to the university of Wittenberg and from that moment was one of Melanchthon's closest friends. Melanchthon got him made head of the Nuremberg College but he spent most of his life at the university of Leipzig which he helped to turn into a very good university while he became the most famous philologist in Germany. A pleasant man with a moderate spirit, a fine scholar, an expert in university affairs, and another peacemaker, Camerarius was uniquely qualified to understand both the ranging mind in Melanchthon and his concern for the unity and harmony of the Church.

Gnesio-Lutherans

In Greek *gnesios* meant born in wedlock and then by metaphor real, genuine, legitimate. So gnesio-Lutherans were persons who claimed to be 'the real Lutherans', ready to defend the authentic inheritance of Luther against compromises. They knew neither the term gnesio-Lutheran nor the term philippist, as history came to know their opponents the followers of Melanchthon. They were stiffer on justification by faith alone and on the real presence in the eucharist. Melanchthon's disciples were readier to accept the part of reason in theology and to think that they were not so far away from the more moderate reformed theology of the Swiss. On both sides the leaders were former pupils of Melanchthon. Apart from Amsdorf all the gnesios were a generation younger than Melanchthon. To them Melanchthon only had weight when he was interpreting Luther.

The argument made it matter much what Luther was like, what he said, what he wrote. They needed his works, his letters, memories about him, biographies. Both sides collected and printed.

The Wittenberg edition of Luther's works was edited by George Major and Cruciger, twenty years and nineteen folio volumes, edited not by chronology but by theme. Major was a choirboy at the elector's chapel and then an undergraduate at Wittenberg and taught by both Luther and Melanchthon. He went into teaching at Magdeburg and was a pioneer in the use of the theatre for schools. At the age of thirty-five he was ordained by Luther to be preacher at the Wittenberg castle chapel and in 1544 became professor in the theological faculty. He returned to the university when it was reopened at the Interim and was therefore attacked by the gnesios (unjustly) as a person bribed by Elector Maurice. No genius, he had the unwavering loyalty to Melanchthon and Luther and the steadiness which brought to completion so large an undertaking.[22] Luther was not easy for editors in an age of controversy. Major found it necessary to delete certain passages.

The ex-elector John Frederick after his imprisonment by the emperor was now an aggrieved duke of a smaller Saxony which had lost Wittenberg. He founded a college at Jena, which soon turned into the university. It was a gnesio place, was determined to find the authentic texts of Luther, distrusted Wittenberg and Major, regarded that edition as an instrument of propaganda, and started its own collected works. They were fortunate to collect Georg Rörer who had started work on the Wittenberg edition and was accurate with proofs. He arranged the material chronologically and tried to correct the faults of Wittenberg, four Latin volumes and eight German volumes 1555–8, faster work because he had the Wittenberg edition as a guide. These two editions were expensive but were bought because church orders ruled that they should be acquired by parish libraries.

But still there were gaps. Johannes Aurifaber was Luther's last secretary and lived for two years in his house. He had earned his living as an army chaplain and in the Schmalkaldic War served the elector John Frederick and shared his prison afterwards. Inevitably he backed the gnesio-Lutherans. Though at first he had nothing to do with the edition of Luther's works, he had a passion for collecting scraps of letters and copies of sermons and after Luther's death went on collecting. The ex-elector John Frederick meant to print only what Luther printed. Aurifaber wanted to print what was unprinted and went round Germany hunting unpublished texts and persuaded the duke to pay for their purchase. He completed the Jena edition after Georg Rörer's death. In 1556 he published Volume I of Luther's letters.

Ten years later he published the texts which were to give him world-wide fame. He found an already existing report of what Luther said at his table. He collected from friends their memories of these conversations and added his own memories. He then inserted pieces from other works by Luther, not spoken at table. He first published this collection at Eisleben, under the title

---

[22] Major's controversy over good works—Major and Bugenhagen (to do good is necessary to salvation) versus Amsdorf and Flacius and Gallus—was part of the argument between gnesios and philippists; for the Interim held that good works are necessary to salvation. Amsdorf even accepted the extraordinary sentence, good works are harmful for salvation. Major was driven to recant his sentence about doing good but he had never believed in merit nor abandoned *faith alone*.

Table Talk or Conversations of Dr Martin Luther (Tischreden oder Colloquia Doct. Mart. Luthers). These records were not in chronological order but were arranged by themes. It was a wonderful record of conversations. Since it had the unedifying as well as the edifying, people who wished to preserve a portrait of a conventionally pious Luther held that it could not be genuine. As it was the only collection published for three centuries, it served a valuable purpose.

Until the nineteenth century historians knew Luther's letters and Table Talk through the work of Aurifaber; the Table Talk they did not know otherwise till 1883. By later standards the methods of editing left much to be desired. In the nineteenth century the notes of others, on which Aurifaber made his selection, were found and printed and so Aurifaber's texts could be dismantled and amended. Though he touched up and made certain texts more pointed or godly, he also kept and wrote down everything even if it was to Luther's discredit. He had no idea of making his hero into a saint. Without him we should know nothing of several of Luther's astounding utterances and the character of the man would be far less vivid. In his service to humanity and literature Aurifaber can justly be compared with Boswell despite the difference of more than two centuries.

The gnesio-Lutherans charged their opponents with turning Luther into a waxwork that he was not, and so had a desire to show him as he was in three dimensions.

The historical portrait of Luther

This now mattered as it had not mattered during his life. It went on mattering through German history—the anchor of intellectual freedom and of the rights of conscience as the Enlightenment saw him, the hero of the German nation as nationalists of the nineteenth century saw him, the bourgeois who opened the gate towards social revolution as Marxists saw him. But present concern is how the second generation of early Protestants saw him.

He was a fascinating commentator upon the Bible especially on the texts of the Old Testament. People could enjoy reading Luther's commentaries and think of them as more than solid tools for study. That kept his influence in the parishes. The doctrinal influence on the development of thought looked great but was not: with the crucial exception that his soul-discovery of justification by faith alone conditioned the development of evangelical theology, with his conviction that Christianity and the Bible demanded a doctrine of real and substantial presence in the eucharist. His work was always directed to a practical end, he was never a systematizer, they drew opinions or judgements out of his collected works—but it was his friends, systematizers like Melanchthon or Brenz or Bugenhagen, who mattered more in creating the structure of evangelical thought. What dominated their minds was the reformer—he had a mission from God to remedy the ills of the Church and bring it back towards its earlier purity and he gave certain ways by which that was best done and we must try to carry them out in our new circumstances. Out of their experience they took it for granted that the origins of reformation were religious and theological, not social nor national nor political; and that one chief thing which Luther had done was to cast down the merely external in religion, the faith that rests only in ritual acts, and to change the idea of the Church from that of an institution of power in the world to that of a community of believers.

When Luther died his close friends Melanchthon, Bugenhagen, Justus Jonas, published obituaries usually preached first as memorial addresses, warm in affection and admiration but, like all obituaries, not considered in a longer perspective. What stood out from them was his courage, and power as a speaker to the people; Bugenhagen thought of him as one who came with a message from God like a prophet of the Old Testament, to overthrow idolaters.

But soon after the obituaries, the ground was occupied. Three years after Luther's death Johannes Cochlaeus, who had dedicated his life to fighting Protestants, published his *Commentaries on the Writings and Life of Martin Luther*.

Cochlaeus was little, full of go, restless, with waving hands, short-sighted and haggard. The only time he met Luther was in the debate at the committee of the Diet of Worms and after that he was sure that Luther was a revolutionary who would destroy Germany and the Church. The fiercer he grew the further Rome moved from him; but he was kept going in various German canonries.[23]

Until 1530 or soon after he dedicated his energies to demolishing Luther. He had not the qualities for the task. He felt theology to be dusty, he was a learned compiler. His books are heaps of quotations without construction or selection.

From soon after 1530 he realized that he might be after the wrong enemy. It was Melanchthon of whom they should be afraid, more than Luther. He was cleverer, not a married monk nor an outlaw. Luther was choleric and openly a heretic. Melanchthon had sense and was a master of pretence. He formed an inflated view of Melanchthon's European weight, respected from Scotland to Poland, the person who made the schools Lutheran and trained the reforming preachers. 'No one is a more dangerous enemy to Rome.'[24]

---

[23] Court chaplain to Duke George of Saxony, 1527; canon of Meissen in the same Saxony, 1533, pleasant house by Elbe; when ducal Saxony went evangelical after Duke George's death, to a Breslau canonry but disliked it; to an Eichstätt canonry, forced to resign 1549; died at Breslau 1552 over his books.

[24] Cochlaeus to Contarini, 20 February 1539, in Franz Dittrich, *Regesten und Briefe des Cardinals G. Contarini* (Braunsberg, 1881), Anhang no. 5.

Just as he entered this phase of promoting Melanchthon above Luther, about 1534, he started compiling annals of Luther's life, from 1517 to that date. It was a collection of documents, selected citations; not precisely a history of Luther because it included only documents which would tell against him. In the preface he wrote that he let the documents speak, without commentary. In a private letter[25] he said that he chose those citations which lead the reader to hate the heretic.

The book was finished by 1534 but he did not publish it and turned to fight Melanchthon with passing assaults on Bullinger and Calvin and King Henry VIII. When Luther died this material lay at hand. Within a few days he added the last twelve years (283 pages, 1517–34; 36 pages, 1534–46). It was published in folio in 1549.

None of his controversial works made the least impression upon the public—except this. It conditioned the Catholic portrait of Luther till the modern age. Despite his hatred of Luther, he recognized the gifts, the power of speech and quality of the sermons, and how he was learned in the Bible, and had been a good monk, and had a true zeal for reform even if it went wrong, and wrote helpful books of devotion. But the bad side came uppermost. No plague of God was worse. The force in it was knowledge. He used Luther's letters and those of other Protestants. This was not vague abuse. Ten years later a German translation appeared at Basel and from 1565 Catholic editions were fairly regular.

The book embittered Luther's friends. They appealed to Justus Jonas to 'stop his mouth'. Jonas said it was a book of lies but he was too tired to answer and one must have faith that truth prevails.

The Strasbourg historian Sleidan took up the cause: *On the State of Religion and Politics while Charles V was Emperor.*[26] It found more readers than any other historical work of that age. Until the opening of the archives Protestants regarded it as the authentic history of the Reformation. It was translated into many languages, and had eighty editions before 1700. It took the research of modern studies to show that it was less impartial than it seemed.

Sleidan did not mention Cochlaeus. But he was provoked by Cochlaeus. Charles V had it read at meals and hated it, and demanded that it be answered and gave access to his state papers but nothing happened.

In 1564 a big person tried to show the wickedness of Luther. Surius was a Carthusian of Cologne famous because during his last years he published the

---

[25] Cochlaeus to Cervino, 11 June 1546, in W. Friedensburg, *Beiträge zum Briefwechsel der katholischen Gelehrten Deutschlands in Reformationszeitallter*, ZKG 18 (1898), 613: many lies are spread about Luther, even about his sanctity; so '*extraxi sane ea potissimum quae in odium notorii et malissimi haeretici lectorem trahere videntur.*' This Cervino is Marcello, future president at the Council of Trent and then pope.

[26] *De statu religionis et reipublicae Carolo V Caesare Commentarii*, (1st edn. Strasbourg, 1555).

first proper collection of the Lives of the Saints since printing. As a student he was attracted by the Protestants but reacted against them. He took a history of the world by Nauclerus, the last world history before Melanchthon's, and added a history of Europe from 1500 to 1564. The work had no merit, and aimed to down Sleidan. Catholics liked it, and for fifty years used it as their textbook of Reformation history.

At long last, seventeen years after Cochlaeus, in 1566 there was published the first biography; still from one of the close circle who had known Luther as friend and table-companion. The richest landowner in Bohemia was an ardent Lutheran and this affected the area. The chief evangelical reformer in north Bohemia was Johannes Mathesius. He was twenty-two before he read Luther's sermon on *Good Works* and was affected and was twenty-five before he first studied in Wittenberg. He was soon head of the Latin school at St Joachimsthal the mining town in Bohemia, where reformers were strong because many of the miners were Saxons from across the border. He went back to Wittenberg and lived with Luther and made notes on the talk. In 1542 Luther ordained him and sent him back to St Joachimsthal as pastor. His sermons were much used as models.

Two series of sermons were important: (1) Sarepta, originally sixteen sermons to miners but in them was a handbook to mining methods, the first adequate handbook; (2) on Luther and his work; these were published after his death and were at once a source of the first rank for Luther's life and had fifty editions till the nineteenth century.

It was well done, graphic, anecdotal, and too lifelike to be pure hagiography, he did not conceal that Luther enjoyed a drink and confessed that God would need to forgive him for coarsenesses; yet it was the discriminating portrait of a friend and disciple. Though he valued Luther as the theologian who gave back truth to the world, the pastor in him valued most the practical reformer who gave them catechisms for the children and the illiterate and taught them to say grace before meals and to say a prayer when they went to bed. Of his doctrine it was the political doctrine—non-resistance—that he most admired since resistance had led the world into wars and troubles and for him one of Luther's supreme claims was as a man of peace.

After Cochlaeus did his killing work on Luther, and then Luther's intimates died one by one, the biographers of Luther changed. They were no longer people who had known him, they needed to use his name as a weapon in propaganda, a counter to the propaganda of the Counter-Reformation. As time faded he became misty, a symbol in legend, if they had thought the idea of a saint respectable they would have given him a halo; and if they thought of him as more like Samson or Moses, they were willing to think of him as a new St Paul. Though they disliked halos, they were willing for a pedestal.

The appeal to history

Catholics said, the reformed must be wrong because they are new, no one in Christian history before them behaved as they do. The reformed said, we behave in a way which resembles the ways of the apostles and their early disciples, with simple ways of prayer, and no excess of ceremony, and a language which people understood, and with no pope and no indulgences and no praying to saints. If that were true, said the Catholics, we should expect to find these apostolic ways appearing in all the centuries of Christian history from St Peter until today. We do not find this. Your historical judgement about the apostles and their disciples must be wrong.

This was an appeal to history. It needed a large answer and from historians instead of propaganda-merchants. They now wanted the evidence on what early Christians believed and how they prayed, and on what happened in the following centuries. Can we see signs of continuity between those first congregations and what came about through Martin Luther? Did true Christianity submerge under corruption about 500, and was it cleansed and purified from 1517? Was there evidence through the centuries of authentic Christianity believed and practised despite various corruptions? They not only needed a study of the New Testament, but of every generation from 300 to the end of the fifteenth century.

While at Magdeburg Flacius conceived the plan in 1552, for a letter shows Catholics hearing of it and trying to keep him out of libraries. In the next year he started to find a team and drafted a plan. From a historian's viewpoint it was not a good plan because its purpose was to confute the Roman Catholic Church.

But it had two excellent principles. First, it was to be written out of original documents. This was a new world for history, to benefit from the resources due to printing, the knowledge of Greek, the relative freedom of enquiry, the new care about libraries, and the dissolution of so many monasteries which pitched valuable manuscripts into the auction room.

Secondly he had realized that the scheme of annals on which history was written did not bring understanding. We need sweeps of events—history by theme and not by one day after the next—life, teaching, worship, errors, divisions, mode of government, and only then eminent people. Therefore this was to be history by centuries, within each century a treatment by subjects.

In Vienna Caspar von Niedbruck was an imperial counsellor with a big private library. He had sat in Flacius' lectures at Wittenberg and become a friend. From Niedbruck Flacius got letters which gained him access to Catholic libraries, to money for buying books, for travel, and help from Niedbruck's own private librarian Wagner. In the hunt for manuscripts

Wagner travelled to Copenhagen and then Edinburgh where he found 'rich booty', then through Austria and Bavaria and Prussia. He went to many monasteries. It was important that this researcher on behalf of Protestant historians came with Catholic commendations. Flacius sent out for other resources. He consulted the great printer Robert Estienne in Geneva, and Oporinus in Basel who eventually printed the book. Agents bought at the Frankfurt book fair. Piles of books from across Europe collected in Magdeburg.

With his dubious reputation as Melanchthon's enemy he found it hard to collect informed persons who would consent to write. Several likely people refused. But he gained the services of two young pastors at St Ulrich's church in Magdeburg, Johannes Wigand and Matthias Judex. By astonishing good fortune this pair turned out to be real historians able to profit from the materials provided so lavishly.

Afterwards this series, so famous under the name the Magdeburg Centuries, was believed to be written by Flacius because his was the first name on the title page. But he knew his limitations and wrote very little of it, except prefaces and editing. The virtues of the plan were his, he paid the secretaries from his pocket, he saw that the books and manuscripts were available.

In 1556 Flacius published a book, *Catalogue of Witnesses*. It was a historian's answer to the charge that evangelical faith and practice were first invented in 1517. It was widely read. He made his work easier by including all the critics of popes, even Machiavelli and Dante.

Three years later the first volume of Centuries (1–3) was published by Oporinus. The Fourth Century (1560) was a huge book of 1,574 columns dedicated without permission to Elizabeth Queen of England France and Ireland. After the Seventh Century Judex died (his widow helped the debts) and Wigand separated from Flacius who grew more impossible. In all the last volumes Wigand was in control. But he became a bishop, first of one see in the north and then of another at the same time, and his hours were taken, and to the last volume, the Thirteenth Century, a short Latin poem was added which might hint that he was worried—for it is a song that the true Church can never be destroyed.

The Centuriators collected a bigger mass of material than was at the disposal of any previous historians. That made their volumes needed. Where a document hurt the Church of Rome they failed to treat it critically. They were happy to believe in the letter which Jesus sent to King Abgar of Osrhoene—a legend with a respectable antiquity even to the third century. When they met a letter from Pontius Pilate to the Roman Emperor Tiberius, another early legend, they accepted it as genuine. They met the famous story of the lady graduate from Athens who disguised her sex and was so learned that in 855 she was elected Pope Joan and after a pontificate of two years gave birth to a child during a procession. This legend had no antiquity, it went back only to the thirteenth century, but in the middle sixteenth century it was widely believed and the Centuriators did not doubt it.

But when old documents helped the see of Rome, the Centuriators turned upon them the guns of a critical rationality. Though the motive was impure, this turned out to be their second service to the study of history. They used true critical methods to analyse the dates of documents—date of the style, texts of the same period, contents in relation to the alleged context, date of first mention in another source, motive of its author. This was not a new method, the Renaissance used it, Lorenzo Valla was a master at it. But now the Centuriators extended it. In the Middle Ages documents were frequently forged. No one had realized how often.

The triumph of the critical doubt came with the Isidorian Decretals. About AD 850 reformers in France created a system of law which would stop lay interference in the Church and block the seizure of church property; and put this law into the orders of old popes and bishops. They used old decretals but freely altered their texts to suit present needs. Since they found no text to meet parts of their needs they wrote whole laws and wove them into the collection of older law. It pretended to be the work of Isidore of Seville who died during the seventh century. Most important were sixty decretals ascribed to the line of earliest popes, all made up for the purpose.

This famous collection had pieces which Renaissance eyes could see to be extraordinary. Valla raised a doubt, so did Erasmus. The Centuriators dedicated themselves to demolishing pseudo-Isidore and succeeded. It was a memorable service to the study of history. Nothing did more to alter attitudes to the early history of the papacy and the development of church law.

No one with a famous career ever died more of an outcast than Flacius. And yet his force and learning and power of work had created a historical movement of the first importance to the growing understanding of the European past.

16

RADICALS

Anywhere in central Europe peasants could demonstrate, or riot, or take up arms and make a civil war, a jacquerie, sudden, emotional, violent. The causes are debated: whether they were desperate and went out for bread to help starving wives and children; or whether they were prosperous as working people and so had go, and enough knowledge to see how inequality ruled the land; whether the State was a little less inefficient and made unaccustomed demands upon people not used to paying. In parts of Germany and Switzerland and Austria where peasants rose the causes and conditions varied, so that it is not easy to determine the same social reasons for different *émeutes*. The territorial State grew more effective and weakened feudal rights which were also rights of the poor and the poor were indignant at the loss of old protections. In these struggles the peasants felt conservative—preserve old rights, freedom to use common land, freedom to cut fuel in the woods, freedom to fish in the streams, freedom to hunt, and very low or no taxes. They had backers among the discontented in the growing towns.

They were aided by the system of mercenaries. Older workers had gone away to serve as hirelings in a prince's army and there saw more of the world and how different things could be, away from their parish pump, and had returned with the training of a soldier. If peasants rose in rebellion, the force could be formidable. The experience of Switzerland, which supplied the best of mercenary fighters and prospered on the incoming revenues, showed that returned mercenaries were not the most contented of manual workers. They had found exciting ways of earning and now were 'unemployed'.

The low reputation of the old church institutions was a new form of provocation. An abbey with wide lands lay in the countryside, with but few monks, and they despised by many of the people, and demanding rent from their serfs/tenants. At times they invited trouble by raising their demands, for a big abbey was expensive to maintain and harder for fewer monks. They invited trouble because they stood there undefended and their storerooms were believed to be full of food and wine.

The abbey of Kempten was an 'imperial abbey' where the abbot was also the prince. The abbot/prince drove the families of free peasants downwards towards serfdom. Inheritance tax from serfs took half the property of the married and from tenants the best garment and the best horse. Annual tax rose twentyfold. The abbey's serfs were sure that this was illegal because contrary to long custom and to justice. They negotiated and got nothing but hard words. The result was the sacking of the abbey in 1525.[1]

But it did not need oppression to stir the common people. In the July of that year, suddenly and without warning, a big mob of peasants gathered at the Carthusian monastery of Ittingen and ransacked the buildings and burnt them to the ground. Rebels at Salzburg were heard to state the motive at its hardest: 'The poor people have to fatten up monks as though they were pigs. These monks are no use either to God or to the world.'[2]

In certain places a link was set up between the social desires of the common people and religious ideals. Early in the year of the indulgence, Joss Fritz, a serf of the bishop of Speyer, raised a little revolt along the Upper Rhine, with the older standard of Bundschuh, the clog or peasant's shoe, perhaps from the painting of a shoe on a peasants' flag. He was a veteran agitator, this was his third attempt to raise peasants of the Rhineland to arms. There was more here than conservative demands against more taxes or loss of rights. Here was one of the early communists. Our best hope is the reconstruction of society. We should abolish princes. All property should be in common—it is easy to see how this call came in a world where the rights to common land, and free fishing, and free hunting, and free cutting of fuel in woods, were being restricted. Serfdom should be abolished. There should be no tithes and no taxes and no lending at interest. They had a slogan, 'Nothing but the righteousness of God,' which was a motto taken from the Hussites in Bohemia.

Joss Fritz went through the Upper Rhine valley and the Black Forest, always just ahead of the police. The peasants ought to kill the knights and the landowners and pay rent to no one but the emperor and the pope. He used sayings from the Bible to justify his politics. His followers ended in executions but he always seemed to be able to slip away. When the war of 1524 came he was a veteran fighter in the Black Forest but no one knowingly caught him and he was never seen again.

There were wandering preachers in the land, orators on village greens. If the law of man is wicked, there is an appeal to the law of God. Was it the duty of the true Christian to refuse to pay tithes? Was it the duty of the true Christian to assail by force the Jews? When the wandering preacher told his serf hearers that serfdom should be abolished, the line between a social preacher and a political agitator was blurred. Why should hunting be private, or fishing? Was class privilege compatible with the gospel? Between

---

[1] Gunther Franz, *Der deutsche Bauernkrieg*, 8th edn. (Bad Homburg, 1969), 114–15.
[2] Franz, *Der deutsche Bauernkrieg*, 168.

the peasant rebels of 1524–5 and earlier jacqueries lay a difference, these later peasant leaders talked as though they had a conscience, they felt justified, or said that they felt justified, by the Word of God. They were not preserving the safeguards of old feudal society against oppressive landlords, they looked forward to a just society where God should be king and rule humanity and they would have this chance to help bring in his kingdom. They would abolish serfdom for, they said, 'God created every human being to be free.' They claimed to be able to prevent their pastor being forced upon them and to elect him for themselves—and to get rid of him by vote if they wished.

During 1523–4 many village communities in south Germany refused to pay tithes. Villagers who disliked their pastor (who might have claimed the tithe too vociferously) drove him out of the village and claimed to find their own pastor.

During the summer of 1524 war began in the Black Forest. They were not a rabble. Among them were ex-mercenaries who had guns and were helped by volunteers out of Switzerland who were trained troops. The small town of Waldshut came over to them. The chief power of the region, the Habsburg, happened to be so extended in money that no one could raise even a squad of cavalry to attack them. They used phrases of evangelical language. They knew of what had happened in Saxony and how the old church there was being overthrown, radical pastors from elsewhere in Germany came to join them. Not many of them could read. But they were affected by the new instrument of propaganda, the printed pamphlet, which came into its own as a revolutionary sheet.

A military commander who was far from a peasant came over to them out of a sense of justice. Florian Geyer was made famous in German history by a play of the late nineteenth century. His family was noble and historic in Franconia, the custodian of two castles. He had fought in the courts a tithe battle against the local canons and because he refused to pay was excommunicated, a fate which did not bother him and which he made no effort to get rescinded. He had fought for the Swabian League in the south-west and then in the war between Poland and Prussia, for he was Albert of Prussia's right-hand man. In 1523 Albert of Prussia went to see Luther about secularizing his order of Teutonic Knights and took Geyer with him and from that moment Geyer was a backer of the evangelical cause. In April 1525, unexpectedly to everyone, he joined the peasant army in Franconia. The peasants did not quite trust an aristocrat but made him a chief adviser rather than a general. He accepted a peasant demand that nobles and churchmen should follow the common law of Germany and give up their privileged status. He was most useful to them as a negotiator or threatener, he brought over to their side several towns, most important of them the free Reich town Rothenburg. When the south Franconian peasants were beaten in two decisive battles at the beginning of June 1525 he was not there but fled northward from Rothenburg and in a wood was stabbed to death by two servants of his sister's husband Grumbach, later so notorious in German history that he needed a two-volume biography to include his crimes.

Florian Geyer was unique among peasant supporters; the only experienced commander (but they did not dare use him thus); one of the very few informed disciples of Martin Luther to be on their side.

In the Tyrol where the miners rose, the leader was a disciple of Zwingli, Michael Gaismair, a secretary from a mining family. He was another who appealed to texts from the Bible: equality before the law, end of the privileges of noblemen and ecclesiastics, banning of capitalist merchants, nationalization of the mines and foreign trade, and much more money to welfare for the poor.

Once the regular armies were organized against them it was a hopeless struggle, and ended in too many executions, mostly in June 1525 but in the Tyrol a year later.

Thomas Müntzer was the educated religious leader who wanted to use these jacqueries for a wholesale reformation in Church and State, to purify the Church from the godless if necessary by blood. He believed that Luther started to follow a noble ideal and then failed to carry it through. Unlike the peasants whom he joined his motive was not social reform. He was a prophet full of religious fervour. He would not have started the rebellion but when he saw it happening he believed that it must be an instrument of God for higher ends.

To this day opinions about Müntzer are divided, whether he was a fanatic or a Christian crusader whose religion included social justice. He was the first person to raise in a coherent way the question whether Christians talk practical truth when they assert that Christianity is a revolutionary religion. He raised a hope which still speaks to nations—'the people will be free and God and none other shall be their Lord'.

He studied at two universities and entered the teaching profession and taught girls. When Wittenberg grew famous he became an evangelical preacher, where the ferocity of his attacks on pope and Franciscans made his sermons known. He wrote difficult German, staccato, with jargon from the mystics, and fascinating digressions; less difficult Latin. The letters show a pastor by instinct, at one end charming at the other a hater.

His foes were not only conservatives but supporters of reform to make the Church better but not unrecognizable. Expelled from Saxony he moved into Bohemia. He was now sure that the teaching of Wittenberg failed; that the teaching of justification by faith was not profound enough for the predicament of humanity especially because it made faith easy. The judgement of God is upon us, and evangelical teaching is only a new form of old error, and

God must send new prophets into the world who will show how it is the last time and how God will at any hour bring his creation into harmony. He knew that he was one of these prophets. He was to tell the world that the elect shall rule the earth.

The Bohemians threw him out and he became a wandering preacher. In 1523 he managed to be back in Saxony as pastor at Allstedt which was where he preached a sermon against princes in the presence of the elector. In the parish he did acceptable things—turned the Latin mass into German, made a reformed breviary for the clergy, translated hymns into German and had congregational singing. The people liked him, the congregation grew. He married a nun from a noble family and it seemed as though he would settle and put away a stormy past. But not all was acceptable. Since he believed in force for the sake of God he formed an armed band, some of the troopers were women.

The State stepped in, shut his printing house, suppressed the armed band and he had to flee. Fatally for him it was the moment when peasants were rising over south Germany. At Mühlhausen in Thuringia he helped an ex-monk Heinrich Pfeiffer to make a radical reform of the town.

In mid-April 1525 the peasants of Thuringia and Hesse rose. By early May they controlled vast areas of central Germany. Müntzer saw that the new world of justice was coming sent by God and identified his cause with theirs. Erfurt opened its gates to them. Even the Saxon dukes had a hesitation whether this movement might be of God. At that moment the elector Frederick the Wise was dying in agony and tormented his mind with the idea that this might be the punishment of God for the sins of princes and that the future might lie with a peasant-ruled world.

Shortly before the battle of Frankenhausen Müntzer signed himself 'Thomas Müntzer with the sword of Gideon'. He behaved like Gideon for he took only 300 picked men with him, with standards of the rainbow and on the flags the motto of the Reformation, 'May the Word of God stand for ever', to join the peasant army at Frankenhausen.

On 15 May 1525 the peasant army of 8,000 met the combined troops of Hesse and Saxony, fewer but better armed, mercenaries because they dare not enlist peasants to fight peasants.

As the armies faced each other Müntzer preached to the peasants that by their aid God was to make the world pure and take power from the upper classes and give it to the lower. The princes' army appears to have broken a truce. Five thousand peasants died and there is only a record of six deaths in the government army.

Müntzer was captured. In a farewell letter he asked the people of Mühlhausen to lay down their arms to spare further bloodshed. He did not alter his opinions. He was sure that he died in the service of God.

Here was the first educated mind to produce a Christian theory of class war. He started from the simple premise that the old Church is corrupt and Luther's way is the right way to make it pure. But he found that to purify a church is also to purify a society; and his reforming ideal was caught up in the tensions of divided humanity. The lower class among his people hated the clergy not because they were clergy but because they were part of ruling society; and for Müntzer Luther was as much one of these clergymen as was the archbishop of Mainz. He discovered that people were moved, socially as well as religiously, by the combination of a mystical idea of God's presence in the soul of every person and the expectation that the kingdom of God is upon us, round the next corner. There was something here of the thought of later German medieval mysticism. The true servant of God, the elect, is the person who makes the soul 'empty' by freeing itself from passions and from the affection for the things of creation that divide it from God, and so to make room within for the living Word to fill the entire being. And we have the signs that God is about to re-create the harmony for which he planned the world, and throw off the yoke of the oppressors, and give the kingdom to the godly.

He divided the human race into two. Here were godless, and chosen. Till harvest wheat and tares grow mingled but now the time of harvest is upon us. It is not only this government—the present pope or the emperor or the Saxon elector—which holds the people away from God. It is government, any government, for all government is due only to the Fall of Man, and when it is overthrown God alone shall be the government. It shall be a democracy ruled by God, or rather a rule of God expressed through a democratic form of society.

The peasants who rose against their lords had more practical cares than this pre-Marxist dictatorship of the proletariat where government is no longer necessary. But in the circumstances of a rising peasantry Müntzer must join them and believe in them. He did believe, he did not doubt for a moment that the common people were on the way to be king by opening their hearts to God. And he did not doubt the right of resistance by force to godless rulers. So far from it being the duty of Christians to disobey tyranny and suffer, it was their duty to disobey and overthrow the tyrant.

He believed that human society could be made perfect and that it was man's mission from God to achieve this happy state. He realized that the mass of people had to be prepared by education for their work. But he taught that everything was in common and was looked upon by modern communists as the hero of the German Reformation even if idealism made him advocate what was impracticable.

During the war the peasants lost up to 100,000 lives. The only victors were the princes, not the towns nor the bishops. The peasants had shown the old feudal lords, whose castles were burnt, that they needed the protection of the prince. For two centuries the working man of Germany had no part in the political quest. In the longer run it was necessary to modern states to have a contented peasantry and soon the states were passing laws to ensure that the poor labourer was not exploited beyond reason.

Northern Germany was untouched.

The Catholics had prophesied that Luther's revolt would end in social disorder. When the revolt broke out they put the blame on Luther. They published pamphlets extracting texts from Luther's works and commenting upon them to prove that he was the cause. Unscrupulous pens accused Luther of drafting the demands of the peasants. Even humanists, above all Erasmus, took the same line. The duke of Lorraine, who was a bigot, understood the war as a war of religion 'against the Lutheran sect'.

For posterity the reaction of Martin Luther was the weighty consequence of the Peasants' War. Peasant leaders hoped that they would get the backing of the leaders of the Reformation. During the spring of 1525 the Swabian peasant bands issued Twelve Articles at Memmingen, which contained their normal demands but were backed by citations from the Bible. Luther answered with a pamphlet of April 1525, *Warning to Peace on the Occasion of the Twelve Articles of the Swabian Peasants (Ermahnung zum Frieden auf die Zwolf Artikel der Bauernschaft in Schwaben)*. He criticized both sides; the princes for the part they played in causing the unrest, the peasants for their uprising. But he allowed that some of their demands were just and right. He was gentle with the peasants and conceded that governments had behaved in such a way as to merit it if God turned them out of their thrones; but this did not justify rebellion. They claim to be Christians but they are not because their appeal is to the sword and they overturn the law of the land. It is the part of the Christian, he said, not to seek out revenge, and not to go to arms, but to suffer. And he did not like it that they put forward social and political programmes and then called them by the name of gospel. Both sides are lost if they engage in this fight.

He next went on a tour of the nearest troubled district, north Thuringia. He was agonized by what he heard, and attributed more to Thomas Müntzer than was right, and believed that he dealt with a mob misled by religious fanaticism.

He therefore added early in May 1525 to the second edition of his pamphlet, the most famous of supplements: *Against the Thieving Murdering Gangs of Other Peasants (Auch wider die rauberischen und morderischem Rotten der anderen Bauern)*. He demanded that the princes restore order. A peasant who dies in battle is a servant of the devil, a soldier who has a clear conscience and dies in the fight against the peasants is a martyr for God. There can be nothing more poisonous, or more devilish, or more pernicious than a rebel.

This writing was the more disastrous because it was soon printed not as an appendix to the *Warning to Peace*, but as a pamphlet in its own right; and since that day has usually been printed separately.

It can be said in his defence that when he knew what the authorities did when they won he hated that also. He appealed to the victors to be merciful to the prisoners. When he found that cruelty was the order of the day he printed a pamphlet against the tyrants who after winning a battle are not satisfied with blood. But he was willing to defend his appeal to the princes to re-establish order.

He has often been accused of writing with such vehemence because he saw how if he was to save the Reformation he must at all costs free it from the charge that it caused popular revolution. But his mind and personality were too ebullient, too little moved by diplomatic motives and by prudent foresight, to make this a probable charge. He was a person who reacted hotly to the shock of events and was not conscious how his person was giant in Germany and that every word that he uttered would be pondered.

Other reformers were tough in their language, but their words did not carry so far. The gentle Melanchthon wrote a pamphlet making the cause of the princes the cause of God, the law of the State is to be respected as a duty from God. He had a very low opinion of the present state of the German people when they could commit such barbarity and pleaded that better education, better schools, were a necessity, for it is the educated who see the necessity of law and order. He was as shocked as Luther by the rebellion and believed that all civil society and all religion were at risk.

Some neutrals were concerned only about themselves. Erasmus in Basel was bored by the Peasants' War, it interfered with his travel arrangements, and he could not get letters through.

Historians argued whether the war hurt reformation or helped it. In parts of the south and especially the south-west princes or city councils suppressed the religious reformation at the same time as they suppressed peasant bands, and a few towns, apparently reformed already, were lost for ever to the Reformation. On the other side governments found that they had new executive powers by reaction against the anarchy and proceeded more swiftly to reform their territories—but this was all across the north and in the area where the peasants never marched. And when they made alterations, they made them cautiously. The German Reformation was a little more conservative after 1525. The days of the artisan orator on the village green were almost over.

This feeling speeded the process by which the reformed Church was organized systematically. Too many of the lower clergy had been found on the side of the peasants. Preachers evidently needed better training, their discipline needed courts, their powers needed defining, the parish system needed law and visitation.

The dissenter—the anabaptist—appeared in south Germany before the war. The extreme left among the future Protestants began now to be found more often. It is possible, though it is not provable and modern enquiries have not made it very probable, that one consequence of the war was to give some peasants a nausea against any official church; or in other words, to turn their old hostility to the Catholic priest into a common hostility also to the reformed pastor. But it is more probable that peasant hostility to the Church of the Middle Ages was simply carried through to hamper the work of a new generation and a new type of clergyman.

The anabaptists

Their variety was not very diverse. From the main churches there were three heads of disagreement.

1. If faith is the key to salvation, it can only be conscious faith. Baptism is not rightly administered to little children who have no consciousness of what they do or is done. In this axiom they were unanimous.
2. Jesus told Christians to turn the other cheek and resist not evil. In a fallen society policemen and magistrates and soldiers are necessary. But Christians must not be magistrates or policemen or soldiers. This axiom was not unanimous among them but was accepted very widely and then interpreted in different ways in varied circumstances.
3. If the Bible is our sole guide, we cannot need the language of the early Church to explain it. This was not unanimous for the reason that most of them had no idea what the early Church taught. Most simply accepted the tradition of the whole Church on the incarnation of the Son of God and his work to save humanity. But among the few leaders who were educated or even trained in theology, there came a doubt or denial that we need language like 'Holy Trinity', or 'of one substance', or that we need any kind of formal creed.

(1) and (2) taken together meant that they must conceive the Church as an elite group within society, or on the fringe of society, not as the religious aspect of a whole society.

It started in several places independently, though chiefly in Switzerland and south Germany. They were not descended from the little radical groups of the Middle Ages though here and there they picked up adherents from survivors of such groups, and might take over a name which a medieval group had used, like True Lovers of God. They were men and women of the Reformation, who then stripped their piety down to simplicity and gathered simple folk around them; and then the simple folk bore the tradition among quiet solitary world-rejecting congregations. They did not call themselves anabaptists or baptists or rebaptizers. They liked to call themselves brethren in the Lord. They were sure that they were the true way and sometimes their names for themselves sounded proud, such as the Children of Light, or the elect saints, or the true disciples of Christ. The name anabaptist which won the day was a term of abuse from enemies. By 1525 the term Wiedertäufer, rebaptizers, was used in Zurich.

At Zurich they were young, middle-class, educated in modern humanism. They wanted private Bible study and were against large services in parish churches and looked back to the upper room of the gospel. From 1523 Felix Manz and Conrad Grebel met to read the Bible and to celebrate their sacrament in a private house; in the evening, like the Last Supper, and with ordinary bread. In learning they were very unlike future anabaptist leaders. Manz was the son of a priest and learnt Hebrew and wanted a college lectureship. Grebel studied at the universities of Basel and Vienna and Paris and had interests in natural science and philology. Soon they believed that the reforming leaders, though they appealed to the Bible, were not faithful to the Bible. They knew the writings of both the formidable German critics of Luther for not going far enough in reform, Thomas Müntzer and Carlstadt.

Conversion they understood as God's work of a moment with lasting moral effects. The Christian community ought to share in charity the property of its members. The Church is not for all the world but is a little group of the chosen. No Christian should be a civil servant with a duty to government which could mean the need to punish. Faith is needed for conversion and the baby cannot profess faith. The baptism of adult believers was the only true way.

Zwingli presented to the city council the biblical arguments for the baptism of infants and the council accepted them. The order was given that parents who under this baptist influence had not brought their children to church to be baptized should do so within eight days, on pain of expulsion from Zurich. In 1525 Grebel baptized George Blaurock, a secular priest from Grisons and a revivalist preacher. Then others were baptized. They regarded their earlier Catholic baptisms as null. But in the eyes of the authorities they were baptizing for the second time, hence the name.

In Zurich this ended in the arrest of Grebel and Manz and Blaurock. They escaped but Manz was caught a year later and on 5 January 1527 drowned in the Limmat. The Zurich city council banned failure to baptize babies, banned private meetings for worship, expelled radicals from the canton.

These ideas of quiet groups soon spread northward, into northern Switzerland and then southern Germany. Grebel taught the doctrine in St Gall. It persisted, and gained the allegiance or sympathy of members of the council, and St Gall was the only canton in Switzerland where evidence for the presence of anabaptists continued over decades. There was a strong community in Appenzell. The teaching was evident in several places in the Tyrol, and spread down the Rhine to Strasbourg and towards the Netherlands. It flourished in Basel and that usually tolerant city did not deal with it tolerantly.

But the place where it made many converts was South Tyrol, especially in the Puster valley running west–east through Bruneck. The chief founder there was the Swiss priest George Blaurock, who travelled round, sometimes with his Swiss wife. His record showed that he started, like George Fox the founder of the Quakers, by interrupting and trying to disrupt services in parish churches. But soon he was effective as a wandering apostle. In the mountain villages he collected private meetings and baptized; hid in mountain huts; travelled by night. He suffered a short imprisonment in Appenzell, and another in Basel. At Berne he attended a disputation between anabaptists and the reformed theologians, for good reformed pastors wanted to bring anabaptists under safe-conducts to such a debate so that they could be taught why they were wrong. The preachers usually wanted gentler penalties than did governments, for which the payment of tithe and taxes mattered.

In the distant future of the anabaptists this work in the Tyrol was of the first importance. Why the evangelists prospered in a Catholic area is not easy to say. At least four or five of the converts had been members of Gaismair's rebellions. But that is not enough to show that the spread of anabaptism was a legacy of the Peasants' War.

Soon Blaurock was too well known by reputation to be safe anywhere and the government at Innsbruck sent out a posse. They caught him in July 1529 and burnt him at Klausen that September.

In what amounted of necessity to a series of secret societies, the sources are hard for historians to judge. The best sources for early members are almost all examinations in prison before execution or other penalty. These disclose much but the accused would try not to incriminate others and slanted the evidence and would give no evidence on a subject about which the examiners did not ask. Sometimes but not often the state archives preserved an original anabaptist source thought relevant to the trial.

But where the groups survived and came eventually into the modern world early records were preserved. These were usually the chronicles of martyrdoms or letters written from prison by confessors or future martyrs and then circulated in the community. Because the Hutterites managed to survive they kept a useful chronicle of this nature. The Mennonites in the north were never forced to disappear and so records remained which helped history to know something of their internal life as churches. Such sources have the inevitable slant that they favour a particular body of people. In this area of archives discoveries may still be made unexpectedly. A 1529 paper in favour of pacifism, copied during the eighteenth century, was discovered in 1946 in the attic of a Mennonite farm in Switzerland; and fifteen years after that a copy of the same paper was found in a former Hutterite cottage in Slovakia.

The number of members who could read and write was not large but they appear more frequently than might be expected and so created written sources which were often destroyed in hunts but which could survive, either because an anabaptist leader wrote down a confession of faith or a sermon or a letter to other churches, or because a law court kept them in its archives. This second was not the best source because a defendant only replied to questions that were asked and it was in his or her interest to say as little as possible even if the little was said in many words. There were several ex-Catholic priests, one of them, Hubmaier, an ex-professor of divinity. There was a well-known municipal engineer, Pilgram Marbeck. Of the 167 leaders known during the 1520s in Switzerland and Germany and Austria thirty-eight were clergymen and eight were schoolteachers, seventy-six were craftsmen and twenty-six were peasants or farm labourers or shepherds. That is a much higher proportion of educated leaders than would be found later in the century despite the greater chance by then to go to school. But most members came from the poor, peasants in the country, proletariat in big towns. The categories are known for 212 anabaptists in Augsburg in the three years from 1526. Six or seven of them were well-to-do. About a third had a little property. The remainder were poor.[3]

Members were likely to be strong-minded and among them were oddities. Claimants to the title of prophet of God and to be under divine inspiration at times talked beautifully and at times talked nonsense. And they had the experiences of charismata, ecstasy, limbs in convulsion, sweat, groaning on the ground, shouts of praise in services, occasional miracles of healing.

They were symbolists in their attitudes to the sacraments. They avoided the word sacrament. Baptism was if anything more important than in the traditional churches. Usually they were near Zwingli's doctrine that the eucharist—which they called the Table of the Lord, or the Supper, or the Testament, or the breaking of the bread—was a memorial of a passion and death but a memorial that was a gift of grace. They used ordinary bread. In certain communities they used intinction, that is putting a piece of bread into the wine and consuming both elements together. Like the Catholic Church of the centuries and like the reformed liturgies, they spoke the biblical accounts of the founding of the Supper before distributing the bread and wine. Some communities practised the rite of washing the feet in connection with the Supper.

[3] C. P. Clasen, *Anabaptism: A Social History 1525–1618* (London, 1972); leaders, 310; Augsburg, 324–5.

Hardly any of them were willing to share prayers or sacraments in the parish churches because they would need to communicate with sinners. This reluctance made them stand out in the countryside and helped to bring on persecution. Some of them did not receive the bread and wine even in their own community for years at a time, and rare communities abandoned the breaking of the bread. The study of the New Testament and their experience as persecuted people led to much talk of suffering as the way to God. Human beings must suffer if they are to be true human beings, if they are to do that for which the creator intended them. Those who used the bread and wine as a symbol were aware of the symbolism of suffering within it, the breaking of the bread which is a sign of body, the cup which contains the symbol of blood.

They refused funerals in church and that must lead to difficulty. If they refused the funeral in the churchyard, they were known. If they were known beforehand they were refused funerals in the churchyard. Tolerant vicars, and even the state of Württemberg, allowed burials in the churchyard without vocal prayer. Berne being a more tolerant canton allowed them to use cemeteries without conditions. But many anabaptists were buried on private land hugger-mugger. In this, however, they were not exceptional for in those days quite a number of countrymen who thought themselves ordinary Christians were put into the ground by their families casually.

They usually expected the end of the world very soon. This easily led to eccentricity because under the power of apocalyptic sensation they felt an obligation to help men and women and avert their destruction, and then they could run through a village or town warning the folk to flee from the wrath to come. When the kingdom did not come, these expectations were confined to a minority whereas at first they were characteristic of the movement.

They met in barns or inns or cellars or fields or gardens or private houses or quarries or derelict buildings like old country chapels or abandoned monasteries. It was not easy to find a house to meet in even if the owner was anabaptist because householders were reluctant to run the risk of discovery. They often changed the place of meeting from Sunday to Sunday and this presented the problem of giving safe notice to the folk where they were next to meet. For this purpose they might use children as messengers. In cities it was not easy for members to find the right house, in forests not easy to find the right clearing or to find the way out at the end of the meeting; especially when as often happened the assembly met at night. At various night-meetings in the countryside they put out sentries or guard-dogs. In a city they dared not be seen to arrive at a house in a large body and must 'stagger' their entrances. Cases are known when they went into a church where they thought that they would not be disturbed. In the mountains of the Tyrol the hosts constructed shacks in the high forest so that the coming people could stay for a meeting that lasted two or three days.[4]

Sometimes they used a bowl or a bucket for a font but more usually they baptized in a stream or a creek or a pond or even a puddle in the road. We know only of one baptism by total immersion and that was in the Rhine performed by Grebel. They used kneeling for prayers. Psalms were sung but this was not universal. They refused organs but as they never had control of an organ this question hardly arose. Some refused to use the formal polite '**you**' in speech but addressed the other in the familiar as '**thou**' or '**thee**',[5] but unlike their Quaker descendants they did not turn '**thee**' into a nominative. They disliked addressing anyone by a title.

The first baptist confession of faith is known as the Schleitheim Confession of 1527. It was written by the Swabian Michael Sattler, who was once a Benedictine prior and accepted the Reformation and came to Zurich and was influenced by the anabaptists and then expelled from Zurich and went to Strasbourg where he created the first anabaptist congregation of that city. The creed was accepted by a secret meeting of leaders at Schleitheim. Because printing was dangerous the creed was spread in handwritten copies.

The creed took for granted the chief doctrines of the Reformation. It laid down where anabaptists differed. Adult baptism; the excommunication of unworthy members; no use of oaths; the sword is an order of God for an imperfect world but the true converted soul can have no part in government or the use of violence; the need for the imitation of Christ. A copy was discovered by Oecolampadius in Basel and sent to Zwingli. The Berne government found a copy on an anabaptist whom they arrested. Zwingli wrote a refutation.[6]

The Schleitheim agreement was among the first of a series of such pacts between various groups. These agreements were not binding because each congregation was supreme over itself, and no other authority existed to enforce an orthodoxy, and many miles lay between groups and they were divided by the difficulty of sending letters. Letters were important, like the letters of St Paul the letters from the leader of one community would be read out at the prayers of other communities. Such exchanges gave them the feeling that across the mountains there existed other groups of the elect who prayed for each other until the Lord came. The pacts were advice, expression of opinion, of right faith and practice. As such they sometimes had a wider influence. But they did not stop frequent 'schisms', that is, the break-up of a congregation through disagreement felt to be on a matter of principle.

---

[4] Clasen, *Anabaptism*, 66ff.   [5] Ibid.
[6] Zwingli, *Sämtliche Werke*, ed. E. Egli and others (Zurich, 1961), vi. 1. 103ff.

During the 1520s they were found in four main areas: the cantons of northern Switzerland; the Inn valley and the southern Tyrol; Augsburg and its region; and in Franconia in the region to the west and north and south of Würzburg. There were a few groups already in their future place of near-prosperity, Moravia. In this very large area they were not numerous. In the whole of it 3,617 anabaptists were discovered in the years 1525–9.[7] Hardly any of the communities had more than thirty members, the smaller had eight or ten or fifteen. Very occasionally for a moment there might be a gathering of 500 or more.

A little group did not need a minister who devoted all his or her time to them. They resented the notion of a pastor or priest who had a salary or an endowment. They hated fees for sacraments. They had a desire for ministers who were not separate from their people and earned their living like everyone else. The congregations could not afford to finance a pastor or preacher. The idea of calling someone doctor was abhorrent, but they sometimes used the word minister, or elder, in places the ministers were called shepherds, a number of congregations had a 'director' (*Vorsteher*). But since the leader of a congregation had pastoral obligations which took time, the people often helped by gifts in kind or supplies of food.

They had no use for learning. Theological expertise was not the quality needed for understanding the Bible. They wanted people who knew the Bible but almost illiterate memories knew the text better than ordinary townsfolk with school-education and less need to use memory. In places the doctrine is met that the only book which it is necessary or right to read is the Bible; and even the doctrine that only the uneducated can be truly of the elect. Where a community chose a leader it was almost inevitable that a member who could read and write was chosen. But a number of congregations chose by lot and believed that any other method had too poor a faith in God. They usually laid hands on the minister's head and so gave the commission. There were members who felt the vocation to be wandering apostles to spread their gospel. Experience proved that at first sight it was hard to distinguish a wandering apostle from a fraud or a mendicant or a mentally deficient, and after a time they required such apostles to bring formal evidence of approval.

Statistics so far as they are known show more male members than female. This might be due to the danger of meeting-places and the risk of travel. They would not commission women as apostles, nor let them vote in the choice of ministers. In Holland anabaptists used women as deacons, that is as welfare officers for the sick and poor. Women occasionally preached and there was one known example of a woman celebrating the sacrament, but all

---

[7] Clasen, *Anabaptism*, 20, with tables and map, cf. 63.

such cases seem to be in moments of crisis and disorder. She who celebrated mass was at Mühlhausen just before the climax of the Peasants' War and she had led the plunder of the church of St Blasius and hunted out the pastor.[8] Normally anabaptists were conservative in their attitude to the need for males as ministers. This may be thought surprising in the light of the history of early Christians with their prophetesses. Few anabaptists knew much history.

Where they were quiet and known, they were respected. To be known was important because flight from persecution and secret meetings at night and itinerants warning of the wrath to come generated legends, so that somehow it was necessary to be known as they were—sober, honest, hard-working, kind, free from cursing, generous to a fault, and careful at their crafts. But it was not easy to know them because to be known might lead to arrest and worse, and because they preferred to keep to themselves, temptations were fewer if they did not mix too jollily in this wicked world.

For the same reason the people of whom we know most were those who stood out to the authorities and might not be typical of the ordinary members. Hans Hut was a pedlar of books between Wittenberg and Nuremberg and met a few radicals. He was touched by the expectation of a coming end of the world and by the ideas of Müntzer and he helped Müntzer to publish.

At the end of 1524 he refused to allow his third child to be baptized and was exiled from his home at Bibra. At the battle of Frankenhausen he fought in the peasant army and afterwards was caught but proved to his captors that he was only a pedlar of reforming books and went into hiding at Nuremberg and Augsburg. After a time he was convinced of peaceful ways and in 1526 had himself baptized by Hans Denck.[9] That summer he travelled round baptizing people who would be the elite in the coming judgement on lords and priests; a dangerous life, moving from mill to farm to hamlet, especially among folk who had fought in the war. He made no congregations, he was content to leave them as individuals cleansed against the wrath to come. The police hunted him for they believed that all this was the preparation for another revolt of peasants. Finally he moved into Moravia to Nikolsburg where Hubmaier presided over a less insecure anabaptist congregation. Hut and Hubmaier could not agree, for Hubmaier as a former Catholic priest with education did not expect the end of the world tomorrow. In May 1527 they held a disputation after which Hut was imprisoned and fled.

He went to Vienna and then westward through the towns to Salzburg and

---

[8] She was the wife of Carl Kreutter, an ally of Thomas Müntzer. *Akten zur Geschichte des Bauernkriegs in Mitteldeutschland*, ed. W. P. Fuchs (Aalen, 1964), ii. 753–4.

[9] Denck, Bavarian, educated at Ingolstadt university; worked in Basel as a proof-corrector and was influenced by Oecolampadius, who got him the headship of a school in Nuremberg. There he became a radical and was ejected. After secret travels he settled again in Basel where Oecolampadius persuaded him to a sort of recantation; and died of the plague.

beyond, still baptizing secretly. In August 1527, by arrangement, many of the anabaptists met in Augsburg and Hut joined them. The authorities arrested him. They soon discovered his link with Thomas Müntzer and the war.

During his wanderings he wrote several books of which three became known.[10] His message was derived in part from Müntzer but he identified himself as a John the Baptist in preparation for the kingdom. It was a gospel of a thousand-year kingdom and of suffering, for through suffering alone can we come to serve the Lord. He did not preach communism of property but expected it to happen in the coming kingdom.

The power in this movement was shown here. Hut was a dreamer who was confident in an end that never came; and since he expected the end next year he did not build congregations or attempt a structure which could make his gospel last. Yet it lasted. Individuals whom he baptized in Austria set up their little groups and so the groups spread through Austria and Bavaria and Augsburg until they merged into other groups. Individuals among them ended not within congregations but in a mystical spirituality of the soul solitary before its Redeemer.

Though the imperial law of Germany said that anabaptists could be executed, and though this law was carried out more systematically in Catholic areas than in Protestant, neither the people nor the local authorities liked to obey the law at all times. If they got to know an anabaptist they might respect him or her and refuse to give anything away. Poor people felt more in common with poor anabaptists than they felt with their rulers or pastors and were unlikely to give them away to the authorities. A judge who was fierce with anabaptists, a pastor who kept attacking them in the pulpit, suffered attacks from non-anabaptists. Minor officials frequently closed their eyes to the existence of anabaptists in their area of duty. This spirit was not always present especially where there was unemployment and peasants wanted the jobs held by anabaptists. Nor was it present if the defence of a town was in question, when the citizens resented anyone who refused to fight. At Markirch in Alsace there was a trade union threat. The miners said that if any anabaptists were employed down the mine they would strike.[11] But usually the human race was more tolerant than its representatives who were appointed to care for public order.

In the Protestant areas after the early years few anabaptists were executed and expulsion was more likely than imprisonment. They were strong (they

---

[10] *Christliche Unterrichtung; Sendbrief*, written from Augsburg before his arrest as an encyclical to the apostles sent out into Switzerland and the Rhineland and Austria; and two hymns. Best description of his work in Gottfried Seebass, *Müntzers Erbe. Werk, Leben und Theologie des Hans Hut* (Erlangen, 1972); summary in *TRE*, s.v. Hut (Gottfried Seebass).

[11] This was 1561; Clasen, *Anabaptists*, 418, from Mennonite Historical Library at Goshen, Indiana, a collection of documents on Alsace.

were few in number, strength was relative) in the state of Württemberg and there the evangelical reformer and leader of the religion of the country, Johannes Brenz, thought it wrong to persecute them with severity. Other evangelicals had no doubt that repression was right but doubted the death penalty. Wolfgang Capito and his Strasbourg colleagues thought that the execution of Michael Sattler, author of the Schleitheim Confession, and others was wrong. Capito was prepared to contend that the defect was more like an illness of the soul which should be treated, than like a crime which deserved to be punished. Some in Nuremberg thought expulsion right but doubted imprisonment. Despite the clarity of imperial law, there were lawyers doubtful whether the death penalty could be justified in equity. The Protestant Schmalkaldic League of German states passed a resolution of 1531 allowing its members to disregard the imperial law insisting on death.[12] But they allowed them to observe it if they wished.

If an anabaptist proved valuable in the labour market, the employer usually kept him for all that he was known to be an anabaptist. The outstanding example of this was the engineer Pilgram Marpeck, who had skills which were rare, and who was known to be an anabaptist leader, and whom the city of Augsburg continued to employ for twelve years as the manager of the water supply.[13] An anabaptist won the respect and affection of his noble employer. When the anabaptist died, the pastor said that he could not be buried in the cemetery. The nobleman threatened the pastor that if the anabaptist could not be buried in the cemetery he should be buried in the noble family tomb in the chancel of the church.[14]

Several governments used long terms of imprisonment, not for all anabaptists but for leaders—until they stopped being heretical which might be a very long time—or until the gaolers got tired and gave up hope of recantation. Prison was an unjust punishment by its inequalities in that some cells were sordid, damp dungeons likely to kill whereas others were dry and reasonably comfortable. Some prisoners could write letters or books, others were allowed no materials. Occasionally the authorities put prisoners on parole. Expulsion also varied as a penalty, from quiet removal after a time of grace for arranging the departure, to throwing across a border. At its worst it was accompanied by whipping. In 1570 the theological faculty at Wittenberg

[12] For Capito, cf. *Quellen zur Geschichte der Täufer*, vii (Leipzig, 1950) Elsass; ed. M. Krebs and H. G. Rott, 1. 80. For the League, *Die Schmalkaldischen Bundesabschiede 1530–1532*, ed. E. Fabian (Tübingen, 1958), 30.

[13] Born in the Tyrol, he rose to be secretary of the miners' union in the Inn valley, and rich. He turned passionate for the Reformation and was dismissed. Water engineer at Strasbourg for four years though he was known to lead an anabaptist group. Augsburg employed him 1544–56. Untrained, he wrote theology but the books were forgotten until the Mennonites rediscovered them in the twentieth century.

[14] Clasen, *Anabaptists*, 417.

formally denounced the whipping of anabaptists. Expulsion also varied in its penalty, from confiscation of all property, or less severely the permission for the family that remained to use the property, or less severely still a permission to sell up and take the money away. (This last was owed to the humanity of the landgrave Philip of Hesse.) But property was not plentiful among anabaptists.

This half-hearted or quarter-hearted leniency towards anabaptists has been seen as an unknowing but decisive step towards toleration. A thousand or more were killed (845 are known for certain) and many more were mal-treated. The groups survived; because they were pious and honest, because ordinary folk disliked the sight of cruel penalties to apparently harmless persons, because working people often sided with them, because the system of government was not tight enough to prevent many escaping the net of repression, and because their faith was often steady.

Meanwhile they divided. Often the splits were local or personal—part of the group thought the teacher's preaching in error, or had a higher standard of self-discipline than he, or wanted to leave for their lives when he was reso-lute that they should stay or were determined to stay when he thought they must move. The splits that most concern history raised basic arguments about the nature of their church polity.

The first and chief was the rightful place of the State. The second was the right way in which excommunication should be inflicted, in other words, when was it right to eject members from the community? The third was how the common property of the congregation should be administered and how spent. And the fourth was, what should happen if a world-rejecting body of people found themselves by political circumstance actually in control of a government?

The State

The most anxious question was tax. They needed a state, to keep open the roads and make life safe. They must not, so the majority thought, be officers of this state. If policemen and road-menders were needed, it must be moral to pay tax when it was demanded. But when the State raised taxes it gave no assurance on how the money should be spent. It might hire mercenaries, or buy guns. It might go to war.

Anabaptist leaders varied. The problem was less pressing because many were either so nomad or so poor that they were not likely to be pressed by tax-collectors or by clergymen for tithes. Most of them held that it was right to pay tax; that they must assume the government to have moral purposes in raising it. But if the government announced that this was a special tax to fight a war then it was a moral duty to refuse to pay. Not everyone was so consistent if the Turks invaded Germany. They were agreed that no one ought to join the army to fight the Turks and if there were conscription they must refuse to serve. But many held that in such a crisis it was proper to pray for the defence of the realm. When a town was besieged, not all anabaptist males could bear to refuse their help. They were willing to do services which did not need gun or pike or sword; and the inconsistent were ready to go further, they would even dress up as sentries on the walls and look as though they were martial though they were determined not to fire a gun.

The State exacted oaths from witnesses in the law courts. Nearly all of them refused oaths. In Hesse they did not mind swearing. A group in Esslingen even allowed that Christians could be magistrates. Pilgram Marpeck was not resolute to tell them that they could not be magistrates, he believed that they could sit provided that they refused to judge in cases which brought in capital punishment or religion. These concessions were rare. Most anabaptists held that it was as unthinkable to be a magistrate as it was impossible to be a policeman or a soldier.

Trained in Catholic theology by Johann Eck and later a doctor of divinity and a professor, Balthasar Hubmaier accepted the reforming doctrines and a parish at Waldshut in the deep south-west. There he realized that he did not believe in the baptism of babies and persuaded the entire town to accept an established church which was, in the modern sense, 'baptist', and where many of the people and most of the town council were (re-)baptized. He gave adult baptism its first systematic defence, *Of the Christian Baptism of Believers* (1525). The Peasants' War broke out and Waldshut joined the side of the peasants, with Hubmaier's full approval, for there was nothing wrong about using force in a cause believed to be godly.

The rout of the cause forced him to flee to Zurich where the Zurichers forced him to recant his anabaptist opinion. So he went off to Nikolsburg in Moravia, created and led the community there, with the same idea as in Waldshut—an established 'baptist' church of the town. He believed that the Christian like any other citizen had the duty to pay taxes for a war if required and do military service if the State needed. Vienna arrested him and the war record left him no chance (10 March 1528).

He had needed to defend these opinions against the Moravian anabaptists who rejected government. He wrote a tract, *Of the Sword* (*Von dem Schwert*) which was a commentary on the texts from the Bible used by the non-resisters, especially those in the Sermon on the Mount on 'resist not evil', 'turn the other cheek'. It is the traditional theory of politics, government was not needed in the Garden of Eden, it is the result of sin, but as such it is necessary and God-given and a good; and Christians are likely to make better kings and better magistrates than non-Christians because they are less likely to become tyrants and, if they need to punish, more likely to feel compassion for the punished. Put at its simplest: non-resisters would say that if a man is about to kill your neighbour and you can stop him only by killing, you may protest but may not use violence—on the contrary, 'the person who fails to stop a good person being killed when he could, is himself guilty of that murder'.[15]

The ban

The pure community was not always easy to keep pure. The earliest Christian Church expected to be a community of the saints and was soon in trouble about a system of penitence, whether or when Christians who had committed an act unworthy of a Christian should be excluded and under what conditions might they be readmitted. Anabaptist congregations had the same expectation of purity and reacted against the penitential system of the churches which seemed to readmit gross sinners on easy terms with the plea that true contrition will be acceptable with God. In general society excommunication carried social penalties, like the refusal of ordinary people to buy at that shop or employ that workman. But anabaptists were not in general society and if they excluded it would not be a public act. The only penalty was exclusion from their own common life—which might mean ejection from an encampment and so homelessness, and might mean loss of generous almsgiving in sickness or calamity. But mostly it meant a simple loss of place in the community.

Where the ban was inflicted, it carried with it the social penalty, the members must no longer have friendly or business relations with the sinners, must not even speak to them nor shake their hands. In a rural community this might not be hard; but even in remote places two members of a community might be working as labourers on the same farm and after a ban they could hardly avoid each other during their daily work. Many of them were craftsmen and that often brought them into the same workshop and then meetings with the banned member must of necessity be endured.

But suppose a wife was banned and the husband faithful? or vice versa? This made the sharp division of opinion. Is marriage so sacred that it crosses the rule that we must not associate with those whom the Church has put out— or, might there be cases where a ban forces also a divorce? One side accused the other of moral laxity, the other side accused the one of moral rigidity.

It came to a full-scale schism. Dutch and north German anabaptists were resolute that the Church must be kept pure. Everything must be done to try to bring a sinner to penitence; but if that was refused the social ban must be

---

[15] Hubmaier, *Von dem Schwert*, in *Schriften*, ed. G. Westin and T. Bergsten (Gütersloh, 1962), 451.

inflicted. One of the largest meetings of anabaptists ever, 600 members at Strasbourg in 1554, voted for charity and against rigidity and then tried to persuade the northerners that this was the right moral attitude. The best of the northerners, Menno Simons, was persuaded that his groups were right. By 1558–9 it was clear that the disagreement had made a breach between the two big groups of communities. But even in the south the Swiss did not finally agree to reject rigidity till 1571.

Community of goods

The anabaptists of the Puster valley in South Tyrol were so numerous and therefore so prominent to the authorities that their life became impossible. One of their leaders was Jacob Hutter, another Hans Amon. In 1529 Hutter heard that at Nikolsburg in Moravia it was possible for anabaptists to live in peace. Moravia was under-populated, with abandoned villages and houses, and under the rule of local lords who wanted immigrants with labour and skills. Nikolsburg was the place to which Hubmaier had fled and where he was now the head of a community, the most educated head of any anabaptist community. Hutter went over to Austerlitz to see the anabaptist community there and admired what he found. The group at Austerlitz did not like Hubmaier's views that it was possible to serve the State and so were separate from the community at Nikolsburg.

Four years later Hutter moved from the South Tyrol and settled in the anabaptist community at Auspitz in Moravia and was soon accepted as the leader there. An emigration was organized from the South Tyrol into Moravia—over the Brenner pass to Innsbruck, down the Inn by river boat to the Danube, down the Danube by river boat but leaving the river before Vienna, and then northward overland into Moravia. It was arranged with skill—which inns were reliable, which ferrymen, how it would be possible to avoid notice. Some 600 anabaptists moved from South Tyrol to Moravia by this route. Ways were found to pay the expenses. For a time it had something of the atmosphere of the later Mormon emigration to Utah—a promised land in a far country, to be won after a difficult journey, but where at the end there were fields to work and a living to make, and people of their own faith to dwell with and freedom from the contempt and persecution of the neighbours in their old land.

From other parts anabaptists heard of Moravia and sent travellers to see what it was like and whether the stories were true and then might decide to risk the journey.

Community of goods was not universal nor even common. The idea came from reading the Acts of the Apostles and finding that the apostles had all things in common. It might be expected that inheritance from the ideal of poverty and community of goods as practised by the monks would have descended into this new form of elite group, but there is no sign of influence from the monastic inheritance.

The intellectuals in Zurich talked about it. In various other groups it was discussed. Most decided that it did not mean an institutional communism, but generous care by the community for any member in need. As institution it was impossible to achieve in a structured way without stability. They were so often in hiding, so often suffering, and what happened was what would happen with any other Christian body in extreme conditions, they helped each other in desperate need. To practise communism of goods needed a certain permanence, which meant that they must not be persecuted rabidly.

Jacob Hutter was the person who organized the system of common goods in Moravia. But in 1536 he was caught on a visit to South Tyrol and his lieutenant Amon succeeded as leader. But because of his work they became known as Hutterites.

There began to be better sources for history. Peter Ryerdeman (Riedermann) was the third head of the Hutterite community. He was an evangelist and went into Hesse to convert and suffered prison for several months and during his enforced leisure wrote *An Account of our Religion* (*Rechenschafft unserer Religion, Leer und Glauben*, 1540). Unlike Hutter he died in his bed. With the exception of a refusal to baptize babies because they cannot have faith, there was nothing uniquely unorthodox in doctrine, for his teaching on the Lord's Supper is almost that of Zwingli. The differences from the other churches were in morals.

All goods are in common, that we may be free of created things. Property is a form of force and causes envy and hatred. Churches built of stone or wood were bad and were hated by God from the beginning. Priests make people obey them by using force—stocks and dungeons—we are not to receive priests into our houses. Proposed marriages must receive consent from the elders of the community. We are to obey a government even though it is godless, unless it commands what is wicked. It is right to pay the taxes which it demands but not if it orders a special tax for fighting a war. No Christian can hold a governing office. In manufactures no Christian can make spears or muskets or swords—we can make knifes and axes and hoes, which can kill, but that is not the purpose of making them. We are not to swear. On clothes there must be no embroidery, braiding. No adornment with jewels. Greeting is good but men and women should shake hands and not kiss. No one may be an innkeeper, though if he gives shelter to a tired traveller he must accept no money. No one may stand another a drink. Children are to be kept away from the state schools and sent only to our own schools. No one may be a trader or a merchant. To make a thing and sell it, that is honest. To buy something and sell it at a higher price, that is exploitation.

The Hutterites did not ask themselves how the things that are made are to reach the buyers who need them. They thought of trade in terms of taking to the village market the cow which one has grown, or the woodworker making a cupboard and carrying it to a local fair. Yet as far away as the celebrated book fair at Frankfurt the Hutterites could be found selling their wares. As Dutch Mennonites were to be famous merchants, so later Hutterites, craftsmen of quality, sold expensive goods to an upper class.

In Moravia the communities flourished, usually protected by a local lord. By 1546 there were thirty-one communities which contained about 5,000 people and practised common goods. They grew astonishingly, to about seventy communities with up to 20,000 Hutterites.

Not only property was in common. Everyone of both sexes must work though the women did more household work than the men who were in the fields or practised a trade. Children were at once in crèches. The ministry was authoritarian, a bishop at the head of the whole, under him some thirty-five 'servants of the Word' and the heads of each community.[16] The bishop was not elected by general vote but by the servants of the Word and representatives of the communities. Since the servants of the Word were chosen by other servants of the Word, government had an element of apostolic succession, choice of leaders by co-option and not by a people's vote. This was unlike the custom of anabaptists generally who gave supremacy to the congregation to accept or reject a leader.

The Hutterites printed material for their own use, sermons, catechisms, forms of service, books of devotion or instruction. Their metalwork was valued though they refused to make weapons. They had a scruple about working for clergymen. They preferred not to do it. When at the end of the century Cardinal von Dietrichstein became one of their profitable customers they devised a casuistical distinction, that they worked for him as a man and not as a bishop.

The Hutterite community was like a medieval monastery. The doctrine that all things were in common did not prevent the members keeping necessary properties for their private use. They drank wine at the main meal. The women sat to eat at a different table from the men. As in a medieval monastery, where the abbot or prior usually had better food and comforts than others, the leaders were allowed special privileges. The idea of equality was impracticable and was not absolute. They also found it useful, like the rest of Christendom, to distinguish their leaders, if not by 'clerical dress' then by a rather more formal costume. Probably most communities were about a hundred people in number including children. There was a large refectory also used for meetings and for worship, and attached to it a kitchen and larder

---

[16] Cf. H. Fast, in *TRE* xv. 5. 753.

and bakery. There were dormitories, communal for the unmarried, in vestigial cubicles for the married. Another building housed a place for washing and lavatories. There was a place for the medical attendant who was also the hairdresser (but all the men grew beards). These medical attendants became well known in their districts for their skill and by the end many Moravian noblemen used Hutterite physicians. Moravian families also sought for Hutterite women as midwives and nurses. One house at least had a printing press. The printers did not appear before the world as a printing firm, that would be risky. There was a ward for women in childbirth. And there was a schoolroom. In short except for the absence of a vast chapel and the provision for childbirth their buildings were very like those of a medieval monastery for they served much the same needs. The community lived by a timetable. Like monks or nuns they looked alike in dress except for those with an office of authority. The clothes were not a special religious habit but of the ordinary working men or women to be seen in the Tyrol or Bavaria. Anyone who appeared in an exceptional or middle-class costume was stopped. On Sundays ordinary members, though still in peasant costume, were expected to be tidy and decent. Holy communion was held only once in the year and then was a feast of the people as well as a sacrament.

Since the young people must marry within the community the choice for either sex was limited. Male or female was given a limited choice in the small selection of the other sex available but really the match was arranged not by the parents but by the servants of the Word. It was possible but not easy for the young to refuse what their elders arranged. If he or she continued to refuse after a few suggested arrangements it would probably mean leaving the community.

The Thirty Years War after 1620 destroyed the flourishing Protestantism of Bohemia and Moravia and forcible Catholic restoration drove out the Hutterite communities. They moved eastward into Slovakia but it was a bad time. One group moved to Siebenbürgen in the Carpathians and later under more persecution moved into the Ukraine. During this time they could not always practise common goods, though from time to time it was possible. When the Tsar's government introduced conscription for military service they emigrated to the United States. American and Canadian democracy was good for them; the small group of emigrants became some 32,000 Hutterites.

A kingdom by force

The majority of anabaptists were souls who thought force wrong—there had to be a government to prevent anarchy and murder and keep the roads in repair, but true Christians should have nothing to do with it because power always corrupts. For obvious reasons the only groups of anabaptists to survive into the twentieth century were of this conviction.

But a minority, not small, had another opinion. For these the kingdom of heaven must be brought to earth by force, that is, by destruction of the wicked.

This second opinion had more than one source.

The commonest was visionary apocalyptic. God brings in his kingdom, the time is ripe. He will use his elite to bring it. His servants must be men (and women) of the sword to destroy his enemies. God, not a body of godly warriors, will bring in the kingdom. But in the bringing the godly warriors are his agents and they are called to destroy the ungodly as his servants. Such looked to the apocalyptic in the Bible, Daniel in the Old Testament, the Book of Revelation in the New. The prophet Elijah's slaughter of the prophets of Baal became a model to be admired and imitated.

The next source was the heritage of the Peasants' War. Had they failed? Was the campaign still possible and if possible must it be right?

The next source was persecution. They were sure that their community was that with Christian truth. Yet for professing that truth they were liable to be burnt, or more usually imprisoned, or flogged, or expelled by the State. There was nowhere in the world where they could meet publicly to pray to God, except in a few estates as in Moravia, or a few towns as in north Germany but then they must not flaunt their presence. Since they had little hope of converting kings or emperors or bishops (though Müntzer had tried to convert the elector of Saxony), this taking of power must come from below, a rebellion of the people.

Such minds did not ask themselves the question, why, if power corrupts, is it safe for us to take it? The only success which they won almost destroyed the entire anabaptist movement. They took it for granted, like some old crusader, that this was so divine a mission that it could not be corrupt. Yet where it did not succeed, a group easily became a robber band, sacking churches because it is virtue to steal from the rich to help the starving and virtue to destroy a building dedicated to misleading the common people.

The name of one theorist became associated with the doctrine, *force is right, slay the ungodly*: Melchior Hoffmann. This belief, attributing wide influence to Hoffmann, was probably false.

A Swabian worker in the fur trade, he was one of the early lay preachers of the Reformation, who took to the heart the doctrine that all the Lord's people are priests. Such people were often wanderers, from the working class, had nothing to lose, were willing to take risks and were against society. They earned their living with their trade. They knew that to be a preacher of the gospel there was no need to be a trained theologian. They were able to express the fears and longings of the common man and woman in words which they were able to understand.

At first leading reformers welcomed such preachers as a sign that the common people were reaching out for God. But soon they realized the singularity and the wildness and fanaticism which went with the wandering untrained soap-box orator. Such speakers had only a chance in the years when no one knew quite what was going to happen, when the jurisdiction of the old Catholic courts was broken and the jurisdiction of the new Protestant courts was forming or not yet formed. As the Protestant states established their church disciplines—and they were more effective disciplines than the Catholic because that was the way of reform—the individualist, the lone evangelist, had to conform or go underground.

Though a south German Hoffmann must soon have moved north because he could speak Low German. The fur trade flourished in the Baltic and Hoffmann went to Latvia and Estonia. It was an unsettled time there, with mobs throwing statues and pictures out of churches, and the people regarded bishops and clergy and the Teutonic Order as foreign rulers who deprived them of their reformation.

Along the Baltic coast he was a wild preacher, at Dorpat he caused a street battle in which the mob sacked the bishop's palace and every church and monastery. Expelled, he went to Wittenberg to learn from Luther and Bugenhagen. Then he went back to the Baltic but was expelled again—and after wandering came to Kiel where for the only time in his life he was given a stable pastorate and a proper stipend. He was important enough to be one side of a public disputation with Bugenhagen in April 1529; his apocalyptic led him into fantasy which the evangelicals could not bear; expelled again, he found in East Frisia a people of anabaptist sympathies and was even able to baptize 200 of them in the sacristy of a parish church. Then he went up the Rhine to Strasbourg where he found two companies of anabaptists. It was now believed that he taught how virtue is not resignation by the elect; that we must prepare for judgement by destroying the godless; that he associated true faith with killing. From the sources it is hard to prove that this belief was correct. It is probable that he was blamed for events outside his control. He had a fanatical mind which expected extraordinary events. When extraordinary events happened he was blamed for causing them. The evidence now suggests that what happened was contrary to his faith which was quietist even though apocalyptic.

Münster

In the far south-west anabaptists with Hubmaier as their minister had succeeded in taking over the town of Waldshut; only to be repressed when they joined the Peasants' War. In central Germany they had succeeded under the leadership of Thomas Müntzer and Heinrich Pfeiffer in taking over the town

of Mühlhausen, only to be repressed when they joined the Peasants' War. But
Münster was a bigger place, well-armed and the centre of a wide region, possessing a college of higher education with a respected humanist tradition
that attracted scholars from elsewhere, an educated and prosperous merchant
class; a member of the Hanseatic League, just the kind of city which would
be expected to become evangelical, not the sort of community to be either
anabaptist or revolutionary. If it had remained Lutheran it would almost certainly have turned its college into a university during the sixteenth century.
Anabaptist success there was in part due to the environment of the north-
west, so near the Netherlands and East Frisia, with Protestants fleeing from
repression by the government in Brussels; in part due to the nominal head of
the State who was the bishop of Münster and whose rights the city had not
yet brought to nothing; and in part due to a single Lutheran minister who like
Hoffmann was a convert to the wrongness of baptizing infants, Bernhard
Rothmann. The anabaptist event made the university of Münster wait till the
later eighteenth century and be the last German university founded with the
historic licences from Emperor and Pope.

Rothmann was another university-trained anabaptist. Son of a smith, he
was sent to Deventer to the famous school of the Brethren. At first he went
into teaching but a canon paid for him to go to the university of Mainz and
in 1529, aged already about thirty-four, he was given a lowly clerical post as
chaplain to a collegiate foundation in his home town of Münster. No sooner
was he in a pulpit than the town discovered him to be a brilliant speaker and
everyone talked about him. The canons of the college were disturbed and
paid for him to receive more education at Cologne. After a year he was back
in Münster as an open foe of the established church and with a following
which included patricians and rich merchants, his centre being the church of
St Mauritz. He went on a tour of Protestant capitals—at Wittenberg he
made friends with Bugenhagen and Melanchthon and won Luther's respect;
at Strasbourg he lived with Wolfgang Capito and fell under his influence—
and then returned to Münster to fight for the reform of the town. In August
1531 the bishop of Münster inhibited him and won from the emperor a man-
date sending him into exile. But the bishop then died.

A committee of thirty-six was established to make the city fully Protestant.
The new bishop Franz von Waldeck declared this illegal and besieged the city
half-heartedly with mercenaries. In February 1533 a treaty was achieved
which gave the Protestants legal rights and Rothmann was their pastor. He
talked like Luther and at that moment was respected in the evangelical world
as the reformer of Münster.

In the Netherlands the persecution of anabaptists was tough. Refugees
fled to the nearest Protestant city, which was either Emden or Münster. The
immigrants into Münster had the triumph of converting Rothmann to the

belief that it is wrong to baptize babies. The council tried vainly to stop him preaching and then to exile him. At the elections of 23 February 1534 his party won the majority. Anabaptists had power not by a coup but through the constitution.

The result was a wave of earnest religious devotion, and 1,400 people received adult baptism. Suddenly the name of Münster was a magnet—a Sion, a place where the persecuted could come to be free and say their prayers in the way that God wished, a sanctuary for the oppressed, its gates open to the downtrodden of Holland and the Rhineland. As hundreds from South Tyrol had trekked to Moravia, now hundreds, probably even a few thousand, set out for Münster in search of a new Jerusalem. Most of them were stopped on the way.

The resulting calamity was partly caused by the bishop. Franz von Waldeck was not a stout Catholic, he had sympathy for Protestants. But the city was doing what so many other cities had done, Nuremberg and Basel and others, and what Geneva was about to do, prise itself away from all authority of its bishop. When Münster was Lutheran it could count on the formidable protection of nearby Philip of Hesse. Now that it was anabaptist it could count on no one. The faith of its leaders became more extreme. God had decided that this was Mount Sion and from it they would go out to conquer the world for the truth and his kingdom and destroy everything and everyone that was bad. They expelled anyone not willing to resist the bishop's ramshackle army.

In a state of siege the government must have absolute power over the inhabitants. One of the Dutch refugees Jan of Leyden seized the authority and defended the walls with courage and afterwards made himself king and a tyrant, and replaced the laws of the city with the laws of the Bible and instituted a reign of terror against the growing number of discontented and abolished money and instituted polygamy because there were so many more women than men in the town and himself took twenty-one wives. Bernhard Rothmann, who once won wide respect as a Lutheran reformer, accepted the office of chancellor under him and wrote a defence of anabaptist Münster which persuades no one.

A capable besieging force would never have allowed all this to go on for so long. Politically the besieged had no hope. They believed or pretended to believe that God would act as in the Old Testament he destroyed the army of Sennacherib without the besieged lifting a hand. But they must hope for other towns to be taken over by anabaptists. If Münster could be changed, it was possible in any city. A wild group twice tried to take over Amsterdam, another group planned to take Wesel, 300 men occupied the Old Cloister at Bolsward and lasted out a siege of eight days against heavy guns; there was talk of taking over Aachen.

Pathetic, misled, fanatic, causing ignorant men to go out and get killed, they were starving in Münster by April 1535 but the city did not fall till June. As Hitler believed that the Germans had been unworthy of him, Jan of Leyden believed that God refused to defend Münster because of the sins of its inhabitants.

The disaster almost destroyed anabaptists totally opposed to what went on in Münster. Even in Moravia, for a year or two, the lords made life very difficult for the peaceable groups there.

Menno Simons

He was converted to anabaptism in 1536 and as an ex-Catholic priest was educated and a year or two after the conversion was persuaded to lead a group as an elder. He began, though so slowly as to seem to be feeling his way, to baptize adults. Since perforce his movements were hidden, history finds it hard to follow his early course. He worked along the border between the Netherlands and East Frisia and in 1541 first appeared in a state document as a dangerous person, with the next year a price upon his head. The soul-predicament was sore. He was building a community and attracting literate people, three more Roman Catholic priests among them. But if he baptized an adult he made that person liable to death. Early in 1544 two whom he had baptized were executed at Amsterdam. He confessed that more than once he was tempted to give up. He asked for prayers that he might not be captured.

By now his wife had borne him several children, for whom a secret life was less possible. It was another part of the predicament when colleagues or disciples recanted. For him the worst was Obbe Philips, who had ordained him in Groningen to be an anabaptist minister. Philips recanted, said that what he had done was wrong, and that what Menno Simons did was wrong. Evidently Philips felt that their work was too near the ideas which led to the calamities at Münster and the Old Cloister. Another colleague David Joris thought that conformity was the way to defend their people against persecution—let anabaptists go to church, even have their babies christened. For Menno this was betrayal. Joris disappeared to Basel where he lived for years under an assumed name and was lost to the anabaptist cause. Then robber bands, relics of Münster's military ideas and now under Jan van Batenburg—kill the worldly, destroy churches, take the money of the rich to give to the poor—kept proving to the authorities that anabaptists were criminals and put into danger the non-violent like Menno Simons.

Menno next appeared at Emden in January 1544 for a public debate, in the church of the Franciscans, to which the eminent reformed theologian John a Lasco, the Pole who inherited Erasmus's books, invited him. Lasco knew enough of him to believe that this was a thinking and devout Christian mind and that if he could be persuaded to accept the baptism of children reconciliation was possible. It was Menno's first chance of legal utterance in public since he ceased to be a Catholic—and almost his last chance. The debate proved that Lasco had judged wrongly, that they were too far apart, both sides came away discouraged. Menno was soon exiled from Emden and moved south, into the archbishopric of Cologne where there were already lively anabaptist congregations.

But the debate with Lasco elevated his status among the members in north Germany. Such debates had happened before in the south under safe-conducts, especially in Berne and Basel. None had happened in the north, that an anabaptist could stand up to a famous Protestant leader. Lasco's act elevated Menno to be a representative leader of his people. Probably in the late 1540s he was at his most influential.

From 1550 he was moving along the towns on the Baltic coast. In June 1555 Martin Micronius wrote from Emden to Bullinger in Zurich to say that the influence of Menno reached all along the German coasts from the frontier of the Netherlands to Danzig (Gdansk). That year a nobleman in Schleswig-Holstein gave him the first secure shelter, on the estate Wüstenfelde, where he lived for the last six years of his life. They were sad years; he was miserable over the schisms, which were made worse ultimately by his conviction that he must accept the more rigid interpretation of the ban.

Menno can be said to have saved the anabaptism of north-west Germany and the Netherlands. If these groups were to continue despite the extermination from governments who believed them to be violent revolutionaries, they must free themselves from the record of Münster, or the Old Cloister, or the robber bands of Jan van Batenburg. They had to be known as men and women of quiet peace and faith who wanted to live in a community of true Christians and could not think it right to christen children. After the Dutch revolt against the Spanish government in Brussels, and the making of Holland and Zeeland into a separate and Protestant state, the government of the Netherlands was not yet tolerant; but its fight against Spain had made it less hostile to the idea, and since it depended for its survival on trade and good craftsmanship, its citizens were hardly prepared to be hostile to good craftsmen wherever they came from, so long as they were not bizarre.

Menno had lived in secret but he had printed what he wanted to say, eighteen and more books under dangerous conditions, sane books, devotional, orthodox in their substance. Unlike some of his colleagues he confessed that it was possible for a government to be a Christian government even if that is very unlikely because of the corruption of power; and therefore he would not compel his members to refuse to be magistrates or force them to resign their office if confronted with a case which involved blood. He even allowed that government, non-Christian government, could have a spiritual work, to try to see that the Land was obedient to God's Word. In earlier years he accepted that capital punishment was allowable for murder and adultery and robbery, but in later years he thought all use of the sword to be wrong and that though government must penalize crime it must not shed blood.

His government of the churches was oligarchic (or apostolic). Elders chose elders. All authority lay with the elders, the congregation had no democratic power. That did not stop schisms, which were elders versus elders, but it was a constitution for survival through a bad time.

The name Mennonite by which we know his later successors was not known for a long time. They were known as Doopsgezinde, literally meaning 'persons in favour of baptism'.

17

TOLERATION

It was an axiom accepted by everyone but anabaptists that a state cannot exist safely unless it contains only one religion—with the large exception that many states allowed hedged communities of Jews.

A second axiom at first accepted by everyone but anabaptists believed that heretics who refused to recant should rightly be repressed. This axiom left two awkward doubts—when is a variant opinion so harmless that it does not matter to Church or State? and what kind of repression is right? Was the object of repression to keep the moral and religious life of the society pure? in which case it was enough to banish the deviant from the society. Or was it like most penalties in the penal system, aiming also to frighten other persons from following the deviant's example? in which case capital punishment, or worse, might be held to be justified.

The argument was affected by three pleas:

1. At present too many doctrines are regarded as of the essence of faith. Make them fewer. This was Erasmus's point of view. The beliefs necessary to true faith are far less numerous than professors at Paris say. If so, penalties for heresy must be inflicted more rarely. But he did not doubt that there were a few religious opinions, at least, for which an obstinate professor of them deserved to be burnt. Yet the argument cast a little shadow over all burning of heretics.

2. Luther was tougher. The bull which excommunicated his opinions selected as one of them this: 'It is against God's will to burn heretics.' He held, in those early days, that since heresy concerns spiritual opinions, only pastors can cope with it and their only weapon is the Word of God—no one should be beheaded or burnt or drowned for heresy.[1] 'The State must stop none teaching or believing what they wish, whether it is gospel truth or false.'[2] Luther accepted the interpretation of the parable of the tares that wrong beliefs and true beliefs exist together until the last harvest and we must not try to eradicate the tares by force.

---

[1] *WA* xi. 268, *Von Weltlicher Oberkeit*, 1523.
[2] *Ermahnung zum Frieden auf die zwölf Artikel der Bauernschaft in Schwaben*, April 1525, *WA* xviii. 299.

It looked as though he had already arrived at what a later age was to call a theory of toleration. But perhaps from the Peasants' War, at least from three years later, he accepted that the heads of states have moral as well as physical duties to their subjects; so that (at least on principle) he would not think modern states unjustified if they legislated to stop the broadcasting of racialist opinions among their people. Hence the sovereign has a duty to see that the preaching is biblical and to silence preachers who teach untruth; to make sure that truth is taught in schools; and to try to make sure that the people hear this truth.

3. Spalatin wanted to stop the canons of his parish at Altenburg from saying mass. He appealed to the elector John of Saxony. The canons said that the State had no right to interfere with religious worship. Spalatin asked Luther for advice. Luther replied with an answer which limited his idea of freedom. Anyone is free to believe what they like. But the State can repress blasphemy and if the mass is that the State may stop it being celebrated.[3] But then he wrote to the elector a letter which put the argument over toleration almost back to the beginning. Preachers preaching different doctrines in one place make for riots and factions. The State should prevent that.

That was not quite back to the beginning because it allowed the possibility that in Munich there should be mass and in Nuremberg the reformed service. And none of the Lutherans suggested that the canons be burnt.

The State did not do what Spalatin and he wanted. The canons of Altenburg kept their mass.

It took civil war in Germany to make this settlement possible in the Reich. By the treaty of Augsburg in 1555 Catholics recognized the legality of Lutherans in Lutheran Lands, and Lutherans recognized the legality of Catholics in Catholic Lands. But each side could expel dissenters. This solution depended upon the federal constitution of the Reich. It meant that no Lutheran, though in Catholic eyes a heretic, could be executed in Catholic Lands and no Catholic maltreated, except by expulsion, in Lutheran Lands.

This half-toleration was not thought to apply to the Reformed states— of which in 1555 there were, officially, none outside Switzerland. But six years after the 1555 treaty the elector Palatine Frederick agreed with many of his people that the Swiss Reformed and not the Lutherans taught truth and the Palatinate became officially a Reformed state. The elector just, but only just, saved its legal right to toleration on the plea that they could accept the Augsburg Confession in Melanchthon's more ecumenical version (the Variata).

---

[3] Luther to Spalatin, 11 November 1525, *BW* iii. 616–17.

In the French Wars of Religion each side aimed to make a wholly Catholic or a wholly Protestant France. So late as 1585 the French King Henry III declared absurdly that Huguenots must convert to the Catholic faith or leave the country. That was an improvement on the burnings earlier in the century but it was far from any idea of toleration.

As the French wars dragged, as peace after peace failed, the weary on both sides reached a practical conclusion. Though it is ideal that in a state there shall only be one religion, if the effort to achieve that ideal destroys the State, we must find a way to allow both religions to exist. This acceptance was not frequent. A majority still believed that a state with more than one religion cannot stand.

The year 1555 was a turning point for other reasons than the treaty in Germany. The burning of Archbishop Cranmer of Canterbury, and of such respected minds as Ridley and Latimer, was a universal shock, not only in England. At that time the French government multiplied its executions of Protestant heretics. But the epoch came when a revered Protestant government astonished many by the same act, of burning a celebrated heretic.

Nothing happened to the *theory* of toleration until Miguel Servetus was executed at Geneva on 27 October 1555.

He was an extraordinary person, unattractive, arrogant, and difficult but an original always trying to say what no one else had thought of. A Spaniard by origin, he developed his uniqueness by knowing something of the thinking among the Jews and Arabs of Spain. Almost all his short melodramatic life, probably of only forty-two years, he lived in France as a practising Catholic. In 1531–2, aged only about twenty or twenty-one, he published two imma-ture books on the doctrine of the Trinity, to the effect that the way the Church used it cannot be proved out of Scripture.[4] This did not endear the unknown author to the authorities of France or Germany. But under a dif-ferent name, Michel de Villaneuve (his Spanish birthplace was Villanueva) he behaved as a devout Catholic while he enquired into astrology and geog-raphy and surgery. Then he turned his mind to writing a riper book on his old subject, the Trinity.

He had no desire to deny that Christ is the revelation of God and shares in the divine nature. With his early knowledge of Jewish and Islamic thought, and now with an interest in Platonism, he believed that the language of the Trinity was an obstacle to understanding between the great religions. Therefore all the main churches were wrong, Rome or Wittenberg or Geneva. He was sure that the world would come to accept his restatement of religious truth. As he wrote the book he tried out the ideas by letter on the

---

[4] *De Trinitatis erroribus* (1531); *Dialogi de Trinitate* (1532).

leading French-speaking theologian, John Calvin. He offered to go to Geneva for debate. Calvin thought his ideas lamentable and declined to invite him.

Early in 1553 he printed at Vienne his new book, *The Restoration of True Christianity* (Christianismi Restitutio). The Vienne Inquisition heard that he was the author and examined him. He denied that he wrote it. Geneva, and Calvin personally, provided the evidence that he was the author; perhaps a unique instance of Protestants providing materials to the Inquisition for a prosecution. The Inquisition arrested him.

They may have preferred to avoid a troublesome process because he escaped easily from their gaol and vanished on 7 April 1553. He seems to have thought of going to Italy but on the way made a detour by Geneva. He went to Mary Magdalene's Church on Sunday when Calvin was preaching. A member of the congregation recognized him and he was arrested.

He probably took this risk on purpose. He knew that Calvin was far the most influential thinker in the French-speaking Protestant world. He had the wild illusion that because his theology was so well based, a reasonable Calvin would be persuaded and so he could change the churches for the better; and that if Calvin was blind enough to reject what was so manifestly true, he Servetus would be backed by the many opponents of Calvin whom he knew to exist in Geneva and he might lead the resistance.

It took the council of Geneva two and a half months, from 13 August 1553 to 26 October, to decide to burn him (*nem. con.* on the final vote).

His heresies, if members of the council understood him, which mostly they did not, were multiple: since Christ was divine he was not a real human being—the idea of original sin is false (therefore the doctrine of predestination is false)—though he did not deny the Trinity, it was false as the churches taught it and so the Council of Nicaea (325) was demonic—children ought not to be baptized, the right age for baptism is thirty years. He claimed the backing of two early Christian Fathers, Irenaeus and Tertullian, and twisted to his own theories what they thought. In addition other ideas floated round his mind, Neoplatonic, Judaic, and personal. Heresy-hunters had an easy time, such a miscellany of notions they could find preposterous or woolly. But—did he do any harm? Would anyone else be influenced by these complex theses couched in long words? Did it matter? Anabaptists were illegal but he was not an anabaptist, he practised as a Catholic, his offence was saying that they were right though he did not do what they did.

The council at Geneva were confused by these subtleties and were not all sure that they understood the argument. Servetus defended himself intelligently though unwisely. He argued that this interference of a state in doctrine was improper; that he had done nothing whatever to hurt the State of Geneva, that he had engaged solely in matters for discussion among the learned, and that a gospel minister (Calvin) had no business to be acting as a

prosecutor in a state court. He made the mistake of adding to these arguments violent personal attacks from the dock upon Calvin, one of the three
worst attacks which Calvin ever experienced.

It was not true that he had not hurt the State of Geneva. By coming into
the town he confronted them with the presence of a notorious heretic, and if
the State did nothing its reputation abroad would suffer, and its reputation
affected its political safety, exposed on a salient towards France.

The council were sure that it mattered. He must be silenced. The question
was whether it was enough to silence him by expulsion, or whether his
mouth must be shut for ever. They realized that opinion outside, especially
in their ally Zurich, would think expulsion a weak penalty. It would also give
their Catholic neighbours the weapon of propaganda, these Protestants care
little for Christian truth.

The council were bothered enough to consult other Swiss churches—
Zurich, Schaffhausen,[5] Basel, Berne; two letters to each, one to the council and
one to the ministers, with appended documents—Servetus's books, Calvin's
extracts of heresies, refutation of Servetus by Genevan ministers and Servetus's
refutation of the refutation, and the works of Irenaeus and Tertullian.

None of the four towns would pronounce on *how* Geneva should treat the
heretic. Zurich had no doubt that he must be suppressed, 'to clear the reputation of the Swiss churches'. Basel said that if he persisted he must be
stopped by force (*coerceatur*). Berne, which disliked Calvin, said that it prayed
the Genevan magistrates might act with wisdom and courage, and save the
churches from this pest, and do nothing unworthy of a Christian magistrate.[6]
None of the four towns asked for a death sentence. These consultations did
not help the Geneva council out of its predicament. But private letters from
ministers or individuals showed them that such private opinion in those
towns as was articulate believed the death penalty to be right.

Calvin wanted a straight execution—the wish does not appear in the
council minutes but his personal evidence cannot be doubted. The council
decided on the traditional penalty of the stake. And so Servetus died on the
hill of Champel with his book tied to him, and instantly became, among a
handful of the compassionate, a martyr for the right to enquire into the truth
even at the risk of being wrong.

The first sign that a different world was in the distance came because
Calvin needed defending from blame for what he had helped to do. He

[5] Schaffhausen, the only Swiss canton north of the Rhine, had grown round the famous
Benedictine abbey of All Saints and allied itself with the Swiss to resist the power of the neighbouring Austrians. It accepted the Reformation in 1524 when it turned the abbey into a college of
secular canons; and five years later secularized it altogether; but the weight of its council was light
compared with those of the other three towns which Geneva consulted. In its answer to Geneva it
copied what Zurich thought.

[6] These letters of the four towns are printed in Calvin, CR xiv. 808–23.

became aware of a tide of feeling which blamed him. Bullinger, not being in Geneva, was still more aware of it and wrote, less wisely than was usual in him, urging Calvin to publish a defence of what had happened. A true question had been raised—not so much, whether the State may repress immoral teaching as in modern times racialism, which no one denied, but whether in its repression of public teachings not recanted, the State may kill. A fortnight after Servetus's death, on 11 December 1553, Calvin asked the Geneva council for leave to write and publish a book on the case, and was given the permission which he sought.[7]

The book was quickly written for it was already out in February 1554, printed by Robert Estienne. In its expressions but not in its underlying thought it was probably the least clear-headed book by this so clear-headed author. Bullinger complained to Calvin that it was difficult to read. It had a long title: *A Defence of the Orthodox Faith on the Holy Trinity, against the Prodigious Errors of the Spaniard Michael Servetus, in which it is shown how Heretics are Rightly Subject to Capital Punishment . . .*; a book normally known by its first three words, *Defensio Orthodoxae Fidei*. The argument may be summarized thus:

There are many offences not capital—there may be exile, or excommunication; there must be efforts to recall the culprit to a right mind. But to defend the glory of God we may need to put aside compassion—as a shepherd defending sheep cannot feel compassion for wolves.

Objection 1. The papists kill heretics. If we kill we cannot blame them. Answer: They kill for the sake of untruth; and they use torture which is cruelty. If papists abuse the capital penalty, that does not stop its use in right circumstances.

Objection 2. No one can be compelled to faith. It is a gift of God. Answer: Of course. Governments cannot reach into people's minds. But they have a vocation to stop venomous mouths.

Objection 3. Christ is compassion—resist not evil, turn the other cheek, let the tares grow with the wheat till the harvest, St Peter's sword in Gethsemane, etc. Answer: Yes; the people who need this compassion are the ordinary people. Compare the cleansing of the Temple.

It was the appearance of this book in defence of the death, more than the death itself, which caused the wider debate on the use of capital punishment for heresy.

Some readers of the book felt doubt or even repulsion. In Basel voices were heard as if Calvin, minister of religion, had made himself an executioner. This was the first effect of the book, to draw the blame, among those

[7] Calvin, CR xiv. 832.

who blamed, away from the Geneva council to the individual chief pastor at Geneva. Viret reported from Lausanne that there was much doubt there about what Geneva had done. The pastor at Worms said that though he backed Calvin many of his people were against him. From Montbéliard Toussaint, a respected leader among the Reformed pastors, was against what had happened and allowed his deacon even to preach against it. In Marburg Hyperius expressed surprise at the execution[8]—but Hyperius was a Lutheran and Lutherans were apt to think the Reformed mistaken.

Basel was the place where the opposition to Calvin mounted. The memory of Erasmus perhaps; the town with the only university in Switzerland; the presence of several scholars who had fled from Italy and remembered their own mortal danger; and the killing of an anabaptist old lady—as the execution of an anabaptist in the Netherlands started the conversion of Menno Simons on the path from Catholic priest to founder of a Protestant denomination, so the execution by drowning of two anabaptists in Basel, one a woman of eighty and her daughter the mother of six children, provoked one of its leading laymen to compassion about the penalty of death for religious error. As he watched their death he could not conceive either why they suffered this death only because they would not allow the baptism of babies, or what conceivable fear there could be that these two poor women could corrupt the human race with their error.[9]

Nicholas Zurkinden was an official in the Berne civil service, a very religious person and a bureaucrat of quality who, seven years later, rose to be secretary of state, the head of the canton administration. Calvin sent him a copy of his book defending the death penalty for heresy. In acknowledging it Zurkinden wrote the most famous of Reformation letters.[10]

It may be my lack of experience or my timidity, but I want to keep to a minimum the use of capital punishment for persons who attack our faith. Sometimes they go wrong out of ignorance, sometimes deliberately . . . I prefer magistrates to commit the sin of being too lenient than to use the death sentence rigidly. Accused people can sometimes be led, not dragged off . . . I would rather spill my own blood than be spattered by the blood of an accused who did not deserve to die . . . We cannot give papists more pleasure than by reinventing their office of executioner. I write what you will much dislike. I put it in a private letter because I want to be frank with you. I prefer to keep my mouth shut as long as my conscience allows, rather than cause quarrels and offence . . . PS. I should have preferred the first part of your book, on executions, to have appeared under the name of the Geneva Council and not under your own name, the Council can defend itself. I don't see that in being a leader in

[8] Gratarolus to Bullinger, Basel, 24 December 1554, CR xv. 354; Waydner to Calvin from Worms, CR xv. 534; Calvin to Toussaint, 15 October 1554, CR xv. 270.
[9] Zurkinden described the origin of these feelings in a later (1556) letter to Calvin, CR xv. 20.
[10] Zurkinden to Calvin, 10 February 1554, CR xv. 19–22.

defending this thesis, which almost everyone hates so far as I can hear, you can win any backing from sober-minded people.

In this letter, commonly regarded as the first great letter on toleration, the author did not deny that there may be some heretics (though far fewer than at present) who might rightly be put to death. And he dared not speak his opinion too publicly. He would tell Calvin privately—yet on a subject where he felt very strongly he would not jeopardize his place in a civil service by doubting a law which was so widely acceptable. The axiom in the general mind, heretics are a terrible blot on the State, could hardly be recognized more emotionally. This fine letter showed how far there was to go before anything like an idea of toleration became public property.

Calvin's reply is lost, but Zurkinden confirmed his opinion in a second letter, not so famous but almost as dramatic:

The evidence of the ancient world proves that you do not get rid of these blots by blood. Killing only makes the opinions spread. But I don't include Servetus, or blasphemers.[11]

Calvin could at least be satisfied that the leaders of opinion approved of him. The only other mind in Switzerland with a European stature, Bullinger, stood wholly on his side. So Farel who tried vainly to minister to Servetus at the stake, and Viret at Lausanne and Haller at Berne. Apart from Hyperius the leading Lutherans thought that he was right. In May 1554 Hyperius met Melanchthon at the colloquy at Naumburg and was lent Calvin's book and when he gave it back was told by Melanchthon, to Hyperius's surprise, that Melanchthon, famous for his gentleness, was on Calvin's side. That October Melanchthon wrote to Calvin to say so—'The Church, and posterity, owe you a debt. Your magistrates did right to try this blasphemer in a regular court and sentence him to death.'[12]

Meanwhile in Basel pamphlets against Calvin appeared. In April 1554 came a reply to Calvin's book: *Ought Heretics to be Prosecuted?* (De haereticis an sint persequendi). For the first time a serious debate on toleration was joined.

The question may be asked why the Basel censorship allowed the printing of such a book against Calvin, and on a subject where even Zurkinden had not dared to speak his mind publicly. Apart from the academic mood of the town, there was its professor of Old Testament in the university: Martin Borrhaus. For a leading teacher in a Reformed faculty he had an unusual background. A friend of the undergraduate Melanchthon when he was an

---

[11] CR xv. 115–16.
[12] Melanchthon to Calvin, 14 October 1554, CR viii. 362; Hyperius to Bullinger from Marburg, 18 September 1554, CR xv. 234.

undergraduate, then a pupil of Reuchlin in Hebrew, then a pupil of Luther at Wittenberg, he lost respectability in Wittenberg by joining the extreme advocates of change and became a wanderer, for a time was imprisoned in Prussia. He was not an anabaptist but thought that they were right about infant baptism and had several anabaptist friends. He found refuge for a time in Strasbourg but that became uncomfortable and he went to Basel in 1536 and made his living in the manufacture of windows and in chemistry. Meanwhile he published academic books which led to a chair of rhetoric at the university and in 1544 the chair of Old Testament studies. Here was an influential person near the heart of the censorship who from his past could hardly be unsympathetic to a debate on toleration.[13]

The book passed the censors; and so Castellio stepped forward as the boldest critic of Calvin's standpoint.

Castellio

Born in the Jura by the name Sebastien Chatillon, son of a barely literate peasant, he went to Lyons to study and there was converted to the reformed faith. There is no reliable evidence how, but he was a member of the local group of humanists and took the name Castellio which a friend gave him in jest. During his undergraduate years he read the second edition of Calvin's *Institutes of the Christian Religion*, the logic and system of reformed religion, its base and structure and aims. It persuaded him. He left for Strasbourg to find Calvin. Welcomed into Calvin's house he soon had to make way for Calvin's new wife and the children by her first husband. He became a member of the French congregation to which Calvin ministered and learnt to know and love metrical psalms. Within a few months Calvin was summoned back to Geneva where after a time Calvin needed a headmaster of the school and invited Castellio for the work. For the school he published his *Sacred Dialogues*, destined for such success in teaching the young both Latin and the Bible.

The biblical work persuaded Calvin that he was not a reliable expounder of the Bible. Castellio thought the Song of Songs a book of sexual passion and not an allegory, and differed with Calvin on the meaning of the clause in the Creed, 'he descended into hell'. Finally he damned himself by contrasting the Genevan pastors with St Paul—Paul was humble they were proud, Paul was sober and they out for their stomachs, Paul was imprisoned and they imprison, etc. It was inevitable that he lost his post.

---

[13] The works were varied. At Strasbourg *De operibus Dei* and a commentary on Hosea which offended Bucer; otherwise, a commentary on Aristotle's book on speech; a textbook on astronomy and geography; a study of jubilee celebrations; and *De censura veri et falsi* (this last, Basel, 1541).

Not expelled, he could find no work so he left for Basel and became a proofreader at the printing works of Oporin who was publishing a famous series of classical texts. On the side he taught Greek to undergraduates. In 1553 the university at last gave him a post worthy of his ability by making him reader in Greek.[14] That was generous because he was known as an enemy of Calvin. Erasmus's friend Amerbach made him tutor to his son.

In March 1554 he published the epoch-making little book on the persecution of heretics. It posed as published at Magdeburg, the Lyons edition in French posed as published at Rouen. Its author was called Martin Bellius. (For a time the doctrine that heretics should be tolerated was called Bellianism.) And its preface disturbed the readers. Suppose there were a prince who went out to visit his subjects and ordered them all to wear white clothes to receive him. But when he arrived he found them all in debate, on whence he would come, and how he would travel, and whether he would have a numerous escort or not; and their debate rose to such anger that they started knocking each other as liars and killing. And he found that some of the violent claimed that they killed by order of the prince.

And is not this what has happened? Christ said he would come again and we are to greet him in purity; and what we find in the world are disputes and sin; and these disputes are on every sort of question about Christ. There is no sect which does not condemn all the others—hence prisons, pyres, scaffolds.

Let us define what a heretic is; and once we have defined that let us ask how we ought to treat such a being? We cannot judge what a heretic is by common opinion for the crowd is moved only by prejudice and wants to put anyone to death who is called 'heretic' without even knowing what it is of which that person is accused. We should never forget that Christ and his disciples were killed because they were 'heretics'. And yet if we then research into the question 'What is a heretic?', I cannot reach any other conclusion but this, a heretic is someone who does not agree with us. For all sects think other sects to be heretical; and if you change your dwelling-place from one state to another you have to change your religion just as you have to change your money.

There are two kinds of people in revolt against the Church: rebels against its doctrines, and rebels against its moral rules. We only give the name heretic to the first kind. And persecution is the proof that we are still in ignorance about truth. We are all agreed that there is one God, it is clear to everyone. If we were as clear about everything else we would not persecute because we should all agree.

---

[14] At Basel he published Latin (1551) and French (1553) translations of the Bible. In the Latin Bible he admitted the Apocrypha to the same rank as the Old Testament.

We do not exterminate Turks or Jews. Why should we exterminate mistaken Christians? The more truth we know, the less we are likely to condemn others. Anyone who cannot bear an opinion which disagrees knows nothing still. If someone wants to be a Christian and sees Christians killing each other will that person not regard Christ as a sort of Moloch, a Baal who wants human lives burnt on its altar?

Castellio ended his preface with a famous apostrophe:

O Christ, creator and king of the world, dost thou see all this? art thou changed from what thou wert, to be cruel? When thou didst walk upon the earth, no one was more gentle and full of compassion. Scourged and mocked and crucified, thou didst pray for thine oppressors. Art thou now changed? I appeal to thee, by thy Father's name, hast thou commanded all these drownings and roastings and beheadings and tortures? The people who order these are they really thy servants? Dost thou eat human flesh? If thou dost, what hast thou left for the devil to do?

His axioms were two. First, the only power of the Church is to excommunicate the impious. Second, the State ought to punish no one unless they trouble public order in the republic. This position looks very strong to a modern. It was problematical in that generation. For to excommunicate someone was then to make the crowd shun the banned and so affect social order. And if someone advocated opinions which the crowd thought scandalous he or she could trouble public order in the republic. The line between the heretic like Schwenckfeld who was quiet and the heretic like Hubmaier who advocated force was very clear to the later analyst but was blurred in that society of the middle sixteenth century.

The remainder of the book was a series of Protestant authorities, more than slightly selected: the early Luther; Johannes Brenz, himself persecuted by Catholics after the Augsburg Interim; Erasmus (very selected); Urbanus Rhegius; Conrad Pellican of Zurich; and others less eminent. Two of these less eminent authorities appear to have been Castellio himself under an assumed name.

Though a short book it was one of the seminal books of the Reformation; not always in a non-Christian world, for in the 1980s a Muslim state issued a death penalty against a British subject for blasphemy, and in 1992 the advanced state of Pakistan passed a law making blasphemy a capital offence. In weighing the argument of the middle sixteenth century over toleration we need to remember such signs of deep feeling still about what were thought to be attacks upon religion.

Two publications continued the debate. Neither made much difference.

First, Castellio wrote an anonymous book *Against Calvin's Little Book* (*Contra libellum Calvini*). This was even more potent than his book by Bellius, and much more personal against Calvin—that he was guilty of a bloody execution—if he kills people who disagree with him he has no chance of teaching them better—and so on. The book did not affect the argument because the Basel censors refused to sanction it and it remained unknown till a Netherlands scholar printed it fifty-eight years later at Amsterdam. Then there was argument whether Castellio could have written it and whether it was not a Dutch fabrication suited to a much later situation. This argument was settled when the original manuscript was found at Basel.

Secondly, Calvin's young assistant Theodore Beza rallied to his defence, that September 1554, with the first 'theological' work that he ever wrote, *On the Punishment of Heresy by the State* (*De haereticis a civili magistratu puniendis*). There was nothing different here from what Calvin had argued. Beza's was easier to read. He made an admission which Calvin had not made: that the opinion—*though exile may be right capital punishment is wrong*—was held by many wise persons and therefore is not a wild view. But he regarded this as care for the wolves and neglect of the sheep.

Castellio was not dismissed from his post at the university of Basel though it was hard for the Genevans to understand why, for his name was disreputable among them and in Zurich. He continued to teach Greek. Zurkinden tried to get him into the professorship of Greek but the opposition from Zurich was too strong. He needed to live a quiet life but that was what he preferred. A few minds in France or Germany thought that he must be taken seriously. Four years later he received an astonishing line of support. A volume of Melanchthon's letters was published. Among them was a letter from Melanchthon to Castellio dated 1 November 1557,[15] a letter which quite disturbed Geneva: 'When I think of your writings I must be your friend though I do not know you personally . . . I should like a lasting friendship between us . . . Let us bear with wisdom a situation which we cannot change . . . If I live long enough I would wish to converse with you personally about many things.' No letter could do more to free Castellio from his disreputable image.

Acontius

This name was the humanist version of the Italian Giacomo Conzio, who came from Milan where he became an expert in the art of fortification. Early in 1557 he was no longer safe because of his opinions and like so many other north Italians crossed the borders into Switzerland. He took with him a work *On Method*, that is on the right way of investigating and handing on the sciences; and printed it at Basel where he must have met Castellio. At this time his doctrine was that of the Swiss Reformed Churches. In Zurich and

[15] CR ix. 359; cf. CR xvii. 133.

Strasbourg he met English refugees from Queen Mary, so Queen Elizabeth of England hired him as a military engineer and he fortified the Scottish border at Berwick-upon-Tweed and dyked the marshes near the mouth of the Thames. He was soon in trouble for defending a member of the London Flemish congregation who wanted to shelter anabaptist refugees from the Netherlands. In 1564 he went back to Basel to publish his main work, *The Stratagems of Satan* (*Stratagemata Satanae*), which he dedicated to Queen Elizabeth. He died soon after, when and where are not known.

The *Stratagems* are another plea for toleration. Despite the similarity it is more probable that Castellio and Acontius thought independently on the same lines than that Acontius derived his opinion from Castellio. Truth is bound to prevail. Therefore a 'freedom of religious opinion', *libertas opinionum de religione*, is not a danger. We have to try to extirpate the spirit of intolerance from the heart of the Church. He was very biblical, but he had a horror for the discipline, and for public penitence and the system of excommunication, and narrow-drawn articles of faith as tests of orthodoxy. If someone teaches an opinion which touches the essence of truth and after wise consideration this is found to be destructive, then the Church must say so—but without hate or anger or bitterness or social penalty. The magistrate should have nothing to do with it.

More than those of Castellio the opinions of Acontius remained isolated. Yet the *Stratagemata* had three editions in 1565 and was placed on the Index of Prohibited Books; twelve more editions before 1664, mainly translations into English, Dutch, French, and German.[16]

Castellio, and Acontius, and the Basel laypeople, and anabaptist denial of state authority in religion, amounted to little enough in the movement of European opinion. Whatever they taught, and it was much that they were able to teach it, Basel continued to think it right to repress heretics. Castellio and Acontius were more read during the seventeenth century than the sixteenth. So something at least began to happen to opinion.

A Christian posterity argued that freedom of opinion in religion unless the opinion created riot, in which case the holder was punished for causing riot not for holding an opinion, was the essence of the Reformation—that is, it was the summit of human intellectual advance towards which the Protest led logically and inevitably. When the French bishop Bossuet wrote his *History of the Variations of the Protestant Churches* (1688) he cried as a term of abuse that the opinion of Castellio was, as it were, 'the bowels of Protestantism'. And from this doctrine appeared the further historical doctrine, that Luther was the real originator of religious liberty in the world. He turned religion, it was argued, from a corporate act, where all conformed, into a private state of the

---

[16] Modern editions by G. Radetti (Florence, 1946) and G. Koehler (Munich, 1927).

faithful soul before its Maker; and after Luther, with his powerful insistence on the rights of the individual conscience, the ultimate in being a Christian was not to be a member of a body in the world but to meet God in faith as a deeply personal and individual act; and 'from this act of faith modern liberty was born'.

This opinion, that the Protest inevitably led to modern toleration, has been far from universal. This much only is certain: the Protest divided Europe in religion and a divided Europe was forced to tolerate or destroy itself.

Toleration of the Jews

During the age just before the Reformation, the Jews were not being expelled from cities as often as in the fourteenth century. But the more effect-ive system of police and courts as towns organized themselves better meant that more Jews were arrested, and more were tortured under the system of enquiry into alleged crime, and so more confessed to crimes which they had not committed. As legal officer of Archbishop Albert of Mainz Ulrich von Hutten took part in the trial of a Jew who was accused of posing as a pastor and a physician and then under torture confessed all the legends, robbery of churches and pollution of the Host and poisoning of Christians and murder of Christian babies. Hutten, educated humanist, with a critical mind and a wide experience, had no hesitation in believing this confession and no doubt that the capital sentence was just.[17]

Prejudice, or the resentment of one people for another people which lives side by side but has different customs of life and a different religion, is hard to explain in historical terms. The disaster was the Spanish fervour, generated by the reconquest of Muslim Spain, which caused the expulsion of Jews if they refused to convert; and Spain had the most numerous and best-educated communities of Jews in all Europe. More Jews appeared in other parts of Europe, especially in Germany and Italy and eastern Europe, as well as in the Turkish empire. Many towns already had Jewish quarters, not always known as ghettos, because Jews preferred to live among their own people. With the increased numbers city authorities preferred to enforce separate residence, and the walls of the ghetto were higher. More people having different cus-toms was likely to lead to more resentment at differences. The ghettos were helped because the towns controlled public disorder less inefficiently; but no force of civic watchmen could prevent lynchings if an enraged crowd was sure that the Jews had stolen a Christian baby to sacrifice it in a devilish rite.

---

[17] F. D. Strauss, *Ulrich von Hutten*, new edn. (Leipzig, 1938), 79.

During the Middle Ages ritual murder, the killing of babies or children for magical purposes, was a widely believed legend. Its origin was not Christian for it was used against Jews in the pre-Christian days of the Roman empire. Early Christian writers condemned the idea but needed to defend themselves, being suspect for secret practices, of such cultic murder. When wild preachers whipped up anti-Semitism in the recruiting for the First Crusade, they appealed to the legend. When Jews were massacred in the Rhineland, Jewish fathers were known to slay their own wives and children before committing suicide, lest worse should befall; and these events horrified neighbours and gave the impression that the Jewish people had a lust after blood. The legend is found in Chaucer's *Canterbury Tales*.

During the later fifteenth century the lawyers of the Renaissance started to save Jews from legendary evidence and pooh-poohed the accusations. Johann Eck tried to keep them going. They continued to be believed in remoter parts and for a long time. In 1946 the legend unleashed a massacre at Kielce of Jews who had escaped the Holocaust.

In comparison with legends the hatred of moneylenders was less likely to provoke mobs. In most places Jews were not allowed to own property or land. They must trade and they were very seldom rich but were poor sellers of goods on carts like costermongers. But a few of them became bankers of substance. Christians were banned from lending money at rates of interest which could hurt the person to whom it was lent and hence must lend at rates which were uneconomic. Jews were under no such ban and stepped into the breach, lending money at higher risks and therefore at higher rates of interest. This was the origin of the conviction that they were natural Shylocks. It contributed to their unpopularity, for usury was a word of abuse like the word capitalism in later socialist countries, but since its impact fell upon the debt-ridden individual it was less likely to cause a mob.

Apart from trade and moneylending they could enter a profession. Because interference with dead bodies was doubtful in Christian morality they produced experienced anatomists and physicians. As the cry for the knowledge of the Old Testament grew louder, so that a university became disreputable without a chair of Hebrew, their men of learning could be an indispensable help.

Governments usually liked them to exist in the State. By long custom they paid a special and higher tax, and they encouraged trade and might give good advice on finance. Princes and town councils were aware that driving them out was bad for prosperity; and ruling elites wanted the best physicians that they could hire. No government would force Jews into sheds, or compel all their young people to manual labour.

The Jewish community at Frankfurt was small but grew all through the sixteenth century until in 1614 a sudden pogrom, which the city tried and failed to control with mounted police, drove 1,400 Jews out of the city. It was caused by a message from Catholic Cologne asking for an enquiry into the alleged murder of a child by Jews. This exodus was fewer than half the Jews in Frankfurt, and during the riot many Christians gave shelter to fleeing Jews; two years later they were all back in the city and it remained the capital of German Jewry until the emancipation of the nineteenth century.

Worms was another town where a Jewish community had lived for a long time. There was an attempt to expel them in 1548 and five years later a crowd stormed over a ritual murder charge. Where they were allowed they lived under strict conditions—the synagogue must be in a private house on a side street and the congregation must be kept small so that singing or prayer could not be heard outside; certain towns had a rule that they must undertake before the pastor not to harm Christians or discuss religion with them. They must stay at home on Sundays unless there was an emergency over food and then they must keep off the streets at time of service. One irritation was whether they were allowed to pay Christian servants to do the work which they themselves were not allowed to do on Saturdays.

Christians liked the ghetto system for it kept the two peoples apart. Jews liked it for the same reason, they wished to maintain their customs and laws and to hamper assimilation with surrounding society. Persons who wished to abolish the ghetto were almost always Christian pastors who wanted Jews to mingle in general society as the best way to get them to understand Christianity and so give a chance of conversion.

One of the Reformation's best gifts to posterity was preparation for a public opinion which accepted toleration, not by intention but by smashing the religious unity of central and western Europe. Voices that called for toleration, for Jews as well as Christians, were heard during the 1550s—first heard in Protestant Basel; voices long before their time but yet not without influence.

There was also a concealed benefit in Protestant attack on Catholic superstition. For one base of the common people's anti-Jewish prejudice was the belief in magic.

The persecution of Jews was not according to the law of the Reich which allowed them at least a minimum of justice. The extent of Reich help was shown by the achievements of Josel von Rosheim. He was of a distinguished family, probably a relation of that personal physician of the emperor who had helped Reuchlin to learn Hebrew. The distinction did not prevent recent members of his family from dying in scandals over alleged ritual murder. He was well educated in the Jewish law and became known to two famous evangelical pastors who befriended Jews, Wolfgang Capito at Strasbourg and Osiander at Nuremberg. He became a moneylender at Rosheim and the banking business gave him enough money to travel in the cause. He appealed to the emperor Maximilian regularly on behalf of Jews who had been arrested for alleged crimes. He would have made an excellent attorney and pleaded cases with brilliance. The victories which he won gave him a reputation with the Jewish communities and one by one they put themselves under his 'protection'. In 1529 they awarded him a title—'the head of Jewry in Germany'. There were Gentile critics who thought this illegal, but Charles V accepted it. Not all the time but every so often he was able to stop Jews being expelled from a town and to secure the release of Jews from gaol. He made himself master of imperial law as it affected Jews and used it to the best results. Among his own people he sought to diminish the ills which provoked Gentiles, for example the abuses of the system of high rates of interest. He wrote works of devotion to help their piety. No such Jewish protector of Jews appeared again in Germany until the later eighteenth century. Yet he could not prevent the 1530 Diet of Augsburg renewing the medieval order that Jews be distinguished by their dress and should work in manual labour.

They were more needed in the poor Lands of the east than in the west and therefore better treated in Lands like Pomerania. Still not allowed to buy houses but only able to rent, they must use rented property as synagogues and every five years or so they must pay big sums for the renewal of their permission to reside. Poland did well out of Jewish settlers coming from the west and by 1570 Poland was becoming the centre of the Jewish people, with the control of important areas of Polish trade. In Breslau their community was weighty in the eastern trade. In Bohemia, even in Prague, the squires freely used them on their estates and for business.

In west German towns it was very different. Not a single Jewish family lived in Ulm for three hundred years after 1500. There was no Swiss canton, no main German city outside Frankfurt and Worms, in which Jews were allowed to live after 1520—but the law was not enforced, so that Jews existed though they were not allowed. Germany was such a chessboard of different jurisdictions that a Jew expelled from a town settled a few miles away and there continued in business. Occasionally there was competition for Jewish settlers, for economic reasons. Members of the educated classes could be more tolerant than the law of their towns. Lazarus Spengler, the Protestant town clerk of Nuremberg, demanded that no Jew be driven to conversion, that their ceremonies be respected and that they be not disturbed. The same ruler might need to be intolerant in one jurisdiction and tolerant in another. Albert of Mainz, by nature easy-going, was archbishop of a city which had expelled all its Jews in 1470, and there he could not tolerate them. But he was a pluralist and in his other sees of Halberstadt and Magdeburg he tolerated several Jewish communities which prospered.

What is celebrated about the Protestants and their attitudes to Jews is the contrast between the friendliness to them of the early Luther and his extremism against them in his last sick years. But Luther was not typical.

In those days few Jews could read Latin. Christian scholars, concerned for the mission to the Jews, translated Christian documents into Hebrew. Sebastian Münster of Basel, the ex-Franciscan, studied under Reuchlin, was friends with Jewish scholars, and tried to know about their intellectual life and ways of worship, became the best Hebraist of his age, and edited at Basel *Biblia Hebraica*, an edition of the Bible in Hebrew with a Latin translation, in which he used the scholarship of the Rabbis. Sure that the Jewish religion was a preparation for Christian faith, he wanted Jews tolerated because this was the best way for them to learn, that is, his motive for toleration was more academic than pastoral, and he objected to the idea of confiscating books on the ground that it was neither desirable nor practicable. He wanted serious dialogue between Christian and Jewish scholars and though he believed that most Jews were not convertible he has been called the father of the Protestant mission to the Jews.

With the same objectives Paul Fagius founded the first Hebrew printing press in Germany. (German name Büchelin, a beech, hence the Latin Fagius.) He studied Hebrew under Wolfgang Capito at Strasbourg and was a friend of Bucer, and was sent to be head of the Latin school at Isny. There he founded his press and used the help of Elias Levita the Jew to print. The most important book was an edition (1542) of Jewish prayers but he brought out some twenty volumes of Rabbinic texts. He wanted Christians to understand the best of Jewish religious sources and desired to translate Christian documents in such a way that Jews would understand them. It was a disaster for this cause when, unable to bear the Interim and therefore an exile, he went with Bucer to England at the invitation of Archbishop Cranmer and taught Hebrew at the university of Cambridge.

Osiander at Nuremberg was another. In Sappenfeld, a village near Eichstätt, a three-year-old boy vanished and three weeks later his body was found in a wood. The modern age is familiar with the cause, an infant straying or a paedophile taking. Since the people believed that Jews murdered babies in ritual, the Jews were at once suspected. The Eichstätt bishop's court enquired among the Jews of the area. Two Jews presented a printed pamphlet denying that Jews did any such thing. The bishop sent this for comment to Johann Eck at the university of Ingolstadt. Eck published a refutation of the booklet, in a heap of allegations which made it one of the most hateful pamphlets of the sixteenth century—all the legends stated as though they were proven: the Jews poison wells, curse Christians in daily prayers, desecrate the Host, practise black magic, need Christian blood to anoint their rabbis. Eck was not a mob. He was a learned professor, but one with an obsession; for as a boy in his teens he had seen the corpse of a baby with wounds, which the community there believed to be perpetrated by Jews, and the memory of this horror stayed with him. He believed that Osiander ('Hosander or another

Lutheran') was the author of the pamphlet in defence and attacked him as a lumpen-Protestant in the pay of Jews. He attributed this new softness towards Jews, of which Osiander was an example, to the disciples of Luther.

Osiander printed the reply: *Whether it is Credible that the Jews Secretly Strangle Christian Children and Use their Blood.*[18] It was packed with modern articles of a devastating criticism; the piety of the Jews and their attitudes to human life—the alleged evidence never available except after torture—and most powerfully for that time, that Jewish converts to Christianity often make grave complaints against their former co-religionists but not one has ever testified to child murder. The depth of popular prejudice is shown by Osiander's need to screw up his courage to print these facts of elementary justice. He felt it to be unwise, for personal acceptability and therefore influence, and yet he could not but speak.

Antonius Margaritha came of a long line of rabbis and his father helped Reuchlin over the cabbala. He became a Christian and then a Lutheran and taught Hebrew at Augsburg. There he published an instruction on the nature of the Jewish religion and its worship.[19] It disclosed what hardly a Gentile knew before, of ceremonies, and prayer book, the way the sabbath was kept, the office of rabbis, the rules about food, clothes, and customs and culture. It was hostile to Jews—representing them as cursing Christians, containing unpleasant anecdotes of usury—but with not a mention of ritual murder. He believed that Jews could only be happy if they assimilated to their environment and the way to this was to become Christian. Josel von Rosheim protested to the emperor and tried to get the book banned. In the longer run it may have helped the Jews by clearing away ignorance.

Two states, one a Land and the other a city, both under a demand from their people that all Jews be expelled, illustrate how governments acted in various ways.

The Land Hesse treated its Jews with leniency. The State demanded that they attended Christian sermons and made no anti-Christian propaganda. This listening to sermons was a common rule, but it hardly helped the Christian cause because not many understood High German and compulsion was hard to enforce; a group came, sometimes in rotation, they usually said they had no children or left their wives behind on the plea that the children needed care, and if they were offended were ostentatious in their inattention. But most states felt they ought to have the rule as a way of bringing knowledge to them and Hesse was no exception.

---

[18] *Ob es war und glaublich sey, dass die Juden der christen kinder heymlich erwürgen und ir blut gebrauchen.* Printed Nuremberg 1540 and in Osiander's *Gesamtausgabe*, vii, ed. Klaus Keyser (Gütersloh, 1988), 223–48. Eck's book was *Ains Judenbüechleins Verlegung.*

[19] *Der gantz Jüdisch Glaube* (Augsburg, 1530), but I have used the edition of Frankfurt am Main, 1544.

But in 1538 a wave of feeling among the people demanded that the government expel all Jews. The landgrave Philip asked for Bucer's opinion. Bucer wrote a memorandum, whether it is right for a Christian government to allow Jews to live among Christians. It is the moral duty of a state to uphold its people in the true religion, on this depends the harmony of society. Yet he thought the Jews could stay under conditions—and the conditions which he commended were such that Josel von Rosheim regarded him as an enemy— no new synagogues to be built, attendance at sermons, to be barred from finance and marketing and to work in jobs with the hands—he suggested stonemasons, coalminers, woodcutters, sweeps, cleaners of sewers. Yet he confessed it to be the duty of the Church to love the Jews.[20]

Philip needed their advice in finance and took little notice of this memorandum. He limited the charging of interest and banned new synagogues. He did not restrict them to certain jobs. The Jews continued in Hesse as before, and attended sermons in the most formal way.

A town which came under this pressure from its people to expel was Brunswick. There was a community of Jews in the town. Suddenly there was rumour among the people that they were blaspheming. The chief reformer of the district at that moment was Urbanus Rhegius (real name Rieger), a south German humanist, once poet laureate, and he had married an Augsburg girl who was expert in the Hebrew language. In north Germany he did what he could for the teaching of Hebrew and held discussions with rabbis, with the aim of showing them that Judaism and Christianity have common roots and should not be such antagonists. His devotional book *The Healing of the Soul* went through ninety editions and ten languages.

Though not one for universal toleration, he pleaded with the city council of Brunswick. Toleration is the way by which some may find Christian truth, and charity demands it. He used biblical grounds: (1) the promise that some Jewish people would become Christian and this could only happen through kindness, persecution must drive them away; (2) St Paul in Romans used the metaphor of the branch which is the Gentiles grafted into the olive tree which is the Jewish people; the early Church tolerated Jews; Brunswick has housed Jews for three centuries—and as for charging excess in interest or blaspheming, let the magistrate stop it.

The plea succeeded for a very short time. He died a year later and five years after his death the last Jews were expelled from Brunswick.[21]

The eastward movement of the Jewish people and their part in trade affected Luther as he aged.

---

[20] Bucer's work in *Deutsche Schriften*, vii, ed. E. W. Kohls (Gütersloh, 1964), 343 ff.

[21] For Rhegius's work for the Jews, an indispensable article by Scott H. Hendrix, *ARG* 81 (1990), 189 ff. Brunswick readmitted them, 1578; expelled again, 1591. Rhegius's much-read book was *Seelenarznei* (1529).

In 1523 he published a civilized tract: *Jesus Christ was Born a Jew*. We spread lies about Jews and accuse them of spilling Christian blood and treat them like dogs—how do we expect to do any good to them? They cannot practise an ordinary occupation so they are forced into usury—how can this make them better? To help them, we have to receive them kindly, and let them work with us, and give them a chance to live among Christians instead of separated.

History has difficulty explaining the contrast between this tract and the Luther of the 1540s, his last few years. The best explanation is the pain which then afflicted him. But meanwhile the movement of Jewish people eastward made them more prominent in Saxony and Bohemia and he did not like the consequences among Christians especially in Bohemia. Then he read more of the rabbis who commented on the Old Testament and felt that they were corrupting its study. And he began to be unbalanced about it—he did not rule out that ritual murder might occasionally be true.

In 1543 he wrote the three tracts which some have seen as a sensational step on the road to the Holocaust for this was no fanatic ex-Jew but revered over much of Germany as its leader in religion; and others have said that bad books by elderly professors can have no such effect on the human race and its small effect is proved since the Jewish people were emancipated in Germany very early by European standards. But it was a sad business, this ageing failure of a once-big mind. Keep them in manual labour; prevent them living in proper houses; confiscate their religious books; ban usury; a capital offence for rabbis to teach; expel those who will not be converted, like the good examples of Spain and France and Bohemia. But—they are not to be hurt physically. His last sermon in February 1546 said the same, be converted or be expelled—yet we must use charity towards them.

His colleagues disliked what he did. Melanchthon was uncomfortable. Justus Jonas praised the work as valuable and then made a translation which removed harsh passages. Agricola the chief pastor in Brandenburg persuaded his elector to continue his tolerance to Jews and take no notice—this was not difficult, the elector needed to borrow much money for his debts. Osiander was upset but did not want Luther to know what he thought. Bullinger said that it was silly and scurrilous and unfitting for a senior theologian.[22]

Even in pain Luther's humour kept breaking in. One of his last letters to his wife was sent when he went to Eisleben. He told her how he caught a cold on the way, or flu—and perhaps it was caused because on the way he passed by a community of Jews and they might have blown at him.[23] But he liked the Naumburg beer.

---

[22] Bullinger to Bucer, 8 December 1543: in *Briefwechsel Landgraf Philipp's des Grossmütigen von Hessen mit Bucer*, ed. Max Lenz, ii (1887), 224.

[23] *BW* xi. 4195.

Witches

It is a world of study which has easily come to grief because it is mixed with the occult and sadism and sex. The state of enquiry varies much in different countries. It has extraordinary features, for example that there is no single case of a witch trial in any of the countries of the Eastern Orthodox Church. Heinrich Himmler, five years before he engaged in another and worse destruction of human beings, and already subject to curious fantasies, started to collect a mass of papers about witch trials. Probably his idea was to use the papers as anti-Church propaganda but nothing that he did was so simple. These papers were seized at the end of the Second World War and are now at Poznan in Poland, but less used so far than might be expected from their reported value. That value is diminished for the historian because the researchers took cases alone and had no interest in the social milieu of the people accused or the witnesses.

Exodus 22: 18: this is translated by Luther 'The sorceresses (*Zauberinnen*) are not to be allowed to live' (modern translation 'You shall not allow a witch to live').

The word is feminine. Many societies have thought certain women to possess secret powers. Roman law made provision for sorceresses. In earlier days they were rare. From the thirteenth century they were thought to be commoner and to be a menace to healthy society. Very few asylums for the mad, the absence of effective provision for poor old women who went gaga and had no family to care for them, cast many women into a state of eccentricity or worse, whether they were known to the public and despised by passers-by, or hidden in the countryside to keep themselves away from mockery or a people's fear.

The decisive point came in 1479 when Heinrich Institoris was appointed inquisitor for Germany. He started to do what he could about women who might have magical powers but found that when he took them to court he met popular resistance. When he tried to prosecute witches in Innsbruck he met strenuous resistance from the bishop. He thought that this could only be due to ignorance of the peril, and wrote a book *Malleus Maleficarum*. It looks as though he faked a recommendation for his book from the theologians at the university of Cologne. What he did not fake was a bull to back him, from Pope Innocent VIII, 1484. He now had authority. Till 1520 the book went on being printed. People did not like it. It was not printed in Germany for sixty years after 1520.

The new code of imperial law under Charles V, the Carolina 1532, adopted provisions of Roman law. In Article 44 it created the witch craze of Reformation and Counter-Reformation Germany. It is the duty of the State, not the Church, to enquire. In cases concerning witches torture may be used. The crime is of exceptional gravity, and so it was *crimen exceptum*, exempt from the lawyers' usual restrictions on the use of torture.

A legend was believed widely. The witch was in a pact with Satan. She was his servant, and his partner in sexual intercourse. She danced with his devils in secret midnight dances. Because she could call upon his invisible power she could harm people: blight crops, strike with illness, cause cows and sheep to die of a plague; but she also had ways to murder. The Carolina code ordered that persons convicted of witchcraft should be burnt.

She or he—quite a number of males were convicted. The Pope's bull assumed that they were of either sex. *Malleus Maleficarum* assumed that they were all female. Females lived longer and so were more likely to decay in mind and behave oddly in their last years. In all Europe the average was four out of five females, in some areas nine out of ten, in other areas two out of three. Nowhere were males a majority of the convicted.

The sources of witch trials were three:

1. The medieval mob which rose against heretics or Jews or sorcerers was still a mob. But most cases were not lynching. They were formal appeals by a group—perhaps friends, or the village headmen, or a trade union, or offended individuals—convinced that a crime had been committed and it must be enquired into and prosecuted. That is, far the largest number of such trials came 'from below', from the people and not from the authorities— though then the authorities needed to assent and to conduct the trial.

A village harvest was destroyed by hailstones. These hailstones were astounding in size, nothing like them had ever happened before. Therefore they were not 'natural', they could only be caused by someone playing the sorcerer. Who has a grudge against the village? We need protection from such a crime or we shall starve.

A healthy baby suddenly dies of a cot death. There was no disease, it can only be murder, and murder by spells from a distance. Who has a grudge against this family? The police must enquire and remove the villain from our midst.

Uncaused deaths; plagues among the cattle or sheep; poison among humans, for there was no protection against poison and no one afterwards had any means of a post mortem on the stomach—there are foul crimes in the world perpetrated by magic, we must find who did it, voice our suspicions about who did it, present our evidence for the suspicion, and formally ask that a culprit be brought to court and tried.

The evidence of informers was liable to its usual awfulness that it opened the door to personal vendettas. A case is known where a daughter hated her father's second wife and took steps to see that she was removed by providing evidence of behaviour as a witch. This was not the only case of false evidence.

The system opened the door to hatred. But in the evidence so far available this cause was rare. The vast majority of cases were started by persons or groups who were convinced that a crime had really been committed. Cases were known where a village went on strike if a government refused to act on the evidence which they presented; or where, if nothing was done, a lynching happened easily.

2. The clergy. It did not matter what kind of clergy—Catholic or Protestant, among Protestants Lutheran or Reformed. That is not so true of the end of the sixteenth century when the worst excesses happened in Catholic bishoprics (Bamberg, Würzburg) which were in the full zeal of the Counter-Reformation. Nor is it easy to tell how many clergy. These are not the illiterate country clergy, they are educated. They believed in the crime of satanic devilry. It was not their business to start prosecutions or to judge, but some felt it their business to warn their people from the pulpit against witches and the horrors which they could wreak, and some felt it their business to add their weight to the pleas of the people that government should act.

There were other varieties of sermon. A pastor might find his people assuming that bad weather which hurt the crops was the result of spells and then needed to warn them that they could not so put the blame for disaster on other people, it was more likely to be their village sins which brought a just warning upon them; and that they would not promote a friendlier climate by lynching an old woman or giving dubious evidence about her in a law court. They would do better to keep the moral law. And there exist sermons which told the people not to be foolish, it was mere superstition to blame natural disasters on demonic or magical agencies. For the informed preachers it was necessary to teach how no witch could hurt anyone by their own magic, they were only the agents of demons and the demons could do nothing against those who had true faith in God.

Calvin expounded the witch text of Deuteronomy 18: 10 and following. In his efforts to deceive humanity Satan plays many tricks and one is bewitching. There are beliefs about witches which are absurd and not be credited—for example the sabbath. But Deuteronomy makes an order which ensures that we must treat witchcraft as a capital crime which a Christian society cannot permit. In this demand for the capital penalty Calvin was unlike himself, accepting a social custom dependent on popular axioms instead of the word of the Bible; for Deuteronomy does not say that witches must be executed, it says that they are an abomination to the Lord and should be driven out. The trouble was that Exodus did not agree with Deuteronomy, Exodus 22: 18: 'Thou shalt not suffer a witch to live'.[24]

[24] Calvin, CR xxvii. 510–11.

Pastors, though they believed in the alleged crime as possible, not seldom tried to influence the courts to justice; as good pastors would have acted in any serious law case; to make sure that the court was not giving way to ignorant mob rule; that witnesses were heard with care (but how could this be when most believed that torture was legitimate in legal enquiries?); that the court was aware of the danger that the evidence was mere gossip, or concocted by private enmity.

3. The lawyers—responsible for courts, fair trials, sifting of evidence. They partly worked in camera, but what they did was public enough. Witches are arrested, tried, proved guilty, and condemned—therefore witchcraft exists. It may now be thought odd that intelligent and educated people could believe this stuff. But in any age popular axioms are also believed by the educated. To take one example, Calvin was one of the most highly educated persons in Europe. When plague hit Geneva he was sure that it was caused by a conspiracy of men and women. He did not know how it was done but believed that the conspirators blended a poisonous ointment which they smeared on the door-locks of houses to infect the people inside with the disease. He had nothing to do with the subsequent punishments, which were in secular law, but did not question them.[25]

Two aspects of the current belief were fatal. The witches had a sabbath, a secret midnight dance with other witches. Therefore a witch knew other witches. This is a group crime. If a witch is caught, the knowledge of other witches can be extracted from her. Secondly, torture was believed throughout the legal system to be a justified way, often the only way, of discovering and of ensuring the truth. They needed to pull out of her not only a confession of her part in these terrible acts, but a disclosure of her associates. We see nothing but horror—an old woman in agony being told to name accomplices as a way of ending the pain and then mentioning names of the only people she knew. This is the most puzzling feature of the human predicament—why it so seldom occurred to trained lawyers or educated clergymen that torture promoted false 'evidence'.

In Germany it did not happen everywhere. It was found in the Rhineland, south Germany but not Bavaria, in the Saxon duchies, and in the extreme north in Mecklenburg. It was rarer in most of north Germany and the west, Spain and Portugal were largely free; it was least in Ireland and England and Scandinavia and Poland and Bohemia and Hungary, and worst in France, Lorraine and Trier, north Italy, Switzerland, the Netherlands, Scotland.[26] Most victims were peasants, rarely of the towns. The 'typical' witch was a peasant of the lowest class but a rejected member.

---

[25] Calvin to Myconius, 27 March 1545, CR xii. 55.
[26] Distribution in Gerhard Schormann, *TRE* (1986) s.v. Hexen, an excellent article.

It has to be asked whether the religious revival contributed; whether the moral discipline, which tried to abolish not only crime but immorality and heresy, pressed harder on the dissentient, especially the willy-nilly dissentient, women with a sexual aberration and dreams of intercourse, women who were drug addicts of the hubble-bubble species with feelings of riding the winds. It cannot be the doctrine that Satan has power to work through humans, or the use of torture (though that belief and that practice were essential to it) because both belief and practice existed before and after the craze. It could be asked whether it was the greater knowledge of the Bible which education brought, since Exodus said 'Thou shalt not suffer a witch to live.' Probably not. The lawyers who drafted the Carolina code were not likely to think about the book Exodus. Their Roman forefathers had made these legal provisions.

In this time of the earlier Reformation the hunt was less oppressive than it became later. It began to get worse about 1550, but not till 1580 can we talk of waves of witch-hunting. That *Malleus Maleficarum* had to be republished in 1580 after a long interval of neglect is a sign of the change.

The campaign had critics. They were very few until the seventeenth century. But an occasional bold person spoke out and published.

From 1550 Johann Weyer was the personal doctor of the duke of Cleves-Jülich in Düsseldorf. Trained at the university of Paris he was one of the ablest physicians of his age. His book on *Medical Observations* contained better descriptions of diseases and their treatment than had so far appeared. His religion was like his duke's, moderate reforming—needing to be moderate because the Spanish army in Brussels was not far away. He published a book *On the Tricks of Demons and Those who Make Spells and Poisoners.*[27] The book was much read: five editions in the next twenty years, and translations. It was famous enough to be accused of heresy and be put on the Index of Prohibited Books. Fierce pamphleteers wrote against him, not all Catholic.

He used his scientific knowledge, but the book was full of compassion. He believed in demons and their deadly work. He thought that witches exist. But what they say in law courts is not their fault and is not true, it is due to imagination put into them by demonic agencies. They are nothing but sad old innocent women. Hence he demanded of the courts that they do not convict on confessions of witchcraft, but have a proper trial if they are accused of criminal acts.

Whether this was cause and effect, there was a stopping of witch cases in the duchy of Cleves-Jülich. (They started again in his old age, under pressure

---

[27] *De praestigiis daemonum et incantationibus ac veneficiis* (Basel, 1563); modern English translation of the last edition by John Shea, Medieval and Renaissance Texts and Studies, 73 (Binghamton, NY, 1991).

from Brussels.) He dedicated an edition to the city of Bremen. The city council accepted its argument and stopped all witch trials. Later in life he was able to write a grateful paragraph:

'The reward of my book *De praestigiis* is that some governments have not only acted gently, but have freed altogether the poor old women whom the populace calls witches, contrary to long-standing law and prejudice.'[28]

But only *some* governments.

---

[28] *De Lamiis* (1577), preface.

18

UNBELIEF

The unbelief of the sixteenth century was not unbelief in the modern western European sense. People breathed religion even if their parents went to church as little as possible or only to avoid fines, and even if in public houses drinking men and in brothels fornicating men made comments which ordinary folk regarded as blasphemous. The anti-clerical ditty of the bar was historic in the custom of the Middle Ages and was not silent because reformers tried to abolish brothels or bars. Meeting in the bar often came after meeting in church.

The weightiest of axioms were rather social than intellectual. No education can be of any use unless it brings to the young person a knowledge of the highest of moral imperatives, God. No atheist (if such exist) can have a conscience, therefore atheists are moral dangers to society, with them our daughters and spoons and freedom are not safe. The new registration books of births and deaths and marriages were kept in the church cupboard. The only place to be married was in church (but many people avoided marriage). Holidays were only on holy days. A majority of the educated men in the state were still parsons—who therefore influenced legislation and the civil service as well as universities and schools. The best places to learn what happened in town and world were in front of the church noticeboard and under the pulpit. If they needed an alarm clock they used a cock, even in the army. The easiest way to know the time of day, for most the only way, was to hear the church bell. The church clock if there was one did not sound out the hours except within the tower, people learnt the time because a church watchman rang the bell when he heard the clock. But they did not mind about the exact time, only the more-or-less time, which they judged by dawn and sun and gloaming; except in sermons when they could see the sand dripping through the funnel on the edge of the pulpit. The only building in a village which could be called well-built was the church (though it often needed repair). If they held a meeting they held it in church usually, their children went to school more often than not in part of the church building.

It has been argued that the ditties of bars were trivial, that if a wassailer shouted 'God's a bloody tyrant' in his cups that had not the slightest importance for the beliefs or unbeliefs of society. The explosion was a meaningless release of emotion by swearing which could have no effect upon other topers in the bar and no influence in propagating a non-Christian view of the world. Yet this is not quite certain. Erasmus was persuaded that proverbs enshrine a truth from the long experience of humanity, and one proverb is *in vino veritas*, people blurt what they really think when drunk.

A preacher is not upon oath in describing from the pulpit the state of mind of the flock; since the object of the words is to propel to action as well as instruct, one-sidedness is not worse than a pardonable sin in the speaker, and experts in persuasion, a Cicero or a Quintilian, would have thought it virtue. This makes the evidence of sermons harder to use. Postulate that a preacher, shocked and depressed by immoralities in his village, thumped the ledge and thundered that they were all atheists, he made no accurate metaphysical statement about their beliefs or non-beliefs, he reproached them that their behaviour was more lamentable than it ought to be.

One thing that came out of the parishes to Luther was the simplest form of practical materialism. He needed good parsons. These needed reasonable stipends, the more because now they had (socially accepted) wives and children. The parish folk should help and give money. In former times they paid out bags for indulgences or private masses or pilgrim shrines, now they grudged paying money to help the pastor. Why? Luther was given blunt answers—the money must go to what is indispensable, we can get on without any pastor in the parish, we cannot get on at all unless we have a parish shepherd and a parish swineherd and a parish policeman. So our money must go to pay the herds and if you close the church we can still live.[1] Or a peasant heard his pastor talking about heaven, and said, like a German Social Democrat three hundred and fifty years later, 'What's the good of heaven so long as we have flour!'[2]

The next doubt reported to Luther from the parishes was that over suffering. If God rules the world, why do agonies happen? They said that if God were sovereign he would not allow the oppression and the injustices that we see about us. Therefore one of two things is true, either God does not exist or God does not care what goes on among mankind.[3] This was the old question with which St Augustine wrestled. But it did not come now as the puzzle of a philosopher (perhaps it never had) but as a gut-feeling from those who saw suffering.

The next doubt which he found among the people was a more bourgeois kind of doubt. The Reformation gave the Bible to the people. But what extraordinary events the Bible is found to contain when it was read by the people! The ark of Noah—now we have it in front of us in German we can

---

[1] Luther, *Comm. in Genesim*, ch. 31, vv. 14–16, *WA* xliv. 15.
[2] Luther, *in Psalm.*, 90, v. 11, *WA* xl. 3. 565.
[3] Luther, *in Psalm.*, 110, v. 1, *WA* xli. 108–9.

work out the consequences and the measurements are not practicable. The dimensions of the ark can only be a miracle. What behaviour is approved in the books of Moses, deeds by Reuben, or by the daughters of Lot, or even by the hero and patriarch Abraham? What trivialities the Holy Spirit thinks it worthwhile to record—why should God waste his time and ours by bothering to insert into his revelation so many details which fascinate but can have no influence on our perception of truth or our conscience in its moral judgement? Can it be possible that the Holy Spirit is the author of everything in the Bible?

Such questions were easy to answer because Luther for one, and many another in his generation, had a more continuous sense of miracle in the world than their later successors. Why do not the clouds drop upon us? How is the River Elbe held on its course through Wittenberg and Saxony? How is it that birds vanish in the autumn, and swallows die and are reborn, and hens can lay an egg and create a chicken, and women bring babies into the world, and dung beetles are generated by horse manure, and carp are generated by pools and lakes, and trees sprout leaves and suddenly flowers are lovely with blossom, and the eye can so magically reproduce a distant vision? So Luther asked as he gloried in the power that upholds the universe. In that context the measurements of the ark were no intellectual problem. The measurements must be wrong. But God did it.[4]

Men who drank in bars were not only the illiterate. Artists, writers, architects, even academic clergymen, were known to solace their solitude in bars. The Middle Ages showed that the anti-clerical ditty could at times be the verse of an authentic poet. What was new about the sixteenth century was due to printing. We have songs from a tipsy world in which now lurch real scholars with information. 'He sets a bad example' recorded the registers of Grenoble in 1540 about one of their lecturers. 'He is a blasphemer against God. He is drunk most of the time. He sets a bad example to students, who carry swords because he is always in a fight with one or other of them.'[5] It was a question whether blasphemy did not promote what it was against. If this language meant anything God must matter.

The enemy of the Catholic Church or of the traditional faith usually ended as a Protestant. But it was possible to hate the Catholic Church and hate Protestants or have nothing to do with them. At moments Erasmus was not far from strongly criticizing Catholic practice but being as hostile to Protestant religious practice. Such minds are not commonly found in historical sources because usually they preferred to neglect religion and get on with

---

[4] See especially *in Genesim*, ch. 1, vv. 21–2, *WA* xlii. 38–40; *in Psalm.*, 111, v. 2, *WA* xxxi. 1. 407–8.

[5] Lucien Febvre, *Le Problème de l'incroyance au xvie siècle: la religion de Rabelais*, rev. edn. (Paris, 1947), 69–70.

other aspects of life and so were not visible in their anti-religion. But on occasion there were natures which enjoyed pricking their neighbours by shock, or by provoking, or, less commonly, had a desire to help the world by getting rid of untruth even at the risk of their comfort—or even their life.

Etienne Dolet was celebrated by atheists during the nineteenth century as a Reformation martyr for their cause. He was condemned and died at the Place Maubert in Paris on 3 August 1546. Precisely three centuries afterwards a monument was unveiled there to his memory as an atheist martyr, not without a demonstration against the ceremony. But was it true? or was it like the vehement preacher, enemies using the word 'atheist' as a term of abuse which bore little relation to what the condemned really thought? Four years after his death John Calvin wrote a treatise *De Scandalis* in which Etienne Dolet was denounced as an atheist. Then others searched for signs in his writings which would justify this verdict and discovered unbelief where a modern critic does not see it. Dolet was a good scholar and produced a Latin dictionary in two beautiful folio volumes which he expected to make him a European name but it was so badly organized, contained such inflated self-laudation and abuse of critics, that it dropped half-dead in the market and he was much hurt and abandoned a planned third volume.

Critics seized on certain definitions, for example Miracle. 'Miracle means any happening at which people are astonished.'[6] In truth the definition had no relation to Dolet's faith or lack of it. He showed the classical meaning of the word, as was evident from his non-quoted next sentence—'While now Christians call miracles events where they marvel, the ancients used the word to mean foul events—like monsters or what gives us horror.'

Under the word *Literae* he inserted a dissertation on the history of literature and its revival in the Renaissance; with a long list of authors from the various countries; and the German list included Reuchlin, Erasmus, Melanchthon, Hutten, Simon Grynaeus and some lesser writers whose names gave the orthodox pause; but the context is about scholarship not about faith.

Dolet's complex mind needs study. Aged twenty-three he came to the university of Toulouse then in such a state of riots as to be compared with the university of Vincennes in the 1970s, and was elected a student leader and found the customs of the place ludicrous, like horses trotting nine times round the inside of St Etienne's church on St George's day to protect their health, or hurling a cross into the River Garonne to protect the town from floods.

In the battle of contending student speeches he was accused of being a Lutheran, but only because that was a general word of abuse. He took up the

[6] *Commentariorum linguae latinae*, ii (Lyons, 1536), 1300.

charge: 'You all know that it is only unquiet and irreligious and inquisitive minds which approve of Luther's ideas. You also know that if anyone shows signs of genius and originality he is at once thought by bigots to be a Lutheran and is hated. Have the Toulouse courts ever acquitted a scholar?' In violent language he denounced the recent burning of a member of the university as gross injustice. He denied the charge on himself. 'I revere nothing but that faith and those rites which have come down to us from the ancient world.'[7]

His provocations brought expulsion. He went to the common resource of the scholarly ejected, proofreading for a printer, and made his home at Lyons. His next step on the road to European unpopularity was to publish a book against Erasmus's Latin style[8] which could have been harmless but contained abuse of Erasmus which only hurt its author. When Melanchthon said that the book should be answered, Dolet's name was more notorious than well known. But Melanchthon had a reason not literary, for Dolet's attack on Erasmus shaded into vituperation of Luther and his followers. All these words—this verbosity—what does it do to religion?—reverence is taken away, opinions are divided, religion is vulgarized—'what of Luther? or Zwingli? or Oecolampadius? or Bucer? or Erasmus? or Melanchthon? or Lambert? or Farel? What religious bilge has been brought by these clear acute commentaries on the Bible . . .?'[9]

More than one of his abusers used of him the word atheist. One said 'impious, Godless, faithless, religionless'—the words were but pebbles in an abusive list of epithets. Nothing that Dolet had yet written gave ground for the judgement; except that he criticized both Catholics and Protestants. When he met the book by Erasmus on patching up peace between Catholics and Protestants, *De sarciendo*, he called it *nugae*, nonsense.

The next year he stabbed an artist to death in the street. They accepted a plea of self-defence. But as his reputation sank, this was a bad memory and not forgotten. At his final trial the artist's widow played a part.

In that city of many printers he became a publisher in his own right, after a time with a privilege from the government. He made money, with textbooks of medicine and Latin texts. But he did not care what he published if it sold; Marot's psalter, a French Bible from Geneva, and Rabelais's *Gargantua* carefully including the passages which Rabelais had omitted out of prudence in his second edition and so earning Rabelais's undying hatred. He liked to ask for trouble, and was one of those characters who enjoys alienating close friends. He was denounced as one who imported banned books from Geneva and when they searched his house they found copies of Calvin's *Institutes*, which he said he possessed only out of curiosity. For a time he had

---

[7] *Orationes duae in Tholosam* (Lyons, 1534), 2.

[8] *Dialogus de Imitatione Ciceronis adversus Erasmum* (Lyons, 1535).

[9] Ibid., 36. The absence of Calvin's name is because he had not yet published on religion.

to flee to Piedmont but soon came back. He went on printing unlicensed books, and finally was strangled on the Place Maubert. In law courts he cheerfully professed Catholic orthodoxy. The evidence shows that he was not an atheist but that he cared very little about religion. He died because he made the world his enemy; by folly, pride, self-satisfaction, willingness for any illegality if it made a profit, abuse of people with high reputations.

Protestant leaders refused to recognize him as a martyr for their cause.

The word atheist misled historians of ideas. Latin had no word for atheist, when Cicero wanted the word he used Greek. When Greeks used the word it did not mean what moderns mean. Socrates was accused of atheism, because he did not believe in the gods of Athens. Sophocles used it to mean a person whom the gods have abandoned. When during the 1550s the word came in as a term of abuse, it could be more moral condemnation than statement of philosophy. When English authors used the word, it was imported. Coverdale (1568) wrote of 'the Italian atheoi'; or they translated Calvin's French.

By the 1550s no one met an atheist and yet the word was commoner as abuse. In 1564, when the Huguenots were in control of Lyons, Pierre Viret was its pastor. He said that he was disturbed at the number of atheists and deists in the place—deists a new word, persons not sure they believe in Christ. He discovered several who said they believed in God as Jews and Muslims do, but the witness of the Gospels they thought fable. They go to church to please their neighbours or avoid fines, but in the heart they despise religion. It is worse because such are among the intelligent and well-educated. Viret found it odd to live in an age when it was more needful to defend against unbelief than superstition.[10]

The Renaissance revived the classics and created speculation by modern historians that classical morality, found inspiring in Aeschylus or Cicero or Seneca or Plutarch, lessened the force of Christian morality; that an educated person who once looked for the source of the moral law in the Commandments and the Gospels, now looked for it in the best morals of the pre-Christian world. Luther misjudged Erasmus by thinking that this was his weakness in understanding faith; but Erasmus could have qualms that the new knowledge of Latin literature, pumped into the heads of schoolboys and schoolgirls, would introduce the young to a paganism with which at their age they were not fitted to cope. In the *Enchiridion* he advised that they should only be introduced to such literature when they were mature and then only with discretion.

Among the ancient texts came Lucretius; noble poetry to declare that gods, though existing and serene, did not affect human beings, that superstitious religion is a calamity for society and that souls are mortal. His book did

---

[10] Viret, *Instruction chrestienne*, vol. ii, preface, 'Epistle to the church at Montpellier'. Febvre, *Problème de l'incroyance*, 69–70.

not please Christian leaders and the Huguenot scholar Ramus was blamed for introducing him to young people. His defenders said that if poetry is literature we ought not to be discouraged from reading it because it contains a philosophy which no one is likely to accept.

Gerolamo Cardano

His father was interested in geometry and had been consulted by Leonardo da Vinci. Gerolamo was brought up with an interest in mathematics and medicine and a good though chaotic mind, not helped by an illegitimate birth and early experiences which helped to explain a deviant psychology. In Milan, though at the time a city much troubled by the wars of Italy, he taught mathematics and won fame as a general practitioner; was for eight years professor of medicine at Pavia and was even hired to go to Edinburgh to cure of his asthma Hamilton who had been made the archbishop of St Andrews after the murder of Cardinal Beaton and was himself later to be hanged on a charge of murder. Though Cardano was no orthodox Catholic, the Inquisition did not begin to take serious notice of him till after 1564 and he was not arrested till 1570. He submitted, destroyed 120 of his books and died in retirement at Rome in 1576, after writing a too frank autobiography not published for nearly seventy years.

It could hardly be expected that an Italian physician and mathematician would affect the ideas of the Protestant north. But he published many of his books at Nuremberg or Basel. He was cheerfully ready to print praise of Protestant theologians—'Osiander of Nuremberg, learned in many languages, a theologian and my friend'[11]—'Philip Melanchthon, a learned man and trustworthy'; or even a Protestant monarch—Edward VI of England—'would that he had lived!' for it is good when philosophers are kings.

His *De subtilitate* was an encyclopaedia of the natural sciences and was successful in both Protestant and Catholic Europe. It was a mixture of information on a range of subjects, in such a way as to cause thought, with credulity. The miracles are wonderful things like animals generated from putrefying carcases, and tightrope walkers and breaking a stone with the fist and candles that no one can put out and Icelanders who see the dead and the demons; and with it all a critical doubt—'if oracles were not ambiguous they would not be oracles'—'everything well-known is despised—so priests have wanted to keep their ceremonies obscure and they would be nothing unless they were shrouded in a cloud of obscurity'.[12] Miracles that are believed are often caused

---

[11] Cardano, *De subtilitate* (Basel, 1557), xviii. 523; xix. 534; *De Rerum Varietate* (Basel, 1557), viii. cap. 40, 286.

[12] *De subtilitate*, xiv. 405; xix. 534.

by pretence or tricks. But at the end he professed faith in God as the creator of all and he thanks God for his help in what he has written.

We cannot say with any certainty that such a book by an Italian had an influence upon the doubts of Protestants. But these books were read in the north. Their effect could hardly be other than to force persons interested in the study of physics to consider the relation between the normal laws of nature and the evidence for these exceptional happenings. On the other hand the attitude of Cardano was an intellectualized form of Luther's conviction—there are so many wonderful things happening all about us in the natural world that we can almost expect miracles to happen. A highly educated and sceptical mind like the Huguenot Jean Bodin was convinced of the reality of the powers of sorcerers and demons. Reformers mocked Catholic miracles as illusions or tricks that promoted superstition. But they accepted biblical miracles and expected wonderful things to happen now though the wonders which they expected were more in conformity with the laws of nature. In the earlier years of the Reformation their Catholic opponents did not dream of accusing Protestant leaders of promoting atheism. Before the end of the century this accusation began to be heard. *If you want to be an atheist start as a Calvinist*—it was a text (before 1583) of the Jesuit Maldonado who had himself been accused of heresy by the university of Paris.[13] The force of this charge is not that Geneva was supposed to be plagued by atheists. It was observation that atheists now existed and were not suppressed.

Of these rare intellectuals one only, François Rabelais, gained a European fame and some rueful affection, because he was a writer of genius and helped to form the French language, but not only for that reason. He took the ribald ditty and used it for messages more profound, so that students have treated his work as though it was a philosophy instead of a joke. For some he was a mocking indifferent disbeliever who conformed to the Catholic Church because there lay his bread and butter. For others he was a hater of Christianity, not at all indifferent, who dare not say what he thought except in veiled form, because he must not risk the stake. For others he was a vulgarized Erasmus, and his onslaught on the Church from his gin-palace, or from the less than sanitary arrangements of the gin-palace, was intended to drive it to reform itself. It must be true that he wanted to make readers laugh but that cannot be all that was true about his purposes.

At the age of nine he was a Franciscan near Angers to get education and remained a Franciscan long enough to be ordained and study Greek. As adult he petitioned the pope to transfer to the Benedictines but soon left their monastery and turned up at the university of Montpellier to read medicine.

---

[13] *Commentarius in S. Matthaeum* (Pont-à-Mousson, 1596, but at least thirteen years posthumous), ch. 26, col. 630.

His copy of Galen in five volumes is held by the university library at Sheffield. The Paris humanists thought of him as a leader in reviving medical science and he is known to have been a good doctor.

In 1532 or 1533, when he was physician to the hospital in Lyons, and aged just over forty, he published *Pantagruel*, like *Gargantua* the name of a giant in folklore. The author's name was not mentioned. Calvin said the book was obscene. He was diverted from his medical career by becoming assistant to Bishop Jean du Bellay who won him papal absolution for his flight from the Benedictines, and a canonry of Saint Maur. Meanwhile *Gargantua*, which probably appeared in 1534, was now republished with *Pantagruel* and he must have thought of respectability because he omitted various passages.

But by 1546 he was notorious and even fled to the hospital at Metz to be over the French frontier, but soon was the incumbent of two French parishes, in neither of which he did anything. He died in 1553 but left additions to *Gargantua* which were published posthumously. This part is fiercer in its anti-clericalism and it has been argued though unconvincingly that he was not the author.

Despite scurrilities, it was reformers who first patronized it for it contained an attack on the Catholic Church in a form never seen before. The Sorbonne at Paris condemned Rabelais's books but associated them with the books of famous Protestants.

In 1550 Calvin published *De scandalis*[14] and gave 'Rabelaysus' a mention as a person 'who took a pleasure in the gospel and then went blind about it'. But five years later, in his course of sermons on Deuteronomy, when he reached chapter 13 verses 6–9 where the author orders the Israelites to kill even a friend or kinsman if they secretly try to entice towards other gods, his experience of Servetus two years before made him more militant.[15] He felt the world to be under attack from unbelief. 'People who mock talk of God—people who mock the Bible as if it is absurd—clowns who put out squibs against the Bible, like the demon Pantagruel—such don't push for a new religion, they are against all religion . . . They have cardinals to back them, we even see the names of cardinals blazoned on their books.' It was a year when Calvin grew gloomier than he needed to be.

Yet reformers hardly minded Rabelais's skit on monasteries. An ex-Franciscan and an ex-Benedictine, he never forgave the system. He treated his past, not like Luther with a rueful respect, but like Erasmus with mockery, though a more salacious and less persuasive humour than Erasmus's. Monasteries have a head and a strict obedience. Rabelais's abbey of Thélème has no one in charge and everyone does what he or she likes. Monasteries have walls and hours of visiting. Thélème has no walls and everyone comes

---

[14] CR viii. 44.   [15] CR xxvii. 262.

in and goes out at will. Monasteries have a regular timetable. At Thélème they climbed out of bed when they liked and ate meals and went to bed when they liked—and could not go to church at a set time for a common service but each had a private chapel. On Sundays and holidays they dress in fashionable clothes. If a monk or a nun enters the house they regard it as a pollution and afterwards cleaned the room. No nuns could be admitted who were not beautiful and sweet-natured nor monks who were not good-looking and courteous. Anyone could leave. No vows to be taken, or if so the opposite of the three old vows, they were to be rich and married and anarchic. Gargantua mocked the old targets of Erasmus—lawyers, etiquette-makers, theologians, universities, confessors, relics, descriptions of purgatory, cardinals, schoolmen, the breviary, pilgrims, indulgences, inquisitors, alchemists, drunken bishops, astrologers, and finally popes. He visited hell and found four famous popes doing menial service.

More important were the skits to make pieces of the Old Testament incredible; genealogies, or the several-centuries ages of the patriarchs, or the measurements of the ark (enough room inside?) and once at least a miracle of the Old Testament, the recovery of the axe from the water, in an air of scepticism hardly paralleled before the eighteenth century. He did not scorn the idea of life after death for there is evidence that he held to this hope. He was strong in the sense for worship, of the individual on the knees before the divine. But this worship was solitary, the soul before its Maker, priests saying their masses are contemptible. Later the pope-mongers were bad but the Calvins were as bad—'demoniacal Calvins, impostors of Geneva', put with herb-stinking hermits and priest-ridden bigots.[16]

Hidden in the comedy is a plea for toleration. God needs no protection from human beings. Chapter 29 of *Pantagruel* was a mockery of the self-contradictions of half-toleration—faith must not be forced but we exterminate those who assail it.

Columbus discovered new lands and peoples in the west. Vasco da Gama and his successors found new lands and people in the east. What light was shed upon the faith by these discoveries? It is odd, but the question was hardly asked during the sixteenth century. Aztecs or Incas seemed to have no means of communication to Europe or Asia. The Europeans might have asked whether it was so easy to attribute a descent from Adam and Eve to peoples so far across the ocean; and if all mankind were not descended from a single pair, it made a difference in theology, for example to the idea of original sin. But they asked no such question. They continued to assume that the Garden of Eden was the first home of all the human race.

---

[16] *Pantagruel*, bk. 4, ch. 32, end.

They might have asked another question. If Christian faith was the way to salvation, was there anything unjust in God that for centuries or millennia so many souls in the Americas or the East had no chance of hearing the good news? This question was asked but only by an exceptional person and in an unusual form.

Francesco Guicciardini was a Florentine with eminent political experience. He had served Florence as an ambassador, the pope as a governor in north Italy, and commanded a papal army which suffered the fatal invasion that sacked the city of Rome. If it were true that the best historians are persons who have made history and know how it is made—a Julius Caesar, a Guizot, a Winston Churchill—Guicciardini was qualified to be a historian. Forced out of power in Florence by a change of government, he dedicated his retirement to writing various papers on his age—a history and a political study of Florence, and what he felt about Spain, and personal reminiscences. In his last years he turned to the history of Italy during his time. He was intimate with his native city, well understood the popes and their Curia, had governed much of north Italy, and held high office in the tragic wars of Italy.

He had not time to finish this book, but left at death in 1540 a bulky manuscript and fragments. According to his wife he had thought of burning it. His family circulated it, cousins printed it, readers found it packed but dramatic.

Two years after the *History* was published, a Latin translation appeared at Basel, by the Italian radical Protestant Curione. The Index of Prohibited Books placed this upon its list. There was nothing that affected fundamental theology. But the popes, for thirty years before Luther won fame, had not lived as model popes and in the book appeared the conviction of the historian that popes were corrupted because they ruled a secular state. Though he was a Catholic and held high papal office, the seventeenth century listed him as a heretic of the first class. Protestant printers enjoyed publishing edition after edition of his history.

In the eighteenth century they studied the manuscript of his history, by then in the library at Florence. They found that the censors suppressed other passages, till then not known. One excised passage bore upon the voyages of discovery and raised the question of theology:

These discoveries put geographers into trouble. They caused anxiety in the minds of interpreters of the Bible. The Psalm (19 verse 4, on the heavens declaring the glory of God) says that *their sound is gone out into all lands, and their words into the ends of the world*. They always said that this meant how the gospel went out into all the world. They must be wrong. No one knew about these lands. Among these newly discovered peoples no sign of a knowledge of the Christian message can be found.[17]

---

[17] Guicciardini, *Storia d'Italia* (Bari, 1929), ii. 132.

Here are two signs of the discoveries affecting divinity, and within the first fifty years after they began. The first is the text of Guicciardini; the second is the act of the Florentine censors in suppressing the passage so that it was not known until near the end of the eighteenth century. That is weighty. Censors would only act if they feared the passage would hurt readers' faith.

Copernicus

The meanest intelligence knew that the sun went round the earth. Anyone who said the contrary was insane for he denied the evidence of everyone's eyes.

But astronomers said that common sense had its difficulties because it did not account for odd movements in the sky which we could observe. There came the first tentative suggestions that perhaps the earth itself also moves. Biblical witness was the only truth about this matter accessible to anyone who was not a mathematician of rare learning. Catholic laymen seldom studied the Old Testament. But the psalms were used in every monastery and often outside and the psalms were clear. Psalm 93: 2, 'The Lord hath made the round world so sure that it cannot be moved.' Psalm 19: 5, 'The sun cometh forth as a bridegroom out of his chamber, and rejoiceth as a giant to run his course. It goeth forth from the uttermost part of the heaven, and runneth about unto the end of it again.' When the evangelicals promoted the study of the Old Testament and the more frequent use of the psalms by laypeople, such texts were well known. And when they promoted the knowledge by laypeople of the Old Testament, even children learnt in catechism classes how Hezekiah king of Judah lay dying and turned his face to the wall and was given a sign of healing that the shadow cast by the sun on the staircase went back ten degrees; and how when Joshua was pursuing the enemies of Israel and there was not enough time in the day to slaughter the retreating Amorites, Jehovah made the sun stand still in the sky and halted the moon. But these scriptural texts meant nothing important in astronomy to those who read them. For it was obvious to all their eyes that the sun went round the earth.

Copernicus was born at Torun on the Prussian–Polish border and after he was famous both Prussians and Poles claimed him but the world has given the advantage to the Poles. His father, who was a merchant, died when he was ten and he was brought up by a priest uncle—who became the bishop of Ermland. He went to the university of Cracow in 1491–6, where they talked Latin and he lived in a humanist atmosphere—and where he collected books on astronomy. Then like so many Poles he went to north Italy for higher education, to Bologna to study canon law, which was the training for a high post in the ecclesiastical administration—but even there he spent a lot of time on astronomy. In 1500 he was in Rome for the jubilee and stayed for a year lecturing on mathematics and astronomy. Then his uncle got him and his brother canonries at Frauenburg, intended as grants to enable them to continue their studies. In Padua he studied medicine and learned Greek, in Ferrara he renewed the study of canon law, and in 1506 was back at Ermland, a highly educated person, qualified to be an administrator in the diocese. He became private physician to his uncle-bishop until 1512 until his uncle died and he occupied his canonry. He was a capable man of affairs not at all a boffin. Among his contemporaries he was more respected as physician than astronomer. He was never ordained priest to qualify for his canonry.

It was during these years that he started redesigning astronomy. In 1512 he wrote down a short and simple account of the difficulties which he met in the traditional scheme. Pope Leo X sent out an appeal for people to help reform the calendar, for there was obvious discrepancy between the way the sun and the moon behaved and the way that they were supposed to behave in the reigning Julian calendar. Looking round for astronomers, the pope appealed to Copernicus, who refused to help. But he began to work at the calendar— and later justified his book because it would further the reform of the calendar and that was why he dedicated it to Pope Paul III.

He made no new discovery, no new observation. There were no telescopes till the early seventeenth century. His instruments and his observations were cruder than those of the old Greeks. He simply worked on the old materials of Ptolemy and his successors in the ancient world, and was not content with what he found and tried to find a more elegant solution for the mathematical problems. What he did have, thanks to the invention of printing, was far easier access to the older treatments of astronomy than any of his predecessors. He had no more material from the naked eye. His object was to take Ptolemy and see how far his system worked and how far his system was self-contradictory. His achievement was not only to offer a less contradictory answer to what was observed but to provide a theory which enabled his successors to make new observations. But the better tables which he produced did help the reform of the calendar and were used in that reform when it came several decades later.

Still the book was unpublished. George Joachim Rheticus (from the Tyrol, for which the Latin was Rhaetia) was well educated by Myconius in Zurich and sent as an undergraduate to Wittenberg where in 1536 at the age of twenty-two, spotted by Melanchthon, he was made professor of astronomy. Three years later, hearing of the work of Copernicus, he arrived at Frauenburg to find out what was happening. Within a few weeks the young Protestant and the ageing Catholic were close friends. Rheticus went with Copernicus on his journeys and as a side-occupation mapped East Prussia and the Baltic coast.

Within a few weeks Rheticus was an ardent advocate of the doctrine that the earth moves round the sun. He studied the unpublished manuscript, asked for explanations, took up points, with the leave of the author he wrote down a short version of the theory, the *First Account* (*Narratio Prima*). This was printed in Danzig at the end of 1539 and so gave the first authentic knowledge which the learned world received of what Copernicus was trying to prove, though acquaintances knew something already and there was talk. Osiander, then still in Nuremberg, and much interested in astronomy, begged him to publish and received a refusal. Osiander tried again and said that it would be possible to pacify objectors by putting forward the theory as hypothesis only. He made the same suggestion in a letter to Rheticus.

Finally Rheticus persuaded Copernicus to prepare the full version for the press. It is probable that but for Rheticus the manuscript would have disappeared.

Copernicus gave it to Rheticus to publish. Rheticus took the book to that centre of printing Nuremberg and gave it to a friend who was a publisher, Johann Petrejus.[18] He did not stay to see the manuscript through the press, because he had to leave to take up a post at the university of Leipzig; but he handed this duty to Osiander, who had corresponded with Copernicus about the question.

In a letter to Copernicus Osiander had given the advice that the book should be given a preface which said that it was only a hypothesis. Since he now had charge of publication he added a short preface along these lines to the book. It was unsigned but could not be taken as written by Copernicus because it praised Copernicus.

This mistaken addition was well-meaning rather than corrupting. It said that astronomers have their special work in observing the movements of the bodies in the sky. We can never know the true cause of these movements. But astronomers must make theories to enable correct mathematical calculations to be made. For this purpose Copernicus's work is distinguished (*egregie*) and shows what follies earlier calculators have committed. The astronomer will go for the best calculations, the philosopher will go for truth. Nothing is revealed about all this by the Bible. It is right that people should look at the new theory as fairly as they look at the older theories which are in no way more probable. And this book contains an admirable treasure of learned observation.

It is a certain inference that Osiander was nervous; that he wanted to smooth the way for the fair treatment of Copernicus's book; and that he much valued it himself. To say of the book that astronomers could not get

[18] Petrejus, MA at Wittenberg, became chief among Nuremberg printers, always a friend of Melanchthon, and much valued by the learned, died 1550.

truth, they could only provide working theories, was sure to make Copernicus cross. It also angered Rheticus. But it appeared at the beginning of the first printed edition of *De Revolutionibus*. The edition was brought to Copernicus on his deathbed but by then his memory had gone and he can hardly have understood what had been done.

In many works of history it has been asserted that the Protestant leaders delayed the reception of Copernicus's theory. In this doctrine there is no truth. Osiander by his preface wished to foster the theory, not to resist it.

Melanchthon, who knew mostly about Greek and the New Testament, taught nearly everything at the university of Wittenberg. He was no natural scientist by inclination and accepted only what he found in the works of Aristotle. In 1549 he published a little book on physics, designed for beginners and Aristotelian, *Elements of Physics (Initia doctrinae physicae)*.[19] He did not believe that the earth went round the sun and mocked those who did. The problem is too difficult, he said, for human minds and in such darkness it is good to consult the Scriptures which refer to a movement of the sun and not the earth; but partly, and this was the weight of his objection, because the arguments of Ptolemy against it are persuasive. He thought that Copernicus was only a restatement of the old error of Aristarchus which Ptolemy refuted. In his later editions he took out the mockery. Melanchthon did not mention Copernicus by name and the only four times he mentioned him he did so with compliments. His colleague as professor of theology, Caspar Cruciger,[20] an intimate friend of Melanchthon, and the founder of Wittenberg's botanic garden, became a dedicated Copernican without any trouble from the faculty as a whole or from Melanchthon.

This is not surprising because both the professors of astronomy at Wittenberg were Copernicans; Rheticus who went off to Leipzig, and Erasmus Reinhold who remained in Wittenberg. There was a historical legend that Reinhold taught Ptolemy to the undergraduates in his lectures and Copernicus to the public in his printed books. For this story there is no contemporary evidence. It is certain that the professor of astronomy all through Luther's later years in the faculty was a Copernican.[21] It is also certain that Melanchthon approved of his work; for the weightiest part was to take the tables of Copernicus and improve them. These tables (1551), called

---

[19] CR vii. 472; xiii. 179 ff.

[20] Cruciger, 1504–48: born Leipzig of a Czech family in the Hussite tradition; by 1523 he was studying at Wittenberg and when he was only twenty Luther married him to an ex-nun. He taught at the school in Magdeburg but from 1533 he was a member of the Wittenberg theological faculty, and one of its Melanchthonian wing. He went with Melanchthon to the ecumenical meetings with the Catholics during 1540–1. With Georg Rörer he started the Wittenberg edition of Luther's works and was one of the revisers of Luther's Bible translation.

[21] For Reinhold, 1511–53, see *ADB*. He studied mathematics as an undergraduate at Wittenberg. He died so young because he caught the plague.

the *Prussian Tables* (*Tabulae Prutenicae*) because Duke Albert of Prussia paid for their publication, were the best tables known till then. They spoke of Copernicus in terms of high praise. Melanchthon persuaded Duke Albert to give Reinhold grants of money.

Four years before the book of Copernicus was published, the sun's movement round the earth came up in conversation at Luther's table. Luther mocked people who thought the earth went round the sun. It was contrary to common sense. 'It is like someone sitting on a moving wagon and thinking he is stationary and that the trees are moving past him; or someone on a ship thinking that the ship is motionless while the coast moves by.'[22] He quoted Joshua and how the sun stood still.

This text of the Table Talk was often cited by persons who supposed that the Protestant leaders were against Copernicus on religious grounds. It does not bear the weight. It was talk thrown out at a private dinner, before Copernicus printed his book. In no book nor letter nor lecture did Luther criticize Copernicus in print.

In the year 1943 Germany celebrated the fourth centenary of the death of Copernicus and the publication of his book. The tone of the celebrations was hostile to Luther and his contemporaries, as religious troglodytes stemming the advance of science. This tone was not scholarly for the managers of the celebration, at that moment of extreme Nazi supremacy, had public reasons for wishing to hold up the churches to scorn as out of date and anti-intellectual. One of the best of Lutheran scholars, Heinrich Bornkamm, answered. He made no open attack upon the nature of the celebrations which would have been neither wise nor possible. But he took the evidence of the sixteenth century and proved how false was the belief, or the propaganda, that the Wittenberg of that day tried to suppress the ideas of Copernicus. He put his article into the last number (before the crash of a war's end and before a later resurrection) of the indispensable journal on Reformation history.[23]

The theory of the earth's motion took about a century to win a way in Europe; that is, it had no effect upon the world-outlook of the Reformation era. In the development of the debate about the firmament the biblical arguments were not important. No one, Catholic or Protestant, wanted to treat Copernicus as Galileo was later troubled. But in 1585 the ex-Dominican from Naples Giordano Bruno, restlessly moving from country to country and university to university, printing book after book as he went, lectured on Copernicus at the university of Oxford. Then for two years after that he lectured at Wittenberg on astronomy, and from there to the new-founded

[22] *TR* iv. 4638 (4 June 1539).
[23] Heinrich Bornkamm, 'Kopernikus im Urteil der Reformatoren', *ARG* 40 (1943), 171 ff.

Brunswick university of Helmstedt, and was grateful to the Germans because they let him say what he liked. The end of his wanderings was Venice, probably because he felt that despite his long experience of the Protestants he was still at heart a Catholic. The Inquisition arrested him. They did not charge him with teaching the doctrine of Copernicus, they had no need, they could use several denials in theology—the Trinity, transubstantiation, virginity of Mary, etc. He defended himself that he accepted all orthodox doctrines in theology but in philosophy he was free. Though Galileo took no notice of him, his execution in 1600 helped to promote the great debate in the seventeenth century about the structure of the universe.

SELECT BIBLIOGRAPHY

Reference—Background—General studies—Renaissance background—The Bible—Erasmus—Reuchlin—Hutten—The city—Luther—Luther's associates—Melanchthon—Bugenhagen—The organization of the evangelical church—Scandinavia—Creeds—Switzerland—Calvin and Geneva—Strasbourg—Huguenots—The Netherlands—Resistance—The development of history—Art and the Reformation—Music in worship—Education—Marriage, home, etc.—Peasants' War—Anabaptists—Antitrinitarians—Toleration—Christians and Jews—Witchcraft—Doubt.

Reference

The Oxford Encyclopaedia of the Reformation, ed. H. J. Hillerbrand, 4 vols. (Oxford, 1996).

At present nothing in the English language is better than this for the purpose. But for one-volume reference see *The Oxford Dictionary of the Christian Church*, ed. F. L. Cross and E. A. Livingstone, 3rd edn. (Oxford, 1997).

In German, *Theologische Realenzyklopädie*, ed. G. Müller (Berlin, 1976 onwards), at the time of writing still incomplete, but not far from completion. Up-to-date specialist bibliographies and fundamental articles of importance.

Martin Greschat has edited, in *Gestalten der Kirchengeschichte* (Stuttgart, 1981–6) a series of excellent short biographies.

Literature of 1965–85 is surveyed in R. W. Scribner, *The German Reformation* (Basingstoke, 1986).

The periodical *Archiv für Reformationsgeschichte* was founded in Germany in 1903 and became the standard tool of research. In the disasters of the Second World War it came to an end, and afterwards its publication could not at first be resumed. It owed its restart to the cooperation of the Reformation scholars Roland Bainton from the United States and Gerhard Ritter and Heinrich Bornkamm from West Germany. A volume edited by Ritter appeared in 1948, but thereafter an agreement was reached which made it an American as well as a German journal, published in Germany by the Verein für Reformationsgeschichte, and in America by the American Society for Reformation Research led by Harold Grimm.

Background

H. A. Oberman, *Forerunners of the Reformation: The Shape of Medieval Thought Illustrated by Key Documents* (Philadelphia, 1981).

Alister McGrath, *The Intellectual Origins of the European Reformation* (Oxford, 1993).

J. Huizinga, *The Waning of the Middle Ages: A Study of the Forms of Life, Thought and Art in France and The Netherlands in the Fourteenth and Fifteenth Centuries*, Eng. trans. by F. Hopman (originally London, 1924; now pb. Harmondsworth, 1976); over the decades much controverted but still a classic. See the discussion by James McConica under the same title (Toronto, 1995).

General studies

Euan Cameron, *The European Reformation* (Oxford, 1991).

Steven E. Ozment, *The Age of Reform 1520–1550: An Intellectual and Religious History of Late Medieval and Reformation Europe* (Yale, 1980; also in paperback).

Robert M. Kingdon, *Church and Society in Reformation Europe* (London, 1985). A collection of essays but making a unity.

Emile Guillaume Léonard, *Histoire générale du Protestantisme* (Paris, 1951).

Renaissance background

L. W. Spitz, *The Religious Renaissance of the German Humanists* (Cambridge, Mass., 1963).

P. G. Bietenholz, *Basle and France in the Sixteenth Century* (Geneva, 1971).

Jean Delumeau, *Sin and Fear: The Emergence of a Western Guilt Culture* (New York, 1990; Eng. trans. by Eric Nicolson of *Le Peur en Occident*, Paris, 1978).

A. Cunningham and O. P. Grell, *The Four Horsemen of the Apocalypse* (Cambridge, 2001). For the expectations of the end of the world.

The Bible

S. L. Greenslade (ed.), *The Cambridge History of the Bible*, vol. 3: *The West from the Reformation to the Present Day* (Cambridge, 1963).

For the Apocrypha among Protestants, S. Meurer (ed.), *The Apocrypha in Ecumenical Perspective* (Reading, 1991).

C. Delano-Smith and E. M. Ingram, *Maps in Bibles 1500–1600* (Geneva, 1991), important for more than maps.

E. M. Eisenstein, *The Printing Revolution in Early Modern Europe* (Cambridge, 1983).

J. F. Gilmont (ed.), *The Reformation and the Book*, trans. K. Maag (Brookfield, 1998).

Erasmus

a) Documents

P. S. Allen (ed.), *Opus Epistolarum Desiderii Erasmi Roterodami*, 12 vols. (Oxford, 1906–47). So personal a writer, letters of the first historical importance.

Opera Omnia, ed. J. H. Waszink and others (Amsterdam, 1969–).

Collected Works of Erasmus, in English translation (Toronto, 1974–).

Selected letters, ed. in translation by H. J. Hillerbrand, *Erasmus and his Age* (New York, 1970).

The more necessary works in *Ausgewählte Schriften*, ed. W. Welzig, 8 vols. (Darmstadt, 1967–).
In translation, the *Colloquies*, trans. C. R. Thompson (Chicago, 1965); the *Adages*, trans. M. M. Phillips and R. A. B. Mynors (Toronto, 1982–).
Biblical work: E. Rummel, *Erasmus' Annotations on the New Testament* (Toronto, 1986), useful for more than the Annotations.

b) Biography

Roland Bainton, *Erasmus of Christendom* (New York, 1969; now pb. Tring, 1988), a little classic.
James McConica, *Erasmus*, in the Oxford series of Past Masters (1991), brief study by an expert.
Cornelis Augustijn, *Erasmus: His Life, Works and Influence*, Eng. trans. by J. C. Grayson (Toronto, 1991).
A. Flitner, *Erasmus im Urteil seiner Nachwelt* (Tübingen, 1952).

c) Enemies and posterity

Useful dictionary in *Contemporaries of Erasmus: A Biographical Register of the Renaissance and Reformation*, ed. Peter G. Bietenholz and Thomas B. Deutscher, 3 vols. (Toronto, 1985).

Reuchlin

J. Reuchlin, *De arte cabalistica* (original 1517; reprinted Stuttgart, 1964; Eng. trans. Martin and Sarah Goodman, University of Nebraska, 1993).
Reuchlin's letters were edited by L. Geiger (reprint Hildesheim, 1962).
J. L. Blau, *The Christian Interpretation of the Cabala* (New York, 1944).
François Secret, *Les Kabbalistes chrétiens de la Renaissance* (Paris, 1964).

Hutten

Opera, ed. E. Böcking, 7 vols. (Leipzig, 1859–69; reprinted Aalen, 1963).
Epistolae Obscurorum Virorum, only partly by Hutten, ed. A. Bömer (reprinted Aalen, 1978). English translation of it by F. G. Stokes, republished with preface by H. Holborn (New York, 1964).
Life, by H. Grimm, *Ulrich von Hutten* (Göttingen, 1971).

The city

Steven E. Ozment, *The Reformation in the Cities: The Appeal of Protestantism to Sixteenth-Century Germany and Switzerland* (New Haven, 1975).
Bernd Moeller, *Reichstadt und Reformation*, new edn. (Berlin, 1987), a revision of the original essay which started the modern debate on the cities.
T. A. Brady, *Turning Swiss: Cities and Empire 1450–1550* (Cambridge, 1985).

Luther

Periodical, *Jahrbuch der Luther-Gesellschaft.*

a) Documents

Werke, critical edn. (Weimar, 1883–1997, indexes 1986–).
Systematic English translation, *Works*, ed. J. Pelikan and others, with scholarly
   notes, 55 vols. (St Louis, 1955–).
Luther's primary works, with his Shorter and Longer Catechism, Eng. trans. ed.
   H. Wace and C. Buchheim (London, 1896).
Famous translation of the Table Talk by W. Hazlitt (London, 1857), but before the
   critical editions.

b) Biography

The hostile life by Johann Cochlaeus, *Commentaria de actis et scriptis Martini Lutheri*
   (originally Mainz, 1549; reprinted Westmead, 1969).
M. Brecht, *Martin Luther*, 3 vols., 3rd edn. (Stuttgart, 1983–7. English translation by
   James L. Schaaf (Minneapolis, 1983–). A fundamental survey of the whole.

c) English lives

Roland H. Bainton, *Here I stand!*, 7th edn. (original New York, 1950; pb. Oxford,
   1994), the classic friendly short study, well based.
Heiko O. Oberman, *Luther: Man between God and the Devil* (original Berlin, 1981);
   English translation by E. Walliser-Schwarzbart (1989; pb. London, 1993), attract-
   ive viewpoint.
Richard Marius, *Martin Luther: The Christian between Life and Death* (Cambridge,
   Mass., 1999). The earlier years to 1526.

Luther's associates

Hermann Barge, *Andreas Bodenstein von Karlstadt*, 2 vols. (Leipzig, 1905); cf. Ulrich
   Bubenheimer, *Andreas Bodenstein von Karlstadt und die Reform von Gottesdienst und
   Leben* (Berlin, 1983).
Gordon Rupp, *Patterns of Reformation* (London, 1969).

Melanchthon

Works in CR i–xxviii (ed. C. G. Bretschneider and H. E. Bindseil, Halle-
   Brunswick, 1834–60; reprint Frankfurt am Main, 1963). Robert Stupperich pub-
   lished a selection of the important works, *Werke in Auswahl*, 7 vols. (Gütersloh,
   1951–75).
The CR edition of the letters is being replaced by Heinz Scheible (ed.), *Melanchthons
   Briefwechsel* (Stuttgart, 1977 and in progress).
Biography in Clyde Leonard Manschreck, *The Quiet Reformer* (reprint Westport, 1975).
Heinz Scheible, *TRE* xxii. 371–410, with bibliography.

Bugenhagen

Hellmuth Heyden, *Kirchengeschichte Pommerns*, 2 vols., 2nd edn. (Stettin, 1957).
H. G. Leder (ed.), *Johannes Bugenhagen: Gestalt und Wirkung* (Berlin, 1984).

The organization of the evangelical church

Documents, illuminating, in E. Sehling, *Die evangelische Kirchenordnungen des 16. Jahrhunderts*, 15 vols. (Leipzig, 1902–77). Guides in *TRE* ii. 553–75, s.v. *Amt* (Holsten Fagerberg), and *TRE* xix. 59–68, s.v. *Kirchenregiment, Landesherrliches* (Hans-Walter Krumweide).
Most Länder have their individual history, usually well done, e.g. H. Steitz, *Geschichte der evangelischen Kirche in Hesse und Nassau*, 3 vols. (Marburg, 1961–77).
H. W. Krumweide, *Zur Entstehung des landesherrlichen Kirchenregiments in Kursachsen und Braunschweig-Wolfenbüttel* (Göttingen, 1967).
H. Hermelink, *Geschichte der evangelischen Kirche in Württemberg* (Stuttgart, 1949).
A. Schröer, *Die Reformation in Westfalen*, 2 vols. (Münster, 1979–93).
Karl Schmaltz, *Kirchengeschichte Meckenburgs*, 3 vols. (Berlin, 1935–52; reprint Leipzig, 1971).
For Prussia, Walther Hubatsch, *Geschichte der evangelischen Kirche Ostpreussens*, 3 vols. (Göttingen, 1968).
TRE under each Land has the modern literature for this purpose.

Scandinavia

David Kirby, *Northern Europe in the Early Modern Period: The Baltic World 1492–1772* (Harlow, 1990).
P. G. Lindhardt, *Die Kirche in ihrer Geschichte*, vol. iii: *Skandinavische Kirchengeschichte seit dem 16. Jahrhundert* (Göttingen, 1982).
N. K. Andersen, 'The Reformation in Scandinavia and the Baltic', in G. R. Elton (ed.), *New Cambridge Modern History*, 2nd edn. (Cambridge, 1990).
Walter Göbell (ed.), *Schleswig-Holsteinische Kirchengeschichte*, vol. iii (Neumünster, 1982). The history of a German Land but with as much importance for the history of Denmark.
C. F. Wisløff, *Norsk Kirkehistorie* 1 (Oslo, 1966). For Iceland as well as Norway.
J. C. F. Hood, *Icelandic Church Saga* (London, 1946).
L. S. Hunter (ed.), *Scandinavian Churches* (London, 1965).

Creeds

Bekenntnisschriften der evangelisch-lutherischen Kirche, 6th edn. (1967).
Bekenntnisschriften der reformierten Kirche, ed. E. F. K. Müller (Leipzig, 1903).
Mark Noll (ed.), *The Confessions and Catechisms of the Reformation* (Grand Rapids, 1991).

P. Schaff, *The Creeds of the Evangelical Protestant Churches* (New York, 1877; reprinted Grand Rapids, 1977–8).

Switzerland

a) Documents

Zwingli's collected *Works*, 14 vols. in CR lxxxviii–ci (Leipzig etc., 1905–).

E. Egli, *Aktensammlung zur Geschichte der Züricher Reformation* (Zurich, 1879; reprinted Nieuwkoop, 1973).

G. W. Bromiley (ed.), *Zwingli and Bullinger: Selected Writings*, Library of Christian Classics (Philadelphia, 1953).

Bullinger's *Werke* only in part as yet (Zurich, 1972–).

b) Treatments

Ulrich Gäbler, *Huldrich Zwingli: His Life and Work*, Eng. trans. by Ruth C. L. Gritsch (Edinburgh, 1986).

G. R. Potter, *Zwingli* (Cambridge, 1976; now pb.).

Fritz Blanke and Immanuel Leuschner, *Heinrich Bullinger: Vater der reformierten Kirche* (Zurich, 1990).

M. W. Anderson, *Peter Martyr, a Reformer in Exile* (Nieuwkoop, 1975).

Cf. also F. Büsser, in *TRE* s.v. *Komander, Johann*, for the effect in the Grisons.

Kurt Guggisberg, *Bernische Kirchengeschichte* (Berne, 1958).

Calvin and Geneva

a) Documents

Opera, in CR, 59 vols., ed. W. Baum, E. Cunitz and E. Reiss (1863–1900).

Selected translations in Library of Christian Classics, especially *Institutes*, ed. J. T. McNeill (London, 1960), and *Theological Treatises*, ed. J. K. S. Reid (London, 1954).

Registres de la Compagnie des pasteurs de Génève, ed. J. F. Bergier and R. M. Kingdon (Geneva, 1962–).

Beza's *Correspondance*, ed. H. Meylan and A. Dufour, 9 vols. (Geneva, 1960–78).

For all the Calvinist world, a useful selection of documents, ed. André Pettegree, Alastair Duke and Gillian Lewis, *Calvinism in Europe 1540–1620* (Cambridge, 1996).

b) Literature

The old biography of Calvin by E. Doumergue, 7 vols. (Lausanne, 1899–1917) is still to be used for the foundations.

Youth: in Alexandre Ganoczy, *The Young Calvin*, translated from the French by D. Foxgrover and W. Provo (Edinburgh, 1988).

T. H. L. Parker, *John Calvin* (London, 1975).

Alister E. McGrath, *A Life of John Calvin* (Oxford, 1990).

Those close to Calvin:

P. F. Geisendorf, *Theodore de Bèze*, 2nd edn. (Geneva, 1967).

J. Barnaud, *Pierre Viret* (original 1911; reprinted Nieuwkoop, 1973).

C. Schnetzler *et al.*, *Guillaume Farel* (Neuchâtel-Paris, 1930).

For Farel cf. also Henri Vuilleumier, *Histoire de l'Eglise reformée du Pays de Vaud sous le régime bernois*, 4 vols. (Lausanne, 1927–33).

Actes du Colloque Guillaume Farel, ed. P. Bartel *et al.*, 2 vols. (Geneva, 1983).

J. T. McNeill, *The History and Character of Calvinism*, 2nd edn. (New York, 1967).

Strasbourg

a) Documents

Bucer's *Omnia Opera* in progress (Gütersloh and Leiden, 1960–).

Selected letters of Bucer, ed. J. V. Pollet, 2 vols. (Paris, 1958–62).

b) Literature

L. J. Abray, *The People's Reformation: Magistrates, Clergy and Commons in Strasbourg 1520–1598* (Ithaca, 1985).

T. A. Brady, *Ruling Class, Régime and Reformation in Strasbourg 1520–1555* (Leiden, 1978).

T. A. Brady, *The Politics of the Reformation in Germany: Jacob Sturm (1489–1553) of Strasbourg* (Atlantic Highlands, 1997).

M. U. Chrisman, *Strasbourg and the Reform* (New Haven, 1967).

Hastings Eells, *Martin Bucer* (New Haven, 1931).

Huguenots

For reference, Eugène Emile Haag, *La France Protestante*. Biographical dictionary of all Huguenots (1st edn. Paris, 1846–59; 2nd edn. by Henri Bordier, Paris, 1877–88 incomplete, so both editions are sometimes needed).

Natalie Zemon Davis, *Society and Culture in Early Modern France* (Stanford, 1975).

Janine Garrisson-Estèbe, *Protestants du Midi 1559–1598* (Toulouse, 1980).

Robert M. Kingdon, *Geneva and the Coming of the Wars of Religion in France* (Geneva, 1956).

Robert M. Kingdon, *Geneva and the Consolidation of the French Protestant Movement, 1564–1598* (Geneva, 1967).

Nancy Lyman Roelker, *Queen of Navarre Jeanne d'Albret* (Cambridge, Mass., 1968).

John Viénot, *Histoire de la réforme francaise* (Paris, 1926–34).

The Netherlands

G. Brandt, *The History of the Reformation in the Low Countries*, Eng. trans. in 4 vols. (1720–3; original at Amsterdam, 1671–1704), fundamental.

Alastair Duke, *Reformation and Revolt in the Low Countries* (London, 1990).

Irwin B. Horst (ed.), *The Dutch Dissenters* (Leiden, 1986).

Resistance

Karl Brandi, *The Emperor Charles V*, Eng. trans. by C. V. Wedgwood (original London, 1939; Brighton, 1980).

Edward Armstrong, *The Emperor Charles V*, 2 vols. (London, 1929).

H. Scheible (ed.), *Das Widerstandsrecht als Problem der deutschen Protestantismus 1523–46* (Gütersloh, 1960).

Quentin Skinner, *The Foundations of Modern Political Thought*, vol. ii: *The Age of the Reformation* (Cambridge, 1978).

a) Huguenots and resistance

P. Benedict, *Rouen during the Wars of Religion* (Cambridge, 1981).

Quentin Skinner, as above.

Kingdon, see under Huguenots.

N. M. Sutherland, *The Huguenot Struggle for Recognition* (London, 1980).

The development of history

A. G. Dickens and P. Tonkin, *The Reformation in Historical Thought* (Cambridge, Mass., 1985).

P. Meinhold, *Geschichte der kirchlichen Historiographie* (Munich, 1967).

P. Polman, *L'élément historique dans la controverse religieuse de XVIᵉ siècle* (Gembloux, 1932).

Sleidan's *Commentarii* (reprinted Osnabrück, 1968).

Wilhelm Preger, *Matthias Flacius und seine Zeit*, 2 vols. (originally Erlangen, 1859–61, and still important; reprinted Nieuwkoop, 1964).

Heinz Scheible, *Die Entstehung der Magdeburger Zenturien* (Gütersloh, 1966).

Art and the Reformation

Hans-Dietrich Altendorf and Peter Jezler (eds.), *Bilderstreit: Kulturwandel in Zwinglis Reformation* (Zurich, 1984). In this may be found the work of Gerold Edlibach, the chief contemporary witness of the Zurich destructions.

F. Buchholz, *Protestantismus und Kunst im 16. Jahrhundert* (Leipzig, 1927).

C. C. Christensen, *Art and the Reformation in Germany* (Athens, Ohio, 1979).

P. M. Crew, *Calvinist Preaching and Iconoclasm in The Netherlands, 1544–1569* (Cambridge, 1978).

C. M. N. Eire, *War against the Idols: The Reformation of Worship from Erasmus to Calvin* (Cambridge, 1986).

Charles Garside, *Zwingli and the Arts* (New Haven, 1966).

Margarete Stirm, *Die Bilderfrage in der Reformation* (Gütersloh, 1977).

L. P. Wandel, *Always Among us: Images of the Poor in Zwingli's Zurich* (Cambridge, 1990).

K. E. S. Zapalac, *'In his Image and Likeness': Political Iconography and Religious Change in Regensburg 1500–1600* (Ithaca, 1990).

Literature in *TRE*, s.v. *Kunst und Religion V*, by Gerhard May (1990).

Music in worship

O. Douen, *Clément Marot et le psautier huguenot* (Paris, 1878–9; reprinted Amsterdam, 1967).
Philipp Wackernagel, *Das deutsche Kirchenlied von der ältesten Zeit bis zu Anfang des 17. Jahrhunderts* (original Leipzig, 1843–7; reprinted Hildesheim, 1964).
Paul Nettl, *Luther and Music*, Eng. trans. (Philadelphia, 1946).

Education

(See also Erasmus, Melanchthon.)
Karl Hartfelder, *Philipp Melanchthon als Praeceptor Germaniae* (Berlin, 1889).
Hans-Adolf Stempel, *Melanchthons pädagogische Werken* (Bielefeld, 1979).
Johann Sturm on Education: The Reformation and Humanist Learning, ed. and trans. Lewis W. Spitz and Barbara Sher Tinsley (St Louis, 1995).
Gerald Strauss, *Luther's House of Learning: Indoctrination of the Young in the German Reformation* (Baltimore, 1978).

Marriage, home, etc.

John Milton, trans., *The Judgement of Martin Bucer concerning Divorce* (London, 1644).
R. H. Bainton, *Women of the Reformation*, i: *In Germany and Italy* (Minneapolis, 1971); ii: *In France and England* (1973); iii: *From Spain to Scandinavia* (1977).
A. Bieler, *L'homme et la femme dans la morale calviniste* (Geneva, 1963).
H. Dieterich, *Das Protestantische Eherecht in Deutschland bis zur Mitte des 17. Jahrhundert* (Munich, 1970).
John F. Harrington, *Reordering Marriage and Society in Reformation Germany* (Cambridge, 1995).
Walther Köhler, *Zürcher Ehegericht und Genfer Konsistorium*, 2 vols. (Leipzig, 1933–42).
W. Lazareth, *Luther on the Christian Home* (Philadelphia, 1960).
Ian Maclean, *The Renaissance Notion of Woman* (Cambridge, 1980).
A. Nowicki-Pastuschka, *Frauen in der Reformation, Untersuchungen zum Verhalten von Frauen in den Reichstädten Augsburg und Nürnberg zur reformatorischen Bewegung zwischen 1517 und 1537* (Pfaffenweile, 1996).
S. Ozment, *When Fathers Ruled: Family Life in Reformation Europe* (Cambridge, Mass., 1983).
Lyndal Roper, *The Holy Household: Women and Morals in Reformation Augsburg* (Oxford, 1989).
Ulinka Rublack, *The Crimes of Women in Early Modern Germany* (Oxford, 1999).
T. M. Safley, *Let No Man put Asunder* (Kirkville, Mo., 1984).

Peasants' War

The collected works of Thomas Müntzer, trans. P. E. Matheson (Edinburgh, 1988).

P. Blickle, *The Revolution of 1525: The German Peasants' War from a New Perspective*, Eng. trans, of 2nd edn. (Baltimore, 1981).

G. Franz, *Der deutsche Bauernkrieg*, 11th edn. (Darmstadt, 1977), classic narrative.

H. G. Goertz, *Thomas Müntzer*, Eng. trans. J. Jaquiery, ed. P. Matheson (Edinburgh, 1993).

Tom Scott, *Thomas Müntzer: Theology and Revolution in the German Reformation* (Basingstoke, 1989).

J. M. Stayer, *The German Peasants War and Anabaptist Community of Goods* (Montreal, 1991).

Angelika Bischoff Urach, *Michael Gaismair* (Innsbruck, 1983).

Anabaptists

Quellen zur Geschichte der Täufer in der Schweiz, ed. L. von Muralt, W. Schmidt, and H. Fast (Zurich, 1952–).

R. Stupperich (ed.), *Die Schriften Bernard von Rothmanns* (Münster, 1970).

Peter Riedemann, *Account of our Religion, Doctrine and Faith*, Eng. trans. K. E. Hasenberg (London, 1950).

Opera Omnia of Menno Simons (1681; reprinted Amsterdam, 1989); in translation by L. Verduin and J. C. Wenger (Scottdale, 1966).

Mennonite Quarterly Review and *Mennonite Encyclopaedia* are indispensable.

M. G. Baylor (ed.), *The Radical Reformation* (Cambridge, 1991).

C. P. Clasen, *Anabaptism: A Social History 1525–1618* (Ithaca and London, 1972).

H. J. Goertz, *Die Täufer* (Munich, 1980).

H. J. Goertz (ed.), *Profiles of Radical Reformers, Biographical Sketches from Thomas Müntzer to Paracelsus*, Eng. trans. ed. Walter Klaassen (Scottdale, 1982).

G. H. Williams, *The Radical Reformation* (Philadelphia, 1962).

Guide to the literature on individuals under their names in *OER* and *TRE*.

For the Vaudois:

Euan Cameron, *The Reformation of the Heretics: The Waldenses of the Alps, 1480–1580*, 2nd edn. (Oxford, 1986).

G. Audisio (ed.), *Les Vaudois des origines à leur fin: Colloque internationale* (Turin, 1990).

For Ochino:

Delio Cantimori, *Eretici italiani del Cinquecento*, 2nd edn. (Florence, 1967).

K. Benrath, *Bernardino Ochino von Siena. Ein Beitrag zur Geschichte der Reformation* (Leipzig, 1875), a ground-breaking book which had an English translation in 1876; but the second German edition was Brunswick, 1892, and this was reprinted Nieuwkoop, 1968.

Antitrinitarians

(See Delio Cantimori and G. H. Williams as above)

Jerome Friedman, *Michael Servetus: A Case Study in Total Heresy* (Geneva, 1978).

J. Raitt (ed.), *Shapers of Religious Tradition in Germany, Switzerland and Poland 1560–1600* (London, 1981).

E. M. Wilbur, *A History of Unitarianism, Socinianism and its Antecedents* (Cambridge, Mass., 1946).

Toleration

F. Buisson, *Sébastien Castellio, sa vie et son œuvre*, 2 vols. (Paris, 1892).
H. R. Guggisberg, *Sebastian Castellio im Urteil der Nachwelt vom Späthumanismus bis zur Aufklärung*, Basler Beiträge zur Geschichtswissenschaft no. 57 (Basel, 1956).
Erik Hassinger, *Toleranz im 16. Jahrhundert* (Basel, 1966).
J. Lecler, *Toleration and the Reformation*, 2 vols. (original Paris, 1955; Eng. trans. New York, 1959–60).

Christians and Jews

S. H. Baron, *A Social and Religious History of the Jews*, 2nd rev. edn. (New York, 1969).
J. Brosseder, *Luthers Stellung zu den Juden* (Munich, 1972).
R. Po-Chia Hsia, *The Myth of Ritual Murder* (New York, 1988).
K. H. Rengstorf *et al.*, *Kirche und Synagoge*, 2 vols. (Stuttgart, 1968–70).
TRE, s.v. *Rosheim, Josel von*, by J. F. Battenberg, with literature.

Witchcraft

Collection at Cornell University, catalogue by M. J. Crowe (1977). Copies of Himmler's Poznan collection are at Coblenz.
Robin Briggs, *Witches and Neighbours: The Social and Cultural Context of European Witchcraft* (London, 1996).
Stuart Clark, *Thinking with Demons: The idea of Witchcraft in Early Modern Europe* (Oxford, 1997), also for literature.
Jorge Haustein, *Martin Luthers Stellung zum Zauber- und Hexenwesen* (Stuttgart, 1990).
R. Kieckhefer, *European Witch Trials: Their Foundations in Popular and Learned Culture* (London, 1976).
E. W. Monter (ed.), *European Witchcraft* (New York, 1969).
E. W. Monter, *Witchcraft in France and Switzerland: The Borderlands during the Reformation* (London, 1976).
Gerhard Schormann, *Hexenprozesse in Deutschland* (Göttingen, 1981), for both archives and literature.
Keith Thomas, *Religion and the Decline of Magic* (London, 1973).

Doubt

Henri Busson, *Les Sources et le développement du rationalisme dans la littérature française de la Renaissance 1533–1601*, new edn. (Paris, 1957).
Richard Copley Christie, *Etienne Dolet*, new edn. (London, 1899).

Lucien Febvre, *Le Problème de l'incroyance au XVIe siècle*, 2nd edn. (Paris, 1988). Eng. trans. by Beatrice Gottlieb, *The Problem of Unbelief in the Sixteenth Century: The Religion of Rabelais* (Cambridge, Mass., 1982, from an earlier edition).

Richard H. Popkin, *The History of Scepticism from Erasmus to Spinoza* (Berkeley, 1979).

INDEX